JOHN BERRYMAN (1914–72) was awarded the Pulitzer Prize for Poetry in 1965 for *77 Dream Songs*. In 1968, *His Toy, His Dream, His Rest* won the National Book Award and the Bollingen Prize for Poetry. Both works were incorporated into his major work, *The Dream Songs*, in 1969. Among his other books are a critical biography, *Stephen Crane*; a book of criticism, *The Freedom of the Poet*; a novel, *Recovery*; and five other volumes of poetry: *Homage to Mistress Bradstreet, Short Poems, Love and Fame, Delusions,* and *Henry's Fate and Other Poems*. His *Collected Poems: 1937–1971* was published in 1989.

JOHN HAFFENDEN is a professor of English literature at the University of Sheffield, England. His publications include *The Life of John Berryman* and *Viewpoints: Poets in Conversation*, as well as a study of poet and critic William Empson. He is a Fellow of the Royal Society of Literature.

BERRYMAN'S
SHAKESPEARE

JOHN

BERRYMAN

BERRYMAN'S

SHAKESPEARE

EDITED AND INTRODUCED

BY *John Haffenden*

FARRAR, STRAUS AND GIROUX

NEW YORK

For Kate

Farrar, Straus and Giroux
19 Union Square West, New York 10003

Copyright © by Kate Donahue Berryman
Introduction copyright © 1999 by John Haffenden
All rights reserved
Distributed in Canada by Douglas & McIntyre Ltd.
Printed in the United States of America
Published in 1999 by Farrar, Straus and Giroux
First paperback edition, 2001

Library of Congress Cataloging-in-Publication Data
Berryman, John, 1914–1972
  [Shakespeare]
  Berryman's Shakespeare / John Berryman ; edited by John Haffenden.
    p.   cm.
  ISBN 0-374-52750-4 (pbk.)
  1. Shakespeare, William, 1564–1616.   2. Dramatists, English—Early
modern, 1500–1700—Biography.   I. Haffenden, John.   II. Title.
III. Title: Shakespeare.
PR2894.B45   1999
822.3'3—dc21
  [B]   98-41000

Designed by Cynthia Krupat

Contents

Preface

BY ROBERT GIROUX

IT STARTED IN THE THIRTIES, when John Berryman and I studied Shakespeare with poet Mark Van Doren at Columbia College. One aspect of Van Doren's greatness as a teacher was his technique of pretending that you were his intellectual equal. Since you knew he expected your best, he got it more often than not. His course covered the thirty-seven plays, the two narrative poems, the sonnets, "A Lover's Complaint," the wonderful songs, and "The Phoenix and Turtle," the amazing poem about two-becoming-one. One of Berryman's best moments in class occurred on the day we discussed *Macbeth*, when he cited Hecate's prediction of overconfidence as the cause of Macbeth's downfall—"And you all know security / Is mortals' chiefest enemy"—and Van Doren asked him to show us the couplet's lines. At first Berryman could not find them, but he did just before the class ended and Van Doren admitted, "Having read the play hundreds of times, I'm amazed I never caught that." Van Doren's high regard for his student was also proved when Berryman became ineligible at the last moment for a Cambridge University fellowship, after an antagonistic professor flunked Berryman and at once sailed for Europe. Van Doren persuaded the Dean to arrange for a special exam in the same subject (English literature); Berryman not only earned an A but subsequently won a prestigious Shakespeare prize at Cambridge. He was a genuine and passionate scholar, who developed into an outstanding poet and critic.

John Haffenden has performed an admirable service for letters in compiling and annotating this book, which required enormous ingenuity and research. One of my favorite sections is Berryman's deferential and knowledgeable exchange of letters, when he was teaching at Princeton, with the great Shakespeare scholar W. W. Greg. "Shakespeare's Reality," printed in the appendix, is a key to understanding Berryman's remarkable insight into the subtle question of a character's identity. The lines he cites from *Richard III* and *All's Well* have an affinity with Shakespeare's assertion in sonnet 121: "No, I am that I am."

Though Berryman's tragic illness (alcoholism) crippled his later years and ended in suicide, I repeat my conviction, as his close friend, editor, and publisher, that biographers have underrated his lifelong torment over his father's suicide, as well as the sinister role of his possessive mother, about which I have set forth my conclusions in "Henry's Understanding" in *The Yale Review* (April 1996). His first "Dream Song" includes a stanza that perhaps sums up his life:

> All the world like a woolen lover
> once did seem on Henry's side.
> Then came a departure.
> Thereafter nothing fell out as it might or ought.
> I don't see how Henry, pried
> open for all the world to see, survived.

Critic Donald Davie got it right, in his review of Berryman's book of criticism, *The Freedom of the Poet*, when he wrote: "The man behind this book was not only one of the most gifted and intelligent Americans of his time, but also one of the most honorable and responsible."

Introduction

BY JOHN HAFFENDEN

IT IS FITTING to open this volume by quoting the preface that John Berryman chose to draft on January 26, 1970, only two years before his death:

As I put this preface together and take leave at last of the work—the third most demanding I have ever done—I come this evening on a Shakespearean note new to me, and I sit up straight with sympathetic pleasure. It is by one of my favourite writers, a man who suffered from many plans. He even managed to lecture and write a good deal on Shakespeare, though never a book. But one day excited he took a sheet of paper (watermark 1796) and set down:

MEMORANDA

for a History of Engl Poetry ------------------------
1. English Romances—compare ----------------------
---------------------- / &c.

and so on thro Chaucer, Spenser, the Ballads, making notes on how each was to be treated, till he came to 5, when all he wrote down was this:
5. Shakespeare!!! ALMIGHTY!*

J.B.

Although Berryman did not manage to bring to a completion his large critical and biographical work on Shakespeare, I became con-

* Compare *Coleridge: Select Poetry and Prose*, ed. Stephen Potter (London: The Nonesuch Press; New York: Random House, 1933), pp. 326–27.

vinced many years ago—judging from the high degree of originality of his writings, as well as their substantial scholarship and their communicative zest for the subject—that his papers should be brought together in a permanent form. I have therefore worked on these papers off and on for over twenty years, and so I am particularly grateful to Robert Giroux, when I showed him samples of these materials a few years ago, for agreeing that the volume should be published by the poet's longtime American publisher, Farrar, Straus and Giroux.

AN OVERVIEW

JOHN BERRYMAN (1914–72) occupies a major place among the outstanding poets of recent times. *Homage to Mistress Bradstreet* (1956) was hailed by Edmund Wilson as "the most distinguished long poem by an American since *The Waste Land*"; and the two volumes *77 Dream Songs* (1964) and *His Toy, His Dream, His Rest* (1968), which together constitute the major work known as *The Dream Songs* (1969), an astonishing modern epic in which Berryman displayed much of his personality and experience, earned him the Pulitzer Prize for Poetry (1965), a Bollingen Award (1967), and the National Book Award (1969). The autobiographical daring of his poetry began in 1947 with *Berryman's Sonnets* (published in 1967), a sequence which charts the fortunes of a love affair.

Berryman's posthumous reputation has been enhanced by *Collected Poems, 1937–1971* (ed. Charles Thornbury, 1989); and his standing as one of the most perceptive critics of the modern period was confirmed by *The Freedom of the Poet* (1976), a collection of essays and short fiction.

Throughout his career, Berryman was also a dedicated and scholarly student of Shakespeare. Understandably, he regarded himself as "lucky" to have been able to study under two exemplary teachers: Mark Van Doren at Columbia College, New York ("the hottest teacher of Shakespeare in the country," Berryman later avowed, "as well as a critic of great & original power"), and George Rylands ("one of the 3 or 4 most acute critics of the 1930s of Shakespeare's *poetry & style*") at Cambridge University, where Berryman held the Kellett Fellowship for the years 1936–38. Thereafter he was keen to acknowledge his primary indebtedness to the scholars E. K. Chambers, John Dover Wilson, and W. W. Greg (whose *The Editorial Problem in Shakespeare: A Survey of the Foundations of the Text* [1942], Berryman had adulated in *The Nation*,[1] and with whom, in the 1940s, he enjoyed a rewarding correspondence on *King Lear* which is included in the third section of this volume)—as well as (to quote from a preface he drafted in the winter of 1970) "to the exhilarating parade of Shakespearean scholars and critics, among whom it cannot be invidious to single out Aubrey & Rowe the pioneers, Dr. Johnson, Malone, Coleridge, the brilliant if unscrupulous Collier, Bradley, the laborious Lee, the subtle but mostly convincing Harley Granville-Barker . . ."[2] I am happy to note too that, more than once among his vast array of notes, he advised himself: "Consider Empson's criticism." Indeed, there is no doubt that he was deeply familiar with the panoply of both primary and secondary writings on Shakespeare; he could even claim to have read a majority of the works that Shakespeare is known to have read, as well as every non-Shakespearean dramatic work published up to 1611.

In 1937 Berryman won the prestigious Charles Oldham Shakespeare Scholarship at Cambridge University (the knowledge that the English critic Arnold Kettle was named "*proxime accessit*" or runner-up, was "a feather in my pompous American cap," he admitted years later). In the same year, he entered himself for the Harness Essay Prize with a seventy-seven-page piece on "The Character and Role of the Heroine in Shakespearian Comedy." Although he did not attain that particular prize (the judges, including Enid Welsford, were so exacting that they did not award a prize that session), he could at least claim to have failed in good company (another critic who went on to win international fame, Ian Watt, also failed in his bid for the Harness that year). In 1944–46 Berryman held a Rockefeller Fellowship while preparing a critical edition, complete with introduction, commentary, and critical apparatus, of *King Lear*. But he put his work into suspension in 1946 almost as soon as he heard the demoralising news that Professor G. I. Duthie was about to publish a fresh critical edition of the play—which eventually appeared from Basil Blackwell, Oxford, after a further three years. In the early 1950s he resumed his researches on Shakespeare with a view to writing a full-length critical biography, but the urgency of his own poetry took precedence; as he was to recall towards the end of his life: "Suddenly, owing to a weird quadrangular conjuncture of diverse events, my *Bradstreet* poem got going and for two or three months nearly killed me daily." The poetry would always come first, and rightly so. In 1951, while working at Princeton University, he delivered the Hodder Lectures on Shakespeare; the following year, he elaborated that series in the form of the Elliston Lectures at the University of Cincinnati. (One of those lectures—"Shakespeare at Thirty"—subsequently appeared in *The Hudson Review* in the fall of 1953.) He also gave a first version of a lecture later published as "Shakespeare's Last Word" (which is also reprinted in this volume). In 1954, at the Harvard University summer school, he delivered an extensive lecture course on Shakespeare's plays. Thereafter, through the 1950s and 1960s, he worked to bring all his various findings on Shakespeare, biographical and critical, into a final form that would satisfy his own high professional standards. Eventually, in 1971, he was awarded a senior fellowship by the National Endowment for the Humanities, specifically to finish his work on Shakespeare in the shape of a book to be called *Shakespeare's Reality*. Sadly, that last and long-desired labour was cut short by his death by suicide in January 1972.

Berryman's notes and drafts of writings on Shakespeare cover many thousands of pages: the typed inventory of his writings on Shakespeare, now housed in the Manuscripts Division of the University of Minnesota Libraries, alone runs to eighty-nine pages. The present volume gathers together the most polished examples of the essays and lectures that Berryman composed between the late 1940s and his final months; though a few of the pieces are regrettably unfinished, none is so fragmentary that it has not established a certain and sustainable argument. Part One represents perhaps the most advanced stage of the popular biographical study on which Berryman was engaged for many years; it dates from the late 1960s. Part Two comprises eight lectures, which he developed, adapted, and cannibalized from time to time (both to suit different audiences and to take stock of the march of scholarship), covering the full life and canon. Part Three takes the form of Berryman's most substantial essays on *King Lear* (text, staging, sources): at once learned and accessible, they are complemented here by his correspondence with the distinguished Shakespeare scholar W. W. Greg, as well as by passages from his letters to his first mentor, Mark Van Doren. Part Four represents Berryman's big excursion into the realm of scholarly speculation: the burden of this substantial but uncompleted enquiry is to demonstrate that the playwright William Haughton might have been Shakespeare's collaborator on *The Taming of the Shrew*, and therefore that Haughton might also be instated as a likely candidate for the role of the "Mr. W.H." to whom *Shakespeare's Sonnets* is dedicated (not by the poet but by Thomas Thorpe, the publisher). Part Five marshals the most notable of his other surviving essays—on Shakespeare's *Sonnets*, the second and third parts of *Henry VI*, *2 Henry IV*, *The Comedy of Errors*, *The Two Gentlemen of Verona*, *King John*, and *Macbeth*. Lastly, an appendix contains a draft section of Berryman's final piece of writing on Shakespeare, "Shakespeare's Reality," written in March 1971.

While the critical essays in this volume really require no further introduction, the writings on *King Lear*, which are based on considerable specialist scholarship, may benefit from being located more fully in critical context; likewise, the detective work on William Houghton/Haughton and his putative collaborative relationship with Shakespeare must also now be placed in the frame with the other important research that has appeared in recent years—most notably, E.A.J. Honigmann's *Shakespeare: The "Lost" Years* (1985) and *John Weever* (1987). The second and third sections of this introduction are therefore devoted to an assessment of Berryman's work on *King Lear* and on Houghton/Haughton, respectively. The fourth section reviews the field of Berryman's studies and writings on Shakespeare in the period from the 1950s until 1971; and the fifth gives a short account of the text and annotations in this volume.

THE LABOURS ON *King Lear*

THE DIFFERENCES between the two major texts of *King Lear* are as subtle and manifold as they can appear to be intractable. Even the titles speak for different generic categories: whereas the quarto (Q), published in 1608, carries the expansive narratorial title (in modernized form), *Mr William Shakespeare: his true chronicle history of the life and death of King Lear and his three Daughters. With the unfortunate life of Edgar, son and heir to the Earl of Gloucester, and his sullen and assumed humour of Tom of Bedlam*, the folio (F) version (1623), published seven years after Shakespeare's death (and ten years after his last known active involvement in the theatre with *Henry VIII*), is given more tersely as *The Tragedy of King Lear*. The quarto runs to 2,986 lines, the folio to 2,890, so there seems to be little in it for length. Although the quarto contains some 285 lines that are not in the folio, and the folio about 120 lines not in the quarto, René Weis, in his very useful parallel-text edition (1993), has worked out that only about one-fifteenth of the whole text differs from one appearance to the other (or 7 percent of the total of the two texts taken together).[3] Yet the considerable alterations of emphasis and implication have far more to do with quality than quantity. If we assume for a moment that the folio copy postdates the copy for the quarto— which is the most appealing (seemingly logical) hypothesis, simply because F comes (chronologically) after Q—we must accept that the folio not only corrected the copy for Q, it also *revised* it. The folio would appear to have "cut" thirty-seven passages from the quarto (nearly 400 lines), for example, as well as one whole scene (IV.iii).

Furthermore, not only is the folio better printed, it was prepared for the press by Shakespeare's trusted associates, John Heminge and Henry Condell (who, incidentally, were remembered in Shakespeare's will), and has therefore been deemed the more "authoritative"—whatever that term may mean. No fewer than three times in their prefatory matter, Heminge and Condell refer to their "care" in presenting the texts. They also mention their annoyance with other "copies" as "stolne and surreptitious," alleging that such texts are "maimed, and deformed by the frauds and stealthes of injurious impostors."[4]

There is also a second quarto (Q2), printed by William Jaggard for his friend Thomas Pavier in 1619, which is now known to have been a fraud: Jaggard sought to pass off a pirated text as the early quarto from which it was copied. Notwithstanding, Jaggard's surreptitious text did incorporate certain emendations, including alterations of spelling and punctuation, and realignments of verse, all of which show that it had been corrected in the printing house (probably being compared with another copy); and it also introduced fresh errors (and missed some big ones in Q1). But it had *not* been corrected blindly and unthinkingly: on the contrary, it was appropriated with a good deal of intelligence. But the central reason why scholars have to *bother* about Q2—the text "stolen" in 1618—is that there is signal evidence that a corrected version of this same pirated text was made use of when the folio was being set up (also in Jaggard's shop) in 1623. Possibly, Jaggard used an annotated or revised copy—and we cannot discount the tantalizing possibility that it had been amended by Shakespeare himself (or some other authorized person, whether producer or editor).

In any event, the consensus among scholars is that the folio—with more than 850 verbal variants from the First Quarto (Q1)—represents a text that is close to theatrical performance: it probably has the advantage of being printed from a quarto annotated from a theatrical manuscript of some kind—presumably a prompt copy.

The First Quarto, on the other hand, the so-called Pide Bull Quarto, was printed by Nicholas Okes and sold at Nathaniel Butter's shop in St. Paul's churchyard—at the sign of the Pied Bull. The play, which may have been drafted as early as 1605, had been performed before King James on St. Stephen's night, December 26, 1606: we know this because it was entered, and so recorded, in the register of the Company of Stationers on November 26, 1607. But the copy for Q, which Shakespeare certainly did not authorize to be put into print, was appalling: so bad, in fact, that it is difficult to credit the assumption that the compositors had in front of them a manuscript that was correctly lined, let alone legible. Whoever wrote (or wrote out) the copy also used many eccentric or archaic spellings. Taxed to the utmost, and sometimes employing sheer guesswork (and ignorance), the compositors perpetrated innumerable misreadings; the verse is poorly set out, making it very difficult to scan, and hopelessly punctuated. Commas were often used in place of full periods, for want of any other kind of pointing, but the commas are as likely to be wrong as right. Jay L. Halio, in a recent edition of the quarto, says, "Some of the verse is also printed as prose": about two-thirds of the verse is correctly printed, and not mislined, he notes (though it is difficult to appreciate the full impact of the matter from Halio's amended edition).[5] In truth, some 500 lines of verse in Q are printed as prose (that is to say, a quarter of all the verse in the play); nearly 400 other lines of verse are in some way misdivided; and, ironically, some 60 lines of prose are given as verse.[6] According to Peter M. Blayney's exhaustive analysis, the printer Nicholas Okes (for whom *King Lear* was a first effort at printing a play text) employed two compositors, B and E, to set the quarto. They began in the second week of December 1607 and had finished the job by the end of the first week of January 1608—a momentous month's work. The printing was done page by page, and supposedly corrected during the process; but this was a curiously casual matter, for the corrected sheets would then be bound up indiscriminately with uncorrected ones.[7] (There may have been as many as 1,200 bound copies, though only twelve now survive— with 167 "substantive" variants distributed among them.[8]) Some lines are hypermetrical, with apparently interpolated matter, that (as some critics have argued) could have been introduced only by actors who were attempting to reconstruct their parts from memory. Alice Walker, writing in 1953, was to suggest (wrongly) that two of the boy actors, specifically those playing Goneril and Regan, reproduced the entire play, so far as their memories served, for the sake of the quarto text.[9] (It may be relevant to know that Okes was not always so careless: even as *King Lear* was being set up, he printed, scrupulously, a sermon by a man named John Pelling, *A Sermon of the Providence of God*, giving it priority over *King Lear*.[10] But he seems to have been almost consistently careless with plays: his shop was to mess up Ben Jonson's *The Case Is Alter'd* in 1609.)

I shall cite some of the simple instances that Berryman raises in his essay on the text of *King Lear* included in this volume. Lear in the very first scene says of his unorthodox abdication, in the quarto version:

> Know we have divided
> In three our kingdom, and 'tis our first intent
> To shake all cares and business of our state,
> Confirming them on younger years.

—and then, a little later, at line 75, he speaks of the third part of the kingdom that he has "confirmed on Goneril." It may be no accident that the word he used "incorrectly" in those two cases anticipates a correct use of the word at l.128, where he says: "Only we still retain / The name and all the additions to a king: / The sway, revenue, execution of the rest, / Belovèd sons, be yours; which to confirm, / This coronet part betwixt you"—the latter being the only proper occurrence of the verb in the play. Similarly, where the folio provides the meaningful explanation from Lear, "To shake all cares and business from our age," the quarto offers only what Berryman took to be this feeble and virtually meaningless variant: "To shake all cares and business of our state" (1.38). Why? Possibly because—given the evident point that the key word is "care"—Q is falsely anticipating F's line 49: "Interest of territory, cares of state" (which is left out of the quarto, with its arguably awkward abbreviation of the speech).[11]

In a later line (Act II.iv), we find in the folio, "Or rather a disease that's in my flesh," and we have to ask what happened (whether first or finally) to cause that searing line to be rendered, in the quarto version, "a disease that *lies within*," which mars the verse. Likewise, the breathlessly mounting exclamation from Lear "Oh me my heart! My rising heart! But downe" (II.iv.110) is reduced to—or maybe started out as—in the quarto: "O my heart, my heart" (1.96).

Are the differences between the two versions merely "incidental and contingent," or are they "patterned and systematic"?[12] Jay L. Halio writes, "The differences between Q and F affect changes in characterisation, structure, thematic emphasis, and to some extent plot"[13]; and many critics in recent years have argued for significant dramatic changes in the roles of Albany, Edgar, Kent, and the Fool, as well as (more obviously) in the representation of Lear, Cordelia, and Goneril (Goneril seems nastier in Q, if only a little less appalling in F).[14] According to some critics, F's omission of the "mock trial" (III.vi.12–49) strengthens and concentrates the dramatic process; others claim the folio is weaker for its absence, arguing that the scene builds tension by anticipation.[15]

To take just two further examples of a more substantive kind: Act III, Scene vi is abbreviated in F. Q contains the actual "trial" scene, and it ends with Gloucester hurrying the King away to safety. Kent laments for five lines the madness of the King, and Edgar closes the scene with a rhyming soliloquy: a recapitulation, a commentary, a labelling, a sign posting. Gary Taylor says the speech gives us "the consolations of sententiousness."[16] René Weis, on the other hand, argues: "The cutting of 'He childed as I fathered' misses out the most explicit recognition by any character in the play of the extent to which the fates of Lear and Edgar connect."[17] That is perfectly true, but one may argue that it is also precisely the reason why it is alienating to have Edgar himself say it: in a way, Edgar's "reading" of the situation seems to insult the intelligence of the audience. Weis remarks too (p. 26) that from this moment Edgar inherits the Fool's mantle, and Edgar hereafter becomes his father's minder, which seems to be a much more relevant critical observation (bearing in mind, for example, that Edgar speaks the final lines of the play—albeit in the folio only).

Act IV.iii (56 lines) does not exist at all in the folio version. Kent and an unnamed gentleman discuss the return to England of Cordelia, now blazoned as "the Queen," at the head of a French army. But the special character of this scene takes the form of an annunciation—I use the word "annunciation" advisedly, as a term often reserved for the Virgin Mary. The Gentleman reports the piteous, weeping Cordelia as "a queen / Over her passion" (13–14), for example, and says "she shook / The holy water from her heavenly eyes" (30–31). As anyone may judge from the full 30-line context, such a representation of Cordelia takes the form of a "narrative prelude" rather than a dramatic action. How to explain it, or explain it away? Grace Iopollo, in "Revising *King Lear* and Revising 'Theory,' " argues that the Gentleman's account of Cordelia establishes her as "an active, foreign queen who exercises strength." Iopollo's thesis is that whereas throughout the quarto Cordelia is presented as a figure of *action*, in the folio she is given to speech more than to action, as indicated in specific modifications: for example, Q: "What shall Cordelia *doe*, love and be silent?"; F: "What shall Cordelia *speake*? Love, and be silent." Iopollo says, "In the Quarto, filial love is tied to action and possession; in the Folio, it is tied to verbal declarations." Whereas in the quarto Cordelia comes across as an active proponent, in the folio her activities are so far redressed that she becomes passive, a voice; so far from being a power in Q, she turns out to be a subordinate in F. In respect of this scene, the argument runs, the Gentleman's report of Cordelia's arrival in England "majestically extends" the portrait of a strong queen, a powerful woman, "one of the play's moral spokespersons." The folio's omission of this passage, on the other hand, diminishes her to the status of a supporting character.[18]

Iopollo's argument is well made. But perhaps it does not take full account of the whole *mise-en-scène*, the theatrical context. For one matter, Q's representation of Cordelia here introduces the promise of a quasi-divine intercession: it smacks of a morality play. Moreover, if the Gentleman functions as a kind of chorus, the play goes on to betray the convention that a chorus tells the truth. Why picture Cordelia in this emblematized way—as redemptive, a transcendent force—only to smash our expectations with a dénouement, an outcome, in savage accord with a pagan Destiny, not the happy ending we are led to expect will follow from this scene?

The ceremonial reverence with which the Gentleman reports Cordelia seems to belong to a different kind of play from the rest of *Lear*. Graham Holderness's response to such a clash of conventions is precisely to celebrate the "diverse generic background" of the play. He points out that even the title of the play in Q claims the work at once for historiography, more legendary modes of historiography, folktale and fairy tale, as well as for romance (and restoration). The quarto swallows all modes: history, romance, comedy, tragedy. Holderness argues that Cordelia figures in IV.iii as "the potential saviour of the romance narrative": she is the subject of "an iconographic idealisation"; she has set out on "a mission of mercy, a crusade of liberation"—in short, she is a redeemer.[19]

Yet, as the plot unfolds, this idealized figure proves ineffectual in the face of evil. In the quarto, Cordelia represents "restorative romance": but the folio evidently decided this scene was entirely out of place. The modern critic, licensed by theories of postmodernism, by polyphony and dialogism, may delight in generic disruptions and inconsistencies; but one may suspect (as an alternative explanation) that it just did not *work* on the Jacobean stage, where all this trumpeting of Cordelia's redemptive virtue and saintliness may have evaporated into bathos. By speaking to a mode of stylistic and generic instability, or mixed virtuosity, the quarto lacks a focused theatrical impact, it can be argued, whereas at least the folio opts for consistency, integrity, and psychological verisimilitude. But—whether we favour quarto or folio, or some sort of admixture, the traditional conflated text—we do have a very interesting problem.

JOHN BERRYMAN officially entered the scholar-strewn lists of *King Lear* by the summer of 1944 (in his thirtieth year), when he was awarded a one-year fellowship by the Rockefeller Foundation to work on an edition of the play at Princeton University. (He had been fascinated by the problems of the text since 1937, when he won the Oldham Shakespeare scholarship—awarded on the basis of rigorous set examinations—at Cambridge.) The Project reproduced in this volume was drawn up in June that year, and on July 24 (as he recorded in his journal) he "really" began work on his edition; he wisely added in his journal that day: "I see why so many academic people pass their lives accumulating but not *doing*. The decision to begin to *do* is a real one, even in scholarship." His preparation had been assiduous to a degree, extending even to the observation that two recent but comparatively minor editions of the play—by Ridley (1935), based on the quarto, and by Kittredge (1940)—differed "in five or six hundred readings."[20] By September 25 he "began *editing*" (that is, tackling the laborious and exhausting business of annotating words, phrases, and cruces), and by May 9, 1945, he had (as he thought) "finished text of *Lear*"—though his work was still only in a fairly early draft. On August 21 of that year, he started "writing critical introd.," he noted. The Textual Introduction (which dates from the second half of 1946), published for the first time in this volume, is the most sustained passage of Berryman's introduction to survive among the diverse drafts of his commentary (which include scores of pieces, together with lists and charts, penned in notebooks and ledgers, as well as on loose sheets). Fortunately, the Rockefeller Foundation had decided in May, in response to his exciting report on work-in-progress, to renew his fellowship for a further academic year, 1945–46. Not only did the fellowship give him free time, it provided the funds to enable him to spend an intensive period scrutinizing the two copies of the quarto and the several copies of the folio at the Folger Shakespeare Library in Washington, D.C.

Given the multiple vexed problems of the texts of *King Lear*—the competing claims of the quarto, in its corrected or uncorrected state, and the folio, outlined above—Berryman devotes what may seem like an inordinately long part of his introduction to the question of provenance and priority (though it is important to bear in mind that what is reproduced below is only a portion of an introduction that was designed to cover all aspects of the play, including language, imagery, structure, characterization, and conjectural staging, in addition to textual issues such as variants, omissions, lineation, dates, and sources). But the archaeology, and the derivation, of the text is a legitimate point of access to a more "true" text; and as a dedicated student of the New Bibliography propounded by W. W. Greg (1875–1959), R. B. McKerrow (1872–1940), and A. W. Pollard (1859–1944) in the early part of this century, Berryman nurtured the notion that one might recover an original or ideal "authorial" text through or beyond the "degenerate" state of the texts as they have come down to us.[21] The folio may have been established to the satisfaction of Shakespeare's executors, but it is not without errors, both slight and substantive. Is it Shakespeare's best final shot, or a playhouse version that falls short of the "ideal" text he must have composed? The quarto is much messier still, but it cannot be dismissed, for it unarguably preserves certain compelling variants—and yet surely it does not approximate to original writ? Does Q therefore stem, directly or indirectly, from F, or do both texts derive from a lost original; or is a stemma, a family tree of texts, just too complicated to reconstruct?

With respect to Q, most modern authorities, since Alexander Schmidt in 1879,[22] allowed, even if they did not advocate, the hypothesis that it was produced not by memorial report but by shorthand taken down (more or less shiftily) during a performance. So many more mistakes in Q seemed to be attributable to a combination of mishearing and scribal error rather than to straightforward graphic error. Both E. K. Chambers and W. W. Greg inclined to a shorthand hypothesis; although neither scholar had any great faith in the theory, both felt stumped for an alternative (and their reverence for the Bard as gospeller precluded any consideration of the possibility that part of the problem might lie with Shakespeare's autograph).[23] Greg could "see no escape from the conclusion" that Q "was based on a shorthand report," he wrote in the 1930s. "If I could imagine how otherwise such a text could have been obtained, I would gladly dispense with the stenographic theory, for . . . it introduces quite considerable difficulties."[24] In 1940 he reiterated his reluctant view that the copy must have been obtained "from actual performance by some method of shorthand"[25]; likewise in his Clark Lectures, *The Editorial Problem in Shakespeare* (Oxford: Clarendon Press, 1942): "I cannot but conclude that some kind of shorthand was employed, however little I like the conclusion" (p. 96). How else can we account for the appearance of the saw "a dog's obeyed in office" (IV.vi.157) in the Q form "a dogge, so bade in office" (Q2366), and "incite" (IV.iv.27) as "in sight"—both of which Greg disdained as "grotesque mishearings"[26] —or "contentious" (III.iv.6) as "crulentious" (or perhaps "tempestious")[27]; and how, in "Striving to better, oft we marre what's well" (I.iv.369), does "oft" come to be printed as "ought," and with the comma placed after it? With the single exception of Madeleine Doran, who proposed in 1931 that the ancestor of Q could be Shakespeare's "foul" papers (a holograph manuscript, though perhaps less than "fair"), no scholar had seriously demurred, for many decades, from the hypothesis that Q must represent some form of report, very likely stenographic.[28] (The tide has decidedly turned in the last twenty years, for orthodoxy now maintains that Q bears an intimate relation to Shakespeare's manuscript; and the postmodern conception of *King Lear* as a legitimately and exhilaratingly "destabilized two-text" work, with authorial revision between Q and F, likewise holds the field of opinion.[29])

Berryman's contribution to this aspect of the problem was to attempt to prove to Greg's satisfaction that certain passages in Q could have come about only by way of shorthand. Such a demonstration would be the tribute of a disciple, since Greg had concluded his monograph of 1940 with this exhortation: "I believe that now the whole of the information is at the disposal of editors, and it appears to be high time that they set about the job of preparing a text of the play that shall be based upon a properly reasoned estimate of the evidence" (p. 190). Berryman put enormous effort into the task, as is evident not only from the Textual Introduction itself but also from the correspondence with Greg and other scholars that accompanies it below. All the same, he never did manage to draw together a conclusive case, in part because he could not get access during the war to the original manuals, most notably John Willis's *The Art of Stenographie* (1602)—the first shorthand system to be based on the alphabet (with a symbol representing a letter or a sound)—let alone samples of authentic shorthand. And yet his inability to get to grips with primary resources obliged him all the more, in a way he relished, to turn from bibliographical analysis to textual interpretation: his analysis of the problem and his consequential critical insights are the really rewarding part of this exercise. Because he himself was taking such mighty pains to explain the text, he would become furious with any scholar who offered a judgement on the basis of unsubstantiated opinion. A small case in point has to do with Edgar's description to his father, Gloucester, of the "fiend" who had supposedly led him to the cliff edge. While Q has "A [he] had a thousand noses, / Horns whelked and waved like the enridgèd sea" (IV.vi.70–71), F gives "enragèd" rather than "enridgèd." One might think the change a matter of no great moment, but Berryman understood that the genuine scholar has a duty to argue a case, with evidence drawn from every possible source, parallel, and analogue, and not just to presume upon the reader's trust. Accordingly, when Leo Kirschbaum published a study with the impertinent (or maybe it was merely provocative) title *The True Text of "King Lear"* (Baltimore, 1945), Berryman pounced on the following telling detail, which he decried as "formula, not criticism":

I am glad to see it because it is the first whole volume (published in this country) to follow Greg's general views—depreciation of the Quarto, &c. But I am sorry to see it because it is not much of a book: the author (Leo Kirschbaum) is Folio-dazzled like Schmidt, uncritical, and quite useless even to an editor, even to me. Three fourths of the book is devoted to sample passages with analyses, of which the following entire-comment-on-one-of-the-play's-real-difficulties is typical: "Q's 'enridged' for F's 'enraged' (IV.vi.71) seems definitely more poetic—but it is a mishearing by the reporter and is not Shakespeare's." The man imagines that this is *argument* (I find in my notes a body of evidence to support "enridged," which is of course necessary anyway by *durior lectio,* and explain the occurrence of "enraged"), and his book is fantastically entitled *The True Text of King Lear.* He too pleads for a new edition: "What is so badly needed" &c. I begin to think my edition will be a best-seller![30]

However, in case it is felt that Berryman might have been controverting Kirschbaum's opinion with an unexampled opinion of his own, part of the body of his evidence on this variant is to be found in footnote 37 of the Textual Introduction to *Lear* below—which I repeat here for convenience: " 'Enridged' in such a context is really not the sort of word that *can* be a corruption; but if a critic should become doubtful, it is readily and amply supported by Nashe's 'ridged tides' (iii.198) and Shakespeare's frequent nonce words, in plays of this period, in 'en-,' esp. enlink'd, entrenched, enclouded. Dr. Kirschbaum should have known this or found it out, but the truth is that he never troubles with evidence nor is troubled by doubt. 'Enraged' is the deliberate sophistication of an unfamiliar word, like too many others in the First Folio. Dr. Kirschbaum knows nothing of this process either, and nothing of misreading . . ." (Despite the availability of such evidence concerning the text and its intertexts, and the author's linguistic habits, no editor has printed "enridged" in place of "enraged.")

As to the possibility that shorthand might serve to account for the peculiarities of Q, Berryman never quite convinced even himself. In 1946 he wrote with remarkable honesty to the British polymath C. K. Ogden (associate of I. A. Richards, and the only begetter of the Basic English system): "What it comes to is that the cumulative evidence for shorthand is formidable, if the method is allowed as possible; but that specific evidence is generally uncertain. Thus, only one line in the play is spoken off-stage: I would expect the reporter to miss this, and indeed Q omits it; but Q also omits other lines—it *could* be an accident."[31] In the very month, July 1946, when he inveighed against the scholarly shortcomings of Kirschbaum, Berryman learned that the reputed scholar George Ian Duthie, based in Scotland, was just about to publish a new critical edition of *King Lear*, together with a separate monograph disallowing the case for stenography. As Laurie Maguire later put it, Duthie's *Elizabethan Shorthand and the First Quarto of "King Lear"* (Oxford: Basil Blackwell, 1949) "cogently disproved" the shorthand hypothesis.[32] Not even Willis's *Stenographie* (the best later Elizabethan system, which Berryman had hoped to vindicate) survived closer examination, despite the fact that its author had claimed in a proem: "He that is well practized in this Art, may write *Verbatim*, as fast as a man can treateably speake." (Duthie spent two pages deconstructing the term "treatable," and decided that it must have meant no more than manageable in moderate conditions.) Notwithstanding, Duthie still considered Q to be a report, not a direct transmission of an authorial manuscript, and chose for a while to adopt a theory that D. L. Patrick had invented in 1936 to account for the text of *Richard III*[33]: that the text is a memorial reconstruction made by the whole acting company (perhaps during a provincial tour, when their prompt book had somehow gone missing), with each actor dictating his own part to a scribe. (By 1960, however, in an essay for the New Shakespeare *King Lear*—edited with John Dover Wilson—"The Copy for *King Lear*, 1608 and 1623," he threw over his 1949 theory in favour of a modified version of Alice Walker's memorial hypothesis, devised in 1953, whereby Q was to be described as the product of a "transcription from foul papers by dictation, the persons involved having had some memorial knowledge of the play"[34]; and in the event that the verbal variants between Q and F were deemed to be indifferent, he preferred, like E. K. Chambers, to follow the so-called better reading in F.[35])

Berryman had noticed that Duthie was due to damn the shorthand hypothesis from a review of a work by Greg that Duthie had published in July 1943; and Duthie confirmed his own inclination in a letter to Berryman of May 22, 1946. In a response to Duthie, Berryman conceded that there were "certainly difficulties" with any shorthand theory; on the other hand, he could see nothing in favour of the quaint idea of actors sitting round a scribe and cudgelling their memories one after another; so he robustly put to Duthie certain acute questions that one might have thought unanswerable in the face of the material evidence: "The difficulties with memorial reconstruction appear to me (so far) practically insuperable, considering both the defects and the excellences of the Quarto. What would be the point, for example, in constructing an illegible prompt-book? How did *all* the actors come to be present, and why is it so long? Why are the letters [which would not normally need to be memorized by the actors, who could recite them from papers carried onto the stage] as well reported as the rest of the text? etc etc. But you will have thought of all this, and I'm eager to see your answers." Duthie was not deterred, though neither his edition of the play nor his demolition of the shorthand argument—when they finally appeared three years later—supplied any answers to Berryman's incisive questions.

All the same, the question of provenance was a relatively minor matter in Berryman's book: if it is accepted that both quarto and folio are (to use the customary moralistic figures of speech) "corrupted," "contaminated," or "sophisticated," the really big issue was how to get beyond the language as embodied in the available printed texts to the original writing of Shakespeare, or at the least to a passable reconstruction.

Nevertheless, after two years of exhaustive work on the texts, the sudden promise of Duthie's edition, which was scheduled for the fall of 1946, deflated Berryman. For some months he had diversified his efforts by undertaking to write a critical biography of Stephen Crane for the American Men of Letters series, which had absorbed some of his energies during the academic session 1945–46, but he never gave up his attention to *King Lear*. By the summer of 1946 he had virtually completed his commentary on the first three acts of the play; but the news of Duthie stopped him in his tracks—even though he distrusted his rival's qualifications as a critical editor. On May 8, 1946, he wrote to Oxford University Press in a way that may appear merely to badmouth Duthie but which was intended to draw an exact distinction between their approaches to the editorial task: "He is a very careful enquirer, and no one I think knows the 'reported' texts better except the Australian [Alfred] Hart. On the other hand, he is a technician primarily, not a literary critic, with little interest I judge in editorial decision. Now in *Lear* to be a technician is not enough, because your data are not fixed (as they are in studying the 1603 *Hamlet*)[36]: they have to be arrived at by editing. The work of J. Q. Adams, Miss Doran, Kirschbaum, is riddled with errors that can only be avoided by a critical editor."[37] Just two weeks later—pat upon his cue—Duthie wrote to Berryman for the very first time to explain his undertaking in terms that candidly confirmed the latter's worst fears: "My sole aim has been to produce a sound text: I am not concerned with problems of exegesis unless these are connected with textual problems."[38] Of his own venture, Berryman told Duthie in turn: "I've been concerned from the beginning more with recreating, justifying and explaining the text itself than with the possibly desperate uncertainties of provenance."[39] And in a letter of the selfsame date to Oxford University Press, he emphasized that he hoped in his edition to achieve more than Duthie in his by stressing the very term "exegesis" that Duthie had just confessed to treating with negligence: "Mine wishes to be, though *not* a variorum, much more minutely critical than any edition of a Shakespearean play has been hitherto. I have paid as much attention to exegesis as to establishment & justification . . ."[40]

In time, he was appalled to discover that Duthie offered no gloss, for example, on Lear's throwaway remark "This a good block" (IV.vi.171)—not even to point out the elision of "This is" or the possible meanings of "block" (the omission was rectified only a dozen years later in the Duthie-Wilson New Shakespeare edition of the play).[41] Even small and seemingly indifferent variants merited careful explanation, Berryman believed. A case in point arises at IV.vi.157, where Lear observes (in the Q version), "Through tottered raggs, smal vices do appear"; for there is a real, yet not perfectly obvious, difference between that line and F's version, "Through tattered clothes great vices do appear," which does require analytical attention. In the following notes toward an uncompleted review of Duthie's edition, Berryman's indignation becomes apparent in the awkward pomp and faltering grammar of his prose: "At IV.vi.162 Q has 'tottered,' F 'tattered,' and Dr. D not quite intelligibly comments on Q that the first 'o' is doubtless a misreading of 'a.' The judgement raises the question of how responsible we consider an editorial decision can be that fails to weigh a word in one text against what in another text is only imagined to be a misprint. Surely one would expect a critical editor to recognize as words things in his substantive texts that are words. Shakespeare uses 'tottered' in *Richard II* and *I Henry IV*, as the 'good' quartos attest, and F in one case, F3 in the other, sophisticated it to 'tatter'd.' He also uses it in the sonnets twice—cf. 'tottering' in *King John* and 'totters' in *Hamlet* Q2 (sophisticated by F to 'tatters'); indeed he never uses 'tattered' unless once in the textually v. poorly attested *Rom[eo and Juliet]*."[42] In sum, if Duthie had been more sensitive to Shakespeare's linguistic range, he would not have dismissed a common word quite so lightly: it is a poor critic who finds the fine, telling detail unremarkable—merely a matter of a compositor's mistake.

A further crucial example occurs at the notorious passage, IV.i.10, when Edgar comes face to face with his newly blinded father. The uncorrected Q has him cry out, "My father poorlie,leed" (Sig. H2ʳ), which both Q2 and the folio compositor (who could not have seen a corrected exemplar of the relevant sheet of Q1) chose to normalize, unimaginatively, to "My Father poorely led?"—presumably after noting that Gloucester is led by an old beggar. For the corrected state of the quarto, however, the press corrector must have been troubled by the dreadful inadequacy of the phrase and tried anew to decipher what must have been an intolerably ill-written passage in the copy: he came up with "my father, parti,eyd"—which many modern editors have favoured, pausing only to modernize the phrase to "parti-eyed" (meaning "parti-coloured," or blood-patched).[43] Professor Duthie, having settled in his 1949 edition for the folio's "poorely led?" (along with the timid comment "There seems little doubt then that 'parti,eyd,' is an emendation gone wrong, and that the real reading of the copy is now irrecoverable"[44]), elected for his second editorial attempt in 1960 to make use of a fresh phrase, "poorly eyed!"—accompanied by this pathetic gloss: "=with something wrong with his sight!"[45] William Empson, one of Berryman's heroes as a critic, consequently remarked in his notes on Duthie's edition: "A very proper exclamation mark. He has no ear or taste."[46] Berryman had felt irritated in a similar way by the editorial insufficiency of Duthie's earlier edition, which he criticized as "merely 'textual' " and therefore "inadequate in the recording of conjectures." He wrote of Duthie in 1949: "He is the newest victim of the notion that you can fix a text without explaining it (which involves language, grammar, sources, theatrical history, literary criticism)."[47] In another place, anticipating Duthie's production, he insisted too: "Above all, it isn't the introductions that edit your text . . . What counts most in Textual Criticism is the individual's day to day decisions, based on everything he can summon . . ."[48] He had long suspected himself of feeling too much respect for what he now denigrated as "textual technicians": he had felt obliged to bow down to what Paul Werstine later styled the "scriptural status" of New Bibliography.[49] What he had learned in the two years during which he had been labouring as an editor was that an evidently corrupt text will not yield all its answers to supposedly objective bibliographical criteria, for the editor must bring to bear the full armoury of the literary critic before he can claim to produce what Duthie called "a sound text." His rumblings and grumblings amounted to a new rationale, a challenge to the putatively "scientific" principles of Greg and his compeers.

On March 22, 1945, while still in his first year on the text of *King Lear*, Berryman was to try out for the crux at IV.i.10 the emendation "bloody-eyed." Accordingly, in the earliest state of his commentary, written at about that date, he ventured this fuller entry:

As Greg says, "one of the worst cruxes of the play." The weakness of the F reading, evidently derived from the uncorrected Q sheet, must always have been felt by readers and actors as grotesque; QF "authority," however, has perpetuated it. But it cannot be right: the character of the Q corrector's changes shows that he was trying seriously to correct what he saw to be a misreading (or a misprinting) of the copy before him; no guess, such as he indulged elsewhere, would have given a reading so difficult. Greg concludes: "There seems little doubt then that 'parti,eyd' is an emendation gone wrong, and that the real reading of the copy is now irrecoverable."

I suggest that behind both the Q readings stood a poorly formed "bloody-eyd!," the hyphen being read twice as a comma; the Corrector made out "eyd" correctly the second time, but did worse on "oo" than the compositor (or the word may have stood "bloodi-eyd"). NED's only quot. for "bloody-eyed" is from Byron, but its materials for "obvious combinations" were often deficient.

Shak. has "bloody fac'd," 2 *Henry IV*, I.iii.22 (line only in F), and "bloody-sceptred," *Macbeth*, IV.iii.104. I do not think the anticipation, by more than 40 lines, of "Bless thy sweet eyes, they bleed" is an insuperable objection to the emendation. Edgar's terrible outcry "World world" shows that he sees at once his father's plight (consisting solely, indeed, in blindness) and with much less graphic justification I believe the present reading would be defensible.[50]

He further noted, on the same page of his draft, the analogous usages "parti-coated" (from *Love's Labour's Lost*, V.ii.776) and "hollow-ey'd" (*Errors*, V.i.240), as well as Spenser's construction "so watchfull and well eyed" in *The Faerie Queene* (IV.iii.7). All in all, it was a creditable first effort, exploiting the resources of his critical reading, which he was to explain more fully in a letter to Mark Van Doren of May 17, 1945 (see text below). But he would not relinquish the problem without deeper reflection; by February 16, 1946, as he told W. W. Greg, he had pored over "six conjectures seriously entertained for 'parti,eyd' at various times, but I have been able to discard more or less conclusively four of these and all I am certain of is that the word ended '-ey'd' (cf euill-eyd *Cym*, sad-eyed *Henry V*, thicke eyde *I H. IV* etc), a hyphen being twice misread, perhaps, as a comma. Since this savage passage has come up, what do you think of 'emptie-ey'd'? Cf v. 3. 189–90; 'empty-hearted' i.i.155; 'A carrion Death, within whose empty eye' *Mer*. This conjecture aims at Shakespeare, of course; it doesn't pretend to know exactly what chaos the copy had, although the second syllable is precise: *lie* Qa : *ti* Qb : *tie* conj." In writing so, he was risking a dual assault on such a crux, blending material evidence (the possibility of graphical misreading, the mistaking of hyphen for comma) with interpretative analysis ("its general dramatic relevance"—as he explained to Van Doren—or "Edgar's terrible outcry" and "at once perceived by Edgar"). He was also risking a gambit, the real possibility of a confrontation with Greg, who had purported throughout his own scholarly writings to deal virtually without exception in "objective" or bibliographically verifiable evidence.

What was perhaps Berryman's last attempt at the "poorly led/partieyed" crux figures in another letter to Greg, dated four months later. In 1960 G. I. Duthie was to record John Dover Wilson's undeveloped, and promptly rejected, conjecture that Shakespeare's elusive term might have been "pearly"—meaning "with cataracts, cf. *Gent.* 5.2.13. But [Dover Wilson] now feels it too definite for the context, though the white plasters provided at 3.7.105–6 might suggest cataracts."[51] Unknown to Duthie and Wilson, fourteen years earlier Berryman had independently expounded this fuller and more persuasive case for "pearly-ey'd?"—adducing graphic, contextual, dramatic, and intertextual evidence, and all with a fine critical flourish—in his letter to Greg (given in full on p. 246), from which I extrapolate here for convenience:

Pearl was "a thin white film or opacity growing over the eye: a kind of cataract." Nashe has it, and Middleton, and there is a dialectal combination "pearl-blind." The "flax and whites of eggs" applied to Gloucester's eyes might give, at first glance, precisely such an appearance. Shakespeare has the word himself in *Two Gentlemen* (unrecognized by Schmidt & Onions but known to Wilson):

    [*Proteus*] Blacke men are Pearles, in beauteous Ladies eyes.
    [*Julia*] 'Tis true, such Pearles as put out Ladies eyes (V.ii.11).

Pearly I take as analogous to "gouty" (*Troilus, Timon*), meaning "afflicted with a pearl"; and the combination one of Shakespeare's sixteen with "-eyed," similar to "gouty-legg'd" (which occurs, as a matter of fact, in Cotgrave).

On this conjecture, the compositor got the first part nearly right (allowing *oo:ea*), whereas the press-reader messed it up (the compositor perhaps helping) but got the second part exactly except for the hyphen, which he thought a comma. The Folio scribe, I agree, emended Qa; Shakespeare's reading, if I am right, being one he would probably have disliked, I don't think it necessary even to suppose the playhouse manuscript illegible here . . . More-over the reading has singular imaginative interest. It enriches the destruction of sight imagery (dart your blinding flames into her scornful eyes—the web and the pin—squenes the eye—I'll pluck ye out—turn our imprest lances in our eyes—see thy cruel nails Pluck out his poor old eyes) which embodies a chief moral theme and supplies the context of Gloucester's actual blinding. Then the weeping & pearls nexus is so frequent that it may suggest Glouces-ter's weeping. And considering the quibble in *Two Gentlemen*, it does not need a Blunden to imagine that Shakespeare remembered in the last Act, when describing this scene, his language in it, and with a meaning of his own hovering under Edgar's, wrote of "his bleeding *rings*, Their *precious stones* new lost."

I wonder. What do you think?

Berryman knew he was dangerously tempting the bibliographical beak, for—as he observed in March 1946—Greg was "as eloquent on the necessity for emendation as he is resolutely skeptical of any par-ticular emendation which comes to his attention."[52]

PETER W.M. BLAYNEY, in the introduction to his majestic *The Texts of "King Lear" and Their Origins*, Vol. I (1982), finds it nec-essary—in order to clear the ground for a fresh analysis of the texts—to take Greg severely to task on two specific points. His first complaint is that Greg muddles his definitions of the areas of study that consti-tute "bibliography." There are in fact three related areas of study: (i) "pure" bibliography (dealing with books as material objects), (ii) textual criticism, which is strictly non-bibliographical, and (iii) the "metacritical" form of textual criticism, which includes the science or art of conjectural emendation.[53] Greg's misleading, and indeed damaging, answer to the problem was to collapse the first two of those three distinct disciplines when, in "Bibliography—An Apologia" (1932), he coined the term "critical bibliography" to cover the whole case and subsequently to argue, in his influential lecture "The Func-tion of Bibliography in Literary Criticism Illustrated in a Study of the Text of *King Lear*" (1933), that in any case bibliography and textual criticism are "the same." The word "critical," Greg maintained, might just as well be dropped from the reckoning, since critical prob-lems are "essentially bibliographical." Thus, because he proposed to subsume textual criticism within his definition of bibliography, Greg left no room at all for any definition of the third discipline—the "metacritical"—which would have allowed into the study the poten-tially subjective and wayward methods of literary interpretation. Naturally, Greg sought to account for every textual problem with a bibliographical demonstration. Consequently, Blayney's second charge relates to the major error that Greg committed with regard to *King Lear* because of the false logic of his bibliographical judgement: a "presupposition in the guise of a conclusion": that the folio represents an "earlier" text, and that therefore the Q text is nothing more than a corrupt reconstruction of the F text. As far as Greg was concerned, it was a truth universally acknowledged that Q was always to be found guilty of altering F.[54] Indeed, Greg's stance on this question amounts to an utter "prejudice," since there is in fact no evidence whatever to show that F existed before Q. "The differences between Q and F are not—most emphatically not—primary evidence for Q's origin," Blayney insists (p. 6); and again: "What Greg offers as an assessment of the Q text is not in any sense a bibliographical argument . . . Nor is it really a *textual* argument as such, but the polemical defence of a presupposition founded on a purely metacritical judgement" (p. 7). In terms of both definition and practice, therefore, Greg has much to answer for in misleading the course of study of the texts of *King Lear*—not least because of his ruling that bibliography is not concerned with the contents of a book "in a literary sense" ("The Function of Bibliography," p. 243). It was in just that respect that John Berryman, even as early as 1946, had begged leave to differ from Greg: bibliography (or textual criticism), he proposed, unduly hampered itself when it purported to cast out literary criticism.

More recently, Laurie E. Maguire, in *Shakespearean Suspect Texts: The "Bad" Quartos and Their Contexts* (1996), has launched an entertaining but similarly unsparing assault on the pretensions of W. W. Greg. The trouble with Greg, according to Maguire's eager argument, is that he was constantly passing off personal critical judgements (which are essentially optative) as bibliographical (scientifically deictic) facts. "Textual criticism offers explanations which may be true; bibliography finds an explanation which must be true."[55] Thus, though he posed as the unwaveringly objective bibliographer, in truth Greg was very often the partial critic, so that—as Blayney had remarked—"material analysis and textual interpretation" came to be "subsumed under one heading."[56] It is best to acknowledge that any critical edition is inescapably a work of interpretation, Maguire insists. The hankering for demonstrable fact is necessarily constrained by the strengths and limitations of individual critical skills—and so it should be—whatever New Bibliography professed to the contrary.

It was just such a reckoning with the potentially overweening claims of bibliography (particularly as embodied in G. I. Duthie's work on *King Lear*) that Berryman arrived at in the mid-1940s. Impersonal and supposedly scientific criteria, he came to believe, were not adequate to the task in hand, which required excellent literary criticism to underpin the material resources of bibliography. On such a basis, Duthie fell short, because he confessed himself to be what Berryman termed "a textual technician"; Duthie's edition, Berryman wrote, was "merely 'textual,' not exegetical, not illustrative, not critical and not aesthetic."[57] To achieve what he wanted for his own work, Berryman realized, he would have to outface the majesty of the great Greg, who had laboured all his life to lift bibliographical scholarship out of the polluting hands of subjective criticism. He therefore knew that he was to some extent affronting what he himself regarded as the supreme court of appeal when he boldly wrote to Greg in February 1946—his recourse to the rhetoric of the courtroom betrays as much—"I submit that the mechanical standards for acceptance of an emendation should not, even must not, be so rigid as is customary and right in other texts. I hope you can agree with this; the necessity for emendation is so widespread in *Lear*, as you have said, that the principles involved seem to me very important. In a sense one must emend through the error to the copy, and through that to the actor, hoping to reach Shakespeare. Unhappily the uncertainty of the limiting conditions tends to open the field to alternatives; one can only hope that if one works hard enough and long enough, and keeps one's head, the competitors will prove unworthy."[58] Greg promptly replied, later the same month—"In view of the multiplicity of possible agents of corruption in Q, the legitimate field of conjecture and emendation is, as you say, very wide, and it is difficult to assign relative importance to the several agencies"—but in view of the fact that in his very next sentence he connected his comment directly with the problems of the handwriting of the copy for Q, it seems quite evident that he had not taken anything like the full force of Berryman's challenge to the "mechanical standards" of bibliography and textual criticism. Greg's response to Berryman might well appear to have been permissive, but Berryman was actually bespeaking more than his old hero would have cared to concede.

"Editing I cannot but think a job for literary critics," Berryman wrote elsewhere, which was as much as to say that he admitted himself to be a better literary critic than a bibliographical analyst.[59] It is exactly what any reader of his criticism would wish, for we ultimately look to the poet not for exact scholarship but for imaginative insight. Notwithstanding, it is greatly to be regretted that Berryman never found the occasion to finish his edition of *King Lear*—or to publish portions of his introduction in the form of articles—for a good part of his critical and textual commentary has a lasting validity, illuminating and invigorating our understanding of a vexed text. Randall McLeod was to write, as late as 1983, "Even now, Duthie's edition remains the only thorough, editorially explicit commentary on the variants between Q and F *Lear*, and the most conscientious defence of the conflationist position."[60] Berryman's *Lear* is the rival that Duthie required—and it still makes a significant contribution to the critical debate.

However, even if we did not get Berryman's edition of *King Lear*, we have gained his first masterpiece, *Homage to Mistress Bradstreet*, which took inspiration directly from *Lear*—though critics of Berryman have not yet evaluated to the full the degree to which his poem is fired by Shakespeare.[61]

WILLIAM SHAKESPEARE, WILLIAM HOUGHTON, WILLIAM HAUGHTON

BERRYMAN MADE FINE but quite exhausting use of his Guggenheim Fellowship for the year 1952–53. His intentions were to undertake creative writing (of which *Homage to Mistress Bradstreet* was the eventual issue) and a critical biography of Shakespeare, for which (as he told the foundation in an outline)

It would be necessary to assemble, select from, and adjust to each other the results of many broad enquiries: documentary, historical, paleographical, bibliographical, editorial, theatrical, linguistic, genetic (sources), critical (including questions of value, comparison, style, form, substance, versification, image-study, etc.), psychiatric and psychoanalytic, ritual, symbolic . . . The biographer must be capable of a book . . . neither unduly confident nor perpetually reserved, presenting an image unified and acceptable.[62]

He was not unaware that his plans were idealistic, but it was only after some months that he realized the true dimensions of his project. "Oh my god!" he wrote in October 1952, "Shakespeare. That multiform & encyclopedic bastard." His friend Elizabeth Bettman has vivid memories of his anguished efforts to recover the personalities of both Shakespeare and Anne Bradstreet (for the poem) during his residence in Cincinnati early that year:

The six months he was here, he was . . . obsessed with the idea that he, John Berryman, could uncover the truth of Shakespeare's identity. It would appear that on this score he confused imaginative reality and the goal of a biographer. I used to kid him about his necrophilia, and in truth he did seem intent on recapturing the lives of these two poets in the sense of trying to relive their experience. He identified personally with the period of Shakespeare's tragedies, and would speculate at length on the subject of the personal tragedies that induced the "dark period." To use his own expression, John talked "like fire." Sometimes one had the feeling he was talking through his speculations, trying them out on diverse friends.[63]

He began a systematic study later in 1952, working first on *Two Gentlemen of Verona* and the *Henry VI* plays and proceeding with formidable amounts of groundwork. In particular he aimed to read all the plays known to have been written between 1570 and 1614, to digest in chronological order those works that Shakespeare read (bringing H. R. Anders's *Shakespeare's Books* of 1904 completely up-to-date), and to pay special attention to the matter of when he read them. At some time in the autumn, however, he began to itch for "discoveries," being incited principally by the conviction that, if Shakespeare really did have a collaborator on *The Taming of the Shrew*, his identity should finally be unearthed.

By January 22, 1953, he felt sufficiently confident of his work as to place on record some tentative disclosures, and abstracted three findings:

1. I think it probable that the William Houghton praised by John Weever in 1599 for his beauty, war-practice, and wit, is, like the other Houghtons praised by Weever, a Lancashire man, and is to be identified with the playwright William Haughton (the name being identical), whom I consider then, as connected with Shakespeare earlier in the Lancashire end and from 1597 in the London theatre, to be the best candidate ever proposed as the young man to whom most of Shakespeare's sonnets were addressed.
2. I think it possible on many grounds that the very early play *The Rare Triumphs of Love and Fortune*, which was produced before the Queen by Derby's men in 1582 and which 30 years later influenced so extraordinarily Shakespeare's last three plays, may be by Shakespeare himself.
3. I feel quite sure on many grounds that Shakespeare's collaborator in *The Taming of the Shrew* was William Haughton (who also wrote, of plays that survive, not only *Englishmen for My Money* and *Grim*, but also *Wily*

Beguiled and *Wit of a Woman*) and therefore the Friend of the Sonnets of Shakespeare.[64]

It is not evident why Berryman enumerated his findings in such an order, since items 1 and 3 are obviously interlinked, whereas the attribution to Shakespeare of the anonymous *The Rare Triumphs of Love and Fortune* would seem to be another matter.[65] However, in respect of 1 and 3, Berryman desired, as he said, to link two possibly distinct persons, William Houghton and William Haughton (both of whom were almost certainly known to Shakespeare), whose names were virtually identical. Were they in fact the same person? And do the initials of that individual deliver the identity of the "Mr. W.H." to whom *Shakespeare's Sonnets* was dedicated by the printer?

The William Houghton in question (it is relevant and useful to preserve the difference of spelling) is addressed by John Weever (1576–1632), an aspiring man of letters who has recently come down (though perhaps without a degree) from Queen's College, Cambridge, in his volume of *Epigrammes* (1599), "In Gulielmum Houghton":

> Faine would faire *Venus* sport her in thy face,
> But Mars forbids her his sterne marching place:
> Then comes that heau'nly harbinger of *Ioue*,
> And ioyns with Mars & with the queen of Loue
> And thus three gods these gifts haue given thee,
> Valour, wit, fauour, and ciuilitie.

Weever is speaking, it would seem, to a young man of beauty and wit who might at some time have been a soldier. Since Weever's volume of so-called epigrams also addresses verses to prominent figures in the main theatrical companies, including Shakespeare and his late patron Ferdinando Stanley, Lord Strange (who gets two poems), Drayton, Jonson, and Marston, and the actor Edward Alleyn, as well as the poets Daniel, Warner, and Spenser (who had died on January 13, 1599), Berryman thought it was natural to infer that the William Houghton addressed in the epigram could be happily identified with another playwright, William Haughton, who had begun writing for the theatrical manager Philip Henslowe by the important date of 1597.[66] R. B. McKerrow, when editing Weever's *Epigrammes* (1911), had not sought any connection between the Houghton of the epigram and the playwright; though A. C. Baugh, in his fascinating

edition (1917) of Haughton's *Englishmen for My Money*, indicated
that he was cognisant of the possible connection but did not set store
by it.[67] The slight difference in the spellings presents little problem,
since the dramatist Haughton's autographs in Henslowe's diary are
always "a," while his will in 1605 is "o." Henslowe calls Haughton
"yonge" in 1597. Accordingly, since John Weever is known to have
been a Lancashire man, Berryman set out to rehearse the evidence
for connecting the William Houghton of the epigram with a notable landed family, the Houghtons of Lancashire; and thence, to
strengthen the possible links between Houghton and Shakespeare, to
pursue the perilous theory (first bruited by Charlotte Stopes in 1914)
which holds that a certain "William Shakeshafte" named in the will
of Alexander Houghton, master of Lea Hall in Lancashire, in 1581,
could be identified with our Shakespeare.[68] (The dramatist's grandfather Richard is recorded as "Shakstaff" in one document of 1533
—which E. K. Chambers understood to read "Shakeschafte"—and it
is reckoned that there were as many as 83 variant spellings of the
family name; though it has also been demonstrated that Shakeshafte
was a well-established local surname in the Preston area.)[69] E. K.
Chambers, in his *Elizabethan Stage* (I, 1923, p. 280), had raised the
tantalizing implications of the will of Alexander Houghton—"Was
then William Shakeshafte a player in 1581?" he mused—but unaccountably forgot about this matter in *William Shakespeare: Facts and
Problems* (1930); though he would return to it in *Shakespearean
Gleanings* (1944), where he built in part on the intervening work of
Oliver Baker, *In Shakespeare's Warwickshire and the Unknown Years*
(London: Simpkin Marshall, 1937).[70] Berryman was therefore tread-
ing in 1952 on fairly fresh ground; and it is only in the years since
his death that it has been more closely gone over—most assiduously
by E.A.J. Honigmann.[71]

The will of Alexander Houghton, executed on August 3, 1581, and
proved on September 12 the same year, was first printed by the Rev.
G. J. Piccope in the second part of his *Lancashire and Cheshire Wills*
(Chetham Society, LI [1860], p. 237). It included in its provisions
this conscientious (and yet curiously conditional) bequest to his half
brother, Thomas Houghton:

all maner of playe clothes yf he be mynded to keppe and doe keppe playeres.
And yf he wyll not keppe and manteyne playeres then yt is my wyll that Sir
Thomas Heskethe knyghte shall haue the same . . . playe clothes. And I
most hertelye requyre the said Sir Thomas to be ffrendlye unto ffoke Gyllome and William Shakeshafte now dwellynge with me and eyther to take

them vnto his Servyce or els to helpe theym to some good master as my tryste ys he will.[72]

The putative player Shakeshafte was to be given an annuity of "ffortye shyllings": it was a generous legacy, quite enough to endow the recipient with legal and economic status—and enough, it is suggested, to give the eighteen-year-old Shakespeare (if it was he) the leisure to return the following year to Stratford, where he would woo, impregnate, and marry Anne Hathaway. Still more, if Shakeshafte was Shakespeare, Houghton's will provides remarkable evidence, as it has also been argued, to suggest that this wholly unexpected Lancashire patron so enabled the young player to enter the service (perhaps in the first instance) of Alexander's heir, Thomas Houghton, who is understood to have maintained players at his residences, Lea Hall and Hoghton Tower.[73] Whereupon, at the latest by Thomas Houghton's death in November 1589, and almost certainly a good while before, Shakespeare might have joined the entourage of Sir Thomas Hesketh, who assuredly kept a troupe of players and enjoyed taking them on tour. Hesketh's residence at Rufford Old Hall in Lancashire was only ten miles from the Houghton residence at Lea, and just a few miles also from both Lathom and Knowsley, country houses of the Earl of Derby (Lord Lieutenant of Lancashire and Lord High Steward) and his son, Ferdinando, Lord Strange, to whom Hesketh was related by marriage. (Lady Strange, incidentally, was a direct ancestor of Diana, Princess of Wales.) The Derby Household Books preserve this tantalizing entry for December 30, 1587, at Knowsley: "Sr. Tho. hesketh plaiers went awaie"; and so it has been fondly conjectured that perhaps Shakespeare had made one of that company.[74] In addition to their social contacts, these families were in any event allied by virtue of the fact that they formed the heart of a redoubtable network of Catholic recusants; and research is gradually being adduced to reinforce the old theory that Shakespeare was probably introduced into this Catholic circle because of his own father's continuing recusancy in Stratford-upon-Avon.[75] John Cottam, who was master of the Free Grammar School at Stratford between 1579 and 1582, hailed from Lancashire, where his family were neighbours and business associates of the Houghtons; his brother, Thomas, who became a Jesuit priest, was apprehended in 1580, arraigned with Thomas Campion in 1581, and executed at Tyburn in May 1582—at a date coinciding with brother John's departure from Stratford (it has been inferred that John would no longer conform in religious observance). Even though Shakespeare was fifteen by the time John Cottam arrived to take up his post at Stratford, and might have already left school to help with his father John's business, Cottam and his convictions would have been known to John Shakespeare, whom we now understand to have been a lifelong recusant (and in any case, Cottam would have taught Shakespeare's younger brothers). Moreover, one of Cottam's predecessors as schoolmaster, Simon Hunt, who certainly did teach William Shakespeare between 1571 and 1575, had quit his post in Stratford precisely to join the Jesuits on the Continent.

As for Shakespeare's career in the theatre, it would have been a ready step for him to move on from Hesketh's players to Lord Strange's Men (who took possession of the Rose Theatre in 1591). On the death of his father in 1593, Ferdinando Stanley, Lord Strange (who was Shakespeare's first authenticated professional patron), became Earl of Derby; and at Strange's premature death in April 1594, his company was taken into the service of his brother-in-law, the first Lord Hunsdon, Lord Chamberlain. (Shakespeare was quite well enough reputed in the London theatre by September 1592 for the acidulous and dying Robert Greene to berate him as an "absolute *Iohannes fac totum*, . . . in his owne conceit the onley Shake-scene in a countrey.") Thus Shakespeare's progression from Lancashire to London is a beguilingly logical one; and Andrew Gurr has recently marshalled a wealth of corroborative evidence to show that Shakespeare must have progressed from Strange's/Derby's Men briefly to Pembroke's Men and thereafter to the Lord Chamberlain's Men.[76] The Lancashire connection may help to explain among other curiosities why Shakespeare selected as one of two trustees for his interest in the ground lease of the Globe in 1599 a London goldsmith named Thomas Savage. The reason could well have been because the Savage family were friends of the Houghtons in Lancashire; and Thomas Savage himself, a native of Rufford, was even related by marriage to Lady Hesketh, a Catholic recusant (he was to leave her twenty shillings in his will).[77] Berryman noted with fascination Keen and Lubbock's showing that a descendant of Thomas Savage "married a relative of the 18th century antiquary William Oldys whose unfulfilled undertaking 'to furnish a bookseller in the Strand . . . with ten years of the life of Shakespeare unknown to the biographers' has always baffled enquiry."[78] Perhaps there was really something in it. If Shakespeare did follow such an unusual route to the London theatre in his early manhood, it would help us also to solve certain other outstanding puzzles or legends, including the antiquarian John Aubrey's report in 1681: "He understood Latine pretty well: for he had been in his younger yeares a Schoolmaster in the Countrey." As scholars now understand the situation, he could have been both schoolmaster and player while enjoying the patronage of either Thomas Houghton at Lea Hall or Sir Thomas Hesketh at Rufford Old Hall; indeed, he might have tutored Thomas Houghton's sons Richard (who was to succeed his father as head of the family in 1589) and William—whose date of birth, though not officially recorded, must have been about 1571 (he was the second of a terrible total of seventeen children born over a period of nineteen years), which would mean that by the close of the 1580s he would have attained a suitable age to be the friend and addressee of Shakespeare's sonnets.[79]

However, to fillet a red herring, this particular William Houghton, the second son of Thomas Houghton (who inherited the Lancashire estates from his half brother, Alexander Houghton, the benefactor of "Shakeshafte"), settled for what must have been a fairly private but well-endowed life on his estate at Grimsargh Hall, just six miles from his older brother's larger estate at Lea. He married, presumably in the 1590s, Grace Sherburne (the daughter of a sturdy parliamentarian, Sir William Sherburne), who bore him six children; and he died in 1642, at about the age of seventy. Apart from the possibility that Shakeshafte/Shakespeare may have known him as a child in Lancashire, that his age would be about right for the "friend" of the *Sonnets*, and that his initials are for scholars to die for, there is nothing further to link him with Shakespeare at any time in his life. The case seems slim, except for the information, or the impression, conveyed by John Weever's epigram 6.4 (published in 1599), which certainly appertains to this particular William Houghton. (For one matter, the epigram in question is obviously a pendant to 6.3, which takes the form of an elegy for William Houghton's father, Thomas; and 6.1 likewise hymns the recently deceased Sir Richard Houghton, William's older brother who has therefore departed the "gold-gilded tower" of his home in Lancashire.) Blessed by the gods, William embodies "Valour, wit, fauour, and ciuilitie": the eulogy could be purely flummery, a gesture of flattery towards a sweet-favoured, fine-mannered youth. (The title page of Weever's volume may suggest some self-approval: *Epigrammes in the Oldest Cut and Newest Fashion*.[80]) There is no doubt but that Weever was acquainted with the members of the Houghton family, and he took care to extol the living and the dead. The entire collection of epigrams is dedicated to "the Right Worshipfull and worthie honoured Gentleman Sir Richard Houghton of Houghton Tower, Knight: Iustice of Peace, and Quorum: High Sheriffe of Lanchshire, &c."; so it seems fairly evident that he has already benefited to a degree from the family's favours, and presumably anticipates further patronage. But we cannot be sure that he knew them well, or was more to them than a grateful client.

Nor is it easy to argue that he had even met Shakespeare, let alone knew of a long-standing relation between the playwright and his patrons (despite the fact that the bulk of the epigrams apropos the Houghtons is neatly balanced by epigrams addressed to Shakespeare and his fellows). Yet Professor Honigmann has made the keen point that, alone among the numerous epigrams in his book, Weever's verses to Shakespeare take the form of a "Shakespearean" sonnet, which might cannily intimate that he had conned a few of the unpublished sonnets to which he otherwise makes no direct reference (if he knew Shakespeare's sonnets to be in surreptitious circulation, he was showing a creditable but probably uncharacteristic self-restraint). This transcription corrects some undisputed spelling mistakes, and expands abbreviations:

Honie-tong'd Shakespeare when I saw thine issue
I swore *Apollo* got them and none other,
Their rosie-tainted features cloth'd in tissue,
Some heaven born goddesse said to be their mother:
Rose-chekt *Adonis* with his amber tresses,
Faire fire-hot *Venus* charming him to love her,
Chaste *Lucretia* virgine-like her dresses,
Proud lust-stung *Tarquine* seeking still to prove her:
Romeo Richard; more whose names I know not,
Their sugred tongues, and power attractive beuty
Say they are Saints although that Saints they shew not
For thousands vowes to them subjective dutie:
They burn in love thy children *Shakespear* het them,
Go, woo thy Muse more Nymphish brood beget them.

Leaving aside the arguable merits of the sonnet as literature (the sestet in particular declines into a gawky struggle between syntax and rhyme, and a desperate effort to sustain the extended metaphor begotten by the pun on "issue": Shakespeare's works, he is flailing to say, seem like the product of a supernatural agency), there is no indication either that he knew the man or that he had seen any of his plays produced on stage. The nub of the argument that Honigmann so impressively set out in the 1980s vis-à-vis John Weever (the nub of which Berryman was likewise trying to persuade himself in 1952) is that *Epigrammes* affords strong circumstantial evidence to support the theory, supposedly intimated in Alexander Houghton's will, that

Shakespeare spent some of his apprentice years in Lancashire. But to judge from this sonnet, Weever had surely not met Shakespeare: after mentioning (as Honigmann conceded in his *Shakespeare: The "Lost" Years* only in a footnote[81]) works that were already in print by 1598 —*Venus and Adonis, The Rape of Lucrece, Romeo and Juliet,* and either *Richard III* or *Richard II*—Weever candidly, or modestly, admits that he does not know the subjects of any other works, though his phrasing seems to imply that he at least knows of their existence. Accepting Honigmann's point that the sonnet to Shakespeare dates from 1598, a year before his volume of epigrams saw print, it is possible that certain phrases Weever deploys in lines 1 and 10 derive from Francis Meres's oft-quoted *Palladis Tamia* (1598): "The sweet witty soul of Ovid lives in mellifluous and honey-tongued Shakespeare, witness his *Venus and Adonis,* his *Lucrece,* his sugred sonnets among his private friends, etc." Of course, it may also be possible that it was the other way round, but that is frankly unlikely: Weever patently gets in a muddle somewhere between "honie-tong'd" and "sugred tongues," losing the point of his sweet conceit; and even though "honey-tongued" was available in *Love's Labour's Lost* (V.ii.334), it is irresistible to believe that if Weever had read that play he would have hastened to mention it and not simply confess he did not know of other "names" in Shakespeare's works, whether protagonists or titles.[82] After all, Weever is nothing if not a name-dropper, seeking status by association (he later became, appropriately enough, a good antiquarian). In sum, it is almost certainly coincidental that he comes from Lancashire, where he is a suitor to the Houghton family, and that simultaneously he seeks to cultivate Shakespeare and other theatre folk. The proximity of the epigrams dedicated to these several individuals tells us nothing at all. Nevertheless, it is vaguely possible that his panegyric to William Houghton, to the degree that it rises above convention, may just tell us something about the inherent qualities of a youth who grew to be loved by Shakespeare.

Berryman was always worried that some other scholar might beat him into print with an announcement as to the identity of William Houghton and William Haughton, or the latter's possible involvement in the writing of *The Taming of the Shrew.* At the bleak hour of five o'clock in the morning of June 18, 1955, he wrote the following memo to himself: "I've waited long enough, & too long. Somebody is going to catch on either to Houghton—W. *Haughton* or to *Engl.—X-Shr* [the affinity between Haughton's *Englishmen for My Money* and the non-Shakespearean passages of *The Shrew*], or both, and wreck me." He had been persuaded of his case, he noted in a hectic hand, for two and a half years. With regard to the status of William Houghton as a plausible candidate for the role of Mr. W.H., the first scholar to declare himself in a published article was Frederick J. Pohl, just three years later, with "On the Identity of 'Mr. W.H.' " (*The Shakespeare Newsletter*, December 1958, p. 43), though surprisingly he made no mention of Weever's helpful epigram. (The only further evidence that Pohl brings forward in his book *Like to the Lark* [1972] is the unconvincing notion that Shakespeare embedded syllables of the name William Houghton in Sonnets 80, 81, and 95 —as in "AltHOUGH in me each part WILL be forgOTTEN"—which speaks for a sad recrudescence of the silly old cipher school of criticism.[83]) It is greatly to Berryman's credit that he admitted to himself that the evidence for the Lancashire W.H. was not in itself enough to convince the serious scholarly community: his sense of that grave insufficiency in the evidence was what drove him on to seek to link Lancashire and London, where the name Houghton (in either spelling) was disconcertingly common.

WILLIAM HAUGHTON was not, it is safe to say, the same person as one Mr. William Houghton, son of Thomas Houghton, of Lea in Lancashire. But if, as we may suppose, the provincial Houghton lived out his fairly long life in relative obscurity, his namesake, who must have been born at roughly the same date (in the early 1570s), exercised his not inconsiderable talents as a dramatist for a highly productive period of five years during his mid-twenties, 1597–1602. Indeed, he became very famous for at least two generations, though he is now virtually forgotten. He wrote principally for Henslowe, who first makes reference to him in his diary on November 5, 1597, when advancing to "yonge Horton" the sum of ten shillings for "a boocke," or playscript. (He is actually the first writer to be specifically named in Henslowe's diary, and the fact that thereafter Henslowe refers to him by a number of different spellings—he is Harton, Horton, Hauton, Hawton, Haughtoun, Howghton, Haulton, Harvghton, as well as Haughton, the spelling favoured by the dramatist himself (though never, as chance would have it, Houghton)—is of no account. It was merely a matter of orthographic whim, since spelling had not yet been standardized. Aside from Haughton's writings for the stage, almost nothing is known of his life. From allusions in the work to philosophy and classical antiquity, it is inferred that he went to Oxford or Cambridge, but no documentation survives to confirm the case.[84]

His best-known play (now quite comprehensively neglected) is also the only work he is known to have written on his own: *Englishmen for My Money, or, A Woman Will Have Her Will* (1597–98), produced for the Admiral's Men at the Rose, which was almost certainly better known at the time of its production by its subtitle (and Philip Henslowe, who commissioned the work, knew it by that title). It was a huge success, and hugely influential. But Haughton found his forte, or was especially valued, as a collaborative writer, principally for Henslowe's play factory: among a considerable body of plays in which he had a hand (more than twenty works, of which some were never printed, while others are no longer extant) were as many as ten written with John Day, and a number with Anthony Chettle, Thomas Dekker, and Wentworth Smith (the last of whom would also serve to witness Haughton's will in 1605[85]). It has been reasonably surmised that one play in particular, *The Spanish Moor's Tragedy*, co-authored with Marston, Day, and Dekker in 1599–1600 (but perhaps never finished), was intended to be a counterpart to a certain Moor's Tragedy by Shakespeare—although, if it was ever completed, it may have anticipated Shakespeare's play.[86] A. C. Baugh, in his invaluable though sparsely annotated edition of *Englishmen for My Money* (1917), remarked that at the peak of his productivity, that is, in the ten months ending in May 1600, Haughton "was working at tremendous speed and produced either alone or in collaboration with others no less than ten plays. At times in this period he produced as many as three plays in one month and on occasions must have had three or even four plays under way at the same time. True, only four (or five) were his unaided work, but with all necessary allowances such a burst of industry is remarkable and is safe evidence of the fertility and facility of the man when he was in the mood."[87] All his known plays were written for the Admiral's Men, though it is conjectured that he worked also as a freelance for other companies. If Shakespeare had needed a collaborator in the period around 1597, he could hardly have done better than to turn to William Haughton.

Baugh further noted that Henslowe in 1600 advanced to Haughton a sum for a book to be called "the devell & his dame," though no such play seems to have been completed by Haughton (and indeed Henslowe some time cancelled the entry); in 1662, however, there appeared *Grim the Collier of Croydon; or, the Devil and his Dame . . . by I.T.* Whoever I.T. was, according to Baugh, he was unlikely to have been William Haughton, despite sharing with him certain characteristics of style and plotting (most especially the form of the induction): "Evidence of Haughton's hand in *Grim the Collier of Croydon* is slight and is hardly sufficient to establish the authorship of the play."[88] Nevertheless, F. G. Fleay (1891)—"the industrious flea"—who is otherwise best known as one of the great "disintegrationists" of the Shakespeare canon,[89] believed the later published play to be Haughton's, as did Walter Greg (1904); and so did E. K. Chambers (1923), even though he was writing not long after Baugh entered his limiting judgement. But the business of literary detection has made some advances in the last half century: notably, in 1978, William M. Baillie adduced evidence, based on tables of usage frequencies prepared two years earlier by David J. Lake in connection with the work of Thomas Middleton, to confirm the attribution to Haughton. "In a wide range of stylistic features—structure, characterization, parallel speeches, versification, function-word frequencies, and spellings—the play closely resembles *Englishmen for My Money*," Baillie adjudged.[90]

Using similar, very detailed lists and tables of his own devising (covering everything from linguistic features to verse style), Berryman had reached exactly the same conclusion in the early 1950s—though as with most of his findings on Shakespeare and his contemporaries, he was never to publish them. In some respects he had gone further than Baillie (and Lake) and included in the equation similarities of proverbial usage, since he recognized that Haughton was addicted to proverbs: he noted, for example (among many examples), the closeness of the following passages:

Grim "Why am I fair, but that I shd be loved / And why . . ." 432
Engl "Why was I made a maid, but for a man? / And why . . ."

Grim "I can no longer linger my disgrace . . . whore . . . You'll prove a soldier!" 440
Engl "I can no longer hold my patience . . . lascivious . . . You'll be no nun!"
    (both speakers suddenly emerging from concealment; and scornfully quoting fragments of conversation just heard)

Writing in 1919, H. Dugdale Sykes had expressed his conviction that Haughton showed "no tricks of repetition or pronounced mannerisms of any kind"[91]; so Berryman took pains to remark, among numerous examples, the following linguistic preferences:

    Grim "I am an old dog at it" 418, *Engl* "I am a dog at this"
    Engl 4 times ends sentence w. "and so forth"; *Grim* 459
    Grim market . . . marr'd 401, *Engl.* ditto

Grim helping hand 410 *Engl* ditto
goose & giblets: *Grim* 462, *Engl*
the flesh is frail *Grim* 916, *Engl*
shadow & substance (good!), thrice in *Engl.*, *Grim* 421

Baillie, in a substantial later publication (1984), has noted too that *Grim* evidently "served as an important source for the anonymous comedy *Wily Beguiled*, which was written about 1602 . . . This ragged but highly popular play—it ran through six quarto editions and was often alluded to—includes a character named Robin Goodfellow and a subplot centered in a rustic lover, Will Cricket, who is patterned closely after Grim the Collier. Goodfellow in this play is not a devil-turned-goblin but a very human rogue."[92] A. C. Baugh had not been so persuaded that *Wily* represented such an important achievement, despite noting the kinship of what he called the "usurer motive" and a related closeness of theme between the two plays ("the attempt of a mercenary father to marry his daughter for wealth against her inclination"), and albeit that he readily allowed *Wily* to be "the nearest approach to the plot of Haughton's play that is to be found before 1598."[93] On the other hand, K. M. Briggs, in *The Anatomy of Puck* (1959), was to credit *Wily Beguiled* as "particularly interesting because it is a rationalised fairy-tale"; and she went on to stress the sophisticated originality of the work: "Though Robin Goodfellow is euhemerized in this play, it yet remains the extreme example of his treatment as a devil, for he is a more disagreeable character than even the devil in many of the folk stories."[94]

Berryman was anyway of a mind in the early 1950s to assign the very popular *Wily Beguiled* also to Haughton. Not surprisingly, the author of *Wily* (whether or not he was Haughton) knew his Shakespeare—for example, he makes what Greg called "obvious imitations of *The Merchant of Venice*"; also, possibly, allusions to *Romeo and Juliet* and to *A Midsummer Night's Dream*[95]—so the attribution might appear to be of no great moment, albeit tidy. No great moment, one might think, except for the fact that on sig. D3 (ll.817–22) the character Lelia bewails:

What sorrow seiseth on my heauy heart?
Consuming care possesseth euerie part:
Heart-sad *Erinnis* keeps his mansion Here,
Within the Closure of my wofull breast;
And blacke despaire with Iron Scepter stands,
And guides my thoughts, downe to his hatefull Cell.

As T. W. Baldwin was to point out in 1950, and as Berryman had independently noted, Shakespeare employed a similar conceit to the fourth line quoted not only in *Venus and Adonis*, 1.782 ("Into the quiet closure of my breast") and in *Richard III* (III.iii.11)—"Within the guilty closure of thy walls"—but also in Sonnet 48: "Within the gentle closure of my breast." Moreover, it seems likely that Shakespeare's development of the conceit followed that very order of composition, since in *Venus and Adonis* the "closure" is not yet a prison but only a bedchamber, and it becomes a gaol only by way of *Richard III* and the sonnets.[96] Thus the author of *Wily Beguiled* may have derived his turn of phrase (which Baldwin did not pick up), with its unambiguous reference to a closure-prison, either from *Richard III* or, much more excitingly and intriguingly, directly from Sonnet 48 —and yet Shakespeare's Sonnet 48 was not to be published until 1609. As Berryman noted when he realised this possibility, "HAUGHTON knew the Sonnets long before publication!" Of course, even if Haughton was not actually the dramatist of *Wily Beguiled*, as Berryman so fervently wished him to be, it remains a strong possibility that whoever actually was the author had private access, perhaps in the late 1590s (the parameters of *Wily* would appear to be 1596–1606, and an early date in that range is likely), to Shakespeare's unpublished work; was indeed one of the friends to whom (as Francis Meres said) Shakespeare circulated his "sugred sonnets."

Haughton (whether or not he wrote *Wily*) naturally knew those dramatic works of Shakespeare that had been produced or in some sort published (that is, in unauthorized quartos) in the period: for example, in line 616 of *Englishmen for My Money*—"His heart was not confederat with his tongue"—he seemingly makes allusion to *Richard II*, V.iii.53: "My heart is not confederate with my hand." But Berryman believed he had detected that Haughton in *Englishmen*, like the author of *Wily* (whether or not it was Haughton himself), borrowed too from Shakespeare's sonnets, specifically numbers 29 and 128. What is perhaps every bit as striking—there is no record that Berryman noted this supportive evidence, but it is difficult to imagine he missed this telling intertext—is that *Englishmen* alludes in the following quotation not only to *Dr. Faustus* ("Earth gapes") but also to Shakespeare's Sonnet 30:

> But now debard of those cleare shyning Rayes,
> Death for Earth gapes, and Earth to Death obeyes:
> Each word thou spakst, (oh speake not so againe)
> Bore Deaths true image on the Word ingrauen;

Which as it flue mixt with Heauens ayerie breath,
Summond the dreadfull Sessions of my death.

(ll.1956–61)

Compare: "When to the sessions of sweet silent thought / I summon
. . ." Such an obvious allusion reinforces the idea that certain of
Shakespeare's sonnets had somehow been made available to Haughton (as to the author of *Wily*, who may have been one and the same)
by 1597.

Shakespeare, for his part, seems to have been thoroughly familiar
with Haughton's works. M. M. Mahood was to point out, in 1966,
for example, that Sir Toby Belch's use of the imprecatory phrase
"*Castiliano, vulgo*" (*Twelfth Night*, I.iii.39), with its general sense of
"Talk of the devil!," must be a reference to the name assumed by the
devil Belphegor when he comes to earth in *Grim the Collier of Croydon*.[97] As for Haughton's major theatre piece, G. K. Hunter has called
Englishmen for My Money a "run-of-the-mill comedy" that exploits
"the usual New Comedy type of intrigue and counter-intrigue"[98]; but
the play is a much more combative, innovatory, and influential work
than that description would have us believe. Modern scholarship has
shown, for example, that both *Englishmen* and *Grim* represent chal-
lenging innovations in the development of the device of the bed trick
in Renaissance drama. The convention is well known, but the major
issues raised by it have to do with gender and power in sexual rela-
tionships. Both plays feature versions of the bed trick arranged by a
father; but Haughton's boldness with this new device is especially
controversial in *Grim*, wherein the character Honorea (as Marliss C.
Desens remarks in a recent study) "is, in effect, raped in a bed-trick
sanctioned by her father." As Desens further explains, such an action
is not called, or even regarded as, a rape—precisely because it is
approved by the father: "While Haughton's choice of the father as
that authority figure satisfies the legal requirement, it may have elic-
ited too much anxiety among dramatists and audiences over the father's intrusion into his daughter's sexual life. On one point we can
be certain, no other play survives in which a father arranges a bed-
trick that deceives his daughter."[99] (In Shakespeare's *Measure for
Measure*, of course, the Duke in his guise as a "Father" also sanctions
a bed trick; but his morally dangerous motive is assumed to be a
decent one: to help Mariana to a husband she unaccountably loves.)
In any event, it is very likely that Haughton was the first dramatist to
exploit the bed trick on the Renaissance stage: the presence of such
provoking plays behind *Measure for Measure* and *All's Well that Ends*

Well is obvious. As Berryman put it in his notes, Haughton's work "bit into" Shakespeare.

While Berryman may have taken such factors into account, he was concerned first and foremost with his determination that Haughton could have been Shakespeare's collaborator in *The Taming of the Shrew*. There is a long-standing tradition (though more or less suspended for the last fifty years) which, for want of scholarly or other supportive evidence, has been little more than an impression, that Shakespeare wrote only certain portions of the play—this tradition of disintegration goes back to the eighteenth century—and that, in particular, the subplot may have been the invention of another dramatist (or more than one). At the height of the Victorian period, J. Payne Collier went so far as to surmise: "We are, however, satisfied that more than one hand (perhaps at distant dates) was concerned in it, and that Shakespeare had little to do with any of the scenes in which Katherine and Petruchio are not engaged. The underplot resembles the dramatic style of William Haughton, author of an excellent comedy, *Englishmen for My Money*, which was produced prior to 1598."[100] Responding to such a suggestion, the poet and critic A. C. Swinburne—who incidentally thought *Englishmen* "a spirited, vigorous, and remarkably regular comedy of intrigue, full of rough and ready incident, bright boisterous humour, honest lively provinciality and gay high-handed Philistinism"—sought to burlesque the excesses of the New Shakspere Society[101] with the proposition that in Sonnet 143, line 13—"So will I pray that thou maist haue thy *Will*"—Shakespeare was hinting that he himself had been joint author with Haughton of *Englishmen for My Money, or, A Woman Will Have Her Will*.[102] (Whichever way you turn the joke, it may still contain a truth; certainly, Shakespeare may be alluding to Haughton's play in that line of his poem, though it seems more likely that he was citing the popularly punning proverb.) Sir Edmund Chambers was not reluctant even to spell out the exact portions of *The Taming of the Shrew* to be ascribed to Shakespeare and his co-author(s).[103] (Berryman agreed in the main with Chambers's apportionment of the work, though he wanted to give Shakespeare just a smidgen more, including I.ii.200–10.

Granting the controversial proposition that parts of *The Shrew* were penned by another dramatist, Berryman found several areas of style and form to support the suggestion of an affinity, if not an identity, between that putative playwright and William Haughton. Some points of diction are (as he admitted to himself) matters of common parlance, or they can be put down to the likelihood that Haughton was a close follower of Shakespeare. What impressed Berryman above all else was the tally of proverbial parallels: his copious lists include "Honours change Manners" (*Englishmen*, l.1642), for which M. P. Tilley's recent and authoritative *A Dictionary of the Proverbs in England in the Sixteenth and Seventeenth Centuries* (Ann Arbor, 1950)[104] provided no examples in the drama apart from the following comparable usage in *King John* (for which a date of 1595–96 has been conjectured), I.i.187: "new-made honour doth forget men's names." *Englishmen* (l. 2139) has "weele plucke a Crow together," which occurs in the same sense only in *The Comedy of Errors*—and yet the latter play went unpublished in Shakespeare's lifetime (though it was probably performed in the Gray's Inn Revels at Christmas 1594). Tilley (C855), as Berryman noted, gives the latter idiom "only in Lyly of dram[atist]s otherwise, & there different." Among the many other proverbs that *The Shrew* and *Englishmen* deploy in common are: "I must dance barefoot on her wedding-day, / And for your love to her lead apes in hell" (*Shrew*, II.i.33–34): "I may lead Apes in Hell, and die a Mayde" (*Engl.*, l.1273); but such correspondences are almost bound to be coincidental, since proverbs are (by definition) in common use. Of the proverbs in Shakespeare's part of *The Shrew*, Berryman calculated, "11 are in *1597–8 plays* and *all* the rest (6 or 7) are in *later* plays. His part really *cannot* be supposed pre-Meres [1598] then . . . The non-Shakespearean part of *Shr.* has 13 proverbs (of 36) with Shakespearean parallels, some of these being v. likely their *sources* . . . Therefore the company is the Chamberlain's & the *date* 1598 or so." His next sentence, however, shows he had not altogether convinced himself: "Well, of 36 proverbs in the non-Shakespearean part of *The Shrew*, 14 have no relevant parallels." Just so: as much as Berryman seems to be on the brink of leaping to still debatable conclusions, he constantly and candidly reminds himself: "Haughton, then, *could* have written X-*Shrew*. But how are we to decide that he *did?*—that these two easy, featureless, unmoral dramatists [Haughton and the author of X-*Shrew*] were the same. The game of verbal parallels has rightly fallen into contempt."

More substantively, therefore, he remained alert to the evidence of all possible sources, analogues, allusions, and intertexts. Urging himself towards a perhaps predetermined conclusion, Berryman claimed in his notes: "W. Ha's . . . imit. of Sonnet 48 seems to prove he knew them and so *doubly* knew Shakespeare & in fact was Mr. W.H." (Of course, one crucial problem with this neat packaging of William Haughton as Shakespeare's "friend" is that in the dedication to *Shakespeare's Sonnets* Thomas Thorpe wishes "all happiness" to Mr. W.H., who might therefore be assumed to be alive at a date (1609) when William Haughton had been dead for four years. "Sonnets then 'posthumous' as to the one mainly addrest?" Berryman flatly queried in his notes. The best explanation he could devise, in another note, was still an unpersuasive gambit: "Haughton's death makes Thomas Thorpe's dedication odd but explains Shakespeare's publication of them—the friend could not be injured & *he* was retiring." (But in his heart he knew it would not do.) On other days, Berryman suffered extreme misgivings about his quest, as in this honest entry in his screeds of notes: "*Mon. night*—at end of tests on this Act I sheet & the three previous—no doubt about it: my random testing has so far given small support to my impression of Haughton's *Shr.* collab'n." And yet, without ever committing himself to a publication on the subject, he nurtured for many years his conviction as to the correspondences between Haughton's work and *The Shrew*, and his proposition that the younger dramatist, who was at once prolific and highly adept as a collaborator, may even have helped Shakespeare with *The Shrew*. To judge in particular from the proverbs, Berryman believed, Shakespeare's part of *The Shrew* "belongs, just as one would expect, with *Ado* and *Merry Wives*," that is, to the period 1597–98. The borrowings back and forth between the playwrights are certainly compelling. But Berryman found the likeness between the opening soliloquies of their respective plays the most astonishing point of evidence of all. In his notes he wrote, with an authority won through sustained critical enquiry: "Of 115-odd plays extant 1594–1605 I have examined, no comedy begins like these—except Haughton's *Grim*."[105]

Again, in a fragmentary essay on "Shakespeare's Collaborator in *The Shrew*, and Mr. W.H.," he begins with another dash of uncharacteristic confidence: "Shakespeare's collaborator in *The Taming of the Shrew* seems to have been William Haughton. Why this has remained so long unsuspected I wonder, since it will be perfectly obvious to anyone who reads one after the other the opening scene of *The Shrew* and the opening scene of *Englishmen for My Money*, an Admiral's play of 1598 by Haughton which held the stage for 40 years, that in situation, themes, setting, characterization, dramatic planning, length, versification, clowning, proverbs, and diction, they are the product of one talent."

One difficulty with any attempt to locate *The Taming of the Shrew* in about 1598 (the year in which Shakespeare acted in Jonson's *Every Man in His Humour*) is that Francis Meres's seemingly comprehensive list of Shakespeare's plays, in *Palladis Tamia* (published that year), does not mention *The Shrew*[106]—"despite," as Berryman put it, "the plain close relation, in material, style, energy, and excellence, between the Induction and *Henry IV* and *Merry Wives* and between the taming scenes and *Much Ado.*" If *The Shrew* is the same play as the unknown *Love's Labour's Won*, which Meres does include in his list, Berryman's suggestion that it was written in 1598 may look paltering. However, even if those plays are one and the same, there is no final argument, Berryman believed, for supposing it earlier than that date, because it seems logical to figure that *Won* would have followed hard on the heels of *Love's Labour's Lost*, which was subject to redaction late in 1597. (Roslyn L. Knutson lent weight to that opinion when she remarked in 1988, "*Love's Labour's Lost* and *Love's Labour's Won* may have been genuine sequels. If Shakespeare changed the title of *Love's Labour's Won* to that of a now-extant play such as *AWW* [*All's Well That Ends Well*], his doing so was at odds with a commercial practice that encouraged title echoes whether warranted or not."[107]) Furthermore, if authority insists that *The Shrew* must needs be *Love's Labour's Won*, Berryman's last nice point with respect to Meres's list was that as far as he could see in 1953, conclusive evidence was still wanting to demonstrate that the play antedates 1598. There were further grounds, he insisted, for "proof" of what he tentatively termed his "discoveries."

THE PROBLEM OF WHETHER or not Haughton could have had a hand in *The Taming of the Shrew* is compounded, and perhaps put out of court, by a big prior problem: the date of *The Shrew*. Peter Berek has recently, and rather strangely, observed: "No one seems to fuss much about the date, to be sure," which blithely ignores what has been the most vexed issue relating to this play for most of this century.[108] At least since Peter Alexander's influential article *"The Taming of the Shrew"* (*TLS*, September 16, 1926, p. 614),[109] a formidable consensus among editors has determined that the quarto, *A Pleasant Conceited Historie, called "The Taming of a Shrew"* (*A Shrew* for short), performed by Pembroke's Men, and then by the Admiral's and Chamberlain's Men in June 1594, and registered and printed by Peter Short the same year, must be a "bad" quarto—a memorially reconstructed and presumably pirated version (not unlike the Q1 of *Romeo and Juliet* and the Q1 of *Hamlet*)—of Shakespeare's *The Taming of the Shrew*; and that therefore the latter must have been written (and produced onstage) at some time in the early period 1588–92. Such is the majority opinion of scholars since Samuel Hickson in 1850, including Richard Hosley and the editors J. Dover Wilson, G. R. Hibbard, Brian Morris, H. J. Oliver, and Ann Thompson.[110]

However, part of the difficulty with weighing the claims for precedence is that the text which is believed to be Shakespeare's was first printed, so far as we can tell, only in the posthumous folio edition of 1623. Scholars hold too that the unpolished and even self-contradictory state of that text of *The Shrew* indicates that it was taken from Shakespeare's "foul" papers: a virtually finished authorial draft (not a transcript), albeit with some evidence of a book keeper's (prompter's) hand—as if it had been rather inconsistently prepared for performance. Alternative arguments, such as that both *The Shrew* and *A Shrew* stem from a (now lost) earlier play, a so-called Ur-*Shrew*, or that Shakespeare fashioned his text as a reply to the (earlier) *A Shrew*, or even that *A Shrew* might be an early draft of the play by Shakespeare himself: all such arguments have been firmly set aside by most scholarly authorities in recent decades.[111] According to Oliver, Morris, and Thompson, all the textual and contextual indicators point to the truth that Shakespeare wrote his version of the play by the early 1590s: they are not impressed by any countervailing argument. This situation seems peculiar, to say the least, especially in the knowledge of the recent fashion among scholars to seek to reinstate the so-called bad quartos as Shakespeare's own versions of plays that he himself revised at later dates (most notably in the case of *King Lear*). *A Shrew* has to be a derivative text, the regiment of editors of *The Shrew* maintain, so the version that Shakespeare's colleagues and first editors, Heminge and Condell (the compilers of the First Folio in 1623), acknowledged as his—their best available "copy"—must have been written by the beginning of the 1590s: the indebtedness runs all in one direction. Even an allusion in a poem entered on the Stationers' Register on June 16, 1593, *Beawtie Dishonoured written under the title of Shores wife*, by Anthony Chute—"He calls his *Kate*, and she must come and kisse him"—must be put down solely to Shakespeare's *The Shrew* (V.i and V.ii), they argue, because a culminating kiss clearly does not take place in *A Shrew*: and therefore Chute must have seen a production of Shakespeare's very play by June 1593.[112] Yet such a nice inference ignores the fact that obvious dramatic action need not always be written into the text.

For the most part, as the *Riverside Shakespeare* acknowledges, it makes little difference if *The Shrew* is Shakespeare's chicken to another man's egg, or vice versa: "Textually, *A Shrew* is of little value to an editor of Shakespeare's *Shrew*, since, whether or not we accept it as a 'bad' quarto of *The Shrew*, there is only some occasional verbal correspondence between the texts."[113] Kathleen O. Irace, who has studied the issue still more recently, has come to the conclusion that "the connections between the two texts are not nearly so numerous as a description of the plot or a sampling of verbal parallels might indicate . . . Fewer than one percent of the lines in *A Shrew* as a whole closely correspond to parallel lines in Shakespeare's play."[114] It has become a habit in the last twenty years for critics not to read or heed the findings of their predecessors, but Irace need not have been surprised: the count of quarto-folio correspondences remains as E. K. Chambers had reckoned it sixty-four years previously: "The verbal parallels are limited to stray phrases."[115]

Stanley Wells and Gary Taylor, in *William Shakespeare: A Textual Companion* (1987), have allowed that the folio text might "derive from collaborative foul papers . . . Dual authorship might account for some of the evidence of textual cross-purposes and revision."[116] Even though they feel duty-bound to go on to say, "In the absence of a reliable and thorough investigation of authorship one must assume that the whole play is Shakespeare's," they do not thereby debar all consideration of *The Shrew* as a possibly co-authored work which might date from the late 1590s or even the early 1600s. Could it be, as Berryman argued, that it was Haughton who grafted George Gascoigne's *Supposes* onto *The Shrew*?

However, if *The Shrew* is not proven to be an early production, the argument for dual authorship also rests on the say-so of personal opinion. In the opinion of recent editors, old articles by Ernest P. Kuhl (1925) and Karl Wentersdorf (1954) made a fast case for the authenticity of the play. Their judgements have to be weighed in the balance with those of several other scholars—beginning with Grant White in 1857—who were persuaded that a collaborator must have supplied the romantic underplot. Sir Edmund Chambers took a while to commit himself on the question, but when he did, it was in no uncertain terms: I think, he wrote in 1930, "Shakespeare had, exceptionally for him, the assistance of a collaborator . . . On my view, his share amounts to about three-fifths of the play [1,556 lines], and includes all the Sly and Petruchio-Katharina scenes. The other writer is responsible for the subplot of Bianca's wooers [1,091 lines]. I do not know who he was. His work, although not incompetent, is much less vigorous than Shakespeare's."[117]

It is not difficult to believe that Haughton's dramatic devices were inspired (as Berryman believed), whether directly or indirectly, by George Gascoigne's *Supposes*, which was first published in 1573 and reprinted in *The Whole Woorkes of George Gascoigne* (1587). Of course, this argument runs against the evidence of a scholar such as H. J. Oliver, who insisted, as recently as 1982, "Nobody but Shakespeare used *Supposes* as a source."[118] But who first took the cue from Gascoigne, Shakespeare or Haughton, it would be hard to say. Haughton, though the lesser playwright, was a tremendous innovator, with a gift for languages, mimicry, and parody: the foreign speeches in *Englishmen*, both "authentic" and pretended, are very exactly attuned to both diction and accent, such that even someone who only reads the text can easily *hear* the pastiches and the parodies. Equally, he had a quick ear for borrowing tricks from other dramatists.

Though Portuguese by birth, Pisaro in *Englishmen* is fundamentally the Merchant of London, and so naturally a usurious Jew to boot (the word "Jew" is never used, but he is called "Signior Bottle-nose"). Yet he is not a stock character but richly characterized as a personality. In his opening soliloquy he explicitly compares himself to Judas; he finds gold "sweet" and declares that he must "work the ends" of "English Gentlemen," who are "unthrifty" Christians; later, by way of a proverb, he is likened to the devil. Yet his calculating and pernicious conduct does not cut him off from a comprehension of physical passion and impulsive behaviour; and he also shows an astute understanding of the psychology of the frustrated woman. Though part of the conception of his character obviously owes a fair deal to Barabas in Christopher Marlowe's *The Jew of Malta* (c. 1589)— "Mine, mine owne Land, mine owne Possession," he crows at one point (1.2326)—Haughton's high achievement with the otherwise commonplace "usurer plot" has to be seen as more closely associated with Shakespeare's nigh-contemporary *The Merchant of Venice*. Again, Haughton might have got there first, though by a small margin: whereas Henslowe made out payments for *Englishmen for My Money* between November 1597 and May 1598, Shakespeare's "book of *The Merchant of Venice* or otherwise called *The Jew of Venice*" was entered in the Stationers' Register on July 22, 1598, and eventually appeared in print, having been "divers times acted by the Lord Chamberlain his servants" in 1600. Maybe Haughton did after all show Shakespeare the way. A. C. Baugh, who was not given to making exaggerated claims in his 1917 edition of Haughton's play, yet remarked that the usurer motive "is used in several Elizabethan plays later than Haughton's and is allied to the Jessica-Lorenzo story in *The Merchant of Venice*. In its fully developed form, however, it is not found anywhere in Elizabethan drama before *Englishmen for My Money*."[119]

And so perhaps, whether or not Haughton did ever collaborate with Shakespeare (and was perchance the "onlie begetter" of the sonnets),[120] the most important service that Berryman performed for us, when he started this hare in Haughton, was to revitalize an interest in the achievements of a woefully neglected dramatist (who has not even been given an entry in *The Oxford Companion to English Literature*). Berryman well knew that he was onto an important subject in Haughton. On a table of contents that he typed out for a projected book, *William Shakespeare's Friend: An Investigation*, he added by hand against the headings for Haughton and his works: "If *Shrew* no go, this would be the book." What we clearly need now is an up-to-date and thoroughly annotated edition of *Englishmen for My Money*, as well as a professional production. But perhaps A. C. Baugh still deserves the last word on this subject:

Important as *Englishmen for My Money* is in relation to the usurer play and important as is its place in the comedy of London life, it is by no means only because of these historical considerations that the play is interesting today. Judged by absolute standards it is one of the sprightliest comedies that we have.[121]

Berryman never gave up on the possibility of identifying Haughton as Shakespeare's collaborator on *The Shrew*. As late as April 23, 1971—nine months before his death—he began to type out the opening sentences of what he hoped would become the final version of "Shakespeare's Friend."

LOOKING FOR THE LIFE: THE LAST YEARS

"ONLY I HAVEN'T GOT any verse written—just Shakespeare, another hundred pages," Berryman wrote to his first mentor, Mark Van Doren, on June 1, 1952, at the end of his tenure of the Elliston Chair of Poetry at the University of Cincinnati (where his immediate successors in the post were Stephen Spender and Robert Lowell). Although his work on *King Lear* faltered by the close of the 1940s, he nevertheless immediately entered upon a more wide-ranging approach to the canon, which would be sustained until his death more than twenty years later. In the spring of 1951 he delivered the prestigious Hodder Lectures at Princeton, embracing aspects of Shakespeare's life and work from first to last: his audience there, he later said, would not have settled for elementary material, since they were "advanced Humanities students, faculty members including two nationally-known Shakespeareans, people from the Institute of Advanced Study, and writers in town; so I permitted myself various liberties unsuitable to essays or a book." (All the same, then and later, he was concerned as much with scholarly exactness as with critical conjecture: he would write in a preface for a biographical volume proposed in August 1960, "I expect . . . or I would not publish it, that some of its results will be allowed.") The next year, at Cincinnati, he recast that first series of four lectures into the sequence of six lectures that feature in the second section of this volume; the first of the Elliston lectures was then expanded in 1953 for periodical publication as "Shakespeare at Thirty." He also delivered a first version of the lecture "Shakespeare's Last Word," which he would give again, in revised form, at the University of Minnesota in 1955. In addition, when invited to teach the graduate summer school at Harvard University in 1954, he would give a remarkable thirty-four lectures covering no fewer than twenty-two of Shakespeare's plays—"idiotic, but that was what I did," he recalled many years later.

The prospect of such hefty lecturing enterprises, as well as the hearty encouragement of friends, including Edmund Wilson and Malcolm Cowley, convinced him that he should undertake a large-scale study of Shakespeare's life and oeuvre. In the fall of 1951 he was to sign such a contract with Viking Press, which was replaced four years later by another two-book contract at Farrar, Straus, signed by his old college friend Robert Giroux. The new contract embraced both *Shakespeare: A Critical Biography* and the poem *Homage to Mistress Bradstreet*—the latter being published to wide critical acclaim in 1956. "Some familiarity with Shakespeare's work is desirable," he wrote in a draft preface for the biography, "but it would be desirable if the reader will look on Shakespeare, at the outset of this book, simply as the author of most of forty plays (some 70,000 lines of verse, and 30,000 of prose) & certain poems—freeing his mind as far as possible of received conceptions about Shakespeare's thought. His most familiar pronouncements on human life, it will be remembered, in context are *ironic*." In 1956 he was also to undertake, with a contract from Thomas Y. Crowell Company of New York, an edition of between four and six plays to be issued as *Plays of Shakespeare*, which was in turn superseded in June 1958 by a commission for *A Shakespeare Handbook*. The latter volume was to include sections on "The So-called Facts: Geography, History, the Throne," "The Life of Shakespeare: The Theatre," and "Publication and Chronology: The Canon," as well as discussing "The Work" in what Berryman called "46 articles": that is, critical digests of forty plays and the non-dramatic works. By October 1958 he estimated that he had drafted some 250 pages of the biography, and 50 pages of the *Handbook*. Certain of the essays included in Part Five of this book—on

Henry VI, *The Two Gentlemen of Verona*, *The Comedy of Errors*, the
Sonnets—were drafted at that period for inclusion in the latter volume. The other occasional essays in Part Five date from slightly later
periods: *Macbeth* (1960), *King John* (c. 1960), and *2 Henry IV*
(c. 1969–70). "I am working on Shakespeare from ten to fifteen hours
a day and am very happy," he wrote in June 1958, along with a
tantalizing postscript: "I have *fixed* the mysterious date of *The Two
Gentlemen of Verona* in the past week. It is late 1592–early 1593 and
I can prove it."[122] (See the uncompleted essay in Part Five.)

More and more, as his career progressed, Berryman made efforts
to bring together Shakespeare's life and work, to highlight areas of
probable interanimation, to essay the risky business of reading the life
in (or into) the work. He was exasperated, he said, by academic critics
who scanted the known facts of Shakespeare's experience which informed the creative work, and who therefore treated the human being
as an abstract cipher. The robustness of this critical tendency in Berryman can be seen at work in a preface for the putative *Shakespeare
Handbook* that he drafted in July 1958. It was absurd and insulting,
he insisted, for Professor C. J. Sisson to have produced a well-known
essay entitled "The Mythical Sorrows of Shakespeare," maintaining
as it did that the proven experiences of the man Shakespeare are of
no account to criticism:

Shakespeare was a man whose son died, who was publicly ridiculed and
insulted, who followed a degrading occupation, whose mistress got off with
his beloved friend, whose patron was condemned to death and imprisoned
for years, whose father died. He wrote many personal poems about some of
these things. But even the sonnets are regarded by many critics, though no
poets, as mere literary exercises . . . J. W. Mackail, a sensible man upon
other authors, once thought he had written a "Life" of Shakespeare—and so
entitled it—in eight pages, dismissing everything not there as "exercises of
fancy," including, I suppose, such fancies of history as the fact that Shakespeare's younger brother Edmund, also an actor, fathered a bastard (both
died in 1607), and the fact that, during his retirement, his elder daughter
was defamed for adultery. The fact that Shakespeare was go-between for a
marriage during the time he was writing *Measure for Measure* is not to be
found in Mackail's complacent little piece either . . . These fools are happy
with Shakespeare; *non ragionam di lor*, to quote another poet who never
suffered anything.

Moreover, with respect to his proposed biography as such, a publication such as E. K. Chambers's compendium of 1930, *William*

Shakespeare: A Study of Facts and Problems, did its job brilliantly as "a work of record, argument, and reference," but it did not really attend to "aesthetic questions except very incidentally." Likewise, no single critical theory or methodology would be enough to illuminate the manifold genius that was Shakespeare; the whole modern tool kit of approaches had to be brought to bear. In a "Plan of Work," dating from the 1950s (which I have already quoted, but it is useful and relevant to read a brief passage again in this place), he maintained— beginning with a future conditional tense that might have given his publishers pause—"It would be necessary to assemble, select from, and adjust to each other the results of many broad enquiries: documentary, historical, paleographical, bibliographical, editorial, theatrical, linguistic, genetic (sources), critical (including questions of value, comparison, style, form, substance, versification, image-study, etc.), psychiatric and psychoanalytic, ritual, symbolic. Each of these fields is large . . . The biographer will require also the broadest possible experience of other literature, critically, and of men's lives, biographically . . . The biographer must be capable of a book, a constructed and written book, clear, neither unduly confident nor perpetually reserved, presenting an image unified and acceptable to a reader sick of quarter-Shakespeares."

Notwithstanding the echoes in that wishful-thinking manifesto of Whitman's rhetoric in his prefaces to *Leaves of Grass,* there is no doubt that Berryman could have brought to completion a very important critical biography of Shakespeare—if only his own life had allowed it. He had done the job on Stephen Crane in the late 1940s, and his psychobiographical study of Crane remained in print for many years (it is notable too that serious critics of Crane, including Daniel Hoffman and J. C. Levenson, accepted Berryman's arguments on the sources of the poetry). But the postwar years, when he might have brought his Shakespeare into full and final focus, were also the years when he came into his own—and came into his fame—as a poet: most splendidly, after the consummate success of *Homage to Mistress Bradstreet,* he was to dedicate the next thirteen years to one of the great epics of our time, *The Dream Songs,* which was completed only three years before his death. Furthermore, by the close of the 1960s, he was very ill with alcoholism. Yet he never relaxed from the largely hidden work on Shakespeare: he devoured and took copious notes on everything that appeared in print, both books and articles, and was continually drafting passages of criticism and biography. In December 1969 he began a fresh draft of what he then called, perhaps ominously, "Shakespeare: An Attempt at a Critical

Biography"; but it was the experience in 1970 of teaching at the
University of Minnesota a seminar that served to scrutinize *Hamlet*
that rekindled his full fervour for Shakespeare, his work and his life.
Notes dating from January 1970 illustrate the energy (and verbal vo-
raciousness) of his approach to the subject:

Hamlet, as we have him in Shakespeare's longest play, is noble, fearless,
energetic, highly intellectual, honest, idealistic, passionate, extremely popular, a devoted son & friend, a profound enquirer, a sharp dramatic critic,
a ready poet, a man of philosophic wonder, a Renaissance Prince. He is also
wildly impulsive, hysterical, half-deranged with hatred & sexual nausea, melancholy, bitter, malicious, unscrupulous, and suicidal. Such the character
seems to me, after enough experience and enquiry. A. C. Bradley and Ernest
Jones between them, in the first decade of this century, disposed of the
numberless inadequate & exaggerated views of him proposed in the last
century; and I follow them as far as I can in what they report of their own
final impressions of the Prince. This is not all the way in either case. Bradley's great weakness lies in his supposing that we have two Hamlets, the man
of the play and the true Hamlet, whereas the truth, widely recognized in
the critical overreaction against Bradley, is that we have only one, the first,
with indications merely as to the nature of the second.

On a separate page he pinpointed what he saw as the intimate link
between Hamlet and his author, in this graphic form:

The terrible sex nausea and cosmic loathing which afflict us so painfully in
Prince Hamlet, and which critics have not hesitated to ascribe to the poet
himself, continued to afflict him for four long years, dominating all three of
his plays of this dreadful period: *Troilus and Cressida, Othello, Measure for
Measure.* Traces of the feelings survive then in the madness of Lear and the
misanthropy of Timon. But from *Macbeth* and *Antony and Cleopatra* they
have disappeared, and evidently the poet was in some degree himself—if I
may put it so—again; though the horror and utter disillusion of these two
later tragedies tell us plainly that whatever unknown experience or experiences originally produced the feelings in 1600–1, they had left him a permanently altered man.

One last word on this crucial, mysterious subject. Some of Shakespeare's
most intensely felt sonnets . . . seem to reflect the same nausea & loathing
(and the insane jealousy) that characterize his work in the tragic period. The
sonnets cannot belong to the same time . . . so apparently we must conclude
that Shakespeare *twice* in his life—during his late twenties possibly and in

his middle thirties—underwent a kind and degree of suffering that few men are called on by fate to experience at all.

The intense experience of analyzing *Hamlet* motivated him to turn yet again, for the fifth time—the final time, as things turned out—to the project of writing a full-length study of Shakespeare's life and work. He had recently read a stimulating work on the subject of "identity confusion" by the psychoanalyst Erik H. Erikson, *Identity: Youth and Crisis*—"Erikson knows what society does to men and vice versa," Berryman remarked at the time, "most writers haven't a clue"—along with a kindred study by an old friend from Cincinnati, the classical scholar Alister Cameron, called *The Identity of Oedipus the King*. Such ambitious, intelligent, and thrillingly perceptive works encouraged him to frame his own enterprise in terms of a bold analysis of Shakespeare's genius. By harnessing the instruments of psychoanalysis to his long training and professional practice as textual critic, biographer, poet, and literary critic, he would essay a major account of the poet's personality and philosophy: it would be entitled *Shakespeare's Identity*. "If [E. K.] Chambers's great work of 1930 might be comparable to Thayer's *Beethoven*, though it will never be revised as that has been," he wrote in June 1971, "I hope mine may be comparable in certain limited respects to J.W.N. Sullivan's book on Beethoven's 'spiritual development'—*not*, mark, by a composer but by a creative scientist, as I am myself not a playwright but a poet and prose-writer." This was not a novel notion: for many years, he had been fascinated by the application of psychoanalysis to the creative imagination, and as early as July 1958 he determined that at the heart of his biographical study of Shakespeare would be the concept of disturbed identity. That conviction had been given a decisive boost by Chambers's observation, in *William Shakespeare: A Study of Facts and Problems* (I, p. 254), that "the favourite device of concealed identity runs through the plays from beginning to end." Berryman's Shakespeare was not to be a figure of facile genius; he was to be a man struggling with his demons, like all men, and overcoming them through the power of art. This biography would aim beyond the plays and poems to the philosophy, as is apparent in some of the memoranda Berryman penned during 1971. In one note he invoked Shakespeare as "the great inventor—the great expresser—the great judge," with the comment that "even Shakespeare's keenest admirers incline to see him only as the second of these." However, when issues of judgement do come to the fore, as they do with regard to Shylock, to Malvolio, and to "Claudio in all the tragic part of *Measure for*

Measure, and so on, are we not inclined to resent it & find him *heartless?*"[123] On another loose sheet of paper Berryman urged himself:

Consider . . . Shakespeare's extreme insistence upon at least 2 *things*, both formidably illustrated in his worst play, *All's Well that Ends Well*:
1. the values of *friendship & service*
2. the necessity, *under any conditions*, no matter what disgrace, what losses, what infamy, of mere *survival* into another time.
The first is moral, the second is not; the second is metaphysical.

So absolutely committed did he feel to the prospect of devising what he called his "large psychosocial critical biography" that he applied in June 1971 for a senior fellowship from the National Endowment for the Humanities: the book would be written between June 1972 and June 1973, and he would expect to do more research at the Folger Shakespeare Library in Washington, D.C., and at the Huntington Library in Los Angeles. The biography was now to be called, controversially—after the example of Erik H. Erikson's *Gandhi's Truth*—*Shakespeare's Reality*.[124] However, although he was in due course awarded a fellowship, which was to afford him both the time and the expenses he needed, he would not live to take up the final challenge of his career as Shakespeare's critic and biographer. The only portion of the projected work he did write was a new beginning, albeit still a rough draft, as he told the foundation in his application form, called "Some Problems: Points of Entry" (which he had sketched in March):

I focus first on one line, from the final soliloquy of Richard III, then on the King's speeches to Bertram about his father in *All's Well*; redate both plays, one his first masterwork, the other probably his last failure (G. B. Harrison alone is with me in putting it about 1608 instead of 1603); rehearse by way of enquiry all the people Shakespeare is known to have known well during a public & gregarious life—and am under way with Chapter II "Beginnings Altogether Extraordinary."
    I don't feel like describing the book, frankly. I will simply write it.

(The surviving part of that typescript is given as an appendix to this volume.)

ONE OF HIS REFEREES for the fellowship, Mark Van Doren, who offered his full support to the application, privately and rather shockingly told Berryman: "You will never finish the Shakespeare book. There will always be metal more attractive: poems, novels, a memoir, a collection of pensées—God knows what else. You have this illusion that you're a scholar, but you know damn well you are nothing of the sort, any more than I am. Scholarship is for those with shovels, whereas you're a man of the pen, the wing, the flying horse, the shining angel . . . You're for the masterpieces . . . " If Berryman had been going to write a critical biography, Van Doren added with shrewd severity, he would have written it by now; all the same, he hoped Berryman would go on to "confound" his scepticism.[125]

Berryman rushed to refute Van Doren's assessment. After all, he had completed certain large-scale undertakings: witness his *Sonnets, Stephen Crane, Homage to Mistress Bradstreet,* and *The Dream Songs.* And yet, he conceded, there were factors which could inhibit his achievement—but having recently struggled through to sobriety, he devoutly believed he could overcome them—one such being "*some* bone-laziness but mostly DOLDRUMS, proto-despair, great-poets-die-young or at least unfulfilled like Coleridge & Co., all that crap." Another real problem, he sorrily admitted, was "temperamental grandiosity." When he embarked on a work of critical scholarship, as with the Shakespeare, he felt it essential to master everything there was to be known: "to present, or explain, as the case may be, *everything.*" The combination of over-ambitiousness and high anxiety could be staggering for him, he allowed. On the other hand, he categorically denied one part of Van Doren's charge: "I have seldom known you wrong about anything but you couldn't be more wrong about me as a scholar. Mark, I am it, Dr. Dryasdust in person. The man I identify with is Housman, pedantic & remorseless (though with a lyric style far superior to mine), a really bifurcated personality—and I mean to deal with him some time."[126] The evidence of the earlier essays on Shakespeare, including his enquiry into the problems of the text of *King Lear,* attests to the truth that he was indeed a genuine and passionate scholar, as he claimed—though he was always even better as a critic.

Biography, it is said, is a mode of self-exploration; the biographer's picture of the subject always turns out to be, in some sort, a self-portrait. What is revealed by Berryman's final writings on Shakespeare, I would argue, is that in searching for Shakespeare's "spiritual status" (Berryman's own phrase) he was in reality questing for an ultimate meaning to his own life experience—battered as he had been by loss, grief, illness, and despair. The question of a disturbed or concealed identity, as he admitted, spoke as much to his own experience as to Shakespeare's. It was, he said, "an important theme" in his work, especially in *Bradstreet* and *The Dream Songs*. Just so, in his last months, the biographical project was threatening to go beyond criticism and scholarship as such: it was seeking out a philosophy. Nonetheless, the expression of this quest is worth recording here, because it stands for a moving bid for a spiritual affirmation of his own—what we might term a mission statement—as in these notes dating from November 1970, which he headed simply "*At last!* . . . after 18 years at it":

Shakespeare's most *promising* plays are on the light side the *Errors* (though it does not tell us the *direction*(s) he would take in comedy, as the inferior *Two Gentlemen of Verona* does), on the "serious" side the chronicle history we know as *2 Henry VI*, and his almost immediately following first master-piece was *Richard III*, and all three works are prominently concerned with —or wind up in—Confusions of Identity. The heroes undergo crises of loss of self-recognition.

Other ambitious writers have found the theme so important that they based their gravest explorations here. Oedipus' ordeal of self-discovery: Dante's "mi ritrovai per una selva oscura" (by which he means *not* that he "found himself in a dark wood" but that he came to in there to find himself *lost*, and remained lost until he was taught to undertake the 15,000-line ordeal of self-discovery); Don Quixote's loss of identity at the outset (symbolized in his adoption, having become mad, of a new *name*—which after 900 pages he renounces, becoming sane & resuming . . .—these towering instances may convince the reader of the centrality of this mere play-monger's intel-lectual & spiritual commitment, which in fact ended only with Prospero's renunciation of *his* identity (his powers as Magician—cf. Oedipus' powers as Criminal, Dante's as Sinner, the Don's as Knight Errant = Saint). I see this also in the lifelong effort of Rembrandt's self-portraits, in Anne Frank's development, in Saul Bellow's heroes (Augie, Henderson, Herzog—esp. Her-zog), and elsewhere in high art. I've devoted the last twenty years to the subject myself (in *Homage to Mistress Bradstreet & The Dream Songs*) which, I found last night (November 25, 1970), a contemporary student of person-ality sees Identity as "both a persistent sameness (self-sameness) & a persistent sharing of some kind of essential character with others." It is true that Prof. Erikson does not have in mind here works of art, but I do, and I find true for some of the most important of them what he finds true of human life in general. This was encouraging. Now the mystics of many persuasions have sought abolition of self-consciousness as an avenue to union with the Divine—in fact, every moderately devout Christian & Jew does so daily (with the prayer, e.g., "that my will may be attuned to Thy Will"). There is nothing grandiose about this, though there *is* something serious enough to aim at salvation ("In la sua voluntá è nostra pace"), and I locate here William Shakespeare's permanent obsession.

He added at the foot: "I expect some highly organized readers will despise or hate the word 'spiritual' & indeed the subject (they should: it's a threat to their comfortable ignorance of who *they* are)." Then he wrote out a famous quotation from André Marivaux: "On parle toujours de l'art religieux. L'art *est* religieux." And on a separate sheet of paper he added what we may reckon to be his statement of faith: the grand narrative, the final word:

This is emphatically not the same thing as self-acceptance; a psychological & practical concept. What I have in mind is first more active and second more philosophical: self-*discovery* (a process) leading to self-*recognition* (an ultimate *state*). It was Sophocles' subject in *Oedipus*, and leads there to tragedy. But in his final work, on the same subject, *Oedipus at Colonus*, it is accompanied by something new: which let me put shortly as a magical, god-protected, beneficent power—produced in the rare hero, not accidentally, by ultimate & incomprehensible *suffering*. We find this in the last act of *King Lear*, in the ecstatic & recovered King:—until a worse abyss is opened before him by the remorseless artist, when, then, at last he is allowed a transfigured death.

Berryman's resources may have failed him at the last, but we are fortunate to be able to recover his earlier writings on Shakespeare, albeit that some of them are insufficiently developed. No one who reads this volume will be looking for permanent scholarship: they will be looking for the poet's reflections on another artist, and for the poet's critical insights, which I believe are here in abundance. All the same, Berryman as both critic and popular biographer of Shakespeare is surprisingly learned, and his analyses often attain the highest level of scholarship. But the most appealing aspect of these writings is that—as another scholar (and Berryman's friend), the philosopher Ralph Ross, told the National Endowment for the Humanities in 1971—Berryman's literary criticism is always judicious and wise, and above all fresh and exciting.

What the collection adds up to is a confirmation and extension of Berryman's status as a critic; and it is remarkable for presenting a very large amount of scholarly material with ease and readability. It is striking, too, to see how closely it matches up to the observations he made about the book that he first planned as long ago as 1951: "I ought to mention, perhaps, that the book, while making no particular claim to originality, will nevertheless not much resemble I think any previous book on Shakespeare, and certainly will contain a good deal that will be new to any possible reader, however expert."[127]

TEXT AND ANNOTATION

THE TEXT OF THE MAJORITY of the pieces in this collection is taken from Berryman's own typescripts (all of them carrying holograph emendations and additions which I have attempted to incorporate wherever possible). The texts of "On *Macbeth*" and the two-part essay "Shakespeare's Last Word" are taken from the collection *The Freedom of the Poet* (1976); so too is "Shakespeare at Thirty." However, after much thought and with great reluctance, I have made the decision to cut from the text of "Shakespeare at Thirty" certain fairly substantial passages which were cannibalized from the series of lectures as given at Cincinnati in 1952, as well as others which were replicated in an advanced biographical piece, entitled "Youth," which is cited in the first section of this volume. Notwithstanding, I have allowed one sizeable paragraph to stand in "Shakespeare at Thirty" —on Robert Greene's assault on Shakespeare's reputation.

W. W. Greg's letters to Berryman are in the Berryman Papers; so too are carbon copies of Berryman's letters to Greg. The letter from Mark Van Doren to Berryman is likewise in the Berryman Papers, as is Berryman's correspondence with the Rockefeller and the Guggenheim Foundations. Berryman's letters to Mark Van Doren are in the Rare Books and Manuscripts Department, Butler Library, Columbia University; I am most grateful to Mr. Kenneth A. Lohf—twenty-five years ago!—for making a microfilm available to me.

"Things needn't be annotated to be thoughtful," Berryman once remarked in his notes. I have tried to heed that wise observation while editing these pieces. Berryman himself supplied a full apparatus of annotations to the largest essay in this collection, on the texts of *King Lear* (Part III); and in the knowledge that he spent two hard and dedicated years in composing that piece, I have taken it as a substantive contribution to this area of Shakespeare scholarship: I have therefore been at pains to supplement Berryman's contemporary notes with further references (supplied in square brackets in the notes) to most of the major studies of *King Lear* that have appeared in recent years, including *The Division of the Kingdoms: Shakespeare's Two Versions of "King Lear,"* eds. Gary Taylor and Michael Warren (Oxford, 1983, 1986), separate studies by scholars including Blayney, Stone, and

Warren, and editions of the play including those by Foakes, Halio, and Weis. My aim has been to show how the argument goes on, and to locate Berryman's effort in the context of this living debate about *King Lear*.

Most of the remaining essays do not carry such a heavy load of annotation, and indeed Berryman supplied only a handful of footnote references in his typescripts: I have therefore limited myself, for the most part, to giving references to major sources—though I must plead guilty to furnishing a further riff of references here and there, when the subject seized me, or else when I just happened to know some more about it. Berryman's quotations from Shakespeare are invariably left just as he wrote them out. He used many and variously reliable editions over a period of more than thirty years, and tended to favour a relatively unmodernized text. In one of the several prefaces he drafted for the critical biography he projected—this one, perhaps the last, dates from the winter of 1970—he wrote:

My quotations from Shakespeare's work are taken from facsimiles of the earliest substantive texts, sometimes as emended; except in the case of *Richard II*, for which I used A. W. Pollard's facsimile of Q3, and in the case of the *Sonnets*, which I quote in the almost unexceptionable text established by W. G. Ingram and Theodore Redpath (1964).

But that was a statement of intent rather than achievement (since some of the essays which mention the *Sonnets*, for example, were written before 1964): he had not yet attempted to standardize his quotations. After tinkering with the quotations for a good while, I decided to review the situation and after all to respect the time and occasion of each piece—and so to leave well alone. As to the dates and sources that Berryman produces from time to time in the essays, so much of the business of establishing the chronology, sources, intertexts, and analogues of Shakespeare's works is a matter of informed conjecture that I have not attempted to insert any specific corrections or warnings with regard to Berryman's speculations, even in a few cases where scholars now tend to discount the evidence he adduces (for example, on the *Henry VI* plays). Berryman's arguments and conclusions can readily be compared with the evidence cited in recent editions, such as the New Cambridge or the Arden Shakespeare, and in the second edition of the *Riverside Shakespeare* (1997). The bulk of the biographical facts (some of which still remain speculative) is furnished in the late S. Schoenbaum's *William Shakespeare: A Compact Documentary Life* (Oxford, 1977) and his *Shakespeare's Lives* (new edition, Oxford, 1991); and some records, allusions, and documents are made available also in the *Riverside Shakespeare*; documentary evidence can also be checked in specialist publications, including *Shakespeare in the Public Records* (London: Her Majesty's Stationery Office, 1985) and Robert Bearman, *Shakespeare in the Stratford Records* (Stroud, Gloucs.: The Shakespeare Birthplace Trust/Alan Sutton Publishing, 1994). Critical developments may be followed in Stanley Wells (ed.), *Shakespeare: A Bibliographical Guide* (new edition, Oxford, 1990). E.A.J. Honigmann's *Shakespeare: The "Lost" Years* (1985) is an important addition to the great enterprise of getting to know Shakespeare; and Gary Taylor's *Shakespeare Reinvented: A Cultural History from the Restoration to the Present* (London, 1990) contains a lesson for us all.

FOR ALL SORTS OF invaluable help and encouragement over the years, I am deeply indebted to Kate Donahue (Mrs. John Berryman); Robert Giroux; Professor Richard J. Kelly, Wilson Library, University of Minnesota; Alan J. Lathrop, curator of the University of Minnesota Libraries' Manuscript Division, and his assistant Barbara Bezat; Austin J. McLean, former curator of the University of Minnesota Libraries' Rare Book Division; Kenneth A. Lohf, Librarian, Rare Books and Manuscripts, Butler Library, Columbia University, New York; and to Professor E.A.J. Honigmann and Lord Morris of Castle Morris (Professor Brian Morris, my former head of department), for their good advice after reading a very early draft of the third section of my introduction (on Houghton, Haughton, and *The Taming of the Shrew*). Letters by W. W. Greg are published by kind permission of his daughter and executrix, E. Joy Greg. For a period in the summer of 1997 I was a Visiting Scholar at St. John's College, Oxford, where I was at last able to gather myself together and write much of the introduction to this volume: I am grateful to the president and fellows for their invitation, and for the lovely generosity of the college. I am indebted also to the Research Fund of the University of Sheffield, which assisted my passage to Minneapolis at a time when I could not finish the job without it.

Sheffield
November 11, 1997

PART ONE

Shakespeare's Early Comedy

THE DRAMATIST'S GRANDFATHER was probably a Richard Shakespeare, who farmed in a small way at Snitterfield in Warwickshire, renting from the wealthy Robert Arden of Wilmcote, the other grandfather. The surname had long been common in the Midland counties, since one William Shakespeare [Sakspere] of Gloucester was hanged for robbery in 1248.[1] Richard had at least two sons: John, who moved four miles to the market town of Stratford-on-Avon about 1551, and Henry, who remained at Snitterfield farming and died there poverty-stricken in December 1596, his widow, Margaret, following him six weeks later. By the time Richard died in 1560, John Shakespeare was prospering as a glover and butcher, had married above him, and purchased two freehold tenements in Henley Street (next door to the building now known as the Birthplace) and Greenhill Street, both with gardens. Mary Arden brought some property with her, not much, belonging to a lesser branch of one of the county's most influential families. The couple's third child, William—two daughters had died in infancy—was baptized on April 26, 1564.[2] The father cured and dressed skins, sold barley and timber; he slaughtered, and dealt in both wool and malt, the town's chief commodities. He was active in civic life. When his son was four, he was elected bailiff (or mayor) of two thousand souls. He signed with a mark and kept the Corporation accounts for years; scarcely anyone now thinks he could not write.[3] (Christopher Marlowe's father was supposed illiterate, because he signed his will with a mark, until an excellent signature—prior to the will—turned up in 1937. A mark, originally a

[*3*]

cross, was ceremonial.) Other children followed William—Gilbert, Joan, Richard, Edmund; Anne died at seven, when her most gifted brother was fourteen.

Whether William Shakespeare entered the free Grammar School at five or seven is a mystery for all Professor Baldwin's thousands of pages.[4] The least inhuman enquiry into his schooling is still Baynes's[5]; it consisted of handwriting (the English "secretary" hand) and Latin —William Lily's grammar, the *Sententiae Pueriles*, Mantuanus' eclogues, Ovid, Virgil, Horace, Cicero, Terence, etc. French he must have picked up by himself at some point, enough to use it obscenely in *Henry V*. Some critics think he knew Italian. He certainly read the Bible, in the Genevan version of 1560, from an early age. He certainly read, all his life, everything he could get his hands on. He played games, fished, hunted, observed rural life as it has rarely been observed by anyone else. Baynes also wrote the most pleasing summary account we have of the influence of the Stratford country— woodland north, champaign south—on senses and a spirit supernaturally keen. How long the boy lived there is doubtful. When he was twelve his father's way of life altered. Having missed only one Corporation meeting in thirteen years (that is, before January 23, 1577), during the next ten years he attended just one, and he did not attend church services. Circumstantial argument lately has failed to shake the evidence that his business affairs were declining[6]; but new evidence has made it clear that he had remained a Catholic. A testament of faith in his name found under the roof tiling of his house in the eighteenth century, transcribed and lost, is now shown to be a translation—brought to England by Jesuit missionaries in 1580—of an Italian testament [by St. Charles Borromeo] composed in Milan shortly before.[7] As of a man who had married near the end of Mary's reign, Catholicism must not disturb us, and many Ardens were Catholics. But the heterodox loyalty helps to explain John Shakespeare's withdrawal from public life; and with regard to his eldest son's training it is of real importance, as arguing an alternation of Catholic influence at home and Protestant influence at school—the latter being further complicated, as de Groot has shown, by an alternation of Protestant and more or less Catholic schoolmasters.[8] The profound balance of sympathies which became one of this writer's marked characteristics had thus an early root. By thirteen or fourteen it may be doubted that William Shakespeare had any more to learn from the one of his masters [Simon Hunt] about whom we know almost nothing, and the tradition that his father—with five younger children to support—withdrew him from school to help in the business is plausible enough. To this age, nothing has been transmitted to us about the boy except that he was eloquent at a dramatic stunt called "Killing the Calf" (you go behind a curtain and act both calf and butcher).[9] He had also, now or later, unless John Aubrey was misled, a friend his own age as talented as himself, and another butcher's son, who died young.[10]

Now, I think, begin the so-called lost years.

Why it should be thought a conservative notion that Shakespeare stayed in Stratford until his marriage I have no idea. Throughout life he returned there from time to time, and very little time is required for either a marriage or the consummation of a marriage. We lose sight of him perhaps at about fifteen. His marriage, in fact, at eighteen, to a woman twenty-six from a hamlet near Stratford, was hasty and probably forced: six months after a bond against impediments was registered at Worcester [November 28, 1582],[11] a daughter was christened Susanna [May 26, 1583]. A nuptial pre-contract amounting to marriage, such as Shakespeare actually mentions in *Measure for Measure*, has been conjectured, and it is true that both practice and law were opposed, in this matter, to ecclesiastical teaching. In any event, from the likelihood that he *had* to marry it does not follow that he was unwilling to.[12] Anne Shakespeare's impressions of the poet have not survived. He did not make a faithful husband, and was seldom at home, but he was after all a husband of whom it is not too much to suppose that a wife could readily be proud, and in time he would flourish. As for Shakespeare's feelings: his portraits of wives are not notably sympathetic except for Hotspur's, Imogen, Hermione, and they include a shrew in *The Comedy of Errors*, Gertrude, Goneril and Regan, and Lady Macbeth. A young Shakespearean student in *Ulysses* insists that the poet's wife was unfaithful to him, probably with one of his brothers back home in Stratford. But his notorious bequest to her of their "second-best bed" is not evidence against the quality of the marriage.[13] She had been an old maid, and loose; more we cannot say. There is no evidence that she ever joined him in London or elsewhere, for instance on tour. But he always returned to her, and one hopes their last years together were happy. Twins followed the daughter by twenty months, early in 1585, and were named after Hamnet (or Hamlet) Sadler, a baker in High Street, and his wife, Judith. There were no more children.

About a century after these events, the son of an actor who had been with Shakespeare's theatrical company in 1598 told Aubrey that the poet "had been in his younger yeares a Schoolmaster in the Countrey."[14] This would be as an usher, presumably, not a schoolmaster proper, and not necessarily for long. A reflection of the supposed experience has been seen in *Love's Labour's Lost* (where Holofernes strikes me as imagined from the point of view of a victim rather than that of a colleague—not to mention his immediate origin in the Pedant of the *commedia dell' arte*). It may be. Failing historical support, this remote assertion is on little better footing than modern theses that he was a soldier, a law clerk, a traveller, a printer, an apothecary, and so on. Possible, any of them, or even several, but I can imagine nothing more futile than pinning one's faith to a hypothesis which does not even bear upon the fundamental problem: the transition from provincial obscurity to prominence by 1592 in the London theatre. A tradition that he began by holding gentlemen's horses at the stage door is worth mention.[15]

The deer-stealing episode which has fixed itself in the public mind is doubly attested and may represent actual experience. Nicholas Rowe, Shakespeare's first editor and biographer, wrote in 1709:

He had, by a Misfortune common enough to young Fellows, fallen into ill Company; and amongst them, some that made a frequent practice of Deer-stealing, engag'd him with them more than once in robbing a Park that belong'd to Sir *Thomas Lucy* of *Cherlecot*, near *Stratford*. For this he was prosecuted by that Gentleman, as he thought, somewhat too severely; and in order to revenge that ill Usage, he made a Ballad upon him. And tho' this, probably the first Essay of his Poetry, be lost, yet it is said to have been so very bitter, that it redoubled the Prosecution against him to that degree, that he was oblig'd to leave his Business and Family in *Warwickshire*, for some time, and shelter himself in *London*.[16]

A late-seventeenth-century Gloucestershire vicar, Richard Davies, adds that Sir Thomas had the poet "oft whipt & sometimes Imprisoned,"[17] for which Shakespeare satirized him as the foolish Justice Shallow of *The Merry Wives of Windsor*, who comes to make a Star Chamber matter of a deer poaching and whose "old coat" bears a "dozen white luces" (pikes, that is, punning on louses), Lucy's arms being "three luces hauriant argent."

I indicate now briefly the four other lines of possibility most attractive in the present state of our knowledge.

The first and vividest is Northern. In the autumn of 1581 died Alexander Houghton, a Lancashire gentleman who kept players; leaving to his brother Thomas if he will keep players—if not, to Sir Thomas Hesketh—instruments and costumes, and specially commending to them William Shakeshafte and another, who now live with him at

Lea, evidently players; and leaving to this pair of servants also annuities of two pounds. Now one of the variants of the name used by Shakespeare's grandfather was Shakeshafte. Sir Edmund Chambers, who noticed this will in 1923 and forgot it in his great work of 1930, *William Shakespeare: A Study of Facts and Problems*, later on—jogged by Oliver Baker—took up the matter again.[18] The Houghtons, and Hesketh at Rufford, were on close terms with the Stanleys, whose great house, Knowsley, lay nearby. Hesketh almost certainly kept players and had them there with him in December 1587.[19] He died a year later. Both the Stanleys—the fourth Earl of Derby and his son Ferdinando, Lord Strange—of course kept players who made up one of the leading English companies, sometimes under one name, sometimes the other.[20] I must enter a little on their history. They performed at Stratford in 1578–79 and 1579–80; may have been the unnamed players at Knowsley thrice in 1588–90 when Lord Strange was there; were eighteen months at the Rose Theatre in London with Philip Henslowe, the manager, early in 1592: giving twenty-three plays, mostly old ones by Marlowe, Robert Greene, George Peele, Thomas Lodge, Thomas Kyd (ten performances of *The Jew of Malta*, thirteen of *The Spanish Tragedy*), but five new ones including "harey the vj" (evidently *1 Henry VI*, fifteen performances)[21]; for several weeks early in 1593 they were there again, and five men who were next year to join Shakespeare in the most famous company of the age (William Kemp the clown, Thomas Pope, John Heminge, Augustine Phillips, George Bryan) were with him when they were given a special license in May and left on tour. Derby died that September, and next spring, during the week before Shakespeare's thirtieth birthday, Derby's son died, April 16, 1594. The company used the Countess's name at Winchester on May 16, 1593, but in the summer reshuffled (Edward Alleyn, remaining personally the Lord Admiral's servant, had been at their head for some time) and dispersed. If the William Shakeshafte of 1581 is Shakespeare at seventeen, it is clear that he might have passed readily thence to Strange's Men, where most critics used to locate him and some (among them Sir Walter Greg) still do. Possibly in the present paragraph we have seen him lose three, four, or even five patrons.[22]

This Houghton will is the first document ever to emerge suggesting, what many have hoped, that he may have been early familiar with a distinguished house; where, they fancy, he acquired the knowledge of books and manners that his plays evince. I see myself no difficulty in his reading almost anywhere, and I think with H. Granville-Barker that he learnt about life from writing plays about it. But this Lancashire avenue is undeniably interesting. The first thirty-five years of George Chapman's life were a total blank until 1946, when we learnt that he was long attendant on a member of the Privy Council, Sir Ralph Sadler, whether brought up by him, as Michael Drayton was by Sir Henry Goodere, or domesticated later in life, as was Samuel Daniel at Wilton.[23]

A frailer line of enquiry has opened up even more recently. An imperfect copy of Edward Hall's chronicle has come to light containing some four hundred marginalia (3,600 words) which are claimed as Shakespeare's; this is the edition of 1550, which he is known to have used. They occur mostly over the reigns of Richard II, Henry IV, Henry V. It wants critical examination, paleographic and linguistic.[24]

The third line was suggested at the end of the last century by Judge [D. H.] Madden and has been developed by Caroline Spurgeon, in appendices to their pioneering studies (*The Diary of Master William Silence and Shakespeare's Imagery*).[25] Shakespeare in 2 *Henry IV* knows Gloucestershire remarkably well: games, husbandry, the "sedgie" Severn. By then, if not long before, he had travelled over half England playing; but he names people (who we find lived there) at places near Berkeley Castle, which he also knows not only well (in *Richard II*) but *emotionally*, as Miss Spurgeon has made clear with an analysis of his martlet images; and both he and his wife appear to have had relatives there in the Cotswolds. Berkeley's Men played at Stratford in the year before he married and again in the year after he married.

A fourth surmise concerns the Queen's Men, the most powerful company of the 1580s. A. W. Pollard points out that Shakespeare took over later the substantive materials of at least three of their extant plays, handling them not so much like a man who had merely read the plays as like one who had acted in them years before, with a strong grasp of situation but negligible verbal congruity. The objection that he might equally have just seen them acted is more satisfactory, I venture to think, with respect to *The Famous Victories of Henry the Fifth* and *King Leir* than with respect to *The Troublesome Reign of King John*. This company mostly broke up on the comedian Richard Tarlton's death in 1588.[26]

DRAMATIC BEGINNINGS

WE DO NOT KNOW whether Shakespeare began literary work for the stage with original plays or with collaborations or by revising existing plays; and we do not know whether he started with history or comedy. It is not very likely that all his early dramatic work is preserved or has been recognized as his. Only twenty-five plays by anybody survive now assignable to the crucial decade, which was *not* the 1590s, as most modern authorities suppose, but the 1580s. The chief contenders in the canon, for his initial surviving efforts, are probably the Plautine farce *The Comedy of Errors* and the chronicle known to us by the misleading title given to it long afterwards by the editors of the Shakespeare Folio in 1623, *2 Henry VI.* Later it will be convenient to deal with it [*2 Henry VI*] and *3 Henry VI* together, as a two-part history, but the first part is so much more impressive and inspired than its sequel that I want to consider it first alone. It has not been often praised by critics—Coleridge never mentioned it, nor Edward Dowden, except to canvass in a footnote the division among scholars up to his time in regard to authorship[27]; only E.M.W. Tillyard devotes fifteen pages to it as "a fine piece of construction . . . a fine whole."[28] It is little read and seldom performed. But I took a friend, the poet and playwright Louis MacNeice, to a production at the Old Vic in 1953 and he agreed with me afterwards that it is a damned good play. It is also, in its extensive Shakespearean part, one of the most *original* plays of the decade, preceded—so far as we know—only by the miserable *Famous Victories of Henry the Fifth* (about 1586). The English chronicle play sprang out of nowhere, without either classical or native models. We must abandon the long-established view of Shakespeare as a mere perfecter, though rehandling here, it is true, the work of other men: Greene, Peele, and perhaps Marlowe, collaborating in the original version of the play. Dover Wilson finds Shakespeare's hand in eighteen of its scenes, and thinks he wrote three alone.[29] Chambers's dating, 1590, is certainly too late. Perhaps it belongs to 1588 or earlier, just after Marlowe's *1 Tamburlaine* of 1587, to the *verse* of which *2 Henry VI* in its heroic speeches (only) is clearly indebted. Marlowe's influence on Shakespeare, though real, has long been greatly exaggerated; the judicious Clark Lectures of F. P. Wilson, published as *Marlowe and the Early Shakespeare* (1953), embodied and strengthened a reaction to the traditional view.

How to characterize this new, frequently unmistakable voice? Already in fluent verse he can reason, mourn, exult, rebuke, curse, quarrel; already his prose, in the Cade scenes of Act IV, is flexible, vigorous, individual. Already his persons are distinct beyond their actions. Already both pathos and irony are ready to hand. Already a bewildering, unprecedented variety of human experience is deployed without confusion: intrigue, ambition, pride, penance, a raving death, wrangling, the supernatural, the amusing inconsequence and brutality of the common people, hawking, murder, domestic life, treachery, nobility, resignation, the businesslike (curt, natural, manly), the ominous, the contemptuous, the exalted. Already he is a young master of both the amplitude and the expressive conciseness in which he was to outdo almost all other writers, rivalling in the one the poet of the *Iliad* and in the other the poet of the *Commedia*. I take from the wealth of the play two tiny strokes, the first of understatement, the second of Shakespearean psychological inwardness. When the Duchess of Gloucester's resort to black magic is discovered in I.iv, her exposer comments on the disastrous consequences to her husband, the most powerful man in the realm, with one satisfied, grim line: "A sorry breakfast for my Lord Protector."

My second instance also follows on an exposure—a telling dramatic device to which Shakespeare would be devoted throughout his career. In the next scene (II.i) the royal party is introduced to a "miracle": a beggar, with his wife, pretends to have been blind and to have recovered his sight. When Gloucester exposes him and orders their punishment, the poor wife moans: "Alas Sir, we did it for pure need." This gratuitous touch of the playwright's sympathy does not save her, but a glimpse of helpless suffering has been afforded.

As we enjoy this well-invented episode, we are also aware that the secure and penetrating Gloucester and *his* wife, as high as the beggars are low, are just about to be disgraced and punished. The play is rich already in foreshadowing, double awareness, contrast, out of the reach of his contemporaries. His rendering of death scenes shows, I think, enjoyment as well as skill: an evil cardinal's deathbed babbling (III.iii), the spoiled and mighty Suffolk's lonely, ignominious end (IV.i). The author's dawning, enthusiastic ability to convey complex character I reserve till later in the chapter, when we come to his first major achievement, *Richard III*. The personality of this vivid man seems to have engaged Shakespeare from the outset, his sudden introduction in V.i:

> *Rich.* Oft haue I seene a hot ore-weening Curre,
>
> Run backe and bite, because he was with-held,
>
> Who being suffer'd with the Beares fell paw,
>
> Hath clapt his taile, betweene his legges and cride,
>
> And such a peece of seruice will you do,
>
> If you oppose your selues to match Lord Warwicke.
>
> *Clifford.* Hence, heape of wrath, foule indigested lumpe,
>
> As crooked in thy manners, as thy shape.

His leaps-and-bounds development through 3 *Henry VI* is one of that play's keenest strands of interest.

2 *Henry VI* intertangles four themes: Suffolk and the Queen, Gloucester's dominance and fall, York's claim to the crown, Cade's rebellion; three of which are brought to a conclusion, the Yorkist third dominating then the second play, where Warwick is the unifier of the contention, insofar as one can be found in a rather random performance that looks forward to *Richard III* even more explicitly than the preceding play looked forward to it. Richard is the focus whenever he appears. He teases the hesitant York onward in I.ii:

> How sweet a thing it is to weare a Crowne,
> Within whose Circuit is *Elizium*,
> And all those Poets faine of Blisse and Ioy.

His announcement of and wrestling with his own ambition, in the long fine soliloquy that concludes III.ii, provides midway the play's high point:

> I, *Edward* will vse Women honourably:
> Would he were wasted, Marrow, Bones, and all,
> That from his Loynes no hopefull Branch may spring,
> To crosse me from the Golden time I looke for:
> And yet, betweene my Soules desire, and me,
> The lustfull *Edwards* Title buryed,
> Is *Clarence*, *Henry*, and his Sonne young *Edward*,
> And all the vnlook'd-for Issue of their Bodies,
> To take their Roomes, ere I can place my selfe:
> A cold premeditation for my purpose.

And the difficulties multiply upon him, until:

> And I, like one lost in a Thornie Wood,
> That rents the Thornes, and is rent with the Thornes,
> Seeking a way, and straying from the way,
> Not knowing how to finde the open Ayre,
> But toying desperately to finde it out,
> Torment my selfe, to catch the English Crowne:
> And from that torment I will free my selfe,
> Or hew my way out with a bloody Axe.

His confusion, in this middle of his speech, accommodates itself to the weak King's confusion over his identity. The polarity of the two characters is the single most salient element in what form Shakespeare has been able to impose upon the play. Henry gives himself credit for royal virtues—before the battle of Barnet (IV.viii) he says of his people:

> my meed hath got me fame:
> I haue not stopt mine eares to their demands,
> Nor posted off their suites with slow delayes,
> My pittie hath beene balme to heale their wounds,
> My mildnesse hath allay'd their swelling griefes,
> My mercie dry'd their water-flowing teares.

—but he is aware that these are not the proper qualifications for rule in the turbulent world he inhabits, and when this grievous reflection calls into question his very self-image (III.i) he can only, in reply to their questioning, say that he is

> More then I seeme, and lesse then I was born to:
> A man at leaste, for lesse I should not be . . .

Whereas Richard, by the end of his soliloquy, has thrown off his irresolution and is himself again:

> Why I can smile, an murther whiles I smile,
> And cry, Content, to that which grieuves my Heart,
> And wet my Cheekes with artificial Teares,
> And frame my Face to all occasions.
> Ile drowne more Saylers then the Mermaid shall,
> Ile slay more gazers then the Basiliske,
> Ile play the Orator as well as *Nestor*,
> Deceiue more slyly then *Vlisses* could,
> And like a *Synon*, take another Troy.
> I can adde Colours to the Camelion,
> Change shapes with *Proteus*, for aduantages,
> And set the murtherous *Macheuill* to Schoole.
> Can I doe this, and cannot get a Crowne?
> Tut, were it farther off, Ile plucke it downe.

Later on, when all is won with his murder of Henry, the theme is made still more explicit:

I haue no Brother, I am like no Brother:
And this word (Loue) which Gray-beards call diuine,
Be resident in men like one another,
And not in me: I am my selfe alone.

1 Henry VI BELONGS several years later on: Chambers puts it in 1592.[30] . . . It was extremely popular, no doubt for the patriotic ranting of the Talbot scenes, but it is not much of a play and Shakespeare had very little to do with it. Most critics find him only in the Temple Garden scene (II.iv) and one Talbot scene (IV.ii), both of which Chambers thinks he inserted only in 1594 or even later.[31] The original play was probably by Peele and somebody else, possibly Marlowe, splitting between them the native and the French actions. It has done Shakespeare's reputation more damage than anything except *Titus Andronicus*.

But with this other inferior canonical play the case is different. Attempts to prove it a collaboration have failed, in spite of a stage tradition (reported by Ravenscroft in 1687) that it was the work of a "private author," to which Shakespeare "only gave some master-touches to one or two of the principal parts or characters."[32] This is very slight evidence against the great weight of the folio attribution, which is moreover supported by Francis Meres's list of Shakespeare's plays down to 1598.[33]

Three main critical views seem available to us. The first is best put by Mark Van Doren: "a conscious parody of the tragedy of blood considered as a current form."[34] I feel very little confidence in this. The second is that of Hardin Craig: "In spite of Shakespeare's masterly motivation in his rearrangement of scenes, and in spite of excellent invention and noble rhetoric, *Titus Andronicus* remains a relatively unpleasing work. We may say that the subject is impossible, unsuited to Shakespeare's wise and gentle genius, and these things are true; but it is the change in our race and its *mores* which is to be blamed, or it may be to be congratulated, that *Titus Andronicus* has lost its charm . . . The play is indeed horrible with a horror that nobody but Shakespeare could have given it."[35] A third, rather attractive view is M. C. Bradbrook's, that it "seems a first crude attempt to portray some experience that Shakespeare was only to recognize, understand and embody in a 'lively image' at a much later stage."[36]

Dating the play is exceptionally difficult, partly because of our ignorance of its relation to a lost *Titus and Vespasian* of 1592. But the anonymous *A Knack to Know a Knave* (1592) obviously alludes to it with

As Titus was vnto the Roman Senators,
When he had made a conquest on the Goths
[ll. 1490–91]

so it cannot be later than that.[37] It may be much earlier: Ben Jonson in 1614 refers to it as extant "these fiue and twentie, or thirtie yeeres,"[38] taking us back to 1584. Taking the lesser figure in this loose expression of memory, we get 1589, which will have to do. A few lines in IV.i sound like Shakespeare at about this date:

And come, I will goe get a leafe of brasse,
And with a Gad of steele will write these words,
And lay it by: the angry Northern winde
Will blow these sands like *Sibels* leaues abroad,
And wheres your lesson then.

THE BEGUILING, unpredictable, terrible Richard III has been done justice by audiences and critics alike as Shakespeare's most brilliantly drawn character earlier than Shylock half a dozen years later. To make a monster attractive was the poet's problem, and he brought to it, not indeed the spiritual insight and the dramatic resource available when he created Macbeth, but all his considerable theatrical ingenuity of 1590—the date I follow Dover Wilson in accepting for the play. His success with the *play* is limited because nothing is allowed to compete with his hero's personality, except Clarence's dream: it is otherwise an interminable, tiresome railing by bereft ladies. But the work done with Richard is enough.

It was necessary above all to humanize him, make him credible, and this was accomplished mainly by inventing for him a tone, an idiom, verbal and psychological, to contrast with the rhetorical convention that informs almost everything else in the play. A mere trick of iteration was helpful here. "How hath your Lordship brook'd imprisonment?" he asks Hastings in the opening scene:

Hast. With patience (Noble Lord) as prisoners must:
But I shall liue (my Lord) to giue them thankes
That were the cause of my imprisonment.
Rich. No doubt, no doubt, and so shall *Clarence* too . . .

In I.iii Queen Margaret is rebuking Dorset for being "malapert" with his "fire-new stampe of Honor," which he may lose: "*Rich.* Good counsaile marry, learne it, learne it, Marquese." In III.v, as the Lord Mayor leaves, "Goe after, after, Cousin *Buckingham*."

These are slight touches, and nothing is made of them such as the poet will make of the same mannerism when he comes to Falstaff and Hamlet, but they help enforce the sense of an *individual* speaking. The invention of a psychological idiom for him is more important. To the crucial conference in the Tower, III.iv, where the chief nobles of the kingdom are seated around a table anxiously awaiting his decisions, he enters late, remarking, "I haue been long a sleeper," addresses the affectionate lines to Hastings (whom he is about to destroy), and then suddenly says:

> My Lord of Ely, when I was last in Holborne,
> I saw good Strawberries in your Garden there,
> I doe beseech you, send for some of them.

His malicious pleasure here is to lull his victim into security, and Hastings in fact presently says with satisfaction, when Richard has left the room for a moment, "His Grace looks chearfully & smooth this morning . . ." But Shakespeare is up to something else also: a deepening of the audience's view of the character: the abrupt revelation of a man with a life of his own apart from history and the plot, an easygoing, self-possessed lover of strawberries.

Very well: this diabolical Duke, this tyrannical King, regarded by all as not merely inhuman but animal, called variously hedgehog, toad, dog, spider, tiger, cockatrice, wolf, hell-hound, and boar, especially boar, is a human being like ourselves, having virtues as well as vices, complicated, convincingly real. We must try to assess his character. Coleridge, with his taste for philosophical simplification, once told an audience at Bristol that Richard's chief characteristic was "pride of intellect."[39] I agree that this is an element. But can we really see it as central to Richard's outrageous conduct? I would rather find a center in his inspired, daring, and flagrant *hypocrisy*, intimately and ironically accompanied by what has to be called brutal *sincerity*.

Nothing less than this double formulation, it seems to me, will do for Richard's ghoulish, sprightly procedure in what has always seemed to me his finest scene, the wooing of Anne. He intercepts her in a London street as she is conveying the body of her slain father-in-law, King Henry VI, to Chertsey for entombment; hears out her curses; parries her thrusts. Gradually he becomes more and more ingratiating, and then he counter-attacks: her eyes, he says, "kill me with a liuing death" and made even *him*, who never wept for Rutland or for his father, weep for her beauty.

She lookes scornfully at him.
Teach not thy lip such Scorne: for it was made
For kissing Lady, not for such contempt.
If thy reuengefull heart cannot forgive.
Loe heere I lend thee this sharpe-pointed Sword,
Which if thou please to hide in this true brest,
And let the Soule forth that adoreth thee,
I lay it naked to the deadly stroke,
And humbly begge the death vpon my knee.
He Layes his brest open, she offers at (it) with his sword.
Nay do not pause: For I did kill King *Henrie*,
But 'twas thy Beauty that prouoked me.
Nay now dispatch: 'Twas I that stabb'd yong *Edward*,
But 'twas thy Heauenly face that set me on.
    She fals the Sword.
Take up the Sword againe, or take vp me.

This is too much for her, and presently she is saying helplessly, "I would I knew thy heart." Then she actually accepts his ring, he dismisses her and the burial party go their separate ways, and he is left alone to his gleeful self-congratulation:

Was euer woman in this humour woo'd?
Was euer woman in this humour wonne?
Ile haue her, but I will not keepe her long.

But this rapid and sinister foreglancing at her death gives way at once to droll (and scornful) rejoicing over his victory. Note that he never shows the slightest sympathy, respect, or even liking for her: at the same time he is wholly in earnest, wholly *sincere*, about getting her hand. Probably it is his daring that wins both her and the audience: nobody thinks she will strike, but the gesture is melodramatic and engaging. It is *not* plausible, apart from Shakespeare's imposition upon his audience of the character he had invented for his hero or villain. A deeper seizure of personality, an advanced craft, when he comes to represent the implausibilities of Macbeth, will be both necessary and attainable.

Richard is only first-class journeyman work, a performance we admire rather than feel with. For instance, he never exhibits either affection or remorse. But even in Act IV the dramatist is still working at his development: we have learnt from his poor wife, twice, of his continual nightmares, and his mother mourns out to him a short history of himself:

> Thou cam'st on earth, to make the earth my Hell.
> A greeuous burthen was thy Birth to me,
> Tetchy and wayward was thy Infancie.
> Thy School-daies frightfull, desp'rate, wilde, and furious,
> Thy prime of Manhood, daring, bold, and venturous:
> Thy Age confirm'd, proud, subtle, slye, and bloody,
> More milde, but yet more harmfull; Kinde in hatred:
> What comfortable houre canst thou name,
> That euer grac'd me with thy company?

Richard replies to this with a contemptuous pun. His startling loss of self-possession is finely conveyed in IV.iv, and the agitated soliloquy of V.iii, after the coming and going of the ghosts, is the effective end of him, where Shakespeare has saved for the character his most piercing, pathetic line: "*Richard* loues *Richard*, that is, I am I."

This brings to a close the identity problem of 3 *Henry VI*, and corresponds, at its lesser level, to the "miserable conceit" and self-cheering-up that Dr. Johnson and T. S. Eliot found characteristic of Shakespeare's greatest tragic heroes.

The other achievement of the play, more remarkable perhaps even than what is done with Richard, is of course Clarence's dream. Here for the first time in his dramatic work Shakespeare brings his full powers as a *poet* into play. With Clarence's terrible lines,

> What scourge for Periurie,
> Can this darke Monarchy affoord false *Clarence*?

we might think ourselves in the night world of the tragedies or the *Inferno* itself. And the romantic beauty of the lines just following look forward to the poetry of *Romeo and Juliet*:

> Then came wand'ring by,
> A Shadow like an Angell, with bright hayre
> Dabbel'd in blood . . .

Not much is made of Clarence otherwise—we have the King his brother's penetrating characterization, "his fault was Thought"—but two new dimensions have been added to Shakespeare's armory.

King John HAS BEEN generally and rightly regarded as one of the playwright's weakest performances. He found the reign chaotic, and chaotic he left it; despite his pains taken with the unattractive monarch, the "blunt" and "sprightfull" Bastard Faulconbridge, and Arthur. For John himself, the best word that has ever been said is Walter Pater's, who thought Shakespeare "allows" him "a kind of greatness, making the development of the play centre in the counteraction of his natural gifts—that something of heroic force about him—by a madness which takes the shape of reckless impiety, forced especially on men's attention by the terrible circumstances of his end, in the delineation of which Shakespeare triumphs, setting, with true poetic tact, this incident of the King's death, in all the horror of a violent one, amid a scene delicately suggestive of what is perennially peaceful and genial in the outward world."[40] This, we may feel, is to do more than justice to the poet's intentions and achievement in what for Chambers and others is "hardly more than a bit of hack work,"[41] lacking both unity and coherence.

If anything is to be found worth comment here, it is the patriotic energy of the Bastard, whom Shakespeare obviously intended to make a focus for the sprawling action, and the situation and fate of the young Prince. For the second, where a certain pathos is barely secured, we need only quote his mother's lines:

> And so hee'l dye: and rising so againe,
> When I shall meet him in the Court of heauen
> I shall not know him: therefore neuer, neuer
> Must I behold my pretty *Arthur* more.
>
> (III.iv.86–89)

But the Bastard is complicated. He serves not only as a proponent but as a critic of the action: "Mad world, mad kings, mad composition," he begins his splendid soliloquy on "Commoditie" at the end of II.i. He is even a critic, like Hotspur and Hamlet after him, of the inflated language in which the action is conducted:

> Zounds, I was neuer so bethumpt with words,
> Since I first cal'd my brothers father Dad.

The peculiarities of his character, however, are laid aside when he comes to pronounce the dignified concluding lines of the play, foreshadowing the exalted patriotism of Shakespeare's later histories:

> This England neuer did, nor neuer shall
> Lye at the proud foote of a Conqueror,
> But when it first did helpe to wound it selfe.
> Now, these her Princes are come home againe,

Come the three corners of the world in Armes,
And we shall shocke them: Naught shall make vs rue,
If England to it selfe, do rest but true.

(V.vii.112–18)

"Later," I said; but how much later? The dating of *King John* presents us with a problem more vexed than any other in the whole canon, exception made for the similarly perplexing *All's Well that Ends Well.* The received modern date used to be 1596, which was argued for at length by G. B. Harrison in 1930 and independently accepted by Chambers in the same year.[42] These are high authorities. But their date was violently disturbed by J. Dover Wilson in his careful New Shakespeare edition of the play in 1936, where he proposed and defended the year 1590, reversing moreover the traditional view of the relation of Shakespeare's play to the anonymous two-part play *The Troublesome Reign of King John,* published in 1591: he asserted, on the basis of an analysis of the texts more searching than anyone before had given them, that instead of being Shakespeare's source, as critics mostly had hitherto thought, the anonymous play(s) derived from *King John,* of which they were merely an inept expansion. Wilson was joined in both these revolutionary conclusions by E.A.J. Honigmann when he brought out his admirable new Arden edition in 1954.[43]

The specific internal evidence is slight and ambiguous. "Basilisco-like" [I.i.244] refers to a character in *Soliman and Perseda,* a play assigned by Kyd's editor, F. S. Boas, to 1588 or later. Very likely "An Ate stirring him to bloud and strife" (II.i.63) is indebted to Spenser's *Faerie Queene* (1590), II.iv, stanza 42:

For all in *blood* and spoile is his delight.
His am I Atin, his in wrong and right . . .
And *stirre* him up to *strife* . . .

Samuel Daniel's *Complaint of Rosamund* (1592) probably echoes II.ii.52, and H. Constable's *Diana* (also 1592) is in one passage too close for coincidence to IV.i.61–66: see Honigmann's notes. Everything really turns on our decision as to the relation between *John* and *The Troublesome Reign,* and this is a matter of cumulative evidence, except for one important general consideration, which I have never seen put with proper force or perhaps put at all. How can it be supposed, and why was it ever by anyone supposed, that Shakespeare would at any date rewrite a play so bad, *adhering so closely to it?* All his extensive practice with early plays—with *The Famous Victories of Henry the Fifth*, with George Gascoigne's *Supposes*, with George Whetstone's *Promos and Cassandra*, with the old *King Leir*—forbids absolutely, in my opinion, any such supposition; and I have no doubt that Wilson and Honigmann are right. One striking difference, though, noted by Wilson, is worth remark: for Shakespeare the King is a usurper, whereas the author of *Troublesome Reign*—whether Marlowe (Malone), W. Rowley partly (Pope), Peele (H. D. Sykes),[44] or S. Rowley partly (Honigmann)—makes him into a legitimate and native hero.

One final and fascinating matter must be summarized. Alfred Harbage drew attention in 1941 to an Elizabethan play, *Guy Earl of Warwick*, first printed in 1661 as "by B.J."[45] Act II of this contains the following passage:

> *Rainborne.* . . . prethe where wer't born?
>   *Sparrow.* Ifaith Sir I was born in England at Stratford upon Avon
>   on Warwickshire.
> *Rainborne.* Wer't born in England? What's thy name?
>   *Sparrow.* Nay I have a fine finical name, I can tell ye, for my
>   name is Sparrow; yet I am no house Sparrow, nor no
>   hedge Sparrow, nor no peaking Sparrow, nor no sneaking
>   Sparrow, but I am a high mounting lofty minded
>   Sparrow, and that Parnell [his mistress] knows well
>   enough, and a good many more of the pretty Wenches
>   of our Parish ifaith.

When we juxtapose with this a curious little interchange in *King John* it seems likely that the two plays are connected.

> *Bast.* *Iames Gurnie*, wilt thou giue us leaue a while?
> *Gour.* Good leaue good *Philip*.
> *Bast.* *Philip*, sparrow, *Iames*,
>   There's toyes abroad . . .

Now just five lines earlier, the Bastard has cited "*Colbrand* the Gyant," who was Guy's final opponent in the other play; and the clown Philip Sparrow presently is saying, "There's *rumours* abroad." The multiple combination of the Guy legend and "Philip" and "sparrow" and "There's . . . abroad," taken in conjunction with a clown from Stratford-on-Avon with a "fine finical name . . . high mounting" (like "Shakespeare"), cannot be coincidental. *Guy* must be later than

John, but only a little later, and there must be a satire on the poet as (1) a clown, (2) of stated provincial origin, (3) with a high-sounding, perhaps ridiculous name, and (4) twitted with lechery. One would certainly like to know who wrote this play. It was a "young" playwright (Time says in the final chorus, "For he's but young that writes of this Old Time"), but there seem to be no other indications of authorship; the monosyllables are against Thomas Nashe, whom otherwise "Martiallist" and "apprehensive" and "dolent" might point to.[46]

BY 1591, IF NOT EARLIER, William Shakespeare was a figure in the London theatrical world, with active friends and at least one bitter enemy. To this year belongs what may have been the first public compliment paid to him, and to the year following, the first public insult. Queen Elinor in George Peele's *Edward I* (1591) says with some awkwardness to the Scottish King:

> Shake thy spears, in honour of his name,
> Under whose royalty thou wear'st the same.[47]

The likelihood of an allusion here, discovered by A. W. Pollard, to Shakespeare as the actor of the part is reinforced by the tradition that the poet regularly played kingly parts.[48] A pleasant outset for his reputation, if so.

The next year the celebrated Robert Greene lay dying, warning—in his last work, *Greenes Groatsworth of Wit* (1592, S.R., September 20)—Marlowe and apparently other university playwrights away from actors:

Those Puppets (I meane) that spake from our mouths, those Anticks garnisht in our colours. Is it not strange, that I, to whome they all haue beene beholding . . . shall (were yee in that case as I am now) bee both at once of them forsaken? Yes trust them not: for there is an vpstart Crow, beautified with our feathers, that with his *Tygers hart wrapt in a Players hyde*, supposes he is as well able to bombast out a blanke verse as the best of you: and being an absolute *Iohannes fac totum*, is in his owne conceit the onely Shakescene in a countrey.[49]

Quite apart from the impudent parody of one of Shakespeare's lines in *3 Henry VI* ("Oh Tygres Heart, wrapt in a Womans Hide," I.iv.137), here was a congeries of contempt and slander that might enter into the soul. To the savage scorn for Shakespeare as an uneducated, base (and insolent) actor is joined an intense resentment and envy of Shakespeare's dramatic success.[50] Whether the injured

poet made any reply to this deathbed attack is a question I postpone.
But he resented it to the public effect that within three months the
young playwright and printer Henry Chettle was apologizing to him
and Marlowe in an Epistle to his own *Kind-Harts Dreame* (1592, S.R.,
December 8). He names neither man, but no scholar has doubted
their identities. Apparently they have accused him of writing the libel
himself, which he disclaims, speaking of

a letter written to diuers playmakers, is offensiuely by one or two of them
taken; and because on the dead they cannot be auenged, they wilfully forge
in their conceites a liuing Author: and after tossing it to and fro, no remedy,
but it must light on me . . . With neither of them that take offence was I
acquainted, and with one of them I care not if I neuer be [obviously Marlowe, with his atrocious personal reputation]: The other, whome at that time
I did not so much spare [while editing Greene's papers for the press], as
since I wish I had, for that . . . I am as sory as if the originall fault had
beene my fault, because my selfe haue seene his demeanor no lesse ciuill
than he exelent in the qualitie he professes: Besides, diuers of worship haue
reported his uprightnes of dealing, which argues his honesty, and his facetious grace in writting, that approoues his Art.[51]

Observe how explicit and comprehensive is this witness in repudiation. To Greene's libel of egotism, Chettle replies with his experience
(just recently) of Shakespeare's civility; to Greene's contempt for the
actor, with his judgement not alone of Shakespeare's excellence but,
by implication, of the worth of the profession or "quality." To dispose
of what many contemporaries (among them Barnabe Riche, renewing
Greene's attack in a work of 1594)[52] seem to have taken as a charge
of plagiarism, owing to a misunderstanding (possibly) of the "feathers"
phrase, Chettle then invokes general honourable witness to Shakespeare's moral character, and not only to this but to the elegance
("facetious" meaning polished) of his work for the stage.[53] Courtesy,
professional excellence, integrity, artistry. A most unusual apology, I
think, especially when viewed in the light of an independence, on
Chettle's part, that refused to make any amends whatever to the most
famous playwright of the moment; and a vivid introduction to the
subject of the present biography.

EARLY COMEDY

WE SAW THAT in the best modern opinion Shakespeare had largely
to break ground for himself in the English chronicle play, and we

will see later that something of the sort was his necessity also when he came to essay tragedy. But four main avenues already to some degree explored lay open before him in comedy; and he took, quickly, all four. There was Roman comedy, and *The Comedy of Errors* adapts Plautus' *Menaechmi*, with an addition from the *Amphitruo*. There was the bombastic, often obscene element in the Morality or "Interlude," and he adopted this tradition not only into his comedies but into his history plays: Richard actually says,

> Thus, like the formall Vice, Iniquitie,
> I morallize two meanings in one word—

on which the best gloss is A. P. Rossiter's, that "Barabas, the Jew of Malta, Aaron in *Titus Andronicus*, Richard III, and Iago has each his devil's shadow; and the tricksy malice and jocularity of each of them derives from the tradition of the old Vice, but for whom no villain need have been a comic."[54] There was the native low comedy of *Ralph Roister Doister* (1553) and *Gammer Gurton's Needle*, and he was to make much use of this. Finally there was native elegant high comedy, on the Italian model, in the court plays of John Lyly, who may certainly be regarded as one of Shakespeare's masters, with his mark unmistakable on *The Two Gentlemen of Verona* and *Love's Labour's Lost*.

The *Errors* is nothing much to read, perhaps, but it has one commanding merit, which was put admirably by the veteran Ashley Thorndike. "Where Shakespeare's play," he writes, "surpasses Lyly's and all other imitations of the Roman comedy is not so much in the ingenuity of the plotting as in its adaptability of the stage . . . The farce itself moves with unwavering attention to the dramatic possibilities of comic situation. In comparison with the best plays of the time, 'Mother Bombie' included, there is astonishingly little in it that is incidental and adventitious. The action never wanders off into byways and never stops—even for a song. Characterization and witty dialogue never delay the movement. As a result it was funny on Shakespeare's stage and has been just as funny on every stage where it has been acted."[55] In fact, fitted out with music [by Rodgers and Hart] and called *The Boys from Syracuse*, it was a smash hit on Broadway some years ago [1938]. One great reason for this effectiveness, in which none of his contemporary playwrights at all rivalled him, is certainly the *specific* character of Shakespeare's play-imagining. I take two instances. The part of Pinch was evidently written for the actor John

Sincler or Sincklo (who perhaps also played Robert Faulconbridge in *John* a year later)[56]:

> a hungry leane-fac'd Villaine;
> A meere Anatomie, a Mountebanke,
> A thred-bare Iugler, and a Fortune-teller,
> A needy-hollow-ey'd-sharpe-looking-wretch;
> A liuing dead man.

And Baldwin has proved beyond doubt that the play was written for either the Theatre or the Curtain, both only a few yards away from the old Great Gate of Holywell Priory in Finsbury Fields just north of London, and adjacent equally to one of London's principal places of execution:

> the melancholly vale;
> The place of death, and sorrie execution,
> Behinds the ditches of the Abbey heere.

He notes eight points of description for Act V's abbey of nuns: its abbey gate opens onto a street which leads to a nearby place of execution *in a vale* which is *behind the ditches* of the abbey, which are on the opposite side of the procession approach. He goes on to think Shakespeare witnessed the hanging here of a priest, William Hartley, on Saturday morning, October 5, 1588; but has not I think made out his case sufficiently for conviction.[57]

Two able passages may be cited as a sort of makeweight against the absence of any Shakespearean character-drawing. One unites the play's dominant Quest theme and the Identity theme that we found prominent in Henry VI and Richard III:

> For know my loue: as easie maist thou fall
> A drop of water in the breaking gulfe,
> And take vnmingled thence that drop againe
> Without addition or diminishing,
> As take from me thy selfe, and not me too.

The other is a spirited crescendo of dialogue illustrating, even so early, Shakespeare's unique ability to *put pressure on* and then suddenly *apply* it with an unexpected turn. Adriana explains to the Abbess that her husband has gone mad only recently, and the Abbess makes tranquil enquiry into the cause: lost wealth, a buried friend, "vnlawfull loue"?

> *Adr.* To none of these, except it be the last.
> Namely, some loue that drew him off from home.
> *Ab.* You should for that haue reprehended him.
> *Adr.* Why so I did.
> *Ab.* I but not rough enough.
> *Adr.* As roughly as my modestie would let me.
> *Ab.* Haply in private.
> *Adr.* And in assemblies too.
> *Ab.* I, but not enough.
> *Adr.* It was the copie of our Conference.
> In bed he slept not for my vrging it:
> Alone, it was the subiect of my Theame:
> In company I often glanced it:
> Still did I tell him, it was vilde and bad.
> *Ab.* And thereof came it, that the man was bad.

And she crushes the jealous wife with a violent speech.

But there is little enough of this excitement, even the four women are without character, and most critics have thought the *Errors* Shakespeare's first comedy. I follow Fleay and Baldwin in assigning it to 1589. "France . . . arm'd and reuerted, making warre against her heire" (III.ii.126) alludes to Henri IV, who became entitled to the throne on August 12 of that year, as a result of a spectacular opportunistic conversion which electrified London—he is supposed to have said, "Paris vaut une Messe." Spain's "Armadoes of Carrects" just earlier refers to the year before. The name Menaphon (V.i.368) is borrowed from Greene's new romance of that name (1589 also),[58] which twenty years later the poet made into *The Winter's Tale*: perhaps Aegeon's reunion with his Abbess wife at the end was suggested by a similar reunion in *Menaphon*, though his general source for the enveloping action is Gower's *Confessio Amantis*. I do not know where he picked up the Greek cities' trade war.

THOUGH LESS EFFECTIVE than the *Errors*, *The Two Gentlemen of Verona* is more *like* the comedies Shakespeare would write after these, in three ways worth our notice. He is much interested, throughout the play, in an ideal of gentility—the perfect courtier, well-born, handsome, skilled, travelled, scholar and lover and ideal friend. This was in the High Renaissance air all about him, for the

listening: but he very likely read at some point Hoby's translation of
Castiglione's *Courtier* (1586), and scholars are surely right in thinking
that he was strongly influenced, both here and later, by Sir Thomas
Elyot's admirable treatise on the education of the statesman (and "any
other Christian gentleman," as Canon Ainger added), *The Governour*
(1531).[59] Proteus' treachery to his friend Valentine follows closely
Titus' treachery to Gysippus (II.xii), except that we may feel Elyot
has drawn Titus more plausibly than Shakespeare has been able to
draw Proteus. Certain passages also remind one verbally of Elyot, and
I will mention two when we come to *Hamlet* and *The Tempest*,
though as usual with him Shakespeare transforms what he remembers, so that it is hard to be sure of his borrowings.

A second point is the sudden emergence of the dramatist's ability
to represent women. Her maid brings Julia a suitor's letter; she thrusts
it back unopened and sends the maid away and says:

> And yet I would I had ore-look'd the Letter:
> It were a shame to call her back againe,
> And pray her to a fault, for which I chid her.
> What 'foole is she, that knowes I am a Maid,
> And would not force the letter to my view?
> Since Maides, in modesty, say no, to that,
> Which they would haue the proferrer construe, I.
> Fie, fie: how way-ward is this foolish loue;
> That (like a testie Babe) will scratch the Nurse,
> And presently, all humbled kisse the Rod?
> How churlishly, I chid *Lucetta* hence,
> When willingly, I would haue had her here?
> How angerly I taught my brow to frowne,
> When inward ioy enforc'd my heart to smile?
> My pennance is, to call *Lucetta* backe
> And aske remission, for my folly past.
> What hoe: *Lucetta*.

(I.ii)

Here's a good deal done with a girl's soul in seventeen lines, and the
poet never rivalled it again till Juliet herself. Notice the emotional
organization. An introductory line of pensive regret: then three distichs, one with "shame," a second with "foole," the third an accu-
satory *generalization* on "foole," leading to the climax "Fie, fie,"
which begins the *three*-line unit that is the centre of the soliloquy;
then three more distichs of *self*-reproach, leading to *action* taken in

the final half-line, standing alone as an outcome of the debate announced in the opening line. Novice work, perhaps, but what talent. A promising beginning for the character; but this is all we get: she never develops—and Sylvia, the other heroine, is negligible. Still, the dramatist is under way with women.

The third point is the sudden endowing of a clown—against our expectation—with a voice of his own. Speed in Act I is nothing, any more than the Dromios were (and he continues to be nothing throughout). A second clown comes onstage alone at II.iii.1 and begins to talk to himself, or rather he begins to confide in the audience:

Nay, 'twill bee this howre ere I haue done weeping: all the kinde of the *Launces*, haue this very fault: I haue receiv'd my proportion, like the prodigious Sonne, and am going with Sir *Protheus* to the Imperialls Court: I thinke *Crab* my dog, be the sowrest natured dogge that liues: My Mother weeping: my Father wayling: my Sister crying: our Maid howling: our Catte wringing her hands, and all our house in a great perplexitie, yet did not this cruell-hearted Curre shedde one teare . . . Ile shew you the manner of it. This shooe is my father: no, this left shooe is my father; no, no, this left shooe is my mother: nay, that cannot bee so neyther: yes, it is so, it is so: it hath the worser sole: this shooe with the hole in it, is my mother . . . I am the dogge: no, the dogge is himselfe, and I am the dogge: oh, the dogge is me, and I am my selfe: I; so, so . . .

Here we attend, for the first time in English comedy, to a definite and irresistible *personality*, absorbed in its delicious subject to the exclusion of all else; confused, and engaging. The writing is completely professional, aimed at leaving to the actor as much play as possible. One would like to have seen the young playwright directing the part.

But Launce apart, and the entrancing song (so far superior to all the verse dialogue) "Who is *Sylvia?*" in IV.ii, *The Two Gentlemen* is a poor affair—"one of Shakespeare's worst plays" (Theobald), "certainly one of the weakest and least satisfactory of all Shakespeare's plays" (Fleay),[60] "Shakespeare's first essay at originality . . . sentimental bankruptcy . . . an infallible sign of an early play" (Chambers), "intention at its crudest" (Charlton),[61] "it minces uncertainly to an implausible conclusion . . . at best half-grown" (Van Doren).[62] There is no convincing evidence for dating. It must be later than the *Errors* and as much earlier as possible than *A Midsummer Night's Dream.* Malone put it in 1591. The source is a Spanish story by Jorge de

Montemayor [*Story of the Sheperdess Filismena*, in *Diana*, 1542], translated by Bartholomew Yong about 1582; this was not published till 1598, so Shakespeare saw either a manuscript [Yong's translation is known to have been completed by 1582] or read the French translation of 1578 or saw the Queen's Men play *The History of Felix and Filiomenia* [which is now lost] at court in 1585.[63]

1969–70

PART TWO

The Lectures

Shakespeare at Thirty

We must be content, then, in speaking of such subjects and with such premises to indicate the truth roughly and in outline . . . In the same spirit, therefore, should each type of statement be received; for it is the mark of an educated man to look for precision in each class of things just so far as the nature of the subject admits.
—Nichomachean Ethics

I am able to make from the springboard the great leap whereby I pass into infinity, my back is like that of a tightrope dancer, having been twisted in my childhood, hence I find this easy.
—Fear and Trembling

SUPPOSE WITH ME a time, a place, a man who was waked, risen, washed, dressed, fed, congratulated, on a day in latter April long ago—about April 22, say, of 1594, a Monday—whether at London in lodgings or at a friend's or a tavern, a small house in the market town Stratford some hundred miles by miry ways northwest, or at Titchfield House a little closer southwest, or elsewhere, but somewhere in England at the height of the Northern Renaissance; a different world. Alone at some hour in one room, his intellectual and physical presence not as yet visible to us although we know its name, seated or standing, highlone in thought. He is thirty years old today and few enjoy this jolt from decade to decade. It would be an error to imagine him very young. He has been married almost twelve years, has (at least) three children, and Elizabethans age fast. He follows several occupations or trades; "professions," we call them, just as we call each other upon no evidence "gentlemen," but in this age they stand low; in two of them, moreover, his future must look at the moment to William Shakespeare problematical. In the third he is now sensationally settled and he may not know that he is about to abandon it.

He is first an actor; this must be how he has chiefly got his living so far. In a book soon to appear students agree that it is he who will be described as an "old player," and possibly he has been a player for fifteen years. He may thrice have been alluded to in print as one. Let us put aside the two earliest "contemporary allusions" given by Sir Edmund Chambers (who does not believe in them either) as referring not to Shakespeare but to John Lyly ("Willy"), Michael Drayton ("Aetion"),[1] and substitute for them George Peele's vapid couplet in *Edward I*, a chronicle history published in 1591, wherein Queen Elinor says rather gratuitously and very awkwardly to Baliol, just named King of Scots by Longshanks:

> Shake thy spere in honour of his name,
> Vnder whose roialtie thou wearst the same.

This phrase is known elsewhere and the text of this play is morbidly corrupt; nevertheless, I follow hesitantly the late A. W. Pollard in thinking we appear to have here a punning compliment by the play-wright to the actor of the part, especially in view of testimony (1610) that Shakespeare had acted kingly parts. Then from another university wit, Robert Greene, we learned that in 1592 Shakespeare was a player who, intolerably, had set up also as playwright. And from an apology for Greene by his associate, the playwright-to-be Henry Chettle, that same year, we heard an opinion of Shakespeare's acting: it is "excel-lent." John Aubrey later will tell us that he "did act exceedingly well"—and all this is worth more emphasis than it has received, owing to a tradition that he wrote better than he acted.[2] An unilluminating tradition, for he also wrote better than anyone else has ever acted.

A player then; he plays kings—not Longshanks but Baliol—and other dignified parts (perhaps, as a boy actor, he once took female roles). Those parts that will be indicated are still unconceived, Adam in *As You Like It*, the Ghost in *Hamlet*.[3] In the latter play the Prince will have much to say against some current styles of playing, much to say for "a temperance, that may giue it smoothnesse," and he implies, in part of his advice to the Chief Player, a remarkable opin-ion of the philosophical and social importance of acting, which it will not be very daring in us to suppose that his creator will then hold also: "oresteppe not [says Hamlet] the modestie of nature: For any thing so ore-doone is from the purpose of playing, whose end both at the first, and nowe, was and is, to holde as twere the Mirrour up to nature: to shew vertue her feature, scorne her owne Image, and the very age and body of the time his forme and pressure." The history of theatrical apologetics contains no encomium or admonition more intense and lofty. But this sentiment, like the style, may lie veiled seven years in the future. So far William Shakespeare must have been apprentice and then "hireling" (not "sharor," or part owner) in whatever his company or companies were, rising to six shillings a week. Actors, by an ancient statute often renewed, are legally vagabonds—men who if caught masterless are to be branded and put to forced labour—except as they have status being servants to some nobleman or gentleman who protects a company. Just now we do not know that Shakespeare is a member of any company. The theatre is still in such ill repute that a young gentleman has vexed his mother by settling this month in Bishopsgate near the Bull Inn, where plays and players may corrupt his servants. Some private feelings of Shakespeare upon this occupation of his I postpone a little. But he must wonder as he reflects here late in April of 1594 whether he is going to be able to continue to be an actor at all. For a year and a half London's worst plague in generations has forbidden any playing except for one month in winter and a few court performances. Opening hopefully this month, the Rose had to close on the tenth, a Privy Council order of yesterday has again restricted access to court, and Shakespeare does not know that the plague is at last over now for nearly ten whole years. Of course the companies survive by travel in the provinces during plague time. But this disorganization, notable already from 1588 on, has deepened since 1592. Shakespeare can hardly suppose that an entire new period of stability is at hand. Indeed, he has taken up, during this period of protracted theatrical adversity, a new occupation.

For second he is a poet. I do not mean that he wrote early in his twenties perhaps a large number of sonnets, which he has not printed and which will not be printed for fifteen years more: nor that he writes songs. This is private expression, diversion, not occupation. The Elizabethan poet, too, has status only when attached; as the poet who greeted Elizabeth for the Earl of Hertford in the entertainment several years past at Elvetham, amid fantastic pageantry, was booted, lest he be imagined "a loose and creeping poet." With the 1,200-line *Venus and Adonis*, published a year ago with a dedication to the dazzling young Earl of Southampton, Shakespeare became a professional poet. He seems not to have known Southampton much. "Right Honourable," he wrote, "I know not how I shall offend in dedicating my vnpolisht lines to your Lordshop . . . onlye if your Honour seem but pleased, I account my selfe highly praised, and vowe to take advantage of all idle houres, till I haue honoured you with some grauer labour. But if the first heire of my inuention prove deformed, I shall be sorie it had so noble a god-father; and neuer after eare so barren a land, for feare it yeeld me still so bad a haruest." Poets dedicated often at random, fishing. A few months after, Thomas Nashe dedicated his novel *The Unfortunate Traveller* to Southampton, imitating Shakespeare ("these vnpolisht leaues of mine"), but with so little success that in a reprint of this year (1594) he has withdrawn the dedication. Shakespeare's stress upon a coming work suggests, behind conventional modesty, both self-confidence and calculation; a sort of threat, even, being implied (if you do nothing about this honour, you will not hear from me again). His experience must have contrasted with Nashe's, for he is now engaged on the "grauer labour." One reason for our pitching on the present date is that for the first time in his professional life we know exactly what William Shakespeare is doing. He is finishing a second, longer poem, *The Rape of Lucrece*. Just over a fortnight hence it will be registered for printing with a dedication to Southampton widely different in burden and tone from the first: "The loue I dedicate to your Lordship is without end . . . The warrant I haue of your Honourable disposition, not the worth of my vntutored lines makes it [the poem] assured of acceptance. What I haue done is yours, what I haue to doe is yours, being part in all I haue, deuoted yours." What "warrant" the poet has already received, his silent figure does not tell us. But the assurance of this address is as rare, among Elizabethan dedications spanning a social gulf, as was the self-possession of the first, and I think we must take it that a social and financial status never before, perhaps, very promising, has been by the Earl decisively improved. *Venus and Adonis*, meanwhile, has become one of the celebrated poems of the age; Thomas Heywood, down from Cambridge, is busy with the earliest extant imitation of it (*Oenone and Paris*). *Lucrece* will make its mark instantly. In an elegy upon a lady who died ten days ago, somebody signing himself W. Har. will urge Lucrece's poet (and also Cornelia's Thomas Kyd) to call home from the foreign past their pens for women's virtues and praise Lady Branch. For the wife of the Lord Mayor of London, one of the players' most persistent adversaries, Shakespeare we can hardly expect to respond; but it is instructive that he will only once or twice respond to such occasions and entreaties, which must have come thick henceforth. Through an age brimming with eulogy and lament, his friends will publish and die, his son will die, Essex fall, Southampton languish in the Tower and emerge, the Queen lie speechless sweating and perish, James be crowned, without poems from Shakespeare. He will begin or has already written a third long one, *A Lover's Complaint*, compose a single magnificent enigmatic occasion-poem, "The Phoenix and Turtle," throw off six crude lines of epitaph for a wealthy brewer, perhaps some squibs. These are all and more than we are sure of. *Lucrece*'s dedication promises nothing further. But a change will take place immediately in his affairs; whether at the moment he plans a career as a poet, we can hardly say.

For third he is a playwright, and although there is more to be said for his poems than mid-twentieth-century criticism will find to say, this last is certainly the reason we are looking at him. He sits here as the author of a good many plays, including probably three comedies, *The Two Gentlemen of Verona, The Comedy of Errors, Love's Labour's Lost*, much of a double chronicle called *The First Part of the Contention between York and Lancaster*, and *The True Tragedy of Richard Duke of York* (known to us misleadingly as the second and third parts of *Henry VI*), and *Richard III*. It is most improbable that all of Shakespeare's early work has survived. For excellent reasons, his escaped the general mortality of plays. Of 250 surviving plays from the three decades 1581–1611 that he might have seen or acted in, one-sixth are his own; two of his are the only survivors we can place readily in the busy theatrical year 1595. But one of his very late collaborations is known to be lost (*Cardenio*), and no doubt some apprentice work is lost to us, particularly in its original form. Tantalizing among many plays mentioned later as his are *Love's Labour's Won* (part or most of which may survive under another title), *Iphis and Ianthe* (a subject from one of his favourite works, the *Metamorphoses*, and a form of title he liked), and *King Stephen* (a reign, fully treated by Holinshed, which has points in common not only with John's but with those of Henry VI and Richard II). He has doubtless, like other authors, started things and laid them aside. Some of his casual work survives in plays by other men. He has written at least two scenes (II.iv, IV.ii) into a stage success, known to us unfortunately as *I Henry VI*, worked up by Greene and Nashe to capitalize on the popularity of the "Contention" plays by dramatizing the earlier part of Henry's reign; he may have helped an imitator with *Edward III*; and he has lately done a general job of revision, with mocking enthusiasm, on somebody's bloody *Titus Andronicus*. The point of revising plays is that double admission can be charged for plays billed as "new"—an elastic term —and the special point in plague time is that the impoverished companies can seldom then afford wholly new plays. Plays in fact have been swapping about desperately, as companies go on the rocks and have to sell playbooks, costumes, anything. For the same reason, plays are coming this year in numbers into printers' hands; normally, of course, the company that has bought a play from its author wants its use exclusively and so objects to its printing. *Titus* was registered for printing two months ago, on the day of its last performance by Sussex's Men (it had belonged earlier to Derby's Men, and to Pembroke's). Ten days ago without his knowledge began a raid on work dominantly Shakespeare's, with the registration of a mutilated version of *I Contention* (or *2 Henry VI*), constructed probably from memory by a minor actor with Pembroke's Men last autumn, when that company broke up, for sale to a printer. A similar, vulgarized "report" of *2 Contention* (*Richard Duke of York* or *3 Henry VI*) will follow the next year; and meanwhile, ten days hence, will be registered for print something called *The Taming of a Shrew*, of which the less said the better, though criticism is finally beginning to agree to regard it as a memorial reconstruction of a lost play which stood behind the later *Shrew* play, part Shakespeare's—the lost play having been itself perhaps part Shakespeare's.

So nearly half his visible dramatic work to date may have been botched. How will Shakespeare feel about it? Philistine biography has an easy answer: he will be indifferent, or concerned at most with the financial loss represented in case he is still associated with any of the companies involved. Why not otherwise take authentic versions (of the long poems) to his own printer, Richard Field? In passing: the poet's relation with Field, a Stratford contemporary who married well, may just now be deteriorating; it is John Harrison the elder who will enter *Lucrece*, and though Field will print it for him, he will also transfer to Harrison the next month *Venus and Adonis*; Field, for that matter, seldom prints poetry for himself. But the real reproof is different and double. Companies own plays, not authors, and anyway, the printers of the pirated versions now control the copyrights. Shakespeare could be wild and helpless. Note also that no *original* work of his is yet involved. Later, when his power has increased and original work is infringed, more often than not we will find him active enough when this sort of thing happens. I have been trying so far to avoid general conceptions or preconceptions. But now that the complacent image of an Apollonian Shakespeare has threatened to disturb our patient enquiry into the situation of this gifted veteran thirty years old, it seems time to draw nearer. It is a question whether we have not found him angry and helpless—but active as well—already.

His manifest public career begins for us with an onslaught by the dying Greene two years before. Greene was a vain, irritable, red-headed character of thirty-four who when young had written a series of mellifluous romances, which are still half readable and which strongly engaged Shakespeare—their mark is early plain on *The Two Gentlemen*. Greene plastered his title pages with his university degrees. Interested by the triumph of Marlowe's *I Tamburlaine* in 1586–87, he took up playwriting. Then he turned to realistic pamphlets on sharp practice in London, having deserted his wife for the sister of an important thief named Cutting Ball. Presently he underwent a spectacular and unevenly convincing repentance, displayed in various new pamphlets; of which it is the snarling close of one of the last, written shortly before his pathetic, almost desolate death of a surfeit of wine and pickled herring, that we care about. In order to estimate the force of Greene's attack on Shakespeare, we must take note of several conditions: Greene's fame, the publicity of the affair (such that Barnabe Riche, in a work registered soon before Shakespeare's birthday now in 1594, renews the attack), Shakespeare's highly probable sensitivity upon the educational score, the social score—and just possibly also upon the score of his name.

The name seems to have been a Middle English formation, after the Norman model, for some blustering warrior or overactive sergeant of the law: an imperative nickname.[4] It is immaterial that the first known Sakspere, a William from a village south of Stratford, was hanged in 1248 for robbery, and that the first known Warwickshire Shakespeare was a felon who fled the country. But it is not immaterial, either, that just a century before our date a Merton College Shakespeare changed his name to Saunders, *"quod vile reputatum est,"* or that the poet himself may have had recourse as a boy to one of his grandfather's variants, Shakeschaft. Greene, who felt himself deserted by the actors, his inferiors (though it is not clear what they owed him and he had even on one occasion cheated them by a double sale of a play), was warning Marlowe and other university playwrights away from them, "those Puppets (I meane) that spake from our mouths, those Anticks garnisht in our colours." The worst of them, Greene pursued, is "an vpstart Crow, beautified with our feathers, that with his *Tygers hart wrapt in a Players hyde*, supposes he is as well able to bombast out a blanke verse as the best of you: and being an absolute *Iohannes fac totum*, is in his owne conceit the onely Shake-scene in a countrey." Quite apart from the impudent parody of one of Shakespeare's lines in *2 Contention* ("Oh Tygres Heart, wrapt in a Womans Hide"), here was a congeries of contempt and slander that might enter into the soul. It is far from clear to me that this is not a main slander handled in the sonnets of Shakespeare, particularly the last two of the extremely bitter trio 110–111–112. 110 speaks with self-contempt of his "motley" occupation, but in 111 the emotion has swung to an access of self-pity, with a special complaint:

O for my sake doe you with fortune chide,
The guiltie goddesse of my harmful deeds,
That did not better for my life prouide
Then publick means which publick manners breeds.
Thence comes it that my *name* receiues a brand,
And almost thence my nature is subdu'd
To what it workes in, like the Dyers hand,
Pity me then, and wish I were renu'de.
Whilst like a willing pacient I will drinke
Potions of Eysell gainst my strong infection . . .

And 112 begins:

Your loue and pittie doth th' impression fill
Which vulgar scandall stampt upon my brow,
For what care I who calls me well or ill
So you *ore-greene* my bad, my good alow?

Though not much addicted to cryptograms, I feel the suggestion as
plausible which sees in the otherwise unknown word "o'er-greene"
an allusion to the name of his tormentor,[5] somewhat as in "out-
Herod," the meaning of the clause then being: If you wipe out
Greene's insult to what *is* ill in me, my occupation . . . In these
excruciated poems no resort is had to the veneration for playing that
will be expressed by Hamlet; instead, a proud nature seems stung to
a writhing assent to what is true in Greene's charge. This is Shakespeare helpless, in private with one friend. In public he resented the
attack so effectively that, within three months Chettle—whom Shakespeare and Marlowe (he says)[6] accused of writing the thing himself
—had apologized in the Epistle to a book of his own. Not to Marlowe,
whom he does not care ever to meet. But to Shakespeare, whom
Chettle when he was preparing Greene's posthumous papers for the
press had not met either, but since has met, and is now "as sory [for
not having changed the passage] as if the originall fault had beene
my fault, because my selfe haue seene his demeanor no lesse ciuill
than he exelent in the qualitie he professes: Besides, diuers of worship
haue reported his uprightnes of dealing, which argues his honesty,
and his facetious grace in writting, that approoues his Art." Observe
how explicit and comprehensive is this witness in repudiation. To
Greene's libel of egotism, Chettle replies with his experience of
Shakespeare's civility; to Greene's contempt for the actor, with his
judgement not alone of Shakespeare's excellence—by implication, of

the worth of the profession or "quality." To dispose of what many contemporaries seem to have taken as a charge of plagiarism, owing to a misunderstanding (possibly) of the "feathers" phrase, Chettle then invokes general honourable witness to Shakespeare's character, and not only to this but to the elegance ("facetious" meaning polished) of his work for the stage. Courtesy, professional excellence, integrity, artistry. A most unusual apology, I think; especially when viewed in the light of an independence that refused any amends whatever to the most famous playwright of the moment. It suggests that William Shakespeare had become more favourably known, was more imposing by 1592, than some careful students allow. And it introduces us to his character.[7] "His character," somebody will exclaim like Tesman in *Hedda Gabler*. "But, good heavens, we know nothing about his character!" No; but there is a thing or two more to be said about it all the same.

What is your physical image for this man I don't know. The first authentic image surviving is the fatuous bust at Stratford, perhaps made from a mask, but conventionally made as a sepulchral affair and since butchered (let's mean: brought to resemble a butcher) by incoherent repaintings over the stone. The third and last authentic image surviving, engraved by a young Fleming in London, half a dozen years after the man's death, for a collection of his plays in folio, you will have seen there or elsewhere and probably hardly admire. If opposite the present page were placed the second authentic image surviving, which is less well known, I think you would be interested. It is again recognizably Martin Droeshout's "immortal piece of inferior engraving," though the head alone, say, without the vile-drawn dwarf's doublet; but if you looked at it with care, the other two presentments of the man would fade. This is the first state (or "proof") of the folio portrait, known in just four copies.[8] Spielmann describes it as that of a frank young English face, with firm delicate features, a gaze calm and observant under fair eyebrows set low. The forehead is bald—perhaps prematurely, perhaps shaved either in a fashion (as were the monks of Iona) or for ease in playing venerable characters; it is broad and massive but lacks entirely the bulbous appearance you are familiar with, and the dark hair grows naturally down from each side of it. There is a slight downy mustache, a small lip-beard above a strong smooth chin. Spielmann speaks also of a "characteristic aspect of large sympathy held in control by critical judgment, the strong reserve of individuality." One sees clearly why Aubrey was told that he was "a handsome well shap't man." Beautifully oval, the forehead wide, high, prominent, the jaws not prominent except as rondure, the chin large but round, the face might alone have inspired Mantegazza's catalogue of the characteristic appearance of intelligence. The nose, however, which dominates it is singular, a little broader at the nostrils than down the straight, solid bridge. The upper lip is deeply bowed, the lower full. But what is visible of one ear is so misshapen that I wonder how far we can trust Droeshout in detail. Spielmann believes he worked from an outline drawing of the poet, with flat washes of colour, made when Shakespeare was about thirty.

This, then, is the man we have been looking at. Whether Spielmann's impression of "frankness" will do, I doubt. Years of studying the image off and on have not diminished my contrary sense of its enigmatic character. There are faces that seem *merely* reserved. This speaks, it is all but ardent. Yet, proud without assertion, harmonious, formidable, less than any face I have seen does it yield you up any secret. The ambivalent impression is enforced, perhaps, not checked, by the one anecdote transmitted to us about Shakespeare's father. Somebody once saw the "merry cheekt" old man in his shop—he was a glover—and heard him say that "Will was a good Honest Fellow, but he durst have crackt a jeast with him at any time."[9] With a son only "gentle," companionable, "witty," as his contemporaries tell us Shakespeare was, there would have been no question of "daring" to crack a jest.

Now turn back from this face to the second state of the portrait and see what poor Droeshout has done in his attempt to give it proper age and status as the frontispiece to a folio. He has made the skull hydrocephalus by multi-management of light, lifted the hair like a wig, eradicated a mole on the left cheek, stubbled the chin, puffed and hollowed the under-eyes, achieved at last that hard, foxy, *false* appearance which has gravelled us all and sent so many weak-minded persons scurrying about in search of the "real" (the titled) author. I will not suppose that a poet looks like a poet necessarily, whatever that appearance may be. But if he does—as Virgil did, we know from the unrivalled mosaic discovered in Tunisia in 1896, and as Shakespeare (it seems) did—it is not only as well to know it but important not to suppose that he didn't. My point, of course, is an analogy. Just as you forget the Stratford bust and Droeshout's rehandling, so it will be helpful if, while recalling as vividly as possible everything you have experienced of Shakespeare's work, you can put out of mind all that you have hitherto known of his character and life. You may know, for example, that Shakespeare was relatively uneducated, his parents illiterate, that he matured very late after a long period in regard to which one guess is as good as another about what he was doing, that he commenced playwright by rewriting other men's plays, that Marlowe was his master, that he followed literary and theatrical fashions, that he did not deal with contemporary events, that he was indifferent to the fate of his work. These are fancies. Some may be true fancies, some false; I think most are false; but all are troublesome because they interfere with the reception of an image which has to be created slowly. At thirty men think reluctantly back over their lives, and we must try how far we can follow him.

THROUGH THREE AND A HALF centuries up to the publication of Hyder Rollins's enormous variorum edition of the sonnets in 1944, hardly anything was discovered about when they were written, and Rollins overlooked the shrewdest suggestion perhaps ever made, that of Fripp's about "o'er-greene," which, a few pages back, I tried to strengthen. This is in accordance with a fatality that seems to dog Shakespearean study. Of "the most expressive man that has existed," the item of correspondence that has survived is a loan-begging letter to him, which was never sent. Of England's most effective dramatist, the surviving manuscript is part of a play that was never produced. But from two known circumstances it has never been likely that the sonnets could be much later as a whole than the poet's thirtieth birthday—the last line of Sonnet 94 being quoted in *Edward III* (printed 1595) and Shakespeare's "sugred Sonnets among his priuate friends" being a familiar fact to Francis Meres at some time before September 1598. Into the currently hot controversy (which is weirdly neglecting these two circumstances), I enter here only to explain and a little assist Leslie Hotson's position. Three years ago Hotson took Sonnet 123, of which nobody had ever made any sense whatever, and, proving "pyramid" a regular term for obelisk, argued that the sonnet probably refers to the famous obelisks disinterred by the Pope's order and re-erected at Rome, one each year during 1586–89. Their celebrity was European; strangers just off the ship, we are told, ran to see the first, the marvelous Needle. Not the poet.

> No! Time, thou shalt not bost that I doe change,
> Thy pyramyds buylt vp with newer might
> To me are nothing nouell, nothing strange;
> They are but dressings of a former sight:
> Our dates are breefe, and therefor we admire
> What thou dost foyst vpon us that is ould . . .

The "dated" sonnet so-called (107), about the "mortal moon," had been here and there asserted to refer to the Armada and its defeat in 1588, but assertion is nothing. If the Spanish fleet did not in actuality approach in crescent form, as Hotson supposes, yet that the English thought it did he proves with five quotations calling it a moon (to which, since, others have been added). More cogent still, since 1475 European prophets, Protestants, astronomers had been predicting a doom, a wonder, for '88; and for decades afterwards England would rejoice over the catastrophe (designed by some "to be the end of the world"—1631) prophesied and avoided.

> Not mine owne feares, nor the propheticke soule
> Of the wide world, dreaming on things to come,
> Can yet the lease of my true loue controule,
> Supposde as forfeit to a confin'd doome.
> The mortall Moone hath her eclipse indur'de,
> And the sad Augurs mock their owne presage,
> Incertenties now crowne them-selues assur'de
> And peace proclaimes Oliues of endlesse age.
> Now with the drops of this most balmie time,
> My loue lookes fresh . . .

In view of the immediacy of the last six lines, it is useless to deny the possibility that Sonnet 107 was composed in the late summer or early autumn of 1588. Hotson fancies Shakespeare waited until the year ended, but that balmy rain feels like a summer rain and news of the Armada's conclusive dispersal came early in August. Sonnet 123 follows very well in 1588 or 1589; 124—we will see presently—in the latter half of 1589. But except for two odd sonnets (125, 126), these two last end the sequence; all those to Shakespeare's mistress (127–52, followed by two more odd sonnets) having been collected at the end, probably by the 1609 printer, in order to spare the reader as long as possible a story unedifying, the woman being married and also having seduced at one point the poet's young friend. More explicit and savage than those to the friend, these twenty-six belong with Sonnets 40–42. To 107, moreover, is linked backward 106, and to it 105; 104 is the sonnet celebrating three years of friendship with the young man, and I think we may take it, on the present evidence, that Shakespeare wrote most of his sonnets during 1586–88. A few are no doubt later. 110–12 I have placed tentatively in 1592, 125 I should suppose much later. These are misplaced, then. I expect others are. But on the whole the received order is more acceptable than critics (except Chambers) have inclined to allow. The sonnets do not tell a story, still less do they follow a fashion, though a habit of sonnet writing will produce occasional exercises; they reflect interests, pieces of living, two passions. About twenty-five of them contain passages that lodge them among the most beautiful or most energetic short poems in English. Three or four challenge perfection.

But most of them are very moderately good or bad, and I think their mediocrity has been insufficiently appreciated by those critics who feel strong resistance to an early dating for the sonnets. On the other hand, one reason for the resistance is probably the excellence of certain sonnets. The critic cannot imagine lyric verse of this quality proceeding from an author who is simultaneously writing dramatic verse so inferior or no dramatic verse at all that has survived. Here we stumble, I believe, on a misunderstanding of the differences between lyric and dramatic verse. Let the critic consider the superiority of the song "Who is Sylvia?" to almost all the verse dialogue of its play, *The Two Gentlemen*. A similar misunderstanding of the differences between dramatic and narrative verse has led scholars either to set the beginning of Shakespeare's dramatic career much too late or to fancy *Venus and Adonis* written long before it was printed and to brood painfully over the turgidity of *Lucrece*. Scholars troubled by the poet's allusions to his aging must underestimate either the Renaissance convention or the actual feelings of oldness endured by some young poets, or both. With another reason for resistance to Hotson's discoveries I confess less sympathy. The critic has made up out of nothing long ago, or borrowed, a view which evidence distresses. A man with a distinct idea of what the other side of the moon is like will naturally be disturbed when he arrives. Hotson's case, though itself very difficult, far from being conclusive, and inadequately argued by him, is not only much less unsatisfactory than Professor Harbage's, say, who tries to place in 1603, in the teeth of likelihood, the two sonnets I have discussed; it is the best case we have.

We have arrived, of course, only at some dates, not at identities. Who the dark-haired woman was God knows; her husband was named Will. There has been no small speculation about the identity of the friend, "Mr. W.H.," to whom the 1609 printer dedicated the sonnets as their "onlie begetter." This he was not, but Thorpe was willing enough to keep the woman out of sight. I neglect the considerations positive and negative which ought always to have made it inconceivable that the friend was an earl; since Southampton (and of course Pembroke, forlorn hope) we can dismiss on the score of date. Any gentleman was far enough above an actor. Now we enter the jungle. In the autumn of 1594 will be printed a tedious work in fluent stanzas, ostensibly by one Henry Willoughby, about how various suitors including himself assail with words the virtue of an innkeeper's faithful wife, Avisa. It is implied that she lives in Sherborne, Dorsetshire, where her husband keeps the George, and she may have been a real woman named Avis. I doubt if she was; it has not been noticed that the name "Avice" was considered by some "detorted from *Hilveg*, that is, Lady-defence" (Camden's *Remaines*). Willoughby, when his turn comes, seeks the advice of his "familiar friend," and "old player," "W.S.," who "not long before" fell in love himself and is just over it. Shakespeare, if this is he, gives some unexceptionable advice, in dull stanzas.[10] The whole work is so earnest and dull that it is hard to see it as aggressive, but aggressive it must have been, considering much hocus-pocus impossible to describe briefly, an even duller counterattack by one Peter Colse in 1596, and an order of suppression in 1599. I am not sure "Henry Willobie" is an actual Henry Willoughby, who went up to Oxford at sixteen in 1591. But his stated initials are H.W. Now Southampton's initials were H.W. (Henry Wriothesley) and Pembroke's W.H., and Southampton may conceivably be satirized in "Willobie." But as of the Friend of the Sonnets, both I believe are irrelevant. But we have seen another W.H. ("W. Har.," actually) addressing Shakespeare in verse in 1594, and there is a limit to the amount of coincidence I am willing to *conjecture*. Some of these friends and poets ought to be the same. If they are not, perhaps we might declare further coincidence inadmissible. Shakespeare's young friend of the sonnets was certainly named Will, and I see "Will" in "Willoughby," and further, without evidence, we can hardly go. Of the "rival poet" nothing can be said except that Marlowe is currently leading Chapman in that ghostly race; from which, I think, Kyd ought not to be excluded.

Hotson's case for a third dated sonnet, 124, is less striking in itself than his others, but more significant still when we link its two parts to two topical features correspondent to them in *The Comedy of Errors*. Again, both religion and politics are implicated; Shakespeare is coming to seem a more allusive poet, perhaps, than we thought him. The scene for the execution threatened at the end of the *Errors*, Baldwin has contended, fits point to point the execution stand set up in Finsbury Fields, near the Theatre and Curtain north of London, where a priest was executed in October 1588 (his initials, I note with horror, were W.H.). If Baldwin exaggerates the psychological correspondence between history's scene and the dramatist's, he makes it appear very possible that Shakespeare's Act V was designed for one of those two theatres at no long interval after the execution, which presumably he witnessed. Now, his subject in Sonnet 124 is the difference between his love and other enthroned things such as monarchs: *their* subjection to change of fortune, weakness-in-power, assassination political or religious, *its* invulnerability—"It feares not policy that Heriticke . . ." In view of this line, Hotson is undoubtedly justified in referring the couplet to the Jesuit-inspired, devout, futile attempts to cut down Elizabeth:

> To this I witnes call the foles of time,
> Which die for goodness, who haue liu'd for crime.

Yet a sympathy is impressive here behind the theme and verbal condemnation, of interest as our first glimpse of Shakespeare's mature spiritual feeling. We recall his training in balance between the religious parties, as his father had been (and he would be) suspended between social classes, as he stood balanced in some sense, in his twenties, between the sexes (the theory, by the way, that he was ever a practicing homosexual is of course untenable). But the earlier part of the sonnet is still more definite than this allusion to Jesuits executed. It uses for metaphor Henri III of France, the "childe of state": whose people rise against him in support of the Duke of Guise in May 1588 ("might for fortunes bastard be vnfathered"), who for the rest of the year endures affably a contemptuous, pro-Guise States General and even news that Guise intends to kill him ("suffers . . . in smiling pomp"), who murders the Duke and is himself monk-murdered in the summer of 1589—"falls under the blow of thralled discontent, Whereto th'inuiting time our fashion calls . . ." He had named Henry of Navarre his heir, civil war revived, and to this there is explicit allusion in the *Errors*. "I could find out," confides a Dromio, "Countries" in the kitchen wench, and to "Where France?": "In her forehead, arm'd and reuerted, making warre against her heire." A minute later we hear of "Armadoes of Carrects," and anyway, this quadruple topicality is irresistible; both sonnet and play ought to belong to 1589.

Shakespeare, then, would seem to have begun writing comedy *at the latest* directly after the sonnets. This chronology would account incidentally for what has always seemed to me one of the sonnets' anomalies; he speaks of writing sonnets, of acting, of travelling, of his mistress, of scandal, of a book he gives the friend (77), of a memorandum book the friend gives him (122), but never of writing plays. Perhaps he began in 1588, at twenty-four. Baldwin and Hotson reinforce each other more impressively, of course, by not knowing each other's work. The trouble with this view of Shakespeare's dramatic outset is that it raises as many difficulties as does the "conservative" modern view that he began only about 1590 with 2 and 3 *Henry VI*, and in the face of these difficulties the positive evidence is by no means mandatory. I don't believe we can yet say confidently whether he began with comedy or history.

But the conservative view has for a long time been entangled with a most serious error, the clearing up of which does perhaps enable us to form a more satisfactory image of his dramatic outset than has ever been possible before, if he did not begin with comedy. I feel sure, that is, that the editors of the Henry VI plays, H. C. Hart and Dover Wilson, are right in regarding them as not originally Shakespeare's, while current authority is wrong in thinking the two important plays are. What is intolerable about the conservative view is that they are patently by several authors, among these dominantly Shakespeare, but the ground plan seems in both 2 and 3 *Henry VI* to have been laid by somebody else, probably Greene. The difficulty with this is that they are so greatly superior to plays of the period by Greene or anybody else (except Marlowe's *Edward II*, which follows and imitates them). Consider the superiority alone in theatrical address, the setting up of a story. 2 *Henry VI* springs into being as ceremonial, joyous, expectant—the King's bride, whom he has never seen, is about to arrive—everything looks splendid—then a fact, which we feel as odd, is introduced: she comes without dowry—the King pays no attention—but he is shrinking in our sight as the peers grow tall—a qualm—and suddenly, as the author looses the peers, power is pulling exactly seven ways—in Scene ii, power pulls an eighth way—and under this comparison, none of Shakespeare's rivals seem to have a story to tell at all.

I think the key may be found in the length of these plays. One of the things Shakespeare was to revolutionize was play length. Of thirty-six plays belonging to 1590–94, the average length is 2,250 lines; of four by Greene, 2,200. I expect, as originally written, 2 and 3 *Henry VI* were typically inept and strengthless, psychologically primitive, usual-length Greene plays—which Shakespeare expanded into these outsize astonishing dramas (the first over 3,000, the second just under) that gave the theatre after *Tamburlaine* its fresh and true start. Now the hard questions have always been, *why* and *how* the young actor did any such thing. How came he to? Who let him? Who but the other actors? What actor would not have in his part, rather than Greene's inexpressive lines, Gloucester's to the Keeper of his disgraced Duchess:

> Entreat her not the worse, in that I pray
> You vse her well: the World may laugh againe,

And I may liue to doe you kindnesse, if
You doe it her . . .

or a weaver's honest testimony to something not relevant: "Sir, he
made a Chimney in my Fathers house, and the brickes are aliue at
this day to testifie it: therefore deny it not"? It was on the big "parts,"
especially York's, and the rant, and the comic scenes, that Shakespeare did most work—if that can be called work which seems done
so easily—but before he finished he had rehandled or written fresh
half the play. Maybe he really just began casually doing it, dissatisfied,
like his fellow actors, with the script they had bought; discovering in
himself, as he went, feelings that would not let him dismiss even two
flagrant impostors without the woman's parting "Alas Sir, we did it
for pure need" (which will not soften their sentence), and powers—
a diction, say, such that even in this early work he probably uses more
words than all his early dramatic rivals taken together—not to speak
of an intellect, an imagination, a structural sense, a wit, a sweetness
and energy of versification, a syntax, gifts equally for plenitude and
concision, all incomparable with theirs. He did much the same to
3 *Henry VI*, but with a dwindling interest perhaps (the first play is
better), until the figure of Richard rekindled it and drew him then
on his own into the masterwork of the opening period. Our taste is
uneasy, I think, with the malignant and beguiling Richard; the most
sufficient account of the daring manifested in his creation is that of
an eighteenth-century Scot, William Richardson. But this daring
throws a broad light forward to Shakespeare's achievements—the
greater the difficulties, the more active he is—and he was master here
already of the unique stroking of presentment that drove Coleridge
to one of his deepest conceptions, that of an "ensouling of experience
by meditation":

Richard loues *Richard*, that is, I am I.

Richard's opening soliloquy, which seems crudely explicit (ugly and
therefore unfit for love, I'll be a villain) and yet is so far from being
repellent that it fascinates, instead merely hints at what really matters
to Richard: his feeling that since wrong has been done him by nature,
he is justified in doing wrong—a sentiment which escapes our critical
coolness precisely because it is not expressed—unwittingly our similar
feeling about ourselves unites with Richard's, and we sympathize and
admire. Shakespeare, as Freud put it in an analysis of the speech,
"obliges us to supplement, he engages our intellectual activity, diverts

it from critical reflections, and keeps us closely identified with his hero."

This work was written, presumably, hard on *Henry VI*, and perhaps in 1592, before playing went under restraint for plague on June 23. Then the English drama reached full psychological stature in Shakespeare before Marlowe, whose *Dr. Faustus* followed *Richard III*. Shakespeare's predecessors in comedy determined the character of his work even less: Lyly as a remote model in elegant prose comedy, Henry Porter with some form of *The Two Angry Women of Abingdon* about 1589, Peele possibly, others no doubt unknown. *The Comedy of Errors* is a classical farce based on Plautus' *Menaechmi*, with touches in situation from the *Amphitruo*; but it is more complicated and elegant than Plautus and it adds an enveloping action that is romantic. *Love's Labour's Lost* is a classical comedy, likewise observant of the unities of time and place; no source is known for the plot, such as it is. *The Two Gentlemen of Verona* is related rather to the romantic action of the *Errors*, and its sources were romantic: a Spanish romance probably through the medium of a lost Queen's Men's play, *Felix and Philiomena* of 1585, perhaps a French tale translated by Henry Wotton in 1578, Aldington's *The Golden Asse of Apuleius* (1566), Arthur Brooke's poem *Romeus and Juliet* (1562), etc. This is Shakespeare's emptiest work—his only comedy, for instance, I've not seen performed—and ought for this reason, as well as for its interest in the conflict between love and friendship, a chief theme of the sonnets, to precede *Henry VI* and *Richard III*, though it may not have. Whether he began on the classical or romantic side, farcical or comedic, we can hardly yet say. But he developed towards the use of rhyme in comedy; *A Midsummer Night's Dream* will have as much rhymed as blank verse; and it may be instructive that in *The Two Gentlemen of Verona* this proportion is less than one-tenth, in the *Errors* one-third. The *Errors*, at least, cannot be later than 1594, because it was produced in notorious confusion at Gray's Inn at the end of the year. *Love's Labour's Lost* is peculiar in everything, partly because a great part of the end of the only version we have was rewritten by the poet about 1598. But the diverse strands of mockery blended in this first triumph of Shakespearean comedy were put at the service of an artistic method he never used again, to the end of polemic.

His wit rather than his heart is everywhere, I think, in *Love's Labour's Lost*, except in the revised portions. The first dramatic labour ever fully to engage Shakespeare's *heart* was his next. Here, I suppose, most readers would identify the author with his hero, if anyone, and

Mercutio. But among the most personal lines in the play seem to be some unnecessary lines of old Capulet, who has indeed already just welcomed his guests and will shortly welcome them again:

> Welcome gentlemen, I haue seene the day
> That I haue worne a visor and could tell
> A whispering tale in a faire Ladies eare:
> Such as would please: tis gone, tis gone, tis gone.

A moment later among meaningless chat we hear, for no reason, of somebody unidentified and indifferent: "His sonne is thirtie."

Shortly after his thirtieth birthday in 1594, a company was formed under the protection of the Lord Chamberlain, in which he bought a share; probably by a gift from Southampton, which may have been of £100.[11] In October, Hunsdon was instructing the Lord Mayor to let "my nowe companie" play again at the Cross Keys in Gracechurch Street, and William Shakespeare was one of three payees, with Richard Burbage and Will Kemp, for December performances at court. Perhaps the ambitious *Romeo and Juliet* was his first play for the Chamberlain's Men—as his one other tragedy before *Hamlet* will be written five years hence for the opening of the Globe. Shakespeare's field has strangely cleared: Lyly had long ceased to write for the stage, Peele was ill and to die, Greene and Marlowe and Kyd were dead. And so, on to his wilderness of dramatic literature, or garden, or palace, to be created in the six years coming—*Richard II, 1* and *2 Henry IV, Henry V, King John,* comedies of the *Dream,* the *Merchant,* and *Shrew, Merry Wives, Much Ado, As You Like It, Twelfth Night,* and *Caesar;* and beyond.

1953

Pathos and Dream

THE PROBLEM WITH Shakespeare, in discussing what we may call his Second Period, is to make him seem real. During the first six years of his thirties, 1594–1600, he invented the following plays: *Romeo and Juliet, Richard II, A Midsummer Night's Dream, King John, The Merchant of Venice, 1* and *2 Henry IV, The Merry Wives of Windsor, Much Ado about Nothing, Henry V, Julius Caesar, As You Like It,* and *Twelfth Night.* That's twelve; it must have been of this period that John Ward, vicar of Stratford fifty years after Shakespeare's death, heard he "supplied yᵉ stage with 2 plays every year,"[1] for this prodigious rate was not true apparently of his First Period, which I treated in a summary fashion, so far as its achievements have survived to us, and it will not be true of his Third and Fourth (or tragic and final) Periods. This blinding and deafening array of dramatic work, which is able by itself to make pale the entire life effort of most great artists, constitutes what I am calling his Second Period, or the period of normal maturity, to which this and the two following lectures will be devoted. Today my discourse will be (unlike last week's) chiefly critical, the third lecture chiefly political and ethical (but there is Falstaff), and the fourth again critical, leading however through the convulsion of the English state towards the personal catastrophe of the spirit that ended his Second Period.

But the disconcerting rapidity of his production during this period is merely part of the general problem. He did so much well—his gifts were so various, his energy so great, he created so many persons, so many worlds—he produced alone, in a few years, such an anomalous proportion of the supreme dramatic literature of the whole world, in all ages—that not unnaturally Shakespeare is hard to believe in, either as an author or as a man. I have some hope that my account last week may have helped him to seem more credible as a man; but for the *author* everything is still to do. Our incredulity, to tell you the truth, does us small credit. It savours of what Kierkegaard called "playing the game of marvelling at world history." It betokens inexperience, and perhaps it is a little unmanly. At the highest levels of artistic understanding—in Coleridge, Baudelaire, Melville—you will not find it. Up there, admiration for Shakespeare strengthens, but incredulity about him evaporates. We judge of others by ourselves. On the other hand, before not only the grand mass of this creation but before some detailed triumph of imaginative design *within* a play, we do reasonably pause with astonishment. Sometimes, without warning, in a short speech, the soul of a man seems indeed to surface, for an instant, before it returns forever to the depths. Sometimes a series of this poet's phrases will drag at our profoundest thought as if, truly, we overheard the soul of the world murmuring truths to herself. In the face of this fundamental problem, which I think it better to admit candidly than to take for granted, I think I must offer you some general reassurances. It is reassuring to consider that Shakespeare wrote four failures, plays that, notwithstanding the immense attractive power of their author's name, few have ever cared to produce and mostly scholars read. These failures are *The Two Gentlemen of Verona, King John, All's Well that Ends Well,* and *Timon of Athens.* If we accept, with some modification, the established division of his work into four periods, you will notice that his four failures fall one in each period; and this, I think, is reassuring too. The reasons for his failure in each case were different, but at least he was always capable of failure, and it is pleasant to know this.

Also, against the bewildering plasticity which we correctly attribute to Shakespeare, but which will badly mislead us if we suppose it his governing characteristic, it will be useful to discriminate one personal and strong theme in his work which recurs from start to finish. Call it the *Utopian* theme. It dominates the choice of subject, again in four plays: *Love's Labour's Lost, As You Like It, Measure for Measure,* and *The Tempest;* and again these plays fall one in each period. The theme of withdrawal from the world into a perfect society, and the criticism then of that society, is treated differently in each period— which may be why no critic seems to have remarked the persistence of this preoccupation of Shakespeare's. But the theme is perfectly distinct, it is not one that engaged other contemporary playwrights, and it matters heavily in the development of his thought. This is the first time I have referred to Shakespeare's "thought." By this term I mean rather more than R. G. Moulton did or Alfred Harbage does. I mean the whole articulate attitude towards the world, both systematic and incidental, expressed as a developing understructure in his work dramatic and lyrical; and not in his work only, but in his life; and not towards the world only, but towards himself and towards God; a body of thought practical, psychological, ethical, and metaphysical, which we can not only *relate* to Renaissance thought in England but *distinguish* from it. Slowly I hope, in the course of this and the following lectures, to lay out the burden of the successive phases of his thought; meanwhile, it will be helpful to realize that some of its important elements, such as the Utopian theme, were permanently active under his reflection and speculation—that he did not by any means select the subjects for his plays at random. It is a fact that nearly *all* the subjects later employed by Shakespeare as dramatic subjects were familiar to him at thirty; and for instance, a passage in *The Two Gentlemen* already imitates a passage in the long poem that he later used as his substantial source for *Romeo and Juliet.*

A third reassurance is to be discovered upon consideration of the writing itself. One may admire more, but one wonders less, after a difficult feat has been investigated successfully, and let us put aside for a moment our vague sense that Shakespeare wrote extremely well, and wrote better and better, while we see just *what* he did better. I take first a poetic, and then a dramatic example. The poetic I borrow from the most sensitive living German critic of Shakespeare, who points out in the earliest histories *a development from simile to metaphor.* Henry VI compares himself to a ship:

> Thus stands my state, twixt Cade and York distressed;
> Like to a Ship, that having scaped a tempest,
> Is straightway calm'd, and boarded with a Pirate.

When Richard III compares himself to a ship, he *is* the ship. The passage comes in Act III, when he is pretending to refuse the crown that he has arranged to have offered to him:

> . . . so much is my pouertie of spirit,
> So mightie, and so manie my defects,
> That I would rather hide me from my Greatnesse,
> Being a Barke to brooke no mightie Sea,
> Than in my Greatnesse covet to be hid,
> And in the vapour of my glory smothered.

The gain both in immediacy and suggestiveness is great, but particularly the gain in emotional colouring (here: coyness); and in the last line, a lovely one, you see metaphor throwing a cloak over even the abstract. This direction was irreversible. To the end of his life Shakespeare used simile on occasion, but more and more, metaphor supplied the sinew of his style, advancing in subtlety of expressiveness.

My dramatic example is very short. "Genius at first," so the wisest of English novelists once wrote, "is little more than a great capacity for receiving discipline." The basic discipline for a playwright is the necessity of *writing for the actor*. A play is material for actors. Shakespeare used as few stage directions as Beethoven used emotional directions, in which other playwrights and composers are so prolific. It may be that Shakespeare, with the Chamberlain's Men, produced his plays himself, governed rehearsals, that is; we are not sure; almost certainly he had a hand in it. But the real, continuous control of the actor had to be *built into* the dialogue: e.g., of Titania, III.i.118: Bottom is singing—one can imagine his voice—and she says, "What angel wakes me from my flowery bed?" But Shakespeare was an actor himself. He knew intimately the abilities of the men he was writing for: the nine regular members of the company, the few hired men, and the boy actors. He knew that the actor has not only to be controlled and guided but he has to be *left free*. The human voice is far more expressive than any musical instrument, it has capacities—not to speak of the powers of stage position, gesture, facial expression— beyond any governable by the written word. We must think therefore of Shakespeare, by the time he came to write *Romeo and Juliet*, as accomplished in supplying materials to actors which both guided them and left them free, all the way over a broad scale of which the opposite limits would be Berowne's great set piece, "Have at you then, affection's men-at-arms" in *Love's Labour's Lost*, and the tiny dialogue which is my example. One of my favourite early dialogues in Shakespeare consists of just two words. The braggart Spanish courtier Armado, whom we know to be in love, meets Jaquenetta the country wench.

Armado Maid.
Jaquen. Man.

I am not an actor and cannot pretend to speak these lines adequately, but how much they imply! The two hardly know each other, but both are deeply interested. Armado is aware of his condescension in loving beneath him, but he is very tentative too. The girl's reply simplifies him to what she can deal with.

The fourth assurance I think we can have is a little surprising, and less easy to formulate. It is this: that as soon as Shakespeare attained, in 1594, a certain professional security, he seems to have worked *along the lines of major resistance*. The three plays we want to consider, that is, written that year and the next—a tragedy, *Romeo*; a history, *Richard II*; and a comedy, the *Dream*—either strike out afresh (when considered in relation to his previous work) or develop from its weakest, least successful part. Consider: his smash hits had been *The Comedy of Errors* in its farcical aspect and, in chronicle history, the trilogy culminating in *Richard III*—almost solely "energetic" history, we might call these plays. His artistic triumphs so far, to our view, had been *Richard III*, with the daring, "radiant hypocrisy" of its villain-hero, and *Love's Labour's Lost*. But *Romeo* and *Richard II* and the *Dream* are all rather less like any of these plays than they are like the romantic failure, *The Two Gentlemen*; and despite their different categories, they are all much more like each other than they are like anything else earlier. It is as if the poet deliberately turned his back upon all that at which he had shown himself most brilliant. Of tragedy he had had experience only with the Senecan melodrama *Titus Andronicus* and the Marlovian Gloucester (Richard III)— scarcely one element of either surviving to *Romeo and Juliet*. In history he turned to "pathetic" history; and here he had a model, the different Marlowe of *Edward II*, whom he utterly and instantly surpassed. In comedy he abandoned Lyly and, probably with influence from Henry Porter's *Two Angry Women of Abingdon*, concentrated upon strengthening and refining the romantic comedy he had initiated, without effectiveness, in the frame part of the *Errors* and in the *Two Gentlemen*. But in comedy he turned his back upon more than Lyly. In order to see what, we will have to look in some detail at *Love's Labour's Lost*.

A cluster of allusions and likelihood seem to locate the play (the revisions apart) late in 1593, perhaps December—a few months before Shakespeare's thirtieth birthday[2]; and its special air marks it as designed for private performance. Some ten thousand persons died in London again this year of plague (as if half a million New Yorkers were swept away); playing was restrained. Midway between his long poems, Shakespeare was fully in the favour of Southampton; the play must have been done for him, perhaps at Titchfield.[3] We are within a few months of the point where we began in April of 1594. Now I must invite your attention to some matters that interested the poet. We have seen how he followed French affairs. Despite Navarre's conversion, war dragged on in France between his forces under the young

Duc de Biron, Longueville, and others, and the League's under Mayenne; English troops were now engaged, and I suppose curiosity was active about the French lasciviousness—the King's notoriously, and Longueville had been one of his rivals for Gabrielle the year before, Mayenne had been prostrate with debauchery at Rouen. The young Earl of Essex stood very high at court, Southampton his intimate in one of the deepest friendships of the age. Essex's rival Sir Walter Ralegh, still in disgrace for the affair with a maid of honour in 1592 that had sent him to the Tower, had retired sulking to Sherborne and was occupied with study and speculation, surrounded by a small group of learned and literary men of whom the mathematician-astronomer Thomas Hariot was chief. The action of *Love's Labour's Lost* also takes place in retirement. The King of Navarre and three young lords, Berowne, Longaville, Dumaine, withdraw from the world to study for three years, vowing to see no women, fast, watch. Their austerity is to be relieved only by a fantastic strutting Spaniard named Armado, and incidentally a schoolmaster, Holofernes, and the clown Costard. But the Princess of France with three ladies comes visiting on a political embassy. In secret all four men love, breaking their vows; they discover each other and join forces; after a Farce of the Nine Worthies, Armado, who began the play by accusing Costard of breaking the retreat's laws with a country wench, is found to have got her with child himself; the ladies impose a year's penance upon the lords for vow breaking and part, agreeing to accept them afterwards.

The initial situation is very much that of a musical comedy in which Malenkov, Beria, and Tito agree to give up public life and retire together in silence to study theology.[4] But this satire is not developed, and I think that recent investigation, however disputable its details, has made good its claim that the general object of the play's satire is Ralegh and his group. Armado must in some degree be a caricature of Ralegh himself. He is melancholy, a "tough signeor" (Ralegh was over forty to Essex's twenty-six), poor, an orator and writer. "His humour," says Holofernes, "is loftie, his discourse peremptorie: his tongue fyled, his eye ambitious, his gate maiesticall, and his generall behauiour vaine, redicilous, and thrasonical . . . too picked, too spruce, too affected, too odd as it were, too peregrinat as I may call it." This is probably a fair Essex-Southampton image of Ralegh. To make him a Spaniard is merely the last straw. Armado cannot multiply one by three—"I am ill at reckning," he explains, "itt fitteth the spirit of a Tapster." The mathematical and astronomical satire is intermittent. There may be hits at Hariot in Holofernes, and

odd hits elsewhere, as at Nashe in Armado's page Moth, perhaps also
in Holofernes at Gabriel Harvey of Cambridge and John Florio (later,
at least, Southampton's tutor in Italian, but incompatible with him
politically).

Our knowledge of the makeup and interests of Ralegh's group is
imperfect. Shakespeare seems, however, to have taken Chapman's
poem *The Shadow of Night* as a statement of its doctrine, and this is
his real butt. Chapman called for solitude, contemplation, the Furor
Poeticus—

> No pen can any thing eternall wright,
> That is not steept in humor of the Night.

Berowne, throughout a critic of the others' proceedings, is Shakespeare's hero, and he replies directly in the opening scene:

> So ere you finde where light in darknes lyes,
> Your light growes darke by loosing of your eyes.

Of course Berowne is a fearful euphuist, too; he only surpasses the
others in self-knowledge and eloquence; and when he is converted
to plain speaking, when he rationalizes all their vow breaking with
an appeal against affectation and for *experience*, his author is as usual
in this play both serious and not serious. Shakespeare's position, as
against Chapman's, is a genuine one, but his heart is not in polemic.
He might have used Berowne's words, to Chapman:

> I haue for barbarisme spoke more
> Then for that Angell knowledge you can say . . .

Shakespeare's playful, imperturbable superiority must sometimes have
galled more dogmatic intellectuals.

But reflect now: how entirely all this political and literary satire,
this partisanship, this up-to-the-moment intellectual brilliance have
disappeared from his next three plays, pathetic and dreamy, *Romeo*,
Richard II, and the *Dream*. Although the personality that created
these works is clearly in many respects continuous with the personality that created *Love's Labour's* (and *Richard III*), it is at the same
time so different from them that the further transformations we are
to see it undergo should leave us unsurprised. In these opening plays
of the Second Period—in all of it, indeed—however the characters

may be feeling, we feel in the poet no angry desire, no acrid scorn, no fury of repudiation, no misery of endurance, no terrifying drift: emotions all familiar to us earlier in the sonnets, and emotions that will return. *Romeo and Juliet* is a tragedy of *pathos*, and curious as the denial may appear of what has long since taken rank as the chief love tragedy of Western literature, several responsible critics have denied that it is a true tragedy at all. I think they are wrong, but I see what they mean. A modern critic has called it an *experimental* tragedy. Let us ignore H. B. Charlton's exposition, of which the less said the better, and adopt his term for our own.[5]

Experimental in subject—as *Hamlet* for instance will not be—*Romeo and Juliet* certainly is.

Tragedy meant to the Elizabethan in 1594 the fall of princes; *The Mirror of Magistrates* had determined the sense. Senecan revenge melodrama, initiated by Kyd, and the tragedy of private monsters whose affairs were important to the state, initiated by Marlowe's *Jew of Malta*, had become familiar exceptions, and another exception had been provided by theological tragedy in *Dr. Faustus*, but none of these offered a model for *Romeo*, which is a domestic tragedy, as only *Othello* among Shakespeare's later works will be. Setting, characters, and action had neither historical nor mythological prestige; they are taken simply from a long poem by Arthur Brooke of the generation before, and whatever *status* Shakespeare wanted for them he had to give them himself. That the lovers' story in various forms was centuries old in Italy is immaterial.

Status is a product of, among other things, *structure*. It goes without saying that Shakespeare compressed Brooke's languid narrative from months to days. He fortified Romeo in two ways: by creating a foil for him in Mercutio, who hardly exists in Brooke, and by letting him kill at the tomb Paris, who just disappears from Brooke. But the major cross-actions of the love and the families' feud remained what they were: a sequence of accidents, beginning with the masquerade. The dramatist, experimenting, took two courses with them. He introduced order into them of a sort, by emphasizing the two motive personages (I follow now Moulton's analyses, which are never likely to be surpassed for lucid and comprehensive simplicity): "reconciling: Friar Laurence: honest herb wonders" and "destroying: The Apothecary: dishonest herb wonders."[6] And he struggled towards an enveloping action, so far as his style and experience permitted, by means of omens of impending fate. But Moulton's characterization of this as "rudimentary" is just, when we compare with it the cathedral structure of the hastily written *Merry Wives* two or three years later. Shakespeare's instinct must have told him how defective it was, how wanting in necessity. He put choric sonnets before Acts I and II. He distracted attention by working up Mercutio and the Nurse as high as he could. But he took direct steps also.

If he could not make the fate seem inevitable, at least he would make the love passionate and secure, so, an allusion of what was irresistible. This was less easy than it may seem. No previous play of his had contained, or demanded, passionate love. And it will be remembered that he was writing for male actors; neither could their bodies move the audience, like Miss Linda Darnell's, nor their faces, like Miss Elizabeth Taylor's, and not much physical love-making was feasible. It had to be done verbally—luckily for us. He decided, experimenting, on a dual campaign, which we may separate into what he did with Romeo and what he did with Juliet.

So that Romeo's real love would be recognized, when it appeared, for what it was, the playwright gave him an unreal first love (for Rosaline, who never appears), artificial and moony. This simple device was overwhelming as it worked out. When his speeches like

> Love is a smoke rais'd with the fume of sighs,
> Being purg'd, a fire sparkling in lovers' eyes,
> Being vex'd, a sea nourish' with lovers' tears

are superseded by speeches like "It is my lady, O it is my love," we are made aware that a fantasy, unexpectedly, has turned into the real thing.

The passage from convention to passion is symbolized, and concentrated, in the exquisitely soft, formal stanzas of his wooing at the masquerade. Juliet participates here. But for her Shakespeare had more ambitious plans. He reduced her age from Brooke's fifteen to thirteen, bringing her nearer the age of his elder daughter, Susanna, who was eleven or twelve; you recall that it was to some lines of her father's that we attributed a strong personal feeling in the last lecture. For Juliet there was to be no single transition out of convention. She was to mature before our eyes. From the submissive child of her opening scene, who to her mother's question about marriage answers only: "It is an honour that I dream not of," and the enchanted but witty partner at the masquerade, "You kiss by the book," her qualities open swiftly to us, governed all by her love—generosity, desire, candour, resolution—until she sounds, or is, full mistress and wife:

> Wilt thou be gone? it is not yet near day,
> It was the nightingale, and not the lark,
> That pierced the fearful hollow of thine ear . . .

By then, she was already Shakespeare's first great feminine creation. He took her, however, to further points. It was the impact of uncontrollable terror *upon this developed character* that he imagined in the soliloquy over the potion. This soliloquy is nervous beyond anything in *Richard III*; it is the tragedy's height. It contains the seed of powers unexplored by the poet for years to come, and I must quote it all. Her mother and the Nurse go out.

> Farewell! God knows when we shall meet again.
> I have a faint cold fear thrills through my veins
> That almost freezes up the heat of life,
> I'll call them back again to comfort me,
> *Nurse.* What should she do here?
> My dismal scene I needs must act alone.
> Come, vial. What if this mixture do not work at all?
> Shall I be married then tomorrow morning?
> No no, this shall forbid it: lie thou there.
>
> (*She lays down a dagger.*)
>
> What if it be a poison, which the friar
> Subtly hath minister'd to have me dead
> Lest in this marriage he should be dishonour'd
> Because he married me before to Romeo?
> I fear it is—and yet methinks it should *not*,
> For he hath still been tried a holy man.
> How if, when I am laid into the tomb
> I wake *before* the time that Romeo
> Come to redeem me? there's a fearful point.
> Shall I not then be stifled in the vault
> To whose foul mouth no healthsome air breathes in
> And there lie strangled ere my Romeo comes,
> Or, if I live is it not very like
> The horrible conceit of death and night
> Together with the terror of the place
> As in a *vault*, an ancient receptacle,
> Where for this many hundred years the bones
> Of all my buried ancestors are packed,
> Where bloody Tybalt, yet but green in earth,

Lies festering in his shroud: where, as they say,
At some hours in the night *spirits* resort:
Alack, alack, is it not like that I
So early waking, what with loathsome smells
And shrieks like mandrakes torn out of the earth
That living creatures hearing them run mad:
O if I wake shall I not be distraught,
Environèd with all these hideous fears
And madly play with my forefathers' joints?
And pluck the mangled Tybalt from his shroud?
And in this rage, with some great kinsman's bone
As with a club, dash out my desperate brains?
O look, methinks I see my cousin's ghost
Seeking out Romeo that did spit his body
Upon a rapier's point: stay, Tybalt, stay:
Romeo, I come: this do I drink to thee.

This speech lacks the marvels of versification, imagery, and diversity that we will meet in the much later tragic soliloquies, but its theatrical power is scarcely less than theirs, and one of its profoundest psychological merits may not be at once apparent. Her lover appears only incidentally until near the end—this agony is her own—when he appears as the *cause* of all this that she is suffering: his crime is, as it were, furiously recited: *then*, a superior terror, born of her hysterical vision—lest harm come to him—overcomes the lesser, and her love, unmentioned throughout, drives her to the potion. Her delusion forces her to act under the original, forgotten, basic motive.

What was in her heart we learn from her first words on awaking; like a yawn and attention: "O comfortable friar: where is my lord?" He is dead, and Shakespeare has yet one more level of dignity and self-realization to thrust her to, with her magnificent line to Friar Laurence, who dares not stay: "Go, get thee hence, for I will not away . . ."

The experiment with Juliet, then, succeeded, and made the play a genuine tragedy. Romeo is a mere rhetorician compared to her, if a fine one. But the poet never again risked developing a tragic heroine beyond the hero; he was not eager for she-tragedies, like his first editor, Nicholas Rowe; and it was many years—it was not until *Antony and Cleopatra*—before he once more let a woman even *approach* his tragic hero in range or intensity.

How far Juliet was based on observation we can hardly say; at any rate, the observation was private. An advance, however, notable in the play, in exquisiteness of social manner, over his earlier work, and then over it in A *Midsummer Night's Dream* and *The Merchant of Venice*, I think we may safely relate to the playwright's increased opportunities of public and private social observation. His theatrical patron, the first Lord Hunsdon, was a coarse fellow, as a matter of fact. But apart from the Southampton association and performing at court, Shakespeare and his fellows increasingly in other connections kept exalted company. They did *The Comedy of Errors* on a confused night of revels at Gray's Inn after Christmas of 1594, perhaps at Southampton's instigation[7]; Shakespeare must have known henceforth many Inns of Court men. A year later, December 9, 1595, they did *Richard II* at Sir Edward Hoby's [house in Westminster] before Robert Cecil. I remind you again that the manners Shakespeare was observing, and using, were not ours. Let me read you Hoby's letter of invitation to Cecil:

Sir, finding that you were not conveniently to be at London tomorrow night, I am bold to send to know whether Tuesday may be any more in your grace to visit poor Canon Row where as late as it shall please you a gate for your supper shall be open: and King Richard present himself to your view. Pardon my boldness, that ever love to be honoured with your presence, neither do I importune more than your occasions may willingly assent unto: in the meantime, and ever, resting at your command, Edward Hoby.[8]

Cecil's one-word endorsement is quite as impressive: "Readily." The correspondence, say, of Justice Holmes and Pollock, or of President Roosevelt and Churchill—gentlemen all four, and highly placed— exhibits no such courtesy.

Rising confidently into this world, or towards it rather, Shakespeare learned from it. Perhaps he taught it also. The *Dream*, I think, was composed for the celebration of the marriage of the Earl of Derby and Elizabeth Vere, at Greenwich, January 26, 1595.[9] The Queen was present, and the play contains one of this poet's rare theatrical compliments to her, as well as one to the bride. Not only does the play contain, in the figures of Oberon and Titania, a wonderful instruction on how *not* to conduct a marriage, but it is certain that no one watching it had ever seen such manners before, in either art or life, as grace Theseus and Hippolyta. Meanwhile, Shakespeare pursued his concerns. Darkness had done very well in *Romeo and Juliet*; a high proportion—a little over a third—of that tragedy was laid in darkness; so he laid the *Dream* all but entirely at night. The fairy speech of Mercutio had given him an idea: and he fills the stage with real fairies. Magic potions are drunk again. The only villain is introduced thus:

> I know a bank where the wild thyme blows,
> Where oxlips and the nodding violet grows;
> Quite over-canopied with luscious woodbine,
> With sweet muskroses, and with eglantine:
> There sleeps Titania some time of the night,
> Lull'd in these flowers with dances and delight;
> And there the snake throws her enamell'd skin,
> Weed wide enough to wrap a fairy in;
> And with the juice of this I'll streak her eyes,
> And make her full of hateful fantasies.

It is worth all possible emphasis that nowhere in his plays of this Second Period did Shakespeare create a real villain.

The nearest he came was Shylock, who snarls like a cur through the music of *The Merchant of Venice*, until he succumbs to it. He is like a bad dream the elegant others have. Probably he was intended to surpass Marlowe's Jew, which he easily does, even in the context of a comedy of manners; but that he was intended at the outset to master the whole centre of the play as he does I doubt.[10] Everyone who has read Shakespeare's work in anything like its order is familiar with an increasing tendency on the part of certain characters to take over the plays in which they occur, Falstaff and Hamlet being the ultimate instances. Mercutio is usually cited as the earliest, and Dryden tells us that Shakespeare "said himself, that he was forc'd to kill him in the third Act, to prevent being kill'd by him. But, for my part," Dryden goes on, "I cannot find he was so dangerous a person: I see nothing in him but what was so exceeding harmless, that he might have liv'd to the end of the Play, and dy'd in his bed, without offence to any man."[11] I am bound to say that I agree with this and think Shakespeare's view—if it was his—very odd. But Shylock is another matter. Here we do for the first time see a creature, not designed as central, intensify and enlarge under the dramatist's absorption until the work is threatened. Only threatened. A sound Antonio and a first-class Portia (such as I have never in fact seen) should hold a first-class Shylock in the play's frame. The noble Shylock we know is hardly eighty years old, a sentimental production, and worse if anything than the low comic Shylock, nose and all, visible at Lincoln's

Inn Fields in the early eighteenth century. We pay heavily for him:
in an enfeebling of Act V, usually in Portia, who was Shakespeare's
second great feminine portrait (after Juliet), and always in the Merchant himself. Antonio is an interesting figure. He opens the play:

> In sooth I know not why I am so sad,
> It wearies me, you say it wearies you;
> But how I caught it, found it, or came by it,
> What stuffe tis made of, whereof it is borne,
> I am to learne: and such a want-wit sadnesse makes of me
> That I haue much adoe to know my selfe.

For over a hundred lines he and his friends discuss this, they chiding
and questioning; but his finances are well, and to the question of love
he says "Fie, fie"; a long time, for the subject is never to return or
be solved. Only at Bassanio's entrance does Antonio rouse, to ask
about the love suit his friend has in hand and to offer every help; he
is energetic enough then with Shylock about the help, and conducts
his farewell with Bassanio as if it were final. Then he leaves the play
to the Jew and the lady. Homosexuals had been seen on the stage
before—Marlowe's—grossly; to which this portrait bears no relation.
But after full allowance for the convention of Renaissance friendship,
dilated already by Shakespeare in his sonnets and *The Two Gentlemen
of Verona*, this seems an all but clinical study of the mild, insistent
depression experienced by a continent homosexual on a friend's marriage; as a fairly able psychiatric account published some years ago
makes clear—a demonstration the weightier because the critic infers
nothing about the poet himself except that he has treated the subject
with respect and admiration, which is certainly true.

The thrusting of Shylock into this delicate comedy was much like
the thrusting of Bottom into Fairyland—both rather the work of a
poet who liked things difficult than one who liked things easy, as we
are continually told that Shakespeare did. Shakespeare may have
thought instead: the bolder you are, the safer. The fun, somebody has
said, is in the difficulty. So he supplied this Bottom then with an ass's
head and had the Queen of Fairies woo him in magical speeches.
There must have been a great deal of *pure* fun—it is hard not to
suppose the dramatist a happy man in 1595, when he had Bottom
and the "rabble" (as he calls them in a stage direction) burlesque his
Romeo and Juliet of the year before. Upon any nonsense or invented

tracery, the world can return in a moment, serene and broad—"My love," says Theseus,

> My loue shall heare the musicke of my hounds,
> Vncouple in the westerne vallie, let them goe . . .

But with Shylock Shakespeare had tasted blood: he went straight to Falstaff.

The World of Action

IT IS A FAMILIAR PRAISE of Shakespeare that he is the most *natural* of great dramatic authors. That is rather vague, but it ought to mean: the least *conventional*. Partly, this judgement is an outcome of Dryden's views, transmitted then to eighteenth- and nineteenth-century critics. Dryden was imperfectly acquainted with Shakespeare's later dramatic contemporaries, hardly knew at all his early contemporaries, and instituted misleading comparisons with the dramas of Greece and France. Partly the judgement responds to something really felt in Shakespeare: a spontaneity of articulation, best described once by Coleridge [on March 5, 1834] when he remarked that "Shakespeare's intellectual action is wholly unlike that of Ben Jonson or Beaumont and Fletcher. The latter see the totality of a sentence or passage, and then project it entire. Shakespeare goes on creating, and evolving B out of A, and C out of B, and so on, just as a serpent moves, which makes a fulcrum of its own body, and seems for ever twisting and untwisting its own strength."[1] But this view of his unconventionality takes in more than a unique capacity in dialogue, and I don't know whether anyone has observed that it is sharply at variance with the impatience or wonder, sometimes expressed by critics and intellectual historians, that a mind so powerful should have been—so conventional, commonplace even. It is sometimes forgotten that Descartes was not born until 1596; still, English thought was alive and one certainly runs over its accepted leaders without coming on Shakespeare. We have seen that he was far more original in his early literary practice, both of poetry and drama, than is imagined, and we will see something similar again in regard to the period of crisis. But I want to adopt the view that during the six years of his supreme *normal* achievement, from 1594 to 1600, his literary practice *was* conventional, and perhaps his life was.

A man's life (like his spiritual convictions) may differ from period to period. Shakespeare was acting with his company, the Lord Chamberlain's Men, and supplying them with at least two plays a year, for their house the Theatre in Shoreditch (and the Cross Keys Inn, their winter house, and a few court performances each year, and provincial touring), until shortly before the Globe was built on the Bankside in 1599. Something Aubrey was told, plausible in itself and contradicting the usual testimony about the poet's conviviality, relates apparently to these years. It contains one of the few surviving scraps of his correspondence. "The more to be admired," says Aubrey, because "he was not a company keeper—lived in Shoreditch, wouldn't be debauched [as of drinking parties, that is?] & if invited to, writ he was in paine."[2] At some point before October 1596 we know from a negligence about taxes that he was living in St. Helen's Passage, Bishopsgate, and probably this address comes to the same thing. Image of a man occupied and private, so far as his business permitted. Not quarrelsome, and so we hear little about him—the only record of this sort tells us simply that once in the autumn of '96 Shakespeare was in company with the owner of the Swan theatre, Francis Langley, and two women, when Langley quarrelled violently with one William Wayte, the creature of a powerful and sinister Surrey justice named William Gardiner. Whether Shakespeare took part we don't know, nor who his "date" was.[3] A lucky thing, this character, when men wore steel about them. Marlowe was stabbed in the brain; another pioneer of the tragic drama, Charles Tilney, was executed for treason. The sole known active survivors, except Shakespeare, of the first generation of playwrights were Peele, who died of the plague in '96, and the talented, mysterious Henry Porter, who was killed by a rival playwright, John Day, in 1599, a few months after Ben Jonson killed the actor Gabriel Spencer (who had himself killed a man several years before) and was branded, escaping the rope with Latin. Shakespeare seems to have spent part of each year at Stratford, perhaps riding there twice a year, but must have been mostly in London. Sometimes he toured. His plays contain a wealth of affectionate and knowing allusion to children, unparalleled in the work of his contemporaries; and in *Richard II* we hear also this:

> The pleasure that some fathers feed vpon
> Is my strict fast, I meane my childrens lookes . . .

Much evidence shows that William Shakespeare meant to found a family. In February of 1596 his son Hamnet was eleven, and in August he was dead. The two girls were left; Shakespeare was thirty-two. But his wife was forty. His sonnets in the past, many plays in the future, display a man entirely capable of responding with despair and horror to the world; I would suggest that his activity at present was such that the real force of this stroke did not reach him for a long time, for years, though it must have thrown an irony over the grant of a coat of arms two months later [October 20, 1596] (nominally to his father) by the College of Heralds, and his own purchase in the following year of the most substantial house in Stratford—New Place. It perhaps helped to ruin *King John*, if that directly followed it, and the lamentations for young Arthur's death reflect—as some critics have thought—the poet's grief for his son. But this is incidental compared to what will come. The rising tide of his personal consequence, an increasing involvement in large financial and public affairs, as the Chamberlain's Men gathered importance and he did, must have combined to assist in the translation of the poet of *Romeo and Juliet*, *Richard II*, *A Midsummer Night's Dream* into the dramatist of the major historical plays of England and *Julius Caesar*.

Neither the old *schema* applied to Shakespeare's histories nor the analysis of such critics as Tillyard quite fits the evidence. Tillyard, the best modern expositor of the histories, sees two tetralogies: the three parts of *Henry VI* and *Richard III*, and then *Richard II*, the first and second parts of *Henry IV*, and *Henry V*. The initial trouble with this is that scarcely any scholar any longer thinks Shakespeare *wrote* the first part of *Henry VI*.[4] We have left, then, a first trilogy: the plays we know as 2 and 3 *Henry VI* and *Richard III*. But *Richard II* itself appears to be an isolated work, a pathetic history; it does not at all lead into *Henry IV*, as 2 *Henry VI* leads into 3 and that into *Richard III*. The first part of *Henry IV*, on the other hand, does so lead into the second part, and that into *Henry V*; and so we seem to have a second trilogy—suggested, no doubt, by the sequel to the events in *Richard II*, but not including that play. This is interesting, because it indicates a broad, repeated artistic pattern; and the links are impressive. The first trilogy is concerned in its first two parts with the Wars of the Roses, out of which rises an all-dominant villain, Richard III, to whom the third play is devoted. The second trilogy is concerned with the much earlier civil wars under Henry IV, during its first two parts, out of which rises the all-dominant hero Henry V, to whom the third play is devoted. This is as if a contemporary American playwright were to construct in his late twenties a trilogy on the Civil War, culminating in a third play on Lincoln, who for this purpose would have to be presented as a universal villain—one of the nation's supreme evildoers, if only the American temperament admitted to the conception of such persons; and then, in his early-middle thirties, wrote a trilogy on the American Revolution, culminating in a third play on George Washington seen as national hero. Between them, meanwhile, Shakespeare wrote two isolated plays, *Richard II* (like a pathetic discourse on a doomed-to-failure Samuel Adams) and then *King John* (like an incoherent but nationalistic discourse on a much more important Captain John Smith). Small wonder, if with *Henry V* Shakespeare had had enough of English history, and never afterwards resorted to it unless for legendary, even earlier, tragic figures like King Lear, except in the spectacular collaboration, at the very end of his career, on *Henry VIII*. It is a further point of relation between the two trilogies that the first two plays are more closely knit in each than the second is with the comparatively independent third, and that the opening play of each is much more satisfactory than the second—I can cite Dr. Johnson for this judgement with me in the first trilogy, and all theatrical and literary history as of the second.

So much for the chronological design. To the content, as to the broad aspects of Shakespeare's thought during this Second Period, probably the isolated history of *Richard II* affords the best introduction.

Shakespeare prepared this play very carefully, more carefully perhaps than he had ever done a play before, though even for his early work we are coming to learn that he went to more sources than used to be thought. Besides the chroniclers Hall and Holinshed, for *Richard II* he consulted the English translation of Froissart's, one or two other French chronicles, a French poem, Daniel's *Civil Wars*, and an old play about Richard's uncle Thomas of Woodstock; no casual job of research. Yet the play begins strangely—strangely in this sense: though one understands exactly *what* is being done, one has no idea *why* it is being done. Theobald, indeed, cut out the first two acts for his eighteenth-century version. Let us look at what happens from the point of view of a man in the pit and a gentleman in the gallery at the Theatre in 1595. Mowbray and Bolingbroke accuse each other, lengthily, of treason, before the King, who tries to reconcile them, fails, and appoints them a day for trial. It is far from clear who is right; both strike one as right, or in the wrong rather, and neither inspires more sympathy. Richard seems more sympathetic towards Mowbray than to Bolingbroke, who is his cousin, but not clearly so, and his character is not clear either; it shows, for example, no weakness and no special strength. In the second scene the Duchess of the

The World of Action

King's murdered uncle, Thomas of Woodstock, laments to John of Gaunt, another uncle of the King and also Bolingbroke's father; she calls down vengeance on Mowbray. Well, the accusers are to meet in the lists—long speeches—when abruptly the King forbids the combat, exiling both, Bolingbroke for some years, Mowbray forever; they take very lengthy farewells. A small scene follows at court, in which it develops that Richard did not like Bolingbroke at all, especially his popularity—this still does not endear Bolingbroke to us; also that Richard is hypocritical, surrounded by flatterers, extravagant, and tyrannical with his subjects' money—news being brought of Gaunt's illness and desire to see him, the King prays that he may die immediately, so that his wealth can serve for the Irish wars. Now all this is admirably written, and to the auditors of 1595 both the recent and coming history were better known than they are to us, but one's sympathies are still absolutely at sea. It is with no consuming anxiety that we enter Act II, to find old Gaunt sick, waiting to breathe his last in wholesome counsel to the King, when he comes, and talking meanwhile to his brother the Duke of York. We can imagine very well what he will say to the King, more or less, and how ineffective it will be. His tone to York is high—

> Oh, but they say, the tongues of dying men
> Inforce attention like deepe harmony . . .

and

> Methinks I am a prophet new inspirde,
> And thus expiring do foretell of him,
> His rash fierce blaze of riot cannot last

—but, though we recognize the Renaissance doctrine that a soul near death may be capable of divination, as he proceeds we are hardly prepared for anything remarkable; we do not expect to *learn* anything:

> With eager feeding, foode doth choke the feeder:
> Light vanitie, insatiate cormorant,
> Consuming meanes, soone prayes vpon it selfe:
> This royall throne of Kings, this sceptred Ile,
> This earth of Maiestie, this seate of Mars,
> This other Eden, demy Paradice,
> This foretresses built by nature for her selfe

Against infection and the hand of War,
This happie breede of men, this little world,
This precious stone set in the siluer sea
Which serues it in the office of a wall,
Or as a moate defensiue to a house,
Against the enuie of lesse happier lands:
This blessed plotte, this earth, this realme, this England,

and it is ten lines more before the sentence ends in

Is now leased out, I die pronouncing it,
Like to a tenement or pelting farme.

It didn't matter how the sentence ended. Now this is staggering, and
still to us staggering, but it is not only staggering: as the skins in the
pit are crawling with awe and rapture and pride, the gentleman in
the gallery (whose skin is crawling too) has experienced an unusual
satisfaction: the clearing up, with splendour, of an oppressive and
legitimate and deliberate mystery, namely, where his sympathy ought
to lie. These lines embody the second half of the convention of which
everything that has preceded them constituted the first half. All that
went before was defections from the ideal here announced. Their
eloquence, in short, is a fraction merely of their greatness; and when
we call this apostrophe conventional, as it is, or its sentiment conventional, as it is, we do the poet and dramatist some disservice. His
convention was larger, Shakespearean.

I must pursue this a little, to the heart of the play.

The object of the auditor's sympathy established, Shakespeare is
rougher still with Richard, until he is ready for him, on the return
from Ireland. Then bad news rushes in on the King after bad news,
and he embraces despair. Note that we have meanwhile had a chance
to despise his parasites *by themselves*, as they agree to desert him; also
that, upon the moment of his disembarking, Shakespeare has with
one stroke allied Richard himself with the patriotic sentiment: "How
brooks your Grace the ayre," somebody asks,

After your late tossing on the breaking seas?
—Needes must I like it well, I weepe for ioy,
To stand upon my Kingdom once again.

This is a beginning. But the passage towards full sympathy takes a
strange way: I think it does through the *ridiculous*. From Maurice

The World of Action

Evans's recitation of the part, one would never suspect this, indeed, nor from other Richards. But a great actor gave the play as the first of his season at the Queen's Theatre in London in 1937, and his playing of this scene exhibited an intellectual and emotional tempering such as I have *never* seen from him in New York and seldom in London. The King, you remember, sits upon the ground to "tell sad stories of the death of Kings": how Death, the antic, allows his King "a breath, a little scene" and then

> Comes at the last, and with a little pin
> Bores through his castle walles, and farewell king . . .

John Gielgud played this so exquisitely, so weakly, with such self-pity, such grotesquerie, so *ridiculously*, that the proper young lady with me threatened to leave me in my stall if I did not stop laughing.[5] Dumb fascination and pathos were all right in the pit—Shakespeare wrote for them too; but I suspect that some of the gentlemen on the stage edge or in the gallery half-suffocated with nervous laughter at this absurd—this existential—spectacle, and I think the poet did when he wrote it—as a preparation for the development then of pathos proper and the increasing fantasy of Richard's grief, towards the Deposition scene and his cadenzas before the mirror, the shattering of the mirror:

> Was this Face, the Face
> That euery day, vnder his House-hold Roofe,
> Did keepe ten thousand men? Was this the Face
> That like the Sunne, did make beholders winke? . . .
> A brittle Glory shineth in this Face,
> As brittle as the Glory, is the Face . . .

We are not, in *Richard II*, dealing with Shakespeare's greatest powers either poetic or dramatic, but we *are* dealing with a fusion of those powers, at a level seldom attempted by other authors, in conventions hardly conceived except by Shakespeare.

We have also arrived, in this fervid and monumental nationalism, at a resting place of the author's thought. The nation is not simply an area of residence, nor a collection of values, nor even an object of allegiance, but an Idea, which has its representative in England. In accordance with Professor Lovejoy's formulation [*The Great Chain of Being*, 1936] of what he has termed the principle of plenitude— "the thesis that the universe is a *plenum formarum* in which the range of conceivable diversity of *kinds* of living things is exhaustively exemplified"—the idea of the Nation takes its station somewhere along the range of the Platonic Ideas of which the representatives in our knowledge form "the great chain of being." I say "somewhere along," and I confess that in any case I am adapting a metaphor, from the chain *full, continuous,* and *unilinearly graded,* of the forms of natural existence, the conception of which the Middle Ages and the Renaissance (for that matter, the eighteenth century) inherited from Plato and Aristotle. In the spiritual realm, for Elizabethan belief, stood God's three persons, the angels in their nine orders, lesser spirits, man's soul; and in a system of perfect correspondence to this—so that *analogy* was the chief means of intellectual investigation—stood in the material realm the heavens, the solar system (which included the fixed stars and centred in the earth), the earth itself in four elements, man in his orders under church and nation, animals, plants, metals, minerals. We ought to be able here to follow the chain *up,* in Shakespearean thought, from the nation, and *down* through the individual person to the "meagrest existents." But it is a question of a *stage* of Shakespeare's thought, and up—just now—we cannot go. Nothing is clearer in the thought of Shakespeare's Second Period—of the practical works we will now be examining—than a virtual indifference upward beyond the nation. Otherworldliness, as a motor, does not exist. What could be less vivacious, for example, than the King's exhortation in the opening speech of *1 Henry IV?*

> Therefore, friends,
> As far as to the sepulchre of Christ,
> Whose soldier now, under whose blessed cross
> We are impressed and engaged to fight,
> Forthwith a power of English shall we levy,
> Whose arms were moulded in their mothers' womb
> To chase these pagans in those holy fields
> Over whose acres walked those blessed feet
> Which fourteen hundred years ago were nailed
> For our advantage on the blessed cross . . .

The *opening* speech, mind; languid and perfunctory, and the arms and feet almost recall Costard. Shakespeare writes thus when he is bored. Even of the hierarchy within the nation, conceived as necessary—though it is foreshadowed in the Garden scene of *Richard II*—we get explicit, vivid statement only in the tragic period, after this conception has been tortured; in Ulysses' familiar speech on Order [*Troilus and Cressida*].

On the other hand, consider an extraordinary relation between the two trilogies. In the first, the condition of the nation is disorder, and the governing person of its opening two plays is Warwick, the king-maker, whose nature, duty, and delight it is to install a sovereign. In the second, the condition of the nation is order, and the governing person of its opening two plays is Falstaff, whom we might call a King-*un*maker, he who unfits the Prince of Wales, so far as possible, to be a king—the enemy of all authority, Falstaff. Both Warwick and Falstaff *fail*. The first is killed, the second rejected. The first has prepared the way for that exponent of Nihilism, Richard III, and the second has simply diversified the experience of the all-conquering exponent of Order, Henry V—so that that prig feels more keenly for his common troops than otherwise he would have done. So broad, and so organic, was Shakespeare's Idea of the nation.

I descend now to the Individual. And here we encounter like the Rockies a difference of opinion, over which no plane flies. Shake-speare has been studied as a judge, a distributor of rewards and pun-ishments to his characters, a nemesis. It has also been indignantly denied that he had any such interests: he has been claimed simply as an expresser of life, the non-judicating recorder of what he found or imagined. Edward Dowden speaks to us for the first view, John Butler Yeats for the second. These are high authorities. Dowden was learned, thoughtful, and assiduous, the leading Shakespearean per-haps of the second half of the nineteenth century, the first man to take a *general* view of Shakespeare's development. John Butler Yeats was a man of *superior* calibre, one of the gayest old men, and one of the most penetrating upon artistic questions, who ever lived—and incidentally the father of the greatest poet in English of the first half of the twentieth century. I am happy not to have to choose between them. I think they are both wrong; and both right.

Against Dowden first. The elder Yeats was right: there is something irritating in the extreme, to anybody really familiar with Shakespeare's work, in the notion of him as a fussy moralist, eager to get things right. Dowden's analysis is fatuous before it has got well under way; and particular examples make nonsense of it. Dowden I said was learned, but he had not attended to the plays' sources—and what biographer has? The bare-faced imposture of Simpcox and his wife in Shakespeare's earliest surviving history is in the source chronicle just that: the man, pretending to have been born blind, claims to have recovered his sight at a shrine, and his wife supports him, and Duke Humphrey—in a handsome inquisition—exposes him, and they go to punishment. But Shakespeare puts in a little sentence. After they are hopelessly exposed, the wife cries: "Alas sir, we did it for pure need." They go straight to punishment all the same. But it is not all the same. The poet has made you feel that it is dreadful that they should be punished—so absolutely punished; and then, however, he has punished them (or allowed them to be punished) instantly nevertheless. There were areas both of sensitivity *and* of callousness in Shakespeare, as in any great artist, of which Dryden knew nothing.

On the other hand, Dowden was right, and Yeats dangerously wrong. Shakespeare had a tracking mind. Throughout *Henry IV* the image of the wronged (and assassinated) Richard recurs with a beauty, dignity, and pathos which makes spaghetti of the peace of mind of the usurper King. *Not* of his son. But observe with what iron judgement the dramatist elaborated the story of the son's *stealing away* the crown physically before his father's death—thinking his father dead —and the being recalled and rebuked and forgiven (image of the ancestral usurpation), before the dying King can say (upon one hint from Stow):

> *God* knows, my son,
> By what by-paths and indirect crookt ways
> I met this crown, and I *myself* know well
> How troublesome it sat upon my head:
> To thee it shall descend with better quiet,
> Better opinion, better confirmation,
> For all the soil of the achievement goes
> With me into the earth . . .

Justice, then, has to be satisfied: justice of some sort, even if only justice to the feelings, even if only a symbolic justice. When *no* justice could be achieved, Shakespeare was at a loss. The late John Palmer, with lovely insight, accounted for the weakness of the play *King John* by supposing that Shakespeare simply could not make anything of the reign, both in its fundamental disorder and in the refusal of the King to accept responsibility for the worst act of his reign, the death of the boy Arthur.[6] It was not that the poet did not take pains. He took the Protestant hero of the source play and made him an ignominious usurper, re-creating his England very much like Richard II's, with Faulconbridge however as the patriotic champion. But he did more. In a hundred ways Shakespeare destroyed anti-Catholic prejudice in the transmitted materials. This he may perhaps have done on his own account; both at the beginning and at the end of his life we hear of Catholicism. But it was a shrewd guess of Liebermann's that he did it also on Southampton's account, whose parents were

Catholics, himself a sympathizer.[7] Probably on account of the Earl
of Essex, whose cousin Southampton married in 1595, his like-named
ancestor Essex's prominent, rebellious part in the original is cut to
three lines. Under the disadvantages of this basic antipathy, and the
religious and political expedients, all Shakespeare could do was create
in the Bastard Faulconbridge a resolute self-critical character a little
recalling Richard III—a focus of energy, at least—and let him phrase
his author's consternation: "Mad world, mad kings, mad composition
. . ." The Bastard stands out from the play almost as Falstaff will do.
But Shakespeare had got sick of history. I think it was Hotspur who
drew him back, besides the imagination of Falstaff.

On the most amusing character ever created, not much can be said
in a few minutes; but I want to indicate one or two lines of reflection.
Dover Wilson [*The Fortunes of Falstaff*, London, 1943] I think is
wrong in regarding the two parts of *Henry IV* as one play, for the
plain reasons, first, that they are radically different, though continuous
works, and second, that in Part I Hotspur and Falstaff cannot possibly
be understood apart from each other until they have been considered
together. A play is not an ethic. Poor [Maurice] Morgann, who, in
his attempted vindication of Falstaff's courage, begged leave to defer
consideration of the robbery until after he had tried to explain the
"whole" character, went hopelessly astray.[8] Hotspur we hear of, impressively, before we hear of Falstaff; we see him marvellously in
action directly after we first see Falstaff; the play is inconceivable with
him—in some sense he is its hero. His stunning speeches upon honour early on are answered later by Falstaff's soliloquy:

Honour pricks me on. Yea, but how if honour prick me off when I come
on? how then? Can honour set to a leg? no. Or an arm? no. Or take away
the grief of a wound? no. Honour hath no skill in surgery then? no. What
is honour? a word. What is in that word honour? what *is* that honour? air.
A trim reckoning.

Observe that no neutralization of Hotspur's thought has occurred.
Two views have each had a place.

Falstaff is a prose creation, Hotspur (though he speaks prose too)
a verse creation, and in other respects too—except for the superlative
wit, brilliance, energy they share with each other and no one else—
they stand opposed. At the same time—little as I incline to yield to
anyone in my opinion of Shakespeare's ability to discriminate his
characters—they are opposed aspects of a single mind and must be
seen so. Let me illustrate this congruity in their creation. "An olde

Lorde of the Councell," Falstaff remarks to the Prince, "rated me the other day in the street about you sir, but I markt him not, and yet he talkt very wisely, but I regarded him not, and yet he talkt wisely and in the street too." Hotspur walking up and down, reading a letter from a lord he has sounded on his conspiracy and commenting to himself: "Say you so, say you so, I say vnto you againe, you are a shallow cowardly hind, and you lie: what a lacke braine is this? by the Lord our plot is a good plot as euer was laid, our friends true and constant: a good plot, good friends, and full of expectation: an excellent plot, verie good friends; what a frosty spirited rogue is this? . . . Zoundes and I were nowe by this rascall I could braine him with his Ladies fanne." The illusion of naturalness in either case can go no further, but there is more than prose style here: Shakespeare's other major characters do not talk this way—Hamlet almost alone has even the iteration—there is correspondence between the projected minds.

Nor can Falstaff possibly be understood in Part I apart from the Prince. I agree with Knight[9] that Prince Hal is comparatively a poor stick (and by the way a heartless one) when Falstaff is not by. But he is Falstaff's reason for being. Many conventions and much observation went to the making of Falstaff, but in all save the mere braggart soldier, coward, buffoon, he is inseparable from the Prince. As of the older drama, Falstaff is the "Vice," the Prince's corrupter; but he is also a foster father; from observation, he is the rare man in whose presence everyone is enchanting and vivid; most important of all, he is the Prince's Fool—irresponsible, privileged, criminal, and (as Lord Raglan has shown)[10] sacred. The critic's task, then, would appear to be to interrogate the character first in these functions and relations, and afterwards in himself, whatever that is—all this in Part I. In the delightful but quite different world of Pistol and Shallow, in Part II, Falstaff will have to be seen as a development entirely free of these dominating relations, and weaker for it, though still marvellous. The Epilogue to that play tells us that Shakespeare intended to carry him forward into Henry V. But Shakespeare was in trouble over Falstaff. He had called him originally Sir John Oldcastle, after a similar character in an old play on Henry V, and had to change the name after production, when Henry Lord Cobham (whose ancestress had married this historical personage) protested.[11] The name clung popularly to the character and the play, and Cobham was known privately to the Essex-Southampton set as "Sir John Falstaff" for at least two years. Moreover, midway through the composition of the second part of Henry IV, Elizabeth ordered Shakespeare to write a play showing Falstaff in love (so a tradition tells us which even Chambers accepts) and this he did in a fortnight[12]—taking, I suspect, a play of 1592 called *The Jealous Comedy*, which he rewrote in prose so completely that whether the original play was his it is impossible to say. Thus *The Merry Wives of Windsor*, his only Restoration comedy, with a Falstaff again so different that I think Shakespeare must have wearied of his triumph; in *Henry V* he only reports his death.

I want to make one further suggestion, which will appear to some of you farfetched and must certainly be regarded as speculative, for I must advance it concisely. Falstaff stands as a sort of foster father, an ill father replacing his own, to the Prince; as the King himself seems to be uneasily aware. Perhaps the intimacy and intensity of the representation of Falstaff are best accounted for by regarding him as what psychoanalysts call a father image, a *debased* father image. I am struck by the scene in which Falstaff actually plays the father, the King.

> *Fal.* That thou art my son, I have partly thy mother's word, partly my own opinion, but chiefly a villainous trick of thine eye, and a foolish hanging of thy nether lip, that doth warrant me. If then thou be son to me, here lies the point: why, being son to me, art thou so pointed at? Shall the blessed sun of heaven prove a micher and eat blackberries? a question not to be asked. Shall the son of England prove a thief and take purses? a question to be asked. There is a thing, Harry, which thou hast often heard of, and it is known to many in our land by the name of pitch: this pitch (as ancient writers do report) doth defile, so doth the company thou keepest . . . and yet there is a virtuous man whom I have often noted in thy company, but I know not his name.
>
> *Prince.* What manner of man, an it like your majesty?
>
> *Fal.* A goodly portly man, i' faith, and a corpulent, of a cheerful look, a pleasing eye, and a most noble carriage, and as I think his age some fifty, or by 'r lady, inclining to three score. And now I remember me, his name is Falstaff . . .

This would be suggestive even if the King were not the Prince's father, a king representing often a father symbol. But there are other indications. The things we chiefly know about Shakespeare's father are that his name was John, that he often *jested with his son* ("merrycheekt," you remember, is our only description of him),[13] that his affairs had gone downhill and he was in legal trouble. These features are all reproduced in Falstaff. John Shakespeare had lately been raised to the gentry, where he occupied a status as humble or ambiguous as Sir John Falstaff's among the nobility. A relation is conceivable between the name of the imposing new Shakespeare residence, New Place, and the name the poet originally gave to Falstaff, Oldcastle; both neutral names. It is remarkable that Falstaff gets himself involved, as soon as the political action permits, with provincials such as John Shakespeare would have known—the first character in Shakespeare's work, since the induction to *The Taming of the Shrew*, who does; and it is more remarkable that, having to get up at short notice a play showing Falstaff in love, Shakespeare lays it not in London but in a town scene [Windsor] among burgesses much like Stratford's. Of course we cannot take Falstaff as a *portrait* of the poet's father. My contention is for the possibility that among the impulses that united in his creation, one of the deepest sprang from the mingled love, amusement, and resentment that a son like William Shakespeare must evidently have felt towards a father like his own. Not necessarily a *conscious* impulse, this. A good deal is known now about the degree to which some artists represent their parents (however disguised) in their work, and it would be very surprising if Shakespeare had never done this. But not much is known about how often Shakespeare did. I am unable to attach this suggestion to a strong established pattern, as it ought to be attached. But much *has* been written about Shakespeare's father in relation to the play that contains the other most fully elaborated character the dramatist created, Hamlet. When we come to this work, I think you will find the present suggestion about Falstaff considerably, if indirectly, strengthened. The truth seems to be that Shakespeare's inspiration for the two most overwhelming characters he ever imagined came, first, from his father, and second, from his son; as well as, indirectly in both cases, from himself.

WE SAID THAT Shakespeare wearied of Falstaff. *Henry V*, the play in which the King fulfils the destiny of Hotspur's "honour" tempered with Falstaff's, shows itself no weariness, but it shows two very striking kinds of impatience. The first is with the English language as then constituted. Throughout *Henry IV* the scope of Shakespeare's material had broadened his diction by a good deal, but in *Henry V* for the first time he begins to strain, with words like rivage, vaultages, sternage, sonance, legerity, pocky, womby, cowarded—all used by him only here, and many of them coinages. Nearly 550 words are used by him only in *Henry V*, and something like this will be true from now on. Of his whole employed vocabulary—he knew of course many words he never used—about a *quarter* occur only *once* in his work, or 6,000 words, more than Dante needed altogether for the *Commedia* and nearly as many as would do shortly for the King James Version of the Hebrew Bible. Much of his diction takes on henceforth a strongly exploratory cast. Yet he was an unpredictable author. Directly after this play he wrote *Julius Caesar*, in which a sobriety determines against any elevation of diction more completely than in anything else he ever did—the price inevitably paid being an occasional meanness. One might suppose this (and I do) a deliberately classical intention, though with his next classical subject, *Troilus and Cressida*, he ran wildest in language. But by then a general change had overtaken his work.

The other impatience is with the theatre. The descriptive choruses of *Henry V* evince an anxiety for effects that the Elizabethan theatre could not get and probably no theatre ought to want: scenic and narrative effects like Tolstoy's. It is the chorus to the last act here, which, very exceptionally, hopes for the triumphal return of Essex from Ireland, so that we are in the spring of 1599. Lately the Theatre had been pulled down and borne to the Bankside, where its materials were being used for the Globe. Whether this artistic impatience has reference to the Curtain, being used meanwhile, or to the Globe itself in prospect, and whether the Globe at all satisfied Shakespeare, we enquire in vain; but it is a fact that after one more public play, *Caesar*, and two or three comedies, his work moved inward.

He was reading North's translation of Plutarch's life of Caesar while writing *Henry V*, so that he must have prepared his first classical play, and his second tragedy, after some thought. Shakespeare now knew more about turning history into plays than anyone else has ever known before or since. From two sentences he made his opening scene, otherwise (as MacCallum says) "an entirely free creation."[14] But in Plutarch he had a mind, and in North a style, superior far to those of any source he had worked from before; and he borrowed more and contradicted less. The result is a Renaissance Rome, naturally, but an action unusually simple, orderly, and clear, for an Elizabethan play even of less calibre—as conventional, in sum, as he could make it. The young actor, playwright, and classical scholar Shakespeare had taken up the year before, Rowe tells us, introducing him to his company and getting a rejected play accepted, Ben Jonson, seems to have been irritated by it and unable to forget it.[15] Perhaps friendship with Jonson helped to move Shakespeare, tired of English history, to the great Roman subject, though very likely he had meant to treat it for years. In Brutus he had a man of conscience and power far beyond Romeo. The quarrel scene is the most hair-raising thing of its sort he ever achieved before the interviews of Lear with Regan and Goneril. Hair-raising in a profounder way are one or two passages where stir powers dormant since *Richard III*:

> Betweene the acting of a dreadfull thing
> And the first motion, all the *Interim* is
> Like a *Phantasma*, or a hideous Dreame:
> The *Genius*, and the mortall Instruments,
> Are then in councell; and the state of man,
> Like to a little Kingdome, suffers then
> The nature of an Insurrection.

One almost incredible fact about this play, as it emerged from Shakespeare's mind, I must postpone to my discussion of the crisis. But he went back to comedy for 1600, with the twin masterworks *As You Like It* and *Twelfth Night*, in which much is malicious but nothing is more ominous than Malvolio's name.

All's Well

THE LAST ACT OF *The Merchant of Venice* returns to Portia's seat at Belmont, where we find Lorenzo and Jessica, the first of the play's three pairs of lovers to be united, conversing in music. "The moone shines bright," Lorenzo begins.

> In such a night as this,
> When the sweet winde did gently kisse the trees,
> and they did make no noyse, in such a night
> *Troylus* me thinks mounted the Troian walls
> And sigh'd his soule toward the Grecian tents
> where *Cressid* lay that night.
>
> *Jessi.* In such a night
> did *Thisbie* fearfully ore-trip the dewe,
> and saw the Lyons shadowe ere him selfe,
> and ranne dismayed away.
>
> *Lor.* In such a night
> stoode *Dido* with a willow in her hand
> vpon the wilde sea banks, and waft her Loue
> to come againe to Carthage.
>
> *Jessi.* In such a night
> *Medea* gathered the inchanted hearbe
> that did renew old *Eson.*

They fall then to talk of themselves, and presently Lorenzo calls for actual music.

How sweet the moonlight sleepes upon this banke,
heere will we sit, and let the sounds of musique
creepe in our eares. Soft stilnes, and the night
become the tutches of sweet harmonie.
Sit, Iessica, looke how the floore of heauen
is thick inlayed with pattens of bright gold,
there's no the smallest orbe which thou beholdst
but in his motion like an Angell *sings,*
still quiring to the young-eyde Cherubins;
such harmonie is in immortal soules,
but whilst this muddy vesture of decay
doth grosly close it in, we cannot heare it.

Then the music comes. But this real music has thus been given a merely *representative* character before it comes. So, love in Shakespeare has increasingly, henceforth, a merely representative character, for Order, as well as its actual character; that is, love returned; and I want, with these two citations, to establish not only the legendary but the philosophical setting for the poet's supreme work in love comedy, *As You Like It* and *Twelfth Night,* written both at the turn of the century, in 1600, when he was thirty-six—supreme, I say, setting aside *The Tempest,* where the love *comedy* is entirely subordinate to a ritual with a different end. Of course these two plays are much unlike each other. *As You Like It* is pastoral, and critical. It is in the last degree significant that its only allusion to the Platonic doctrine of the Music of the Spheres, handled by Lorenzo, is disruptive, negative. "If he," the outlawed Duke says of Jaques,

> If he, compact, of jarres, grow Musicall,
> We shall haue shortly discord in the Spheares . . .

Twelfth Night is courtly, and more accepting. They are more like each other, however, than either is like any other work earlier or later. A. C. Bradley, the greatest critic so far of the major tragedies, selected—not one of them but—*As You Like It* as the most completely characteristic work by Shakespeare.[1] *Twelfth Night* stands on towards *Hamlet.*

You perceive that although it is Lorenzo who handles it, the earthly representation of Plato's doctrine could be only, really, within the governance of *women;* as in the catalogue, after Lorenzo's introduction to Troilus, it is women only who occur to both Lorenzo and Jessica as love's exemplars. Women can destroy the harmony, but they alone create it; as we see in the benign machinations of Rosalind. (Men, by the way, for unrequited love, just run off: Orlando 259, Silvius 263.) *The Merchant of Venice,* in fact, is dominated upon all but its complicating side by Portia, and there, too, in the event—*she* puts down Shylock. And yet it must be felt, on reflection, that this domination by women of the two supreme comedies was hardly to be expected. Shakespeare had created, besides Portia, only one great feminine portrait: Juliet; unless you call Beatrice so, whom for a moment I postpone. In comedy and history alike, men had governed. Now, fluent, thriving, all-sufficient, this poet who was amusing and instructing England turned away to make Rosalind, and Viola and Olivia.

Observe that he was still creating his own exemplars, adapted from contemporary narratives and stories. As of Lorenzo's catalogue, Shakespeare had indeed already parodied Thisbe, but it would be several years still before, in a mood of indescribable bitterness, he would take up Troilus and Cressida. As for Dido, Marlowe had treated her, and no Elizabethan handled Medea (who appears anyway not as a lover but as a sorceress). Of two catalogues in *As You Like It,* Shakespeare had treated Lucrece in his poem, and would treat Helen (incidentally) and Cleopatra—Atalanta he neglected, as not precisely a theatrical subject; Troilus, again, in the second, he would come to, and Hero and Leander had been pre-empted by Marlowe. I think we may take it that, notwithstanding this persistent citation of analogues, Shakespeare probably did not yet regard himself, *as a dramatist,* as part of the great line of love poets stretching from Euripides through Virgil and Ovid to Chaucer and so down. The third catalogue, in fact, is playful and critical—the work of a man into whose soul the iron has not yet wholly entered. "Leander," says Rosalind,

he would have liu'd manie a faire yeere, though Hero had turn'd Nun; if it had not been for a hot Midsomer-night, for (good youth) he went but forth to wash him in the Hellespont, and being taken with the cramp, was droun'd, and the foolish Chronoclers of that age, found it was Hero of Cestos. But these are all lies, men have died from time to time, and wormes haue eaten them, but not for loue.

Since later, in agreeing with himself to re-create two of the chief pairs of lovers of antiquity, Troilus and Cressida and Antony and Cleopatra, Shakespeare plainly *did* regard himself as entering that great line, it has sharp interest that here in 1600, at the height of his powers, he seems still to have seen his dramatic work primarily as entertainment.

We are approaching, then, some grand watershed of ambition, on the other side of which all will be different.

I say, of course, "primarily" entertainment. *Much Ado about Nothing, As You Like It,* and *Twelfth Night* are always considered together, and share even a name familiar in criticism, as Shakespeare's "golden" comedies. I have never been able to see any justice in this. *Much Ado* is a fine play, and wonderful on the stage; but it is not as the other two are, and moreover it is very different from them, in that it works towards no larger issue, whilst *they* make worlds—we attend in them to a *greatly* increased burden of moral and social reflection, almost absent from *Much Ado,* which was written a year or so before them. Troubled by this heretical opinion of mine, I once consulted Coleridge's "Notes on the Comedies of Shakespeare," where, in the standard edition by Raysor, are assembled all his notes on the individual comedies that are not merely part of an argument in some lecture. But there *are* no notes on *Much Ado*; though we know from allusions elsewhere that he had, of course, read it attentively (not quite appreciating, perhaps, Dogberry); and this is the only comedy so slighted. This silence is significant. For the next fifty or hundred years we might try separating *Ado* from its superiors to come, and seeing it backwards, rather, in relation to *The Taming of the Shrew* and *The Merchant of Venice,* with which its affinities seem to me stronger.

Much Ado possesses a lovely organization, Don Pedro plotting agreeably downward to bring together as lovers the two sparring champions, while his brother plots malignantly upward to separate the milder betrothed lovers. But Don Juan is a tedious, empty villain, who never at any moment fulfils the promise of his opening speech, when upon being made welcome he replies: "I thank you; I am not of many words, but I thank you." His crumby associates are no more interesting. The opening intrigue, wherein Claudio supposes the Duke to be wooing for himself, is rather feeble. And something went wrong with the momentum. The major, less engaging plot developed too fast, so that the disgracing of Hero, I think, has somehow cheated us of one *most* marvellous wooing scene between the deluded Benedick and the deluded Beatrice—which could hardly follow the disgrace, and Shakespeare couldn't get to before. Without Dogberry, just here, the comedy would languish utterly—and here, of course, he comes, the supreme and triumphant enemy of the English language. The dramatist's instinct seldom fails when it matters. Leonato's impatience, for instance, at the marriage itself is handsomely set up in the preceding scene, and dazzlingly heightens the drama of Act IV.

But I suspect that Shakespeare found the plot oppressive to the love and wit, as I do, and therefore disburdened himself in *As You Like It*, where in the forest anyone can meet anyone at any time and say what he likes, without an artificial structure of events impending to be satisfied. This was not, I should observe, to take it easy, but to find a form adequate to what essentially was to be done. Among other things, he had not, in *Much Ado*, to deal with much general life. One of the very few general observations in the play is a simile which I hope you will have in mind when we get towards the close today. Hero, with unusual force, speaks of

> honeysuckles, ripen'd by the sun,
> [that] Forbid the sun to enter, like favourites,
> Made proud by princes, that advance their pride
> Against that power that bred it . . .
>
> (III.i.8–11)[2]

I have ventured upon *Much Ado* in some detail, partly in order to substantiate what may appear an eccentric judgement and partly because it seems unfortunately to be true that this work is more familiar, both educationally and on the stage, than either of its great successors; but I have not touched Beatrice yet. Let me close first with the distinction of merit. This seems to me best to be symbolized in the clowns. Dogberry was created for the clown Will Kemp—as we know from Shakespeare's speech prefixes in the quarto of 1600; the playwright had in mind so strongly the actor who was to play the part that he often wrote "Ke" instead of "Dogberry" or "Constable" (as he sometimes substituted the name of the actor Cowley for Verges).[3] In 1599 Kemp left the Lord Chamberlain's Men and was replaced by an actor much subtler, Robert Armin, for whom Shakespeare created the courtly fools Touchstone and Feste.[4] The difference will not be due, of course, solely to the actors. We learn from John Aubrey that Shakespeare "took the humour" of Dogberry from an actual village constable at Grendon (in Buckinghamshire), where he happened to lie one night journeying between Stratford and London; Sir Edmund Chambers objects that this is off the main road a bit, but I think we must hesitate to regard the poet as a crow—very likely, like other men on their way home from work or on their way back to work, he might loiter.[5] This is the only clear evidence we have of a character drawn from life, but others obviously must have been also. The gain in refinement of Touchstone and Feste may reflect an increased acquaintance with actual Fools, even Queen Elizabeth's, including per-

haps the one who so girded at Ralegh that one evening Sir Walter
got in masons and bricked him up to the eyebrows in a corner of the
apartment. Certainly, there had been foreshadowings, especially in
Love's Labour's Lost, of the cat-and-mouse technique of Touchstone
with the countryman whose girl he has taken away; but its new exquisiteness seems to contain some residue of delighted experience.

Clo. Good eu'n gentle friend. Couer thy head, couer thy
    head: Nay prethee bee couer'd. How olde are you
    Friend?

Will. Fiue and twentie Sir.

Clo. A ripe age: Is thy name *William*?

Will. *William*, sir.

Clo. A faire name. Was't borne i'th Forrest heere?

Will. I sir, I thanke God.

Clo. Thanke God: A good answer: Art rich?

Will. 'Faith sir, so, so.

Clo. So, so, is good, very good, very excellent good: and yet it
    is not, it is but so, so: Are thou wise?

Will. I sir, I haue a prettie wit.

Clo. Why, thou saist well. I do now remember a saying: The
    Foole doth thinke he is wise, but the wiseman knowes
    himselfe to be a Foole. The Heathen Philosopher, when
    he had a desire to eate a Grape, would open his lips
    when he put it into his mouth, meaning thereby, that
    Grapes were made to eate, and lippes to open. You do
    loue this maid?

Will. I do sir.

Clo. Giue me your hand: Art thou Learned?

Will. No sir.

Clo. Then learne this of me, To haue, is to haue. For it is a
    figure in Rhetoricke, that drink being powr'd out of a
    cup into a glasse, by filling the one, doth empty the
    other. For all your Writers do consent, that *ipse* is hee:
    now you are not *ipse*, for I am he.

Will. Which he sir?

Clo. He sir, that must marrie this woman: Therefore you
    Clowne, abandon: which is in the vulgar, leaue the
    societie: which in the boorish, is companie, of this
    female: which in the common, is woman: which
    together, is, abandon the society of this Female, or
    Clowne thou perishest: or to thy better vnderstanding,

dyest; or (to wit) I kill thee, make thee away, translate thy
life into death, thy libertie into bondage: I will deale in
poyson with thee, or in bastinado, or in steele: I will
bandy with thee in faction, I will ore-run thee with
police: I will kill thee a hundred and fifty wayes,
therefore tremble and depart.
Aud. Do, good *William.*
Will. God rest you merry sir.

As this ridiculous, and yet meaningful, gaiety of expression got incorporated with the play's emotional structure, in Feste, and above
all in the Fool of King Lear, even Shakespeare's range acquires a
fresh dimension.

With the heroines, we discern a similar development.

It is striking that Beatrice is at her height, she is never better than,
when the *other* plot reaches its first climax: when Claudio and Hero
are betrothed. You remember the scene: she acts as a positive chorus
for the dumb lovers—"Speak, cousin; or, if you cannot, stop his
mouth with a kiss, and let him not speaker neither." "In faith, lady,"
says Don Pedro, "you have a merry heart." "Yea, my lord, I thank it,
poor fool, it keeps on the windy side of care"—and so for thirty lines
to his "out of question, you were born in a merry hour"—"No, sure,
my lord, my mother cried; but then there was a star danced, and
under that was I born." Shakespeare then, with one of his least inobvious contrivances, has to have her uncle say blankly, "Niece, will
you look to those things I told you of?" not only that the good-natured
plot against *her* may get broached, but simply, too, to get her offstage
and shut up. There is an incongruity here between the action structure and the personality structure, which has never prevented *Much
Ado's* being an infallible item in the English theatrical repertory, but
which the playwright was concerned, henceforward, to abolish. When
Rosalind talks thus, the action is being advanced, what action there
is. There is no story of Celia's that is being impeded.

Now for "character." Without soaring into the over-elaboration of
"character," and especially the character of the heroines, that vitiated
much nineteenth-century criticism, we may certainly distinguish between the higher, lighter tone of Celia and Rosalind's free intensity.
Here is Celia: "You know my Father hath no childe, but I, nor none
is like to haue." Here is Rosalind: "Come, wooe me, wooe me." No
critic, I think, however churlish or wedded to our imperfect understanding of Elizabethan stage conventions, can fail to recognize here
a difference in created character. These tones are not interchange-

able. So for the types: Hero, clearly, is Celia's prototype, Beatrice Rosalind's. But with *Twelfth Night* the pattern disappears, as the weaker, lighter plot heroine disappears. Viola stands as a representative, transformed, of the Beatrice-Rosalind type; far more Rosalind than Beatrice, and yet not Rosalind either. As for Celia, she is new. *Her* sole prototype, I think, is Portia, and I will come back to Olivia.

It ought to go without saying that the tones are not absolutely maintained. Most human speech is shamefully neutral; most things people say, that is, might with equal propriety be said by somebody else. This humiliating fact has not failed to exert an influence upon dramatic art in dialogue even at its most exalted, as in the comedies before us. And it is also known to many in our land (as Falstaff would say) that Homer has been observed to nod. "Scratch thee but with a pin," a character says in *As You Like It*:

> Scratch thee but with a pin, and there remains
> Some scarre of it: Leane vpon a rush,
> The Cicatrice and capable impressure
> Thy palme some moment keepes . . .

I am afraid this is Phoebe speaking, the shepherdess—most learned shepherdess. Shakespeare does not run straight out of his character, thus, often; but no commentator (except Dr. Johnson) seems very willing to mention it even when he does do it—the present instance having never, so far as I know, been exposed to the harsh light before.

If a heroine is to be built so high, clearly somebody must suffer, all the more if Touchstone and Feste, Jaques and Malvolio and Sir Toby are to have full play, and the sufferer is of course the hero. An actor like Laurence Olivier can do a great deal with Orlando, but the moments of real invention in the part are few. You remember when Charles the wrestler calls out: "Come, where is this yong gallant, that is so desirous to lie with his mother earth?" "Readie Sir, but his will hath in it a more modest working." That is wonderful, and conceals beneath the wit a characteristically Shakespearean rebuke to the bravado. Shortly, however, Rosalind will be saying, as if against her pride and will:

> Sir, you have wrastled well, and ouerthrowne
> More than your enemies.

To this tone, Orlando must yield primacy; and after his vivid cry, following the final couplet, when he is left alone at the end of the

wrestling scene ("But heauenly *Rosaline*"), there is not much more
in him than there has been in Le Beau. Le Beau, by the way, illustrates what the poet could do by way of presentment in a few lines
when he cared. Orlando has to be got back home, so a courtier has
to be made friendly—out of mere goodness—to warn him. But the
complex of sorrow and honour in Le Beau's short speeches go well
beyond the necessity of the situation:

> The Duke is humorous, what he is indeed
> More suites you to conceiue, then I to speake of . . .

and

> Sir, fare you well,
> Hereafter in a better world then this,
> I shall deserue more loue and knowledge of you.

As You Like It we said was a pastoral. You observe, however, that
those who possess power in the play misuse it: the usurping Duke
and Oliver. Even in the Forest of Arden, we first hear that Jaques has
been lamenting the tyranny of the hunters (themselves refugees) over
the deer; we then, as in a musical recapitulation, learn that Corin
can do little to relieve Rosalind and Celia because *his* master too

> is of churlish disposition,
> And little wreakes to finde the way to heauen
> By doing deeds of hospitalitie . . .

and then we see Phoebe tyrannizing over Silvius. To keep all this
misorder under scrutiny, in preparation for the waves of conversion
that will end the play, there are three major instruments of criticism:
Rosalind herself, Touchstone, and of course Jaques.

The play is inconceivable, I suppose, without Jaques. And yet it is
quite possible, and even likely, that Shakespeare first wrote the play
without him. As John Wilcox pointed out in 1941, if you take away
just 250 lines from five scenes, and change the speech-heading "Jaq."
to a "1st Lord" on ninety mechanical lines in five scattered scenes,
Jaques disappears.[6] Shakespeare's major characters can seldom be detached in this fashion. Moreover, the 45-line description of Jaques is
rather excessive to his introduction in Act II, Scene v, and he is
described *again* in II.vii and waited for. Finally, the middle brother
of Oliver and Orlando, when we hear of him, is named Jaques, but

when he actually appears at the end of the play he has no name, he is just "Second Brother." All this suggests irresistibly that Shakespeare at least conceived and planned the work without Jaques (he has no parallel, by the way, in Lodge's romance, the source), and probably wrote it too. Whether it was produced so or not, we can hardly guess. Then he built up the First Lord's part into Jaques. I can imagine three possible reasons. First, a discontent felt by the playwright with the play as not full enough; to this possibility a very close parallel can be discovered in Theseus' famous lines about the poet in A Midsummer Night's Dream, which Dover Wilson has shown (from mislineation in the quarto) were certainly inserted by Shakespeare into a rather tame speech on just the madman and the lover *after* he had written it. Second, Jaques may have been enlarged (created, really) for some important actor who joined the company. (Baldwin thinks Thomas Pope played Jaques, but Baldwin thinks many things[7]; we simply don't know. Nor, stable as the company evidently was, can we say with confidence who did not enter when.) The third possibility is that Shakespeare suddenly decided to satirize, and employ, the current convention of the Melancholy Man, the malcontent, the cynic. His name was pretty clearly pronounced, not "Jake-weez," as we have it, but "Jake-iz" or (shorter) monosyllabically—not quite like the French name it *is*, but more like. The name was contemporary in Warwickshire, incidentally, where it was often spelt (and no doubt pronounced) as a monosyllable.

G. B. Harrison suggested some years ago that his name was a pun, arising out of Sir John Harington's recent scatological treatise, *The Metamorphosis of Ajax* (or *a jakes*) [1596], which contained instructions for making your privy odourless.[8] This suggestion could only hang in the air and worry us vaguely, until Professor Kökeritz of Yale made some alarming discoveries about Jaques's language and incidentally about Shakespeare's, which seem to show that Harrison was right.[9] You know the lines—American schoolteachers are peculiarly fond of them—

> And so from houre to houre, we ripe, and ripe,
> And then from houre to houre, we rot, and rot,
> And thereby hangs a tale . . .

Well, they are a perfect labyrinth of obscenity. "Hour" you say as it's spelt, a pronunciation of "whore" that survives; of the verb "ripe" you employ a second meaning—to search out, to examine; "rot" you mispronounce a little; and so on, and you have nothing less than

And so from hour to hour we ripe and ripe
And then from hour to hour we rut and rut
And thereby hangs a tail . . .

It's amazing. Of course the actor of Jaques, Henry Condell or whoever, did not read the lines so broadly as I have just had to in the
service of historical truth, and I do not in the least suggest that the
centuries' old homiletic reading of the lines is wrong. There are two
meanings simultaneously. The actor no doubt just slurred the words,
so that quick ears and quick wits would pick up both, and feel, with
some justice, that nothing was ever wittier. I want to distinguish this
entirely from the sort of work done by James Joyce laboriously; this
could not be done laboriously—and also from Joyce's work is lacking
just the homiletic meaning that strikes instantly and lasts for 350 years
all by itself.

Less covert examples of this sort of thing have long been familiar
in Shakespeare's work, and bothered the eighteenth and nineteenth
centuries very much. He was either accused of pandering to the gross-
ness of his audience or excused on that ground. But in recent years
much has been learnt about his audience. Not so much from *direct*
contemporary testimony, nearly all of which, as Harbage puts it, "expresses a social attitude ("The theatre was a democratic institution in
an intensely undemocratic age") or comes from disappointed poets,
disgruntled preachers, wary politicians, or spokesmen for threatened
commercial interests."[10] But from indirect testimony; and what has
been learnt suggests on the whole an audience far more responsible
than has ever been supposed—certainly one with powers of attention,
and a verbal and symbolic intelligence, well beyond those of any large
modern theatrical audience, stupefied with newspapers, radio, and
the conversation of their friends. Exactly the audience, in fact, for
which one would *suppose* these extraordinary comedies written. In
London, in 1600, a city of about 150,000, some 20,000 people, or
two in fifteen, went to the theatre every week. Shakespeare, as not
only the most popular but far the best playwright working, plainly
commanded the superior element of that audience; and commanded
them not once, but many times, for each play; and then again for
his next play—the old play, however, as a rule remaining for two or
three or four or five years in the repertory. Writing two plays a year,
Shakespeare—as Harbage points out—was the first playwright to be
oppressed by the Shakespearean repertory. His plays competed with
each other. Perhaps it would be more correct to regard him as the
master of his audience, rather than its creature. Similarly, I think most

scholars suffer from a tendency to minimize what must have been his enormous independent power in his own company. The commercial difference between the play that was a failure, with three performances, and the play that was a success, with dozens and for years, was nearly as decisive then as it is now. He wrote successes. No doubt he took suggestions—as perhaps for the subject of *As You Like It*, which was clearly written to surpass Anthony Munday's two Robin Hood plays for the rival company, the Admiral's Men; and he certainly wrote for the audience. But I am afraid we must face the likelihood that he wrote bawdy, not because the audience insisted on it, nor his fellow actors, nor even the aristocratic followers of his work, but just because it amused him. In other respects he was beginning to do as he liked. Jaques is unreconciled. Malvolio is unreconciled. Look at the titles of these comedies: *Much Ado about Nothing*, *As You Like It*, *What You Will* (which is the alternative title of *Twelfth Night*). Under the guise of wooing the audience—these last two—the titles are really self-confident, indifferent, a little contemptuous.

The truth is, he elevated his audience, and he probably worked his actors to the bone and nerve. He gave them better materials than they had ever had before, but materials requiring a perfection of execution less continuously necessary earlier. I want to take two instances from *Twelfth Night*.

Nothing could be higher in tone, courtlier, more musical or imaginatively love-lorn than the opening scene of this great work, devoted to the Duke's praise, with his courtiers, of the lady Olivia—who will not be visible to him, we learn, for seven years, cloistered that long to mourn a dead brother. In the second scene Viola is shipwrecked on the shore of Illyria, and hears from the Captain of this Olivia, virtuous, noble, and retired. In the third scene her qualities are conned by, in their way, Sir Toby, her thirsty uncle, and his preposterous candidate for her hand, Sir Andrew Aguecheek. In the fourth scene, Viola has become, in male disguise, the Duke's confidential servant and promises to try to win access (on his behalf) to Olivia. The fifth scene begins with Maria and Feste; at last Olivia herself appears, and into the grand, beautiful, luminous, melancholy image of her so long a-making is inserted like a corkscrew her first speech: "Take the foole away." This is character creation with a vengeance, and if it presented the actor with opportunities, it also surrounded him with complexities and risks. When Olivia first receives Viola, Viola runs through fifty tones with her before Olivia finally opens up into the justification of the initial image we had of her:

> Your Lord does know my mind, I cannot loue him.
> Yet I suppose him virtuous, know him noble,
> Of great estate, of fresh and stainless youth;
> In voyces well divulg'd, free, learn'd, and valiant,
> And in dimension, and the shape of nature,
> A gracious person; But yet I cannot loue him:
> He might haue took his answer long ago.

And what can happen now?—there is a danger in utterance so perfect: it satisfies perfectly. And *now*, from this, *sets off* the most demanding and character'd love discourse the poet had ever written. Instantly upon Olivia's last line, he makes Viola a full character—forcing us to hear, what never strongly mattered to us, that she *loves* Orsino:

> If I did loue you in my masters flame,
> With such a suffering, such a deadly life:
> In your deniall, I would finde no sence,
> I would not vnderstande it.

Olivia is understandably amazed by this intensity.

>   Why, what would you?
> Vi. Make me a willow cabine at your gate
> And call vpon my soule within the house,
> Write loyall cantons of contemned loue,
> And sing them lowd euen in the dead of night:
> Hallow your name to the reuerberate hilles,
> And make the babling Gossip of the aire
> Cry out *Oliuia*: O you should not rest
> Betweene the elements of ayre, and earth,
> But you should pittie me.
> Oli.   You might do much:
> What is your parentage?
> Vi. Above my fortunes, yet my state is well:
> I am a Gentleman.
> Oli.   Get you to your Lord:
> I cannot loue him: let him send no more,
> Vnlesse (perchance) you come to me againe,
> To tell me how he takes it . . .

Something takes place here, in this sudden and multiplied access of reality, comparable to the shift by which Shakespeare, forced to rely upon boy actors for his women, disguised them then as boys and men—defeating the convention's unreality by multiplying it. Olivia *falls in love* upon her intuition that the person before her is capable of love.

My other example, from this play, in which all the male lovers are sticks, is not in Malvolio, of whom too much would have to be said for the allotted space, but in the topers, and it relates to *timing*. You saw, even in my reading of the Touchstone-William scene, how profoundly Shakespeare was coming to rely upon timing, rather than verbalism, for his humour. This is in accordance with life: the things at which we have laughed hardest are hardly ever worth repeating— it was *when* they were said, *after* what, by whom. I once saw Laurence Olivier as Sir Toby Belch, surprisingly. His Sir Andrew was Alec Guinness, since celebrated and then equipped with a blond upstanding forelock exactly like Laurel's (of Laurel and Hardy). They played their drinking scenes together so slowly that they might almost have been dead. First one, then the other, would rouse himself, Toby from all fumes, Sir Andrew from his brainlessness, and make a remark and lapse back. A remark like Sir Andrew's, "Methinks sometimes I have no more wit than a Christian, or an ordinary man has," made you *hurt* with laughter. But I am not an actor and only refer to this.[11]

HE HAD MOVED TO the Liberty of the Clink, near the Globe. In this theatre Shakespeare owned a share, so that his income—at which we can only guess—had increased. Even before the erection of the Globe it had been so considerable that a Stratford friend in the City on town business, Richard Quiney, would write confidently for a loan of thirty pounds; the letter survives, of October 25, 1598, and apparently it was never sent—he must have met Shakespeare.[12] "Master Shakespeare" bought a book in Stratford three years before, but whether the poet or his father, and what book, who knows?—it had belonged to the sister of his London printer, Richard Field.[13] And so the book most authoritatively supposed to survive from the poet's library is an early example of Anglo-Saxon printing [William Lambarde, *Archaionomia*, 1568], now in [the Folger Shakespeare Library in] Washington, perhaps never opened by him though he wrote his name in it.[14] His own dramatic work had legitimately come to print in some quantity, beginning with a quarto of *Richard II* in 1597 printed from his manuscript. A "bad" actors' version of *Romeo and Juliet* was pirated the same year—this was replaced by a "good" edition, again from manuscript, in 1599.[15] *Love's Labour's Lost* is also thought to have been pirated in a version of which no copies survive,

and similarly replaced by a good one of 1598. The same year followed
1 Henry IV (of the first edition of which just one sheet survives), also
probably from Shakespeare's manuscript. It is inconceivable that the
dramatist did not consent to, or actually arrange, most of these transactions, but he never read proof and he must have been somewhat
careless, because Richard III had had a curious fate. On tour in the
summer of 1597 (it is conjectured) the company found themselves
without the prompt book but wanting to play it, so they sat around
and reconstructed it from memory, pretty well, but with endless minor variation from the original; back in London, the improvisation,
being of no further use, was sold to a printer.[16] About this Shakespeare
did nothing that we know of. A "staying" order in 1600 saved As You
Like It from pirating, but not Henry V,[17] and this year came four good
texts, 2 Henry IV, Much Ado, A Midsummer Night's Dream, and The
Merchant of Venice; thereafter during his lifetime, never but two good
ones, one to replace a bad version and one over which he had no
power.

The fortunes of the two major companies, the Chamberlain's Men
and the Lord Admiral's Men, seem to have faltered a little in 1600.
For one thing, they had some competition from the Children of
Paul's, who had mocked the adult companies in Histriomastix, and
in September the Children of the Chapel began to act at the
Blackfriars—a more serious matter. For another, the Admiral's Men
were between theatres, waiting for a new one a-building, the Fortune.
Henslowe's playwrights meanwhile had no work, and three of them
(Anthony Munday, Henry Chettle, Thomas Dekker, with perhaps
Heywood) tried apparently to sell to the Chamberlain's Men a play
they had written together, Sir Thomas More. This would be about
January 1601. It had to be revised, and even then, in the restless state
of London after a year and a half of anxiety over the discontents and
ambitions of the Earl of Essex, the Master of the Revels was dissatisfied with the crucial Insurrection scene. So Shakespeare rewrote it.[18]

The manuscript of this play is in the British Museum [Harleian
7368].[19] After thirty-five years of very entertaining controversy [since
Sir Edward Maunde Thompson's Shakespeare's Handwriting, Oxford,
1916] there is no longer any serious doubt that the Insurrection scene
is a rough draft in Shakespeare's hand—various lines of evidence con-
verging, paleographical above all, orthographic (from spellings in the
good quartos), stylistic (diction, imagery, versification), and what I
suppose we have to call ideological, the treatment of the mob and of
More, of political ideas, and the characteristic, conventional insistence upon degree, order, unity.[20] It is about 150 lines, on two long

leaves, and paleography suggests that he wrote the first two pages at one sitting, the third at another, quite possibly because he only had one sheet of paper with him the first time. The hand is swift, with few corrections, all made while writing. Punctuation is scanty. Once or twice diction is altered up or down. Thus "what's [a watrie] a sorry parsnip to a good heart" (9), and "marry, the removing of the strangers which cannot choose but much [helpe] advantage the poor handicrafts of the city" (70). (The London apprentices are rioting on May Day for the banishment of foreigners.) There are a few false starts and slips of the pen. Once Shakespeare got somewhat confusing, and the book keeper who went over the manuscript before it was shown to the censor again crossed out three lines, substituting "Tell me but this" (114). The style is hasty, but it has been badly undervalued because all the dating, till lately, has been far too early except Schücking's: it is the style of which the next product will be *Hamlet*.[21] For a particular reason, I want to quote a good deal. The mob has been tossing, hardly willing to listen to its own leaders, much less to the Lord Mayor and the Earls. More the Sheriff stands silent, then comments:

> Whiles they are o'er the bank of their obedience,
> Thus will they bear down all things
>
> (39–40)

Hearing, a leader, Lincoln, cries, "Shrieve More speaks. Shall we hear Shrieve More speak?" Doll says, "Let's hear him. 'A keeps a plentiful shrievaltry, and 'a made my brother Arthur Watchins Sergeant Safe's yeoman. Let's hear Shrieve More." Cries: "Shrieve More, More, More, Shrieve More!"

> *More.* Even by the rule you have among yourselves,
> Command still audience.
>
> [*Cries and so on.*]
>
> *More.* You that have voice and credit with the number,
> Command them to a stillness

"A plague on them," Lincoln says, "they will not hold their peace. The dev'l cannot rule them."

> *More.* Then what a rough and riotous charge have you
> To lead those that the dev'l cannot rule.
> Good masters, hear me speak

Doll. Ay, by th' mass, will we, More. Th'art a good housekeeper
and I thank thy good worship for my brother Arthur
Watchins.

All. Peace, peace!

More. Look what you do offend you cry upon,
That is the peace; not one of you here present,
Had there such fellows liv'd when you were babes,
That could have topp'd the peace, as now you would,
The peace wherein you have till now grown up
Had been ta'en from you, and the bloody times
Could not have brought you to the state of men.
Alas, poor things, what is it you have got
Although we grant you get the thing you seek?

Betts. Marry, the removing of the strangers . . . [and so on]

More. Grant them removed and grant that this your noise
Hath chid down all the majesty of England,
Imagine that you see the wretched strangers,
Their babies at their backs, with their poor luggage
Plodding to th' ports and coasts for transportation,
And that you sit as kings in your desires,
Authority quite silenc'd by your brawl,
And you in ruff of your opinions cloth'd,
What had you got? I'll tell you: you had taught
How insolence and strong hand should prevail,
How order should be quell'd, and by this pattern
Not one of you should live an aged man,
For other ruffians, as their fancies wrought,
With self-same hand, self reasons, and self right,
Would shark on you, and men like ravenous fishes
Would feed on one another.

Doll. Before God, that's as true as the gospel.

Lincoln. Nay, this' a sound fellow, I tell you, let's mark him.

More. Let me set up before your thoughts, good friends,
One supposition, which if you will mark
You shall perceive how horrible a shape
Your innovation bears: first, 'tis a sin
Which oft th' apostle did forewarn us of, urging obedience to
      authority,
And 'twere no error if I told you all you were in arms 'gainst
God.

At this point Shakespeare broke off, having crowded his last lines
together at the bottom of the second page. Taking it up again:

All. Marry, God forbid that!

More. Nay, certainly you are,
   For to the King God hath his office lent [and so on]
      . . . what rebel captain,
   As mutines are incident, by his name
   Can still the rout? Who will obey a traitor?
   Or how can well that proclamation sound
   When there is no addition but a rebel
   To qualify a rebel? You'll put down strangers,
   Kill them, cut their throats, possess their houses,
   And lead the majesty of law in lyam
   To slip him like a hound; alas, alas, say now the King,
   As he is clement if th' offender mourn,
   Should so much come too short of your great trespass
   As but to banish you, whither would you go?
   What country by the nature of your error
   Should give you harbour? . . .

The speech is extended but the peroration abrupt:

     What would you think
   To be thus us'd? This is the strangers' case
   And this your mountainish inhumanity.

All. Faith, 'a says true. Let's us do as we may be done by.

Lincoln. We'll be rul'd by you, Master More, if you'll stand our friend
   to procure our pardon

More. Submit you to these noble gentlemen,
   Entreat their mediation to the King,
   Give up yourself to form, obey the magistrate,
   And there's no doubt but mercy may be found if you so seek
    it.

I have illustrated this scene at length because it displays the intensity of Shakespeare's opinion just on the eve of the most important political event of his lifetime—which put *Sir Thomas More* out of question, by the way, so that it was shelved and never played. This man must have contemplated the rising of Essex with strongly mixed feelings. On Saturday, February 7, 1601, his company were asked by some of Essex's friends and gentlemen to play *Richard II* and refused because it was old, but they had forty shillings extra and played it that afternoon.[22] Next morning the Earl imprisoned four officers of state, went on his futile progress into the City, returned fighting and by water to barricade himself in Essex House, where he and Southampton treated with the Lord Admiral from the leads, and surrendered. On the nineteenth the Earls were tried in Westminster Hall and condemned to death. On the evening of the twenty-fourth Shakespeare's company gave a Shrovetide play before the Queen, who retired then to her private apartments, and next morning, Ash Wednesday, Essex went to the block. With this event ends the Elizabethan period.[23] The Queen lingered two years, with the feelings of a grandmother who has been betrayed by and destroyed her favourite, with a failing interest in life, but the mood of men at once soured and darkened. Southampton's fate, as others were executed, remained in doubt; he was ill in the Tower. The Lord Chamberlain's Men went on tour, and Shakespeare was writing a long play, in an outmoded category, and a new kind, very long and a tragedy, about a northern prince.

The Crisis

IT SEEMS LIKELY THAT Shakespeare in middle life underwent at least two nervous crises that shook his work to its heart. Later it will be interesting to see what we can make of the second, the concert of exhaustion and rage that broke off his tragic period, the crisis of *Timon*. But certainly that coeval with its onset, with *Hamlet*, had consequences larger still, and among others that it governed the traffic at a crossroads on the metamorphosis whereby the author of *As You Like It* turned into the author of *King Lear*.

We think now of Shakespeare as a tragic dramatist, with reason. But he was not naturally a tragedian, like Marlowe and Kyd. He became one.

He was thirty before he undertook the completion of his first tragedy, more or less properly so called, *Romeo and Juliet*, in 1594. Perhaps this ambitious work was his first play designed for the Lord Chamberlain's Men; as probably his next tragedy five years later, *Julius Caesar*, was designed for the opening of the Globe. They would have been substantial incentives, the formation of the new company, the erection of the new theatre. In the interim he made many more comedies and histories.

It is reasonable to enquire what happened to the man who during 1599 and 1600 probably wrote *Henry V*, *Julius Caesar*, *As You Like It*, *Twelfth Night*, who in 1601 wrote *Hamlet* and followed it during the next five years with *Troilus and Cressida* and *Measure for Measure*, with *Othello*, with *King Lear*, with *Macbeth*. A more difficult subject does probably not exist in critical biography, but let us see what we can do. Observe at once that Shakespeare's rate of composition has slackened; instead of two plays a year he writes one, and for a year or so after *Hamlet*, at thirty-seven, it may be that he wrote nothing. But it is the change in the character of his work which is decisive. I must say something of the temper and substance of this new work.

From the exquisite temper of the great comedies, even of *Caesar*, we proceed in *Hamlet* to the torture of outrage—an outrage of incest and of a murdered father, brother-murdered. Critics have noticed a heavy incidence in this play of what they call sexual nausea, which is indeed staggering in its generality and force, but which let us see as a response to the outrage and call by a more genetic name, sexual loathing. This emotion is new in Shakespeare's dramatic work; how new will be clear if you will contrast with its expression Claudio's reproaches to Hero in *Much Ado about Nothing* (IV.i), the tone heretofore most like. In *Othello* we attend to a malignant brilliance of evil matchless in classical or modern literature, producing a torture of jealousy, that expresses itself in—not nausea—anti-sexual frenzy. In *King Lear* the whole of nature is assembled to a torture of undergone ingratitude, to which one grand reply is Lear's articulation of sexual horror. In *Macbeth* a man and his wife suffer the torture of *acting* ingratitude—a king-murder—and the torture of guilt. It is remarkable that the sexual feeling livid in its predecessors has disappeared, ostensibly, from *Macbeth*. This last of the greatest tragedies is the most terrible of them, lacking the variety of *Hamlet* and *King Lear*, more continually dreadful than *Othello*; one would suppose that the presentment of torture could go no further, and it did not. Resisting the temptation to pursue these themes into the later tragedies, I turn back to note that they dominate also the two comedies, so termed, composed between *Hamlet* and *Othello*. *Troilus and Cressida* is not unlike a sketch for *Othello*: a torture of sexual doubt, the hero's jealousy being here justified and he forbidden even the dignity of death. This painful, inconclusive play conveys some sense of a persistent, disgusted spitting upon honored images. In *Measure for Measure*, on the other hand, morality runs riot. The Duke of a corrupt Vienna attempts to establish (by proxy) a utopia where irregular sexual indulgence will be punished, as it deserves, by death, and only a contemptuous or flippant happy ending keeps this play from being a (most unsatisfactory) tragedy. Giant powers are visible certainly in both works, but powers flickering, intermittently in control, at the mercy of obsession. (Much special pleading in the last twenty years has failed to persuade me that these were his least successful plays since *King John*.) We distinguish, then, three phases of Shakespeare's

critical period: the triumphs of *Hamlet* and *Othello*, the disorder of
the comedies of corruption, the triumphs of *King Lear* and *Macbeth*.
But I want to make it plain that I am speaking of dramatic and poetic
triumphs, not of any return to normality in substance or temper.
When we first hear Prince Hamlet alone, we learn that he wishes to
die. The train of loathing and disillusion thus initiated will advance,
so far as we seem to experience the *general* mood of the author,
through every degree of exasperation, without any broad rest (except
in one play) until Timon's prayer: "Destruction phang mankinde!"

Very likely, in sum the celebrated poet, playwright, actor, and gentleman in his late thirties strolling about London during these opening years of the seventeenth century, or playing or rehearsing, or
writing in his orchard at Stratford, spent part of his time in a ferocious
or even a desperate frame of mind, which did not fail to display itself
elaborately in nearly everything he composed. No one doubts this
except a few scholars and literary historians, Oxfordians, Dyerians,
and so on. But the cursory view we have taken so far has wished
especially to begin to discredit at once the conjectures that we are
dealing *merely*, in this tragic period of the greatest poet known to us,
with a normal literary development, or artistic ambition, or with literary influences, or with a certain qualified disenchantment with life
which very many reflective men undergo after the age of thirty-five.
Ambition is undoubtedly relevant; it is amusing that the scholars who
insist upon *ambition* as the dominant motive of the tragic period
never think of relating the occasions for Shakespeare's two earliest
tragedies, as we saw them, to the occasion of an unusual leisure for
Hamlet provided by the inhibition of playing in 1601; but hardly
dominant? Any candid hearing for the mood of these plays recognizes
a voice as restlessly special as the titanic works it uttered. The poet
who, never before having taken up a lunatic, for years sends his heroes
and heroines mad—Hamlet in craft to avoid the reality, Ophelia,
Othello in delirium, Lear, Edgar feignedly in self-protection, Lady
Macbeth—is not himself as we know him in earlier work, and he will
never be again. Ambition no doubt, literary influence to a degree
much slighter than scholarship has usually supposed, but essentially
we must look for other things.

There seem to be two roads of enquiry open, by way of the poet's
life and by way of the pivotal play itself, *Hamlet*. I propose to try both.
Neither road is at all smooth, and upon the first we must be prepared
to push patiently past a good deal of uncertainty. What goes wrong
with a man?

Money—lack of it, that is, generally accompanied by things called debts. We can suppose none for Shakespeare. His income, from both the Chamberlain's Men and his share in the Globe, seems to have been excellent. I had better be specific. Already in 1597 he had purchased for £50 ["sexaginta libras sterlingorum"] one of Stratford's largest houses, New Place. Upon his father's death in the autumn of the critical year, 1601, he inherited presumably the Henley Street houses. Next year he extended his properties with a purchase of freehold land in Old Stratford for the large sum of £320, also renting a cottage in Chapel Lane for a servant, and three years later he bought for an even larger sum, £440, a ninety-two-year lease on a parcel of tithes in Stratford which had once belonged to the Stratford College; this gave him a fifth of *all* Stratford tithes.[1] Instead of owing he was owed money—for which he sued now and then, injuring his character with certain scholars indifferent, I suppose, to whether people repay them loans or not and inadequately alive to the truth that Elizabethans went to law at the drop of a hat. Socially: Shakespeare was still an actor, but the position of actors had improved, and he himself had technically, through a grant of arms to his father (arranged doubtless by the son) in 1596, the status of a gentleman.[2]

Other forms of objective failure or disappointment seem inapposite also. He was the chief playwright of the most powerful London company. All his early rivals had disappeared long ago, and against the new dramatists—Heywood, Chapman, Jonson, Dekker, Marston, Middleton—Shakespeare appears easily to have maintained supremacy, as his company did against the Lord Admiral's Men. For an involuntary entanglement with Essex's rebellion of February 8, 1601 (they had been paid by followers of his to revive *Richard II*—"I am Richard II, know ye not that?" said the Queen to William Lambarde),[3] the Lord Chamberlain's Men were quickly exonerated.[4] Suffering under the inhibition of public London playing after the revolt, it was they who had the macabre privilege of performing for Elizabeth on the worst night she ever passed, the eve (February 24) of the Earl's execution; and they were as often as usual at court the following winter. Upon the Queen's death in March 1603, within two months the company was licensed as the King's Men, Shakespeare with others being made a Groom of the Chamber in ordinary. There is a teasing record of a letter, now undiscoverable, written evidently towards the end of this year from Wilton House by the Countess of Pembroke to her son, telling him to bring the King from Salisbury to see *As You Like It*; one sentence is quoted: "We have the man Shakespeare with us."[5] The court was in fact at Wilton from late October for a time and James at Salisbury on November 1. During the single winter of

Shakespeare's career for which our notices are detailed, 1604–5, out of a dozen court performances by the King's Men, eight were of his plays, James liking so well *The Merchant of Venice*—now years old—on Shrovesunday that he commanded it again two nights later.[6] The royal favour, in short, that probably ordered *The Merry Wives* written in 1597 continued through 1601 and through the whole tragic period. Besides royal patronage, and an active aristocratic and large popular following, Shakespeare had critical standing. As early as 1598 he was singled out by the clergyman Francis Meres, in *Wit's Treasury*, as "the most excellent in both kinds for the stage" (comedy and tragedy, calling the histories tragedies). This superlative strikes us as well enough; what was thought then of Meres's judgements is unknown, except that he stung Jonson by finding another man [Anthony Munday] "our best plotter." But more flattering still, he actually named twelve or fourteen of Shakespeare's plays, nearly all we know up to that date—he names none by others—and remarked that the "sweete wittie soule of *Ouid*" lived in him as a poet, adducing both the famous long poems, "his sugred Sonnets among his priuate friends, &c."[7] Of an author thirty-four, a remarkable citation. Other allusions, mostly by poets, attest his standing, and at least one notorious critic, Spenser's friend at Cambridge Gabriel Harvey, approved *Hamlet*.[8]

Whether all this quite rules out a subjective artistic dissatisfaction is less clear. One might suppose such feelings impossible to the author of the last few plays of Shakespeare's Second Period, but such feelings depend not upon achievement but upon state of nerve. A great poet may fall as readily subject to a sense of inadequacy, gloom, self-contempt, as a poetaster to wild self-esteem. Traces are visible indeed of a related dissatisfaction in *Henry V*, an impatience with theatrical form—a longing for epic or a shameless longing for the thing itself. But his work then turned inward, with *Hamlet*; the impatience died; and I think the prolific, devoted attention lavished on the theatrical profession and dramatic art in *Hamlet* enables us to regard the bearing of this possibility as slight. What may have been the personal feelings *later*, of a playwright accustomed to mastery, about his failure comparatively with the comedies of disillusion, is another matter. But that is beyond our point.

Then there is the possibility of definite illness, which *Hamlet*'s stunning energy seems to exclude, but there are many kinds of illness. For a reason some other time to be canvassed, I am afraid it will be a mistake not to bear in mind among the rest syphilis,[9] and I pass to other matters that evidence does not enable us to bar from consideration.

Current experience shows with what intensity the state of the world can affect writers. As the Queen aged, successorless, an acrid melancholy is discernible in Elizabethan writing, which thickened after the fall of Essex. It is clear that this might have influenced *Hamlet* either directly, in the time's mood, or indirectly, by way of literary influence. But the truth is that that commonplace of criticism, the Elizabethan Melancholy Man fully developed, seems rather to have been created by Hamlet than to have produced him. There are interesting sketches, such as Chapman's Dowsecer of 1597 (*An Humorous Day's Mirth*). The only tragic figure, however, really resembling Hamlet in some traits so distinctly that borrowing one way or the other is certain, Marston's hero in *Antonio's Revenge*, has been too easily taken by scholars as earlier. To say nothing of the possibility that Shakespeare had composed a Hamlet-play before 1601 which he then revised (for which Granville-Barker[10] and others have accumulated impressive evidence of some of its features in the corrupt First Quarto, 1603, of *Hamlet* proper), Marston's dating has not been handled critically enough. His tragedy is the second part of a two-part play of which the first part, *Antonio and Mellida*, is a comedy. This belongs to 1599. *Antonio's Revenge* displays a marked, unpredictable change in both mood and material. The plays were published in 1602. Now two other plays of Marston's, *What You Will* and *The Fawn*, most scholars have found impossible to date except upon the conjecture that he revised them shortly after their first production, either for revival or for publication. Marston was a man of letters, like Marlowe, who scholars now think revised *Tamburlaine* just before publication in order to insert passages from a new work on fortifications and to borrow passages from the just-issued *Faerie Queene*. I suggest in the light of the extraordinary discontinuity between his two parts as we have them that Marston revised *Antonio's Revenge* in 1602 with *Hamlet* sounding in his mind[11]; and his latest editor, who has done so little for Marston's text, has found an allusion to monopolies at the end of IV.iii that would not have been safe before 1601— Shakespeare himself first ventured on the topic in *King Lear*—and helps remove the play from its original composition about 1600. The aching fusion, then, in Hamlet, of sexual, political, and philosophical melancholy, seems less indebted to known literary influence than critics have imagined. About an influence from events, however, scepticism can go too far. Shakespeare's sympathy with Essex was sharply qualified, no doubt, by his own political philosophy, as we see that in his histories and (just before Essex's outbreak) the riot scene he wrote into *Sir Thomas More*. If he had saluted in a chorus of

Henry V "the Generall of our gracious Empresse," he had warned already in *Much Ado*—a passage of astonishing weight—of

> favourites,
> Made proud by princes, that aduance their pride
> Against that power that bred it . . .

But the universal anxiety about the succession to Elizabeth we have every reason to suppose he shared; his livelihood, for one thing, might depend on the succession. I think it as reasonable to see this anxiety playing some slight part in the formation of *Hamlet*, and the career of the brilliant, unstable, out-of-favour, ill-fated Earl playing some slight part in the reconception of Hamlet, as it seems to me fatuous to imagine the Prince his portrait, or a portrait of any personage of state.

Of Essex's intimate the Earl of Southampton we can say less. It is a fact that during the composition of *Hamlet* he lay in the Tower under sentence of death, and a fact that seven years before they had been on terms of (to Shakespeare) extremely satisfactory patronage. But we can do nothing with these facts, since nothing is known of the men's relations in between. We can only guess that the Essex-Southampton group followed the poet's work (but it would be surprising if they had not), for they nicknamed somebody at court Sir John Falstaff and both Essex and the Countess of Southampton joke about him. Southampton was never executed, but never by Elizabeth released; under James he was restored at once to his honours and shone at court thenceforth. Nothing is known of his relations with Shakespeare hereafter either, except indirectly through an extant note of 1604 from Sir Walter Cope to Robert Cecil, sent by Burbage, saying that according to Burbage, "ther ys no new playe that the quene [Anne] hath not seene," but the company has revived an old one, *Love's Labour's Lost*, which will please her exceedingly and "ys apointed to be playd to Morowe night at my Lord of Sowthamptons."[12] On the other hand, Southampton may have remained Shakespeare's patron from 1593 to 1616, in which event the disaster of 1601 can hardly be irrelevant. The dedication by Heminge and Condell of Shakespeare's plays to the Earl of Pembroke and his brother in 1623, rather than Southampton, tells us nothing; Pembroke was and had been for years the company's master, as Lord Chamberlain.[13]

If the poet was not in distress over his patron, he is conjectured to have been depressed by the death of a friend, say Richard Quiney, who died at Stratford in May of 1602—a year too late for the passage about Horatio, spoken to Horatio (III.ii.67–69), which is thought to memorialize him. It is a striking passage. A passage not less striking, in *All's Well that Ends Well*, is so little known that I had better quote it. The play is usually assigned to the present period with *Troilus* and *Measure*, but seems to contain much earlier writing, as well as much later writing, including the lines in question; wherein, although the matter is to our purpose, the versification is probably that of Shakespeare's final period. I should mention that the source, a story in Painter, contains no hint for this matchless meditation, not even a suggestion that Bertram's father and the King were friends, nor does the passage accomplish anything for Shakespeare's play except beauty.[14] "Youth," says the King,

> Youth, thou bear'st thy Fathers face,
> Franke Nature rather curious then in hast
> Hath well compos'd thee: Thy Fathers morall parts
> Maist thou inherit too: Welcome to *Paris*.
> *Ber.* My thankes and dutie are your Maiesties.
>   *K.* I would I had that corporall soundnesse now,
> As when thy father, and my selfe, in friendship
> First tride our souldiership: he did looke farre
> Into the seruice of the time, and was
> Discipled of the brauest. He lasted long,
> But on vs both did haggish Age steale on,
> And wore us out of act: It much repaires me
> To talke of your good father; in his youth
> He had the wit, which I can well obserue
> To day in our yong Lords: but they may iest
> Till their owne scorne returne to them vnnoted
> Ere they can hide their leuitie in honour
> So like a Courtier: contempt nor bitternesse
> Were in his pride, or sharpnesse; if they were,
> His equall had awak'd them, and his honour
> Clocke to it selfe, knew the true minute when
> Exception bid him speake: and at this time
> His tongue obey'd his hand. Who were below him,
> He vs'd as creatures of nigher place,
> And bow'd his eminent top to their low rankes,
> Making them proud of his humilitie,
> In their poore praise be-humbled: Such a man
> Might be a copie to these yonger times;
> Which followed well, would demonstrate them now
> But goers backward.

Ber. His good remembrance sir
    Lies richer in your thoughts then on his tombe:
    So in approofe liues not his Epitaph,
    As in your royall speech.
K. Would I were with him! He would alwaies say,
    (Me thinkes I heare him now) his plausiue words
    He scatter'd not in eares, but grafted them
    To grow there and to beare: Let me not liue,
    This his good melancholly often began
    On the Catastrophe and heele of pastime
    When it was out: Let me not liue (quoth hee)
    After my flame lackes oyle, to be the snuffe
    Of yonger spirits, whose apprehensiue senses
    All but new things disdaine; whose iudgements are
    Meere fathers of their garments: whose constancies
    Expire before their fashions: this he wish'd.
    I after him, do after him wish too:
    Since I nor waxe nor honie can bring home,
    I quickly were dissolued from my hiue
    To giue some Labourers roome.

I refrained from warning you of its length because its unwonted, absorbed protraction is a capital point. It is personal; but it is to be contrasted, rather than compared, with the youthful lines in Sonnet 30:

    Then can I drown an eye (vn-vs'd to flow)
    For precious friends hid in deaths dateles night,

which preceded it probably by twenty years. Shakespeare somewhere in maturity certainly lost a lifelong friend, another "coetanean" such as Aubrey tells us he lost in youth.[15] But who, we enquire in vain. "Master W.H."—if he and the poet were still friends—seems to have been alive as late as 1609, if the printer Thorpe was well informed and candid, and with Shakespeare's other contemporaries such evidence as we have, though it suggests amiability, has nothing to say to fullness of relation. The circumstances of the beautiful poem now called "The Phoenix and Turtle," written in *Hamlet*'s year to lament the death of a childless couple, are enigmatic; it may be significant of the poet's frame of mind that their "married Chastitie" is celebrated. Shakespeare was the first of a dozen fellow players named as legatees in Augustine Phillips's will in 1605.[16] All three of his Lon-

don associates remembered in Shakespeare's own will, John Heminge, Henry Condell, Richard Burbage, named sons William. In 1604
he had rooms in the house of a Huguenot tire maker (a creator of
elaborate head-dresses for women of rank) in Silver Street, Cripple-
gate, and good-naturedly, at the wife's request, arranged a marriage
between the daughter, Mary Mountjoy, and her father's apprentice
Stephen Belott, which was duly celebrated.[17] It is impossible to doubt
that his acquaintance in literary and theatrical London was wide
(though the Mermaid Club, with which besides nothing adequately
associates Shakespeare, belongs a decade later); but we *hear* of no
special friend save Ben Jonson.

About women we are a little wiser. His betrayal by his dark-haired
mistress with his friend of the sonnets has often been cited in relation
to the tragic period, but this experience seems now to have occurred
and been digested many years before, in his twenties. Other affairs
had perhaps followed. In March of 1602 one student at the Middle
Temple told another [John Manningham], who put it in his diary,
the only contemporary personal anecdote of Shakespeare. "Vpon a
tyme when Burbidge played Rich. 3. [it runs] there was a citizen
greue soe farr in liking with him, that before shee went from the play
shee appointed him to come that night vnto hir by the name of Ri:
the 3. Shakespeare overhearing their conclusion went before, was
intertained, and at his game ere Burbidge came. Then message being
brought that Rich. the 3.[d] was at the dore, Shakespeare caused returne
to be made that William the Conquerour was before Rich. the 3.
Shakespeare's name William."[18] This is amusing enough to be suspicious. Duller stories are more plausible, and anyway, our records
are so imperfect that no performance of the play can be dated later
than (perhaps) 1595: "upon a time" does not sound recent. It is likely
that during the critical years, and possibly thereafter, he broke his
annual journeys between Stratford and London at Oxford, where he
was either the private guest of or a lodger with a taverner named John
Davenant, a melancholy man who treated the poet with great respect.
His wife, Jane, "a very beautiful woman, & of a very good witt and
of conversation extremely agreeable," was perhaps kind enough to
bear the poet a son named William in 1606. So the son, later Poet
Laureate, intimated, and there is general agreement that he was
Shakespeare's godson; whether more, perhaps only Jane Davenant
knew, if she knew.[19] I mention in passing that a fellow actor, William
Sly, had a bastard the same year, and Shakespeare's youngest brother,
Edmund (also an actor), a bastard the following year. Later report
gives Shakespeare an illegitimate daughter, and there is no judging

the truth of any of this. Though none of it is improbable, none of it is verifiable. His legal daughters were eighteen and sixteen in 1601, and we know nothing about them yet, nor anything about their mother's character.

Shakespeare's father was buried on September 8, 1601. It would be convenient, psychologically, if *Hamlet* followed this loss; as *Coriolanus* may have followed shortly on his mother's death eight years later. But by a historic agreement between Sir Edmund Chambers and Professor Dover Wilson, the best we can do at present for the composition of *Hamlet* is either the summer or the autumn of 1601, and we know nothing of his father's last illness, so that the death may have followed by a coincidence on the writing of the play. I will come back to this. Meanwhile, however, we have here undoubtedly reached the gravest and most plausible event along the biographical road of enquiry, and perhaps it too has failed us. We shall have to turn now to *Hamlet* itself. But I wonder whether you have not become increasingly conscious of a certain want of adequacy in the possibilities we have been considering, unless in some terrible unknown *degree* or *combination* or as thrust into an *already completely unusual* spiritual state, to explain the sudden development of the tragic substance and temper which we summarized at the outset. It is the cause of a revolution in the soul that we are seeking; which a straw might set off—but we know something of Shakespeare's capacity to digest experience. Since his son's death five years have passed, without a trace of that grief in his work, unless the critics are right who see it influencing the lament for young Arthur in *King John*. I am doubtful about this myself. But I observe that the best dating we have for the play is G. B. Harrison's, on political grounds, in June–September 1596, and that Hamnet (or Hamlet) Shakespeare was buried in mid-August; and I am struck by the fact that if this is coincidence, it is odd. If Mary Shakespeare's death [1608] followed by chance upon *Coriolanus*, the coincidence is odder. If John Shakespeare's death [1601] followed by chance upon *Hamlet*, we may as well conclude that there is nothing reasonable in nature. The dogmatic sceptics in these matters really give us more to explain than they trouble to notice. (I even find it interesting that the man from whom Shakespeare bought New Place died shortly thereafter by poison, and was presently proved to have been murdered by his heir [eldest son], who had since died himself; unfortunately the transfer of property had been incomplete and there was a question of forfeiture to the crown, avoided when the murderer's younger brother, Hercules Underhill, came of age in 1602 and was allowed to inherit and complete the transfer to

Shakespeare.)[20] But let me mention further, before entering on *Hamlet* critically, three remarkable and undeniable points of relation between the play and Shakespeare's life.

The first is that its hero, the poet's most fully imagined character, strangely bears the name of his dead son. The second is that this play written close upon the death of the poet's father is a work

> whose common theame
> Is death of fathers:

not Hamlet's only, but the death of Fortinbras's father is related in the opening scene, and the death of Laertes's father follows, all slain. The third is a disturbing similarity of phrasing between the Spiritual Last Will and Testament of John Shakespeare, lately rehabilitated and proved genuine by Dr. de Groot,[21] in which Shakespeare's father calls to mind "that I may be possibly cut off in the blossoms of my sins," and the outcry Shakespeare gave the Ghost to Hamlet: "Cut off euen in the blossomes of my sinne . . ." It seems hardly too much to say that old-fashioned words like "demonic" and "unnatural" cough gently as we address ourselves to his dramatic masterpiece.

That it is a dramatic masterpiece appears to me to be comfortably attested by its records of performance for 350 years and by my experience every time I see or read it. That it is a strange dramatic masterpiece appears to me to be uncomfortably attested by the library of controversy produced by it in the last two centuries. I begin with these impressions. Critics have not failed to attack the first impression with the second, and two schools of these are too plausible to be ignored. One school tells us that *Hamlet* is a failure, because of Shakespeare's imperfect imposition of a psychological drama upon a simple Revenge play by Kyd. Panoply of learning by this school, much reference to Kyd's surviving work, deep familiarity with the lost source play. However, the inference by which (from a passage of Nashe's) Kyd was supposed to have written a Hamlet play has been rejected by both R. B. McKerrow and W. W. Greg, the most astute judges of such evidence who ever lived. Of the lost pre-Shakespearean *Hamlet* we know nearly nothing except that it was Senecan, but by someone who (unlike Kyd) knew almost no Latin. Whether it imitated or was imitated by Kyd's *Spanish Tragedy* (about 1589) we do not know. We do not even know that it was not by Shakespeare. But of the way in which Shakespeare treated his occasional source plays we know a great deal—not only in the mid-1590s, when (for once) he rewrote the old King John play to produce one of his feeblest works, but later in his mastery, when from the old *King Leir* he takes the King and his unkind daughters, borrows a hint for the character of Kent, a theatrical business of Lear kneeling to Cordelia, some phrases, and nothing else. From the point of view of the old play, *King Lear* is practically all invention. Our reasonable inference is much clearer than these critics' was. In the false teeth of suggestions about the Ur-*Hamlet*, about the later German *Fratricide Punished*, about the First Quarto, we are on firm ground in supposing that whether Shakespeare wrote the play twice or not, he was intellectually, dramatically, and poetically responsible for *Hamlet* as we have it (in Q2 and F) from beginning to end.

The other school is blunter and even less gullible. To the fundamental question about Hamlet's delay in prosecuting his revenge, it answers wisely: No delay, no play. I am at a loss to account for the prestige of this stupefying explanation, unless we imagine many of Professor Stoll's readers for thirty-five years as little able to bear the effort of reflection as he is. *Hamlet* is a very long play, Shakespeare's longest, thrice *Oedipus the King*, twice *Macbeth* nearly. Shakespeare—let us withdraw to an elementary idea—knew what he was about at least as well as we do, in stagecraft, in theatrical organization. It is mere fatuity, a pomposity of professorship, to suppose a work so protracted by this great dramatist crudely and insubstantially without being felt as protracted so by him. He could have made it half as long. About this protractedness there are some unusual features. As Coleridge truly observed, this is "almost the only play of Shakespeare, in which mere accidents, independent of all will, form an essential part of the plot."[22] It is an exaggeration only of a truth to say there is no plot. After the first act, we hear nothing whatever of the Ghost or Hamlet's duty again until the very end of the second, when we are indebted to the accident of the players' arrival for the resumption of the central action; the Play scene is arranged to test what we thought we knew Hamlet had not the slightest doubt of, namely, Claudius's guilt (this loss of faith in the Ghost then is a plot element, yet how little insisted upon); his one opportunity to kill the King arrives by pure chance; the Bedroom scene is a perfect digression, disobeying moreover the Ghost's injunction

> (nor let thy soule contriue
> Against thy mother ought, leaue her to heauen);

Hamlet, upon the accident of Polonius's slaying, is sent and goes like a mouse to England, is rescued by accident, and then by wills not his own is drawn into the action that proves fatal. Embarking upon a drawn-out drama sorry with delay, why did Shakespeare not lay out a *plot*? He seldom made up plots, but he was a genius at adapting them. The old *Leir* he found empty and filled his play not only with closely relevant invented material but with a whole new second action worked up out of a story in Sidney's *Arcadia*. *Macbeth* again has surprisingly little plot; and he made it short. A related strangeness was noticed by Dr. Johnson, that "Hamlet is, through the whole piece, rather an instrument than an agent." An instrument; though the point of the play is his agency of revenge, and though, unlike Shakespeare's other tragic heroes, he has no peer in the play, no other character at all similar in importance—two of the others indeed being mere foils to him, Laertes and Fortinbras. The delay, then, is that of a hero singly important, in a work of enormous length, where everything ought to depend upon his actions but where instead he does almost nothing except by accident, with no precautions whatever taken by Shakespeare to disguise these curious facts.

On the contrary, of course, Shakespeare insists upon them. It might be thought not easy to kill a king; but so far from emphasizing the difficulties, Shakespeare never mentions them and Hamlet never gives them a thought. It is when he is on his way to England, for the first time, without *any* chance of accomplishing his revenge, that he exclaims

> I doe not know
> Why yet I liue to say this thing's to doe,
> Sith I haue cause, and will, and strength, and meanes
> To doo't . . .

Now what he had said when he *could* do it, when he came on the King alone trying to pray, after the Play scene, was this, whipping out his sword: "Now might I doe it . . ." But these opening words already warn us that he has no intention of doing it, even before he thinks of a reason (an excellent bloody reason) for not doing it.

Nor did Shakespeare create Hamlet a fellow unfit for this sort of work, as Goethe and Coleridge imagined. In the last minute by himself, before he comes on the King thus, he was muttering:

> now could I drinke hot blood,
> And doe such bitter busines as the day
> Would quake to looke on . . .

That he is not wrong about himself is proved shortly by his unceremonious spitting of Polonius, his Italian murder of Rosencranz and

Guildenstern. Werner's view, echoed by Dowden and some modern critics, that Hamlet represents a moral force incapacitated by the evil nature of his world, ignores this activity of his *in certain directions*; and the support invoked for the view from the play's disease images has been destroyed by Clemen's recent demonstration that these originate all from the impressions made upon Hamlet by the Ghost's terrible description of its poisoning and the fact of his mother's incest.[23] This prince of conscience shows no scruple of remorse for any of the deaths he causes, any more than for his ferocious treatment of Ophelia.

It is true that Hamlet is in a most unusual state throughout the play. At the outset he feels so far "sullied" by the incest of his mother's marriage with his father's brother that he wants to die. When first we meet him alone after his interview with his father's ghost, he is contemplating—not revenge, which he never mentions—but suicide, and he seems to have forgotten all about the Ghost. His death-will has only been intensified, not changed, by the revelations of his mother's adultery and his father's murder. His setting out for England (no protest made or escape attempted) is a patent example of his willingness to be destroyed; his accepting the challenge of Laertes, whom he knows hates him, is clearer still. Further, he treats Ophelia like a whore, though there are many and strong indications that Shakespeare wished us to believe that Hamlet *had* loved her, and one always does believe this, correctly, in the theatre. *Now*, he says not a word about her in either of the first two soliloquies and seems to regard her with suspicious horror. She has not changed. But he has. He is not mad—though he pretends to be. But something so dreadful has happened to him that he knows himself not responsible for much that he does. In the wonderful plea to Laertes, for pardon near the end, the deaths of whose father and sister he has caused, Hamlet disclaims those deaths. He lays them to his "madness," the best term he has for the mysterious affliction, the "sore distraction," with which he has been "punnisht" throughout. On the other hand: the sexual revulsion, life-loathing, in which he is suffering when we first meet him, hardly seem, from his tone when the Ghost first tells him of the murder, likely to inhibit his vengeance upon whoever was the murderer.

> Hast me to know't, that I with wings as swift
> As meditation, or the thoughts of loue
> May sweepe to my reuenge.

The Crisis

It is when he learns upon *whom* he must take revenge that he becomes the man of pause we know.

The psychoanalytic explanation of the play suggests itself as the most comprehensive and reasonable that has been offered. According to it, Hamlet cannot bring himself to kill his uncle precisely (without knowing this) because his uncle has accomplished two of his own infantile fantasies: the killing of his father and the enjoying of his mother. These fantasies have already been thrown into disruptive life again—accounting for his initial loathing—by the suggestive spectacle of incest following on the unsettling experience of his father's death. To kill his uncle, with respect to whom he feels "the jealous detestation of one evildoer towards his successful fellow," is impossible because he cannot be sure as to his motive for killing him; he may simply be disposing of a second rival; and (one notes with a shock) it *is* not until his mother is dead of poison that Hamlet is free to kill the King, when he kills him instantly. Until then, he drifts, flailing, amongst apathy, hysterical and irrelevant emotions, self-questionings, sexual disgust, torture of mind, yet able to do everything but that which is necessary and *this* able actually to forget, to let sleep in "bestial obliuion," seeking always his own death.

One of the strongest minds of the modern period opened this view in a footnote of his great work on dream interpretation of 1900, but Freud's opinion was certainly unknown to Bradley when he published his classical account, *Shakespearean Tragedy*, in 1904. Here, in a passage that may be held rather to foreshadow than to supplement psychoanalytic findings, we come on an acute admission. "Possibly [Bradley wrote] we may be baffled because [Shakespeare] has illustrated in [the character of Hamlet] certain strange facts of human nature, which he had noticed but of which we are ignorant."[24] Now that something like this seems really to be the case, except that we are no longer ignorant of these particular strange facts, we have to ask whether "noticed" is proper. The same enquiry arises, in regard to the *Oedipus the King* of Sophocles. I do not think it possible to decide what these men knew. But it would be wide of our point to attribute to Sophocles and Shakespeare any discursive knowledge of the action of the psyche under the Oedipus complex. What we are bound to suppose is narrower and less doubtful: that Shakespeare's instinct for the operations of human nature simply detected them latent in the materials of the Hamlet story as these came to him, and elaborating them, he obeyed his instinct. One detail of elaboration will instance the process: of the three fathers whom we mentioned as dead in the play, one is killed by Hamlet himself, the father of his

foil Laertes, in his mother's bedroom. The question is, what this obedience and this elaboration may have cost Shakespeare in anxiety or
pain. But close as we are at this point to the possibility of a general
solution to our enquiry as a whole, I must interrupt it to insist upon
the *unconscious* character of this aspect of the play's truth. I can best
enforce this by looking briefly at two other very different aspects of
Hamlet, the first a source of unconscious power, the second an en-
actment of unconscious gratification. Not entirely unconscious, any
of the three, but essentially so.

It is not only in terms of psychology that we have taken centuries
in getting at certain depths of Shakespeare's mind. Just yesterday some
light was thrown there by Miss Levy's study, authoritative so far as
our knowledge extends, of the persistence of human religious conceptions from the Cave period forward to Greek tragedy.

In the tragic cycles of Orestes and Oedipus [she writes] the battle for the
New Year, and the New King, and mimed then, as now in the crude folk-
plays, itself provides the plot. It was used long afterwards for one more masterpiece. Shakespeare's *Hamlet* . . . In all three instances the old king is
dead before the hero's drama begins, and he himself returns to, and from,
banishment, disfigured, black-robed, and feigning madness or death, like the
bleak "winter" fighter of the folk-plays who struggles for supremacy with his
bright double . . . The plot was so firmly established in human memory,
that the vacillations of Hamlet and Orestes, and the spiritually blinding ignorance of Oedipus . . . became more important than the very horrible
action."[25]

Small wonder if Shakespeare's critics have brooded sometimes over
an imagination so deep that it seems to include all human history.

With the other aspect we are drawing back towards our enquiry.
The bewildering, unexampled richness of presentation of human experience in *Hamlet*, directed all upon one character, and that character bearing the name of the poet's lost son, decidedly urges upon
us a likelihood that the commentators' usual identification of Shakespeare with Prince Hamlet is only half the truth. He must have imagined himself in King Hamlet, the father, also; the part in fact that he
is said to have taken at the Globe and it was (Rowe gathered) "the
top of his Performance."[26] From this point of view, the play is an
imagined *life* for his dead son, a life supreme in imagination and
abilities, in social position, in experience, lovingly and interminably
dilated. I mention one feature of it that seems suggestive: the Prince's
exceptional interest in, kindness towards, and respect for, the players—he renders a speech himself even, he even writes a speech. Is it

to enquire too curiously to find here a syncopation of every ambitious man's desires (thwarted in Shakespeare) to advance his son beyond himself without forfeiting his esteem? But it was also a life, under the general necessity of the materials and above all under the special necessity of Shakespeare's psychological recognition, dreadful. And in the end he lost his son all over again.

We have then the divisive strain of a dual identification, gruelling both ways, besides the burden of the creation of mysterious guilt and repulsion, incomprehensible paralysis, all protracted through an enormous and exhausting work, beginning and ending in loss, loss. How far is it not justifiable to conjecture that all this, the creation itself of *Hamlet* in its conditions, helps us to understand the appearance of the tragic substance and temper? But into this creation moreover was thrust, so far as we can now judge, a tragic and apposite event; or it closely followed it. Shakespeare's letters are lost, but a remarkable letter by Freud upon his father's death has lately come to light. The two men were nearly of an age, thirty-seven and forty. "Somewhere on the dark roads behind the official consciousness," Freud wrote, "the death of the old one has touched me deeply . . . Inwardly all of the past seems to have been awakened again now. I have the feeling of being utterly uprooted."[27]

The death of a man's father removes the barrier that always heretofore stood between infantile fantasy and its achievement. Worse, more disruptive still, is a father murdered, because here the other old fantasy is enacted *for* one. But king-murder is a familiar representative, in psychoanalytic terms, for father-murder; and Shakespeare had once already dramatized this aspect of the centre of *Hamlet*, in the play not quite inevitably called *Julius Caesar*. Craik noticed long ago the lifelong fascination exerted by the figure of Caesar upon William Shakespeare's imagination.[28] As for Brutus, everyone has noticed his similarity to Prince Hamlet, the man of reflection unwillingly impelled "by honour" to murder, king-murder. What few have noticed is that Caesar thought Brutus was his son. "For when he was a young man," we read in North's translation of Plutarch, "he had bene acquainted with Servilia, who was extreamelie in love with him. And bicause Brutus was borne in that time when their love was hottest, he perswaded himselfe that he begat him."[29] This fact, fundamental to Caesar's feelings, is entirely suppressed in *Julius Caesar*. But Shakespeare was not therefore unaware of it. He alludes to it as fact in his earliest surviving history, *1 Contention* (or *2 Henry VI*):

> *Brutus* bastard hand
> Stab'd *Iulius Caesar*.

It is striking in the last degree that Laertes's father, whom we were remembering is killed by Hamlet in his mother's bedroom, was saying to Hamlet shortly before, as if announcing to the future understanding his symbolic role, "I did enact *Iulius Caesar . . . Brutus* kild mee." For the catastrophic effect upon Shakespeare of his recurrence to this theme in *Hamlet* we may look to the comparatively open and terribly combinative representation.

Not entirely open, for one king-murder is carried out by a substitute, the uncle, and a father-murder by a substitute son. In *Macbeth*, where Macbeth and his wife will stand for some purposes as aspects of the same character, the dramatization is in detail more open still, the disguise frailer.

> Had he not resembled [says Lady Macbeth]
> My Father as he slept . . .

Here there is no longing for a vanished son to linger out the play, no elevation of moral quality to postpone the deed, and the work is rapid and horrible. I suppose the strain on human nerves, displayed in their conversation after the murder—when one unconscious gratification stands complete, and the superego instantly forbids, does it not, the other, the "sleeping"—has never been exceeded. Macbeth, who adopts the whole burden, is all but mad, his voice swelling with hysteria, over the hurried efforts of his wife, sensible, deeper, to calm him.

> *Macb.* One cry'd God blesse vs, and Amen the other,
> As they had seene me with these Hangmans hands:
> Listning their feare, I could not say Amen,
> When they did say God blesse vs.
> *Lady M.*   Consider it not so deepely.
> *Macb.* But wherefore could I not pronounce Amen?
> I had most need of Blessing, and Amen
> Stuck in my throat.
> *Lady M.*   These deeds must not be thought
> After these wayes: so, it will make vs mad.
> *Macb.* Methought I heard a voyce cry, Sleep no more:
> Macbeth does murther Sleep, the innocent Sleepe,
> Sleepe that knits vp the rauel'd Sleeve* of Care,
> The death of each dayes Life, sore Labors Bath,
> Balme of hurt Mindes, great Natures second Course,
> Chiefe nourisher in Life's Feast—

*Sleave: raw or floss silk.

Lady M.   What do you meane?
  Macb. Still it cry'd, Sleep no more, to all the House:
          Glamis hath murder'd Sleepe, and therefore Cawdor
          Shall sleepe no more: Macbeth shall sleepe no more.

Just beyond this *ought* to lie madness. Just beyond it lay, for the control of this author, *Antony and Cleopatra*.

Meanwhile, that control, artistically, went off badly for two or three years after *Hamlet*. With *Othello*, much the least strange of these gigantic works, it was resumed, I suggest, because in Iago he created a thorough satisfactory external opposite, and evil got free play unmixed with virtue. But to the convulsion of *Lear* the poet brought new elements of human chaos—misanthropy, spiritual pride—of which the raving end lay beyond *Antony and Cleopatra*.

The Tragic Substance

I HAVE TRIED TO ACCOUNT FOR the appearance of the tragic temper in Shakespeare's work by seeing it as a product of certain forces: the strain of representing—at enormous length in *Hamlet*—mysterious and frightening truths about human life probably not verbally understood by the dramatist, the simultaneous excitation and despair of imagining a life for his dead son which unfortunately had to embody these truths, and the dishevelling experience of the loss of his father, which happened also to bring into play in his own life the truths.

I considered immaterial the order in which these events occurred. But as we turn now to enquire into the nature of the substance upon which the tragic temper worked, I want to resume our usual chronological concern; and there will have to be *several* other important differences between our investigation last week and its present sequel. Then we cared chiefly to discover what happened to Shakespeare; now we wish to see what he did. Depth psychology, moreover, is not the only science which has developed since Bradley wrote.

The essential condition of the tragic substance, I think, is the Displacement of the King. This is the actual condition under which the whole of *Hamlet* takes place, and accounts for the intolerable burden falling upon the Prince—that of himself displacing the new King. The virtual displacement of King Agamemnon by Achilles and others is what has produced the political disorder in *Troilus and Cressida* and what Ulysses castigates in: "The specialty of *rule* hath been neglected." Lear, in fact, displaces himself. The Displacement of the

King is the story of *Macbeth*. The Duke of *Measure for Measure* pretends to displace himself, and rules from underneath. You note that I have omitted *Othello*, of which something will be said presently. But the condition is uniform otherwise, and significantly it does not recur once in the three later tragedies, which every critic has felt as radically different from the works of 1601 to 1606. It is in the light of this condition, rather than of the so-called tragic flaw, that I want to examine Hamlet's meditation on the tragic flaw. He is on the parapet with Horatio and Marcellus, waiting for the apparition, when they hear the ordnance for the King's brawl:

> This heavy headed reueale east and west
> Makes vs tradust, and taxed of other nations,
> They clip vs drunkards, and with Swinish phrase
> Soyle our addition, and indeede it takes
> From our atchieuements, though perform'd at height
> The pith and marrow of our attribute . . .
>
> So oft it chaunces in particuler men,
> That for some vicious mole of nature in them
> As in their *birth* wherein they are not guilty
> (Since nature cannot choose his origin),
> By the ore-growth of some complextion
> Oft breaking down the pales and forts of reason,
> Or by some *habit*, that too much ore-leauens
> The forme of plausiue manners, that these men
> Carrying I say the stamp of *one* defect
> Being Natures liuery, or Fortunes starre,
> His virtues els be they as pure as grace,
> As infinite as man may vndergoe,
> Shall in the generall censure take corruption
> From that particular fault: the dram of eale
> Doth all the noble substance of a doubt
> To his own scandle.

This last clause is almost certainly corrupt, but the meaning is fairly clear: the tiny evil works the man's whole "noble substance" to his undoing. Here we seem to be presented by Shakespeare himself with a formula for the tragic hero: Hamlet, with his excess of reflectiveness; Othello, with his excess of trust (I am reporting standard critical opinion, not mine); Lear, with his irascibility; Macbeth, with his ambition or—better—imagination. The quality of habit would be the tragic *accident* of the "noble substance." But this view may seem itself a little accidental in appearance, and perhaps it neither conforms exactly to what Hamlet says nor at all represents the genuine substance of the tragedies. Hamlet *set off from* the Danes' drunkenness, which is destructive of their whole reputation; that is a *habit*; but he moves far, beginning well *behind* any habit, with *birth*, and passing beyond it to "Fortune's star," or *Fate*. Birth is, for men capable of being conceived as tragic heroes, birth *into a predicament*, and Fate is the *imposition* of a predicament. Observe that it is at this exact moment, as this speech ends, that the Ghost appears, the Displaced King, and his predicament is in fact imposed upon Prince Hamlet. Fortune's star suddenly and horribly shines, and only in its light is the hero born.

We are far, here, from merely a "tragic flaw," and perhaps the tragic substance can now be formulated in a way that will not neglect psychoanalytic and anthropological claims any more than ethical and literary. Let us regard it as the conflict between loyalty and necessity, its condition being regularly the Displacement of the King.

Loyalty is the attribute of the "noble substance" lamented by Hamlet as subject to necessity: "Being Natures liuery, or Fortunes starre." The necessity is invariably a product of Nature *and* Fortune, character and fate. Foreshadowed in Juliet, we find the conflict first full-blown in Brutus, as he paces in his orchard in the darkness, thinking:

> It must be by his death: and for my part
> I know no personal cause, to spurne at him,
> But for the generall. He would be crown'd:
> How that might change his nature, there's the question?
> It is the bright day, that brings forth the Adder,
> And that craues warie walking . . .

It is as the guardian of the commonwealth that Brutus suffers necessity. Hamlet's necessity—the duty of revenge—is laid upon him against his loyalty to Claudius, not only as kinsman, but as King. But in *Hamlet* everything is handy-dandy, to anticipate Lear's great term. Hamlet's loyalty, on the other hand, to his *father* is in conflict with psychological necessity—the moral impossibility (not understood) of killing his uncle before his mother is dead, inaccessible. The highest natures, *only*, feel loyalty so fully that necessity can make them heroes. In *King Lear*, where all is mirrored upward and downward, Kent dies with his loyalty—its victim alone, apparently, and its fatigue's—and even an Oswald, faithful to a Goneril, dies for his loyalty; but

Lear, outraged doubly by Goneril as a subject and as a daughter,
forsakes *his* loyalty to her, under the necessity of her faithlessness and
his temper, the worst ever imaged in drama, with a speech so terrible
that even a mediocre actress knows enough, physically, to wilt under
it. It has the form of a prayer:

> Heare Nature, heare deere Goddesse, heare:
> Suspend thy purpose, if thou did'st intend
> To make this Creature fruitfull:
> Into her Wombe conuey stirrility,
> Drie vp in her the Organs of increase,
> And from her derogate body, neuer spring
> A Babe to honor her. If she must teeme,
> Create her childe of Spleene, that it may liue
> And be a thwart disnatur'd torment to her.
> Let it stampe wrinkles in her brow of youth,
> With Cadent Teares fret Channels in her cheekes,
> Turne all her Mothers paines, and benefits
> To laughter, and contempt: That she may feele,
> How sharper than a Serpents tooth it is
> To haue a thanklesse Childe . . .

The conflict in Macbeth hardly wants illustration, but I should mention that *his* necessity, called up by the witches, to be worked on by
his wife, first makes itself overwhelmingly felt in the extraordinary
speech, short like everything best in the play, and like much else in
it in producing an uncanny sense of *inversion*, as if the speaker
thought himself on the way up and we in our perspective saw him
instead on his way down:

> Two truths are told:
> As happy prologues to the swelling Act
> Of the imperial theme . . .

This affects one like demonic exultation in a man about to be
executed—a theme by the way in the imagery of *Macbeth*, as we are
to see.

Even in *Measure for Measure*, a work tragic mainly for Angelo, the
conflict (though undeveloped) occurs precisely between his loyalty to
his own life and the absent Duke, and the necessity of his passion—
a passion still for saintliness, notice, such was Shakespeare's irony, in
the person, however, the very physical person, of the saintly Isabella.

"Heaven keep your honour safe!" she says to him; "Amen," he says aside,

> For I am that way going to temptation
> Where prayers *cross* . . .

In *Troilus and Cressida* the conflict politically has no representative; but this play is double, and the great crucial speech of Troilus *is* representative, his loyalty to Cressida fighting fact—the utterance of a man on the rack, tortured by co-existent possibilities:

> This she? no, this is Diomed's Cressida.
> If beauty have a soul, this is not she;
> If souls guide vows, if vows be sanctimony,
> If sanctimony be the gods' delight,
> If there be rule in unity itself,
> This is not she. O madness of discourse,
> That cause sets up with and against itself;
> Bi-fold authority! where reason can revolt
> Without perdition, and *loss* assume all reason
> Without revolt: this is, and is not, Cressid.
> Within my soul there doth conduce a fight
> Of this strange nature, that a thing inseparate
> Divides more wider than the sky and earth;
> And yet the spacious breadth of this division
> Admits no orifice for a point as subtle
> As Ariachne's broken woof to enter.
> Instance, O instance! strong as Pluto's gates;
> Cressid is mine, tied with the bonds of heaven:
> Instance, O instance, strong as heaven itself,
> The bonds of *heaven* are slipt, dissolvd and loosd;
> And with another knot, five-fingertied,
> The fractions of her faith, orts of her love,
> The fragments, scraps, the bits, and greasy reliques
> Of her o'er-eaten faith, are bound to Diomed.

I said that this was a *representative*; but we might say with great plausibility that the whole general tragic conflict is only a representative of *this*—and psychoanalysis would support us. *Troilus* may have been written directly after *Hamlet*. I have spoken of its relation to *Othello*—as a sort of sketch for that full tragedy of jealousy—and Chambers puts it between *Hamlet* and *Othello*; but Chambers thinks

Othello was written rather later than it was—it was written apparently (upon evidence by the Australian scholar Hart in 1935) in the year after *Hamlet*, 1602.[1] *Troilus*, in any event, for us is a stage on the way to *Othello*, the stunning success of which I must now try to explain, as well as its variation from the tragic pattern.

The key to *Othello*, perhaps, from the poet's point of view, is to be found backwards in the character of Ophelia. Recalling the revulsion with which Hamlet treated Ophelia, let us imagine the poet looking about, in the following year, for a dramatic subject—or trying, rather, probably, to decide which of the several subjects he has been wanting to treat he *will* treat next; and more probably still, what we will be describing is what pitched him at this moment absolutely and without reflection upon the subject. He knew the substance of an Italian story of thirty years before, [*Ecatommiti*, 1565] by Giraldi Cintio, about a Moor who is led on by his ensign to jealousy of his Venetian wife and her murder. Whether he knew this story directly, or from the French translation or some lost adaptation, is uncertain. He may have been reminded of it by hearing from some traveller of the murder in fact by a Venetian nobleman of his wife this year exactly, 1602. I suspect that Shakespeare was aware—whether consciously or not is immaterial—of something unsatisfactory and incomprehensible (from the normal theatrical point of view) in the way he had dealt with Ophelia. In his next part for the same actor—the actor, too, no doubt who also created that piece Cressida—he wanted to handle it differently. She had to die—somehow she *had* to die—she was the second in the series Ophelia-Desdemona-Cordelia; well, this was the climax of the Venetian story. But the deepest point was that, although a virtuous woman (like her sisters past and to come), she had disgraced *herself* in the fact of her unnatural marriage. *Already* degraded, she was to be protected thus from the Ophelia-treatment and could be handled with the respect and admiration with which Shakespeare liked to handle women, instead of the despairing and brutal horror that had had to be visited on Ophelia (or the contempt spent on Cressida). We are speaking of psychological necessity—obsession—in the poet. I suggest that he reflected with strange satisfaction on the opening of Cintio's story: "There was once in Venice a most valiant Moor who had shown great judgement and brilliancy of mind in war-like affairs and who was much beloved by the Councillors of Venice, which in the recognition of ability excells all other republics. It happened that a virtuous lady of great beauty named Disdemona, won not by feminine appetite but by the worth of the Moor, became en-amored of him, and he also of her, subdued by her beauty and noble-mindedness, and their love was so happily mutual that they were married, although her parents did all they could to make her take another husband."[2] Here was a situation whereon the poet's sense of *outrage* could be transferred from the adultery and incest and father-murder of *Hamlet* to the relation of a Moor and a white woman, and normalized, spent on a marriage—though it is striking that it *is* again a marriage (like that of Claudius and Gertrude) that is the object of the—largely suppressed—outrage. I mention three capital circumstances. The first is that although Shakespeare *knew* Othello was a Moor, he sometimes imaged him as a Negro—rendering the union, of course, more degrading still to Desdemona. (I speak, naturally, from his point of view in 1602, not from mine in 1952.) This accounts, I think, for such allusions as that of "thick-lips," which has troubled many critics and is better explained psychologically than as a mere insulting distortion by Roderigo; no such terms are found for Aaron the Moor in *Titus Andronicus*, who is also the lover of a white woman. The second is that the jealousy which reigns suppressed in *Hamlet*, that of Hamlet for Claudius, continues unabated and increased, imaged *in Othello*—it is the major theme—but now it is *baseless*; and besides, there can now be given full admiration to the violating figure (Othello)—Shakespeare's obsessions were the same, but they could be dramatized at a safer distance. The third suggestive circumstance is that the protection of Cordelia from the Ophelia-loathing, of which I spoke earlier, is far from complete. Many have been offended by Iago's loose talk to Desdemona in Act II, as they all stand anxious for the Moor's arrival. It is fair to observe that ninety years later a playwright named Charles Gildon was "assur'd from very good hands, that the Person that Acted Jago was in much esteem for a Comoedian, which made *Shakespear* put several words, and expressions into his part (perhaps not so agreeable to his Character) to make the Audience laugh, who had not yet learnt to endure to be serious a whole Play."[3] And it is an odd coincidence, perhaps, that part of Iago's loose talk exactly has parallels in a book by Nicholas Breton [*Choice, Chance and Change*, 1606] published four years after *Othello* was written and has thus been sometimes regarded as an interpolation.[4] But ninety years is a long while, and Breton may have been the borrower. In any case, the whole play is a staggering dramatized assault on Desdemona's name for chastity, and for the detailed survival of the feelings about Ophelia we need only recall Iago's insolent and fantastic obscenity about the marriage in the opening scene.

After Desdemona's situation, the second grand attraction of the story was certainly the possibilities of the character of the ensign, whom Shakespeare named Iago. Here could be developed a real, full-scale hypocrite-villain; and I think this goes far to account for the notable steadiness and thematic concentration of the play as contrasted with *Hamlet* and *Troilus and Cressida*. How satisfactory this was to the poet will be realized when you think back on the makeshift appearance of the villainy in *Hamlet*: the ambiguity of Claudius, whom Hamlet hates well enough but is also forced to envy, and the triviality of Rosencranz and Guildenstern. Even Polonius and Laertes are drafted as villains, a role for which they were plainly not cut out; as if the poet were trying again and again, with dissatisfaction, to find some *reason*, some worthy agent, for the ill that has befallen Hamlet. He even accuses his mother, at one moment, of his father's murder —of which she cannot possibly, as he knows very well, have been guilty—and Shakespeare takes the accusation so lightly that he does not have Gertrude explain or explicitly repudiate it and Hamlet never recurs to it. Imagine then the satisfaction with which the poet must have contemplated the working out of the perfect malignity of Iago, who *is* responsible alone for the horror that overtakes Othello.

Under these two immense attractive forces, we might conjecture that Shakespeare's imagination found itself ready to forgo in his second great tragedy the condition of the Displacement of the King which governed the first and will govern the third and fourth. But in that case I should expect in the play a symbolic representation of the condition so powerful that it would be hard to say whether he had really forgone the condition or not. This is precisely what we find. The action occurs, in Act I, in a *republic*, and Shakespeare is even careful to emphasize the Duke (so he calls him) at the outset by having Iago say to Othello (before we come on the Senators):

> the Magnifico is much belov'd [that is, Brabantio]
> And hath in his effect a voice potentiall
> As double as the Dukes . . .

The general then, particularly in the existing military crisis, has virtually the status of a king: the state depends on him. For the rest of the play, the action occurs on Cyprus, which Othello rules in fact and absolutely. Othello is the King, master of himself, and Iago displaces him, until

> Your power, and your Command is taken off,
> And *Cassio* rules in Cyprus.

It might be thought, at least, that there is a displacement of the tragic conflict *from* this condition, which the other tragedies do not exhibit; but even this is not so. In this respect, as in certain crucial others, *Hamlet* and *Macbeth* form a pair, and the two written between them form another. The conflict in Lear between loyalty to his daughters and the double necessity of his nature and of the evil of two of them and the obstinacy of the third, finds a parallel in the conflict in Othello, which is between his loyalty to his wife and the double necessity of *his* nature and the experimental evil of Iago. Both go mad under the conflict. But there is no tragedy in madness, and so both recover—to be overwhelmed.

I cannot leave *Othello* without remarking that it seems to me to exemplify more perfectly and more continuously than any other work of this author's that characteristic which Coleridge, in one of his most profound passages, placed *first* among the characteristics of Shakespeare. "Expectation in preference to surprize. 'God said, let there be *light*, and there was *light*' . . . As the feeling with which we startle at a shooting star, compared with that of watching the sunrise at the pre-established moment, such and so low is surprize compared with expectation."[5] In the largest as in the least things this work was constructed to dazzle the mind and break the heart. One tiny, vivid opening chord in Shakespeare's magisterial structure of expectation in *Othello* is Iago's opening words:

> S'blood, but you'l not heare me.
> If euer I did dream of such a matter,
> Abhorre me.

"Abhor me," and the intensity of the hatred he evokes, into which our admiration for his intelligence enters simply as a screw, is perhaps incomparable with that evoked by any other character ever imagined by man. The scene in which his work is finally done, the last, drew from Dr. Johnson an unusual confession when he was editing Shakespeare. "I am glad," he wrote, "that I have ended my revisal of this dreadful scene. It is not to be endured."[6]

Some critics consider Act III of *Othello* the dramatist's highest achievement, but I want to illustrate in the opening scene of *King Lear* the address now at his command, such that this work seems different not simply in degree but in *kind* from the attempts and achievements of all other dramatists. Its magnitude appears in an instant, when we reflect that to the successor of Ophelia and Desdemona, Shakespeare has added *two* sisters, and all three are extensively displayed. For the first time, moreover, and for the last time, he has mirrored the tragic action with a large and continuous and harrowing sub-action. It is as if *Antigone* and *Oedipus Rex* had been built into *Agamemnon*, and fused. What it meant at the outset, in terms of theatrical composition, was that no less than *nine characters* (*Hamlet*'s first large scene has five) were elaborately necessary in the *opening* scene—which the King must dominate completely, which must proceed with well-nigh incredible expedition unless it is to last for a thousand lines (it has just over 300), and which must be, besides, extremely passionate, the King alone becoming *twice* overwhelmingly angry, so angry that he disowns onstage his best-loved daughter and banishes one of the chief peers of the kingdom. As for the facts to be represented, other than those already mentioned, they are nothing less than these: the partition of the kingdom into three among his daughters and their husbands, and the ensuing arrangements, the deciding on a husband (among several suitors) for the youngest daughter, a final courtship and acceptance under a cloud, as events turn out, all the farewells, and the beginning of the elder daughters' intrigue against their father. As for the emotional colouring, an unhesitating sympathy must be secured for Cordelia and Kent, while at the same time *nothing must estrange the audience from the King,* who violently mistreats them. But there is another entire action that has not even been mentioned. It will hardly do—it is inconceivable at this stage of Shakespearean flexibility and meshing—just to start this blankly, fresh, in the second scene. Moreover, that is mechanically impossible, unless Edmund—the motor of the sub-action—is to introduce *himself* to the audience like a character out of the drama of the eighties; for he has to *set up*, in Iago-esque soliloquy, the sub-action, before he can go to work on his father and then his brother —and this too must proceed in high key, unvexed by exposition. Any sensible playwright confronting all this would adopt another trade. But what sensible playwright would have imagined all this? Perhaps we touch, here, in Shakespeare, the moment of self-confidence supreme in the craftsman's portion in human art.[7]

He made two initial decisions: to take a risk and to pay a price. The risk was considerable: to treat the partition of the kingdom as *already decided*, and even a matter of gossip. (Scholars who treat this part of the story as familiar to the audience must have failed to ask themselves enough questions about either the story or the audience; I should say, after a long experience of Elizabethan and Jacobean literature in terms chiefly of this play, that only a negligible fraction of the first audience at the Globe would know the story at all, whether from Geoffrey of Monmouth, Holinshed [*Chronicles of England, Scotland and Ireland*, 1577, 1587], *The Mirror of Magistrates*, the *Faerie Queene*, or the long out-of-date, boring play by Peele or who-ever.) The price was slight: some opening speeches as characterless as anything in his first-rate work. What happens is that two noblemen of importance come on—this you can tell by their dress—neither young—and with them a young man of no importance. "I thought," says one, "the King had more affected the Duke of *Albany*, than *Cornwell.*" "It did always" (says the other) "seeme so to vs: But now in the diuision of the Kingdome, it appeares not which of the Dukes he valewes most, for qualities are so weigh'd, that curiosity in neither can make choise of either moity." Not a trace of individuality here. But then at once the first asks the second if the young man is not his son, and in a winking bantering way the second admits he is, but a bastard, reminisces about his getting, affirms a fondness for him not inferior to that he feels for a legal son he has, and introduces them: Edmund and the Earl of Kent. Edmund, who (we feel) must have been galled by this chat, is very smooth. Thirty lines, prose; and witty. Enter court and King: "Attend the Lords of France and Burgundy, Gloster." Verse, regal authority of a peremptory king, the identifica-tion and dismissal of the Earl of Gloucester (and Edmund, who has no more status here than an ape). Kent is our one acquaintance left, and Lear is in charge. With him two lords, obviously Albany and Cornwall, both immediately named as the kingdom is formally with a map divided; each stands by a wife, and these two women, with a third, are identified in sequence as daughters to the King, as Lear proceeds straight to the inquisition about their loves for him. The youngest (for whom Lear has told us France and Burgundy are rivals) has asides to help fix her before she is formally questioned, the first identifying her: "What shall *Cordelia* speake?" We are prepared then for her answer's failure to satisfy the King; we understand that she cannot compete with her sisters' antecedent insincere hyperbole, which her careful honesty cuts into like a knife. But nothing has prepared us, except perhaps the whim of splitting the kingdom and certainly a heightened exchange, for the King's outbreak of alienation. Kent with some difficulty halts him and protests, and is himself ban-ished, bids farewell, and departs. Gloucester brings in the Continental suitors. Morose now, Lear frightens away one, but France is as ob-durate as Cordelia had been—their link—and insists on her. Exit Lear, Burgundy, Gloucester, the court. In the farewell of Cordelia to her sisters, her bluntness speaks again: "I know you what you are . . ." The blank verse formalizes again into couplets, as at Kent's farewell, and then the two successful sisters are left alone. In Komisarjevsky's celebrated and ridiculous production of *King Lear* at Stratford before the last war, a fine actress played Goneril—Joyce Bland—and her drop here into rapid and sinister prose rendered the close of this scene extraordinary.[8] Shakespeare made the prose and contrasted the speeches with the fulsome public professions of the daughters earlier, but Miss Bland, controlling the brainless actress of Regan as Goneril was intended to control Regan, invented a tone low, quick, and awful, which foreshadowed everything inhuman to come.

> Sister, it is not little I haue to say of what most neerely appertaines to vs both, I thinke our Father will hence tonight.
>
> Reg. *(leaning forward)*: That's most certain, and with you: next month with us.
>
> Gon. You see how full of *changes* his age is, the observation we have made of it hath not been little; he always loved our *sister* most, and with what poor judgement he hath now cast her off appears too grossly.
>
> Reg. Tis the infirmity of his age, yet he hath ever but slenderly known himself.
>
> Gon. The *best* and soundest of his time hath been but *rash*, then must we look from his *age* to receive, not alone the imperfection of long-ingrafted condition, but therewithal the unrule waywardness that infirm and choleric years bring with them . . .
>
> Reg. We shall further think of it.
>
> Gon. We must *do* something, and i'th' heate.

These monsters depart—the scene is over—and here comes Edmund, chafing still from his father's satirical remarks to Kent about his begetting, with his prayer to nature after Machiavelli, and his Iago-like plan against his brother. The *only* persons of consequence we have not met are Edgar, who will be on before this second scene is over, and Lear's Fool, who even in the fourth scene of Act I is delayed that we may hear of his sympathy and pining for Cordelia gone into France and expect his coming. This fourth scene begins with Kent disguised, ready to offer his service to Lear dispossessed; he spurns out Oswald; and the Fool, as loyal (we are to learn) as Kent, enters mocking him.

We have been looking at craftsmanship, administration of a refractory and proliferating material. But the two high moments of the opening scene of *King Lear*—one reaching up out of the other—were products not of craftsmanship but of inspiration, like the exquisite matching of a slight excess in Cordelia (an excess of contempt for her sisters' extravagant replies over her filial emotion) against a decided prematurity in Lear's ungovernable rage against her thereupon. The first high moment was of course this one, the repudiation of Cordelia. The second high moment, with Kent, *seems* merely to affirm the first—Kent, in her behalf, being articulate, whilst Cordelia is not, and Lear's second rage crescendoing out of his first; but in *theme*, and on the stage—if ever producers or actors (or, for that matter, editors) understood the lines—it is the second one that matters. Kent has tried to get a word in before and been silenced by Lear. When Lear's exasperation with his daughter has spent itself and he has returned to business, Kent takes advantage of a pause for an address entirely uncharacteristic, extended, servile, and ironic:

> Royal Lear,
> Whom I have ever honor'd as my King,
> Lou'd as my Father, as my Master follow'd,
> As my great Patron thought on in my praiers—

The original actor must have made the irony clear (it is that, exactly, of Kent's later mocking of Cornwall that earns him the stocks), and Lear, who knows Kent, smells falsity with an acrid interruption: "The bow is bent and drawne, make from the shaft." Kent becomes more elaborate and mock-insincere than ever (as much as to say: If you act the tyrant, I will address you as one):

> Let it *fall* rather [the arrow of your metaphor], though the forke inuade
> The region of my heart, be *Kent* vnmannerly
> When *Lear* is made, what wouldest thou do old man?

This paralyzing informality must have jolted the Jacobean audience more than it can ever do us, but at least it is certain that the King can never before have been addressed as "old man." What this really means is that he is not King anymore. Kent, never wrong, has sensed the vanishing of the actuality with the power; he is indifferent to the *name* of King, which Lear stipulates to retain; and the poet has dramatized in this shocking line the Displacement of the King—foreshadowing, also, the King's madness. Kent's loyalty, later, is to the *person*, whom he knows will suffer. His irony towards Lear disappears, and is taken over by the Fool. More than one agent for the irony, which

Lear undeniably deserves, would seem to us vicious, when the heavens themselves, in Act III, appear to have joined forces with his daughters.

But this voluntary relinquishment of power by Lear, following directly the pretence of giving up power by the Duke in his play of the year before (*Measure for Measure*), suggests a theme in the author's mind: at forty-one he must already have been longing for retirement; and four years later we *know* that he planned to retire and then changed his mind or yielded to importunity. Meanwhile, after *Lear*, he collected himself for an effort in many ways even more formidable.

Thanks chiefly to Mr. Paul of Philadelphia, whose work appeared recently, the actual composition of *Macbeth* is clearer to us than is the composition of any other work by the poet.[9] It is the summer of 1605, and probably *King Lear* is not quite finished yet. Perhaps Shakespeare was in love this summer. The son William, whom I mentioned earlier, will be born to Jane Davenant at the beginning of the following March, and there are some other indications that the poet was in Oxford this summer. He was not in Stratford, at any rate, as one would expect, because on July 24 his solicitor, Francis Collins, had to sign for him the assignment of a lease. Oxford was the scene of sedate but intense and multiform preparation for the visit of King James. Perhaps Jane Davenant leaned on the arm of the author of *King Lear* in the throng outside Oxford as the King with his train approached on August 27 and was greeted by scholars of St. John's who performed for him there a Latin playlet by Matthew Gwinn about James's ancestor, Banquo, and the women's prophecies.[10] It was very short, only thirty lines, they repeated it in English for the Queen, and James liked it. It was the only play he did like in Oxford. Richard Burton's *Alba* he was with difficulty persuaded not to leave in the middle; he disliked a Latin *Ajax*, slept through Gwinn's *Vertumnus*, and escaped an Arcadian play by Samuel Daniel by visiting the university library. James was proud of his learning, but he was primarily a hunter, and sleepy in the evening: he liked *short* plays. All this interesting evidence as to the King's theatrical opinions was available to Shakespeare through his acquaintance Sir George Buc, the Acting Master of the Revels, who was of course in Oxford and then back in London, and who seems himself to have consulted Shakespeare about the authorship of anonymous printed plays from time to time. Shakespeare told him that *George a Greene* [1599] was written by a clergyman who played the Pinner's part himself, and Buc wrote this information (ascribing it to Shakespeare) on his copy of the play—a document so obviously resembling a forgery that it was only rehabilitated a few years ago[11]; but it is interesting that William Shakespeare's only surviving attribution of an Elizabethan play has been rejected by nearly every scholar.

Whether the dramatist had planned a play specially for the King prior to this occasion at Oxford we don't know, but when he got back to London he must have looked hard in his Holinshed and been thinking from that time of a short play about Macbeth that would include five characters from whom King James was directly descended, that would culminate in a great necromantic scene wherein all his royal ancestors would be shown, that would centre (though very indirectly) in *conscience*, a subject upon which James had strong views that were known because he had published a book on it [*Daemonologie*], and that would include of course witches, of which James had had absorbing experience in Scotland, also published.

The King's Men were paid ten shillings in Oxford on October 9.[12] Four days before, plague closed the London theatres, and they stayed shut for over two months, until December 15. Shakespeare was probably writing in his lodgings in Silver Street. He found one nerve-racking change. An ancient citizen named Robert Dow, troubled about the sinners dying reprobate all the time at Newgate, had given fifty pounds the previous May to endow the midnight ringing of a hand-bell at Newgate, and the midnight tolling of the great bell at St. Sepulchre's, for the condemned. Within easy earshot, the poet shuddered like others, and both went into his play. Lady Macbeth rings her little bell, the signal for the murder, and Macbeth mutters:

> Hear it not, Duncan, for it is a knell
> That summons thee to heaven or to hell.

Then she is saying:

> Hark! Peace.
> It was the owl that shriek'd, the *fatal* bellman,
> Which gives the stern'st goodnight.

Paul thinks, with plausibility, that Shakespeare began his play at line 40 of the third scene in Act I, and wrote with great rapidity, in one blast of envisioning, straight to the cauldron scene at the beginning of Act IV. Then he had to study for this scene, especially the King's *Daemonologie* of 1603, and lost momentum. Later he wrote the short witch-prelude and the opening of I.iii, but he seems not to have taken up the play seriously to finish it until he heard that King Christian of Denmark was to visit James in the summer. This play would obviously be perfect, and since the end of it, long foreseen, was not going to be very interesting, he made it as topical, introducing both into it and earlier allusions not only to the Gunpowder Plot of November and the equinoctial storms of the end of March and two statutes of May but to an uproar of July 31, and it was produced evidently in the great hall at Hampton Court August 7, 1606. As Paul says, much of this could have been put in in an hour. He took other pains also. Since a King of Denmark was to see it, he made Siward, a Dane, prominent beyond necessity, and he transformed into Norwegians the Danes who had been defeated by the Scots; he also worked into the Bleeding Sergeant scene (I.ii), which seems to have been the last written of all, references to the Danish King's cannonade and a largess of 10,000 dollars. The elaborate flattery of James in the scene laid in England I need not remind you of. Paul thinks Shakespeare saved the end of his play with the ninety lines of the Sleepwalking scene: a *second* involuntary self-revelation of crime, in prose and very simple, as against the ornate verse of Macbeth's hallucinations; and this is one of the best suggestions of recent years. This unbelievable work, then, was conceived and executed from first to last under conditions the most local and (one would have thought) *cramping* possible.

But the condition of brevity is of the essence of its power. Being short, it had to exert the utmost *suggestiveness*. Three urgent means were darkness (much of the play is laid at night and all of it seems to be), the supernatural (now first invoked since *Hamlet*), and a fantastic compression and pregnancy of style, ranging from the dense physicalness of

> By the pricking of my thumbs
> Something wicked this way comes

out to the extreme, all but philosophical generality of the mysteriousness of much of the diction:

> If it were *done* when tis done, then twere well
> It were done quickly; if the assassination
> Could trammel up the consequence, and catch
> With his surcease success, that but this blow
> Might be the be-all and the end-all here,
> But here, upon this bank and shoal of time
> We'd jump the life to come.

By that word "assassination" Macbeth just means assassination, killing, but everything so consistently stands for much more than itself that it takes a while to realize it. In the last line, the daring of the thought (for the "life to come" is not mortal only but immortal) is perfectly characteristic of this play: the ultimate mystery of that jump. But even statements apparently the simplest have mystery in *Macbeth*: "It will have blood, they say: blood will have blood . . ." It is now many years since I began to be bewildered by the humorous lucubrations of G. Wilson Knight on Shakespeare, but I remember with unalterable respect his analysis (in his first important book, *The Wheel of Fire*) of "the fabric of mystery and doubt in *Macbeth*," the continual questions asked in it and not answered, the characters' continual surprise, amazement, and bafflement, the constant "blurring and lack of certainty" of time, movement, motives, the omnipresence of rumour, anxiety, error—functions, all, of the dominance of Evil.[13] Part of the quality of *Macbeth* can be seen in one negative fact. It contains no successor to Ophelia and Desdemona and Cordelia; none. Instead, it contains a successor to *Goneril*. The Evil for which so much search was made in *Hamlet*, which was concentrated then in Iago, which was divided then among Goneril and Regan and Cornwall and Edmund, here usurps the universe. Professor Curry had to employ the phrase "demonic metaphysics" when he was studying the play's black magic.[14] This alteration of nature, together with the dramatization again of the Oedipal desire, the murder of the king-father, go far to explain the mysteriousness that *Macbeth* shares only with *Hamlet* among this poet's works. At the same time, Macbeth himself is warm, whilst Iago was cold: where he was all brain, Macbeth is all passion. What this effort cost Shakespeare we will not know—he made no comparable effort again, at any rate, until his masterpiece of *white* magic at the end, *The Tempest*—and the nature of his work changed immediately after *Macbeth*.

The End

Antony and Cleopatra A N D *Coriolanus* evoke none of the dissatisfaction one feels with the comedies of corruption written in the middle of the tragic period; they are powerful, competent, even, and splendid. Nevertheless, every spectator or reader is made aware of their inferiority to the greater tragedies that immediately preceded them, and it is with the grounds of this inferiority—by no means the same in the two plays—that I begin our witness to the final decade of the poet's life.

In the *Antony and Cleopatra* of 1607 we attend at once to a *relaxation* from the *Macbeth* of 1606: a relaxation affecting structure, versification, material, and manner. There is no true development either upward or downward in the play. For 1,700 lines, up to the action at Actium, the hero's fortunes (and the heroine's) are at their height; then, after an interim of 35 lines wherein the woe is announced by others, for 1,300 lines their fortunes are at the bottom. Great skill is evinced by Shakespeare, it goes without saying, in dissimulating this structure, but so it stands, and it makes a chronicle, not a tragedy. He was resting, in fact. The verse too is loosened. We hear for the first time that resort to a profuseness of extra syllables and run-over characteristic of his final period:

> This common bodie,
> Like to a Vagabond Flagge vpon the Streame,
> Goes too, and backe, lackeying the varrying tyde
> To rot it selfe with motion.

Here and there, when the magnificent diction is in abeyance, Shakespeare's metrical practice produces effects loosened almost to (first-class) prose:

> As for my wife,
> I would you had her spirit in such another;
> The third oth' world is yours, which with a Snaffle
> You may pace easie, but not such a wife.

Fine passages both: details; it is a play of details. The first aspect of the material that strikes us is its normality—the nightmarish lives of the tragic heroes lie behind, like their simplicity; here all is open, elaborate, superb, no one shudders. But its striking second aspect, notwithstanding the disappearance of the evil of *Macbeth*, is a controversion of any idealism far more thoroughgoing than any in the great tragedies. There is much moral reflection, as there was in *Caesar*, but though true enough, it is *never* good-natured. It would hardly be overstating a case to call *Antony and Cleopatra* the most sophisticated work of the human imagination so far. All the same, it is clear that either the author has come free or an overwhelming experience has worn itself out for the moment—leaving only a trace, a profound trace, which I want to try to analyze.

Antony and Cleopatra is extremely unreal. Its characteristic expression is a wild hyperbole, followed by an abrupt shifting of the subject, or a rapid deliquescence. Even a study of the diction confirms this general impression: it is grandiose, thick with words like "world" and "great" (each of these, for instance, occurring forty-two times), but the favourite verb "melt" occurs twice as often as in any other play (always in spectacular contexts) and coinages of like meanings are numerous—dislimn, dispunge, discandy. Everyone speaks matchless poetry, but that is nearly all it is—poetry; undramatic. It is relevant that *Antony and Cleopatra* is almost never seen on the stage. Passages astonish us, not scenes. There are no scenes, or too many. The play has only four scenes of 200 lines or over; leaving out of comparison *Macbeth* for its brevity and unexampled intensity, we remember that *Hamlet* had ten, *Othello* nine, *King Lear* seven. Nobody sticks to anything—for example the leading characters are all models of faithfulness, even Enobarbus. Now the incapacity to organize experience (comparatively, that is) combined with the grandiosity and the rapid alteration of subject suggests to me in the poet not only degrees of fatigue and evasiveness but a remnant of hysteria. The character least the victim of these conditions is certainly Cleopatra, and when she is most herself, a woman muttering, hugging her narcissism, we hear what is not merely poetic but dramatic, for a few lines fully of the stature of the great works gone:

> Hee's speaking now,
> Or murmuring, Where's my Serpent of old Nyle,
> (For so he calls me): Now I feede my selfe
> With most delicious poyson. Thinke on me
> That am with Phoebus amorous pinches blacke,
> And wrinkled deepe in time . . .

But Antony is nearly everywhere the vehicle of these conditions. It is appropriate that one of his greatest passages, which is to be contrasted with that just quoted, though they share a sharp unlikeness to the general style of the play, should be actually an expression of intellectual hysteria. Hysteria is emotion unable to hold its form; Antony defeated does not know what he is. He is brooding:

> Sometime we see a clowd that's Dragonish,
> A vapour sometime, like a Beare, or Lyon,
> A toward Cittadell, a pendant Rocke,
> A forked Mountaine, or blew Promontorie
> With Trees vpon't, that nodde vnto the world
> And mocke our eyes with Ayre. Thou hast seene these Signes,
> They are blacke Vespers Pageants.
> *Eros.* I my Lord
> That which is now a Horse, euen with a thought
> the Racke dislimns, and makes it indistinct
> As water is in water.

But the ultimate mood of these conditions ought I think to be called disillusion. The great tragedies were created under the reassertion of a principle, the Fortinbras principle. Hamlet can be murdered, Claudius reign, Hamlet be slain, King Lear dispossess himself, Duncan be murdered and Macbeth reign, but Fortinbras takes over, or Edgar, or Malcolm, and this strongly matters. The characterless Octavius Caesar taking over does not matter. There *seems* here to be no future—very remarkably for this author; and this disillusion has underlain the brilliance and energy of the work since Antony's opening cry:

Berryman's Shakespeare

Let Rome in Tyber melt, and the wide Arch
Of the raing'd Empire fall . . .

IN SHAKESPEARE'S second play of 1607, Rome is really to be
burnt—by one of her heroes, a warrior patrician exiled by the people's
tribunes for his hatred of the people and come back at the head of a
Volscian army—when upon his mother's pleading he finally relents
and Rome is spared. Whether Rome was worth sparing is another matter, and brings us at once to a fundamental difficulty. The unnatural-
ness of a man's destroying his own city—and Rome: in effect the state,
any state, the human race itself—is so clear that we are forced to hope
Coriolanus will relent. At the same time, the cowardice, insolence,
stupidity, and instability of the Roman people—of human beings in
mass—have been so forcibly demonstrated, and one's sympathy with
the hero's contempt and wrongs is so decided, that one half wishes he
would go ahead. From this hopeless conflict there is no evasion of style,
either, as in *Antony and Cleopatra*. Shakespeare wrote his first Roman
play, *Julius Caesar*, in monosyllables, running the risk of meanness,
into which he sometimes fell; his second ran the risk of grandiloquence
and often succumbed to it. But in *Coriolanus* he has lost all self-
consciousness with the Ancient World: the style is both majestic and
supple, it faces and expresses all. What it faces almost alone is a character remarkably simple when he is compared with any other of Shakespeare's tragic heroes. Coriolanus has been studied lately in terms of
Renaissance psychology, with more plausibility than such studies generally have as applied to Shakespeare's people. Coriolanus' "humour"
is bile, he is choleric. From the first of three types described by Bacon
after Aristotle—sudden anger soon over, wrath nursed secretly, a wrath
also long but violent—he develops into the third; and the familiar sequence pride-wrath-revenge-ruin is fulfilled. From this point of view,
says the critic, the play has a "truly Greek severity of outcome." But I
fear the effect produced by it even in 1607–8 cannot have been so
consistent—I note in passing that modern productions in Paris generally cause riots. Coriolanus' character has three plangent emotions:
hatred of the people, love for his mother, and pride. I neglect the obvious psychoanalytic interest of the second, which has yet to be properly explored, to concentrate on the others.

At Coriolanus' entrance he comes on the mutinous "rabblement"
(Shakespeare's word in the stage directions of two other plays), and
his first words are these, a fellow patrician having greeted him,
"Hayle, Noble *Martius*."

The End

> Thanks. What's the matter you dissentious rogues
> That rubbing the poore Itch of your Opinion,
> Make your selues Scabs.

I see no reason to dissimulate as some have done the poet's profound disdain for the populace. We hear much in the twentieth century about the dignity and even the political sagacity of the common man, the love of the American people for the Chinese people, and so forth. Shakespeare was spared such canting; and so his natural sympathy, though he thought people in mass ridiculous and dangerous, taking pains to exhibit them thus in *2 Henry VI, Julius Caesar, Sir Thomas More*, and elsewhere, his sympathy, unimpaired by nonsense with the prestige of the age behind it, was free always to separate one or two from the mob as capable of thought. Theatrically also this was effective; here, for example, one citizen replies ironically, "We haue euer your good word," opening an occasion for the hero's tirade. But disdain is not hatred, and Coriolanus' hatred itself is not ordinary hatred—it requires a return. As a nameless officer puts it, "Hee seekes their hate with great deuotion then they can render it him; and leaues nothing vndone that may fully discouer him their opposite." Such hatred we have not seen before. It far exceeds any cause in the poor object, which it seeks by the way to exterminate. "Where is the Viper," says a tribune,

> That would depopulate the city, &
> be euery man him selfe?

Here we remember his amazing cry to his soldiers before an assault: "Oh me alone, make you a sword of me . . ." Of course it is pride that is the cause of his hatred, pride so intense that it can bear only his own commendation (and his mother's), shrinking from any other, entirely unable to bear ordinary life, unwilling that anything should exist outside its own order of virtue, and indeed inhuman. The tribune is not wrong when he exclaims:

> You speake a'th'people, as if you were a God
> To punish; Not a man, of their Infirmity . . .

I think it is in the failure even of this dramatist to make a political and secular predicament seem adequate to this essentially morbid spiritual state that we may best find an explanation for the inferiority of *Coriolanus* to *Othello* or *King Lear*, as well as in the unpersuadable nature of the essential detestation. Now Shakespeare made many studies of men—we hear from Aubrey that "Ben Jonson and he did gather Humours of men dayly where ever they came."[1] We might see Coriolanus' partial misanthropy as a study, but that it was immediately preceded by the profound disillusion of *Antony and Cleopatra*, which it outgoes, and followed directly by the total blighting hatred of mankind declared in *Timon of Athens*.[2]

I take all this to be overflow and degeneration out of the original tragic complex which I have tried to survey. Again we have little guide in the circumstances of Shakespeare's life. His young brother Edmund died a few months after his bastard at the end of 1607 and was buried on New Year's Eve in St. Saviour's, Southwark, "with a forenoone knell of the great bell, xx^s," which the poet must have ordered.[3] But the chief event of this year was the marriage at last of one of his daughters, the elder, Susanna, on June 5. She was twenty-three. They were good matches, the two girls of New Place, and from their late marriages I think we may infer that they had small beauty, or that their father was extremely particular about matches in return, or both. Susanna was witty and deep, her father's daughter—it is not clear, as we'll see presently, that her husband could manage her. He was presumably a good match: a Stratford physician named John Hall, an Oxford M.A., travelled, and a writer on medical subjects. Perhaps it was from his parents in the year of his birth (1575) that Shakespeare's father had bought his Stratford houses. A sudden interest in human physiology and the body generally, evident in *Coriolanus* and *Timon*, the poet probably owed to conversation with him. A daughter Elizabeth was christened on February 21, 1608. Six months later, early in September, Mary Shakespeare died. Her son had been working on a new play called *Timon of Athens*, without much success.

The uncouth misanthrope he had found in Plutarch's life of Mark Antony, in Painter, perhaps in Lucian, and in an old play, Shakespeare had made a lord of enormous wealth, culture, learning, and ability, whose insane generosity to his friends at last undoes him. Horribly in debt, refused help by all who had lived on his bounty, he sinks rapidly into revilings unexceeded even by Lear. The first and the fourth and fifth acts are the most fully formed; much that lies between reads more like notes for verse dialogue than like verse or dialogue. There is no record of production, and probably the poet never finished it.[4] The manner everywhere suffers from gigantism, the tone is cold and violent, and the whole play a serious puzzle. In recent years there have been many extended studies of it in the literary technical journals, English and American critics alike calmly ignorant of each other's work, even when, as often, they closely agree. Most of these studies consider it either a treatise on usury ("the social chaos," says Draper, "consequent . . . upon the economic ruin of the nobility"—"the disruption," says Pettet, "of feudal morality"[5] or a morality play; and anything more depressingly half-relevant than these studies can hardly be imagined. Diseases sprawl over the play, it sounds a broken gnashing of rage and horror. Timon is howling to Alcibiades' whores:

> Consumptions sowe
> In hollow bones of men, strike their sharpe shinnes,
> And marre mens spurring . . . Downe with the Nose,
> Downe with it flat, take the Bridge quite away
> Of him, that his particular to foresee
> Smels from the generall weale . . . Plague all,
> That your Actiuity may defeate and quell
> The source of all Erection . . .

For a long time, psychiatric study was no more successful than literary, though persistent reference to syphilis through the play ought to have pointed the road, but in 1934 an American convincingly described Shakespeare's Timon as a paretic dement. You will recognize the play in his account, almost feature by feature. "A common picture today of paretic dementia," Dr. Woods wrote, "is that of a cultured man who becomes careless, unreliable, then irritable and boastful. He loses foresight, neglects his affairs, and wastes his money without concern. Grandiose ideas press him to greater extravagance. Bookkeeping seems slavish. Gusts of anger lead to violence. Maudlin sentimentality alternates with bitterness and hostility. As the dementia proceeds, self-restraint is lost; conversation and behavior are often coarsely sexual. Expansive ideas of wealth and greatness are taken as representing realities. Bodily strength is lost; paralysis and death from apoplexy."[6] You remember that Timon writes his epitaph but that his actual death is mysterious, offstage. Now, as Dr. Woods observes, Shakespeare can have had no knowledge of paretic dementia *as a disease*, any more than Dr. Hall could have; it had not been described. But syphilis both would know—English interest in it was considerable at this date—and all we can suppose is that the poet observed the dementia in some case, as he must have observed the melancholy we observed in Antonio the merchant. The question, of course, is *why* he took up a subject so repulsive and unpromising— or, rather than "took up," *insisted* on it.[7] But he could not handle it, or he lost interest, or he fell ill; and when he took up his pen next, his imagination was well.

Perhaps it was very soon—I think we are still in 1608—and it may very well have been owing to an accident. I resort partly to conjecture. Somebody not named George Wilkins was rewriting for the King's Men an old play on the adventures of Pericles, Prince of Tyre. When a play was about half done, the author would bring it in to read to several members of the company, receive further payment, suggestions, and so on—*if* they were satisfied. The new *Pericles* at the end of the second act seemed fair but old-fashioned, and moreover, it was not getting anywhere. In the first act Pericles woo'd a king's daughter, learnt she was her father's mistress, and fled. In the second act he woo'd another king's daughter and this one he is to wed; but the second act has made so little use of the first act that—is it worthwhile having him go on? What happens next? In a storm at sea (says the nervous author), Pericles' wife is delivered of a child, a daughter, dying in the act, and the sailors' superstition requires her body to be cast overboard immediately; the father and daughter are separated— Shakespeare took over.[8] He took over with a tenderness that had died from *Timon* and *Coriolanus*, almost from every play since *King Lear*—with what one can only call a *restoration* of temper—and with new styles, the final style. Pericles looks down at his wife's body:

> A terrible Child-bed hast thou had (my deare),
> No light, no fire, th'vnfriendly elements
> Forgot thee vtterly, nor haue I time
> To giue thee hallowd to thy graue, but straight
> Must cast thee scarcly Coffind, in th'ooze,
> Where for a monument vpon thy bones
> And aye-remayning lampes, the belching Whale
> And humming water must orewhelme thy corpes,
> Lying with simple shels . . .

Nothing that the poet's imagination had suffered is forgotten in this style, and it is hardly too much to say that nothing is feigned. Of the "ooze" we hear, and "belching," and "orewhelme"—any of these recognitions might have wrecked the passage in another poet; here they are caught into a truth of devotion and music—they are not what they are. Marina passes through the brothel scenes unstained, converting. When she and her father meet at last and know, the actual music that Lear heard when he recovered to face Cordelia now only Pericles can hear—"the Musicke of the *Spheres*," he calls it—not Marina.

The End

Most heauenly Musicke.
It nips me into listning, and thicke slumber
Hangs vpon mine eyes, let me rest.

Probably this play (his last three acts) and certainly the easy weary *Cymbeline* that followed upon this re-establishment of his art were written for the Blackfriars "private" theatre, with its more cultivated audiences, acquired by the King's Men late in 1608. When they began to use it, however, we don't know. There can have been little playing in the city in 1609, when nearly 12,000 people died of the plague in London, though the King's Men gave a dozen plays at court in the Christmas time of 1608 and thirteen a year later. Nor can we determine a priority between *Cymbeline* and the very similar *Philaster* of young Francis Beaumont and John Fletcher. This year *Pericles* was pirated in a "bad" version, which is the only one we have, *Troilus and Cressida* in a "good" one (from a private transcript) with a defiant Epistle implying that it was published against "the grand possessors wills" and discoursing generally upon Shakespeare's comedies, which "are so fram'd to the life, that they serue for the most common Commentaries of all the actions of our liues, shewing such a dexteritie, and power of witte, that the most displeased with Playes, are pleasd with his Commedies . . . And beleeue this, that when hee is gone, and his Commedies out of sale, you will scramble for them, and set vp a new English Inquisition." These two were the poet's last plays published during his lifetime. But this year (1609) also appeared his sonnets, regularly entered by Thomas Thorpe and printed with a dedication (which has not slept in oblivion but may on the contrary easily claim to be the most celebrated dedication in literary history) "To the Onlie Begetter of these insuing Sonnets, Mr W.H., All Happinesse and that Eternitie promised by our ever-living Poet . . ." He was not, in fact, the "only" begetter, but the sonnets to the mistress were collected at the end of the book. There is not a trace of irregularity in any of this. Spelling shows a "copy" close to Shakespeare's. Internal linking and grouping among the sonnets—of which critics have made too little—suggest authoritative copy. Shakespeare moreover is not known to have protested, though three years later Thomas Heywood tells us that Shakespeare "I know much offended with M. *Jaggard* that (altogether vnknowne to him) presumed to make so bold with his name" as to print two of Heywood's poems under Shakespeare's name in *The Passionate Pilgrim* of 1599.[9] Nor did Shakespeare replace Thorpe's book with a true and authentic copy, as I suppose he could easily have done had he been dissatisfied. In sum, until somebody explains away all this, and also explains who besides the poet was likely to have *both* the sonnets to the boy and to the woman, it seems best to abandon the generally received notion that the sonnets were published with Shakespeare's authority and to adopt instead the notion that he probably published them himself. That there are many misprints means nothing—I do not suggest that he oversaw the printing; and that some sonnets are out of order means hardly more—I doubt if he kept a card catalogue. Two things that seem to me important are hardly ever mentioned in this connexion. The exact year of his retirement, if there was one, we do not know; he is found in London at least occasionally for five years more; but with exactly this year, 1609, begins an increasingly steep possibility that at any moment he might see his career as ending and published the poems of his youth to crown it. That he was already contemplating retirement is strongly suggested by the diary of a cousin (Thomas Greene) resident at New Place, who on September 9 notes that he can stay there another year.[10] Finally, there is an explicit statement by William Drummond about 1614 to this effect: "The last [poets] we have are Sir *William Alexander* and *Shakespear*, who have lately published their Works."[11]

TO THE NAME GIVEN USUALLY to Shakespeare's last full plays—the romances—I see no objection so long as we pay no attention to it and distinguish methodically between *Cymbeline* and *The Winter's Tale* (of 1609–10) and *The Tempest* of 1611. As of the two earlier: Shakespeare was often high-handed, but he now outdoes himself—at one end of the scale in the shameless narrations at the beginning of *Cymbeline* and near the end of *The Winter's Tale*; at the other end in the prolific and intolerable complications of the last scene of *Cymbeline*, towards which the whole action has been rather maliciously working and which contains in less than 500 lines enough recognitions and dénouements for the entire career of some long-lived playwright willing to husband his material. There is a perceptible difference between these two plays, the second being much the richer, finer, more energetic, as if the poet were collecting his powers for a final stroke; as indeed he was. But *The Winter's Tale* has not Imogen. I doubt if even Granville-Barker—whose graceful preface to *Cymbeline*, better twenty-five years ago than now in expansion, is the best account of the play we have—makes enough of Imogen.[12] I don't quite know what is to be made of her. Her qualities are high and clear, her career hard, and yet it is not for any of that—for her endurance throughout the play of separation from her husband and then from her father, her almost-not-understanding resistance to Iachimo's ingenuities, Cloten's lust, the Queen's plots, her husband's treachery, her Rosalind-like travel and recovery of her brothers—that we remember her. In Hermione and Perdita, two heroines of the next play, we can put our finger on long-familiar passages and say: Here you are. Imogen is less brilliant than the one, less poetic than the other, but she is poetic and brilliant enough, and it is odd that we cannot locate her even in:

> I would haue broke mine eye-strings, crack'd them, but
> to looke vpon him, till the diminution
> Of space, had pointed him sharpe as my Needle:
> Nay, followed him, till he had melted from
> The smalnesse of a Gnat, to ayre: and then
> Haue turn'd mine eye, and wept . . .

Or

> Why did you throw your wedded Lady fro you?
> Thinke that you are vpon a Locke, and now
> Throw me again
> I would haue broke mine eye-strings, crack'd them, but

To which even Shakespeare's most tedious hero must reply:

> Hang there like fruite, my soule,
> Till the Tree dye.

I saw once a very good Imogen, Joyce Bland, and she was nothing. The remnant power from Cleopatra, purified into fidelity (Fidele is the name she takes disguised)—it is perhaps not to be analyzed.

But *The Winter's Tale* has Autolycus, in some ways the most delicious irrelevance Shakespeare ever created, and its general quality both dramatic and poetic is such as to suggest that the poet was again on the verge of something absolutely extraordinary. That is: neither the bewildering expression given by Leontes to his jealous rage nor the dazzling poetry of Florizel and Perdita quite takes us out of the play, but the powers of imagination involved are obviously too great again to be so slightly involved. Let me try to enforce this; the point is crucial to an understanding of Shakespeare's ultimate development. Perdita's great flower speech in Act IV—twice imitated by Milton for his own very different purposes—seems generally to be taken as a poetic excrescence or cadenza. This it certainly is not. The King (disguised) and the girl have just had an argument, if so it can be called, about her refusal to set flowers produced by grafting, the King standing for art (which he says itself is nature), Perdita for nature. A most interesting and subtle argument, worth more attention than it has ever had. He wins, as it were, but she gives not an inch, and her speech a moment later is a sort of celebration of nature with mild reproof aside to the old man:

> Now (my fairst Friend)
> I would I had some Flowres o' the Spring, that might
> Become your time of day: and yours, and yours,
> That weare vpon your Virgin-branches yet
> Your Maiden-heads growing: O *Proserpina*,
> For the Flowres now, that (frighted) thou let'st fall
> From *Dysses* Waggon: Daffadils,
> That come before the Swallow dares, and take
> The windes of March with beauty: Violets (dim,
> But sweeter than the lids of *Iuno's* eyes,
> Or *Cytherea's* breath) pale Prime-roses,
> That dye vnmarried, ere they can behold
> Bright Phoebus in his strength . . .

The Prince then himself celebrates her in philosophical terms, and we have had a kind of ballet of thought. There is structure. But there is not structure enough for so great ability. One imagines Shakespeare at last restless with licence, dissatisfied, longing for larger and stricter meanings. A less inobvious development is from the cave-life of Imogen's brothers, to the pastoral here, and so away altogether to an enchanted island.

I am not going to be so superfluous as to praise *The Tempest*, a work on the order of *Macbeth*, and indeed its successor in a virtuous magic. But I want to say something as to its temper and design. And first, that the body of criticism treating it (not very effectively) simply as a dazzling and lovely comedy, which it is, or as a utopia, which it is, falls far short of appreciation by not recognizing that, for example, its murder plots are presented not as they would have been in any earlier comedy but just as they might be in *Othello*. I give both examples. As the wrecked King's party lie mostly sleeping about them, the usurping Duke of Milan, Antonio, has been slowly working the King's brother towards the conception of his murder. At last he understands, asking fearfully:

But for your conscience?

Ant. Ay Sir: where lies that? If twere a kybe
Twould put me to my slipper: But I feele not
This Deity in my bosome: Twentie consciences
That stand twixt me, and *Millaine*, candied be they,
And melt ere they mollest. Here lies your Brother,
No better than the earth he lies vpon,
If he *were* that which now hee's *like* (that's dead)
Whom I with this obedient steele (three inches of it)
Can lay to bed for euer: whiles you doing thus,
To the perpetuall winke for aye might put
This ancient Morsell, this Sir Prudence, who
Should act vpbraid but course: for all the rest
They'l take suggestion, as Cat laps milke,
They'll tell the clocke to any businesse that
We say befits the houre.

Caliban's tone is entirely his own, but the murder of Prospero urged by him on the drunkards is not less serious:

Why, as I told thee, 'tis a custome with him
I'th afternoone to sleepe: there thou maist braine him,
Hauing first seiz'd his bookes; Or with a log
Batter his skull, or paunch him with a stake,
Or cut his wezand with thy knife. Remember
First to possesse his Bookes; for without them
Hee's but a Sot, as I am; nor hath not
One Spirit to command: they all do hate him
As rootedly as I. Burne but his Bookes,
He has braue Vtensils (for so he calles them)
That when he has a house, hee'l decke withall.
And that most deeply to consider, is
The beautie of his daughter: he himselfe
Cals her a non-pareill: I neuer saw a woman
But onely *Sycorax* my Dam, and She;
But she as farre surpasseth *Sycorax*,
As great'st do's least.

This extraordinary tragic involvement, both at the state level and at the island level, suggests that the entire mind (not the comedic mind only) of the poet is at work, and is besides much in excess of the plot necessities of so short a play. But if the entire mind of the poet is at work in so short, premeditated, and classical a play, many strange things become even stranger. Gonzalo wonders "That our Garments being (as they were) drencht in the Sea, hold notwithstanding their fresheness and glosses, being rather new dy'de then stain'd with salte water." That they were drenched, we have heard from Ariel ("all but Mariners/Plung'd in the foaming bryne"), and we wonder too; but many things are strange here, and it is only when Gonzalo mentions this cleansing (not staining) a second time, a third time, a fourth time, that we *really* wonder. Of this, as of much else, the best account that has been attempted was that by Colin Still in a book of thirty years ago.[13] He takes this, I think rightly, to be clearly an insistence that the experience was subjective, and equivalent to the pagan "washings" (or the Christian baptism), preparatory to the initiatory rites of a Mystery. The experiences of the court party, he argues in detail, constitute what is called a Lesser Initiation, Ferdinand's a Greater, while Stephano and Trinculo fail to achieve Initiation; aspects of the Fall are represented in Caliban (and his mother), the Powers of Redemption (in their ways) by Ariel, Miranda, and of course Prospero. What is in question is the Christian Mystic Way, the Way of Salvation, but pagan allusion is very elaborate also. It is not a case that can be judged on details. We have always in these matters to allow heavily for coincidence; and the more experienced one is, the more one allows. Take for example the 46th Psalm in the Authorized Version of the Hebrew Bible: the forty-sixth word in from the beginning is "shake" and the forty-sixth word in from the end is "spear," and this translation went to press (at Oxford, a few miles from Stratford) the year before *The Tempest*, 1610, when Shakespeare was forty-six years old. These are facts and they constitute a coincidence.[14] What are we to make of it? The answer is: nothing. But of too many coincidences we have in the end to make something, and so I think it is with Still's enquiry. It illuminates not only much that is difficult but much that seemed perspicuous and is greatest in the play. In the Mysteries, life was conceived as a transmigration from sleep to sleep and from dream to dream, and Still has found the word "revels" used with the technical meaning "orgies" precisely in 1611, throwing light toward

> be cheerefull Sir,
> Our *Reuels* now are ended: These our actors,
> (As I foretold you) were all Spirits, and
> Are melted into Ayre, into thin Ayre . . .

The End

Still links *The Tempest* to the *6th Aeneid* and to the *Commedia*, and to these great ritual works I would add *The Magic Flute*. They have all, of course, an intensely personal signification too, a searching, a cleansing, a testing, a preparation, before the end. At the critics who in Prospero cannot see his creator let us smile. Marrying his spotless daughter to a Prince, he breaks his staff and drowns his book and returns home.

The Tempest was given at court on November 1, 1611, and for a year and a half nothing connects Shakespeare with his company or its theatres. His brothers Gilbert and Richard died, leaving only his sister, Joan Hart, who had three sons. The Halls had had no children after Elizabeth, and Judith Shakespeare, now in her late twenties, had still not married. The one-time apprentice [Stephen Belott] of his old landlord, Mountjoy, had been fighting with his father-in-law about the amount and payment of the dowry, and in May 1612 Shakespeare, who had arranged the marriage, was in London to testify. The case turned on his testimony. But he could not remember[15]; as four years later for his will he could not remember, the name [Thomas Hart] of one of his three nephews.[16]

Next spring, at fifty, he was active again, and I think J. Q. Adams is right in supposing a double reason: the activity of the King's Men in the festivities for Princess Elizabeth's marriage to the Elector Palatine in February 1613, when they gave twenty plays including at least half a dozen of Shakespeare's, and the retirement from the stage of Francis Beaumont, leaving them strapped. With John Fletcher, then, Shakespeare did rapidly three: a *Cardenio* (on a story from *Don Quixote*), which is lost, *Henry VIII* [*All is True*, ? 1613], and *The Two Noble Kinsmen* [? summer 1613].[17] Each of these two last he began and wrote about a third of; journeywork but for moments that take one's breath:

> O Queene *Emilia*
> Fresher then May, sweeter
> Then hir gold Buttons on the bowes, or all
> Th'enamelld knackes o'th Meade, or garden, yea
> (We challenge too) the bancke of any Nymph
> That makes the streame seeme flowers . . .

In March the poet added to his properties the Blackfriars gatehouse (a sort of House of the Seven Gables) and designed an *impresa* (or shield device) for the Earl of Rutland, which Burbage painted, and which was exhibited at the King's Accession Day tilt [at Belvoir Castle] on the twenty-fourth. Sir Henry Wotton complained of the obscurity of some of the *imprese* that day.[18]

On June 29 the Globe burnt to the ground during a performance of *Henry VIII*, and William Shakespeare was dealing with a worse trouble in Stratford. For weeks one John Lane had been spreading word about Susanna Hall, that she "had the runninge of the raynes & had bin naught with Rafe Smith at John Palmer"—whether at Palmer's house is meant, or *and* Palmer, is uncertain. Suit for defamation was brought in the Consistory Court at Worcester in mid-July, witnesses for Mrs. Hall were heard, and Lane, who did not appear, was duly excommunicated.[19] It is less clear to me than to Shakespeare's nervous biographers that his slander was idle. In a world where reputation was much more important than it is today, and particularly to Shakespeare, this must have been a grave matter.

In 1614 a visiting preacher drank some sack and claret at New Place.[20] The year is otherwise a blank except for a visit by Shakespeare to London in November, not worried about a threatened enclosure of some of his Stratford holdings. This matter ran on; in the end he was indemnified.[21] What else? Ben Jonson had been for several years at work on a collection of his plays and masques to be called "Works." Did his friend plan one? To a collection actually published some ten years later, [the First Folio] in 1623, his friends Heminge and Condell prefaced at least one sentence to which insufficient attention has been paid: "It had bene a thing, we confesse, worthie to haue bene wished, that the Author himselfe had *liu'd* to have set forth, and ouerseen his owne writings; But since it hath bin ordain'd otherwise, and he by death departed from that right . . ." [Berryman's italics].[22] Or did he share the feelings of another poet who, before his death, wanted the *Aeneid* destroyed?

Early in 1616 he had a will drafted. A Stratford vicar [John Ward] fifty years later tells us he had a merry meeting with Jonson and Drayton "and itt seems drank too hard, for Shakespear died of a feavour there contracted."[23] On February 10 Judith at last married, at thirty-one, a vintner of a family long friendly with Shakespeare, Thomas Quiney. Celebrated (perhaps because of the poet's illness) in a period forbidden by the Church [Lent], the marriage finally caused the couple's excommunication[24]; but some changes Shakespeare made in his will late in March with regard to Judith seem to reflect his own dissatisfaction.[25] He also wrote a doggerel curse against anyone who should move his bones, which has proved effective.[26] He must have shared the horror of charnel houses expressed by Juliet and Hamlet. On April 23 his mind died forever with its body, its work well done—but in what state of expectation we do not know. A late-seventeenth-century note [by Richard Davies] tells us, "He dyed a papist."[27]

And the name? "Wishers are ever fools," said Cleopatra. Judith Quiney died without issue. Elizabeth Hall married twice and died without issue in 1670, ending the line. But two years before, in the most beautiful critical essay yet written in English, John Dryden had recognized a different posterity:

He was the man who of all modern, and perhaps ancient poets, had the largest and most comprehensive soul. All the images of Nature were still present to him, and he drew them, not laboriously, but luckily; when he describes any thing, you more than see it, you feel it too . . . I cannot say he is everywhere alike; were he so, I should do him injury to compare him with the greatest of mankind . . . But he is always great, when some great occasion is presented to him.[28]

One wonders whether Shakespeare would have cared. Seventeen feet deep the grave is supposed to be.[29]

Shakespeare's Last Word

JUSTICE AND REDEMPTION

THE DRAMATIST'S SCENE FOR *The Tempest* is an "vninhabited island" somewhere in the Mediterranean, where live the exiled Duke of Milan, Prospero, his daughter, Miranda, his slave, Caliban, and spirits, servants to him, of whom the chief is called Ariel. This, with the sea about, is his whole realm and he rules it by magic. By chance his enemies from Italy are delivered into the power of his art, punished with a storm and in other ways, and he regains his original kingdom. The play has sometimes been regarded as a comedy of revenge. But one is made to feel that, except in the interest of justice, Prospero does not much desire his original kingdom ("where Euery third thought shall be my graue"); he never even in the past really desired to rule or administer it: he was interested in *study*. It seems fair to regard him as an unwilling ruler in both the first and the last of the story's three periods of his sway; whether he must be thought of as an unwilling ruler also in the second period—that of the twelve years on the island culminating in the afternoon during which the action of the play occurs (from about two o'clock to about six)—is a question I postpone. Revenge, except as the agent of justice, does not quite name what happens. But revenge is an unsatisfactory characterization for a further reason. It is less striking that he punishes his enemies than that he forgives them, and more striking still is the hope that their natures are altered—most of their natures are altered—by their punishments and his forgiveness—punishments, by the way, obviously symbolic: harmless shipwreck in a magic tempest, mental torture in a magic distraction. Yet what we have been saying has at once to be qualified in two ways. First, Prospero does absolutely rule—no other character in drama is so uncompromisingly in charge of all the presented events; and second, he does certainly not impress the spectator or reader as a naturally forgiving man. On the other hand, it is clear that he rules justly, or on behalf of justice; and he is concerned—as once with the education of Caliban—with the spiritual fate of his enemies. Let us take the play, tentatively, as a tragicomedy of justice and redemption, and look into a curious speech of Gonzalo's.

The unwilling visitors to the island are dispersed, you recall, in four places: Ferdinand alone to meet Prospero and Miranda, Stephano and Trinculo to meet Caliban, the sailors (with whom we are not concerned) on the ship still, and last what we may call the court party—the King, Gonzalo, and the rest. Now Gonzalo's chief topic, considered as one for shipwrecked courtiers, is a little surprising: how society ought to be organized, or disorganized. "Had I plantation of this isle my Lord," he says (that is, colonization)—

> I' th' Commonwealth I would (by contraries)
> Execute all things: For no kinde of Trafficke
> Would I admit: No name of Magistrate:
> Letters should not be knowne: Riches, pouerty,
> And vse of seruice, none: Contract, Succession,
> Borne, bound of Land, Tilth, Vineyard none:
> No vse of Mettall, Corne, or Wine, or Oyle:
> No occupation, all men idle, all:
> And Women too, but innocent and pure:
> No Soueraignty . . .
> All things in common Nature should produce
> Without sweat or endeuour . . .
> . . . Nature should bring forth
> Of it owne kinde, all foyzen, all abundance
> To feed my innocent people . . .
> I would with such perfection gouerne Sir
> T 'Excell the Golden Age.

Now this view is satirized by the others as he develops it, and Gonzalo concedes he spoke mockingly. But this is a respectable, or distinguished rather, sixteenth-century European view of primitive social organization—the dramatist lifted half of it indeed, almost uniquely for him, word for word nearly, from Montaigne's essay on cannibals. Gonzalo too is linked with Prospero, not only as the one notably good man among the court party, but as Prospero's saviour at the time of the usurpation; the Masque of Ceres aims also at the Golden Age when "Spring came to you at the farthest/In the very end of harvest"—that is, a winterless age; and beyond some superficial resemblance between Gonzalo's ironic description and Prospero's actual commonwealth on the island, they present of course radical and imposing differences, by which we may suppose the dramatist to be developing his theme. I take four of these differences.

Clusters of difference they really are, and may form a chain, but the first is absolute. "No Soueraignty," says Gonzalo, and Prospero is an autocrat. The nature of his sway can be suggested by a consideration of some features of his speech. Even among the grand rulers Shakespeare imagined, Prospero commands an utterance of incommensurable solemnity and majesty. When his daughter ventures a question, he answers, robed, erect:

> Know thus far forth,
> By accident most strange, bountifull *Fortune*
> (*Now* my deere Lady) hath mine enemies
> Brought to this shore: And by my prescience
> I finde my *Zenith* doth depend vpon
> A most auspicious starre, whose influence
> If now I court not, but omit, my fortunes
> Will euer after droope . . .

Birth, rule, age, wisdom do not by themselves account for the extremity of this tone; Prospero also is a magician, and sounds it. He speaks himself of his "dignity"; the transition, both in the courtiers and the drunkards, from levity to evil, is in this play an easy one. Then, his ceremonial elaboration is consistent with the most violent or expressive curtness—a curtness of which the next lines of this speech show an overbearing instance:

> Heere cease more questions,
> Thou art inclinde to sleepe, 'tis a good dulnesse,
> And giue it way: I know thou canst not chuse . . .

In the slowing of the final phrase we hear Miranda succumb; we feel the spell as real. The solemnity is executive.

Majesty, activity. Another feature of Prospero's speech worth signalizing is nakedly its power. Consider some lines from his final adjuration to his spirits—

Shakespeare's Last Word

> by whose ayde
> (Weake Masters though ye be) I haue bedymn'd
> The Noone-tide Sun, call'd forth the mutenous windes,
> And twixt the green sea and the azured vault
> Set roaring warre . . .

This hair-raising language is thoughtful, not ornamental. He calls his assistants "weake" but acknowledges them "masters"; whose master he is. He bedimmed (a high-keyed word) the sun at the moment when that feat might be thought most difficult—a fancy borrowed from Ovid, who exaggerates it. Then he called forth (low or neutral key, as for calling dogs) winds that did not want to come (a figure for the reluctant Ariel); however, they come. Then a vast and blazing image: of the ocean and of heaven's arch, and of the space between them—and since a high "azured" is coming, plain "green" is vivid with "sea"; now, into this space, and between these great stages of nature, he "sets"—a detailed, local word, as if he were going to place a salt cellar there—he sets war, and before, or just as you learn "war," it "roars" at you.[1]

Sovereignty, then, as against Gonzalo's anarchy, and a sovereignty of which the hard characteristics, displayed in the style, are ritual solemnity, activity, all-mastering power. Prospero's sovereignty in the world of the play, the island, is founded upon power, and nothing else. His power is founded, however, and here we reach a second difference from Gonzalo's commonwealth, upon learning. "Letters should not be knowne." Prospero's learning—his magic art, his actual books—these are repeatedly insisted on; he even studies a good deal during the rather short course of the play, and in the end he has undertaken to drown his book. Prospero has also attended carefully, we learn, to the education of Miranda; and he and Miranda have taught Caliban what Caliban could be taught. Prospero, indeed, is a real pedant—this is one of the directions in which a risk was taken with the audience's sympathy for him.

The ruler, in short, works. Everyone works under Prospero's commonwealth, he at ruling, Miranda at her education and Caliban's, Ariel and Caliban at tasks fitting their quality. This marks a third difference between Gonzalo's image of universal idleness and the island fact, and it is unusual in drama. The audience has been working itself all day (or the Elizabethan popular audience was exactly shirking work to attend the afternoon performance) and does not care to see people work on the stage. But much of this work, again, is done onstage, feeble indeed from a theatrical point of view, like the log-bearing. The sole visitor to the island with whom its ruler comes immediately into contact, Ferdinand, is put to work immediately. We must distinguish, of course, between on the one hand the unsuitable work done by Ferdinand and Ariel's, and, on the other hand, that done by Caliban. Ferdinand's is a test of character, imposed to determine the quality of his devotion to Miranda. Ariel's is on contract—another feature of society excluded by Gonzalo; it is performed partly out of gratitude to Prospero for having freed him from the pine, partly out of fear of the oak, and partly in reliance upon Prospero's promise to free him wholly in the end. And here we come first upon what anyone must feel is one of the play's dominant themes: the impending freedom of Ariel. The work done by these two is limited in term and teleological: it has an end, which is understood by the ruler—not necessarily by the subject (in Ferdinand's case not), but by the ruler. Caliban's labours are another matter.

A fourth difference between Gonzalo's description and Prospero's state let us describe as an error made by Gonzalo when he speaks of "my innocent people." Neither do most of the court party, nor Stephano and Trinculo, illustrate any such conception of human nature as underlies this (ironic, to be sure) optimism; but them we will come to. On the island already exists a creature able to make mincemeat of Gonzalo's notion, or the later idea, consistent with it, of the Noble Savage. Caliban, however, who is certainly one of Shakespeare's most exquisite creations, crucial to this play, is as complicated as his parentage, and I am anxious not to oversimplify his character, which is at any rate triple. Upon his first appearance he is called "Thou Earth, thou," to Prospero's threats he answers only, "I must eat my dinner," and much of his talk presents nature in its earthiest form:

> I prethee let me bring thee where Crabs grow;
> And I with my long nayles will digge thee pig-nuts;
> Show thee a Jayes nest, and instruct thee how
> To snare the nimble Marazet: Ile bring thee
> To clustring Philbirts, and sometimes Ile get thee
> Young Scamels from the Rocke: Wilt thou goe with me?

Or

> she will become thy bed, I warrent,
> And bring thee forth braue brood.

But it is clear that this is already very poetic, and the contrast between the tone of this last remark and Stephano's response to it ("Monster, I will kill this man") makes it clearer still that faculties far higher than those of the butler and jester have not been denied to Caliban. We are not wholly surprised when the poet places this in his mouth:

> Be not affeared [he says], the isle is full of noyses,
> Sounds, and sweet aires, that giue delight and hurt not:
> Sometimes a thousand twangling Instruments
> Will hum about mine eares; and sometime voices,
> That if I then had wak'd after long sleepe,
> Will make me sleepe again, and then in dreaming
> The clouds methought would open, and show riches
> Ready to drop vpon me, that when I wak'd
> I cride to dreame againe.

The gulf between him and his colleagues yawns again in Stephano's comment upon this:

> This will preue a braue kingdome to me, where I shall
> Haue my Musike for nothing.

But in Caliban's comment upon *this*—"When *Prospero* is destroye'd"—we are reminded of his third nature, or rather of the disposition that governs, for action and in the commonwealth, both his representative (or lower) and higher natures. This disposition (recognized by Caliban himself in "You taught me Language, and my profit on't,/Is I know how to curse") is unregenerate and malicious, extending to designs of rape and murder, which require frustration, demand punishment, and make inevitable his status of slave. He is not master of himself, and therefore the freedom of Ariel is out of the question for him: he must be permanently mastered. One of his lines editors take as drunken nonsense. Caliban is fooling around with his name: " 'Ban, 'Ban, Cacaliban." Shakespeare is not fooling around, however. "Ban" means *curse*, and the first two syllables of "Cacaliban" are suggestive: they suggest "cacodeman" (or devil)—a word the poet had applied twenty years before to Richard III, who is *also* deformed. Prospero finally, in Act IV, calls him "a devil." We may wonder whether Prospero's nature—in the dramatist's intention —has not been soured partly by his failure with the education of Caliban—"on whom my paines Humanely taken, all, all lost, quite lost . . ."

We are ready, perhaps, for a more detailed formulation. Sovereignty is implied by society. It should be based on power, and power should be based on learning. Work is necessary, and it should be work done on contract, with its end in view by the ruler, except where the subject is unable to enter into a contract because he cannot be depended upon to fulfil it; such cases exist, and are not incompatible with the possession of considerable and even elevated faculties otherwise than in the matter of self-mastery. Contract is strongest when triply based: on gratitude backward, present fear, and confident hope forward. Mutiny against a just ruler (such as Ariel's in prospect, Caliban's in practice) is the ultimate social crime and gives rise to or accompanies all other evil. Thus, there is no "freedom" upon this island at all. Even Miranda studies and educates Caliban and solaces Prospero. The ruler's work consists in: education (including unremitting self-education), the administration of justice (including punishment), and redemption. Before passing on to this third work of the ruler, of which we have said almost nothing, I want to notice one broad controlling design of justice dramatized.

A singular feature of the structure of *The Tempest* is that the catastrophe which delivers Prospero's enemies into his power occurs in the opening scene. We do not at the time know this. We see only a storm at sea, rulers on board, a wreck. We learn it during the second scene, suspectingly and slow, then suddenly in the speech that I used to illustrate Prospero's solemnity. But meanwhile we have heard about another "sea-sorrow" twelve years before, of which the near-victims were Prospero and his daughter. Thus, the instant of full recognition of *what* has happened contains a full recognition of *why* it happened. Those tortured by the sea at first were innocent; those who caused that torture are guilty and are now tortured by the sea; justice exists. Deep in the play Ariel makes the vice-like pattern explicit:

> you three . . .
> Exposed vnto the Sea (which hath requit it)
> Him, and his innocent childe: for which foule deed,
> The Powres, delaying (not forgetting) haue
> Incens'd the Seas, and Shores, yea, all the Creatures
> Against your peace . . .

It is owing to this unexampled priority of the catastrophic action, as a German critic has pointed out, that imagery in *The Tempest* has not its normal Shakespearean function of foreshadowing but is used rather to recall, to remind of what has happened (and so, as well, of what it meant).[2] I adduce two morose, disdainful instances of the way in which the persistent sea imagery is linked with the guilty men and with the conception of the ocean as an agent of retribution. When Anthonio is working the inert Sebastian towards the murder of his brother, Sebastian admits:

> I am standing water.
> *Anthonio.* Ile teach you how to flow.
> *Sebastian.* Do so; to ebbe
> Hereditary Sloth instructs me.

Here the water image is forced into a full sea image by "ebbe." The other, the most elaborate image perhaps in this play very scant in imagery, is declaimed by Prospero about the guilty men in Act V when he releases them from their distraction:

> Their understanding
> Begins to swell, and the approaching tide
> Will shortly fill the reasonable shore
> That now lyes foule, and muddy . . .

Here only the two abstract terms keep the subject in sight, all the rest being contemptuous metaphor; this is mercy with a *vengeance*.

Alonso is punished throughout in his grief for his son, and at last by Ariel's instruction is brought to despair:

> The thunder
> (That deepe and dreadfull Organ-Pipe) pronounc'd
> The name of *Prosper*: it did base my Trespasse—

that terrifying pun—and so thence to repentance. His enmity to Prospero was general, his crime against Milan general. With Prospero's brother an intenser course is necessary. Before he is punished, he is made (by temptation—the others' magic sleep) to re-enact his crime by persuading the dull Sebastian to the murder of *his* brother; and this persuasion has almost the tone of Iago—it is hardly comedic. Even the brutal fool Sebastian, when at last he sees Anthonio's drift, is moved to ask, "But for your conscience":

Anthonio. Ay Sir: where lies that? If twere a kybe
      Twould put me to my slipper: But I feele not
      This Deity in my bosome: Twentie consciences
      That stand twixt me, and *Millaine*, candied be they,
      And melt ere they mollest. Here lies your Brother,
      No better than the earth he lies vpon.
      If he *were* that which now hee's *like* (that's dead)
      Whom I with this obedient steele (three inches of it)
      Can lay to bed for euer: whiles you doing thus,
      To the perpetuall winke for aye might put
      This ancient Morsell: this Sir Prudence, who
      Should act vpbraid but course: for all the rest
      They'll take suggestion, as Cat laps milke,
      They'll tell the clocke to any businesse that
      We say befits the houre.

This enforced, hell-like recapitulation—it is the plotters who are lapping the poisoned milk set out—is *justice* with a vengeance. Are we drifting back to *revenge?* An element of vindictiveness discernible in Prospero ought not to make us lose our heads and see him as a vindictive rather than a just man. Besides the twelve years of barbaric exile, take the nature of the crimes: intended murder and, far worse to an Elizabethan or Jacobean, usurpation and intended usurpation. The usurpation, moreover, had been, was to be, by worse rulers against better—self-deprecation is not one of Prospero's foibles—and his native state, Milan, thus became basely tributary. But I think we are bound to confess a sense that Prospero finally forgives his enemies rather from justice (the sense that they have suffered enough, and repent, and deserve his restored esteem) than from mercy. There exist touches of mercy; but even these are apt to be accompanied by *rational* resentment and rational, rather than emotional, redemptive operation:

      Thogh with their high wrongs I am strook to th' quick
      Yet, with my nobler reason, gainst my furie
      Doe I take part: The rarer Action is
      In *vertue*, then in vengeance . . .

And what reconciliation can be heard in this?—

      For you, most wicked sir, whom to call brother
      Would even infect my mouth, I do forgive
      Thy rankest fault . . .

—to which Shakespeare wisely gives Anthonio no reply. The general view taken of human nature here? Not high, not high. To see in the last plays, as recent critics do, a sort of ministry of reconciliation seems to me to sentimentalize them and falsify our experience of their reality. Everybody does by no means kiss and make up—not even in *The Winter's Tale*, which (as villainless) I should call the most charitable of them.

Now virtue for a ruler consists in the production of virtue in himself and his subjects—or, where it exists already, the encouragement, refinement, and maintenance of it, as in Prospero himself, in Miranda, in Ferdinand, in Gonzalo. But where it does not exist, it must be produced in whatever degree is practicable, according to the nature of the subject; and this brings us to the fates of Alonso, Anthonio, Sebastian, of Stephano and Trinculo, of Caliban.

Take the first group. Without insisting upon my term "redemption," I think we need not hesitate over the fact, which is that Alonso, Anthonio, and Sebastian are redeemed—reclaimed, ransomed, delivered from their guilt, and by Prospero, in a sequence of deliberate operations. This makes the situation essentially different from the one in *As You Like It*, where, also, a duke is exiled by his brother to a sort of utopia, his daughter is with him, the usurper comes and is converted—there is even, also, a *second* wicked brother who comes and reforms. The imagination of this author used the same materials again and again, all down its mature working life; but it used them differently. The illuminating and nailing difference, between the conventional comedic reformations in the Forest of Arden and those on the enchanted island, is the thematic hammer in *The Tempest* of the word "free," the central word in the play. This is Shakespeare's word. It first appears as "Libertie," in Ariel's demand—which, with Prospero's promise, alluded to throughout and at last performed, is our metaphorical and dramatic instruction in the play's prime theme. But the constant words are "freedom," "free." Alonso, Anthonio (maybe), and Sebastian are set *free* from their old selves, from their guilt. Even Caliban, whose nature forestalls freedom, is freed, at any rate, from his illusions about Stephano and Trinculo, and undertakes in his final speech (one of Shakespeare's oddest and most attractive notes) to "be wise hereafter,/And seek for grace." How is it that Stephano and Trinculo have or can have no part in this general redemption?

Possibly it is because they are drunk. Amusingly as here their antics are handled, drunkenness is not much a comic topic in Shakespeare's mature plays—in *Hamlet, Othello, Measure for Measure*. The drunkenness of Stephano and Trinculo images their self-slavery and the moral stupidity that allows them to fall in with the suggestions of

Caliban's malice. Their crime too, like that of the men from the top of society, intends not murder only but usurpation—Stephano is to be King in Prospero's place. Irrational, self-set outside reason, they stand beyond the reach of the ruler's redemptive design. *They* think they are "free," of course, as Caliban imagines he is with his new master. "Freedome," he cries, "high-day, high-day freedome, free-dome highday, freedome." The catch sung by Stephano and Trin-culo, adapting a proverb already employed in *Twelfth Night*, certainly embodies one of the dramatist's most daring and schematic ironies: "Flout 'em and cout 'em: and Skowt 'em and flout 'em,/Thought is free."

The theme rules without irony the final line of the play, when Ariel hears at last:

> To the Elements
> Be free, and fare thou well . . .

and in the final line, the final word, of the epilogue, Prospero asks the audience to set *him* "free." Probably we are right to wonder whether Prospero *is* not himself in some way freed in the play or by its action. Prospero we have evidently to see in at least two characters: as the exile, injured and vindictive, and as the great Magician and Judge—God onstage—who rights the wrongs sustained by the exile (himself) and also redeems the exile's enemies, so far as their natures permit. Then clearly Prospero is set free, in both the rules: free from vindictiveness (strongly conveyed, the sense of this, in the fifth act) and from the sense of injustice, and free from his overwhelming power. Perhaps those men only who have exercised formidable power can feel fully what it means to wish to be free of it; but everyone understands both fatigue and the desire to be free of the responsibil-ities of power. But to be free of unruly and discreditable desire is the heart of the play's desire, and even in this does Prospero participate, released from the intoxications of hatred and might.

The scene, wonderful in production, where Ferdinand and Mi-randa are discovered "playing at Chesse," brings them, too, within the conclusion of this theme. Here is a game, as against the work they formerly did. No ordinary game: an exercise ancient, orderly, and intellectual. We remember Prospero's harsh adjuration to them not, before marriage, to

> Giue dalliance
> Too much the raigne; the strongest Oaths, are
> To th' fire ith' blood . . .

and we *see* them holding in check their desires, and perhaps we remember Hamlet's crying:

> Giue me that man
> That is not passions slaue, and I will weare him
> In my harts core, I in my hart of harts . . .

Nobody, I suppose, who had not himself *been* passion's slave could have made the longing envy in these lines so central in his most personal play and their sense so necessary in the design of his final play.

1952–55

THE FREEDOM OF THE POET

The Tempest WAS PRODUCED at court on November 1, 1611. (It may help us through an account unavoidably a bit intricate if you will bear in mind that we are interested henceforth in this year 1611.) This was either its original production or an early one: it makes use of two West Indies shipwreck pamphlets of 1610, besides a letter of the same year, and Trinculo's "dead Indian" is no doubt one of the five American savages—only four of whom then returned—brought to London in 1611 itself by the Earl of Southampton and another; William Shakespeare was forty-seven years old. Apparently he had planned to retire two years before and changed his mind; we infer this from a memorandum of September 1609 by a cousin living in the poet's main house at Stratford, New Place, saying he "perceived I might stay another year at New Place."[3] Also in 1609 were published: the last play that appeared during his lifetime, *Troilus and Cressida*, and his *Sonnets*, which for contemporaries ranked as his "works." I have an idea, considering his whole publishing history and these present circumstances, that he may have been responsible for the issuance both of the first, which judges so diverse as Goethe and Keats have thought his profoundest, most characteristic work, and the second. It looks as if at forty-five he meant to retire but stayed on for two years, writing *Cymbeline*, *The Winter's Tale* (seen by a playgoer on May 15, 1611), and then *The Tempest*. He was wealthy. He had perhaps stopped acting some years before, though he may still have been producing. His company, the King's Men, could rely on younger dramatists, and many of his own plays remained so popular that they were competing with each other. He was tired, conceivably, after two decades (at least) of activity hardly by anyone ever paralleled. His memory may have been failing: so we infer from a lawsuit of

1612, when his testimony about a financial agreement was crucial and he said he could not remember, though it was the dowry of a marriage in which he had been the go-between himself[4]; it's interesting that the good Gonzalo is a "lord of weak remembrance." All this comes to a constellation of motives powerful indeed, apart from what drew him to Stratford—business affairs, a granddaughter now three, his younger daughter, Judith, still seriously unmarried *at twenty-six*, and the orchard that had filled his plays with orchards for five years after he acquired it. Now for an entire year and a half *after* this production of *The Tempest* nothing connects him with his theatrical company; he never again wrote a whole play; and it's likely that only the double strain of 1613 for the company (he was still a principal shareholder, of course)—first of Francis Beaumont's withdrawal, then the demands made on them in connection with Princess Elizabeth's wedding to the Elector Palatine—summoned him back to their assistance, collaborating in three plays with John Fletcher. Everything obliges us to suppose that, at the latest, directly after making *The Tempest*, he entered upon the retirement for several years actively contemplated. And few critics have decided not to hear in the play what Victor Hugo calls "the solemn tone of a testament."

But before pursuing this, let me examine a little the impression it gives of its author.

Solemn and testamental it may be—and it shows that what he was most rereading or remembering was Ovid and the *Aeneid* and *The Faerie Queene*—but it goes in for a good gay final flick at George Chapman, with whom Shakespeare seems to have had a long difference or feud. "Temperance," says Anthonio, "was a delicate wench." In Chapman's comedy *May Day*, of a year or so before, his character Temperance is a foul-mouthed bawd. Most of the other objects of the courtiers' satire have not survived or not been recognized, but *The Tempest*, like Shakespeare's other work, is much and immediately indebted to its theatrical environment. There is a deep influence from the court masque, especially Daniel's *Tethys Festival* of 1610. It picks up phrases from the last act of Fletcher's recent *Faithful Shepherdess*. The Wild Man Bremo in the old play *Mucedorus*, revived by Shakespeare's company in February 1610, is the frantic original of Caliban, and it would not surprise me to learn that Caliban was born when the poet heard the character called Envy in *Mucedorus* speak some lines probably new at this production:

> From my foule Studie will I hoyst a Wretch,
> A leane and hungry Meager Canniball,

Whose lawes swell to his eyes with chawing Malice:
And him Ile make a poet.

Memories of a lifetime spent in the theatre were swarming also: Gonzalo's speech out of Montaigne, by *Isaiah*, is indebted as well to primitive-society speeches not only in *Mucedorus* but in the twenty-year-old *Selimus*. Nor is the style Olympian, outside of Prospero. I would illustrate it—admitting its variety, and ignoring *character*—with the line about "turfy mountains, where live nibbling sheep." The beauty of this I account for thus: one thought the gorgeous "turfy" was finished, just a piece of diction, and then the related, even more actively visual and physical "nibbling" brings "turfy" back to life and incidentally completes the presentation of a pastoral world in one line, thick with excellent life. Nor is the form Olympian, but concise as this style, and methodical. *The Tempest*, unlike most of Shakespeare's dramatic work, especially unlike the romances sprawling through time and space that he had just been writing, is a work expressly obedient to the Elizabethan understanding of the classical unities; and it is hard to agree with Dr. Johnson that the regularity of its plan is "an accidental effect of the story, not intended nor regarded by our author."[5] Prospero looks at his watch too often. It was a demonstration.

Was Shakespeare specially proud of this work? It stands first in the collection of thirty-six of his plays that appeared a few years after his death; that's editorial. But Shakespeare's younger friend Ben Jonson was already by 1613 editing his own plays for a collected volume. Shakespeare lived three years longer, dying in the year Jonson's folio appeared. When his long-time associates Heminge and Condell prefaced the Shakespeare folio they had put together, they "confessed" the "wish" "that the Author himselfe had *liu'd* to have set forth, and overseene his owne writings; But . . . it hath beene ordain'd otherwise, and he by death departed from that right . . ." The priority of *The Tempest* may be as well due to him as to them. Now, authors like their last works best, notoriously. But I want to make two points. This was one of the least didactic major poets who ever lived. *The Tempest* is the extreme exception in the canon, only *Measure for Measure* approaching it, and our whole earlier discussion may be held to support the view that Shakespeare might have held it dear as an embodiment, at a high level enough of compression and expressive art, of his maturest feelings about human organization and duty. That that is not why we value it is immaterial. My other point is also biographical.

The Duke of *Measure for Measure* who, so much in tone, insistence on chastity, and arbitrary management, resembles Prospero, pretends to relinquish his power, and devotes much intrigue to getting married a protégé of his named Mariana. This was in 1604, midway through Shakespeare's tragic period: for all we know, he was dreaming already of retiring, and his elder daughter, Susanna, ought already to have been married at twenty-one. A year or so later, King Lear, who resembles in eccentricity and hauteur both that Duke and Prospero, though he surpasses them in irascibility, does relinquish his power, having married off satisfactorily two of his daughters; both of Shakespeare's legitimate daughters were now marriageable. By Prospero's year, only one had still to marry, like Miranda, and besides, I must point out a curious fact: Prospero does not wholly retire. He only retires from his *art*. When looking well ahead towards retirement, it may seem to a man that it can be complete; when a man in Shakespeare's situation gets to that point, he sees that it cannot. Investments have to be protected and extended, family matters arranged, and so on; he even returned to dramatic writing. But back to Miranda. Her father produces for her a stainless prince, sees them betrothed, and watches them hawk-like with distrust (at the same time one has an impression of him leaning forward waiting for progeny—even Caliban, in both his lustful passages about her, envisages progeny).

Now even if Shakespeare's daughters were freaks, they were good matches. They married, Susanna at twenty-four, Judith at thirty-one —grave ages for this period. Their father must have been choosy, very, and, while being choosy, anxious. With reason: backwards, remembering that their mother at twenty-six had married him at eighteen and borne Susanna in six months (not to speak of his own later infidelities); and forwards, as things turned out. He had got a physician, Dr. John Hall, as husband for Susanna, but for Judith he had to wait until two months before his death, when she married a vintner so rapidly that they were excommunicated. But his sufferings over Susanna must have been keener still, for a young gentleman asserted in 1613 that this "witty" woman (as she is described) "had bin naught with Rafe Smith" and her successful action for slander—he did not appear—tells us rather that her father was influential than that her accuser was a liar.[6] The intense anxiety of Prospero upon this topic of unchastity is one of the clearest features of his creator. Dis's rape of Proserpina—the classic plot on a virgin—must have been familiar to William Shakespeare all his life; suddenly, in *The Winter's Tale* and again in *The Tempest*, it inspired passages, energetic and of ravishing beauty, the beauty of pain.

It is remarkable—in a work rich with the happiness of the exercise of supreme art—how often, and with what longing, *sleep* is invoked. " 'Tis a good dulnesse, and giue it way." "Do not omit the heavy offer of it," one says to Alonso drowsy. Caliban's visionary cadenza on sleep and dream you remember. This longing—for release, for freedom— it is which resolves, I think, a genuine difficulty that I cannot truly remember any critic to have noticed: the coarse discrepancy, to appearance, between Prospero's reassurance, "be cheerefull Sir," to Ferdinand, and his celebrated, magnificent, apparently disillusioned and frightening forecast of universal dissolution that follows.

But there is no discrepancy, and it is neither disillusioned nor frightening, this forecast—though not Christian either. It is radiant and desirous:

> be cheerefull Sir,
> Our Reuels now are ended: These our actors
> (As I foretold you) were all Spirits, and
> Are melted into Ayre, into thin Ayre,
> And like the baselesse fabricke of this vision
> The clowd-capt Towres, the gorgeous Pallaces,
> The solemne Temples, the great Globe it selfe,
> Yea, all which it inherit, shall dissolue,
> And like this insubstantiall Pageant faded
> Leaue not a racke behind: we are such stuffe
> As dreames are made on; and our little life
> Is rounded with a sleepe . . .

1962?

PART THREE

King Lear

Project: An Edition of

King Lear

MORE THAN THREE CENTURIES have passed since the only authoritative text of Shakespeare's *King Lear* was published in the folio of 1623, and no adequate critical edition of the play has yet appeared. A great English scholar, W. W. Greg, was able to write in 1940: "There is no disguising the fact that editors have left the textual criticism of *King Lear* in a thoroughly unsatisfactory state; indeed, one is almost tempted to say that no work worth mentioning has hitherto been done on the subject." The reasons for so interesting a situation are as complicated as one would expect. They fall mainly under two heads: the confusing relations and conditions of the early texts; and the principle of eclecticism in Shakespearean editing.

The relevant texts are three. Composed and produced in 1605–6, *King Lear* was first printed in quarto in 1608. This text is a very bad one—mislined, unmetrical, frequently feeble and perfunctory; it was published unquestionably without authorization, and was obtained probably from a "reporter" who attended performances of the play and took down surreptitiously, in shorthand, what he heard. The twelve existing copies of the First Quarto differ from each other in about 150 readings, owing to sheets having been corrected while printing was in progress. A reprint appeared in 1619, the Second Quarto, also without authorization; having access to no new manuscript or auctorial source, it possesses no further authority than its original, the First Quarto. In 1623 *King Lear* was published, under

[*173*]

the supervision of Shakespeare's friends, in the First Folio. This text represents substantially the prompt copy of the play at some undetermined period between 1605 and 1623, and is generally good, although it is in places corrupt and it omits nearly 200 lines (many of them undoubtedly Shakespearean) which occur in the First Quarto. But it appears to have been printed not directly from the prompt book but from a copy of the First Quarto which had been carefully altered to accord with the prompt book. No manuscript of the play being known to survive, these prints are an editor's only materials besides conjecture.

The difficulties faced by editors of *King Lear* have been formidable. Much of the account of the text just given is a result of modern study and some of its details are still disputed; the eighteenth- and nineteenth-century editors worked in half-light. Further difficulties, of which they were largely unaware, can only be suggested. The 1619 quarto, for instance, is fraudulently dated "1608," and the priority of the First Quarto was long unknown. Until recently no one understood exactly the origins and importance of the variants in copies of the First Quarto. It is now clear that agreement in a reading between the folio and the First Quarto, which editors have taken as strong testimony to the reading's correctness, may mean only that whoever prepared a copy of the quarto for the printing of the folio failed to correct an erroneous reading in it; the play is wide open for emendation, and this has not been realized. But there is no doubt, whatever their difficulties, that the editors of *King Lear* would have given us better texts if their principle had not been eclectic. Ignoring the question of the *authority* of the sources of readings, they have taken from the First and Second Quartos and the folio (and from the later folios— reprints—and from each other) whatever readings struck their fancy as "Shakespearean," as Pope corrected Shakespeare's versification. The whim, for example, of a press corrector of the Second Quarto being pirated three years after Shakespeare's death from a copy of the pirated First Quarto has seemed to the editors to present itself for literary judgement as readily and with nearly the same status as a change in that First Quarto text made deliberately, in accordance with the playhouse copy of Shakespeare's company, by or under the superintendence of men who had worked with him and acted his plays for a generation. They have agreed, vaguely, that the 1623 version is on the whole the best, but they have hardly acted even upon this intuition of its superiority. Without the principle of Authority, and until the relations of the early prints were known and the vari- in the quarto copies analyzed, nothing permanent could be accomplished.

Project: An Edition of *King Lear*

If I have now the temerity to propose an edition of *King Lear* where so many masters have failed, it is because for the first time success is possible. The statement I have quoted from W. W. Greg occurs in the final paragraph (p. 190) of his exhaustive study *The Variants in the First Quarto of "King Lear"* [London: Oxford University Press/ The Bibliographical Society, 1940]. He continues, closing: "This (unsatisfactory state) is hardly surprising seeing that the necessary apparatus was not available. I believe that now the whole of the information needed is at the disposal of editors, and it appears to be high time that they set about preparing a text of the play that shall be based upon a properly reasoned estimate of the evidence." Besides Dr. Greg's studies (long essays in 1928 and 1933, the *Variants* monograph of 1940, shorter papers, his summary in the Clark lectures printed in 1942[1]), the most useful contributions to textual theory have been made by P. A. Daniel, A. W. Pollard, E. K. Chambers, Madeleine Doran. Other materials now available are reliable facsimiles of the folio text (supervised by J. D. Wilson, 1931) and the First Quarto (supervised by Dr. Greg, 1939); the *Oxford English Dictionary* and Onions's *Glossary*; Tannenbaum's concise bibliography of *King Lear* (1940); McKerrow's *Prolegomena for the Oxford Shakespeare* (1939) and Greg's *Prolegomena* (1942).[2] Interesting textual comment on particular passages has been accumulating, unused, in the journals and in such books as Leon Kellner's.[3] All this work, some of it contradictory, will need to be checked by study of the prints; but the justification of my editorial procedure I expect to make as little controversial as possible. Into such matters, for example, as the nature of the system of shorthand by which *King Lear* was taken down in 1608, and the origin of several curious readings in the worthless quarto of 1619, I do not plan to enter at length. My principal aim, on the textual side, is simply to establish a text of the play—to recover, so far as science and imagination can, its verbal substance in the form which will depart least from what the author would recognize as his own work. A definitive text—a text, that is, in which every reading will satisfy every scholar—is unattainable; but the general problems of the text are now susceptible of permanent solution; and the establishment of a text at every point responsible and highly probable is a matter now merely of labour and insight.

The basis of my text will be the First Folio. This will need, in the numerous passages which are faulty, to be emended, by the help of an analysis of the First Quarto, familiarity with the methods of the folio editor(s) and with printing methods, linguistic and graphic knowledge. But the authoritative character of the folio text in general is certain to determine a large difference between previous texts of

King Lear and the present one; and lines which occur only in the quarto will be admitted only after a very much more rigid inspection than they have had to pass heretofore. The play will change—how much, I do not know yet. To conservative readers who may object, plausibly, that *King Lear* is quite good enough as it stands, it may be worthwhile to suggest an analogy: the cleaning of a Bruegel: which was sufficiently remarkable with its dirt but hardly what the artist intended or painted—this Shakespeare has too in part to be restored.

For the accidentals of the text: since I first planned to edit the play, in 1937, I have expected to retain Jacobean spelling, pointing, etc.; but after further study last year of several points, I have now almost decided to produce a normalized text. The circumstances of the printing of *King Lear*, which I have described briefly, are unusual, and render it improbable that a shred of Shakespeare's punctuation or spelling or stage direction remains in the folio text. The folio anyway is heavily edited as to these matters, and it is later by nearly a generation than the composition of the play, in a period when practice was changing rapidly. Also, the progress of the new Oxford Shakespeare, part of which was prepared before McKerrow's death and will be issued as soon as the war ends, means that within a very few years an edition which follows closely the early prints in accidentals will be easily accessible. Then the bulk of Shakespeare's readers, who will always want a modernized text, ought to be considered. Finally, I am increasingly impressed by the uncertainty, if not the uselessness, of most attempts to "recover" or "retain" the spelling and pointing and capitalization if any and speech headings and stage directions of an author who seems to have been almost perfectly indifferent to these things and whose manuscripts, if we had them, could certainly not be printed for readers (as distinct from scholars) as they stood. Perhaps I will normalize—retaining however the old forms of certain Elizabethan words and adopting a lighter pointing (as more consistent both with Shakespeare's negligent speed and with first-rate modern usage) than the nineteenth-century editors used.

The new Oxford Shakespeare, which will give relatively full collations, also spares me the temptation to record those variant readings (guesses) which aside from their interest as entertainment or exacerbation serve no purpose except to satisfy an editor's sense of his thoroughness and to interfere needlessly with a reader's confidence in the authenticity of the main text he is reading. Shakespearean scholarship is now old; it ought to get rid of the baggage of Incredible Possibilities which it properly carried during the eighteenth and nineteenth centuries, when all was still in doubt. When McKerrow writes, "I have recorded the readings of the later Folios more because it is customary and on the whole convenient to do so than because of any conviction of their value" (*Prolegomena*, p. 69n), he confesses really to having practised self-indulgence at the expense of the reader's attention. That a conjectural reading has once been suggested which is *possible* (just in the degree that it is possible that Queen Elizabeth wrote Shakespeare's plays) does not justify an editor's asking his reader—and Shakespeare's—to consider it: which is what the editor does when he records it. I plan to record only variants which have a reasonable chance of being right. Like such emendations as are admitted into my text, but in a lesser degree, they must be consistent with an understanding of how the corruption, or possible corruption, in the text came about. The collations and the textual notes—discussing difficult readings and justifying, so far as they can, the text adopted—will appear on each page below the text to which they refer.

COMMENTARY

MY FIRST MAIN PURPOSE in commentary will be to elucidate the text, which is likely to differ a good deal in the end from the received texts and will need at least in its new parts new treatment. Some familiar passages have never been satisfactorily explained. Others have been explained only in remote corners of unread books and dead magazines—material which wants sifting, condensing, assembling for readers of the play. Elucidation takes two principal forms, answering two questions: *What does the text mean?* and *What is happening?* Notes answering the first question will deal with Shakespeare's language, grammar, phrasing, imagery, reference, symbolism. Notes answering the second will deal with the events of the play, with locality and time, with action on the stage (both Shakespeare's and the modern stage), with other theatrical matter when necessary, with character when necessary; the general interests of Bradley and Granville-Barker, among modern critics, will define this range. Both kinds of explanatory notes will appear with the textual notes below the lines of text on the page; there will be no separate glossary. A reader, when he wants a *question* answered, wants it answered at once.

With broader literary or aesthetic interpretation—my second purpose—the case is different; a reader interested in such notes knows the play already, and they can be printed together at the end of the volume. Criticism of the play's structure, style, imaginative design, essential struggle, essential meaning—at present scattered—can there be ordered and made accessible. I do not plan an omnibus like

H. H. Furness's *New Variorum* edition of 1880. I expect to find the criticism of *King Lear* which is of the first order for penetration and justice and power can be brought into a reasonable compass. The space which Furness expended in his desire to represent the history of Shakespearean taste and opinion, and which W. J. Craig, for instance in his Arden edition, expended in a mass of illustrative quotations, will be saved for such things as the remarks of Coleridge—to my mind the greatest of all Shakespearean critics—whose writings on Shakespeare were for the first time intelligently collected in 1930. How many readers of *King Lear* will buy or look out in libraries for those astonishing and expensive volumes? Between the monster of Furness and the admirable bare small editions done for the Clarendon Press by G. S. Gordon (unluckily he did not reach *Lear*) there is a middle ground in commentary which I mean to find and explore.

The Introduction will consist of five sections: (1) general; (2) textual; (3) the date of composition; (4) Shakespeare's literary sources for the play, with some account of their unimportance and their treatment by him; (5) the stage history of *King Lear*. I may include a short discussion of the Elizabethan playhouses and of Shakespeare's English. One matter usually ignored in editions of single plays I intend to treat at length: Shakespeare's situation and his thought, his life, during the years immediately preceding the composition of *King Lear* in 1605–6.

1944

Textual Introduction

THE HYPOTHESIS

IT WILL BE WELL IF THE READER can discard from the outset the notion that there is in existence *a* text of *King Lear* which we shall be discussing. There was once, certainly, such a text, but it is lost. All we have are two widely different texts, a quarto of 1608 and the folio of 1623, as witnesses to it. They report, with upward of 1,200 serious variations, an event—Shakespeare's manuscript—which both of them have witnessed (at whatever remove) and we have not; what we have to do is to weigh their testimony, in order to reconstruct in its light the lost and important event of 1605–6. They call it indeed by different names—in Q it is *The Historie of King Lear*, in F (more accurately) *The Tragedie of King Lear*[1]—and this is interesting. But there is no reason to doubt that it is the same event and a single event. Shakespeare, so far as my evidence goes, never touched the text after handing either his "foul" papers or a fair copy of them to the book keeper (prompter) of his company. The play underwent alteration of many kinds, including deletion and interpolation, by other hands, as we shall see clearly enough; but it suffered no structural changes, and neither of the texts shows anything that should be called literary revision. Where Q and F differ, one is certainly corrupt; or both are.

Before hearing testimony, we may examine briefly the meagre external evidence as to the character of the witnesses. It speaks unequivocally for the folio. Pollard's classic and necessarily over-simplified defence in 1909 of the "good" quartos of Shakespeare's plays [*Shakespeare Folios and Quartos*, London: Methuen, 1909], which were printed from his manuscripts, has obscured the fact that they appeared during a very short time and then ceased. During 1597–1600 appeared eight "good" quartos, and these are all that were ever published, with four exceptions: the doubtfully Shakespearean *Titus Andronicus* earlier (1594); a Second Quarto of *Hamlet* (1605), issued specifically to replace the pirated and abbreviated text of 1603; a print of *Troilus and Cressida* (1609) prefaced with the publisher's boast that the play was now given to the public against, not by, "the grand possessors' wills" (i.e., the King's Men's); and much later, *Othello* (1622), released after the folio had begun printing. After 1600 the King's Men withheld Shakespeare's work from publication: in twenty years thereafter only two of his numerous and very acceptable plays reached print in obviously "good" texts. From these two, no generalization can reach *Lear*. Of course *King Lear* in 1608 may be exceptional also, and my point here is that whether its text proves on inspection to be good or bad, it *is* exceptional. Neither its registration on November 26, 1607, nor its licensing by Buc says anything to its authenticity[2]; and the men who registered the copy say something against it. John Busby the Elder had already assisted in the pirating of *Henry V* (1600) and *The Merry Wives of Windsor* (1602). Nathaniel Butter, who had been in business only four years, was the first publisher impudent enough to claim flatly as Shakespeare's a play of still unknown authorship, the unregistered *London Prodigal* of 1605, and had brought out in the same year the corrupt, surreptitious edition of Thomas Heywood's *If You Know Not Me, You Know Nobody* (Part One) of which more will be heard later. An unpromising pair. The folio of 1623, on the other hand, was under the superintendence of Shakespeare's only surviving associates in the King's Men, whom he had remembered in his will, John Heminge and Henry Condell (Burbage having died in 1619). Their sense of responsibility is attested by their insistence thrice in the prefatory matter on their "care" in perfecting the texts.[3] They had access to the playhouse manuscripts, and I may anticipate a little to say that in the preparation of F *Lear* they clearly used one. Which way the critic's initial confidence reasonably inclines is obvious. Nevertheless, the folio cuts several hundred lines out of *King Lear*, introduces extensive and inferior minor variation in *Troilus and Cressida*, and fails to make use of the faulty but magnificent Second Quarto of *Hamlet*. We had better hear the witnesses themselves:

Here is Q at its not uncharacteristic worst:

Lear. Ile tell thee, life and death! I am asham'd that thou hast
power to shake my manhood thus, that these hot teares that
breake from me perforce should make the worst blasts and fogs
vpon the vntented woundings of a fathers cursse, pierce euery
sence about the old fond eyes, beweepe this cause againe, ile
pluck you out, & you cast with the waters that you make to
temper clay, yea, i'st come to this? yet haue I left a daughter,
whom I am sure is kind and comfortable, when shee shall heare
this of thee, with her nailes shee'l flea thy woluish visage, thou
shalt find that ile resume the shape, which thou dost thinke I
haue cast off for euer, thou shalt I warrant thee.

Gon. Doe you marke that my Lord?

Duke. I cannot bee so partiall *Gonorill* to the great loue I
beare you,

Gon. Come sire no more, you, more knaue then foole, after your
master?

The first thing to observe of this farrago is that the printing is abom-
inable. (In half the twelve copies of the quarto extant it is even worse,
for the compositor first set up "vntender" for "vntented" and "peruse"
for "pierce"; the press reader altered them by reference to the copy.
This variation occurs in about 150 readings scattered through seven
of Q's ten sheets, the sheets printed off before the corrections were
made being not destroyed but bound up indiscriminately with corrected sheets.) Nicholas Okes, who printed *King Lear* for Nathaniel
Butter, was a young man who had become a master printer only some
eighteen months before, on April 19, 1606. That he could do good
work this early is shown by his careful prints for Butter in 1607 of
John Pelling's *A Sermon of the Providence of God* and Dekker and
Wilkins's *Jests to Make You Merry*. But like other printers he was
careless with plays. His printing of Ben Jonson's *The Case Is Alter'd*
in 1609 is called "vile" by the Oxford editors, "a rare example of a
Jonson text which may be described as thoroughly bad."[4] The criteria
of a Jonson editor, however, are bound to appear somewhat unreal
to a Shakespearean; the 1609 quarto exhibits nothing in any way
comparable with the passage I have quoted or with dozens of others
in *Lear* and the page on which this occurs (D2ᵛ) is faultier than the
whole of *The Case Is Alter'd*. In fact, the comparison suggests forcibly
that the copy from which Okes was printing *King Lear* must have
presented a singular appearance: illegible, confused, perhaps quite
unpunctuated and undivided.[5]

The real comparison is with the folio, but a word first about pointing and line division. The punctuation or unpunctuation of the passage is perfectly characteristic of Q throughout; stops other than commas are very rare, the commas are as likely to be wrong as right, and sentences are jumbled together (thrice here) in such a way as to produce absolute incoherence. This is so far as I know without parallel in dramatic texts and cannot be due to the compositor—that is, the deficiency cannot be; if the copy had no points at all, no doubt he supplied those we find, such as they are. To argue that the pointing of Shakespeare's manuscripts was light and perhaps defective (as undoubtedly from time to time it was) will not do; the "good" quartos are punctuated as *Lear* is not. Moreover, although the passage is plainly verse, it is printed as prose. Now, all the early Shakespearean prints show some mislineation, and several, in other respects excellent, show a good deal; but Q is not in other respects excellent, or even passable, and its mislineation is altogether exceptional. This passage is part of the more than 500 lines of verse which, widely scattered, are printed in Q as prose—one-quarter of all the verse in *King Lear*. Nearly 400 more lines of verse are misdivided in Q, much of it crazily; and about 60 lines of prose are divided as verse. Less than two-thirds of the verse in the play, that is, appears correctly divided in Q. With this chaos may be compared *Macbeth* in the folio, according to the Cambridge editors "one of the worst printed of all the plays, especially as regards the metre"; only some 90 lines are wrongly divided to the end of III.ii, and half a dozen thereafter, or 100 in all out of 1,800 verse lines, against *Lear*'s 900 out of 2,400 verse lines. It is impossible to suppose that Okes's compositor had in front of him a copy correctly lined.[6]

A few lines will illustrate the more reasonable character of F:

Lear. Ile tell thee:/Life and death, I am asham'd[7]
    That thou hast power to shake my manhood thus,
    That these hot teares, which breake from me perforce
    Should make thee worth them./Blasts and Fogges vpon thee:
    Th'vntented woundings of a Fathers curse
    Pierce euerie sense about thee. Old fond eyes,
    Beweepe this cause againe, Ile plucke ye out,
    And cast you with the waters that you loose
    To temper clay.

It is well punctuated, rightly divided, and coherent. The nature of the copy it represents is hardly in doubt. While Q's omission of thirty-five passages removes only 100 lines, appearing to be mainly inadvertent, the same number of omissions in F (thirty-seven passages) remove nearly 300 lines, including one whole scene, IV.iii, and they must be due mainly to theatrical cutting. F's stage directions are full (although not elaborate or descriptive), definite, and business-like; entrances tend to be marked early, noises and essential action (*Stocks brought out. Killes him*) are called for, in the way we have learnt to expect from prompt copy.[8] F represents the prompt book.[9] This is what its provenance also would indicate; the copy for it was supplied to Haggard by Heminge and Condell from the playhouse.

It is a surprising fact of great importance, however, that F was not printed directly from the prompt book or even from a transcript of it. F was printed from a copy of the quarto which had been heavily corrected in order to bring it more or less into accord with the prompt book. Full evidence for this will be set forth presently; here it will be sufficient to adduce a single line of proof, probably in itself conclusive, based on the variations which, as I have mentioned, copies of Q exhibit owing to the corrections made while certain sheets were passing through the press. P. A. Daniel discovered long ago[10] that at V.iii.47 [K4ᵛ; TLN 2990] F reproduces an error of the original state of Q, which reads:

> *Bast.* Sir I thought it fit,
> To saue the old and miserable King to some retention,
> Whose age has charmes in it, whose title more (&c.)

The press corrector deciphered "send," which the compositor had misread "saue," and added to "to some retention" the missing half-line, "and appointed guard." F corrects "saue" also, but it omits "and appointed guard" and has the same impossible long line as Qa.[11] Conversely, Dr. W. W. Greg, advancing independently in 1933 an emendation proposed by Kellner some years earlier (*Restoring Shakespeare*, p. 73), used it to show that the folio reading in I.iv.366 [D2ᵛ; TLN 867] is based on a sophistication in the corrected state of Q. Qa reads: "y'are much more alapt want of wisedome, then praise for harmfull mildnes." Qb inserts "for" after "alapt" and reads "attaskt," though it does nothing about the misreading "praise." F prints as verse, reads "prais'd," retains the "for," but changes "attaskt" to "at task." Dr. Greg writes: "Behind 'alapt' must, on recognized graphic grounds, have been the word 'ataxt'; and *atax'd*, i.e. taxed, is even better in the context than *attask'd*, i.e. taken to task, though as a matter of fact neither word is otherwise recorded. Thus 'attaskt' is a ghost word invented by the press-reader, and when the folio editor or compositor further emended it to 'at task,' he proved that he had before him a corrected sheet of the Quarto, since the word had no other existence."[12]

Postponing enquiry into the striking editorial bearing of this relation between Q and F, I note, returning to our passage, that the discovery that F was set up from an altered copy of the quarto tells us something important about its variants from Q. The bulk of them must be assumed to be deliberate and to represent *a playhouse condemnation of Q*, both in general as a text and in the particular readings altered. We shall find, I think, that this statement will have to undergo a good deal of qualification later, but at present it should have all possible emphasis. It applies with uncertain force to minor variation for which a compositor might be responsible, such as F "which" for "that" (320) and "ye" for "you" (324); and Q's "the worst," "vpon the vntented," "about the old," and "you cast" are recognizable corruptions as soon as we compare them with F (though the passage would tax a Porson if we did not possess F). But F's substitution of the superior reading "lose" for a Q reading "make," not clearly wrong in itself, is a clear condemnation. Where did "make" come from? It may be a scribe's or a compositor's recollection of "make" four lines above, it may be a scribe's or a compositor's unconscious substitution, or it may be due to some other agency. Let us call it a *substantial variant*, excluding from the class of variants which it represents all readings which do not "make sense of a sort," all exclamations, all abbreviations, differences in singular and plural, grammatical variants, omissions, and additions large and small, differences in assignment of speeches, etc. Now it is as well known that scribes and compositors do produce substantial variants as it should be recognized that there is probably some limit to the *number* of substantial variants which they can be expected to produce in a text of a given length—in the number, that is, which can reasonably be attributed to them. Thus the editor of *Hamlet*, Professor Dover Wilson, lists more than 1,300 differences "of any importance" between the Second Quarto (representing Shakespeare's manuscript) and the folio (representing the prompt book), but only 144 of these, which he calls "Variants Proper," are candidates for the class I am calling substantial variants, and some of these belong to classes which I have excluded from consideration in *Lear*, as his figure 1,300 includes several hundred readings which would not be taken into account by my "upward of 1,200 serious variations" for *Lear*.[13] The parallel text of *Hamlet* is also much longer than *King Lear*'s. Yet *Lear* shows some 350 substantial variants between Q and F.

This is an astonishing figure: thrice *Hamlet*'s relatively. The origin of a given substantial variant is likely to remain uncertain studied by itself, as we saw in "make:loose," but so large a body of variation ought to reveal patterns of origin to critical scrutiny. Let me continue the parallel analysis. For Q's "yea, i'st come to this? [I.iv.326] yet haue I left a daughter" F has

> Ha? Let it be so.
> I haue another daughter.

"Ha" is evidently a variant for "yea,"[14] written in the margin by the playhouse scribe who corrected a copy of the quarto to serve for F, but "Let it be so" can hardly be a variant for "i'st come to this," since it depends on the Q phrase for its meaning. Similarly, a transition is lacking between "this?" and the following sentence in Q, which the F phrase supplies. Moreover, both phrases are necessary metrically. No doubt the folio compositor's eye, moving from the deleted "yea" out to the margin of Q, returned to the wrong place. The reason for Q's omission is less clear for the moment. But where did Q's "yet haue I left a daughter" come from? It must be connected with Lear's use of the phrase (in both Q and F) fifty lines earlier in the scene, at I.iv.276. This is too remote to have influenced the Q compositor; nor is it easy to see a scribe, about to copy the straightforward "I haue another daughter," altering it thus in obedience to so distant a parallel. It is impossible not to suspect some other agency, and the obvious agent is the actor of the part.[15]

The end of the passage I have quoted from Q runs thus in F:

> Thou shalt finde,
> That Ile resume that shape which thou dost thinke
> I haue cast off for euer.
>
> (*Exit*)
>
> Gon. Do you marke that?
> Alb. I cannot be so partiall, *Gonerill*,
> To the great loue I beare you.
> Gon. Pray you content. What *Oswald*, hoa?
> You Sir, more Knaue then Foole, after your Master.

Knight (1841) was the first editor deliberately to omit the additions in Q, Lear's "thou shalt I warrant thee"; and Goneril's "my Lord," but Knight had more completely even than Alexander Schmidt a simpleminded faith in F which makes it doubtful whether his individual readings represent critical judgement or only the application of a formula. To Dr. Greg belongs the credit of recognizing these for what they look like, actors' connective phrases, which at once dilute the substance and destroy the verse structure. A scribe or compositor is hardly likely to have produced them. Again one suspects the actors, and I think the two streams of complicated corruption that meet in line 236 will serve as a formal indictment.

For "Pray you content" Q reads "Come sir no more"—both paraphrase and addition. I am interested in the addition. *This is the third time in the present scene that F had deleted "Come sir" at the beginning of a speech in Goneril's part.* Both here and in line 258 the phrase is connected with an omission of "sir" a little later by Q, and is so implausible that even the Cambridge editors (who preserve on principle everything occurring in either text) excluded it. At 240 and 258 it is unmetrical. In all three passages it dilutes Goneril's abrupt severity, and in all three it must be interpolated.[16]

The other stream, although less conclusive, is even more suggestive. Q omits "What *Oswald*, hoa?" here, but has it at 356, where according to F Goneril says, "How now Oswald?" F is proved right by the form of "*Oswald*, I say" at 350 in an intervening passage omitted in Q. Shakespeare had his restless Goneril call for the steward directly her father departs, but delayed Oswald so that she and Albany would have time for the first of their pleasant conversations; the delay emphasizes her impatience and is besides a piece of Shakespearean verisimilitude, like Caesar's deafness. Whether the boy actor of the part, not understanding, consciously ignored the first call and transferred (necessarily) its phrasing, or simply forgot it, cannot be known. The extraordinary fact that in Q Oswald replies at 356 with a "Here Madam" (rightly condemned by editors) perhaps suggests that Goneril forgot. What I wish to emphasize is that this sort of corruption can scarcely be attributed to transcripts and prints.[17]

Can Goneril's *Come sir's*? We should have to suppose that some combination of scribe and compositor supplied the phrase thrice, and thrice only in the whole play, at the beginnings of speeches by a single character in a single scene. It will be a hardy critic who can reconcile himself to this, and an ignorant critic who supposes that an author like Shakespeare writes thus or revises thus. I propose to take the plain course, and imagine that we have to do with the actor of the part—the same actor who in this and the preceding scene vulgarized Shakespeare's accurate verbs "condemn" and "distaste" equally into the vague "dislike" (I.iv.356, I.iii.14).

Let me assemble some other evidence of the same kind. When Lear has "that shee may feele, that she may feele" extrametrically at I.iv.309 for the single phrase in F, we may remember that compositors sometimes set up a phrase twice; but when he has also "I would not be mad" twice unmetrically at I.v.51 (at the same time wrecking a line by omitting a repetition of "not mad"), the explanation of printing for either passage is much feebler; and when I report that these are the only such phrases repeated in the whole text, we are thrown I think straight onto the actor. Some accumulation of evidence is necessary to exclude alternative explanations.

Lear's part is naturally richest in it, being the longest, and Burbage as the principal actor in a repertory company having a memory sorely taxed. Thus, in I.i, when Q [B1ᵛ] gives him "Confirming" (41) and "confirm'd" (84), wrongly, for F "Conferring" and "conferr'd," it cannot be accidental that both errors anticipate his "confirme" at 140, the only occurrence of the verb in the play.[18] Inserting "How," unmetrically before line 92, he anticipates 96, "How, how Cordelia?" (F[TLN 100]), where in Q he has only "Goe to, goe to" [B2]—sounding, as Dr. Greg observes, more like Polonius than himself.[19] This "Goe, to, goe to" he inserts unmetrically again before "Better thou" in 236; as "Why," before I.v.17, III.ii.18, III.iv.105, "Well" before I.i.110, "Now" before II.iv.221 and after 239. At I.i.165 for F "Miscreant" he has "recreant," anticipating 170, where he omits the word. At II.iv.160 his impossible "No" for "Never" anticipates his 172. At I.i.40 his feeble variant "of our state" for the final phrase in F's line. "To shake all Cares and Businesse from our Age" clearly anticipates ("care" being the memorial nexus) his phrase at 51, "Cares of State."[20] At I.iv.311 for F's "Away, away" he repeats his phrase "goe, goe, my people" from 294. Anticipation and recollection are not confined within a scene. When in "Thou old, vnhappy Traitor" Q substitutes "most vnhappy" (Oswald's part, IV.vi.232), the vulgarization may or may not be due to the actor, influenced by "most happy" two lines above, but when in Lear's "Ile talke a word with this same lerned Theban" Q substitutes "most learned" (III.iv.162), the only reasonable explanation is that the actor has been influenced by his phrase "most learned Iustice" two scenes later (III.vi.23 Q, F absent). Burbage's memory failures led sometimes to loss, sometimes to expansion. The most disastrous instance in the part is one cited by Dr. Greg, I.i.84–87, where for F's

> Now our Ioy,
> Although our last and least; whose yong loue,
> The Vines of France, and Milke of Burgundie,
> Striue to be interest
>
> [TLN 88–91]

Q has merely

> But now our ioy,
> Although the last, not least in our deere loue [.]
>
> [B2ʳ]

Shakespeare in his mature work much more frequently alludes to proverbs, or develops and transforms them, than he quotes them; the dramatization of "To put the cart before the horse" as "the Cart drawes the Horse" at I.iv.244 and the savage alteration of "Bray a fool in a mortar, &c." to "tread this vnboulted villaine into mortar, &c." at II.ii.72 are characteristic. Here, in a most moving phrase for Cordelia, he is adapting the proverb he used directly when Antony was addressing Trebonius, "Though last, not least in loue" (*Julius Caesar*, III.i.89). Actors, however, and many editors, do not make these distinctions; as readers correct an obvious misprint without "seeing" it, actors revert to the form with which they are familiar, and they so revert *four times* in the quarto of *King Lear*, twice in Kent's part and twice in Lear's.[21] But in returning in this passage to the proverbial phrasing, Burbage lost syntax; so that he had no vehicle to take him into France and Burgundy, and forgot them.[22] A similar levelling process thirty lines earlier transformed his author's "(Where Nature) doth with merit Challenge" into his "doth most challenge it." In a line, II.iv.225, "Or rather a disease that's in my flesh," his dilution of "that's in" to "that lies within" extracts the nerve from the verse in a way characteristic of actors.[23] More striking still is his expansion of the metrical "Ha! Waking?" into "sleeping, or wake-/ing; ha! sure" (I.iv.249). Now and then his memory for the form of Shakespeare's verse broke down altogether. The nervous, passionate line "Oh me my heart! My rising heart! But downe" appears in Q simply as "O my heart, my heart" (II.iv.122).[24]

The other actors did better on the whole (so far as we can trust Q, and F's correction of it—a matter to which I shall return), but a few citations will show them responsible for the same kind of debasement as Burbage's. Confronted at I.ii.10 with a line which runs in F (correcting "Barstadie" and inserting a comma):

Textual Introduction

Edmund produced something very like the line of Burbage's just quoted: "Why brand they vs with base, base bastardie?"[25] The actor of Kent lost his syntax at the end of III.i, much as Burbage did after "last, not least." The passage is well written, but like most of these I have been quoting, not easy to remember precisely:

> . . . That wen we haue found the King, in which your pain
> That wa, Ile this: He that first lights on him,
> Hollas the other.

After "King" and before "He," Q has only "Ile this way you that." Anticipations are common. Edmund's "further" ("other" F) at I.ii.95 *might* be a printer's anticipation of his "further" in 101; but Cornwall's "offence" ("fault" F) in II.ii.96, anticipating his "offence" twenty-five lines later, hardly can be explained so, and his "This is a fellow" (for F's necessary "some fellow" II.ii.101), his "This is a fellow" (opening a speech also) forty lines later, cannot at all. Nor can Regan's verb "slacke" in "scant her dutie" (F II.iv.142), anticipating her "slacke" in line 248. The fact that Oswald, and Oswald alone, twice in different scenes has "Yes Madam" for the folio's "I Madam" might in another text perhaps be counted coincidence (I.iii.3, I.iv.358); but I think the assumption of coincidence is altogether inadequate to account even for the selection of evidence already assembled,[26] much less for the body of variation this represents.

A final class of debased variants in Q is susceptible, I believe, of only one explanation. Lear in the folio allots Kent "Fiue dayes" for provision and tells him to leave on the "sixt." In Q this is "Foure dayes" and "fift" (I.i.176, 178)—variants which may be thought indifferent until we remember that F is printed from a copy of the quarto corrected to bring it into accord with the prompt book, and that every such change must be presumed deliberate. I take these to be unconscious substitutions: by an actor, because neither a scribe nor a compositor would have the same motive (dramatic sense) to preserve consistency between his substitutions. But in the other three variants of the class there is a clear motive for change. When Shakespeare gave the Fool "there's not a nose among twenty, but can smell him that's stinking," Armin evidently thought the number inadequate, and Q reads, "there's not a nose among a 100," etc. (II.iv.71).[27]

A more dramatic alteration of the same kind occurs in Kent's part (II.ii.64), when he explains why a tailor made Oswald:

> . . . a Stone-cutter, or a Painter, could not haue made
> him so ill, though they had bin but two yeares
> oth'trade.
>
> [TLN 1128–33]

Dr. Greg's comment is accurate: "This is sober sense: Shakespeare knows that art is long. But to the actor and to the groundling two years seems an age: so the quarto substitutes 'two hours,' which is absurd."[28] Even Gloucester, who, on the evidence of Q, departed less from his lines than any other major character, was subject to this theatrical exaggeration, and the fifth variant, which is his (II.iv.305), shows the tendency at its logical conclusion. He is protesting the King's being shut out in the night and storm, and was to add:

> for many Miles about
> There's scarce a Bush.

But even a few bushes, one bush, he felt too many, and Q reads: "ther's not a bush."

What conclusions are to be drawn from all this evidence? I think two.

1. Our initial, slight bias in favour of F, on external evidence, has been justified and greatly extended. In corroboration, a word may be said about the so-called indifferent variants generally. Since the re-action against the uncritical methods of eighteenth- and nineteenth-century editors (their tendency, in Greg's phrase, to treat variant readings as if they were counters in a guessing game) set firmly in, critics have tended to deny that taste is able to make distinctions which as a matter of fact it certainly can make. The denial represents in some, of course, only the human propensity to deny to others the powers which one does not feel in oneself, but in most critics and bibliographers it represents I think an honest doubt that such powers exist; so that it is worth saying plainly and emphatically that they do. To a man sensitive to poetic and dramatic effects, widely and exactly familiar with Shakespeare's plays and with Elizabethan usage gener-ally, and willing to work hard and long with Schmidt's *Lexicon*, Bart-lett's *Concordance*, and Abbott's and Franz's grammars, the number of variants which can properly be called indifferent is very small. For instance, in Edgar's great lines

The Gods are just, and of our pleasant vices
Make instruments to plague vs
(V.iii.170–71)

the Q variant "scourge" would by most critics be thought indifferent, and in fact it was preferred by Theobald, Warburton, Johnson, Capell, and Steevens; but there is no doubt whatever, despite our uncertainty as to where it came from, that it is wrong. Compare III.iv.69 and the characteristic union in Shakespeare (e.g., *Timon* IV.iii.108–10, *Coriolanus* IV.ii.11–12) of the concepts "plague" and "just punishment"; contrast the use of "scourge" in I.ii.115 and the absence of this association in other occurences of the verb—Clarence's powerful lines in *Richard III* (I.iv.50–51) cannot serve for parallel against this array. Now in the overwhelming majority, among 350 substantial variants in *King Lear*, of what are usually called "indifferent" variants, F is similarly supported by critical scrutiny.

2. The inferiority or debasement in the quarto has displayed patterns and a character which make it difficult—I would say impossible—to avoid the conclusion that the actors of the parts were a major agency in its production.

Q is thus a reported text—a text which stands at some non-manuscript, *memorial* remove from Shakespeare's text. At some stage of transmission it has passed through memory, the memories of actors. It is time to state that in adopting this hypothesis, we have luckily the highest authority. Advanced originally by Alexander Schmidt in 1879,[29] the theory of reporting as Q's origin was revived by Sir Edmund Chambers in 1930 [*William Shakespeare: A Study of Facts and Problems*] and has been accepted and reinforced by Dr. W. W. Greg in a series of discussions (1933, 1940, 1942) which have constituted until now almost our whole knowledge of the text of *King Lear*.[30] "Authority" is an ambiguous concept in textual criticism, and I have therefore refrained from invoking it while we were examining the evidence for ourselves. But the coincidence in this judgement of the two living critics most experienced and best qualified to form a reasoned opinion in such matters must be allowed considerable weight.

We have now to consider the much more speculative and less important question of how the actors of the parts could have been reported, how the copy for Q, in short, came into existence. I say "less important" because so long as there are several ways in which the actors *might* have been reported, a decision as to the way in which they probably *were* reported is obviously inferior in consequence to the general hypothesis, here adopted, of memorial-theatrical provenance for the quarto. If we could think of *no* way, we might hesitate to trust our sense that actors were an agency, but fortunately this is not our case. The qualification "much more speculative" needs a word of comment also. Most textual study, like most historical study, is essentially speculative, in that demonstration in the laboratory sense is usually out of the question. But "speculative" is a comparative term. How competently an unknown man three centuries ago could employ an unknown system of shorthand is a subject very different from the three interpolated *Come sir*'s in *Goneril*'s part in I.iv. One is a matter of inescapably divergent opinion; the other is a textual *fact* for which there is probably an explanation, widely acceptable, lying within range of the enquiring mind. I should say that our investigation so far has not been *very* speculative. Before entering the realm of opinion, I want to develop our hypothesis a little, and enter a caveat against it.

The most direct way for the actors to be reported would be for them to report themselves, and it is important to know that this is not plausible in Q. The curious mislineation and pointing tell heavily against it. But it is Q's auditory errors that are decisive. "Haue" is misheard for "of" and "of" for "haue" in the lines "Shall *of* a Corne cry woe" (III.ii.34) and "Why should a Dog, a Horse, a Rat *haue* life" (V.iii.306). "A Dogg's obey'd in Office" [TLN 2602–3; IV.vi.163] appears as "a dogge, so bade in office." In "Striuing to better, oft we marre what's well" (TLN 870; I.iv.369), "oft" was misheard as "ought" and the comma placed after it.[31] Others are almost equally certain: Q has "in sight" for "incite" [TLN 2379], "dialogue" for "dialect," "may know" for "make knowne," "threatning" for "thredding," "with the" for "we the" (IV.iv.27, II.ii.125, I.i.229, II.i.121, V.iii.185), and other nonsense readings much more reasonably explained as mishearings than in any other way.[32]

The fact established, it seems likely that some at least of Q's sixty-odd errors in singular and plural are due to the same cause, and that some of its implausible misreadings and misprints are best explained so. Madeleine Doran tries (p. 125) to explain these mishearings as due to the compositor, either setting from dictation or unconsciously substituting (as he memorized his copy) words of similar sound. But authorities on early printing are doubtful whether setting from dictation was practised at all,[33] and the ubiquitous mis*readings* (often senseless, e.g., "mou't" for "noble") in Q rule it out altogether as an explanation. Memorial sound substitution, on the other hand, certainly occurs, and is found even in F[34]; but it is extremely infrequent—one may read half a dozen plays without finding one—and quite incapable of accounting for what Miss Doran calls a "small number" but is actually a very large number of auditory errors in Q. Actors reporting themselves would not produce them. We extend our hypothesis to include a person whom I shall call the reporter and take to be the direct means of reporting the actors.

Let me recapitulate. The quarto is a memorial-theatrical version of the play, taken by a reporter and based on acting; the copy was extremely illegible, and the condition of its line division and pointing is very dubious; it was treated by the compositor (and press reader, as we shall discover) as few books have been treated. At some time between 1608 and 1623 a copy of it was extensively corrected by a playhouse scribe to bring it into agreement with the prompt book at the Globe, and was then used by Jaggard as copy for the folio.

My caveat is against F. On this hypothesis, authority rests with F, except where it is obviously in error, and the priests of the temple on both sides of the Atlantic may be expected to treat even its errors with reverence. I repeat that the present study is interested in Q and in F only insofar as they are witnesses to a *lost original*. Scepticism is the critic's sharpest weapon, and to any reader inclined at this point or later to spend his scepticism wholly upon Q, I recommend study of what F made of the quarto's "Mastife, grayhoud, mungril, grim-houd or spaniel, brach or him, Bobtaile tike, or trudletaile" (III.vi.71–73):

> Mastife, Grey-hound, Mongrill, Grim,
> Hound or Spaniell, Brache, or Hym:
> Or Bobtaile tight, or Troudle taile . . .[35]

THE METHOD OF REPORTING

SO FAR WE HAVE BEEN LOOKING at the quarto from the point of view of a sound text, and we found it very bad. But we have now to study it as a "report," and from this point of view it is very good indeed. It contains practically the whole play; it contains no, or almost no, non-Shakespearean matter; it is, on the whole, remarkably even in the apparent quality of its reporting; and, with one exception,[36] it does not displace even speeches, much less sections of dialogue or scenes.

It is thus sharply to be distinguished from the Elizabethan texts universally recognized as reports. There are six such quartos of Shakespeare's plays (2 and 3 *Henry VI*, *Romeo and Juliet* Q1, *Henry V*, *The Merry Wives of Windsor*, *Hamlet* Q1), ranging in date from 1594 to 1603, and differing greatly in quality but alike in that they are incomplete, heavily interpolated, uneven, and jumbled. These are "memorial reconstructions"; and this, I agree with W. W. Greg, "the quarto of *Lear* emphatically is not."[37] What then *is* Q?

Two theories not absolutely implausible have been advanced to explain it. The first considers it a report of an actual performance, taken by shorthand. This was suggested by Schmidt in 1879 and then forgotten, except for an interesting unpublished M.A. dissertation of 1914 [*Evidence of Stenographic Work in the First Quarto of "King Lear"*] by Harrison McJohnston,[38] until Chambers mentioned it as a possibility in 1930. Since then it has received a good deal of attention, principally from Dr. J. Q. Adams and Dr. Oskar Stössel, who support it, and Miss Madeleine Doran, who opposes it.[39] Unfortunately, most of the discussion has centered on the earliest of the three shorthand systems known to have been published in England before the date of *King Lear*: Timothy Bright's Charactery (1588). This primitive, non-phonetic system, and Peter Bales's very similar Brachygraphy (1590), may be conveniently studied in a series of expert articles[40] by W. Matthews, who believes both impracticable for play reporting—an opinion shared by Chambers and Greg. Bright gave fixed symbols or "characters" to some 550 common words,[41] and these had to be memorized; all other words had to be expressed as synonyms (and "appellatives") or antonyms of the "Characticall words," by prefixing or suffixing to a character the initial letter of the word intended. Bales's basic signs were different, the letters of the Italian hand but surrounded by diacritical marks in various positions, they produced 530 Brachygraphy words nearly the same as Bright's, and were then similarly qualified by a downstroke or initial to right or left to express all other words.[42] The details are unimportant, since I think there is no likelihood whatever that either system was used to report *King Lear*. It is evident that both would give rise to a characteristic error, namely, synonyms beginning with the same letter as the correct word. Actors, scribes, and compositors can also produce this error, but they could hardly be expected to do so regularly, and if a very large percentage of Q's synonymous variants did so begin, we would be justified, I consider, in deciding that either Bright's or Bales's shorthand had been employed. We find in fact nothing of the sort. The enquiry is perforce uncertain, because what for one critic is a synonym will not be for another (nor even a variant), and decisions have to be guided where possible by Bright's inadequate directions; synonyms like "taske:tax," which appear to have been regarded as alternative forms of one word, have slight evidential value; the Q variant must not of course be clearly right[43]; and a good many are much more plausibly explained in another—as Goneril's "*d*islike:*d*istaste" is weakened for this purpose by her "*d*islike:condemne." But when less than a third of the hundred-odd synonymous variants wrong in the quarto are found to begin with the same letter as the folio's (and shorthand, frankly, cannot critically be supposed responsible for half even of these), Charactery and Brachygraphy have forfeited their only claim to our attention. A radically different and evidently much better system, John Willis's Stenography, was published in 1602, and I will return to this.

The second theory has no such history of investigation, being based upon D. L. Patrick's demonstration (1936) that the 1597 quarto of *Richard III* must be a communal memorial reconstruction by the actors, finding themselves without a prompt book while on a provincial tour.[44] Dr. G. I. Duthie has suggested recently that a similar hypothesis might be adopted for the *Lear* quarto, assuming dictation to a scribe in order to account for mislineation and mispointing.[45]

Both theories, it will be noticed, involve a reporter and the actors, and from my point of view—the editorial point of view—are nearly identical. The King's Men dictating their parts to an authorized scribe are in effect performing the play, as the King's Men playing before James are in effect (according to the shorthand theory) dictating their parts to a reporter scribbling surreptitiously in the audience. Whether the Q version was obtained by the reporter legally, that is, does not matter critically. It doesn't even matter critically whether John Busby and Nathaniel Butter obtained their copy legally or not. Of the memorial reconstruction of *Richard III*, Dr. Greg says that the actors, on their return to London, "would have no further use for the improvised prompt-book: it may have gone astray, or it may have been deliberately sold for publication, perhaps with the idea of forestalling piracy, a fate that overtook *Romeo and Juliet* the same year."[46] Nevertheless I think it will be best to assume that Butter published *King Lear* in 1608 without authorization, because the assumption has consequences for the theories we are weighing and because the evidence appears to require it. After 1600, as I have said, the King's Men withheld Shakespeare's plays from publication[47]; except for Q2 *Hamlet*, released in 1604 to replace a pirated text, and the very late *Othello* of 1622; only *King Lear* and *Pericles* (1609) can possibly be authorized quartos. Both were issued by publishers of doubtful repute[48] and neither contains a good text. Now it is very remarkable, and can hardly be a coincidence, that the evidence recently assembled by Professor Charles J. Sisson to show why the King's Men withheld plays from publication involves precisely these two plays. Testimony before the Star Chamber, in a proceeding of 1614 against Sir John York and others, tells us that when a Yorkshire travelling company, the Simpsons, performed in Gowthwaite Hall (Nidderdale) on February 2, 1610, "one of the playes acted and played was Perocles prince of Tire, And the other was Kinge Lere."[49] These are the words of William Harrison, who played clowns and presumably had taken the Fool in *Lear*, and he goes on to say that their plays "were vsuall playes . . . and such as were played publicly and prynted in the bookes"; evidence by the leading members of the company, Christopher Simpson and Edward Whitfield, makes it certain that they were using printed quartos. The players numbered fifteen on this occasion and could have played even *Lear* unmodified.[50] It is not known whether the King's Men at this period ever got so far north[51]; but what the Simpsons were doing in Yorkshire it is reasonable to suppose other provincial companies were doing elsewhere in the kingdom. Using quartos of new plays as prompt books, it is obvious that they would be formidable rivals to the London companies when they went on tour for the provincial revenue upon which, in the summers and during seasons when plague closed the London theatres, they almost entirely depended. Publishers certainly catered to non-metropolitan players; Henry Rocket's print of *The Fair Maid of the Exchange* in 1607 heads its Dramatis Personae with a come-on: "Eleauen may easily acte this Comedie." In the face of this motive operating on the wealthiest of the companies to keep its most attractive plays from print, I think it would be idle to deny that there is a strong presumption that Busby or Butter came by his copy for *King Lear* surreptitiously.

This has three consequences. First, it appears to bring Q *Lear* to extend the group of six "bad" quartos which modern criticism agrees Heminge and Condell had in mind in their celebrated charge against certain "copies" as "stolne and surreptitious"; this completes our external evidence against the quarto, and brings into prominence the second part of their charge, that these copies were "maimed, and deformed by the frauds and stealthes of iniurious impostors"—a statement which speaks decidedly for the shorthand theory and against the theory of memorial reconstruction by the actors dictating. Second, it provides a powerful motive for piracy, speaking again rather for shorthand than dictation.[52] Third, it offers a difficulty in provenance to the second theory. We must imagine, I think, either that one of the players privately sold the dictated manuscript after the company had ceased to need it or that it was stolen.

A more serious objection to both theories must now be considered. Q contains about 3,100 lines; its copy probably contained some 60 more and would have taken a little over three hours to play.[53] If Professor Alfred Hart was right in thinking that Elizabethan performances were limited to two hours, giving time, by his estimate, for an acting version of only 2,300–2,400, or at most (with a gesture of liberality) 2,700 lines, no text so long as the quartos of *King Lear* and *Richard III* could possibly be a report of the types we are supposing. I feel sure myself that he is not right and that the objection has no force; but he is lengthy[54] and insistent on "fact," and several scholars have been overwhelmed by him, so we must take up a few points. (1) Mr. Hart's presumption of a negative thesis, if established, would fly straight in the face of our major and natural evidence for the performance of Shakespeare's long plays at length, namely, the existence of texts over 3,000 lines bearing signs of playhouse annotation.[55] In view particularly of his confession that he cannot explain this evidence,[56] I cannot help wondering that anyone has found him persuasive. (2) Despite his "fact"-emphasis, Mr. Hart is forced of course like other historical critics to rely upon interpretation, and here he appears at a certain disadvantage. Thus the dozen-odd references to length of performances—mostly in verse, and mostly to "two hours" —are facts; but when he says, "I prefer to take the words of Shakespeare, Jonson, Middleton and the rest in their literal sense, because each one of these poets could always find the right words for anything that he wished to say," this is interpretation, and displays indeed a touching faith that poets write the *exact* truth. Nashe also was a poet; does Mr. Hart take literally his charge that lawyers talk "twoo houres before they come to the poynt"? Dekker also was a poet; yet Mr. Hart, a critic unfriendly to exceptions, has felt free to conceal in his phrase "the rest" Dekker's two references to *three* hours as performance length. But the truth is, as any critic not thesis-ridden can see well enough, that "two hours" is conventional not absolute, as its variations (two poor hours, two short hours) are apologetic not descriptive. Chambers, reviewing this evidence, puts the average length at two hours and a half, which agrees well with the average length, 2,430 lines, found by Mr. Hart for 136 plays of 1594–1616 (but see below), and is reasonable.[57] (3) At least one fact of first-rate importance he omits altogether. He admits that before 1594 "some system of illuminating the stage in the winter months must have existed," but he assumes the system to have disappeared, and even asserts that "we have not the slightest evidence that artificial lighting was used in the public theatres, at least up to 1616." Now, Cotgrave in 1611 defined *falot* as "A cresset light (such as they use in Playhouses) made of ropes wreathed, pitched and put into small, and open cages of yron," and Chambers asked twenty years ago, "Would they not smoke and smell badly, if used indoors?"[58] The question is a good one, and points strongly I think to continuity of stage illumination (which one would expect anyway) from the time when plays began at four o'clock to the period after 1594 when they seem regularly to have begun at two. (4) Mr. Hart's authoritarian attitude towards the whole matter does him little credit. The facts are few and uncertainly significant. To state with an air of defiance that something was not possible is merely fatuous. Moreover, his average length for 136 plays excludes thirty-two of Shakespeare's, averaging according to his careful figures 2,744 lines, and eleven of Jonson's, averaging 3,580 lines. What can an "average" mean which excludes the bulky work of the two dramatists perhaps most powerful and popular during the decade which interests us, 1600–10? Are we really to imagine that men occupying their position among the players could not get their longer-than-average plays produced at unusual length? On what ground? Dekker appears not to have thought this length unusual. But for some future critic, employing this meaningless norm, it will be easy to show that neither Shaw's nor O'Neill's immensely long plays were produced in London and New York without being cut to the period "average"; easy, but not critical. (5) Finally, Mr. Hart scrambles somewhat the evidence for the boys' companies, where performances seem usually to have been shortest, and the adult companies; and he says little of court and private performances. But this last subject concerns us directly, since *King Lear* is known to have been performed at Whitehall on December 26, 1606,[59] and I think I may abandon Mr. Hart, noting only that about three-hour performances at court there is no doubt whatever.[60]

By the date of this performance *Lear* was probably a year old, and it was not entered on the Stationers' Register until eleven months later. This gives some leeway. But if Q is a shorthand report from performance, it will be best to suppose that this was the performance reported, the one mentioned on the title page and the only one certainly known to us. First, Dr. Greg suggests plausibly that in the special conditions obtaining at court a reporter would be "more difficult to detect and also more difficult to remove."[61] Second, I don't think a shorthand reporter in the provinces very likely; and the London theatres seem to have been closed for plague from July to November of 1607.[62] A considerable difficulty arises here for the shorthand theory. Q shows signs that the manuscript from which it was printed, so far from being prepared with any care for press, was crude and illegible, suggesting haste. The play was attractive partly because it was new. Why did the reporter or Busby and Butter let nearly a year elapse after the presumed date of reporting before registration and publication?

The plague situation, on the other hand, is very favourable to Dr. Duthie's theory. The King's Men were travelling during an uncertain portion of 1607, but almost certainly during the five months July–November; they visited Barnstaple, perhaps Dunwich and Cambridge, and were at Oxford on September 7.[63] This year was for the King, despite his daughter's death, a festive one. It is possible that, having mislaid the prompt book of *Lear* or left it in London, the King's Men had suddenly need of one for a royal performance—for example at Henry Wriothesley's seat, Beaulieu Abbey, much liked by James, where he was entertained on August 10.[64] The subject of provincial abridgement is still obscure,[65] but since Q is full-length, the possibility that a prompt book was dictated for royal performance may be important. More important, and in fact indispensable to the theory, is the increased likelihood on such an occasion of all the actors being present. Nothing in Q *Lear* resembles the chaos, for example, of the Murderers' parts in Q *Richard III* (I.iv), which has to be accounted for by supposing that the actors who knew them were absent. It cannot be allowed that other actors or the prompter could have got so right as it is even the shortest real "part" in the quarto. I confess I feel this a major objection against the otherwise (so far) rather attractive notion of provincial reconstruction. At any rate, *Lear* was registered at about the time the players returned to London, evidently, and this is much more satisfactory for dictation than for shorthand.

It is difficult, however, for any notion of reconstruction of the prompt book by dictation *in London*. I may as well say that I think this is too implausible to be entertained. Although prompt books would be carefully looked after by the company, I can imagine one's being lost and later recovered. But most critics now agree that a fair copy of the author's manuscript usually served as prompt book,[66] so that his "foul" papers would be available for use as the new prompt book (either directly or in a copy). If they were not, the "plot" and the actors' parts would be; and although the theory of "assembled texts" has not fared very well at the hands of Sir Edmund Chambers and Dr. Greg, I am unable to believe that the company would have preferred dictation to a scribe to the much more obvious process of setting a scribe to assemble a new prompt book from the "plot" and parts. Dictation we must look on, I think, as a last resort for the company.

Would a manuscript so imperfectly legible as the copy for Q seems to have been—we shall find that the press reader as well as the compositor had extraordinary difficulty with it—would such a manuscript be satisfactory as a prompt book? It might for a single performance (this suggests again the hypothetical royal performance I have conjured up), hardly for more. No doubt its scribe could read it. But this makes the prompter the scribe, and the nature of the mishearings in Q is very hard on the identification; I take it as certain that on the dictation theory the scribe would have to know the play fairly well, since the margin for reporter's errors in Q is not great (a subject we will return to); and a reasonable knowledge is not incompatible with such errors as most persons make frequently in reading or hearing even works they think they know well. But I think the prompter himself extremely unlikely. Of course the dictated manuscript, later to serve for Q, could have been transcribed and corrected; but I don't find this easy to credit—why not take more pains in the first instance and save labour?[67]

In the actual process of dictation, Duthie suggests, "the words might be given out in groups not coinciding with verse lines so that the scribe, unable to distinguish between verse and prose, might simply write everything as prose."[68] This seems to me admirable; but I would expect him to get some of the verse right, and in fact more than half the verse in Q is correctly divided. That a compositor could do so well—particularly Okes's far from bright compositor—I doubt; and I think this counts for dictation against shorthand, because like Dr. Greg I would expect the transcription of a shorthand report to be without line division altogether. Duthie accounts plausibly also for mispointing: "Punctuation would not be dictated and the scribe, working in haste, might simply put in a comma on his own responsibility after every few words." This too seems to envisage a scribe who was not the prompter, and the nature of Q's stage directions is conclusive against the notion. These and its speakers' names require some discussion.

Ignoring such divergence as Q's heading Edmund's speeches *Bast.* and Cornwall's and Albany's *Duke*, Q and F differ in about fifty speakers' names; but thirteen of these are trivial Servant-Knight-Gentleman-Messenger variants, and Q is preferable in eight instances (one being an error in F, the other seven resulting from F's shortened cast).[69] Most of Q's remaining variants are clearly wrong. Two make dead men speak—Lear at V.iii.312 and one of Q's captains at

V.iii.295. These captains are curious. F knows only one, who is sent off by Edmund to hang Cordelia, does so, and is killed by the King. Q had him also, but seventy lines after his exit a "Cap." has an extremely implausible speech: "Sound trumpte?" (V.iii.110), which if genuine (F omits it) certainly belongs to the Herald, as do the following "Againe." and "Againe." which in Q become "Sound? Againe?" and are given to (taken by would probably be more accurate) Edmund. Much later a different—presumably—"Cap." confirms Lear's report of his death! (V.iii.275). In F this line is given to a "Gent.," the same gentleman of course who ran out at 251, urged by Albany and Edgar, to save Lear and Cordelia, and who alone with any semblance of plausibility can report events in the prison. Following Malone, editors have sent Edgar, owing to another wrong prefix in Q (the "Duke" being given Edgar's "Hast thee for thy life") and to the absence of an exit for anyone in either substantive text; but besides being unsatisfactory in itself, this is condemned by the necessity of someone identified with F's "Gent." (275) going offstage for at least a few moments earlier and following Lear (after an interval) back in.[70] Twenty lines later, still another captain enters in Q— a messenger in F—and announces Edmund's death. One has the impression that in these captains an agency imperfectly familiar with the play is at work in Q. This impression is strengthened by the fact that in Oswald's first scene, I.iii (F calls him always Steward, "Ste."), Q knows him only as "Gent." Oddly enough, the vagueness of this last appellation is reconcilable with the often indeterminate speech prefixes of Shakespeare's "foul" papers, but it has been abundantly shown that we are dealing in Q with nothing of this sort, and I find the vagueness or ignorance less easy to reconcile with a dictation by the actors intended to produce a prompt book. A shorthand reporter certainly would produce this kind of error, not knowing precisely who minor characters were; also, writing rapidly, he would frequently omit the speakers' names altogether, and they would have to be supplied later, either in transcribing his notes or in the printing. As a matter of fact, Q at least thrice does omit the name: at II.iv.167, at I.ii.38 (here the press correcter inserted a "Ba.," but whether the copy had a name is very doubtful), and the Fool's reply "Lears shadow" is swallowed up in Lear's speech at I.iv.251.[71] All this is more comfortable for shorthand than for dictation.

Most of the speeches really differently assigned and wrong in Q, however, must be due to the actors. Regan, for instance, takes three lines from her husband (II.ii.158, II.iv.298, 301), and it is striking that two of these involve very similar adaptation. Cornwall's "Come my

Lord, away," spoken near the end of II.ii to Gloucester, who has been pleading for Kent, is continued in Q to her and becomes ". . . good Lord . . ."[72] At the end of the act, after the actor of Gloucester has telescoped his speeches at 298 and 300, cutting off a question of Cornwall's and a phrase of his own, Regan takes her husband's "Tis best to giue him way, he leads himselfe" and changes "best" to "good." So strange is coincidence that at V.iii.81 Edmund, her lover, revenges her husband's losses by taking her "Let the Drum strike, and proue my title thine" and changing "thine" also to "good"!—as Dr. Greg observes, this is meaningless, since "a drum can prove nothing but its capacity for noise," but no doubt it sounded impressive to William Sly (if as Baldwin supposes he really played Edmund). The gentle Albany borrows four speeches from Edgar in V.iii and I am sorry to say that editors have liked the closing lines of the play better in his mouth than in the mouth of Shakespeare's Fortinbras in *King Lear*. The actors' responsibility for I.iv.241 "Lear.:Kent." is much less clear, since Lear never addresses the Fool simply as "foole" and a misreading of "Ken" as "Lea" is possible; either misreading or insertion of the speakers' names afterwards must be evoked to account for the same error at V.iii.312. A final variant is complicated, II.iv.191, where for F: "*Lear*. Who stockt my Seruant?" Q has "*Gon*. Who struck my seruant . . ." How plausible this is, Kent having in fact mauled Oswald; yet I cannot imagine the actors producing it. And there is no need to do so. For Q the verb "stock" does not exist: at II.ii.139 (F "Stocking") the compositor first set up "Stobing" and the press reader emended to "Stopping"; at III.iv.140 for "stockt, punish'd" Q has "stock-punisht." But Greg (*The Variants in the First Quarto of "King Lear*," p. 159) takes "Stobing" as a graphic error for "Stoking," and presumably the Q copy here was right also. Evidently "stockt" was misunderstood as "struck," either the compositor or more likely the press reader saw that the sense was wrong for Lear, noticed Goneril's entrance in the previous line, and either supplied the speech prefix "Gon." where there was none or substituted it for "Lear" and inserted "Lear" two lines below where it was now necessary.[73]

Either shorthand or dictation is capable of producing, I believe, such of these errors as we have assigned to the copy for Q; vagueness being difficult for the dictation theory,[74] and the most serious difficulty for shorthand being, I frankly think, the fact that so few erroneous speech prefixes are really attributable to the reporter. I would expect not only more errors from him but occasionally real confusion. The quarto's stage directions present the worst stumbling block, perhaps, that dictation has had to face. They begin in a promising way with a "Sennet" and close with several "Alarum's," but in between there are only two or three notes which suggest a prompter ("A Letter" twice, "draw and fight"); and my impression is of a body of directions incompatible with theatrical competence. They are so scanty that perhaps they may best be characterized, from the point of view of a prompter, negatively. They omit practically all the noises and action notes found in F (which is typical of prompt books in this respect). Forty-five exits are unmarked; actors, Chambers remarks, might be trusted to find their way offstage by themselves, but the number seems large.[75] Entrances are unmarked at sixteen points. It is not easy to imagine the scribe beginning I.v (F Enter Lear, Kent, Gentleman,[76] and Foole), in a manuscript intended for prompt copy, with "Enter Lear"; and similar simplifications occur at II.i.87 and II.iv.1 (Enter King; Enter Lear, Foole, and Gentleman). Lear's exit and re-entrance at I.iv.311, 314, and Edgar's at IV.vi.285, 291 (with the body of Oswald), pass unnoticed.[77]

But if some faith is required to envisage a prompt copy with these lacunae, they are precisely what one would expect in a shorthand report, the reporter being usually much too busy for stage directions, and perhaps adding the few long ones when he transcribed his notes. These appear to be descriptive of action witnessed and sound more like a reporter proper than a scribe:

Sound a Sennet, Enter one bearing a Coronet, then Lear, then the Dukes of Albany, and Cornwell, next Gonorill, Regan, Cordelia, with followers.

Enter Edmund with his rapier drawne, Gloster the Duke and Dutchesse.

Shee takes a sword and runs at him behind.

Alarum. Enter the powers of France over the stage, Cordelia with her father in her hand.[78]

Enter Edgar at the third sound, a trumpet before him.

Enter one with a bloudie knife.

The bodies of Gonorill and Regan are brought in.

Enter Lear with Cordelia in his armes.[79]

Some others have the same character in degree less marked:

> Enter France and Burgundie with Gloster.
> Enter Bastard and Curan meeting.
> Enter Kent and a Gentleman at seuerall doores.
> Enter Gloster and the Bastard with lights.[80]

[*203*]

> Enter Glost. led by an old man.
> He kneeles.
> He fals.
> Enter Lear mad.
> Exit King running.
> They fight.
> He dies.
> A drum a farre off.
> Enter Edmund, with Lear and Cordelia prisoners.

These can be paralleled, of course, in "good" texts. "Enter Gloster brought in by two or three" is a permissive direction characteristic of authors' manuscripts, though found also in the reported quartos of *A Shrew* and *Romeo and Juliet*; the suspicious-looking "Enter Cornwall, and Regan, and Gonorill, and Bastard" has counterparts in Q *Merchant* and *Much Ado*. But again a negative position is useful: we scan Q in vain for convincing, certain marks of author or prompter, and we find a describer. Moreover, analogies may mislead. When we try to support Q's "Enter Duke, the two Ladies, and others" (V.iii.39), with Shakespeare's generalizations, as "Exeunt Ladies" in Q *Much Ado about Nothing* (V.iv.16), we come flat against the implausibility of anyone but a reporter's so describing the monstrous sisters. The remaining directions of any interest are not many.

> Enter Bastard Solus.
> Exeunt Lear, Leister, Kent, and Foole. (II.iv.289)[81]
> sleepes. (II.ii.180)[82]
> Enter Gloster and Lear, Kent, Foole, and Tom.
> Enter three Gentlemen. (IV.vi.191)
> Exeunt. Manet Kent and Gent.
> Enter Edmund, Regan, and their powers.
> Enter Albany and Gonorill with troupes.
> Alarum and retreat.

Q rarely has the "servants" and "followers" with which F is so prolific[83]; there are no storm directions (F has seven), few sounds, no stocking or releasing of Kent, inadequate entrances and exits; the few real directions are descriptive. If this is a manuscript for a prompt book, it must have been prepared with exceptional negligence and little regard to its end, or have been copied. Unfortunately, neither of these contingencies can be quite ruled out; and the sometimes ambiguous character of prompt-book directions forbids dogmatism.[84]

Something more definite might be expected from analysis of the three scroll pieces in the text: two letters (I.ii.49–58, IV.vi.267–78) and the Herald's proclamation (V.iii.110–15). These were not memorized by the actors but were read out in performance from scrolls; a memorial reconstruction by dictation could be supposed to have them very imperfectly, and the shorthand report of a performance (allowing for some errors of the reporter and printer) perfectly. Of course an actor would remember the purport of his scroll; but that he would be able to reproduce Gloucester's letter (by no means easy in phrasing) exactly save for the omission of "and reuerence" I very much doubt: whereas the phrase, which occurs in hendiadys, might be deliberately cut by an actor even with the scroll before him (I think this explanation better for this instance than inadvertent omission by him or reporter or compositor). The letter read by Edgar, setting aside a puzzling omission in F,[85] displays the same verbal fidelity except for "your:our" and an extra "your" near the end, neither difficult to account for on any hypothesis. In the proclamation, an "at:by" also is easy, but "in the hoast" (for "within the lists") is not; it looks like the variant of an actor, whom we must therefore imagine not attending very closely to his scroll, and this deprives the argument of some of its force. Nevertheless, I think the excellence of these three passages a stumbling block for the dictation theory. What the critic is required to believe is that the actors knew their scroll pieces quite as well as they knew their parts, and no critic can be very happy about this. Of course, here as everywhere, F's correction of Q may be incomplete; and it is not absolutely impossible that the scrolls were somehow available[86]; but I have no confidence whatever in either of these qualifications.

I return to shorthand, and particularly to John Willis's *Stenography*, published in 1602. This has not been much studied, despite its importance in shorthand history as the first of the so-called orthographic systems[87]; but whether any study would answer our questions about it is uncertain. Unlike Charactery and Brachygraphy, it would produce no characteristic error, being "in principle phonetic with abundant provision for various abbreviations."[88] Thus "the word Lionesse . . . may be written 12. seuerall wayes by the Rules of this Booke, Viz . . ." etc. (chapter 11 of Willis's Book I). Everything depends then on the competence of the system, and this is precisely both what experts disagree about and what it is difficult to form an impression of. My own examination, which was as careful and extended, I think, as an amateur's can profitably be, produced results so uncertain that they are not even worth reporting.[89] Moreover, we are not limited for

King Lear to Willis's *Stenography*. (1) It is not certain that we possess even all the systems *published* by 1607; of three registered in 1621, none has survived. (2) Edmond Willis's *An Abbreviation of Writing by Character* (1618) in its dedication to Nicholas Felton speaks of its author's "taking many sermons from your Lordship's own mouth by the space of many years"; Felton was preaching in London from 1596, the second Willis (unrelated to John Willis) is probably the merchant-tailor who married in 1603, and Mr. Matthews reports that a manuscript is extant containing eight sermons preached by Felton from 1599 to 1602 while vicar of St. Antholin's and stating on its title page that these were "taken from his mouth by"—the reporter's name is scratched out.[90] If it was Edmond Willis who took these down, clearly his system must be considered; but he is unlikely to have been using so early the one he published many years later, and we enter again on the unknown systems. (3) That there were several even in 1588 is clear from Bright's remark that "none is comparable" with Charactery. Edmond Willis testifies (1618) that "for these fourteene yeeres past . . . I haue not failed to seeke to all men, that haue made any profession of teaching the same in this city"[91]—which brings us back three years earlier than the date of the reporting of *Lear*. John Willis speaks in 1617 of the "diuers formes of short-writing taught in the citie of London" and says five years later, "There are now so many formes of short-writing . . . that a man can not tell which to follow of them," claiming his anonymous *Stenography* of 1602 as "the first book of spelling characterie that was euer sent forth, since which time many others haue sought to better the inuention." Who the many others were, and who taught the second Willis, we do not know, but I take it that everything intelligent after 1602 would be ortho-graphic—any other system for reporting *Lear* is unthinkable—and would insist that we cannot measure the possibilities by 1607.

All this activity is linked to play reporting by three of the best witnesses imaginable, two dramatists and the Master of the Revels. Heywood complained in the same year Butter published *King Lear* of certain of his plays published in a form "corrupt and mangled, copied only by the eare" (Epistle to *The Rape of Lucrece*, 1608). This suggests shorthand more strongly to me than it does to some critics, and at any rate, there can be no doubt of his charge in a prologue of about 1630–32 [1637], describing his Play of Queen Elizabeth as so popular when it was first produced that

> some by Stenography drew
> The plot: put it in print: (scarce one word trew:) . . .[92]

The names of the early shorthands were used more or less indifferently (that of Bales's, the weakest, most often, perhaps because of his fame as a penman), but we may take this to refer, like the references to come, to John Willis's, as the best extant. The play referred to is certainly Butter's quarto of Thomas Heywood's *If You Know Not Me, You Know Nobody* [Part 1], registered July 5, 1605. Unfortunately, though in the absence of a good text for comparison it is impossible to be sure, this obviously corrupt quarto seems to be a memorial reconstruction,[93] not a shorthand report, and the argument through Nathaniel Butter fails, except insofar as this is a piracy and Heywood may actually have been misled (as to the nature of the text of his own play) by hearing Butter associated with shorthand. As evidence, at any rate, of the employment of shorthand at the date of *Lear* for reporting plays, Heywood's statement is impossible to explain away.[94] Webster's allusion of about 1620 seems to refer to theatrical practice as well as to the trial which is in question: "Doe you heare, Officers? You must take speciall care, that you let in no *Brachigraphy* men, to take notes" (*The Devil's Law Case*, IV.ii.28–30).[95] Sir George Buc asserts of "Brachygraphy" in 1612 or earlier that "they which know it can readily take a Sermon, Oration, Play, or any long speech, as they are spoke, dictated, acted, & vttered in the instant" (*The Third University of England* [1615], chapter 34, 401^r, p. 984).

On the evidence it is as impossible, I think, to assert that shorthand *could not* have been used to report *Lear* as it is impossible to feel very certain that it was so used. I do not take very seriously Willis's disclaimer ("If the speaker be of a treatable and slow deliuery, we may write after him *verbatim*: if hee be slow of speech, we may write faster then hee can speake: but if he be of a swift volumility of tongue, then we cannot doe it," 1628); for, as I have explained, it is by no means clear that we are dealing with his system, and in any case, it is really a question not of systems but of proficiency.[96] Nor does our ignorance of a reporter's opportunities trouble me. Gallants at the play noted down in their tables "sentences" they liked—equally at court and in a theatre as large as the Globe, I should think a circumspect reporter could pass unnoticed. I have argued that *Lear* was probably reported, if by shorthand, at Whitehall on December 26, 1606, but it is possible, after all, that the King's Men returning to London in November 1607 played it at once, it was reported, sold to Busby and Butter, and registered on November 26. Even if the reporter had never seen it before (a popular play, however, was likely to be revived once a week for a time), small matter, since once he was launched, his memory would not help him much anyway. Hearing would present no such problem of course as in a modern theatre, the actors being both closer to their audience and (I trust!) clearer.

But I feel rather keenly three broad internal difficulties with shorthand. First, the margin left for the reporter's errors in note taking and in transcription, after those reasonably assigned to the actors and to the printer have been set aside, is in my opinion astonishingly small. Second, the quarto text does not exhibit the variations in reporting which I should expect from a reporter subject now and then, during a long and tense performance, to fatigue and confusion. Third, Shakespeare's remarkable diction is preserved in the quarto more fully than I should have thought possible. Much of it is corrupted and some is ambiguously preserved (as "out paromord," III.vi.94), but a good deal of this corruption is attributable to the compositor, and the reporter got right a stream of surprising words: revengive, epicurism, out-wall, 'parel, remotion, smilet, impertinency, disbranch, superflux, elbow and knee (verbs), renegue, simular, cullionly, faith'd, minikin, cruels, etc.

To account for these features the critic must posit a reporter extremely competent, so competent that without an analogy I don't think I should venture on it. I believe, however, that we have an analogy. Not in 1 *If You Know Not Me, You Know Nobody* nor in *Pericles*—texts which though plainly corrupt cannot be studied with confidence because we have no good parallel texts—but in the Deposition scene of *Richard II*, which A. W. Pollard long ago suggested was obtained by shorthand.[97] This passage of 164 lines (IV.i.154–318), cut for a political reason from Andrew Wise's "good" quarto (1597), appeared first in the Fourth Quarto, published by Matthew Law in 1608; and its text as compared with the folio text of the passage (evidently from the prompt book) is decidedly bad. There are nine omissions, about thirty-two other variants, and about twenty-five lines are misdivided. Now this mislineation is not extensive by comparison with Q *Lear's*, but it is out of all proportion to (for instance) the 100 lines I have mentioned as misdivided in the whole of *Macbeth*; the pointing of the 1608 Deposition scene is better than Q *Lear's* also, and a minimum of preparation for the press would ensure this—it is certainly not good. The twenty-seven or -eight variants in which I think Q4 inferior to F afford no basis for the kind of analysis possible in *Lear*, except that King Richard twice calls Bolingbroke "Harry" where F has "Henry."[98] No doubt, Burbage played Richard. It is the nine omissions that are most interesting. Not only do they occur, without exception, in Burbage's part, but nearly all are half-lines that vanish without disturbance to the rhetoric.[99] For instance:

> 'Tis very true, my Griefe lyes all within,
> And these externall manner of laments,
> Are meerely shadowes, to the vnseene Griefe,
> That swells with silence in the tortur'd Soule.
> *There lyes the substance:* and I thanke thee King
> *For thy great bountie,* that not onely giu'st
> Me cause to wayle, but teachest me the way
> How to lament the cause.
>
> (F 295–302)

The omissions in this passage will not easily be paralleled in the work of scribes and compositors, and the confining of all omission to one part cannot be paralleled. Nor can this be cutting. We have to do, as in *King Lear*, with an actors' version. When Burbage omits "Giue me the Crown" (180), indeed, one is reminded of his identical omission in changing "Giue me the Map there" into "The map there" (*Lear* I.i.38).

This is our analogy, then. The date is precisely that of Q *Lear*, the copy is mislined or unlined,[100] and the conclusion is that the agency was an excellent shorthand reporter using an orthographic system to report performance.

There is no reason to suppose that this portion of a scene in *Richard II* was dictated, and the extreme implausibility of such a proceeding will probably prevent its being suggested.[101] Dr. Duthie's dictation theory for Q *Lear* rests alone on *Richard III*. This was not dictated, and as I have shown, there are grave difficulties in the analogy: the necessity of all the actors being present for *Lear*, the cutting in *Richard III*, its lack of scroll pieces, the vagueness of *Lear*'s directions, the exceptional illegibility of the manuscript, which was presumably to serve as a prompt book. Q *Troilus and Cressida* and Q *Othello*, the texts presenting the next widest variation from their respective folio texts, offer no help to either shorthand or dictation.[102] I will add a final piece of evidence. Most of the quarto's substantial omissions are due to the actors; like the loss of speech ends at II.i.29 and IV.vi.193, the omission of notes for Edmund's song at I.ii.149, they are powerful evidence for the general hypothesis that Q is an actors' version, but say nothing to either of the theories we have been considering. There is one line in *King Lear*, however, which is spoken offstage, Edgar's "Fathom, and halfe, Fathom and halfe; poore *Tom*" when disturbed in the hovel.[103] I would expect this to be lost by a reporter in the theatre, but I can see no reason why it should disappear in dictation.[104] It is missing in Q.

This is as far, I believe, as the argument can profitably go. Much evidence is still to come in later sections, and more evidence than can be examined in the introduction is scattered through the text, but even the evidence given here can be weighed only by someone absolutely familiar with the texts. The system of semi-research in modern education has produced so many pseudo-students, pseudo-critics, that it may be well to say that their assent or dissent in such matters as this is wholly without meaning. I have therefore made no attempt to persuade; one's only interest is in discovering and setting down as much significant truth as possible. So far as I know, there is no third alternative to shorthand and dictation; Dr. Duthie suggests that the scribe in his theory may even have used Willis's stenography to take down the actors' dictation and this I suppose is not impossible, but it little affects the theories, is to me very unattractive, and violates the principle of criticism which remarks that causes must not be multiplied beyond necessity. If there were a third alternative, I should be happy to try to drive it through the evidence offered by Q and F, because shorthand strains my faith. But dictation breaks it,[105] and I think we are required to suppose that the quarto of *King Lear* is a shorthand report of performance.

The absence of external evidence probably means that we shall never know much better than we do now the exact provenance of the quarto. I don't myself think this much matters; if we find a man with a broken leg, ignorance of the precise way in which he broke it does not prevent our setting it; and our case in *Lear* is rather uncertainty than ignorance. There are also two internal circumstances which hamper the enquiry. First, it is impossible from time to time to know what the Q copy had (e.g., II.iv.90, where I cannot really think "Iustice" either a mishearing or a misreading of "fetches" and it cannot be the actor's word); and it is impossible to allocate a good many of its errors with certainty. Second, there is an ineluctable uncertainty in the correction of Q to serve for F copy. How careful the scribe could be is shown by his restoration of the old possessive without suffix at II.ii.159 and II.iv.133, and how careful he generally was is shown by his restoration of every line missing in Q, I believe, except one.[106] But it is remarkable that very few of the seventy cruxes in the play (the bulk of them being passages, of course, in which F either does not correct Q or "corrects" it wrongly) occur in the long first act; I have an impression that, as one might imagine, the scribe began fresh and conscientious, and that his attention flagged as he wearied. His imagined lapses cannot be invoked for a section (as the part of one actor or the three scroll pieces), but as we evoke them reasonably for emendation, they may be supposed in a general way to blur our view of the second half of the play. What we have to do next is to prove his presence.

1946

Staging[1]

F REPRESENTS A VERSION of the play considerably cut, compared with Q, and it saves several minor roles. Dr. Greg evidently considers the theatrical arrangements of the texts identical; quoting Granville-Barker: "There are one or two signs that the stage to which the Folio version was fitted differed a little from that of the Quarto" (*Prefaces to Shakespeare*, 1927, p. 200), he comments, "I should be interested to know what these signs are, for I have not observed them," and continues, taking F's staging to represent both texts and to be original, "that the play was written, not with the ordinary theatre in view, but for a plain stage with no alcove and probably no balcony, and that the act and scene divisions in the Folio were designed for a similar stage and presumably the same occasion" ("The Staging of *King Lear,*" *RES,* 1940, pp. 300–3).

I agree that the Folio *Lear* envisages no inner stage, and I do not know what Granville-Barker's signs are, but there is evidence that the Q version had an inner stage and was evidently original. The question is important for the date and circumstances of the reporting, as well as for editing.

In the Reconciliation scene (IV.vii), neither text gives an entrance for Lear at the commencement. Cordelia and Kent enter, with a "Gentleman" in F, with a "Doctor" in Q. F has changed Q's "Doctor" to "Gentleman" in the medical conversation of IV.iv, and is certainly wrong again here. It is clearly a physician whom Cordelia addresses in line 19:

> *Cor.* Be gouern'd by your knowledge, and proceede
> I'th'sway of your owne will: is he array'd?

F continues:

> *Enter Lear in a chaire carried by Seruants*

> *Gent.* I Madam: in the heauinesse of sleepe,
> We put fresh garments on him.
> Be by good Madam when we do awake him,
> I doubt of his temperance.
> *Cor.* O my deere Father [. . .]

This text might pass muster if we did not know that a doctor was about, but the Gentleman's speech is oddly broken: it sounds like two speeches. And Q in fact continues, without any stage direction:

> *Doct.* I madam, in the heauinesse of his sleepe,
> We put fresh garments on him,
> *Gent.* Good madam be by, when we do awake him
> I doubt not of his temperance.
> *Cord.* Very well.
> *Doct.* Please you draw neere, louder the musicke there,
> *Cor.* O my deere father . . .

Q was wrong also, then, in omitting an entrance for its Gentleman, and some editing is necessary. Capell transposed Q's speech headings "Doct." and "Gent.," so that line 21 rightly (if a little accidentally) follows F[2]; F authority removes "his" in 21[3]; the pointing is Q's usual chaos. But for the rest I think Q has every mark of originality.

As it is the Doctor, not a Gentleman, who would venture to predict Lear's sanity at all, so he would presumably not wish Cordelia to "be by" if he thought her father would be intemperate or mad. F has therefore omitted "not" inadvertently, unless this is a particularly stupid sophistication[4]; F's movement is inferior also. Cordelia's speech, omitted in F, is metrical and probable. Unless we take it to be genuine, we must suppose that the boy actor would gag in perfect metre. I have no doubt that the line was lost with the line to which it responds, in the cut which removed line 25, which is our crux.

Although no one appears to have doubted the line's genuineness, I may compare the music with which Shakespeare accompanies reconciliations in *The Winter's Tale* (V.iii.98) and *Pericles* (V.i.81 and

231!); it is a form of his thought—to "draw her home with music" (*Merchant*, V.i.68), to wind up the untuned and jarring senses of the insane King. But "draw near" suggests an approach to the alcove, the curtain drawn back while the music rises. No entry for Lear is given in Q: he sat on a chair, arrayed, in the inner stage, whence, at about line 50, he comes forward; that he has been out of his chair, and standing, is clear from Cordelia's "you must not kneel" (58); her "Will't please your Highness walk?" (83) merely means, as often, "go," and is appropriate in both texts.

Q omits an extraordinary number of necessary entrances (twelve outside this scene, in two of which it is followed by F),[5] but none of comparable importance with this, and I think we must assume that the failure to provide for the King's entry (attended, incidentally) is a consequence of his really not having entered in the performance of which Q is a report. Otherwise we must condemn line 25 or assume that F omitted it inadvertently (but F has by my reckoning only three inadvertent omissions of single lines in the whole play). In either event, we must try to imagine why the Doctor would supplement—at Shakespeare's instigation or by gag—her father's entrance with "Please you, draw near" to Cordelia. It will be observed that F omits "music" as well as avoids the alcove. Also, when Edmund calls, "Brother, a word: Descend: Brother, I say" (II.i.21, identical in Q and F), he appears to call to a balcony, and I think that in Q he did so; the passage did not require change in F (which having no alcove would presumably have no balcony), because Edgar entering the stage door would be accepted as coming from upstairs in a house.

I suggest, in short, that in Q we have the original staging, for an inner stage and perhaps a balcony, designed by Shakespeare for performance at court, where the play was actually performed on December 26, 1606. In F we have a much later playhouse revision of the staging, perhaps for a provincial performance, with fewer characters, with no provision for music,[6] and without either inner stage or balcony. A carried chair, as Greg says, is "rather a clumsy way to bring on a sleeping patient, but the only one, if the use of the traverse be denied."

Dr. Greg does not appear to have observed the connection here insisted on between F's cutting "Please you, draw near: louder the music there" and Q's omission of any entry for Lear. He argues at length, however, that the use of "stocks brought out" for Kent in II.ii, in which Q and F plainly agree, indicates that Shakespeare when composing the play knew that no inner stage would be available; and this argument I must consider, because if correct it would weaken the probability of different arrangements in Q and F in IV.vii.

Dr. Greg says: "The Natural thing would be to 'discover' them [the stocks] on the back stage, and have Kent put in them there. Then at the end of the scene the traverse could be closed, Edgar could speak his short soliloquy before it, and it could be withdrawn once more to disclose Kent still in the stocks in the scene that follows." But I am not sure that this is natural. The scene takes place outdoors. And there is some evidence that stocks were not so handled. In a scene, which perhaps imitates this one, in *The Travels of Three English Brothers* (precisely dated in June 1607), a Jailor calls to Sir Thomas, who enters, is put in the stocks, is left alone by the Jailor there, and has a soliloquy not unlike Kent's; then the great Turk and others come on, and Sir Thomas is released obviously from the stocks, and put on the rack—"Where foure and twenty howers he shall remaine," the Turk promises; but in fact the Turk gives an order: "One take him downe and bear him back to prison," and Bullen is clearly right in the direction *Exit Tho.*, since a little later the quarto has another command by the Turk and *Enter one with Sir Thomas*. It seems certain that the inner stage is not used either for the stocks or for the rack,[7] although the Red Bull certainly had one, and although this scene takes place indoors.

Against the adoption of the QF arrangement by Shakespeare unless it were absolutely necessary, Dr. Greg urges two distinct absurdities: first, that of the fugitive "Edgar's appearing by daylight at his father's front door to discuss what disguise he shall adopt; secondly, that of a single scene that begins before dawn and continues till nightfall." But Edgar does not appear "by daylight": II.ii takes place very early, before dawn, when the moon is shining (33–34), and at the end of the scene it is still dark ("Approach, thou beacon" [170] and see my note on the line): Kent bids Fortune "goodnight," and the next line spoken is by Edgar, coming on, obviously, *in darkness*. That this is his father's house before which Kent is stocked would hardly appear to an audience, and one doubts that even Shakespeare remembered it. As for the "single scene" that troubles Dr. Greg, consistency of time is not thus in the theatre. By an exquisite preparation, in Regan's "Till noone? till night my Lord, and all night too," Shakespeare can foreshorten as he likes in the violent and very long scene, II.iv, which in any event does not begin until an undetermined hour late in the morning. Time is mastered at its conclusion: at 286 *Storme and Tempest* begin, and Cornwall says, "Let us withdraw"; at 303 Gloucester has "Alacke the night comes on" (still vague); and at 311 Cornwall completes the illusion with "tis a wild night." The only formal lapse of time upon which Shakespeare counted is between II.iii and II.iv.

Greg concludes, from the continuity of the three scenes (so-called in modern editions) in F, that the act and scene divisions there are original, and none of my other dissent has anything to say against this; although I think it must remain doubtful. They were certainly *played* continuously, but so were the scenes, for instance, of Act III, except in the sense that no one remained onstage throughout. No doubt this was unusual; but to stock Kent offstage (as in *All's Well* IV.iii) or behind the transverse would have abandoned the dramatic advantage of his continuous humiliation, sleep, and the King's entrance. To Edgar's entrance and brief speech I doubt that an audience would have had to make much adjustment.

A general and I think decisive difficulty with Dr. Greg's position has yet to be considered. F was printed from a copy of Q corrected by a playhouse manuscript, presumably the prompt book as it stood in 1622, and it appears that Dr. Greg must suppose for his view that during the seventeen years since *Lear*'s first performance the prompt book had never been altered for performance under normal conditions in the company's regular theatres (or that it had—this is even more unlikely—been so altered, and then altered again, bringing it again fortuitously into theatrical agreement with Q). This seems to me an unreasonable supposition—and the more so since its issue is a hypothetical private performance (where perhaps no back stage would be available). To conclude: we know that *King Lear* was performed at Whitehall (where Chambers and Greg agree in thinking an inner stage would be available—*RES*, 1940, p. 303) in December 1606, and I believe its first performance took place at court a year earlier, and such evidence as the staging of Q gives us is compatible with this. F, on the other hand, appears to represent a provincial version, perhaps a late one. It is rather long, but Chambers wrote in 1924, reviewing Greg's classic study of abridgement: "I do not think that there is anything which shows that the conditions of provincial performance or the tastes of provincial audiences entailed shorter plays than were customary in London. There is not much evidence one way or the other. There are examples of local regulations requiring performances to be over by 5, 6, 7, or 9 o'clock. In one case it is 5 in winter and 6 in summer. A late 'bill' of 1624 advertised a performance to begin at 1 o'clock. Clearly there is margin here for a three-hour play" (*Library*, IV, pp. 245–46). F would take about three hours to play.

A note, finally, on properties. *King Lear* is peculiar, as Greg says, in the simplicity of its demands: a throne, perhaps a table, the stocks, furniture for the "trial" of III.vi, a couch or bench. This could be attributed to the singular transmission of the text, the reporter ignoring properties, and the scribe who prepared Q as copy for F failing to add them. [*Unfinished*]

CAST[8]

IT IS DIFFICULT TO RESIST the impression that F represents, as compared with Q, a version adapted for a smaller cast. Such an adaptation is not easy to prove, because of inescapable uncertainty as to how far the King's Men were willing to double parts, even on tour, but I will set forth the evidence, for what it is worth.

First, I note that F is much more lavish than Q with its calls for "Attendants" and "Servants," adding them to entries at I.i.190, I.iv.8, II.i.38, II.i.87, II.ii.127, III.vii.1, V.iii.1. It is striking, therefore (and especially so when one considers the generally descriptive character of Q's directions), when for Q's *Enter three Gentlemen* (IV.vi.191) F has only *Enter a Gentleman*. At least two Gentlemen are badly needed, one to pursue the King when he runs off and one to remain for a curiously leisurely conversation with Edgar. Is the F entrance simply a mistake? How many actors did F have available?

It would be possible, drawing things tight, for twelve actors to produce the F version of *King Lear*. Lear, Kent, Gloucester, Edmund, and the three boy actors, I assume, would not double speaking parts—indeed, they hardly could—although some of them would be useful as followers. Edgar doubles Burgundy, Oswald doubles France and Curan. Cornwall after his death, Albany during his long intervals, and probably the Fool after he disappears can manage the Gentlemen, Servants, Messengers, etc., who dart in and out during the last two acts. Cornwall could take the Knight in I.iv. The first distinct pinch comes in III.vii, and I will discuss this in a moment. In IV.vi, Lear, Gloucester, and Edgar are on, Oswald is to come; everyone has had a rest, but Kent and a Gentleman are needed in the next scene, so that only two of the actors of Albany, Cornwall, and the Fool are really practicable. I do not suggest that the King's Men would have played with just nine men and three boys (although I do not think this impossible); no doubt they would have had extras, but we are dealing with speaking parts. Finally, with regard to *Enter a Gentleman*, I note that one of Q's three Gentlemen cries, "lay hands vpon him sirs," whereas F's Gentleman says, "lay hand vpon him Sir" as if he were speaking to Edgar.[9] There is no direction in either text for Lear to be followed, but clearly in Q he is (by two Gentlemen). In F it looks as if he could not be, and it looks as if only one actor really was used in a scene requiring two actors and played originally with three.

Second, the conversation between two Servants in Q at the end of III.vii is omitted in F. This saves nine lines, but I have little doubt that the real reason for the cut was inability to supply the parts. Cornwall, Edmund, and Oswald (besides Goneril and Regan, but I am not considering the three boy actors as doubling speaking parts) have been on, and Edmund and Oswald have gone when Gloucester is brought on "by two or three" (Q), by "Seruants" (F). How many were needed? One dies at line 80, one goes out with Gloucester (*Exit with Gloucester* F) at 94, and one must dispose of the rebellious servant's body ("throw this Slaue Vpon the Dunghill" F 96–97), unless Regan can be imagined as dragging it offstage. There must be three, and this is exactly the number that, with some difficulty, the folio cast of twelve can muster: Edgar is impossible, having just gone at the end of III.vi, and entering at the beginning of IV.i. Lear, Kent, and the Fool have been gone only a few minutes (III.vi.109), but the last two must come back, to make up with Albany three servants. One need not wonder that F cut speaking parts for two of them. (It is noteworthy that Q really needs *four* Servants, one to die, one to take Gloucester away, two to remain and talk, take out the body, and "follow the old Earle" [Q 103]; the reporter evidently added the stage directions after, and his memory was faulty for what he had seen on the stage. As we have observed, he rarely troubles about attendants at all: he has "followers" [I.i.33], "and others" [IV.iv.1, V.iii.39], otherwise only "powers" and "troupes" in Act V.)

Third, F cuts the Doctor in IV.vii, giving both his and a Gentleman's speeches to one Gentleman, and then cuts the conversation between Kent and this Gentleman at the end of the scene. The second maneuver saves eleven lines, but the first saves nothing and cannot be the original arrangement (cf. Q *Richard III*'s conflation of the Keeper and Brackenbury in I.iv). F hadn't enough actors. Cordelia, Kent, and a Gentleman (probably the former Cornwall) come on, and then—a drain on the company's men not felt in Q, where Lear is "discovered"—Lear is brought on by "Seruants": at least two, since they carry a "chaire." Who are they? Everyone possible must be reserved for the entrances (as elaborate as possible, although rather scanty, one fears, in the performance represented by F) of Edmund's army at the beginning of the next scene, and Albany's a few lines later. In any event, only Oswald and the Fool seem to be available, and these must be the Servants. The Doctor was impracticable—and with rare consistency the book holder must be supposed to have gone back and cut him out of IV.iv also or, rather, given his speeches again to a "Gentleman." But in IV.vii the Gentleman's talk, whatever his status in the prompt copy's speakers' names, is so clearly and professionally medical that (besides wanting to save time) the book holder may reasonably have felt that his political chat with Kent at the end of the scene was unbecoming. At any rate, it went out.

The cumulative force of these cuts and syncopations in F is impossible to ignore.

The Conceiving of *King Lear*

[*The only one of his "discoveries" that he ever felt "bitter" about in after years, wrote Berryman to the National Endowment for the Humanities (May 31, 1971), "is proof that Shakespeare used Camden's* Remaines *for* Lear, *because the other man who noticed this (S. Musgrove, in "The Nomenclature of* King Lear," Review of English Studies, *VII:27 [July 1956], pp. 294–98) did not also see that in fact both plots of that intricate play formed in his mind* while reading *the few pages of Camden during which occur all the main names of Shakespeare's characters—a circumstance dazzling enough for me to plan a chapter-opening around it . . ."*]

NOT ENOUGH ATTENTION, perhaps, in the long and busy course of Shakespearean study, has been paid to the question of why the poet took up the themes he did when he did. This is a topic interesting in itself and crucial to biography. Perhaps it has been avoided precisely because students felt that nothing could be accomplished here, that our biographical materials were too meagre to make promising any enquiry into the nature and operation of the deep impulses that presumably guide the selection of themes, in an artist, for his most important works. But the general picture that scholarship gives, for it gives one, is very different from any suggested by such hesitation. One is asked to see William Shakespeare looking around for a subject for his next play, either quite at random or at the dictates of opportunism. One is asked to imagine a poet entirely unlike any other major poet we know anything about. It is an unfortunate by-product of Henry N. Paul's valuable study of the composition of *Macbeth* (*The Royal Play of "Macbeth,"* New York: Macmillan, 1950) that a most exceptional situation has the effect of seeming usual. Shakespeare certainly, with this play, planned to hypnotize the impatient King, James, though he had also other concerns hardly touched by Mr. Paul. But what other plays are so explicitly, in part, determined? Possibly: *Love's Labour's Lost*, *A Midsummer Night's Dream*, *The Merry Wives of Windsor*. The bulk of his creation remains, plays coming mysteriously one by one into being. One notices at once that the father-dominated tragedy, *Hamlet*, must have been finally handled by the poet at a time very close to the death of his father in 1600 and that the mother-dominated tragedy, *Coriolanus*, must have been written close to the death of his mother in 1609, but upon examination each of the cases bristles with difficulties. The poet had twin children and in the early *Comedy of Errors* he doubles Plautus' twins, and he shows a certain liking for twins later as well, but this does not take us very far. The lengthy mood dominations proposed by Dowden three-quarters of a century ago, and still largely accepted, tell us little of particular plays. Nor has much agreement yet been reached among critics who would like to see eight of the history plays as two gigantic tetralogies, laid down and carried out as a philosophical history of the English world; other critics see them arriving piecemeal, out of order, fortuitously. Shakespeare never, so far as we know, lifted a play out of (so to speak) the newspapers, like Chapman in the lost *Keep the Widow Waking* and the author of *A Yorkshire Tragedy*. Even if he had done so, we should still want to know whether enquiry was not desirable into *why* he had done this, at this time.

Another thing we really know nothing about is how he conceived his plays, whether over weeks or months of brooding, or with unbelievable rapidity. I think one is more likely to feel comfortable with the second of these ideas, which may also seem to receive a certain tangential support from the tradition that he scratched up some form of *The Merry Wives* in a fortnight; but then that was only *The Merry Wives*, largely a matter of writing—and we know that Shakespeare wrote easily and rapidly: the career tells us so, and his first editors do. But if we like better the second idea (upon no evidence), it may seem more desirable than ever to form some notion of the impulses at whose bidding he abruptly made an immense dramatic work out of some shabby, thin old story known to him for years, like that of *King Leir*—one perhaps already sometimes considered as a subject, one perhaps not.[1]

Wilfrid Perrett was quite clear half a century ago that Shakespeare used [William] Camden's *Remaines* for *King Lear*, but truths are lost more readily than come by, and Kenneth Muir tells us now in *Shakespeare's Sources* (London: Methuen, 1957, I, p. 143) that the evidence is "inconclusive." His evidence may be. It is true that he nowhere notices Perrett's book, the subtlest comprehensive study ever of the sources of a single Shakespearean plot to that date (1904).[2]

The old play (acted by the Queen's and Sussex's Men on April 6, 1594), so long familiar to him that some dozen years before 1605 he had modelled on one of its scenes [no. xix in the Malone Society reprint][3] the scene of Clarence's murder, tells the flickering tale of Leir's determination to resign his crown and divide his kingdom equally among his three daughters. Skalliger suggests the division should be "As is their worth, to them that loue professe." Leir rejects this thought, but suddenly invents a stratagem to get his youngest daughter, Cordella, who has vowed to marry for love, to marry where he likes (he likes a King of Britanny): he will try which of the three loves him best and, while they vie, take Cordella "at the vantage." The plot fails, and the King of France, who has come to woo, carries her off. Sorry to see Leir, deceived by flattery, cast off Cordella, a noble named Perillus pleads for her and is rebuked. When the inheriting daughters have turned of course on their father, this man calls him "the myrour of mild patience" and follows him to France, where all ends well. Contrapuntal to Perillus has been the daughters' murderous messenger.

Shakespeare also knew odd versions of the story, clearly in various books he had read: in Holinshed, in *The Mirror of Magistrates*, in Book II of *The Faerie Queene*, perhaps even in Geoffrey of Monmouth. But the differences between these accounts and the old play make it clear to me, as to the elder [H. H.] Furness [in *A New Variorum Edition of Shakespeare*, V: *King Lear*, Philadelphia, 1880], that the version dominant in his mind when he came to make out his own play was the theatrical one.

As for the story in *Arcadia*, first to be noticed by Mrs. Lennox, is it likely that Shakespeare had waited fifteen years to read the *Arcadia*?—in order, moreover, to find the story in Book II, chapter 10, bitterly paralleling the Leir story, and use it at once? Unsatisfactory and reluctant as our ideas are about Shakespeare's reading, I suppose this will not strike anyone as plausible, and I assume that Sidney's story too had been long familiar to him by 1605. It concerns an old man, once Prince of Paphlagonia, blind, and led by his son Leonatus, who at the instigation of his bastard son, Plexirtus, had once ordered that this legitimate son should be led away and murdered. Leonatus escaped, to serve as a soldier, and now attends his father, who has meanwhile been blinded and driven out by the bastard. Misery and remorse alike make the father beg the son to lead him to the top of a rock that he may destroy himself. This story too ends well, the blind king restored, setting the crown on Leonatus's head and dying at once of "excesse of comfort."

Our problem is when, how, and why these stories fused.

Now, Malone thought, and Perrett agreed, that one detail in the work Shakespeare was to write came neither from the Leir stories nor from Sidney but from a section, "Wise Speeches," in a book brand-new, Camden's *Remaines concerning Britaine* of 1605.[4] Shakespeare is not likely to have been long in coming on or being directed to this book, which praises him by name along with other modern authors. In considering the apparent effect upon him of the following passage, we may need to remind ourselves that he was a man as well as an author; whether he was in search of a subject for a new play we do not know, but he was certainly the father of two supremely unmarried daughters.

Ina, King of West-Saxons, had three daughters, of whom vpon a time he demanded whether they did love him, and so would do during their lives above all others; the two elder sware deeply they would, the yongest, but the wisest told her father flatly without flattery, *That albeit she did love, honour, and reverence him, and so would while she lived, as much as nature and daughterly dutie at the vttermost could expect: Yet she did thinke that one day it would come to passe, that she should affect another more fervently, meaning her husband, where she were married: Who being made one flesh with her, as God by commaundement had told, and nature had taught hir she was to cleave fast to, forsaking father and mother, kiffe and kinne . . .* One referreth this to the daughters of king *Leir*.

This is on page 182. We read on. Page 184: "King *Eadgar* of *England*." 185: "*Edmund* the king of the *East-Angles* . . . forced to seeke his safetie by flight." 187, "*Earle* of Kent." 196, "*Robert* Earl of *Gloucester* base sonne to" and "some English . . . put out his eies." 197, "from the cliffes there in a cleere day discovered the coast of *Ireland* . . . *Merlins* prophecies." 201, "the Duke of *Burgundie*." 204, "Earle of *Cornewall*." 207 (Queene Eleanor, to Edward I, quoted as an example of "a most loving and kinde wife"), "I may reserve other to a fitter place"; cf. Cordelia's still-loving "I would prefer him to a fitter place" than her sisters' kindness. And back on page 65, in the section on names, we find "Oswold, *Ger.* House-ruler or Steward" (on page 37 it is "Oswald").

Here, within two dozen pages, we have every missing name of importance in the play[5]—every name, in fact, except those of the three daughters, long familiar, and those of Oswald, Curan, and Caius, and the source of Oswald's must be the passage on page 65, and even "Caius" is given earlier in the section on names, as meaning "Probus." I take it that there is something here to be accounted for, and confess I do not know what will account for it except what I now suggest—that the reply of Ina's youngest daughter was like a sword in Shakespeare's heart, and that during the ensuing minutes, or hours, he conceived his entire tragedy, except possibly for the Fool, not merely fusing Sidney's characters and situation with those of the old play but naming the new people as he turned the pages—in what state of mind and passion we can hardly imagine, but very very busy, perhaps as busy as any man has been.

[*This essay was not finished; but in earlier passages Berryman explained further:*]

What is new here, and apparently seized his attention, is the reason given by the youngest daughter: that in marrying she will inevitably forsake her father. Shakespeare was forty, both his daughters were too long unmarried though splendid matches; he must have hung on to them as well as *wished* them married; Dr. John Hall, who would two years hence marry Susanna, had been several years settled prominently in his Stratford practice.

Upon this argument—which I do not expect scholars to believe—the time limits for the play are narrow, and I think we have reason to think the play was wholly conceived with extraordinary velocity: in a day, or an evening: at a single reading of a few pages in Camden.

Take Shakespeare's mind as attached strongly here, on personal grounds, to the Lear story, which indeed he may have been thinking for fifteen years of some time dramatizing. Add the singular congruity of the figure of Lear in the story, crotchety, peremptory, with the ruler in his most recent play—(not *Othello*, which is earlier, but) *Measure for Measure* of 1604—who also pretends to give up his power. But the Lear story is empty, for a Shakespearean tragedy of the great period: there is no all-possessing motive, as in Hamlet, nor any grand antagonist, like Iago. A subplot then; and thrust itself into his mind a story from the fifteen-year-old *Arcadia*, of a bastard son usurping and blinding his king-father, who then wandering is succored by the legal son whom he had driven out at the hypocritical instigation of the bastard. Here are two fathers who have favoured the wrong children. More closely, I suspect Shakespeare remembered—or noticed when he looked the story up, as we will find he did—a speech given by Sidney to the Paphlagonian King: "I had left my self nothing but the name of a King."

BUT THE PRODUCT OF this creation (of this impulse and reflexion and linking and elaboration) was a universe seething with ingratitude, with treachery; and I think [. . .] that this ingratitude was the emotional governor of the choice of the Lear story, and of the fastening to it of the Paphlagonian story (the youngest daughter's reply only pressing the button, as appearing to justify what *nowhere else* in the play *can* be justified: betrayal, that is, of the realm by the King, of a loyal nobleman by his King [app'ly: opposite], of father-king by daughters, of daughter by father, of father by [bastard] son, of brother, etc. etc.). Now *why* ingratitude?

1946–52

Letters on *Lear*

(WITH MARK VAN DOREN, W. W. GREG,

G. I. DUTHIE, AND OTHERS)

[*to Mark Van Doren*]

3 October 1944

Dear Mark:

Lear's renovation is going on rapidly & ruins me altogether for anything else. I am willing, however, to be destroyed in this cause: I hope to have some permanent effect, & the play was [? contemporaneous] (III.vii.63) with *Error*.

22 March 1945

Dear Mark:

One of the strongholds of corruption in *Lear* fell I think this morning. The terrible moment when Edgar meets Gloucester on the heath:

> But who comes heere?
> My father poorely led? World world . . .

The uncorrected sheet of the Quarto has "poorelie, leed," taken over by Folio as "poorely led" and so reprinted by every editor—the feeblest phrase in Shak, I suppose. But the Quarto corrector tried again and got "parti, eyd," behind which hides the MS. reading. If I am right, this was: "My father, bloody-eyed? World, World O World."

4 April [1945]

Dear Mark:

I've decided to throw the *Lear* edition together in some form by June, abandoning study meanwhile; and this takes fifteen hours a day. I lose time in New York with a dentist, I'll lose time at Sewanee, more work in Washington, it's the devil; worse I'm much over-tired now. O Prince! give me a second personality!

I hate to see you tormented by "poorly led," though it's companionable to know that someone besides myself can feel the fever. I don't know about that; Greg doesn't like "emptie-ey'd" better than I do, and it's still a crux, with half a dozen recent possibilities fighting for my faith. Let me console you with some passages that are *not* cruxes any more.

> To be a comrade with the Wolfe, and howl
> Necessity's sharpe pinch[.]
>
> (II.iv.213)

This is Collier's brilliant restoration of the Shak. metaphor corrupted into "Owle" by the reporter or the Q compositor, and taken over by the Folio.

> *Glo.* O strange & fastned Villaine: I neuer got him!
> Would he deny his Letter said he? Harke!
>
> (II.i.80)

"I never got him," which follows "Letter" in the Quarto, is omitted in F, which mistook the transposition mark for deletion. "Strange" (which at once guarantees and is guaranteed by "I neuer got him") was misread "strong" (how plausible!) in Q, which also omits "O" & "said he." Editors have divided the lines wrongly also. This pleasant chaos only took me eight months. Another very difficult place has defied emendation because the metre was misunderstood. The passage is omitted in F and should read thus:

> *Edg.* This would have seemed a period to such
> As loue not sorow, but another (woe)
> To amplifie too much, would make much more,
> And top extreamitie.
>
> (V.iii.205)

He then resumes his story with a new line. A word was lost after "another," and *woe* has put down its competitors. "Another," incredibly enough, has been taken as parallel with "such" instead of with "This," or someone wd have diagnosed the loss long since.

The mess in Kent's soliloquy (II.ii.175) does not mean that he is reading out parts of the letter but is the result of two misprints ("time" for *balm*, "From" for *for*) and bad punctuation. He says:

> I know tis from Cordelia,
> Who hath most fortunately beene inform'd
> Of my obscured course, and shall find balm
> For this enormous state, seeking to give
> Losses their remedies.

Rowe & Bailey fixed this; "enormous" (Shakespeare's only use of the word) means disordered. I can't make sense of I.iv.5, by the way, without supposing that here also "from" is an error for "for": "The lamentable change is for the best"; what do you think?

Then there is Perrett's admirable gloss *god's spies* (V.iii.17), Furness' (anticipating me) giving "What do you mean?" to *Cornwall* at III.vii.77, Collier's *Finsbury* for the ghostly Lipsbury of II.ii.10, the NED's *remedial* at IV.iv.16, etc etc etc. Don't feel any need to study over this or answer it.

[*to Mark Van Doren*]

17 May 1945

Dear Mark:

About emending the Folio's "poorely led?": I am not of course so happy about my "bloody-eyed" as on the day it occurred to me, but Greg is certain that F cannot be right, and I don't believe it can. The Quarto compositor first read "poorlie, leed," and the press-corrector, noticing an error, changed it to "parti,eyd"—a reading which must be taken to represent a sincere and new attempt to make out the copy, since no guess would give a reading so senseless; F, printing in this sheet from the uncorrected state of Q, has simply emended by guesswork, omitting the internal comma, reading "led" for "leed." This is an early gloss, in fact Q2 (also printing from the uncorrected state of Q) makes the same changes independently. But if "poorlie led" really stood in the copy for Q, how did the corrector arrive at "parti,eyd"? And the supposition that Q had a reading *not* "poorlie led" and yet so similar to it that it could be read erroneously first as "poorlie, leed" and then as "parti,eyd," and that the editor of F independently supplied the true "poorlie led" from the prompt-book in the copy of Q from which, after correction, F was printed—this supposition is inadmissible. Now "eyd" may be easily supposed right, given its general dramatic relevance (Gloucester's plight consisting except for dishevelment only in blindness, and apparently—from Edgar's terrible outcry "World world O world"—being at once perceived by Edgar). It is not difficult to see a hyphen twice read as a comma, and more sensible than to suppose that nothing stood between the two words; Shakespeare has "hollow-ey'd" in *Errors*. "bloodie" (or bloudi, or a similar spelling) if it is right would mean that the compositor had correctly read the middle of the word, which the corrector then bungled (perhaps desperate, since "poorti, eyd" is insane, and as I will show in a minute "parti,eyd" has an "air" of sense), and that both of them misread "p" for "bl"; first "l" and then "t," for "d" in copy, are impossible. NED quotes "bloody-eyed" only from Byron, but its materials for "obvious combinations" were often deficient. Shakespeare has "bloody fac'd" (2 *Henry IV*, F) and "bloody sceptred" (*Macbeth*). The graphic difficulty in short is not insuperable, and neither, it seems to me, is the anticipation of "Bless thy sweet eyes, they bleed" 40 lines later. One would like a clearer case, however. And unhappily I can't escape a suspicion that "parti-eyed" may have been intended, meaning perhaps "striped with blood" (& egg)—on the analogy of "parti-coloured," which was common, and "parti-coated" (*Love's Labour's Lost*). It is one of the worst cruces in the canon.

I will have more time to think about it, since the Rockefeller Foundation have just renewed my fellowship for another year. I've finished text and commentary in their first form . . .

[*to Mark Van Doren*]

13 June 1945

Dear Mark:

Thanks very much for this book on the text of *Lear*, which I am glad to have since it is the first whole volume on the subject to follow Greg (Van Dam, Doran & Hubler all in love with Quarto with varying degrees of obtuseness) but sorry to see since it appears to contribute nothing and must have cost the author a good deal of labour. He comes out at the point I reached two years ago, is as Folio-obsessed as Schmidt, and has objections to the shorthand hypothesis which do not seem to me sensible, although I will study them carefully. Naturally I don't think shorthand *alone* produced the text: the reporter had a memory also, which most of the scholars have ignored—or I may have begun to incorporate mnemonic analysis (as of stage directions) into my work last year without predecessor, I don't remember. But I hope I can get my text published before *another* book simply on the text appears!—they are a waste of time. Kirschbaum like everyone else howls for *a new text*, and here mine sits in front of me, finished. Alas the whole edition won't be ready for months.

[*John Marshall, John Simon Guggenheim Foundation, New York*]
11 July 1945

Dear Mr. Marshall:

. . . Another book has just appeared—the fifth or so—on the text of *King Lear*. I am glad to see it because it is the first whole volume (published in this country) to follow Greg's general views—depreciation of the Quarto, &c. But I am sorry to see it because it is not much of a book: the author (Leo Kirschbaum) is Folio-dazzled like Schmidt, uncritical, and quite useless even to an editor, even to me. Three fourths of the book is devoted to sample passages with analyses, of which the following entire-comment-on-one-of-the-play's-real-difficulties is typical: "Q's 'enridged' for F's 'enraged' (IV.vi.71) seems definitely more poetic—but it is a mishearing by the reporter and is not Shakespeare's." The man imagines that this is *argument* (I find in my notes a body of evidence to support "enridged," which is of course necessary anyway by *durior lectio*, and explain the occurrence of "enraged"), and his book is fantastically entitled *The True Text of King Lear*. He too pleads for a new edition: "What is so badly needed" &c. I begin to think my edition will be a best-seller!

Yours sincerely,
John Berryman

[*to W. W. Greg*]
14 December 1945

Dear Dr. Greg,

I should have gathered courage and written to you long since to say that I am making a critical edition of *King Lear*, for my work wishes to respond to your challenge at the end of the *Variants in the First Folio* and I look upon its recensional part as based largely upon methods of analysis you have developed, so that I cannot help being as eager for your approval (if the edition finally merits it) as my very great respect for your work makes me diffident about writing at all. Besides, without your study of the Q variants nothing of the sort would have been possible. It was only after this and *The Editorial Problem* came out that I returned to an intention formed while reading for the Oldham Shakespeare examinations at Cambridge in 1937. The last eighteen months (owing to the help of the Rockefeller Foundation) have been given almost wholly to textual work, and it is getting on. How difficult it was at first, indeed still is, I needn't tell you. Some months of recension convinced me that Q is a report as you and Chambers contend, evidently taken by an alphabetical shorthand. Farther I couldn't go without editing. So I constructed a provisional text and apparatus, holding hard to F where I could, and wrote a full commentary. These were very imperfect, although they turned up a good deal of new material. But making them taught me how little an inflexible hypothesis will edit *Lear*, and gave me experience. Now I am working out a much more secure study of the whole body of variation in Q and F, paying special attention to analogies with the other parallel texts, and revising text and commentary as I go. No doubt I shouldn't say so, but I really have some hope that for major problems the edition will reach solutions which ought to be more or less permanent unless new evidence of a surprising kind should appear. Details are another matter, and I should be very grateful for your advice on some of the numerous points of judgment and fact in which inexperience must have led me astray. Is it possible that you would be willing to look through part of the Textual Introduction in typescript? About fifty pages are drafted and more will be before I can hear from you. Having some notion of the claims constantly made upon your energy, I venture to ask only because I have myself spent, partly under your involuntary direction, so much energy in a task for which I believe that such abilities as I possess, though hardly my mechanical training, peculiarly fit me—the making of a reasonable Shakespearean text—that I hope the work is worth helping. Also I hope that some of the discussion, familiar as you are with the subjects, may still interest you. Meanwhile will you forgive a question or so now? I will take up only two or three of the matters on which curiosity as to your opinion especially exercises me.

The first concerns Q's addition, or F's omission, of "Come sir" thrice at the beginning of speeches in Goneril's part in a single scene (I.iv.240, 258, 336). The last two are so implausible that even the Cambridge editors, who preserved on principle everything in either text, excluded them; the first is extra-metrical; all dilute Goneril's abrupt severity, and all must be interpolated. They are 3 of forty such Q connectives condemned by F, but this phrase is added by no one else and by Goneril only here. Would you tell me what likelihood you think there is of this phenomenon alone being produced by a non-reportorial agency?—by anything except the (somehow reported) actor of the part (who elsewhere in this scene and the preceding one levelled Shakespeare's "distaste" and "condemn" equally to "dislike"). *Richard III* shows similar variation, though nothing so striking; I think you and Patrick must be right; some of the corruption is identical with *Lear*'s (as the unmetrical "fellow" for "man" at III.ii.100). Reporting aside, no allowance that I can make for scribes, compositors, or F's tinkering with metre, appears to cover these *Come sir*'s, and revision is inconceivable. Nothing analogous occurs in *Troilus* or *Othello*. Wilson's case for "Burbage additions" in F *Hamlet* I consider much overstated, and they are not anyway properly of this kind. That a scribe remembering performance would treat Goneril's part thus I cannot believe; but what I am anxious to know is whether you can.

Then the question of staging. I think there must be a connection between Q's omission of an entry for Lear in iv.7 and F's omission of the line which prepares for his appearance, "Please you draw neere, louder the musicke there," and I wonder whether you think it can be accidental. Q's dozen omitted entrances include none comparable with Lear in F's chair (the reporter seems to be responsible for the substantial directions, though there are two indications that the press-corrector or compositors added a good many). F omits inadvertently so few lines that it seems to me we are bound to assume intention. I take it that Q *had* an inner stage, on which, as one would expect, Lear was discovered seated at line 25. The music is essential and Shakespearean for reconciliation, harmony, cure. F's omission of the line, as of any direction (the only material direction so omitted), is suspicious. F is shortened and saves minor speaking parts. May it not represent the prompt-book arranged for a late tour (1618–22), adapted to an alcoveless stage and without music? I feel an improbability in your 1940 view in that it must suppose, mustn't it, either that the staging never altered at all (which would be very strange) or that by accident the 1608 and 1623 texts preserve identical arrangements, although these arrangements are inconsistent with all the known probabilities of the Court, the Globe, and the Blackfriars. Also, *if* Q has no inner stage, why should we hold it original?—the date of the reporting must remain uncertain, whereas for the Court performance in 1607 surely some better arrangement than F's would have been adopted. (I know no evidence for Sisson's certainty that the copy for F was a quarto *used as* prompt-book; if Q and F differ as I think they do, the F staging must be much later.) You speak of absurdities forced on Shakespeare in ii. But *The Dutch Courtezan* and *The Travels of Three English Brothers*, of similar date, do not appear to use their inner stages for stocks (G. F. Reynolds' different account of the Curtain–Red Bull play is inconsistent with its text): in each, the prisoner is put in stocks onstage, warned that he will have to stay there, and then in fact released and marched off—to gaol. For the other: at the end of Kent's soliloquy it is still dark, and Edgar comes on at once. His "tree" would be taken by the audience to be nearby, and that, escaping, he should pass by again in the darkness would excite no incredulity. Shakespeare evidently arranged his time-lapse to follow what editors call II.iii, and the following long scene is brilliantly foreshortened to lead to the illusion of nightfall as the storm comes on at its end. What do you think?[1]

Finally—a fraction of one's labour, but indispensable in *Lear*—I'd be grateful for your opinion of two emendations.

> (1)   and wast thou faine (poore Father)
> To houell thee with Swine and Rogues forlorne,
> In short, and musty straw?
>
> (QF IV.vii.40)

Short is violently implausible in either of the senses (chopped, scanty) Craig indifferently assigns to it, as well as in a Devonshire dialectal sense recorded by Chope (for straw from which long-straw has been separated), and there seems to be no connection with the *OED*'s "short dung." I agree with Furness that the word must be a misprint in Q—taken over by F—and suggest that the 1608 copy read, correctly, "fowl and mustie." This is characteristic: foule and muddy, foule and pestilent, noysome musty Chaffe (*Temp.*, *Hamlet*, *Cor.*). Cf Nashe, "they are poore beggars, and lye in fowle straw euerie night." Q is so badly printed that I think less need be made of graphic justification than in most texts (luckily, for I am a novice at this, and await correction), but the misreadings s:f and t:l are frequent in it, and r:w occurs.

> (2) And heres another whose warpt lookes proclaime
> What store her heart is made an
>
> (Q III.vi.57)

No meaning has ever been discovered for *store*, and the text's authority is very slight. Capell's "made on" I call certain. For *store* Theobald's "stone" can be supported, and so in some degree can "stuff," but neither satisfies the necessary relation with *warpt* or with the cluster of ideas Lear associated with his daughters—pride, fierceness, contempt. I suggest that "scorn" may be right. Shakespeare had already joined the words in *All's Well*:

> Contempt his scornfull Perspectiue did lend me,
> Which warpt the line of euerie other fauour,
> Scorn'd a faire colour
>
> (V.iii.48–50)

and Goneril's *scornfull eyes* were cursed by Lear at II.iv.168. If this is acceptable, "store" is perhaps the reporter's mishearing, although t:c is common in the Quartos.

Tossing these to their fate, I beg your indulgence for this endless letter. I would like if I may to congratulate you very warmly on your recent anniversary.

Yours sincerely,
John Berryman

[W. W. Greg to JB]

6 January 1946

Dear Dr Berryman

I am much interested in your letter of 14 December about your projected edition of *King Lear*. More power to your elbow!

That Q is a report I feel tolerably convinced; but as you know I don't like the shorthand hypothesis—though I have not been able to substitute any other—so please do not accept that on my authority.

I should not myself hold too fast to F. We know that in some cases it took over errors from Q, and it very probably did so in many others. Where Q & F agree an editor has, in my opinion, considerable freedom of emendation, and to adhere to the reading whenever sense can be made of it is uncritical. Q + F has not *much* more authority than those passages for which Q is our only text.

If you care to send me your textual introduction it will give me much pleasure to read it. I need hardly warn you *not* to send me your only copy!

Your point about "Come sir" in Goneril's part is interesting. It certainly seems to me highly unlikely that the insertions could have got into the text except through the reporting of an actor's delivery.

The question of staging is undoubtedly difficult. I think that in Q version of IV.vii Lear is "discovered" and the alcove used, as one would expect. This is proved by part of the line omitted in F: "Please you draw neere." This has no sense if Lear is borne in on a chair, and was consequently omitted in F. The omission of the rest of the line may have been due to lack of music, and your suggestion that the promptbook had been marked to suit it for provincial acting seems plausible. I am afraid I have been inconsistent over this. My assumption in the *Editorial Problem* that the ms. used for revising Q to form the copy for F was the promptbook, won't square with my argument in "The Staging of *King Lear*" in *RES*, xvi. 300ff. If the promptbook had been originally written for an alcoveless stage, it must in the course of time have been revised to fit the arrangement at the Globe & Blackfriars. The whole of my *RES* argument breaks down. It would of course have been easier to "discover" the stocks, but there is no reason why they need have been. I should suggest that the stocks were brought in into the inner stage, the traverse closed and drawn again for Edgar's entry—and then the scene-divisions altered again for your provincial tour when the alcove was unavailable.

It was doubtless for this same town that the Doctor & Gentleman were amalgamated in IV.vii. Note, by the way, that in this scene in Q the prefixes to ll.21 & 23 have got transposed. You suggest that "the press-corrector or compositors added a good many" directions. I can imagine the press-corrector doing so possibly, but hardly the compositor.

As for your emendations. It seems to me that if "short" can mean "scanty" the sense fits the passage admirably. But I rather doubt whether it can, except in conjunction with some word meaning "measure," expressed or implied. Straw can be short (i.e. in short supply) but short straw can hardly mean a deficient quantity of straw. Your suggestion "fowl" is a possibility. No doubt w(u):r can be paralleled, and l:t is rather a peculiarity of Q (though generally rare). Also s:f is of course possible: but sh:f is less easy to explain. There is however a double-tailed variety of f (perhaps for ff = F) that might I suppose be misread as sh (*unfinished*).

"Scorn" for "store" also is plausible. Of course sc:st offers no difficulty: the difficulty is to account for n:e. It seems just possible that "scorne" was misread as "storre," for rn:rr is conceivable, though rn: nn would be more likely. As it is Q it *might* be a mishearing: what about an error of shorthand?

Wishing all success

I am yours sincerely
W. W. Greg

P. S. Doubtless you have seen Dr. Kirschbaum's book on "The True Text of *King Lear*"—over-simplified, I think. I have lately been reviewing it for *RES* [see *Review of English Studies* 22 (1946), pp. 230–34].

16 February 1946

Dear Dr. Greg,

I am more grateful than I can say for your helpful and encouraging letter. I work quite alone, my publications have been remote from my present labour (I am not "Dr.," by the way), and I was on the point of becoming very discouraged when it came.

I'm glad you agree about the staging. Certainly Kent's stocks could have been brought onto the inner stage in Q; I hadn't seen this, and it makes Steevens's division of ii original. I don't know what is usual for such cases: may I refer to your view as changed and excise the arguments in my Introduction against the view you set out six years ago?—they are mostly a waste of time now. In the letter I compressed them too much, but how such matters stretch out.

Another statement over-brief, on which you were amiable not to pounce, was one about graphic justification for emending the Quarto—the whole text, that is, except for isolated emendations of F like Theobald's "Plate." I meant that in view of the extraordinarily uncertain activities of *four* agencies—(a) the actors; (b) the reporter, while note-taking and while transcribing; (c) the compositor, considering the evidence of the variants for dropped and intrusive letters (beniz, queues, harte lip), literals, omitted words (eleven, most of them no doubt in the copy), added words (this, the), assimilation, substitution (raging-roaring, seemes-shewes), guessing or taking an impression (vntender, mildie, defences, abdication, to saue thee!), general carelessness (the-his, not-most), as well as for fantastic misreading of some forty words; and (d) the press corrector, as to whom I agree with you that there are about fifteen fairly clear instances of guessing and sophistication—in view of all this, I submit that the mechanical standards for acceptance of an emendation should not, even must not, be so rigid as is customary and right in other texts. I hope you can agree with this; the necessity for emendation is so widespread in *Lear*, as you have said, that the principles involved seem to me very important. In a sense one must emend through the error to the copy, and through that to the actor, hoping to reach Shakespeare. Unhappily the uncertainty of the limiting conditions tends to open the field to alternatives; one can only hope that if one works hard enough and long enough, and keeps one's head, the competitors will prove unworthy. For instance my notes show six conjectures seriously entertained for "parti,eyd" at various times, but I have been able to discard more or less conclusively four of these and all I am certain of is that the word ended "-ey'd" (cf euill-eyd *Cym*, sad-eyed *Henry V*, thicke eyde *I H. IV* etc), a hyphen being twice misread, perhaps, as a

comma. Since this savage passage has come up, what do you think
of "emptie-ey'd"? Cf V.iii.189–90; "empty-hearted" I.i.155; "A carrion
Death, within whose empty eye" *Mer.* This conjecture aims at Shakespeare, of course; it doesn't pretend to know exactly what chaos the
copy had, although the second syllable is precise: *lie* Qa : *ti* Qb : *tie*
conj.

That you think "fowl" and "scorn" plausible cheers me very much;
I still do myself. Thanks for the double-tailed *f* and for "rr:nn." In
the simplest way of writing "store" & "scorne" according to Willis's
1602 shorthand, they are in fact quite similar; but since he provides
half a dozen ways, this must be too uncertain for use. The whole
shorthand subject is uncertain. I am not much more comfortable with
this hypothesis than you are. But it cannot be asserted that it is impossible; and what mainly one needs for editing anyway is the practical certainty of theatrical provenance. This I have. One would like
to know with assurance the method used, but I think it very doubtful
whether in the absence of data we ever can. Certainly we won't find
it out by study of Bright's and Bales's negligible systems (I confess I
wasted some time thus) or by such methods as Kirschbaum employs.
You call his book over-simplified, but is it merely that? I'll be glad to
see your review. I found his thesis nebulous and incredible, the exposition uncritical, the whole book lazy, naïve, and dogmatic. Hélas,
hélas.

You say you wouldn't yourself hold too fast to F. Heavens, I'm not!
Beginning with such crimes in F *Othello* as "acerb: bitter," "nicke:
interim," and the astonishing "He dies" (III.iii.165—this I think must
be a stage direction inserted by someone ignorant of the play or very
thoughtless, and caught by the compositor into the text, making it
"metrical"!)—and Chambers's tentative list for F *Merchant*—I made
what I can safely call a careful study of Folio sophistication, and in
spite of Lear's unpromising textual history the study has been useful.
I make about 50 rather clear sophistications of diction, grammar,
metre, personification, puns, etc., in F *Merchant*, allowing about 52
inadvertent changes (the study of those here and in other texts has
been useful also) and some two dozen acceptable emendations, most
of them anticipated by Q2. One may suppose at least this number in
Lear. But except in vocabulary (reuengive, rash, dearne, etc) it is
difficult equally to be confident of any particular one and to act on
the confidence when I have it—owing of course to the antithetical
concept of "authority." I call IV.ii.17 "armes: names" one, Q being
guaranteed by the "distaff" relation with "Yea distaffe women man-
nage rustie bils Against thy seate" in *Rich II*, despite the plausibility

of graphic error. My latest decision was against F "squints," accepting your "squenes." I can't help suspecting, by the way, that "questrists" is something of the sort, a ghost-word—Q "questrits" being not a misprint for it but a misreading for Shakespeare's nonce "questants" (*All's Well*) which then served as the basis for the scribe's (if the prompt-book was defective) or F's (if the scribe missed it) conjecture. Is not this more likely than that the poet invented two words so different for the same thing, given this known insecurity of F? "Alapt: attaskt: at task" is an analogy. "Ataxt" for this last I've always considered yours, so that I was sorry to find it some time ago in Kellner (p. 73),[2] where I assume that you missed it when preparing the admirable review you wrote. Priority seems to me much, in spite of Kellner's actual form (attaxt) and his usual error in quotation and ignoring of F; but I incline to think I should credit you both, as Wilson sometimes does. Another unwilling report: the basis for conjecturing "spence" seems to me to be weakened or destroyed by the occurrence of the Q copy's phrase "spoyle and wast" twice in a contemporary Kingsmen's play, Wilkins's *Miseries of Inforst Marriage* (B3v, F1v). This is riddled with imitation of *King Lear*, which I think Wilkins may have read as well as seen—indeed, my general impression of him, from the work I had to do last year on *Pericles*, is that he was a sort of protégé of Shakespeare's; and I once thought that his use somehow supported Q against F, though I don't now. The phrase may have been common, and is no doubt the actor's. None of the other "expence"s in the canon show signs of sophistication from "spence."

Again I've written too much to you. My excuse must be that no one whom I see has much understanding of or interest in textual criticism, and the temptation to talk on is great. You are very good to agree to look at my textual introduction. I'm putting some of it on thin paper, because a publisher tells me that a large part of his non-air transatlantic mail is lost, and will send it shortly. The delay of losing even a copy would be tedious. What do you say to "Sea a-wax" for the *Timon* crux I.i.48, the syllables being written separately and "a" being misunderstood, as occurs elsewhere, for a preposition? The word isn't known, and NED is unsatisfactory on "a-wane," but experience with the 400 words peculiar to *Lear* suggests to me that conjecture can be as bold as it likes in this regard. Shakespeare has the verb "wax" thrice with "sea." With thanks and all good wishes for your work and well-being,

Yours sincerely,
John Berryman

Letters on *Lear*

Dear Mr Berryman

As regards the staging of *Lear* you are certainly at liberty to say that I no longer am prepared to maintain the position I took up in *RES* in 1940. I am not sure that I ought not to send them a note withdrawing the argument.

In view of the multiplicity of possible agents of corruption in Q, the legitimate field of conjecture and emendation is, as you say, very wide, and it is difficult to assign relative importance to the several agencies. It is clear that misreading of the copy is frequent, and I should judge it to have been roughly written; the hand must have had some very definite peculiarities, for graphic confusions appear repeatedly that are not in general common. It must of course have been a "secretary" hand to allow of the "alapt" misreading.

"emptie-ey'd" is fairly satisfactory as regards sense: but I think you have to find some explanation of the fact that both the compositor and the press reader thought that the word began *p—r* in the MS.

As you say, I overlooked Kellner's emendation *attaxt*; the form is misleading; he only cites it under *1:t* not under *p:x* (a confusion he does not seem to recognize!); and when I wrote the review I had not yet studied the text of *Lear* closely. Of course you must give Kellner credit for the emendation.

As to *spence*: you will notice that I spoke of my suggestion as a "remote possibility." I certainly should not stick fast by it.

sea a-wax is ingenious and seems to me quite attractive.

I shall look forward to seeing your introduction, all in good time.

Sincerely yours
W. W. Greg

1 March 1946

Dear Mr Berryman

I enclose a copy of a note I am sending to *R.E.S.* This will leave you free to develop your own views on the staging of *King Lear* unhampered by any theories I have advanced.

Good hunting!

Yours sincerely
W. W. Greg

[*Enclosure*]

"The Staging of *King Lear*"

[published in the *Review of English Studies* 22 (1946), p. 229]
Some recent correspondence with Mr John Berryman, of Princeton, N.J., who is at work on a critical edition of *King Lear*, has convinced

me that some at least of the views on the staging of the play that I put forward in *R.E.S.* in July 1940 need modifying. Exactly how much of my theory must be scrapped I am not yet certain; but it seems clear that my contention that the act and scene division in the Folio is original cannot stand. The Folio arrangement could only be original if the manuscript used in preparing that text were Shakespeare's original draft. But in *The Editorial Problem in Shakespeare* (p. 100, note) I argued, on the contrary, that it was the prompt-book, and from this conclusion it is difficult to escape. Both the alternative cutting and the reduction of minor characters (especially the fusion of Doctor and Gentleman in IV.vii) point strongly in that direction. And it would be unreasonable to suppose that, in the course of fifteen years' use at the Globe, the Book, whatever peculiarities of staging it may have once displayed, had not be[en] brought into conformity with the usual practice of the house. It is therefore possible that the Folio division was introduced by the editor, working on the undivided Quarto and an undivided manuscript, and that he merely overlooked the necessity of making Edgar's soliloquy in Act II a separate scene. (That a prompt-book should be undivided need not surprise us: the Folio *Hamlet* was printed from the prompt-book, or from a transcript of it, but only the first two acts are divided, and that imperfectly.) On the other hand, I gather that Mr Berryman is inclined to believe that the manuscript used for the Folio *Lear* had been altered to fit it for a late provincial performance. That may yet prove the more fruitful hypothesis.

2 March 1946

Dear Dr. Greg,

I have sent off to you Bentley's allusion book, not because I think it very good (I don't) but because I see in the R.E.S. that you are interested in it, and I am myself so desperate for books that I didn't like your wanting one which I happened to have and don't need. The analytical volume is a wonderful American waste of time, I should have thought a man who will be responsible for revising Bald's chronology of Middleton in three or four pages would have better things to do than tot up scattered half-meaningful data to reach unacceptable conclusions. But no doubt everyone wastes time in his own way; how many days I've spent at intervals trying to correlate the *King Lear* Quarto's (a) use of narrow and wide measures, (b) mislineation, and (c) variant spellings, I don't like to remember, and since I've come to no clear result I suppose they must be reckoned wasted.

Among several cruxes which I believe have yielded recently is an old foe of yours, IV.ii.57: "slayer begin threats : state begins threat."[3] I would locate the corruption differently from the account in *Variants*. I agree that "state" must be right (the compositor probably thought he saw "slare" and interpreted it); but "thereat" has every appearance of correct syntax, and "threats" is a plausible misprint for it; nor do I doubt "thy." We are left with "begins." That the corrector improved the grammar doesn't show that he could read the copy. I read therefore:

> With plumed helme thy state begirds thereat,
> Whilst thou a morall foole sits still . . .

Goneril has in fact just sent Edmund to "hasten our musters"; and although *begird* was an old word I assume it has here a nonce sense: girds, arms itself. Shakespeare, happily, coined four similar verbs in *Lear* (besort, bemeet, bemonster, bemad). The "ds" may have been illegible. There is a surprising further possibility, in that "gird" had a meaning "move suddenly, start, spring" perhaps known to Shakespeare from Golding ("They girded forth"). "Thy state" is clearly contrasted by Goneril with "thou," and this sense contrasts beautifully with "sits still." I note that "thereat" is parallel with "why does he so?" "Noiseless land" seems to me to offer no difficulty as against Cornwall's "state" (governing forces, officials) girding.

Pray turn your heaviest guns on this if you are skeptical. Q's "thereat" below I think is certainly wrong (an unconscious compensation by the compositor for his blunder above!) and gives so weak a sense against "threat-enrag'd" that its having been universally preferred seems fantastic. Even Schmidt, for whom F was Scriptural, follows Q without a word. Sometimes I really have a sense that the play has never been edited before. But independent critics have done good work. Do you know Perrett's admirable gloss *gods' spies* at V.iii.17? Perfect—"God" is never singular in *Lear* or *Cymbeline*—yet no editor had his wits about him at that point. May I keep mine!

> With v. best wishes,
> Yours,
> John Berryman

21 March 1946

Dear Mr Berryman

It was indeed thoughtful and kind of you to send me Bentley's book. I hope you really do not need it yourself. I shall value it in any case as a generous gesture, apart from whatever use I find in it. I had a suspicion, that you confirm, that its elaboration was a bit fanciful. But, God knows, we all waste time on paths that lead nowhere!

Your tackling of the *state begins thereat* crux is ingenious, and I think you may very likely be right in seeing the seat of corruption in *begin(s)*. What I am doubtful about is whether *begird* in the sense of gird on, arm oneself, can be used absolutely. The quotations seems always transitive, and though it could doubtless be used reflexively, I should expect the object to be expressed. If we could take *begird* in the sense of *gird*: move rapidly, it would give a satisfactory sense; but again there seems no authority and little likelihood for the use. But this suggests something else to my mind. You see there is no hint in the evidence that there was a *d* in the word. But being Q there may have been mishearing. *begins* may be an attempt to make sense of (or be a mere misreading of) *begirs*. Could *begirs* be a mishearing of (or a mere miswriting of) *bestirs*. This would also give (much the same) plausible sense—and Shakespeare does use *bestir* intransitively in *The Tempest*. I only offer this as a suggestion.

With many thanks again for your kind thought, and best wishes for good hunting.

I am sincerely yours
W. W. Greg

[*to Mark Van Doren*]

26 March 1946

I collated 24 copies of the First Folio in Washington last week and am only just able to see my hand in front of my face, ha ha. You know [Mr.] Folger had 79 *copies* & begged the Bodleian to sell him its—if only until his death! when he'd will it back. A strange passion. I wonder whether he misses them where he is.

7 May 1946

Dear Dr. Greg,

Hurrah! I feel sure that with *bestirs* you have reached Shakespeare, and I wonder whether the word didn't stand in the copy: "cagion" must be a g:s misreading, and in a passage obviously very confused is g:st impossible? One other possibility is that the amazing copy simply had *besirs*. But I haven't any doubt of the emendation, which is one of the best in the whole text. Poor "begirds" I whistle off, though I'm happy my analysis helped to the true one. I congratulate you. Can you help with others? NED has no doubt of "bolds" V.i.26, but the syntax makes its sense impossible; only if "bolds" could mean *defies* would it seem all right, and I'd say it can't; but *beards* can (= oppose) and better *braves* can (supposing "ol:rau" if not a curious synonymous substitution by the compositor). Unluckily Albany's exact meaning is concealed in the corruption of this word, but he certainly means that "this busines" touches him as England is invaded and not as he wishes to threaten the King, for he doesn't; "brave" as "threaten, menace" is quot. 1619. Also can you imagine with me, among the Q copy's short phonetic spellings, *waide* for "weigh'd"?—if so, I'm sure this is "my *m*ade intent, My boon I make it," where I don't like either "main" or "laid" much better than the original error; or "made" could be a mishearing or compositor's error for "waigh'd." Then the ghastly "Looke where he stands and glars, wanst thou eyes, at/tral madam" &c., quite the worst crux in the text, because the situation is so uncertain. But I take it that "no" in the line above is really an error for "now" and there is no question yet of the foxes' getting away: they are to be arraigned. The "wanst" might be *canst* or anything, but suppose Q2's obvious (I don't say right) corrections to "wantst" and (less easily corrupted) "at triall" are accepted: is not "eyes" a simple misreading of *oyes* (for the formal commencement of the trial)?—"Wantst [i.e. lackst] thou 'oyes' at triall, Madam?" and then his song is to oyez. Or "Wantst thou 'oyes'?" to the King, leaving "at/tral madam" uncertain. I've spent much time on this last to little effect. Have you any suggestions? Alas, words may even be lost. But I don't like "eyes," especially after *Lear*'s glaring; I've tried *eye 's* also, unsuccessfully so far.

A poor return for a beautiful emendation, here are fifty pages of complicated prose; on which I hope you will act a very Cato. Scribble in the margin, please, if you like. I have abbreviated sharply a good deal of argument, and accumulation of evidence and parallel, formerly very long, wishing to simplify; if you think any of this needs reinforcing, I'd be glad to hear it. Some I couldn't get short, as v[ersus] Hart's crazy views of performance-length[4]; no one else has countered them (Chambers disappointed me very much in *RES*) and I thought I had better try. Do you think I have taken Duthie's dictation too seriously? (I wrote to him in January but haven't heard.) Above all, when my review of evidence suggests to you new things, small or large, I'd be happy to know them, though I know you're likely to be busy and I'll be grateful for any criticism whatever. I hope the discussion will interest you.

Thank you very much for sending the note written for *RES*, it helps. I almost wasn't to be "of Princeton, N.J." by the time the note will appear—Allen Tate wanted me to edit one of our major quarterlies, *The Sewanee Review*, which he has left, and it would have meant moving to Tennessee; but I've accepted a post in Creative Arts at Princeton and will be here another year. I wish I could get across to see you, as I half-planned, this summer. However, it isn't likely now. I hope your work and all other things go well.

Yours sincerely,
John Berryman

22 May 1946

Dear Dr. Greg,

I find that F. P. Wilson in the admirable essay published last year [*Shakespeare and the New Bibliography*, 1945], which I discovered the other day and read with delight, anticipated Dr. Duthie by a year in the application to Q of the *Richard III* theory *cum* dictation; so that some of my phrasing will have to be changed. It was convenient to call the hypothesis Duthie's because I had heard he was working on *Lear*, presumably developing it. I have a feeling you don't take much stock in this: am I right?

The Quarto has proved right so often recently that I have more sympathy than usual with McKerrow's shutting off of speculative recension in the Prolegomena.[5]

I am glad to see that Wilson takes a proper view of your work, and I hope your head is unbowed after all the compliments hurled at it recently.

One statement in my last letter, of which I took a copy, might be misunderstood. I didn't mean of course when my review of evidence brought new things of *mine* to your attention—I'm afraid that will happen seldom enough; it was when, thinking matters over, you came yourself to new conclusions or new possibilities, that I wanted very much to hear . . .

Yours sincerely,
John Berryman

23 May 1946

Dear Mr Berryman

You will be glad to know at once that your typescript reached me safely. I have not yet read your Introduction, but may as well reply to your letter without waiting to do so.

I am glad you like *bestirs*. But I am afraid I have nothing useful to suggest for the other cruxes. V.i.26. I fear "Not bolds the king" is probably a deep corruption. Apparently the subject of "bolds" must be France, since he goes on to say that France comes with others &c. This seems to me to make it impossible to construe it as "Not as it threatens the king." III.vi.21 is I think too uncertain to make anything of—almost every word may be wrong. "oyes" is ingenious, but there is nothing to support it. Lastly IV.vii.10 differs from the others in agreement of the texts. *made* may of course have been taken over by F from Q, but it is not an impossible reading. I think *waide* might quite possibly stand for "weigh'd," and might of course have been converted into *made*: "weigh'd" gives admirable sense. I have a suspicion, by the way, that F may have depended a good deal on Q in this scene. In ll.11ff. I should like to read:

> Till time and I think meet.—Be't so my Lord:
> How goes the King!—Sleeps still.—O you kind gods . . .

omitting *Then* and *good* and *Madam*, all words that an actor would be likely to introduce.

I hope to tackle your Introduction shortly.

Meanwhile good hunting.

Sincerely yours
W. W. Greg

26 May 1946

Dear Mr Berryman

I have read your introduction—or section of it—with interest and some care. To be frank I think that the case might perhaps be put rather more clearly and the evidence marshalled to somewhat greater effect—but no two critics will handle material quite in the same way, and I have no particular suggestions to make.

Since you cannot see your way to disposing of—or dispensing with—the shorthand hypothesis, I am disappointed that you cannot substantiate it more fully. I hoped that you would have found some definite evidence pointing to Willis or at least to the practicality of his system. I shall be interested to see what Duthie makes of it.

I have made a few notes on your typescript—nothing of great consequence.

Thank you for letting me see your work.

Yours sincerely
W. W. Greg

4 June 1946

Dear Dr. Greg,

I wonder if this can be it: "My father, pearly-ey'd"?

Pearl was "a thin white film or opacity growing over the eye: a kind of cataract." Nashe has it, and Middleton, and there is a dialectal combination "pearl-blind." The "flax and whites of eggs" applied to

Gloucester's eyes might give, at first glance, precisely such an appearance. Shakespeare has the word himself in *Two Gentlemen* (unrecognized by Schmidt & Onions[6] but known to Wilson):

> Blacke men are Pearles, in beauteous Ladies eyes.
> *Thu.* 'Tis true, such Pearles as put out Ladies eyes.
>
> (V.ii.11)

Pearly I take as analogous to "gouty" (*Troilus*, *Timon*), meaning "afflicted with a pearl"; and the combination one of Shakespeare's sixteen with "-eyed," similar to "gouty-legg'd" (which occurs, as a matter of fact, in Cotgrave).

On this conjecture, the compositor got the first part nearly right (allowing *oo:ea*), whereas the press-reader messed it up (the compositor perhaps helping) but got the second part exactly except for the hyphen, which he thought a comma. The Folio scribe, I agree, emended Qa; Shakespeare's reading, if I am right, being one he would probably have disliked, I don't think it necessary even to suppose the playhouse manuscript illegible here.

Nothing could be less agreeable to a modern actor or reader, unfortunately, than a phrase—at such a moment—requiring such glossing. But I can see no Elizabethan objection to it. Moreover the reading has singular imaginative interest. It enriches the destruction of sight imagery (dart your blinding flames into her scornful eyes—the web and the pin—squenes the eye—I'll pluck ye out—turn our imprest lances in our eyes—see thy cruel nails Pluck out his poor old eyes) which embodies a chief moral theme and supplies the context of Gloucester's actual blinding. Then the weeping & pearls nexus is so frequent that it may suggest Gloucester's weeping. And considering the quibble in *Two Gentlemen*, it does not need a Blunden to imagine that Shakespeare remembered in the last Act, when describing this scene, his language in it, and with a meaning of his own hovering under Edgar's, wrote of "his bleeding *rings*, Their *precious stones* new lost."

I wonder. What do you think?

Yours sincerely
John Berryman

6 June 1946

Dear Mr Berryman

I should be prepared to accept the communal reconstruction plus dictation theory for Q *Lear* if it could be shown to cover the evidence.

But surely the actors would have known who spoke particular lines. False attributions that can be due to the actors themselves—like Edmund's stealings and the final speech—one would expect; but could they have produced the "Who stocked my servant" muddle? [. . .]

Yours sincerely
W. W. Greg

22 June 1946

Dear Mr Berryman

I think *pearly-ey'd* is quite promising. I don't think it necessary to bring in the egg & flax—the first might give a pearly look but hardly the second. It might mean simply "blind."

And I like the way you connect it up with the imagery and the "precious stones."

Good luck!

Yours
W. W. Greg

7 July 1946

Dear Dr. Greg,

I'm very grateful to you for your trouble over my piece of introduction, and sorry it wasn't better. I trust it will be when you see it next. I shouldn't, of course, have taken your time with a draft, least of all with a part of one; but I didn't realize then how *much* more required to be done to it, and did not intentionally impose on you. Among other things, evidence scattered through the rest of it ought to be brought forward at once, and then the whole discussion wants unifying. I'm sorry to say that parts are not even lucid. Willis too will have to be discussed, since as a matter of fact I have some of the evidence you wanted. For instance, I find it remarkable that what is in some respects the most puzzling variant in the whole text, "Iustice: Fetches" (II.iv.90), is readily explained by his symbols—at any rate in the easiest way of writing them [. . .] Q "deserue" (which cannot I think mean "requite" so late as *Lear*) for "reward" at III.vi.5 is easier to see as a similar Willis symbol mistaken than as a memorial substitution by the compositor. The rather numerous words of which the ending is wrong in Q may be due to the reporter's noting by his system only the dominant syllables; omitted Ys (giving *honest, speed, euer,* & prob. also *men* for *meiny*) may result from the same thing; the impossible *sorrow* for *sorry* (IV.vi.262) and, with the press-reader helping, *sorrowes* for *sorry* (III.ii.73) are similar. (The Q variant *bornet* corrected to *bounty* can be used to argue that the compositor omitted all these endings himself; but on the other hand, the press-reader here may have made out *bount*—all that stood in the copy—and expanded it himself by the context; so with *beniz*!)

But there is no doubt that the reporter, if he used Willis's system, used it very well, or repaired in transcription with his knowledge of the play his errors in note-taking, although in many regards he was careless enough. I was interested to discover yesterday that a writer in *Notes and Queries* (Dec. 1, 1945) who has examined 17th C. Mss. in Willis's system, after noting a dozen chief kinds of error one would expect, says that most of them never occur. Shorthand must thus always remain, I believe, what I may call a resort-hypothesis. Unless indeed it can be disposed of, or a plausible alternative established. Dr. Duthie has just written that he has a large work on *Lear* for publication in the autumn, and I long to see it, though he is bound to anticipate my commentary in 500 points or 5000—I would I had Porson's temperament (not to mention his skill), who wept with joy where Bentley had been before him.

Thanks for sending Mr. Scholfield's note. I posted him the reference at once (Chappell, ed. 1893, I.121). But perhaps it is misprinted. Given Malone's discovery of the link between poor Tom and Bessy, I wonder if Shakespeare can have varied the song deliberately to allude to the custom (though I haven't found it so early) of marrying "over the broomstick," play-marriage.

Yours sincerely,
John Berryman

8 July 1946

Dear Dr. Duthie,

Congratulations on *finishing* your *Lear* work! even from where I am in the text I can scarcely imagine such a happy state of affairs. I long to see it. How far I am myself from being done now depends, I expect, partly on what you have done. I had to invent the arguments for reconstruction-&-dictation (a hypothesis I didn't know of, as advanced by you and F. P. Wilson, when I wrote to you) myself, and I am sure you have made them infinitely better, so that I must wait and take account. If I had known, indeed, several years ago, that a reasonable and acute critic was occupied with the play or was going to be, I doubt very much that I would have tried it, though I've been concerned from the beginning more with recreating, justifying and explaining the text itself than with the possibly desperate uncertainties of provenance. With this last matter I can't imagine anyone better fitted to deal than you. Whether on the other side your work will leave a need for mine I don't know, of course. If not, so much the better, better the much so, as Mozart says.

Of Willis's system, weird as it looks, I venture to take a more favourable view than you say you do. How far we can argue from the absence of expected error I don't know. A writer in *Notes and Queries* (Dec. 1, 1945) lists a dozen principal kinds of error one might expect from use of the system, but then says, "looking at an actual manuscript [he examined Castell's notebooks at Cambridge] one can say at once that most of the difficulties never occur." He also calls the system "very easily written" and "very easily read." This is perhaps farther than I would go, and whether the notebooks are verbatim or précis is unknown, but the testimony strikes me as important. I also think there is some direct evidence, for instance in "Iustice: Fetches," unless you are more hospitable to some other explanation for this variant than I am; the Willis symbols as I write them for these words are very close, and this is perhaps the most surprising variant in the whole text.

There are certainly difficulties. But the difficulties with memorial reconstruction appear to me (so far) practically insuperable, considering both the defects and the excellence of the Quarto. What would be the point, for example, in constructing an illegible prompt-book? How did *all* the actors come to be present, and why is it so long? Why are the letters as well reported as the rest of the text? etc etc. But you will have thought of all this, and I'm eager to see your answers. With every good wish,

Yours sincerely,
John Berryman

[*to Kenneth Sisam, The Clarendon Press, Oxford*]

8 July 1946

Dear Mr. Sisam,

Dr. Duthie writes that he has a large work on *King Lear* for publication in the autumn; he has actually edited the play, made a text that is. This amazes me, pleases me, & plunges me into despair. Editing I cannot but think a job for literary critics, but Duthie being so excellent at other things, I hope he is this also. His advocacy of the dictation hypothesis is bound to be far better than mine; if the recension is plausible, and the text adopted a satisfactory one, there may be no need for my edition.

On the other hand, the editions must be planned very differently. Mine wishes to be, though *not* a variorum, much more minutely critical than any edition of a Shakespeare play has been hitherto. I

have paid as much attention to exegesis as to establishment & justification, in what is probably a vain attempt to satisfy three kinds of
readers: of whom Dr. Greg may stand for one, F. P. Wilson for
another, any unscholarly friend of mine, poet or critic, for the third.
A good deal of observation in the commentary is therefore new, and
perhaps unlikely to be anticipated. Then this has affected the text
somewhat, by way of proverbs, puns, etc.; and in general I take a view
of the Folio's sophistication such that I have made a text altogether
more eclectic (a word often used—as Postgate says—with a tinge of
reproach, the ground for which is not easy to discover) than I should
expect from another critic. And, the transmitted texts being very corrupt, there is emendation. This has absorbed months and energy, not
apparently wasted, since Dr. Greg calls some of the conjectures plausible and an analysis of mine helped him to one of the most beautiful
and true emendations in the text. Finally, I don't believe in dictation,
and neither at present, I believe, does Greg, though open to conviction. I must wait and see what Duthie has done. My own work is not
in fact finished, but it couldn't be anyway, having to take account of
his. I am going North for six weeks to do other things.

By way of thanks for the page-proofs and the offprint of Dr. Maas's
review, I am sending you some unpretending notes on [C. T.] Onions' *Shakespeare Glossary* [1911] which I hope may be useful when
this admirable book is reissued; also, separately, the new Scribner
anthology, not for my work in it, but because despite some injustices
(notably to Pound and Bridges) and some over-hospitality it collects
more good poems than any other critical anthology of modern verse,
perhaps, and may not be issued there. A few American pieces I
thought you might not know & might like I marked, but you can
ignore the marks.

Yours sincerely
John Berryman

[*postcard from* W. W. Greg *to* JB]

19 July 1946

Very many thanks for your interesting letter. I am very glad you have
found what looks like real evidence of Willis [. . .]

W. W. Greg

[*postcard from* W. W. Greg *to* JB]

27 May 1947

Thanks for your letter. I am afraid I have no news of Duthie's work
on *Lear*, which I am as anxious to see as you are. I am glad to learn

you are starting on the play again—but I understand your wanting to know what's doing [. . .] I am very well & have been busy over *Faustus*—my parallel text edition is now practically complete.

Yrs. W. W. Greg

[*to John Marshall and David Stevens, Rockefeller Foundation, New York*]

Princeton, 17 February 1949

Dear John Marshall and Dr. Stevens,

Duthie's *Lear* came last night, and I can't at all just now put my head back into Shakespeare—I am dead still from the *Crane* and writing an opera—but I had an hour with it and want to give you immediately an impression.

It is extremely different from my edition: merely "textual," not exegetical, not illustrative, not critical and not aesthetic. It does absolutely nothing that my edition does not do; and my edition does many other things. It will cost my edition, probably, a good deal of novelty, in which I am as time goes on not much interested; but it makes the whole thing much less speculative, of course, and it will save me I think a great body of tentative explanation-of-definite-error, at which a rough glance suggests that he and I largely agree, so I will perhaps throw most of that out and refer the curious to him. His text preserves the non-Shakespearean Folio "accidents"; mine critically does not. His apparatus is traditional and cumbersome, though inadequate in the recording of conjectures. His 425 pages look to have small interest except for experts; I aimed, as you know, at an edition useful to everyone, not altogether different say from Mackail's *Aeneid* of 1930.

Now for Duthie's edition in itself.

I am grossly disappointed. The truth is that I suffer from a respect for textual technicians which is excessive. Originally, I remember, I was dubious as to Duthie's qualifications as a general editor, but over this lapse of waiting I forgot my doubts and came to imagine that his edition would be marvellous. But as I looked at his text last night my respect faded and my doubts flowered. My impression is that he had no right to edit *Lear* at all, for the following reasons.

1. Ignorance. He does not know that there was a possessive without "s," for example, always emended by editors, but Shakespearean; as in the Folio at II.iv.126, "I would diuorce me from thy Mother tombe" where Duthie follows Q "mothers"; there is another example in F, I forget where (& daren't go into my notes at all), and besides being Shakespearean they prove the extreme care of the Folio corrector. A second instance: he prints F "vpbraides" at I.iii.7 and says

Q "obrayds" "may be an aural error." Like hell it may: it is a variant spelling, recognized in NED, of the word "abraids," which the Folio sophisticated and no editor has ever recognized.

2. Timidity. On V.i.30, for instance, where Q has "these domestic dore particulars" and F "these domestic and particular broils," he mentions with approval Malone's emendation of Q "dore" to "dear" (dere)—an excellent one—and then goes on: "There is no reason to suspect F here: but 'dear particulars' strikes me as a rather remarkable substitution for an actor to make for 'and particular broils.'" It just strikes him as remarkable, that's all, and he follows F. *Edit*, Duthie, edit! Q is no doubt original, and F the sophistication. It never occurs to him to *investigate*, discovering that Shakespeare is very fond (after 1600 only) of the word "particulars," and discovering that Q is absolutely guaranteed by the phrase in *Coriolanus* (v.i.3) "Who loved him/In a most dear particular." Neither in range nor in decision is Duthie a respectable editor.

3. Helplessness. On the crux, admittedly a terrifying one, at IV.ii.57, he quotes at length Greg's inconclusive 1940 analysis and then produces an actual conjecture (the *only* original one I have observed so far), the silliest and most cautious I think I ever saw, of which like a reasonable scholar at last he then says: "I do not advance this suggestion with any confidence whatever; but I can think of nothing else." Now Greg's analysis was not only inconclusive but utterly wrong, as I pointed out to him several years ago, offering an alternative analysis, on the basis of which he then sent me one of the most beautiful and certain emendations in the whole canon. I don't object to Duthie that he is not a genius: I object to what seems to be a general absence of resource, which is unacceptable in an editor of *King Lear* and in fact disqualifying.

Well, here are only four passages after all, and he may prove better than I think him; but I came on these and others in one hour, exhausted and with the play almost wholly out of my head for the thirty months I have been waiting on this damned edition. No; I think he won't do.

It goes without saying that he is not a *fool*, like Kirschbaum. He is simply, as I suspected, a textual technician, not a textual critic, or, of course, a textual editor. But he must have no idea of his limitations or he would never have imposed them upon *Lear*. His edition after all is entirely in agreement with Greg and Chambers, except for his application to Q of Patrick's memorial-reconstruction theory about Q *Richard III* (in which for *Lear* I do not believe). So would *any* decent edition now be. The point is a "critical" edition, which he calls his but which my cursory examination does not suggest that it sufficiently is.

What I do hope is that it will be more useful to me than my glance last night indicated. I only learnt then one fact, of bearing toward a possible error of my own, as I recall it. I hope to learn more, and above all it may be a great advantage to have a check on collation. I am extremely careful, but nobody, nobody is accurate, and every check helps. A trouble is that Duthie practically ignores the editorial tradition, missing thereby *certainly* much valuable material that is in my edition. His study shows little evidence of any research properly at all. He is the newest victim of the notion that you can fix a text without explaining it (which involves language, grammar, sources, theatrical history, literary criticism).

And now I must go back to my opera which fascinates me. I hope I've not bored you with all this. I thought I ought to explain at once that the two years of help you gave me do not seem to have been wasted. They will appear. This letter had better be confidential: it *is* provisional, and then I mean to treat Duthie in public of course with more decorum. Privately I could kick his ass for never informing me about his delay; that was indecent. I am writing you a report shortly.

Yours faithfully,
John Berryman

3 October 1952

Dearest Mother

[. . .] It is the devil: the Quarto text, wretched from any other point of view, is unutterably good from the early stenographic point of view. My new theory is that Shakespeare, disloyal at heart and divided against himself, in a fit of amnesia "reported" his own play, sold the copy to the printer after carefully destroying all the distinctions in it between prose & verse, and is now merry with wicked joy peeping over Olympus at sorrowful scholars.

PART FOUR

William Houghton,
William Haughton, *The Shrew*,
and the *Sonnets*

INTRODUCTION

PEOPLE—EVEN VERY knowledgeable people—imagine there is nothing more to be learnt about Shakespeare, barring an occasional, unlooked-for documentary discovery like Wallace's forty years ago about the poet's residence with the Mountjoys[1] and Hotson's twenty years ago about the poet's unfortunate double date in 1597 with a rival theatre manager (who had enemies) and two women.[2] Considering the number of students who have worked at the subject, and the two hundred years they have worked, this point of view can hardly surprise us. But it is quite wrong. It is wrong perhaps even in regard to documentary discovery. "The plain fact is," Professor Sisson wrote in 1933, introducing his important biographical studies, with Mark Eccles and [Deborah Jones], of Lodge, Lyly, and others, "that we are still only at the beginnings of our study of the Elizabethans"[3]; and it will surprise me very much if, as other figures are gradually investigated, nothing comes to light about Shakespeare. It is in its conception of Shakespearean discovery as restricted to documents, however, that the point of view chiefly is mainly unsatisfactory, and in its overestimation of what has wholly been examined in this immense area of research. An incident will help me explain. Several weeks ago a friend, whose general familiarity with literary investigation will not be questioned (it was Mr. Edmund Wilson), asked when we met what I had been doing; I said, as casually as possible, that I thought I had come on the book Shakespeare was probably reading the day or the night he planned *King Lear*. "I thought," he naturally said, "they had gone into all that."

Of course they have gone into all that. Nearly everything has been read. But the reading is nothing. What matters is who reads it, in the light of what, knowing what, and having lately read what. As a matter of fact, Camden's *Remaines concerning Britaine* [1605]—this was the book—has been suspected since Malone of having contributed to Shakespeare's play, and Perrett in 1904 proved that it did.[4] But in a sense the book had not been read. If it had been read, the reader would have noticed what I noticed.[5] The book appeared in 1605, the year Shakespeare wrote his tragedy. He had known the Lear story for years, from an old play, from Holinshed, and from *The Faerie Queene*. What seems to have set his imagination going is something given only by Camden: the *reason* for the youngest daughter's grudging reply, namely that when she marries, her love and duty will be due to her husband not to her father. It may be as a father with two marriageable but unmarried daughters that this struck the poet first. But my reason for thinking it did strike him is this: he had known the story that he used for the Gloucester plot of *King Lear* for years too—it was the *Arcadia* of 1590—but he rejected all of Sidney's names for the characters, and every name that he gave them occurs within twenty pages of Camden following page 182, where Lear's story is related: Edgar, Edmund, the Earle of Kent, an Earle of Gloucester bastard to Henry I (on the same page, 196, one Wimund has his eyes put out), the Duke of Burgundie, and the Earle of Cornewall—not to mention Fools and Kings of France. As for the steward Oswald, he had learnt earlier in the book that the name "Oswold" meant "steward" in German (page 65). It looked to me as if the poet's mind formed the plan of his play, which possibly he had been meditating for years, with extreme rapidity, welding in Sidney's tale (parallel in so many grievous ways) and gathering up names for it, perhaps unconsciously, as he read forward in Camden's witty and moving anecdotage. Whether or not I was right does not matter here, where I can't enter further on the creation of *King Lear*. The point is that there so obviously must be *something* in this suggestion that one is surprised that it was not made long ago, and examined, and accepted or rejected by scholarship. But one is too surprised.

I have taken the reader into this question for two reasons of general bearing. The first is that it seems to fall midway, more or less, between a thing like Mr. J. W. Lever's demonstration [1952] that the beautiful cuckoo song at the end of *Love's Labour's Lost* borrows its flower details, and indeed has its origin, not from Warwickshire nature, but from a herbal published in 1597[6]—midway between this discovery and the matters to be set forth in the present book. The incredulity which Mr. Lever's discovery, being so particular, does not evoke, and which my *Lear* observation may, and which what follows will, is as unphilosophical as credulity would be. A resolute scepticism, quite different from credulity, is the only proper attitude. On the other hand, the reader has a right to have his questions answered, and in one of my appendixes I shall try to explain why someone else did not write this book long ago.

My second reason begins with something I have not told you yet. Shakespeare is praised as a poet in Camden's book. Apparently he barely made it. Of ten poets named, he is the tenth, the others being Sidney, Spenser, Daniel, Jonson, Campion, Drayton, Chapman, Marston, and Hugh Holland (who lived to acknowledge Shakespeare "*Poets* King").[7] But is he not much more likely than not to have heard immediately of a new book in which he was praised—there had not been a dozen yet; and is not this relevant to the likelihood of his having used it at once for *Lear*? Yet nobody has mentioned this connexion.

Scholarship suffers still from a morbid fear of making connexions, inherited from the reaction against Fleay and other madly-identifying-in-darkness nineteenth-century investigators who flourished and spun fantasies (as well as truths) in the crypts of the New Shakespeare Society. This fear alone, it seems to me, accounts for the following strange and crucial abstinence: that the one general account of Shakespeare's reading appeared fifty years ago. It is a very careful, good account, with much that was original together with nearly all that was then known—*Shakespeare's Books* [Berlin, 1904], by H.R.D. Anders; but it was published in Germany and has long been unobtainable and seems to be astonishingly little consulted. It will not do anymore anyway. Too much has been learnt since, and besides, Anders employed a reasoned, Teutonic arrangement, which wants breaking to pieces in order to determine whether Shakespeare actually read a given work or not. Mr. D. T. Starnes, who seems to be the only living person besides myself deeply interested both in whether Shakespeare read a given book and *when*, gave in 1945 a handsome example when he showed that the poet read, very early on, Aldington's Apuleius and used it in four plays, and then some ten years later read it again and used it in five more plays; not all the details of this will stand, but the structure stands.[8] With a few such exceptions, for all the noise of learned activity, our scholarship seems in this respect curiously inert.

Not in this respect only. It is striking that the most impressive account of the dating of the sonnets apart from Hotson's of three years ago—Harbage's; I think it unacceptable, as the reader will see, but its impressiveness is undeniable—was spurred into existence by irritation with Hotson's.[9] And yet we say we are anxious to discover the truth. So with a matter as important to Shakespearean biography and criticism as thè identity of his collaborator in *The Taming of the Shrew*. Nobody responsible doubts, I think, that he had a collaborator; and the parts are satisfactorily discriminated; but no serious suggestion has ever been made as to who the other playwright was. The night of the Penn-Princeton game [in 1952]—but I should recall for you the game. It was the country's leading game that Saturday. Princeton had gone undefeated for what seemed a generation and looked to go undefeated through the season again if it beat Pennsylvania, the other leading team in the East. The defensive lines were very strong; for a while nothing happened, and the Princeton offence was sluggish. Then Penn scored, and scored again, one conversion failing. Shortly before the half, Princeton woke up and scored and converted. 13–7. Through the second half Princeton outplayed Penn utterly. But whenever they were in scoring position they either fumbled and failed to recover, or passed straight to some interceptor; and so the game ended, nerve-racking, wearying, and discouraging. Princeton did not deserve to win, on stupidity, and no more did Pennsylvania. I went to neither place, but have lived in the town of Princeton for a long time, and I came home gloomy. That night it seemed to me humiliating, and suddenly beyond endurance, that we should have no idea who wrote half *The Shrew*.

1952

THE DATING OF THE *Sonnets*

WHEN DR. LESLIE HOTSON exploded several years ago his *Atlantic* article [December 1949], proving that Shakespeare was "finishing his Sonnets" at a date, 1589, years before most scholars over the last two centuries had supposed the poet had begun them, his conclusions were much too easily accepted, I think. Dr. Hotson did not undertake the responsibility of countering any of the rather formidable difficulties raised by his dating. He simply dated Sonnet 107 (about the "mortall Moone") in 1588–89, referring it to the Armada, 123 (about the "pyramids") at the same time, referring it to the re-erected Roman obelisks of 1586, 1587, and 1588, and 124 (about the "childe of state") at the same time again, referring it to Henri III of France. Sonnet 104 makes the friendship between the poet and the young man addressed three years old, and so, for Hotson, the matter was settled: the sonnets all belong in the 1580s—he announced he was "grooming a candidate" for the Friend, and moved on (after—as reprinted in *Shakespeare's Sonnets Dated* [New York: Oxford University Press, 1949]—just 36 pages) to an unusually fruitless and unacceptable discussion of the identity of Shakespeare's lost play *Love's Labour's Won*, which he thinks is *Troilus and Cressida*. With all the problems thus peacefully out of sight, he had a good press. Dr. McManaway of the Folger Library conceded in *Shakespeare Survey* 3 (1950) that he thought Hotson right about 107 and 123, "and possibly about 124" (though "I cannot agree that the first 126 sonnets were written by 1589 until a satisfactory 'Mr. W.H.' is produced").[10] But Hotson had not even taken the trouble to observe that Sonnet 107 is linked backward to 106 and that to 105, much less to justify the long-attacked order of the sonnets as printed in 1609, and of course enthusiasm cooled. After a year, Dr. McManaway in *Shakespeare Survey* 4 was hardly willing to give Hotson the right time and had fallen back on reporting almost without comment fantasies, born of indignation, like Professor Harbage's location of the first two sonnets [107, 123] discussed by Hotson just fifteen years later, in 1603.[11] In the last *Shakespeare Survey* (1952) another critic observes, truly enough, that "opinion seems to be hardening" against Hotson's dating.[12] After having been too easily accepted, the whole case is being too irritably rejected—because Hotson did not make out the case, and because he was too blindly happy with it. Temperament bulks more in scholarship than the layman supposes. Utterly ignoring the fact that one influential section of scholarship ever since Malone had found Samuel Daniel (with *Delia*, 1592) Shakespeare's master in sonneteering, Hotson can hardly be surprised if Harbage finds himself driven into proclaiming that Hotson must discredit all alternative cases before his own can be accepted.[13] Of course this is ridiculous; a piece of logic that no schoolboy, much less a professor at Columbia (and now Harvard) should accept, much less emit; but the temperature is high. The question is solely that of the *strength* of the individual case in relation to the strength of the evidence against it, the contradictory evidence, that is, because there always *is* contradictory evidence. This is probably—the dating of the sonnets of William Shakespeare—the second most formidable literary mystery of the world (the first being the identity of "Mr. W.H.") and it has not really been so little examined that a merely positive case like Dr. Hotson's can possibly be accepted on its merits. Consider: if we came on a signed and dated statement by Shakespeare about the dating of the sonnets, this would still, legitimately, be an occasion for very serious investigation—with ultraviolet and infrared light and with chemicals for the question of forgery, in regard to the provenance of the document, and by paleographers (to mention no other problems such as Shakespeare's sincerity and the reliability of his memory). All Hotson has done is to provide an attractive and very important theory, *far* better buttressed than any alternative theory, in regard to certain sonnets of the 154 printed by Thomas Thorpe in 1609 when the poet was forty-five years old and was certainly considering retiring from London to Stratford.

But if this is all he has done, he has nevertheless done this. I am not certain when the sonnets were written by Shakespeare. The dating is not even fundamental to the theses that this book is being written to investigate. But I doubt if we need really to be so entirely at sea as Professor Rollins's admirable, know-nothing New Variorum edition of the *Sonnets* (1944)[14] and Hotson's blanket, unconvincing assertion, and his antagonists' even more unconvincing attacks, appear to leave us. After all, this subject has been studied by intelligent men (as well as idiots) for a long time, and the results of their enquiries have been responsibly assembled, and certain *facts* are known. It is true that some of the facts are ambiguous, and that most of the studies have been dominated by prepossessions; but so long as we avoid the prepossessions, and are prepared to submit to the best that we can make of the facts, I don't see why we should not hope to get through to some impression much more satisfactory than a brainless creed.

Most of Shakespeare's sonnets, as I said, were published by one Thorpe in 1609, many years after the Elizabethan sonnet vogue had died down and indeed become ridiculous. Some other sonnets by Shakespeare had been published in *Love's Labour's Lost* a decade earlier, and versions of two of Thorpe's (138, 144) in a collection of stuff mostly not by him called *The Passionate Pilgrim* (1599); it is possible that one called "Phaeton to his Friend Florio," printed in John Florio's *Second Fruits* (1591)—a book that Shakespeare certainly read, by the way—is by him[15]; other sonnets by him not in Thorpe's manuscript may of course be lost. Still, 150-odd is a good many sonnets, and one would expect them to have been written years before they were printed. They were. Francis Meres, who, in his extravagant travelogue of contemporary and earlier English writing called *Palladis Tamia* (or *Wit's Treasury*), displays a stunningly complete knowledge of Shakespeare's dramatic and poetic work up to 1598, when the book appeared, praises his "sugred Sonnets among his priuate friends."[16] Meres himself—a clergyman, one year Shakespeare's junior, of no distinction—seems to have been one of these friends (or to have known one), because one of his most elaborate passages combines the same (well-known) passages from Horace [*Odes* III.30.1–9] and Ovid [the closing lines of *Metamorphoses*, in Arthur Golding's translation (1567), XV.984–95] that Shakespeare imitates in Sonnet 55. (It has naturally been argued that Shakespeare imitated Meres, a notion hardly admissible when the passages are compared.)[17] (It has also been argued, naturally, that Meres refers to sonnets by Shakespeare other than those printed by Thorpe later, and this is the sort of thing I plan to ignore hereafter.) Some of Shakespeare's sonnets, then, including 55, 138, 144, were in circulation by 1598–99. I may as well say at once that (so far as I know) no shred of genuine evidence, not incompatible with better evidence, has ever been adduced in favour of the composition *after* 1598 of *any* sonnet by Shakespeare. It does not follow that none were written after that date. But our attention, for the body of them, and for all the individual sonnets for which we have dating evidence, is directed earlier.

This is as we would expect. The sonnet vogue, which was based upon Wyatt and Surrey, Petrarch and Ronsard, had been dimly foreseen by Thomas Watson in his eighteen-line poems of *The Hekatompathia* in 1582. During the next year or so, Sidney wrote his sonnets. But these were not printed until 1591, and the actual vogue lasted just five or six years:

1591 (*Astrophel and Stella* with twenty-nine unauthorized sonnets by Samuel Daniel included)

1592 (Daniel's *Delia*, Henry Constable's *Diana*)

1593 Barnabe Barnes (*Parthenophil and Parthenophe*), Thomas Lodge (*Phyllis*), Watson (*The Tears of Fancy*)

1594 Constable and Daniel enlarged, Michael Drayton (*Idea's Mirror*), William Percy (*Caelia*)

1595 Richard Barnfield (*Cynthia*), Spenser (*Amoretti*)

1596 Bartholomew Griffin (*Fidessa*), R.L. (*Diella*), William Smith (*Chloris*)

In the last year, clearly, we have been scraping the barrel, and except for sporadic publications this was the end. I do not yet suggest that I think Shakespeare's sonnets fell within this period, but it is pleasant to learn from Meres that we do not have to worry about their having followed it by many years.

Now, who were the "private friends" who saw them? Meres was one, or knew one. Ben Jonson was another; in the same year, 1598–99, in his second play for Shakespeare's company, he imitated Sonnets 128 and 129.[18] A third was the unknown author of *Edward III*, who lifted [for II.i.451] the last line of Sonnet 94 ("Lilies that fester smell far worse than weeds") and borrowed "scarlet ornaments" from Sonnet 142 earlier in the same scene (II.i.10)—unless, as I don't think it was, this was Shakespeare himself.[19] The play was registered for printing late in 1595 and printed the next year as "sundrie times plaied about the Citie of London"; it may be years older, and the argument that the sonnets may borrow from it poorly stands in my opinion the comparison of the passages.[20] Here are three friends. Two others are John Trussell, of whom I will say something in a moment, and the man to whom I think most of them may actually have been written [William Haughton], who, as a later chapter shows, imitated one about 1596. Others, I think, will appear. But Meres's word "private" is important, and apparently the sonnets were kept close. It is striking that unless Barnfield imitated in 1594 and 1595 Sonnets 85 and 98, and R.L. imitated (in his Sonnet 30 [*Diella*, 1596]) the notion in 21 of the stars as heaven's candles—the converse imitations seem less probable still—the later sonneteers in the list above had not got hold of Shakespeare's; and these imitations are very uncertain.[21] The editor of *England's Parnassus* in 1600 could not give one. Spenser himself is another matter, whom I reserve. John Trussell was a neighbor of Shakespeare at Stratford—his uncle lived there, a family long associated with the Shakespeares and Ardens. To his poem about Helen, imitative of Shakespeare, registered for printing in April 1595, he prefixed a dedicatory eighteen-line sonnet based plainly upon Shakespeare's (imitating at least Sonnet 150) and apparently addressed to Shakespeare. The book is not available, except an extract in Rollins's edition of the *Sonnets* (II, pp. 327–28, with references).

This makes four friends. Daniel, Shakespeare's "master" at sonnets, seems to be another. In a long passage added to his *The Complaint of Rosamund* in 1594, he speaks of "the reuenue of a wanton bed," Shakespeare in Sonnet 142 accusing the woman of having "Robd others beds reuenues of their rents." This is the same sonnet from which "scarlet ornaments" two lines earlier is borrowed for *Edward III*, and indeed the complication of Shakespeare's image shows which is original, his or Daniel's: he developed into his from the legal imagery of the preceding line ("seald false bonds of loue"), Daniel lifted it loosely. Here is one sonnet, then, deep in the wretched triangle of betrayal, imitated twice in 1594 and *at least* 1595.[22]

Before setting up any other friends—notably Daniel, Spenser possibly, and Drayton—I want to say something about an aspect of the sonnets that seems to many a stumbling block in the way of an early dating, and about one difficult passage, and then I want to see

whether we cannot more or less locate two sonnets ourselves by methods somewhat different from those we have been pursuing.

You observe that the sonnets have been receding from 1598. We
seem to stand now, with a number of them, *not later* than 1594, and
we are going to have to go, frankly, much earlier still before we have
done. What has outraged people as much as anything else about
Hotson, who wants them all over by 1589 when the poet was twenty-
five, was his ignoring—along with every other difficulty—the passages
about the poet's age, especially one in 62,

> But when my glasse shewes me my selfe indeed
> Beated and chopt with tand antiquity,

and the great Sonnet 73 ("That time of yeeare thou maist in me
behold"). I shall have more to say about these later, but two points
ought to be made here. First, nothing so far prevents our supposing
that these sonnets were in fact written later than the others; we have
been dealing only with the *bulk* of the sonnets and with *individual*
sonnets. But, second, I doubt if we are required to put them later,
since Barnes at barely twenty-two and Barnfield at twenty were com-
plaining of age in much the same terms. This is not merely Renaissance convention, though it is partly that; young poets—as scholars
incline to forget—can feel so much older than a freshman or a soph-
omore, not to mention a senior.

Convention and reality probably combine also to make mysterious
the one sonnet upon which everything ought to hang: 104, celebrating three years of the friendship. Unfortunately, Daniel in 1592 also
has a sonnet (26) lamenting "three yeeres" of his devotion passed in
vain. It is not clear to us yet that Shakespeare did not write before
Daniel. But Ronsard had begun his fourteenth sonnet to Hélène
"Trois ans sont ja passez que ton œil tient pris,"[23] and one of Ronsard's odes is imitated in the line [110] of *Venus and Adonis* (1592–
93), "Leading him prisoner in a red-rose chain."[24] Now Shakespeare
does not merely say three years, he says:

> Three Winters colde,
> Haue from the forrests shooke three summers pride,
> Three beautious springs to yellow *Autumne* turn'd,
> In processe of the seasons haue I seene,
> Three Aprill perfumes in three hot Iunes burn'd,
> Since first I saw you fresh which yet are greene.

The other poets say nothing so detailed and reminiscent. Still, there remains the possibility of Shakespeare's development, merely, of the element of convention; and the printed order of the sonnets we have not discussed yet—many may well have been written after 104; and it is not even positive (I introduce this sad truth gingerly) that all the sonnets to a young man were addressed to the *same* young man. It seems plain that we are not obliged to suppose them all or mostly composed within any three-year period. This discovery has the disadvantage that it rather sets us adrift. But it has the advantage that we can follow with a good conscience where the evidence seems to lead. Now I want to wonder whether we cannot, in fact, locate two of the sonnets, both rather early, but six years apart. [*Unfinished*]

1953

The Taming of the Shrew

Unlike most of his colleagues and rivals, William Shakespeare during the major part of his career seems to have collaborated only once or twice. Early on, he rewrote plays by others now known as the second and third parts of *Henry VI* (I think their editors, H. C. Hart and John Dover Wilson, are more likely right about this matter than the critics who have called them all Shakespeare's) and also *Titus Andronicus*. This is not quite collaboration. The immediately following *1 Henry VI*, so called years later by the editors of the First Folio, may already have been finished, by others, when Shakespeare wrote into it at least two scenes (II.iv, IV.ii). It is possible that at about the same time, 1593–94, he wrote the second act of a chronicle by an unknown imitator of his, *Edward III*. All this was before *Romeo and Juliet*. Towards the end of his dramatic career, a question of collaboration has been seriously raised in regard to the splenetic and chaotic *Timon of Athens*. It is agreed that he then finished the loose work *Pericles*, of which the first two acts had been written by someone else, but whether lately or not we don't know, and this may not quite be collaboration either. After he had formally closed his career with *The Tempest*, retired, and produced nothing for some time, he certainly did collaborate with young John Fletcher in *Henry VIII* and *The Two Noble Kinsmen* and probably a play now lost called *Cardenio*, on a story from the lately translated *Don Quixote*, three years before he died. In mid-career, it is practically certain that about 1600–1 he wrote or rewrote a scene or two for a play by a group of Admiral's playwrights, *Sir Thomas More*, in a vain attempt to render it acceptable to the Master of the Revels for production by his own company, the Lord Admiral's Men. This is outside the canon. Within it, conservative scholarship has regarded everything composed during a dozen mature years—from *Romeo and Juliet* to *Coriolanus*—as substantially Shakespeare's, except *The Taming of the Shrew*. Sir Edmund Chambers gives Shakespeare just half of this comedy: *Ind.* i, ii; II.i.1–38, 115–326; III.ii.1–129, 151–254; IV.i.3, 5; V.ii.1–181; remarking that some critics give him less. I give him somewhat less, and a little more, but what matters is that all the rest of this famous warhorse of the theatre is obviously by someone else. "I do not know," Sir Edmund goes on, "who he was. Lodge, Greene, and Chapman have been suggested on very slight grounds."[25] It is the chief purpose of this paper to suggest that it is quite possible he was William Haughton, the author of *Englishmen for My Money* and many other plays, mostly lost, made for Henslowe during 1597–1602. But I believe Haughton would have been suggested, and perhaps demonstrated and accepted, as Shakespeare's collaborator long ago if it were not for a persisting and discreditable uncertainty about the date of the play. I take up first, therefore, without relation to Haughton, the question of the date.

SHAKESPEARE'S COLLABORATOR is rather a neutral fellow, stylistically—"not incompetent," as Chambers says, but "much less vigorous" than Shakespeare (*WS*, I, p. 324). He writes as much like Shakespeare as he can, but he does not write like Shakespeare, much less Shakespeare in 1598 or 1599. I expect it is the confusion about his work—let us call him X, and his part X-*Shrew*—that is responsible for uncertainty about the date, which has wavered between 1594 and 1598, despite the fact that Meres in 1598 does not mention *The Taming of the Shrew* in his thorough catalogue, and despite the plain close relation, in material, style, energy, and excellence, between the Induction and *Henry IV* and *Merry Wives*, and between the Taming scenes and *Much Ado*.

Meres, however, is irrelevant to my argument, for the following reasons: Unless *The Shrew* is the unknown *Love's Labour's Won*, which seems a possible subtitle for it although implausible in the face of the celebrity of the name of the old (source) play which one would expect to have continued[26]—unless these two are the same, we cannot really think *The Shrew* earlier than 1598. Meres names every single play by Shakespeare that is known to us, up to his date (except *Henry VI*, which was before Meres's time and is besides not really by Shakespeare). But if *The Shrew* is *Love's Labour's Won* we still have small reason (too weak to stand before other evidence) for supposing it earlier than 1598; for the *Won* play must have followed close on the *Lost* play, and *Love's Labour's Lost* is not known (upon solid evidence too complicated to assemble here) to have been revised and enlarged late in 1597. Only if the bulk of other evidence points to an early date would it be plausible to conjecture that the *Won* play followed the first writing of *Love's Labour's Lost*. How little that is so, we will see. To conclude with Meres, it seems to me idle to suppose *Love's Labour's Won* to be *The Taming of the Shrew*—since the chief reason for so supposing (we may as well admit) was to get *The Shrew* into Meres's list; and it seems to me inadmissible to imagine that such an identification, even if made, will necessarily put *The Shrew* before 1598.

The reason it cannot be earlier than this date is that X continually imitates plays by Shakespeare that had only by then come into existence—especially *1* and *2 Henry IV* and *Much Ado about Nothing* [. . .]

WILLIAM HOUGHTON

A FEW PAGES AFTER his poem to William Shakespeare in his little book *Epigrammes*, published in 1599, John Weever has one addressed to William Houghton, "In Gulielmum Houghton"[27]:

> Faine would faire *Venus* sport her in thy face,
> But Mars forbids her his sterne marching place:
> Then comes that heau'nly harbinger of *Ioue*,
> And ioyns with Mars & with the queen of Loue
> And thus three gods these gifts haue given thee,
> Valour, wit, fauour, and ciuilitie.

From these lines we learn several things about Houghton. He must have been extraordinarily handsome; nowhere else does Weever write of male beauty in this way. He must at one time have been active in private conflict or in military service; but he is not a soldier at the moment or he would have been addressed as "militem" like the actual soldiers Weever writes to. Mercury is the god of wit. Weever seems to have patronized both the main theatrical companies: he addresses not only ["Honie-tong'd"] Shakespeare and Ben Jonson of the Chamberlain's Men but the leading actor of the Admiral's, Edward Alleyn, and two of their playwrights, Henry Porter and John Marston. If we knew nothing more of William Houghton than what we learn from the epigram, it is hard to see why he would not be identified immediately and more or less confidently with a third playwright for the Admiral's Men, William Haughton, who had begun writing for Henslowe at least two years before and was still at it. The names are the same, exactly; thus Haughton's autographs in Henslowe's diary are always "a" but his will in 1605 is "o." Moreover, he was young, as Weever's Houghton obviously is; Henslowe in 1597 calls him "yonge."[28] Of course the two men may not have been the same, if we had evidence to tell us they were not, but everything so far suggests that they were, and this is an obvious identification. It is hard, further, to see why we have not already here the most plausible candidate who has ever appeared for "Mr. W.H."[29] It seems likely in the highest degree that Shakespeare would have known him personally, in the small theatrical world of London, as one of the half-dozen leading playwrights of the rival company; which is more than can be said for any previous candidate except the impossible earls. He was notably handsome, he was young, and we hear of his *civility*—which squares with the *gentleness* Shakespeare repeatedly attributes to his friend in the sonnets.

I do not say that he *was* the friend; I only wonder whether anything short of documentary evidence to the contrary can make it seem unlikely that he may have been. Meanwhile, there is much more, however, to be known about this William Houghton of Weever's.

Weever was a Lancashire man. His editor, McKerrow,[30] dates some of the epigrams cautiously back to 1595, and there can be scarcely any doubt that, as Haughton's editor, Baugh, suggests, the lament directly preceding this tribute to William Houghton, "In tumulum Thomæ Houghton Armig.," refers to the Thomas Houghton murdered at Lea, Lancashire, in 1590. And here I come on a point of some interest. The general dedication of the *Epigrammes* is to Sir Richard Houghton of Houghton Tower, High Sheriff of Lancashire this year (1599) "but not otherwise [as McKerrow says] a person of much note" (p. 113), in very peaceful language, that they may, Weever hopes, "drive away the tediousnesse of time" and "refresh your wearied mind, continually exercised in matters concerning the common wealth." The epigram but one preceding that on the death of Thomas Houghton, "Ad Richardum Houghton Militem," and a later one to the same man "Militem," have invariably been supposed to be addressed to Houghton of Houghton also, but of course that is impossible. Weever now calls on "great *Houghtons* name" and wishes "my Muse could keep thee stil from death" and hopes not to offend "thine heroicke spirit." This is the Richard Houghton, also of Lancashire, who was fighting in Ireland this year with Essex and knighted by him (1599), who was to perform in Jonson's *Hymenaei* in 1606 and get two sons by the daughter of a tenant of Sir Thomas Hesketh of Rufford (Chetham Society, XIV, 6ff.). Weever knew several important Houghtons in Lancashire.

But the names Lancashire and Houghton in conjunction are electrical for Shakespearean students at present, or some Shakespearean students, among them the most careful.

Sir Edmund Chambers, in his great work *The Elizabethan Stage* of 1923, noted that the will of a Lancashire gentleman, Alexander Houghton of Lea, made in 1581, left to his brother Thomas "if he will keep players" and if not, to Sir Thomas Hesketh of Rufford, the properties and costumes of his private company, recommending to them also especially William Shakeschaft and Fulke Gyllom, clearly players: "Can this be," Chambers asked in a footnote, "the boy William Shakespeare at 17?"[31]

SHAKESPEARE'S FRIEND

SINCE THE EIGHTEENTH CENTURY it has been a standard opinion in Shakespearean scholarship that a large part of one of the dramatist's most effective and popular plays, *The Taming of the Shrew*, was written by someone else. Sir Edmund Chambers, the supreme authority in our century upon this sort of topic and a foe of the critics who in the 1920s desired to parcel out Shakespeare's work among other writers, stated in 1930 his opinion thus: "I assign to Shakespeare Ind. i, ii; ii. 1. 1–38, 115–326; iii. 2. 1–129, 151–254; iv. 1, 3, 5; v. 2. 1–181. Possibly he also contributed to the Petruchio episode in i. 2. 1–116. Some critics give him less than I have done. On my view his share amounts to about three-fifths of the play, and includes all the Sly and Petruchio-Katharina scenes. The other writer is responsible for the sub-plot of Bianca's wooers. I do not know who he was. Lodge, Greene, and Chapman have been suggested on very slight grounds."[32]

Chambers does not appear to regard these men as contenders; and who could? No reasoned attempt, in fact, has ever been made to discover who the collaborator was. The curiousness of this neglect may strike non-Shakespeareans; but there are two reasons for it. In the first place, the date of the play is exceptionally uncertain, and in the second place, its relation to the anonymous *The Taming of a Shrew*, printed in 1594, is even now a subject of controversy. Two scholars argued independently, some fifteen years ago, that *A Shrew* was neither the source play for *The Shrew* nor a corrupt version based upon *The Shrew*, as had variously been held, but instead a "report," or "bad" quarto, of a lost play which was itself the source play of *The Shrew* and in which Shakespeare may already have had a hand. I have no idea whether this view will stand; but here, at any rate, the topic engages us only as it may be held to affect the date we assign to Shakespeare's final participation in *The Shrew*, and in the present uncertain state of opinion it can hardly do that.

The play was put by Chambers in 1593–94, partly on the ground that it "may quite well be" the unknown *Love's Labour's Won* referred to as Shakespeare's in Francis Meres's list of 1598, which is very full and yet says nothing of *The Taming of the Shrew* (WS, I, p. 324). Petruchio certainly wins a wager. But we can scarcely argue from *Love's Labour's Won*, which may quite as well be an early *All's Well that Ends Well* and is now asserted to be an early *Twelfth Night* and now asserted to be an early *Troilus and Cressida*; Meres may have omitted the play as not all Shakespeare's, anyway, even if it was in existence and known to him. Many critics put it at much the period of Meres's list. As C. H. Herford wrote: "The affinities of its most Shakespearean portion, the Taming itself, connect it on the whole with the work of the last five years of the century. Petruchio's wooing is what Henry's and Hotspur's might have been, had their Kates resembled his. The same boisterous, militant, unromantic conception of love pervades them all."[33] This sort of remark, though even harder to deal with, is as important to the establishment of chronology as metrical statistics are. Nothing could be more unlike *Romeo and Juliet* and *The Two Gentlemen of Verona*, in their dominant atmospheres, than the atmosphere of the *Taming* and of Shakespeare's work of 1597–98. "Undoubtedly," Herford goes on, "the whole scheme of comic effect is, for the Shakespeare of 1595–99, astonishingly elementary. On the other hand, the technique is, within its limited scope, wonderfully sure and firm. So far as the piece betrays Shakespeare's hand at all, it suggests not immaturity but preoccupation. It is the offhand sketch of a mature artist, whose serious energies were concentrated upon greater tasks."[34] An intimate relation has been noticed also, and is indeed striking, between the provincial atmosphere—the Warwickshire atmosphere even, with place-names and the names of actual living people—of the Induction, and that of *2 Henry IV* (1597–98). As for statistics, the very small amount of rime in Shakespeare's part of *The Shrew* (38 lines only in 1,443, according to Chambers's admirable tables) would seem to link it definitely with the plays of 1597–99, in which he suddenly lost interest in rime; but would one expect Petruchio to use rime? A valuable refinement on

Chambers's work was introduced at once [1931] by H. D. Gray, who insisted on an average of the three percentages of double endings, run-on lines, and speeches ending in-line.[35] The Shakespearean part of *The Shrew* works out at 11.07, which ought to put it among Shakespeare's earliest plays; but how far do we have to account for this result (surprising, I imagine, to everyone) by rapid composition and Petruchio's characteristically plain end-stopped harangues?

All we seem able to say is what we knew to begin with, that the play must be a work of the 1590s, perhaps rather later than earlier. Greene, then, who, besides being Shakespeare's enemy, died in 1592, and Lodge, who ceased writing for the stage at or before the same time, look less probable than ever.

But *if* the play was written in the later 1590s, then the fact of its being the result of a collaboration is surprising and becomes very interesting, for William Shakespeare was not in these years, so far as we know, collaborating with anyone. He was the major playwright of the most powerful company in London, producing *Richard II, A Midsummer Night's Dream, The Merchant of Venice,* the two parts of *Henry IV, Much Ado about Nothing, Henry V, Julius Caesar, As You Like It*—before proceeding anguished into the strangest areas that the human spirit had inhabited with writing implements since the composition of the *Iliad,* the poem of Job, and the *Commedia.* He introduced protégés, like Ben Jonson, but he did not collaborate. Earlier he appears heavily to have revised the plays known as 2 and 3 *Henry VI,* and put some scenes into the play now known as 1 *Henry VI,* and worked up (Peele's?) *Titus Andronicus.* At the beginning of the period he may have put seven or eight hundred lines in *Edward III,* unless an imitator did[36]—that's 1593–95; at the end of it he clearly wrote a brilliant Insurrection scene, and perhaps a soliloquy, into *Sir Thomas More,* to try to make it producible—that's 1600 or so, Schücking in the end being right, I think.[37] And after the tragic period, he took over the last three acts of a most unpromising play called *Pericles,* went on to do the romances alone, retired, and came out of retirement to help his company out in a crisis by setting up two or three plays which John Fletcher filled in. That looks like a good deal of collaboration. In Elizabethan or Jacobean terms it was not.

We seem to have *The Shrew* and *Sir Thomas More* as isolated cases over, say, thirteen years. But *More* he cared nothing about. It was a multi-authored affair, all done when it came to him and nearly all bad (by Munday, Chettle, Dekker, besides probably Heywood and others), by men for the chief rival company, currently down-at-heels.

The Shrew was a genuine collaboration. The New Cambridge editors are unfriendly to the skill with which the authors worked together, but Dr. Johnson thought "the two plots are so well united, that they can hardly be called two without injury to the art with which they are interwoven"[38] and Chambers is willing to suppose that "the collaborators may well have agreed upon a common conception of Petruchio" (WS, I, p. 324).

SO FAR THIS INVESTIGATION has been reasonably cautious, I believe, and I hope that at any rate a very strong probability has been established as to the identity of the collaborator in *The Taming of the Shrew*. He is hardly likely to have been an enemy of Shakespeare's and cannot have continued a stranger; hence my title, using the word "friend" very generally. (It may and will be said by friendless professors that "acquaintance" would be less hazardous. I agree: "acquaintance" is a sound term for somebody who has collaborated in a five-act play with a busy professional man—actor, playwright, courtier, businessman—with hundreds of acquaintances, in London, in Stratford, everywhere in England the company toured, all of whom collaborated with him in the two or three collaborative plays of his mature career.

We enter the second phase of the enquiry, which is more speculative and will ask whether on the evidence we are justified in regarding it as possible, or even (in whatever degree) probable, that the word "friend" may be understood in a closer and specific sense. It will have escaped no one's notice that William Haughton's initials are initials on which has long been centered the chief biographical problem in the history of English literature.

Now it is not *certain* that W.H. were in fact the initials of the young man to whom most of the sonnets were addressed. All we know is that evidently the publisher thought so. This has been enough for most scholars, and will have to be enough for us; since if Thorpe was wrong, any enquiry is idle. I mention this inevitable though slight doubt at the outset by way of illustrating a truth sometimes forgotten: most of our knowledge of the past is in one degree or another uncertain, resting upon assumption, the assessment of likelihood, inference, and trust. Where Thorpe got his information it is useless to ask. Greg thought once that perhaps all he had to go on was a sheet inscribed "To Mr. W.H." with the manuscript. But inasmuch as we do not know how he came by the manuscript, this suggestion does not take us far. Moreover, it neglects the extremely confident tone of the dedication, which runs:

TO . THE . ONLIE . BEGETTER . OF .
THESE . INSVING . SONNETS .
M^R . W.H. ALL . HAPPINESSE .
AND . THAT . ETERNITIE .
PROMISED .
BY .
OVR . EVER-LIVING . POET .
WISHESH .
THE . WELL-WISHING .
ADVENTURER . IN .
SETTING .
FORTH .

T.T.

This is the publisher, Thomas Thorpe, to whom the copy was properly entered on May 20, 1609; it was printed by G. Eld, to be sold by John Wright (and, according to some copies of the title page, William Aspley). Aspley was legitimately concerned (with Andrew Wise) in the 1600 quartos of 2 *Henry IV* and *Much Ado About Nothing*, the rights to which Chambers thinks had remained with him, though neither apparently had been reprinted. Here may be a link. Did Shakespeare insist, at some intermediate point, on a privilege for Aspley? (These are "good" quartos, and since Pollard's and others' work almost half a century ago the "good" quartos have been thought of by scholars as published with the company's and author's consent.)

I notice, first, in the dedication, its complacency: Thorpe seems sure of his fact, and appears to want nothing in return for the dedication; and second, that of course the dedication is wrong. "Mr. W.H." was not the "only" begetter of the sonnets, if we take "begetter" to mean: inspirer, addressee. Attempts have been made to have "begetter" refer merely to the man who procured the manuscript; a fancy which the tone of the dedicatory address enables us safely to ignore, as we are going happily to ignore many other fantasies in the long argument that follows.

How shall we account for Thorpe's error? There appear to be two main possibilities, neither very attractive. Thorpe carelessly took the chief addressee to dedicate to, or he carefully omitted the woman—the implied tale being unedifying. In support of the second conjecture, I notice that all the Dark Lady sonnets are huddled together at the end; yes, but Shakespeare may have put them there. (Shakespeare's relation to all these matters will occupy us shortly.) The word, the powerful and false word "onlie," has not had enough attention.

I would say that it not only rules out the first of the possibilities, and weighs for the second, but it is polemical in itself—as if claims had been made, which Thorpe now refutes, that *several* persons were addressed in the sonnets, whereas in truth that glory belonged to one, or one young man, only. Looseness on the part of the poet—weirdly, it's true—is repudiated. I think we are on thin ice here, but surely the word "only" is very unexpected? That Shakespeare's sonnets had been circulated (and, of course, chatted about) we know from Meres more than ten years before this publication, and that the poet's sexual life was gossiped about we know from Manningham's *Diary* [Camden Society] seven years before.[39] I won't pursue this, except to say that for me Thorpe's credit, apart from the absurd claim, seems not only not to have suffered in the discussion but to have improved from the *prima facie* status. He could—perhaps?—have suppressed the Dark Lady sonnets. A distinct possibility has emerged: that he speaks in the dedication for the poet—who could hardly, in this case, as a respectable married man and father, have spoken for himself. Why otherwise the insistence?

Perhaps at the insistence of the man W.H.?

1960

THE DEPOSITION: LETTERS ON THE "DISCOVERIES"

22 January 1953

Henry Allen Moe, Esqr.
John Simon Guggenheim Memorial Foundation
551 Fifth Avenue
New York 17, N.Y.

Dear Mr. Moe:

The opinions I wanted to put privately on record, which you were kind enough yesterday to agree to receive, are these:
1. I think it probable that the William Houghton praised by John Weever in 1599 for his beauty, war-practice, and wit, is, like the other Houghtons praised by Weever, a Lancashire man, and is to be identified with the playwright William Haughton (the name being identical), whom I consider then, as connected with Shakespeare earlier in the Lancashire end and from 1597 in the London theatre, to be the best candidate ever proposed as the young man to whom most of Shakespeare's sonnets were addressed.
2. I think it possible on many grounds that the very early play *The Rare Triumphs of Love and Fortune*, which was produced before the

Queen by Derby's men in 1582 and which 30 years later influenced so extraordinarily Shakespeare's last three plays, may be by Shakespeare himself.

3. I feel quite sure on many grounds that Shakespeare's collaborator in *The Taming of the Shrew* was William Haughton (who also wrote, of plays that survive, not only *Englishmen for My Money* and *Grim*, but also *Wily Beguiled* and *Wit of a Woman*) and therefore the Friend of the Sonnets of Shakespeare.

I hope I was not incoherent about all this yesterday. I had just had an abscessed lateral opened which I was calming with gin, after I left you I talked twelve hours straight with Robert Lowell and went to bed exhausted but with these things off my mind which have been oppressing it for months.

Yours respectfully,
John Berryman

[*to Professor Gerald Eades Bentley*[40]
Princeton University]

16 February 1953

Dear Jed,

I write to you under the disadvantage of complete absorption in my poem [*Homage to Mistress Bradstreet*], of which I've done 250 lines in the last month (based, however, on five years' work) and from which I can only take today off to write you & Mr. Moe. The reason I am bothering you with all this is that I am applying for a Guggenheim renewal and can't bring myself to register in an open letter to the Committee of Selection my "conclusions" when they are so tentative still as not even to be conclusions, but only subjects of investigation, and so Mr. Moe suggested that I write them in skeleton to you; but I hope they may interest you *in posse*, even in this form. I take it that Moe doesn't want from you, of course, a judgement as to their validity, no such judgement being formable even by me with hundreds of pages of notes & statistics & genealogy before me here on the desk; but only an opinion as to whether the subjects are worth investigating and whether, from my short account here, you think that they are being reasonably investigated. Well; what I am going to digest for you anyway is a book, and a complicated one, and one only partly written, every part of it still incomplete; and as I say I can't leave my poem enough even to go into the notes, so I write off the cuff, with stanza 31 facing me tomorrow, like a rack.

The main topics are three.

Please let all this be confidential absolutely.

Houghton, Haughton, *The Shrew*, and the *Sonnets*

I was going about my regular work, studying the *Two Gent.*, study-ing *Henry VI* in the light of Wilson's new views, and getting on with three jobs, namely folding the annual bibliog.'s etc into Ebisch & Schücking and my other registers, proceeding with a chronological reading of everything dramatic extant from about 1570 down to 1614, and digesting chronologically & critically Anders's *Sh's Books* and everything learnt about his reading in the 50 years since, into a large alphabetical notebook of my own (paying special attention to *when* he read a book and then when he re-read it: for instance he read as soon as they came out Daniel (*Civ. Wars*) '95, Ralegh or Keymis '96, Gerarde '97, Holland & Cornwallis 1601, Harsnett 1603, Camden 1605, and this sort of thing is interesting to know)—when one evening it struck me as humiliating that we should agree that he had a col-laborator in *The Shrew*, and know almost to a line (I agree almost exactly with Chambers about this) what the collaborator wrote, and not have the faintest notion of who the collaborator was. So I set at once to work, and very shortly I had an excellent idea, and presently I felt sure I was right, although like all the rest, this part of the study is not complete yet either. I don't think this subject of attribution is as mysterious as critics make out. They don't take into account enough evidence. Here is what I take into account:

I   1 Statement, or external evid. if any (as top)
    2 Date of compos./production; or dates
    3 Theatr. company (known; prob., poss.)
    4 Publisher & date of printing
    5 Familiarity with play in question, by projected author; espe-cially if multiple or long-delayed
II   6 Kind of play; source, plot, characters (names); frame? structure
    7 Statist. relation of prose & verse; verse-forms, rime.
III 8 Compar. of *analyzed* indiv. passages 7 lines
    9 Technical devices, as stichomythia, soliloquy etc
  10 Proverbs
  11 Images — esp. clusters if any; esp. odd or elab: & statist. rel. of image-sources
  12 Compar. diction (esp. indirect, as aye-during/aye-remaining), incl. aphetic & compound, negative & superlative, & neol-ogisms
  13 Syntax & idiom
  14 Puns
  15 Foreign lang.'s & classical allusions; Bibl. allus.
  16 Topical allusions: number & kind
IV 17 Where does the play come to life? Wit; passion

18 How conventional (for date)?
19 Moral reflexion, degree & content.
20 Satire, degree & content
21 SD's, if a "good" text
22 Spelling, if a "good" text
V 23 Compar. imitations of what authors and plays
24 Negative: if no other *known* author "possible"; *nor* the author of any surviving date-related "anon." play
25 Opinions of previous critics

You see there is nothing very subjective about this, although I think my judgement of style as sound as another man's. Well, I began with proverbs and passed to item 6 and moved to statistics and it rapidly became clear that William Haughton *could* have written X-*Shrew* (the non-Shak'n part of *The Shrew*) and that practically nobody else known could have; and further study convinced me that he probably *did*. There are two reasons this has not been recognized before: misdating of *The Shrew*, which belongs about 1598, as I can prove on entirely different grounds, and a most surprising neglect of Haughton since Baugh edited very well his *Englishmen . . . 35* years ago. (By "proverbs" above, by the way, I don't mean selected proverbs: I mean every one recognized by Tilley 1950 in X-*Shrew* and every one recognized by me or Tilley in *Englishmen* and Haughton's other recognized extant play *Grim the Collier of Croydon*; but my study of many of these items is still incomplete—all the work I am touching on in this letter I did in about three months.)

At this point I became much interested in William Haughton or Houghton (the names are identical). He was one of Henslowe's star-workers, off and on, at least from 1597 to 1602 (dying several years later, and he was "young" in 1597). Intermittent with Henslowe and with no other known profession—but wait a moment—it is likely as Baugh says that he wrote for other companies also. In my opinion *Wily Beguiled* and *Wit of a Woman* are by him. Now why McKerrow did not recognize in the William Houghton praised by John Weever (1599) for his beauty, war-practice, and "wit" this playwright is a puzzle to me, since Weever also praises Alleyn and Shakespeare, Henry Porter, Marston & Jonson. But McKerrow's editing of Weever was for once curiously slipshod: he did not even distinguish the two Richard Houghtons addressed by Weever, one in this 1599 the peaceful High Sheriff of Lancashire and the other knighted this year by Essex for fighting in Ireland. Both were Lancashire men, however, and Weever was, and so was the Thomas Houghton whose death is lamented in the epigram immediately preceding (on the same page with) that to

William Houghton. There is at least a probability that Wm Ho was also a Lancashire man, and allied to one of these families. There is further evidence I can't go into now; but nothing has been known about the playwright's origin. Now: I don't know how much you have followed the Lancashire possibility for Shakespeare, which was opened by Chambers in 1923, forgotten by him in 1930, canvassed by Oliver Baker in 1938, and studied by Chambers again since the War in *Sh'n Gleanings* (even the maniac Alan Keen has contributed something). The Alexander Houghton, died 1581, whose young player Shakeschaft may have been Shakespeare under one of his grandfather's variant names, was the brother of this Thomas; to whom he commended Shakeschaft in his will, if he meant to keep players, and if not (we don't know that Thomas did) he commends Shake-schaft to Tho Hesketh, who *did* keep players and had them with him at the Earl of Derby's in the 80's. Linked to Shakespeare in 1598 as a young collaborator, linked to him perhaps years earlier in this Houghton-Lancs. business, and beautiful, William Ha/oughton seems to me to be clearly the most plausible candidate yet produced for the Mr. W.H. to whom most of the sonnets of Shakespeare were addressed. Into all the difficulties of this I can't enter here: nor into the problem of the dating of the Sonnets, on which I have spent a great deal of work. I just report the possibility as a subject of study. But one recent discovery I must tell you: a line in *Wily Beguiled* (printed 1606, of uncertain date after 1596) imitates Sonnet 48, "Within the gentle closure of my brest": "Within the closure of my wofull breast" (D_3). (It goes without saying that I determined the authorship of *Wily* and *Wit* on the basis of (as much as I've been able to manage so far of) the 25-part schedule I gave a while back, and I was electrified by this.) Naturally, as a collaborator, Haughton might have known Shakespeare's sonnets without being their addressee; but I think this striking; and my work is not done.

The third topic I will just indicate, because my study is not even midway. The play *The Rare Triumphs of Love and Fortune* (printed 1589) strongly influenced Shakespeare's last three full plays, as individual editors, such as Dowden of *Cymbeline*, have recognized, *and* it was produced by Derby's men before the Queen in 1582, the year after Alexander Houghton's death; and it does not seem to me altogether impossible on internal grounds that it may not be a play by Shakespeare himself when he was eighteen. It is an interesting play anyway, in some respects the first real Elizabethan play, and I mean to go into it. I have already made a full study of the diction, which promises. But some of the style is even more promising. You remember Juliet's "O comfortable friar, where is my lord?" Hermione's "O comfortable words, were they but true!" might be an accident. But Bomelio's Lear-like distractions—sexual, and "Come, Bess, let's go sleep. Come, Bess; together, together"—that does not sound to me like an accident at all, but either the closest imitation (at how many years' distance) or the same mind. And why should a 30-year-old play have obsessed the end of his career, as no other play in his entire career ever did? The mere possibility, at any rate, of its being his, seems to me to deserve investigation along the lines listed before.

Of course, if either of the 2nd or 3rd possibilities should prove ultimately acceptable, the whole Lancs. connexion would be enormously strengthened.

Jed, forgive my troubling you at such length, and I'll be grateful if you'll send me a note, and bless yr work & Esther.

17 February 1953

Henry Allen Moe, Esqr.
John Simon Guggenheim Memorial Foundation

Dear Mr. Moe:

I write to request a renewal of my fellowship for 1953–4, but before I say anything about that let me describe shortly what I have been doing.

Since you added "creative work" to the description of my project, I begin with that. I have been lucky altogether in my fellowship but above all in this. Last summer I spent several months on the long poem called *Homage to Mistress Bradstreet* that I had had helplessly in hand since 1948, and still could not make it move, and so went on to Shakespeare. Then last month when my wife came out of hospital after an operation it suddenly began to move, and since then I have written above 250 lines or more than half of it. I send you the first of its three parts, complete, together with an exordium of 4 stanzas and the opening lines of the second part: 25 stanzas. As a matter of fact, 30 are finished but the whole second part has to be read as an emotional unit. I ought to say two things about what I am sending. First, it is not a draft but extremely finisht. Second, the artistic quality of the whole ought therefore to be clear in this first part; but the passional and spiritual range cannot hope to be, nor the character of the poem's ambition. Mr. Allen Tate and Mr. Robert Fitzgerald, the only poets who have seen any of it, have expressed high opinions of it. I can ask either of them to write to you if you like. I hope to have the poem finished in another month.

Houghton, Haughton, *The Shrew*, and the *Sonnets*

I have written to Professor Bentley, as you suggested, about the nature of the Shakespearean "discoveries" (I put the word in quotes because I am not yet in a position to determine myself whether to consider them valid or not—only of the identity of Shakespeare's collaborator in *The Taming of the Shrew* am I fairly sure) which interfered in the Fall with the quiet progress of my biography; and I enclose a copy of the letter, for your own eyes only, not for the Committee of Selection. These "discoveries," which will at any rate require a book for their exposition, still require extensive investigation. The most important result of my direct, planned work is a manuscript volume called *Shakespeare's Reading*, well advanced, which will presently incorporate, but in chronological order and critically, the whole substance of Anders's *Shakespeare's Books*, now 50 years old, and everything learnt since and everything I have learnt myself—I have been gradually reading every book Shakespeare read.

Meanwhile my critical biography of Shakespeare, although it has moved forward in this and other ways, and nine chapters of it are now drafted, is really not having this fellowship devoted to it, and the new Shakespearean work has prevented my getting abroad, as it is more than ever necessary for me to do. So my application for renewal is for this again, and for the completion of the new studies, and for the finishing, with renewed heart, of the long sequence-poem on the Jewish dead called *The Black Book*.

Yours most gratefully,
John Berryman

PART FIVE

The Essays

The *Sonnets*

THE EIGHTEENTH CENTURY'S antipathy to the sonnet form
—"I am one of those," said Steevens, "who should have wished it to
have expired in the country where it was born"[1]—extended to Shakespeare's sonnets, and there is little doubt that their vogue since is
bound up partly with the delightful biographical problems to which
they give rise. For the same reason, perhaps, judgement of them
among their admirers has been more uneven than one would expect
over poems latterly so familiar. Quiller-Couch, from the twenty he
admitted to *The Oxford Book of English Verse*, managed to exclude
one of the most magnificent, "Not mine own fears" (107), and one
of the most nearly perfect, "No longer mourn" (71); as do Auden and
Pearson (*Poets of the English Language*) from their twenty-five, of
which, indeed, hardly half are given also by Q. Along with these two,
the finest, I think, are 18, 30, 73, 106, 116. Concern with the sonnets'
problems should be resolutely postponed by the reader until he is
familiar with these seven. None of them evinces the intellectual reach
of Milton's sonnet on his blindness ["To Mr. Cyriack Skinner Upon
His Blindness"], but then this is the greatest sonnet in the language.
These are the sonnets of a young man, probably; their chief defect a
certain indifference to how things wind up, so that most of the couplets are weak; their chief virtues expressiveness and violent power.
Some of the very simplest, like "Being your slave" (57), are among
the best; and in general, despite their tiresome (though justified)
claims to immortality, they strike one as proceeding from a man more
or less without a pose—roughly, naked; not to speak of the humili-

ating privacy of some of their subject matter, which is quite different from the matter of all the other Elizabethan sonneteers.

Their manner too is plainer and more natural than that of any other real poet who wrote sonnets except Sidney. But before taking up the question of influences, dates, and identities, it will be well to summarize what they are about. Their overriding *theme* is Time; I mean their ordinary subject matter.

There are more than 150 sonnets in all, written evidently over a number of years; they tell no single story, and it is convenient to see their subjects as five.

1. Seventeen (1–17), addressed to a handsome young man, or boy, urge him to get a child and so perpetuate his beauty; he seems to be unmarried and presumably the plea is that he should marry also, first.

2. The bulk of the sonnets (most of 18–126) describe the poet's "love" for a young man, apparently the same one, for already in 10.13 and 13.13 the word "love" has been used. This love is platonic—as is proved by the obscene Sonnet 20—and is returned. One learns very little about the young man. He seems to be of better birth than Shakespeare; he is fair-complexioned; his father may be dead; perhaps he gives the poet a portrait of himself (46), certainly the poet gives him a table-book (77) and receives one in return and gives it away (122). He likes the sonnets very much (72.14, 110.7) and seems to have complained so vividly when they stopped coming that four in a row (100–3) make excuse for a long silence; but other poets praise him also (78–80, 82–86). The one look we get at his personality (93–94) suggests a boy narcissistic and inexpressive. He and the poet are often separated. He is unfaithful to the poet with the poet's mistress, but let's make this a separate subject. Shakespeare is confident, happy, proud, jealous, reproachful, forgiving, ironic, prostrate, gloomy, resentful, hopeless, as lovers are. He is older than the boy, narcissistic also (62), hates wigs and cosmetics (68, etc.), now says his verse will live forever, now says it is far below the rival poet's or even no good at all. It is not possible to form an opinion as to how the relationship wound up.

3. Some twenty sonnets (in 127–54, 153–54, however, being variations on a theme originally Greek, not addressed to anybody and perhaps not even Shakespeare's) are love poems to the poet's mistress, a married woman with black hair. These are mostly very bad poems indeed, contemptuous, trivial, and obscene.

4. Ten or so sonnets grieve over a love affair between the boy (known in sonnet literature as the Friend) and the poet's mistress (known, absurdly, as the Dark Lady). With 133–37 probably belong

40–41, and perhaps 33–36 by the Friend. One gets the impression that she seduced him, that his name is Will (like Shakespeare's), and that perhaps her husband's name is Will also. Some of these are addressed to her, but whether they were ever shown her must be doubtful; one calls her "the bay where all men ride," another (135) is among the most indecent formal poems in English.

5. Some dozen or so sonnets are so self-concerned that it seems worth abstracting them from 2, 3, 4 as having a separate subject, the poet himself. Among these are two of the sonnets' greatest achievements, the ferocious invective against lust (129) and the grave spiritual poem numbered 146, which are not addressed to either the Friend or the Woman; the bitter, insulted outcries of 110–12, though these call to the Friend for consolation, and the life-weary 66, though there is a flick of jealousy in the last line of this.

It is worth saying at once that all five of these subjects figure also, or find reflection, in Shakespeare's long poems and his early and middle plays, and two generalizations connected with this fact should find place here, before we dive into problems. In the first place, Shakespeare's sonnets, taken as a whole, do not make an *artistic* impression—as do those of Michelangelo, say, whether addressed to the young Roman Tommaso dei Cavalieri, to Vittoria Colonna, to Our Lord, or to Love; the poet's effort differs wildly in degree, there is no steady attention to craft; numerous as they are, the best like the worst appear to be thrown off, impulsive. Second, they follow no general *model*. Since Malone and then Dowden mistakenly thought Samuel Daniel their model, let me quote two experienced modern authorities.[2] "The definite element of intrigue that is developed here," Lee wrote in 1898 of 40–42, "is not found anywhere else in the range of Elizabethan sonnet-literature."[3] "The essential originality of these lyrics," Rollins summed up in his invaluable New Variorum edition of 1944, "is astonishing to most hardened students of Elizabethan sonnet cycles."[4]

The sonnets were not published until long after they were written, towards the very end of Shakespeare's career, in 1609, when the publisher Thomas Thorpe brought them out, as "Never before Imprinted," with a publisher's dedication to "Mr W.H." as their "onlie begetter." They, or some of them, had had a certain currency in manuscript, however, at least a dozen years earlier; one [no. 94, l.14: "Lilies that fester smell far worse than weeds"] had been quoted in *King Edward III* [II.i.41], pr. 1596, several [including nos. 138 and 144] had been printed in *The Passionate Pilgrim*, 1599. Hypnotized by the idea that Mr. W.H. is the Earl of Southampton, who was

Shakespeare's patron in 1593–94, most scholars have wanted to date most of the sonnets in the early-middle 1590s and later. Leslie Hotson's revolutionary demonstration, therefore, that three of the most mature probably were written in 1588–89 has been slow to gain acceptance, after some initial enthusiasm.[5] Perhaps his solidest argument concerns the "pyramid" sonnet, 123, which, proving "pyramid" a regular term for obelisk, he takes to refer to the famous obelisks disinterred by the Pope's order and re-erected at Rome, one each year, during 1586–89; these were a European marvel, by which Shakespeare was not impressed. Then, showing that the year 1588 was a year of which the coming had been feared for more than a century, he refers the "mortal moon" of 107 to the terrible Armada of that year, which seemed to approach in crescent shape and was happily dispersed ("hath her eclipse endur'd"). These two datings are accepted by McManaway (1950).[6] Hotson's third argument, taking 124 to be about Henri III of France and the Jesuit priests executed for their supposed intrigues against the life of the Queen, puts this sonnet at the same time and ought to be related to Baldwin's dating of *The Comedy of Errors*. It is Sonnet 104 that celebrates three years of friendship with the young man (this I think not a conventional but an actual period of time, whatever may be quoted from Horace, Ronsard, etc.). If we could have more faith in the publisher's order for the sonnets, wrong though it obviously is in some respects, it would look as if most of them were written during the late 1580s. At any rate, they are early. The insulted sonnets, 110–12, seem a response to Greene's attack on Shakespeare in 1592, and I fail to understand why this was never noticed until Fripp pointed out the pun in "o'ergreen"[7]; compare Greene's insolent "Shake-scene" with the poet's "my name receives a *brand*." Of course this is too early for Southampton (as the recipient), whom it is clear that Shakespeare hardly knew in 1593.

As for the identity of the Friend, we are at the mercy of Thorpe's dedication. If it was a product of gossip or is wrong, the problem closes before it has begun. Various circumstances and details suggest that Thorpe's publication, though duly entered, was unauthorized: the dedication's being his, brackets being placed (as if for two missing lines) after the obviously complete (though only 12-line) couplet-poem 126, the fact that the book caused no stir and was therefore conceivably suppressed, the improbability of the middle-aged respectable Shakespeare's releasing such poems. It is an unsolved mystery where Thorpe got his copy: who would have had *both* the Friend's poems and the Woman's?[8] But the dedication has a confident air

("TO THE ONLIE BEGETTER OF THESE INSVING SON-
NETS M^r. W.H. ALL HAPPINESSE AND THAT ETERNITIE
PROMISED BY OVR EVER-LIVING POET") and some support
is given to the first initial at least by the name "Will" in 135.

Even so, no plausible candidate has ever been suggested. For
Southampton there was never anything except his admitted patronage
of Shakespeare and the fact that many other poets dedicated work to
him (78.3–4). But his initials (Henry Wriothesley) have to be re-
versed, and his name is not Will; like Gray and Reed, I find it incredible that a nobleman of high rank is addressed in 20^9; like Alden
I think it preposterous to imagine an actor speaking of "leaving
alone," through his death (66.14), such a personage[10]; and Hotson's
dating now puts him out of the question. For William Herbert, Earl
of Pembroke, there was never anything worth mentioning.[11] Behind
the widespread desire to have one of the chief men of the kingdom
addressed in the sonnets of Shakespeare, one is bound to suspect the
same kind of snobbery that would like to father Shakespeare's plays
on somebody of like rank.

Thorpe's phrase "onlie begetter" is wrong anyway, a product of the
same impulse that led him to hide the sonnets to the Dark Woman
at the end of the book. Who she was, nobody knows. There are several
indications that George Chapman may be the chief Rival Poet, but
they are slight and uncertain.[12]

Shakespeare's sonnets take the easy, alternating-rime form, as
against the severe Petrarchan octet-and-sestet, and a deliberate aesthetic is audible in 21, 76, 82, 130: anti-Petrarchan, realistic, plain-
spoken. Insofar as they have a master, it seems to me to be Sidney.
We are thinking now of style, not material. Certain features may be
noted. "O" is a mannerism, occurring some fifty times.[13] Feminine
rime is rare (20 and 87 are exceptional), the average being just over
one to a sonnet.[14] Shakespeare is very fond of monosyllables; Rollins
makes the number of lines entirely monosyllabic about one-tenth of
the whole, noticing that Nashe as sternly reprehended their use as
Gascoigne (*Certain Notes of Instruction*, 1575) recommended it:
"The more monosyllables that you use, the truer Englishman you
shall seeme, and the lesse you shall smell of the Inkehorne."[15] The
poet's blunt force is in good measure due to this practice, almost
never to something else he goes in for, legal quibbling. His form is
sometimes loose; 66 and 129 are not real quatrain sonnets, as [H. C.]
Beeching observed.[16] Certain anomalies occur: the mediocre couplet
of 36 is repeated, perhaps by an error, at the end of 96[17]; 99 has
fifteen lines; the tinkling 145 [in tetrameters] may not be Shake-

speare's; 61 and 120 employ inexact rime. Shakespeare's weakness in couplets has been mentioned; 87 is a brilliant exception, and there are others.

As for the sources, of idea and language, the sonnets contain few allusions and make no show of learning. The indebtedness of a batch of middle sonnets (44–45, 59–60, 63–64) to Book XV of Ovid's *Metamorphoses*, in the translation of Arthur Golding [1567], is exceptional. Shakespeare must have been reading this as he wrote—sonnets can be written three or four a day if one has the habit—or have pretty well memorized the fifty lines (250–300) mostly drawn on. Sources for the major symbol of the sonnets—the beloved as Rose—and their chief symbolic preoccupations—with Time, with Truth-and-Beauty, with substance and shadow, with the lovers as One—can hardly be identified with precision in the welter of neo-Platonic and Renaissance thought, especially since even these large themes are taken up and then laid down again by the poet. They form no solid substratum. The very meagre influence of Christian thought is noticeable. Sonnet 4 uses the parable of the Talents [Matthew 25:14–30]; there are real references to the resurrection of the body and to "my heaven" in 55.13 and 110.13; and twice Shakespeare complains that his friend's infidelity has laid him on the "cross." This is all, and little enough, except for 105, which is decidedly blasphemous (it three times parodies the Trinity, and as one critic [G. G. Loane] has pointed out, the extraordinary line "To one, of one, still such, and ever so" is a doxology)[18] and 121, which sounds as if it had been written by a villain. On the staggering "I am that I am" in 121, adapting God's name (Exodus 3:14), Mackail says: "These words are in effect Shakespeare's single and final self-criticism . . . beside them even the pride of Milton dwindles and grows pale: for here Shakespeare, for one single revealing moment, speaks not as though he were God's elect, but as though he were God himself."[19]

The sonnets' glories are not from books, and rather from instinct than thought. Here is 73, in the original spelling and pointing (one error corrected, one spelling altered for clarity):

> That time of yeeare thou maist in me behold,
> When yellow leaues, or none, or few doe hange
> Vpon those boughes which shake against the could,
> Bare ruin'd choirs, where late the sweet birds sang.
> In me thou seest the twi-light of such day,
> As after Sun-set fadeth in the West,
> Which by and by blacke night doth take away,

Deaths second selfe that seals vp all in rest.
In me thou seest the glowing of such fire,
That on the ashes of his youth doth lye,
As the death bed, whereon it must expire,
Consum'd with that which it was nurrisht by.
　This thou perceu'st, which makes thy loue more strong,
　To loue that well, which thou must leaue ere long.

The fundamental emotion here is self-pity. Not an attractive emotion. What renders it pathetic, in the good instead of the bad sense, is the sinister diminution of the time concept, quatrain by quatrain. We have first a year, and the final season of it; then only a day, and the final stretch of it; then just a fire, built for part of the day, and the final minutes of it; *then*—entirely deprived of life, in prospect, and even now a merely objective "that," like a third-person corpse!—the poet. The imagery begins and continues as visual—yellow, sunset, glowing—and one by one these are destroyed; but also in the first quatrain one heard *sound*, which disappears there; and from the couplet imagery of every kind is excluded, as if the sense were indeed dead, and only abstract, posthumous statement is possible. A year seems short enough; yet ironically the day, and then the fire, makes it in retrospect seem long, and the final, immediate triumph of the poem's imagination is that in the last line about the year, line 4, an immense vista is indeed invoked—that of the desolate monasteries strewn over England, sacked in Henry's reign, where "late"—not so long ago! a terrible foreglance into the tiny coming times of the poem—the choirs of monks lifted their little and brief voices, in ignorance of what was coming—as the poet would be doing now, except that this poem *knows*. Instinct is here, after all, a kind of thought. This is one of the best poems in English.

The Comedy of Errors

ABOUT THE DATE OF THE PLAY there is more difficulty than can leave us comfortable in our impression of when it was, and with what, that Shakespeare began his work for the theatre. Many critics have thought the *Errors* his first play, by which they mean his earliest surviving play. Chambers (1930) put it in 1592–93, and this is probably too late.[1] The case made out by Baldwin (1929) for 1589 is not so strong as one would like, but it will have to do for the present. He thinks Act V reflects the execution of a Jesuit priest, Father William Hartley, on October 5, 1588, in Finsbury Fields, near the Theatre and the Curtain, at one of which, or both, the play will have been performed.[2] Hotson has independently shown that Sonnet 124 probably alludes to the executions of Jesuits and is of the same date, which lends Baldwin some support. A reference to "armadoes" and the borrowing of a warrior's name from Greene's *Menaphon* of 1589 suggest that the play cannot be earlier. Borrowings from it, by Nashe in 1593 [*Four Letters Confuted*] and in *Arden of Faversham* (1592), suggest that it cannot be much later; a negative point just worth mention is that no trace of *The Faerie Queene* (1590) has been found in it. Unfortunately, the well-known topical allusion to the French heir, at III.i.122, is variously interpreted; but a consensus makes it refer to Henry of Navarre, appointed successor by Henry III on August 12, 1589, and that autumn ought to be our date, in the light of the rest of the evidence.

There was a celebrated performance of the play on a chaotic evening at Gray's Inn, December 28, 1594. It may be that some of the expert legal quibbling in the dialogue was worked up and inserted by Shakespeare for this occasion.

But here and there the dialogue makes a distinctly mature impression; and there seem to be not one but two borrowings (IV.iii.81, II.ii.190) from Harsnet's *Declaration* of 1603—a book he later drew on for *King Lear*—as well as a phrase ("Soul-killing witches") echoed from Christopher Middleton's *Legend of Humphrey Duke of Gloucester* of 1600. I have little doubt myself that Shakespeare went over the play before its performance at court on December 28, 1604, when the King's Men were playing their first version before King James. Quite possibly, then, we are dealing with the play in its third version, after ten years (critics are agreed that the folio text was printed from Shakespeare's "foul" papers, or original manuscript, on which therefore he must have done such revision as is visible). As evidence for his dramatic practice in 1589, it may leave something to be desired.

But his main sources were all available at that date, and their assembly looks like a job of one inspiration. They seem to be five. The basic twin-seeking situation, with a shrew-wife, courtesan, and gold chain, comes from Plautus' *Menaechmi*, where it is the whole play. The hint—a hint to twenty-five-year-old Shakespeare, who clearly was ready for anything—to make the servants twins too, he found in another comedy of Plautus, the higher-spirited, more fantastic *Amphitruo*, from which he also borrowed the situation of III.i and developed the travellers' doubts of their own identity. The scene was shifted to Ephesus, probably, because the wife of Apollonius of Tyre floats there in the story on which he based the Aegeon-Aemilia action that frames his play (her name is Lucina—compare his "Luciana" for the sister he introduced to replace Plautus' Senex as confidante); this story may have come either from Twine's history or from Gower, both of which he used long afterwards for *Pericles*. For his characterization of Ephesus he went to the New Testament (Acts 19; Ephesians 5, 6); and for the trade-war idea he was indebted to Gascoigne's *Supposes*, the translated Italian play that stands somewhere behind *The Taming of the Shrew*. Whether or not he had seen in manuscript William Warner's translation of the *Menaechmi*, done long before but not printed till 1595, matters little, since he read Latin. Of course he had read other things also. Aemilia's name comes probably from Chaucer (the Knight's Tale—an important source some years later for *A Midsummer Night's Dream*), and "Aegeon" from the name of Theseus' father (Aegeus, also separated from his son most of the son's life) in the opening biography in North's Plutarch, one of the supreme books of Shakespeare's life. "Dromio" is a servant in Lyly's recent comedy

Mother Bombie, of 1587–90, "Antipholus" modified from a name in Sidney's *Arcadia* (dated 1590 but registered October 3, 1588). The Duke is called Solinus after the Roman compiler of that name, much interested in twins, whose ridiculous book, having misled readers for 1,300 years, was Englished by the poet Golding in 1587.

Sources, however, are not influences. The first thing remarkable about *The Comedy of Errors* is how little like Plautus it is. To a far more than Plautine complexity it adds a more than Terentian elegance. By the standards Shakespeare gave us with his later comedies, the *Errors* looks crude now, but it was the most brilliant piece of its sort since Aristophanes. Calmly doubling the twins, he forbids us to jib at the preposterousness of this by establishing it in the emotionally strongly modulated tragic exordium. The old father's fate hanging over the action throughout, the travellers' nightmarish bewilderments do not indeed come to much, but they evince an ambitiousness in the writer that reminds one rather of Euripides than of any previous comic playwright.

The next remarkable thing is how little it owes to Lyly's Euphuism, familiar as it certainly is with his romance and his prose comedies. This play is in verse, and is far plainer, faster-moving, and more *business-like* than Lyly, besides handling more diverse materials than he ever attempted. Shakespeare was perfectly willing to imitate Lyly, and did, later on, in *The Two Gentlemen of Verona*; but not here. Whom was he imitating? So much of the early drama has been lost that it is not possible to be confident about any answer to this question, but my feeling is that the answer may be: as a general model, no one. (Compare F. P. Wilson's opinion [in *Marlowe and the Early Shakespeare*, 1953] on his chronicles.) His verse is influenced by Marlowe. But he was already so much superior to anyone else in the management of plot, apparently by instinct, that it seems idle to look for one broad influence here. Something may come from George Peele and Lyly, something perhaps from Henry Porter (whose *Two Angry Women of Abingdon* H. C. Hart dated in 1589), but what Shakespeare did essentially was to unite three elements, initiating a new form: Roman comedic management, Marlovian blank verse for history and tragedy, and lyric verse—see, for instance, Adriana's nostalgic cadenza at II.ii.111–17, which George Rylands quotes as an example of what he calls "*stanza movement.*"

I have been using the term "comedy." The *Errors* is really a farce, "a legitimate farce," as Coleridge puts it, "in exactest consonance with the philosophical principles and character of farce, as distinguished from comedy and from entertainments. A proper farce is mainly distinguished from comedy by the license allowed, and even required, in the fable, in order to produce strange and laughable situations. The story need not be probable, it is enough that it is possible. A comedy would scarcely allow even the two Antipholuses . . . farce dares add the two Dromios, and is justified in so doing by the laws of its end and constitution."[3] But this is said rather too strongly. Along with Shakespeare's rejection of the ethics of Roman comedy (for example, the traveller's insistence on paying Angelo for the chain, or his brother's insistence earlier on his innocence vis-à-vis the courtesan) go touches of colouring that point forward towards romantic comedy: the frame-action, the wooing of Luciana. Pure farce the *Errors* is not. Shakespeare seems already dissatisfied, and in fact he never worked in farce again except once, in his part of *The Taming of the Shrew*.

He was bound to be dissatisfied, quite apart from aesthetics. One strong sense conveyed by the play is the moral necessity of subordination—of the servant to the master (see esp. II.ii.26ff.), of the wife to the husband, this latter injunction dramatized largely in Luciana but producing also, near the end, the play's vividest passage, when the Abbess leads the shrew on, to crush her at last out of her own mouth with: "And *thereof* came it that the man was mad." The powerful sense, here just glanced at, of man preparing his own fate for himself, is altogether inconsistent with farce and characteristic of Shakespeare, leading in one direction towards the tragedy of *Macbeth* and in another towards the comedy of *The Tempest*.

1590: *King John*

[*This unfinished essay was announced to the publisher T. Y. Crowell on December 2, 1959: "I have a staggering matter up my sleeve, a play called* Guy of Warwick *of the early 1590s, part Nashe's, with an attack on Shakespeare not Nashe's, which I've been studying for years . . . Please do not speak of this, though the real point is its connection with Sh's* King John."]

King John, AS A PLAY OF 1596 OR SO, founded closely upon an anonymous play called *The Troublesome Reign of King John* printed in 1591, has not for a long time attracted readers or its infrequent audiences. It is a perfectly characteristic work, and for a hundred years, from Garrick to Kean, the Bastard, the King, and Constance were continually done by the chief figures of the English stage, but a critic's characterization of it the other day as "a tiresome, gritty play" is likely to be seen now to deal with it. By 1596, however, Shakespeare was writing plays like *Richard II* and *The Merchant of Venice. King John* is not up to them, and has been fairly regarded as a puzzling failure, the character of the Bastard apart, and perhaps the big scene of Hubert with Arthur (IV.i). But two careful editors of the play, though they disagree about its relation to the *Troublesome Reign,* have placed it firmly in 1590. This is early in the English drama; *Tamburlaine* was three or four seasons old; possibly, just one other surviving play entirely Shakespeare's is so early; and from this point of view, established in Ernst Honigmann's solid edition (1954), *King John* has much to tell us about the materials and method of the dramatist's mind at the age of twenty-six. It will hardly do to see him as a novice; he may have been writing plays for years. But we have never before been securely so far back.

We would like to know, in the degree that we can, how he wrote it and even why he wrote it, as well as what it is like and how it is related to other men's work, but let us begin with an observation of Moulton on its structure. The play swings, said Moulton, like a pendulum of fortune, between England and France (initiating, in this, the historic alternation of all Shakespeare's history plays), and the starting point is an evenness, emphasized in the defiant triple refusal of Angiers' citizens to decide between the claims of John, who holds the crown, and Arthur, whose title is better and is backed by France and Austria. Each claimant has also his passionate mother with him; this comes from Holinshed, Shakespeare's general source. (I think Honigmann's view of the *Troublesome Reign* as a vulgarization of *John* must hold the field until it is controverted.[1]) Nearly everything else for the structure is imposed. As the playwright has it, the Blanch-Dauphin alliance swings all for John, the papal legate swings all against, battle swings all for; in his security, John's practice on Arthur's life produces his nobles' desertion and the French invasion, then his submission to Rome allows the Bastard to waken English resistance, the French treachery intended to the treacherous nobles sends them back to their allegiance; the pendulum's swings shorten and hasten as the action narrows; half the Bastard's forces are lost by accident and the King is poisoned, but the French are withdrawing and Prince Henry is ready. The action narrows to the soul. When the Bastard enters, the King says to him dying:

> all the shrouds wherewith my life should saile
> Are turned to one thread, one little hair;
> My heart hath one poor string to stay it by . . .

This thread in the King, really guilty of Arthur's death and burning for it, is that thread with which the Bastard had threatened Hubert if he was guilty of it, who was really (by a last-moment repentance) innocent:

> if thou want'st a cord, the smallest thread
> That ever spider twisted from her womb
> will serve to strangle thee . . .

It is not a complex pattern, but it is a good one. Almost nothing like it is discernible in Holinshed's annuary recital of this confusing and depressing reign. Shakespeare altered sequence, syncopated, resurrected, invented; in no other historical play is he so free. This does not mean, oddly, that he was indifferent to accuracy. Besides looking up the half a dozen pages in the first volume of Foxe's *Acts and Monuments* (a woodcut captioned "The monke lyeth here burst of the poyson" yielded V.vi.29–30)[2] and a dozen pages in Matthew Paris's *Historia Maior*, he pretty clearly glanced into at least two Latin manuscript chronicles, using Ralph Coggeshall's for the near-blinding scene (Holinshed put him on to this in the margin) and noting in the *Wakefield Chronicle* that Elinor died on the first of April. As his editor says, the tone of this bit of information (IV.ii.120) is very different from the hesitation he evinces (e.g., III.ii.7) when his sources are uncertain, and no doubt he felt some satisfaction in it. All this comes to no great job of research, over the weeks or months needed to write a play; it might take two hours; still, the suggestion even of this industry would have found scholarship incredulous until the last two decades. It is beginning to be admitted that Shakespeare could read, and would. Where did he get books? I suppose he owned some, like other authors (one of them, Lambard's Anglo-Saxon grammar in Latin [*Archaionomia*], 1568, is in the Folger Library at Washington, signed)[3] and, like other authors, borrowed; there were bookshops; within three years a dazzling courtier [Southampton] would be his patron. He was influenced also, in *King John*, by one of the Coeur-de-Lion romances (perhaps that printed by Wynken de Worde, 1528), which handed him the vices of King Philip (treachery) and Austria (cowardice), and pointed to his telescoping of two of Richard's enemies—Leopold, Archduke of Austria, Widomar, Viscount of Limoges. Shakespeare calls him Limoges, Duke of Austria, quite deliberately. Sometimes one sees the author playing a sort of game with himself. Without hesitation he makes almost guilty of Arthur's blinding a man so noble, Hubert de Burgh, that the chronicle tells us he defied the offers of the French before Dover Castle, not only to hang before his eyes his brother, whom they had, but even to hand over a great sum of money; and then, as if by way of symbolic amends, he has Melun expose to the English barons the threatened treachery for "love of" Hubert. But Shakespeare's chief character he invented.

One can follow him going about it. John's reign was familiar, and he must have seen before he began that among these shoddy shadowy figures he would want a focus of sympathetic strength as well as (Arthur) of weakness. A sentence in Holinshed began it, reporting that "Philip bastard sonne to king Richard . . . killed the viscount of Limoges, in reuenge of his fathers death." We hear of him no more. But just before this report, another Philip, Earl of Flanders, has disliked the fifty-day truce for John, and just after it he dislikes also the peace. The amalgamation gave the playwright a warlike man, half-related to John and so imperturbably loyal, while his real link is with the prior, decent reign. The man's surname, Faulconbridge, may have started from Faukes de Breauté, a bastard whom John made a general towards the end of the reign (Honigmann, p. xxxii: Holinshed 1587, p. 189 and—wrong—*John* V.ii.77), and Shakespeare may have known of a Philip de Falconbridge, who succeeded (as Archdeacon of Huntingdon? Honigmann, p. xxv) William Cornehill, one of John's right-hand men; or the name may be topical, for there was a prominent Yorkshire family of Falconbridges, and the playwright was fond of this name. I will come back to this.

How far the special tone Shakespeare created for this character was original it is impossible now to say, so many early plays have been lost, but it is a fact that no character in any surviving play up to 1590 has a tone so individual. Tamburlaine, Barabas even are organs for Marlowe. The Bastard is comparatively an individual, jocose, blunt, ironical, uniformly self-assertive, but incapable of self-congratulation without irony, a mind working, so rapidly established that after a dozen speeches he can be given a cadenza not in the least like his usual tone and still characteristic, when the Queen recognizes in him a Plantagenet spirit and says she is his grandmother: "call me so."

> Madam, by chance, but not by truth*; what though?
> Something about, a little from the right,
> In at the window, or else o'er the hatch;
> Who dares not stir by day must walk by night;
> And have is have, however men do catch.
> Near or far off, well won is still well shot;
> And I am I, howe'er I was begot.

This might be Sancho Panza. Note that the semi-lascivious is not very easily reconciled, as here, with the forthright; that the stanza (later to be used for *Venus and Adonis*) leaves undisturbed the naturalness of the scene, nearly all blank verse and couplets; that the insistence in the last line upon identity of personality, though not characteristic exactly of Shakespeare but of certain of his later characters, Richard III, Parolles, at moments of intense illumination—it is not Senecan ("Medea superest": a remnant of reassurance)—is what we call Shakespearean. Without the three fine set pieces (I.i.182–

*Honestly.

216, that on "Commodity" ["profit"] which closes the long second act, and IV.iii.140–59), the Bastard would be less impressive than he is, but he would still exist; and the imagery in particular of the third is so maturely handled that one wonders whether it can be a later insertion of the author's:

> England now is left
> To tug and scamble, and to part by th' teeth
> The unowed interest of proud-swelling state.
> Now for the bare-pick'd bone of majesty
> Doth dogged war bristle his angry crest
> And snarleth in the gentle eyes of peace . . .

No, this is in the style of *John*—his style, it seems, in 1590. A Continental critic [Clemen 76] points to the passage as an instance of Shakespeare's imagery not interrupting his thought but carrying it forward; and one might almost already be reminded of Coleridge's remarkable formulation of a difference between the style of Shakespeare and the style (far in the future) of Beaumont and Fletcher.

Almost, but not quite; and as with style, so with character. The Bastard does not develop; nobody here does. He is an intuition, a tone. Critics are excusably vague about this notion of character development; I can say better what I shall be meaning by it when we come to some. But let us not mean, for instance, what happens to Hubert. Honigmann is on good bibliographical ground in restoring to Hubert all the speeches headed "Citizen" in the folio and modern editions; so his part is longer than we knew and passes from what is merely official, as a spokeman of Angiers, to what is personal, with the King, and thence to his dilemma. He means to blind the boy, and re-decides; but the decision is not *registered* for us, in us: it is only said by him: "Well, see to live; I will not touch thine eye . . ." The distinction might be like a sly definition of poetry by Robert Frost, that it consists in the difference between what happens to you and what occurs to you. The pathos of Arthur is static, though real, and the boy is the play's only character achievement apart from Faulconbridge, simple as its elements are. Self-possession, first: Hubert greets him, "Good-morrow, little Prince."

> As little prince, having so great a title
> To be more prince, as may be. You are sad.

Second, sympathetic insight—that last sentence. And third, a certain intensity of imagination on behalf of his threatened eyes:

> O heaven, that there were but a mote in yours,
> A grain, a dust, a gnat, a wandering hair,
> Any annoyance in that precious sense!
> Then, feeling what small things are boisterous there,
> Your vile intent must needs seem horrible.
> Or Hubert, if you will, cut out my tongue,
> So I may keep mine eyes.

This is something—Shakespeare had halved Arthur's age from sixteen or so, on Holinshed's remark about his "being but a babe to speake of" in relation to John, and perhaps the playwright's son, now five, had taught him how little childish children are; but this is all. The Bastard indeed, as a character, subsides, becoming choric and the Patriotic Man. He rounds off the play with lines, suddenly impressive, that are its best known:

> This England never did, nor never shall,
> Lie at the proud foot of a conqueror,
> But when it first did help to wound itself.
> Now these her princes are come home again,
> Come the three corners of the world in arms,
> And we shall shock them. Nought shall make us rue,
> If England to itself do rest but true.

If. The theatrical emphasis distinguishes this from the Englishman's couplet the poet probably recalled from the beginning of Andrew Boorde's amusing *Introduction of Knowledge* (? 1542/7):

> I had no peere, yf to my selfe I were trew
> Bycause I am not so, dyuers times I do rew.
>
> [ll.19–20]

THE QUESTION HAS BEEN ASKED, and asked, how William Shakespeare learned to write. It is an idle question if all that is intended by it is incredulity that he did learn to write—that his work was written, say, by somebody else, somebody probably titled; but insofar as answers to it will tell us a great deal about his beginnings as an artist, it is a good question and opens enquiries that are valuable.

These enquiries, as they regard comedy, tragedy, chronicle plays, and poems, are rather different, although related. Here I want to consider only the chronicle, so that our answers, for the present, will be partial. But something can be said first for the question as a whole. Shakespeare, and the author of *King John*, was an actor, and he was a poet. About the first fact I will say something presently; it comes in here just as a fact. By describing him as a poet, I mean not so much that *King John* is written entirely in verse (the only play entirely Shakespeare's that is) as that its author was a lyric poet. Lewis, asked by his father whether he can love Blanch and told to look in her face, makes reply:

> I do, my lord, and in her eye I find
> A wonder, or a wondrous miracle,
> The shadow of myself form'd in her eye;
> Which, being but the shadow of your son,
> Becomes a sun, and makes your son a shadow.
> I do protest I never lov'd myself
> Till now infixed I beheld myself
> Drawn in the flattering table of her eye.

This passage does not rime and is (in diction, iteration, conceit, style) perfect lyric, as the Bastard contemptuously recognizes, commenting in rime:

> Drawn in the flattering table of her eye,
> Hang'd in the frowning wrinkle of her brow,
> And quarter'd in her heart—he doth espy
> Himself love's traitor. This is pity now,
> That hang'd and drawn and quarter'd there should be
> In such a love so vile a lout as he.

The author, we may say, is so securely a poet that he can mock his own poetry, in poetry of just another sort. Now, that an actor, accustomed to performing in plays, who was also a poet, should become a playwright—this can surprise no one; and particularly is this so as we are concerned with the very loose, novel, chronicle play.

Since we possess so far no comprehensive account, however imperfect, of the formation of Shakespeare's style (or styles) and art, it will be as well to deal at once with a view which has hypnotized criticism. The author of the only general survey we have of Shakespeare's reading, now fifty years old, declared without qualification that "Marlowe is Shakespeare's master alike in dramatic and non-dramatic poetry." This will hardly do. It ignores the following problems: (1) what is perhaps Shakespeare's earliest surviving play, *The Comedy of Errors*, is in form and style entirely unlike anything Marlowe ever tried; (2) we do not know when the sonnets, which may owe nothing whatever to Marlowe, were written; (3) it is now generally agreed by critics that Shakespeare's first masterpiece, *Richard III*, preceded not followed *Edward II* and *Dr. Faustus*—without indeed influencing them greatly, for Marlowe was also an original and ambitious dramatist moving very hard and thoughtfully from one problem to another. Marlowe's most considerable influence on Shakespeare was exerted, evidently, after his death, on the two long narrative poems and *Richard II* and *The Merchant of Venice*, where Shakespeare was dealing with subjects like Marlowe's, and in particular he was fascinated by *Hero and Leander*. On Shakespeare's prose, of course—it is two-thirds of all his work—Marlowe had no influence. And here in *King John* no trace of indebtedness to Marlowe has been discovered, unless in one passage in 1 *Tamburlaine* (see Honigmann's note on II.i.312), beyond the general obvious post-Marlovian character of the verse. But the versification is post-Marlovian, not Marlovian; it stands in reaction to *Tamburlaine*, four years later, as indeed one would expect.

The truth is that the same influences were available to both playwrights, and the most important of them was not from the commercial stage but from academic plays and the entertainments of the Inns of Court. That this influence reached Shakespeare directly, and not through Marlowe, is clear when we set a line from the first real Elizabethan play, *Gorboduc*, beside a line from *The Comedy of Errors*:

> That longer could he not refraine from proofe
> (IV.ii.110)
> But longer did we not refraine much hope

Here is no question of random imitation of effect or of isolated memory. The second line is as characteristic of Shakespeare in (probably) 1589 as the first is of Thomas Sackville nearly thirty years before; there is no such lifting or ignorant adapting as we find in *Arden of Faversham* (pr. 1592) out of *John*, where the nonsense

> Zounds I hate them as I hate a toade,
> That cary a muscado in their tongue

came from

> He gives the bastinado with his tongue
> . . .
> Zounds
>
> [II.i.463–66]

Shakespeare's early style owes much to *Gorboduc*; rather to Sackville's last two acts, as more energetic in versification and in syntax more elaborate and dramatic, though in diction more old-fashioned, than Thomas Norton's first three. The Queen's and Marcella's lamentations lead on to Constance's and those of *Henry VI* and *Richard III*, alas. And *Gorboduc* contained designs of visitation from heaven of reprisals, Trojan down through Brute and Morgan into British history, and of Order as violated by civil war, unknown apparently in the popular theatre; there was even a controlling image, Phaeton. Through a whole generation its successors, *Cambises* and others, refined this style, until a writer of no rare ability, Thomas Hughes, in another play of ancient British history, *The Misfortunes of Arthur* (1587), wrote easily a neutral style that in passage after passage might be Shakespeare.

But these Senecan productions, of dumbshow and chorus, debate, wailing, and messengers' recitals, could not of themselves lead to *King John*, and *Locrine*, to which I will come back, may be classed with them. When we turn, however, to the English chronicle histories on the popular stage from which Shakespeare is supposed to have learnt, we find only eight that present any possibility of pre-dating *John*, and only two that are actually thought by scholars to have done so, *The Famous Victories of Henry V* and *The True Tragedy of Richard III*, possibly of 1585 and 1590, but they may be later. Both have come down to us in poor texts, and the first play can never have been much, though it supplied eventually some of the design for *Henry IV* and *Henry V*. The second was clearly superior to most of the non-Shakespearean work of its period; it displays its quality at once in what Shore's wife, upon learning that the King is dying and her position is lost, says to her maid:

> Ah *Hursly*, when I entertained thee first,
> I was farre from change . . .

This must be that very uneven genius George Peele, and the play was helpful to Shakespeare when he wrote his own *Richard III*. But that was later. Belonging possibly to 1591 and 1592 are Robert Greene's sad *James IV* and Peele's unworthy *Edward I*, the corrupt *Jack Straw*, the old *Leir* (which is perhaps by that bore, Thomas Lodge), and Marlowe's *Edward II*; *Edmond Ironside* cannot be dated within ten years. Shakespeare's predecessors have disappeared. He may have been, with *King John*, absolutely the first to draw for the popular stage on the tradition, inconceivably improving it, of learned dramatic representation of English history. But so many plays may have been lost that we can hardly say. And I am leaving the important *Contention* plays (2 and 3 *Henry VI*) over to another chapter [*not written*]. Two things, though, are striking: how much he made use of, first, in one way or another; and second, how little he could have learned from it—just how little will be clear when we come to *Richard III* and *Henry IV* and *Lear*. It was only almost-raw material, encountered in his youth, plays acted in. There was no question of a John Lyly. It is extremely interesting (Kreyssig pointed this out[4]) that Shakespeare invented the whole first act of both *King John* and *Richard III* without source, historical or theatrical.

From what we may call the exotic chronicle play—a vogue initiated by *Tamburlaine* to which he never contributed, apparently—he had learnt more, or something. It must not be supposed that he learned only rant.

> Amongst us men, there is some difference
> Of actions, term'd by us good or ill:
> As he that doth his father recompense
> Differs from him that doth his father kill.
> And yet I think—think others what they will—
> That parricides, when death hath given them rest,
> Shall have as good a part as [have] the rest:
> And that's just nothing . . .

Of course this is Marlowe himself, though few critics have seen it, in a superb speech of 150 lines in *Selimus*. The comic mode apart, Marlowe taught Shakespeare to think, really to think, in dramatic verse. Passages are to be found more effective than this in *John*, but none so reflective yet. The only play quite certainly alluded to in *John* is another Turkish affair, *Soliman and Perseda* (1589? by Kyd?), which has a braggart named Basilisco who, even while being thrashed by a clown and made to repeat an oath, hopes to be called knight: "Knight, good fellow; knight, knight," but is "knave" all the same. In a passage that no one will ever smile at again, Shakespeare took this up, as the Bastard is scolded as "knave" by a mother unaware of his new dignity: "Knight, knight, good mother, Basilisco-like."[5] Perhaps the same actor, no doubt Burbage (see later), played both parts; and this trick Shakespeare lifted from the same play, where Amurath is called "Aristippus-like" after the character in *Damon and Pythias*. A minute before, something strange happens, in relation to another play.

The mother has an attendant, with one of the shortest parts, for a named, non-historical character, in the whole canon.[6] Here is the dialogue:

> *Bast.*   James Gurney, will thou give us leave awhile?
> *Gurney.* Good leave, good Philip.
> *Bast.*   Philip?—sparrow! James:
>   There's toys abroad, anon I'll tell thee more.
>   [I.i.230–32]

And he goes, never heard of before or again. The point is double: (1) Philip was the common name for a sparrow, and the Bastard means "Philip? Call a sparrow so, (2) but not me: I am Sir Richard Faulconbridge now and 'Philip' is dead"—referring to Skelton's familiar mock-elegy *Philip Sparrow*. Very well, but "toys" has been explained not only as trifles (like his knighthood) and entertainments (= you'll be amused to hear about it) but also—by Furness, Schmidt, Onions —as *rumours*; and five lines earlier occurs the only reference in Shakespeare's work (unless *Henry VIII*, V.iv.22 is his, which nobody thinks) to the story of Guy of Warwick. It is ironic as well, the Bastard wanting to know if his mother is looking for his (physically insignificant) brother, "Colbrand the giant, that same mighty man?"[7] Now in the play *Guy Earl of Warwick*, to which Alfred Harbage drew attention some years ago, though without relating it to *King John*, and dated tentatively in 1593, Sir Guy's attendant is named Philip Sparrow.[8] He is a clown, a sneak thief, and has left a girl pregnant in the town that he comes from. This town he tells Rainborne the name of when he asks:

> I' faith Sir I was born in England at Stratford upon Avon
>   on Warwickshire.
> *Rainborne.* Wer't born in England? What's thy name?
> *Sparrow.* Nay I have a fine finical name, I can tell ye, for my
>   name is Sparrow; yet I am no house Sparrow, nor no
>   hedge Sparrow, nor no peaking Sparrow, nor no sneaking

Sparrow, but I am a high mounting lofty minded
Sparrow, and that Parnell [his mistress] knows well
enough, and a good many more of the pretty Wenches
of our Parish ifaith.

Sparrow, as Harbage says (p. 47), is not really such a "fine finical"
name as all that, but "Shakespeare" is, considered with little names
like Greene and Kyd and Peele and Lodge.

The double connexion of the Guy story and Sparrow, in passages
so ironic from the two plays, seems to me rather strong, though
Honigmann only finds it "curious" [p. 17]. But what removes this, I
think, from the plausibility of the accidental is something quite different. The five-stroke attack upon Sparrow is identical in four of its
points with the famous onslaught against Shakespeare by Greene in
1592, and what is clear about the author of this attack is that he was
a young imitator of Greene. Here are the sorry points: low origin,
thievishness (plagiarism in Greene), Shakespeare's name, and his ar-
rogance. Lechery alone is not charged by Greene. That the author
of *Guy Earl of Warwick* was a beginner he tells us himself in Time's
lines that end the play:

> For he's but young that writes of this Old Time.
> Therefore if this your Eyes or Ears may please,
> He means to shew you better things than these.

But that he was an imitator of Greene can be shown shortly. Oberon's
lines to the creatures dancing round Sir Guy asleep on the ground,
while music plays, "Nymphes, Satyres, Fawnes," etc., begin just as a
translation of Melissa's lines (*Orlando Furioso*) to the creatures dancing round Orlando asleep on the ground, while music plays, "O vos
Siluani, Satyri, Faunique," etc.

1960

2 Henry VI

THIS PLAY, WHICH WAS ORIGINALLY called *The First Part of the Contention between York and Lancaster* and formed, as Shakespeare handled it, the first part of a formidable trilogy (the other parts being *The Second Part of the Contention*, now known as *3 Henry VI* and *Richard III*), has never received its critical due, owing to its being preceded in F by the later, inferior play there called *1 Henry VI*, and the problem of its authorship is still not settled. Until recently its study was clouded by a misunderstanding of the relation between this folio text and that of the quarto printed in 1594. In the light of Robert Greene's accusation of plagiarism, apparently involving *3 Henry VI* and presumably also *2 Henry VI*, Malone took the quartos* of these plays to be versions by Greene, known as *1* and *2 Contention* (1594, 1595), that Shakespeare revised into the plays we have in the folio. (Wilson thinks: of earlier versions of the plays as we have them.) It was shown, however, by Peter Alexander in 1929 that the quartos were never independent plays at all, but derivative: " 'bad' quartos" —memorial reconstructions—of the plays as we know them in F. At the same time, Greene's attack was reinterpreted as not one of plagiarism at all, and the way was open to see *2* (and *3*) *Henry VI* as entirely and originally Shakespeare's, which is what A. S. Cairncross does in his New Arden edition (1957). Even so, the editorial difficulties are immense, F not having been printed entirely from manuscript but partly from a corrected (imperfectly of course) copy of Q;

---

*2 *Contention*, 1595, is in octavo actually.

parts of F are therefore hopelessly corrupt, and also Q preserves some passages that are genuine though omitted in F, such as four speeches after II.i.39 in the quarrel between Gloucester and the Cardinal. Cairncross's is thus somewhat longer than any previous text, and we have not as yet anything like a standard text.

But it is far from certain that the play is all Shakespeare's. H. C. Hart in his careful edition of 1909 was working on the basis of a mistaken view of the relation between Q and F, but his work is not thereby discredited, and he regarded George Peele as the chief original author. Dover Wilson, in his even more careful edition of 1952, regards Greene as the main author, with Nashe. His views as to Shakespeare's part are not easy to determine, but he seems to think that about 1,800 lines, or more than half the play, were rehandled by Shakespeare, particularly in Act III; this rehandling he sees as running all the way from just touching up to full-scale revision, as of I.i.130–257, and insertions such as the lameness and whipping in II.i.

There is no agreement about sources either. Hart and Wilson consider as the major source Grafton, which Cairncross denies was used at all. Hall, he says, is the chief source, used side by side with Holinshed (second edition, 1587); but Foxe's *Acts and Monuments* and either Fabyan or Harding were consulted also. There is a good deal of fundamental invention, such as the intimacy between the Queen and Suffolk. A play of unknown date, *The Life and Death of Jack Straw*, perhaps by Peele, influenced Act IV (the Cade scenes) or was influenced by it. Ovid is frequently imitated. The phrase "bona terra, mala gens" (IV.vii.52) is from Andrew Boorde, who influenced the final couplet of *King John*.

The date universally agreed on for the play is 1590, without much specific justification. Unfortunately, our knowledge of Pembroke's Men, who had the play before the Chamberlain's Men took it over in 1594, is negligible for a date this early, and purely speculative even for 1591. Very probably there was some later revision by Shakespeare, affecting Young Clifford's superb outburst at V.ii.31–65, which Chambers thought clearly later in style than the rest; II.iv.81–84 might be added; revivals of the play are strongly suggested by the final chorus of *Henry V* (1599)—"Which oft our stage hath shown."

Criticism more specific than Dr. Johnson's—who remarked on the superiority of *2 Henry VI* to the other Henry VI plays—is hardly possible without a hypothesis. The difficulty with the Alexander-Chambers-Cairncross view that it is wholly Shakespearean is the diversity of styles that most critics have noticed. The difficulty with Wilson's view is that it neither accounts for the strategic power of the play nor at all explains how Shakespeare came to be concerned in it. The present writer attempted in 1953 a partial explanation of the anomalies (*The Hudson Review* VI, 198–99)—[see "Shakespeare at Thirty" above]—: "2 *Henry* VI springs into being as ceremonial, joyous, expectant—the King's bride, whom he has never seen, is about to arrive—everything looks splendid—then a fact, which we feel as odd, is introduced: she comes without dowry—the King pays no attention—but he is shrinking in our sight as the peers grow tall—a qualm—and suddenly, as the author looses the peers, power is pulling exactly seven ways—in scene ii, power pulls an eighth way—and under this comparison, none of Shakespeare's rivals seems to have a story to tell at all.

"I think the key may be found in the length of these plays. One of the things Shakespeare was to revolutionize was play length. Of thirty-six plays belonging to 1590–94, the average length is 2,250 lines; of four by Greene, 2,200 (Alfred Hart, *Shakespeare and the Homilies* [Melbourne: Melbourne University Press, 1934], II, part ii). I expect, as originally written, 2 and 3 *Henry* VI were typically inept and strengthless, psychologically primitive, usual-length Greene plays—which Shakespeare expanded into these outsize astonishing dramas (the first over 3,000 lines, the second just under) that gave the theatre after *Tamburlaine* its fresh and true start." Perhaps he reworked them everywhere, but particularly in structure, in the big "parts," and the Cade scenes—the vivacity and richness of Act IV alone would do for an ordinary play. These plays have seldom been performed since 1600, but Douglas Searle's productions at the Old Vic in the summer of 1953, with Sir Barry Jackson's Birmingham company, showed how little 2 *Henry* VI deserves its theatrical neglect.

A few points of special Shakespearean interest may be made. The technique of foreshadowing is already well developed, producing a *woven* texture that minimizes the loose four-story chronicle structure (Gloucester's, Suffolk's, Cade's, York's). Thus Humphrey is at his administrative best, in the miracle at St. Alban's, just before his fall; and the real claimant, York, has his reaching soliloquy just before the murder of the pretended claimant Humphrey. Henry's complaint about being King is followed directly by Iden's satisfaction in his country obscurity. This, however, is taken away from Iden, as a reward for his killing of Cade, in a characteristic Shakespearean irony not underlined at all. The acute feeling-*with*-his-people that will be one of Shakespeare's chief marks is most striking in his inability to dismiss even two flagrant impostors with the woman's desperate "Alas, sir, we did it for pure need"—which will not soften their sentence. On the other hand, he seems to have moved very slowly, in these early plays, towards his supreme capacity for delineating women. "The poet," said Dr. Johnson, "has not endeavoured to raise much compassion for the duchess, who indeed suffers but what she had deserved. Shakespeare's two earliest women, if these be they, are not attractive." Nor are the women of *King John*, nor the shrewish wife and the vague sister of *The Comedy of Errors*. The brutal, amusing Cade and his colleagues touched the dramatist's imagination much more closely, and it is clear from Richard's first line (V.i.140) that Shakespeare was already interested in the character with whom, two plays later, he would achieve the first psychological triumph of the English drama.

1958

3 Henry VI

THE SITUATION OF THIS PLAY with respect to authorship is similar to that of the first part of the trilogy, *2 Henry VI*, except that Greene's charge of plagiarism affects it more directly, just as his parody of I.iv.137 vouches more directly (*pace* Chambers, I, p. 287) for the Shakespearean authorship of the passage in which the line occurs. That is, *2 Contention* (octavo, 1595) is not a source play but a "report" of (an earlier version of, according to Dover Wilson) *3 Henry VI*, perhaps by the book keeper (prompter), as Chambers suggests. The present orthodox view, apparently, is that the whole play is Shakespeare's. Chambers endorses it, without much enthusiasm, pointing in particular to the high proportion of feminine endings and "the numerous similes and metaphors from natural history and country life." Hart and Wilson are again in opposition to this view. Hart, who thought *2 Contention* the source play, saw in it "a little of Marlowe, less of Greene, more of Peele and much more of Shakespeare," and in *3 Henry VI* "yet more of Shakespeare and yet less of the others." Wilson's views are as usual difficult to summarize, a task he seldom undertakes himself. Act I he calls Greene's, drastically though hastily revised by Shakespeare; II.iii, iv, v he thinks Shakespeare revised pretty thoroughly; IV.iv, v not at all; V.i "entirely recast," etc. The Recording Angel could not say how much of the play Wilson believes is Shakespeare's, and he expresses frequent doubt as to whether a given scene (II.i; III.iii; V.ii, iii, vii) was originally Greene's or Peele's. These complicated and uncertain views reflect the genuine difficulty of the problem, which is perhaps rather insensitively brushed aside by the proponents of a single authorship.[1]

As for dating, all indications are that the composition of the play followed directly on that of *2 Henry VI* and directly preceded that of *Richard III*. 1590 or 1591 this makes it.

There is considerable uncertainty about the sources. Only II.ii, III.i, and V.vii seem to be invented. The most careful study so far is Wilson's, who finds Holinshed behind I.i, IV.vi, and V.v, but hesitates between Hall and Grafton for most of the rest, and thinks Commines (not translated until 1596) may be responsible for the material of V.ii, iii.

Artistically the play has no independent existence, being merely a way of getting from *2 Henry VI* to *Richard III*, and it is the most tiresome play in the canon, notwithstanding the baiting of York (I.iv), King Henry's pastoral (II.v), and some touches by or connected with Gloucester. Nearly all momentum is lost halfway, at the end of Act II; and Richard's huge soliloquy (III.ii.124–95) hardly brings the action to life again. Some of the most leisurely and boring work is plainly Shakespeare's, as when the Queen is permitted to torture a nautical figure for thirty lines at the beginning of V.iv. The best writing is very brief. "He's sudden, if a thing comes in his mind," says Edward on hearing that Richard has run off to murder Henry. Not all of the very well-sustained choric stichomythia in III.ii may be Shakespeare's, but Clarence's line "He is the bluntest wooer in Christendom" must be. Edward in general is well drawn, in IV.i: he is self-indulgent, foolishly secure, disdainful, yet at the end of the scene he is made plausibly acute and frank with Hastings and Montague; the scene then at his camp shows him still foolishly secure but both stoical and brave, and his unshaken pride when he is captured completes the picture. Whether Shakespeare drew it all is uncertain, but the images of Edward as the sun (V.iii.5, V.vi.23), looking to the opening lines of *Richard III*, must be his. Warwick, the king-maker, is less interesting than in the earlier play. Richard, full of proverbs, energy, and envy, gets most of the attention Shakespeare afforded to this dreary production.

1958

The Two Gentlemen

of Verona

THE PLAY HAS PROVED UNUSUALLY difficult to date, because there is no record of performance (it is first mentioned by Francis Meres in 1598) and no precise topical allusions have been found in it. Chambers (1930) put it "early in the season of 1594–5" (WS, I, p. 331) and McManaway (1950) thought "about 1594" was "safe."[1] But evidence that will date the play better has long been available, unanalyzed, in the notes of R. W. Bond's admirable edition (1906). Backward: from Thomas Nashe's *Pierce Penilesse*, 1592 (S.R. August 8), Shakespeare picked up a phrase, "cunning drift" (IV.ii.79), in Nashe's passage in defence of plays, which claims that they anatomize "all cunning drifts" (*Works*, ed. McKerrow, I, p. 213); it is the previous page that celebrates the Talbot play—*1 Henry VI*, perhaps without any of Shakespeare's work in it yet—produced by his company, Lord Strange's Men, in the spring of 1592. Forward: two lines in Valentine's forest soliloquy:

> And to the nightingale's complaining notes
> Tune my distresses and record my woes
> (V.iv.5–6)

are echoed twice by John Lyly in *The Woman in the Moone*, an attractive comedy put by Lyly's editor, Bond, in 1593[2]: "Where warbling birds *recorde our happines*" (III.i.79) and "*And* we will sing *vnto the* wilde birdes *notes*" (III.ii.168). If, then, seeing no sufficient reason to think the *Two Gentlemen* was ever really revised by Shakespeare,[3]

we give it a single date, our best guess is in the theatrical season
1592–93.

Lyly is the general influence on the play, and this date satisfies also
its indebtedness to works of his that came into print in 1592, while
keeping it remote from the plays most like it, *Romeo and Juliet* and
A Midsummer Night's Dream. The immense aesthetic distance between this and those needs no emphasis if you will compare Julia to
Juliet or the clowns here to Bottom and his fellows. Perhaps this was
Shakespeare's final apprentice work for the stage, before he turned to
narrative poetry. Perhaps he was rather dissatisfied with this play.

We may ask whether his sources are compatible with the new date.
No broad source for the play has been discovered. What is cited as
one gave him only the Proteus–Julia outline, and of that just three
scenes: the letter (I.ii), the serenade (IV.ii), the Julia–Silvia interview
(IV.iv). This was a tale in the celebrated *Diana*, importing the Italian
pastoral novel into Spain, by the Portuguese Jorge de Montemayor,
and it came to Shakespeare in one or more of three ways: by a lost
play *Felix and Filiomenia* performed at the English court in 1585, by
a French translation of the novel (Rheims 1578, Paris 1587), by an
English translation made by Bartholomew Yong about 1582, though
not printed until 1598—this he would have had to see in manuscript,
but Shakespeare's later connections with the Middle Temple, of
which Yong was a member, do not suggest the possibility is remote.
The friendship theme, and its conflict with love, may have come to
him in part from an old play, *Two Italian Gentlemen* (or *Fidele and
Fortunio*), translated from the Italian and printed in 1585; he borrowed a name from this play later for *Cymbeline*. In fact, his whole
relation to this play is interesting. Of course he had read Lyly's romance *Euphues*, and was no stranger in his own experience to the
conflict between friendship and love, having (probably) written many
sonnets about it. Perhaps there is also influence from two chapters
on friendship (xi, xii) in Book II of Elyot's *The Gouernour*, a work he
knew well.

On the other hand, Valentine's notorious offer of his beloved to
the twice-evil Proteus, who has just tried to rape her, "All that was
mine in Silvia I give thee," which modern critics have tried to explain
away in vain, is firmly grounded in English as well as Continental
romantic ethics. Gysippus, in the parallel situation in Elyot's *Gouernour*, says to Titus, "Here I renounce to you clerely all my title and
interest that I nowe have or mought have in that faire mayden"
(G. Bullough [ed.], *Narrative and Dramatic Sources of Shakespeare*,
I, p. 216). Shakespeare had yet to reconcile romantic ethics to the
actual world.

The *Two Gentlemen* is decidedly, I think, Shakespeare's weakest play, of interest now (apart from its weakness, to which we will return) mostly as an anthology of motives and devices which he would re-handle later, better, and as an early example of his remarkably complicated instinct for form. Here is Moulton's analysis of its plot scheme.*

MAIN PLOT: With Atmosphere of the Gay Science
Original Situation

Disconnected Triplet { Friendship of Proteus and Valentine
Love of Proteus and Julia
Thurio's suit to Silvia [in Milan]

First phase of the Complicating Action: Journey of Valentine

Connected Triplet { Friendship of Proteus and Valentine
Love of Proteus and Julia
Rivalry of Valentine and Thurio for Silvia

Second phase of the Complicating Action: Journey of Proteus

Triple Intrigue { against Love: Proteus false to Julia
against Friendship: Proteus false to Valentine
in Social Life: Proteus false to Thurio

Third phase of the Complicating Action: Journey of Julia in disguise

Triple Irony { in Love: Proteus wooing Silvia in presence of Julia
in Friendship: Silvia drawn unconsciously to Julia
by the falseness of Proteus to Ualentine
in Social Life: Proteus mocking Thurio, with
Julia's asides

Resolving Accident: The Outlaws: stopping successive fugitives
bring about final clash and Final Situation

Harmonised Triplet { Friendship of Proteus and Valentine
Love of Proteus and Julia
Love of Valentine and Silvia

UNDERPLOT: Relief Atmosphere of Abandon. [Saucy servants—farcical word fencing—Dog sentiment parodying sentiment of Gay Science.]

While feeling some doubt about the propriety of the third "Connected Triplet," I think one is bound to be surprised by the evident symmetry in this analysis of Shakespeare's thin action, which often appears, as one reads the play, merely to be wandering. It is true that the notion of "parody" from the underplot may appear hardly ade-

---

* Richard G. Moulton, *The Moral System of Shakespeare* (New York: Macmillan, 1903), p. 341.

quate; but what the word partly does describe is rather a function of dramatic *movement*—which Moulton's analyses, never bettered in their kind, deliberately ignore—than of story multiplication and balance. This kind of analysis does not help one to read, for the same reason, but it is invaluable after one has read. Shakespeare's mind was from the beginning more orderly than the mind of any other dramatist since Sophocles.

His power, however, depends upon his movement, not his sense of order, and of this the *Two Gentlemen* has only faint touches. When Julia bids Proteus farewell, or should do, she is too overcome with emotion to speak, and immediately in comes Launce with his dog, who alone refused to shed a tear for *his* master's departure. There is parody here, but the essential dramatic operation is more serious than parody. The dog, unknowing, does not grieve. Julia, unknowing, does grieve; she has no idea, that is, of Proteus' nature—which his servant, Launce, knows well enough (see III.i.261–63)—or she would be silent, not from passion, but from indifference. That is, the dog behaves according to his nature; she does not behave according to hers; and the point made about human nature is ironical. This irony deepens when (IV.iv) Launce explains how he takes his dog's sins on his head and suffers punishment for them: "How many masters would do this for his servant?" And in comes Proteus with Julia disguised to become his servant and be sent wooing for him to Silvia. The upper world of the play, in both its women and its men, undergoes a contemptuous depreciation in its contrast to the animal level and the servant world.

But there is very little of this in the play, and its chief merits are lyrical: the famous lines

> Oh, how this spring of love resembleth
> The uncertain glory of an April day
> (I.iii.84–85)

which might be spoken by any character; the fine song, "Who is Sylvia?" in IV.ii; the interesting passages, excrescences both, on poetry and on acting (III.ii.68–81, IV.iv.154–68). Except to some extent with Julia early on, Shakespeare seems not to have been able to identify himself successfully with anyone but Launce. Both the lovers are unreal, the injurer and the injured; almost any speech of Richard III's brought him to wicked, humorous, overdrawn but realistic life as these sticks Proteus and Valentine never come [to life] at all. The playwright was trying out Continental romanticism, but he did not feel natural in it yet and is not effective.

1958

On *Macbeth*

IF A DRAMATIST IS UNFREE in comparison to other kinds of authors, Shakespeare was specially unfree, writing as he did for a particular company (in which he was also an actor), and a repertory company at that. Further, when he wrote *Macbeth* the company was called the King's Men, and his plays had to please not only the London public, the nobles who would occasionally command a performance, the young lawyers of the Inns of Court, and the provincial audiences the company played for when they went on tour in the summer, but the court and the King himself.

It is certain that in *Macbeth* Shakespeare made an extreme effort both to interest and to please King James. The play is very short, for one thing; the King tended to sleep during long plays, and his taste was well known. For another, the play is laid in Scotland, James's country—he had succeeded to the English throne only two years before, in 1603. It is elaborately attentive to certain of his special interests, such as witchcraft (on which he had written a book); and its major spectacle—the procession of the Scots kings at IV.i.111—is addressed directly to James's vanity and pride of family: these are the King's actual ancestors. Among all these limitations upon the dramatist's freedom—some imposed, some voluntary—it may seem that an artist could not do his own work at all. Yet scarcely any work in world literature strikes one as more characteristic or freer than *Macbeth*. This freedom is above all a freedom of *language*. It is through his incomparable language, more than any other feature of the work, that Shakespeare communicates his vision. This is also the feature that a spectator cannot study at all—he can only feel it and only feel part of it correctly: thus, when he hears

> violent sorrow seem[s]
> A modern ecstasy

it is hard to know what he will think, but he will not be very likely to know that "modern" meant for Shakespeare and his actor and his audience, not "up-to-date" with admiring connotations, but "ordinary, commonplace" with bored and (here) despairing connotations. In the sketch that is possible here of some of the play's salient qualities and meanings, language is the topic we take first.

IN THE WITCHES' SCENE that begins Act IV (Hecate's little speech and the extra witches and their song were very probably added to the play after Shakespeare's death), one of the witches says:

> By the pricking of my thumbs,
> Something wicked this way comes.

There is an allusion here to the ancient superstition "that all sudden pains of the body, which could not naturally be accounted for, were presages of somewhat that was shortly to happen." But she might also have said: "It is suggested to me, by a sensation of pricking in my thumbs, that an evil man is on his way here." The difference between Shakespeare's intense two lines and this rather general, unconcentrated alternative is, first, a difference in the quality of the sound, as there is a difference between what you hear at the beginning of Beethoven's Piano Sonata, Opus III and what you hear from a jukebox. The word "wicked" keeps the sound of "pricking" going; the reader's experience of the pricking of the witch's thumbs intensifies. In other ways, too, the two lines are built very closely into each other: "*Some*-thing" half rhymes with "thumbs," and the four short-*i* sounds that measuredly follow (*-thing, wick-, id, this*) carry on the two short-*i* sounds of "pricking" as well as they convey powerfully the sense of movement, something coming, marching. There is an unusually intimate association between the lines, and perhaps we ought to understand the word "by" has quite a different sense from the way we first took it (By means of this sensation, I know, etc.): In accordance with the pricking of my thumbs, something is on its way here, obedient or at any rate *consonant* to my sign. One gets an impression of a fated *assignation* entirely lacking from our paraphrase of the witch's couplet. This sense is greatly strengthened by the alliteration in the second line: "wicked this way"—as if there were something very natural about the wicked man's coming the witches' way, as indeed there is. One thinks of the two ways, of good and of evil, of the Sermon on the Mount (Matthew 7:13–14); and one does not think of them by accident, for the porter in II.iii winds up his hell discourse with "I had thought to have let in some of all professions, that go the primrose way to the everlasting bonfire." This play is certainly about Good and Evil, and we learn so partly from the aural organization of this couplet.

A second difference takes us outside the couplet—as indeed the word "way" has taken us already. The combination of the concept "thumb," in this witch context, and of the particular rhyme that binds the couplet, reminds us irresistibly, if we are careful readers, of four lines earlier in Act I (I.iii.28–31):

> *First Witch* Here I have a pilot's thumb,
> Wrack'd as homeward he did come.
> *Third Witch* A drum! a drum!
> Macbeth doth come.

The same rhyme (here thrice repeated) heralds each of his interviews with the Weird Sisters, and each time there is a thumb. Now this pilot is the second of the adventuring figures (the first being the sleepless sailor) in whom the dramatist is foreshadowing the fate of his hero: Macbeth, for *his* wife's greed, is to suffer from lack of sleep, and he is to be wrecked as he comes home, both in the literal sense home (where he will do the murder) and in the metaphorical sense (as he achieves the crown, what he aims at, home). The calling up in Act IV of this foreshadowing passage, deepens the drama of the couplet, making present, for its suggestiveness, the moral wreckage that had been foreshadowed. But in addition to this general usefulness, there are two or three specific points that claim our attention. It is not possible to be certain about the first one, because we do not know how clearly Shakespeare differentiated the witches in his mind, or whether his speech prefixes for them have been faithfully preserved. According to those we have, it is the first witch who has a pilot's thumb and the second whose thumbs prick; but in the light of the fact that presently Macbeth will be saying, "Had I three ears, I'd hear thee"—a striking speech that will interest us again later— there is an eerie chance that Shakespeare was thinking of *three* thumbs pricking, one of them not joined to its body.

Macbeth is announced, at his first coming, by a military drum; it is open, public; he is a hero, a man with a name. At his second coming he is announced by the pricking of a witch's thumbs, his resort is secret, and he comes not as a hero but as a tyrant; we must imagine as suggested also a terrible diminishment, from the booming of a drum to a slight physical manifestation, corresponding to a removal of the real scene from the objective world to the subjective. But this is not all, or even the main thing. It is as "Macbeth" that he first comes, to be saluted by three prophetic titles. It is with his three titles that he next comes, but not called by them, or even described as a man, but only as "something wicked." His nature has changed —not his characteristics merely, but his essential nature. He has become, perhaps, a demon; and the form, and sound, and allusive value of the couplet help to suggest this as no paraphrase could do.

A modern critic [William Empson, in *Seven Types of Ambiguity* (London, 1930), pp. 2–3] speaks of the exquisite line about wintry trees, in Shakespeare's Sonnet 73: "Bare ruin'd choirs, where late the sweet birds sang," as suggesting marvellously the devastated monasteries and chantries of post-Reformation England, where the choirs of monks had sung for centuries. If a line in a short lyric poem can give, in addition to doing superbly its practical, literal work, this sort of perspective, it need not seem surprising that the analysis of a couplet in a play takes us into complex problems of characterization and theme. Macbeth himself opens the question that leads at last to "something wicked" when he says to his wife (I.vii.46–47):

> I dare do all that may become a man;
> Who dares do more is none.

This is variously glossed by the commentators as "superhuman," "subhuman," "devilish"; but the meaning is clear: that there is a possibility other than the human for Macbeth—the demonic. His next formulation of this subject, at III.iv.59–60, is a little different. "Are you a man?" Lady Macbeth asks him as he stands appalled at the Ghost of Banquo:

> Ay, and a bold one, that dare look on that
> Which might appal the Devil.

The daring here has expanded, is "more"; and the claim that he is still a man does not convince. Then we hear "Something wicked this way comes" and we know where we are. Later the non-human diabolic terms applied to Macbeth, "hellkite," "hellhound," confirm our sense, and one's impression of his standing, or boiling, outside human life is crowned by his horrifying expression "Whiles I see lives," not men but *lives*, as if he had not one himself or only one so different that for human lives he could just say "lives" (like targets merely for his sword) and aim at destroying them (V.viii.2).

A SEPARATION OF the critical elements in *Macbeth* into plot, characterization, imagery, and theme is highly artificial. All are interwoven; the play is a tissue of suggestion. The reason for this is that man's nature is complex. The *ambiguity* of Macbeth's nature is perhaps the play's major subject. This is the shortest of Shakespeare's tragedies; it is barely half the length of *Hamlet*. It follows that the intellectual and artistic work that is being done in the play is being done, even more than is the case in the other tragedies, in terms not of statement but of suggestiveness.

At the same time, it is useful to describe the essential action, because it is that to which everything else contributes and on which everything else depends. The action is extremely simple. A man is tempted, falls, suffers, his nature changes, and he is killed. Such a statement does not tell us very much about the play. But it does suggest to us at once the fundamental difference between *Macbeth* and a mystery novel. Here there is no question of suspense about who has done the deed; the suspense is about how *Fate* will work itself out. And of course Macbeth is not the only person in the play.

Elizabethan Englishmen, including King James, did not feel as we do about the supernatural. They regarded it as a serious topic—just as the American philosopher William James did, for that matter, three hundred years later. The witches are fundamental to the play. Technically, they form an enveloping action, oracular in nature. But the element they represent, the supernatural, reaches and operates inside the action also; so that our description of the plot can hardly leave it out.

In fact, we must begin with it. Act I consists of: an initial statement about the fundamental ambiguity of nature ("Fair is foul, and foul is fair") by the witches; an external war which turns out also to be a civil war, owing to the treachery of the Thane of Cawdor; a prediction to Macbeth, the hero of this war, that he will inherit the (sinister) thaneship of Cawdor, and then become actually King; a debate within himself, like the civil war, conducted on progressive levels—first silently, as he stands enthralled with the Cawdor news of the Scottish lords, next in soliloquy (I.vii.1ff.; the dialogue with his wife at the end of I.v shows him so taciturn that it is best grouped with the silence and asides of the heath), then in controversy with his wife, winding up first in a declaration that he will *not* go on, then in a statement of their plan. You will have noticed already the alternation of outer and inner struggle. And the feast, or supper, for Duncan— as victorious and kindly King, as kinsman (first cousin to Macbeth), and as guest—in a society where the relation of host to guest was a grave ethical matter (during which the debate between the murdering couple takes place) already symbolizes the concord of the state which is to be wrecked.

The ironic and terrible concord of murderer and victim is symbolized by the banquet in Act III (where the chaos of the state is openly dramatized). These are the fruits. Meanwhile, the uncertain weather of Act I (moral weather for the witches, made physical weather by Macbeth in his first line, "So foul and fair a day I have not seen") has settled for *night* in Act II, which is about the deed. It begins with Banquo's ambitious, troubled dreams about the Three Sisters, and its supernatural phenomena are the apparitions of the dagger and the voice—one leading to the deed, the other forecasting its consequences.

In the Murder scene several points need emphasis. The succession of short, nervous questions exchanged between husband and wife, directly following the murder, suggests the uncertainty of the new world they have just entered by committing the murder. But this is only the most tense passage of this sort; critics have remarked on the fact that no other play of Shakespeare's is so *full* of questions—of doubt, of mystery. Then the terror of the offstage deed needs expressive outlet somehow, and gets it in Macbeth's terrible, crescendoing speeches about the voice. *This* is the new single certainty: that sleep is gone. Macbeth clearly is hysterical in these speeches (reaction after murder), and the tone lifts so high that relief is necessary. It is provided at once in the hell soliloquy of the porter. But this is not merely comic relief, of course; it is very rare in Shakespeare to find anything that serves one purpose only; and what is probably the most famous essay in all Shakespearean criticism is devoted to a study of this passage, Thomas De Quincey's "On the Knocking at the Gate in *Macbeth*" (1823).[1] The *noise*, after the terrible silence, like a re-entry into the play of the real world, suspended during the murder, is staggering in the theatre; but a good reader will hear it also for himself in "Knock, knock, knock!" And Lady Macbeth's confident "A little water clears us of this deed" is succeeded by "the primrose way to the everlasting bonfire." The essential irony of the passage is simple: the porter thinks that he is just joking about "hell-gate" and "this place is too cold for hell," whereas the audience sees that with Macbeth's deed hell has been let into the world.

With Act III we see Macbeth seated in power, and learn at once his sense that he has accomplished nothing at all:

> To be thus is nothing;
> But to be safely thus.

He sets at once to his new purpose, the murder of Banquo and Fleance. Note that he does *not* employ, or even fully confide in, Lady Macbeth, and that he sets a third murderer to watch his original two. These are the beginnings (or continuations, for already Malcolm and Donalbain have stolen away) of the situation of universal distrust, which comes to a climax in the scene in England in Act IV and the denudation of Macbeth in Act V. After Duncan has been murdered by Macbeth, who can trust anyone? Macbeth is now fully in alliance with the powers of darkness, and fully at the mercy of his own nerves. The very strange tone created for him by the poet in this act partly accounts for one cardinal mystery of this most demonic of tragedies: that he does not lose the audience's or reader's sympathy.

"O! full of scorpions is my mind, dear wife," he says, and "be thou jocund," and

> Be innocent of the knowledge, dearest chuck,
> Till thou applaud the deed.

This combination of the domestic with the terrible is unbelievably sinister and grotesque. But it is also pathetic, when we hear it in connection with his fierce suffering and hopeless longing:

> Better be with the dead,
> Whom we, to gain our peace, have sent to peace,
> Than on the torture of the mind to lie
> In restless ecstasy.

His strangeness, then, and his suffering, and also the fact that he is *not profiting* from his crimes, help to explain the fact that he does not alienate us.

Notice that the feast of Act I has moved onstage to become the banquet of Act III, so that we now *see* the atrocious linkage made by Macbeth between hospitality and murder. The fact also that it is

Banquo murdered, who was declaring, "In the great hand of God I stand," is striking: God seems altogether remote here in the central act—a place of the witches, the tyrant, the murderers, the Ghost.

Act IV is much lower in key than any of the first three acts, as is usual in Shakespearean tragedy. Such tension cannot and ought not to be sustained. First there is the witches' spectacle, hard only on the nerves of Macbeth, an ironic or sycophantic pleasure to its first audience; then the short pathetic scene of the killings at Fife; then the long—very long—scene in England of the tempting of Macduff. Clearly there is nothing high here. But the scenes are not unrelated: the first ruins Macbeth's dynastic hopes, the second completes the ruin of his moral claims, the third looks to the ruin of his security. The essential subject, then, is still Macbeth. About the long third scene certain points are worth notice. Its length—how *long* it takes for Malcolm to become assured of Macduff's sincerity—is itself a profound instruction in how deeply trust has been corrupted under Macbeth; as Macduff's sturdiness under Malcolm's progressive "revelations" tells us how low hopes have sunk under the tyrant. It is hard now for men to believe each other, and they expect little or nothing; the realm is chaos. Against this chaos in the North is set a realm in concord, England, such concord that the King, instead of being himself a thing of evil, is able to cure evil by "touching" (IV.iii.140ff.)— as James I had in fact been doing. This manifestation of a *benevolent* supernatural force is set by the dramatist against all the supernatural evil that has preceded it; critics who take the passage as a gratuitous compliment to King James have hardly done it justice. It looks forward, too, to the discrediting of the witches' guarantees (about the wood moving and "no man *born*") which takes place in the final act.

After this long respite—if it is one—from the Scottish horrors, we are returned in Act V *not* to Macbeth directly but to his wife, in the most ghastly scene of all, where truth, after all the deception and pretence, emerges in the delirium of the Sleepwalking scene. Except for this deep inward look, and several magnificent speeches, Act V is huddled, exhausted, and external—evil has worn itself out; the great final gestures of Hamlet, Othello, Lear are not possible here, and Macbeth can only die in a warlike parody of himself as the fighting hero we first met in Act I.

MOST OF US NEVER GET TO KNOW many other human beings very well—even our closest friends, even our husbands and wives, above all our children, even ourselves. Our experience of them is discontinuous, our attention uneven, our judgement and understanding uncertain. We know people, perhaps, chiefly by their *voices*—their individual, indescribable, unmistakable voices—and the creation of an individual *tone* for each of his major characters is of course one of the clearest signs of a good playwright. In this particular strength Shakespeare is agreed to be peerless. But the playwright has also two immense advantages over life—"clumsy life," as Henry James put it, "about its stupid work." Even when someone *wants* to reveal himself to another person, he is usually not very good at it, and probably most people spend most of their lives in self-concealment; but self-revelation is a large part of the creation of dramatic character. Moreover, in life we seldom enjoy really informed, highly focused comment by others *on* the person who interests us; and this in drama is the rest of the essence—unless we add that *significant* action plays at least as striking a role in the revelation of character in drama as it does in life, while *insignificant*, distracting action is excluded altogether, enforcing a kind of concentration very rare in ordinary experience.

Not much action, after all, occurs in *Macbeth*. There is some fighting, some eating, no doubt some walking up and down. Plays consist of *talk*; and only one person is talking—the author—*through* his characters, *about* them, to the audience. Therefore, there is, as there is not in conversation, one absolutely continuous subject, which is the characters and the action. (It has been convenient to distinguish between the characters and the action or plot, but really this is misleading: the actions of Macbeth are not more meaningful apart from his character than his character would be apart from them.) Everything said, in short, is, ideally, functional—as very few things indeed are in life; so that the connotations of the word "dialogue" are remote from those of the word "conversation." Even when a line of dialogue is so unstylized, or "natural," that it might occur in conversation, it is easy to show that the purpose it serves in its play is quite unlike the purposes of conversation. For instance, Olivia in *Twelfth Night* is the subject of a good deal of dialogue before we see or hear her: we learn that she is young, noble, wealthy, beautiful, and living secluded, in mourning—she is always spoken of, as it were, *upward*, with love, admiration, longing. Then she enters and says brusquely, "Take the Fool away." The purpose of this unexpected remark is to naturalize, so to speak, the large and gracious image one has formed of her—to give it a voice different enough from expectation to show the audience that that image was only the *beginning* of our understanding of her, though not so inconsonant with the image as to contradict it, and to create for her a tone that convinces, makes an illusion of life. (Elizabethan noblewomen no doubt said, from time to time, "Take the Fool away"—meaning nothing but "Take the Fool away.")

We might approach the characters of Lady Macbeth and Macbeth through one of her observations about him in her soliloquy (I.v.21–22):

> what thou wouldst highly,
> That wouldst thou holily . . .

Here is a remark unlike any ever made by an actual human being since the beginning of speech—as unlike life as a great work of music is unlike anyone's humming. Its *subject* is life, but the means is high art, *just as* the means—the true means—of "Take the Fool away" was. What is Shakespeare telling us, through Lady Macbeth, about Macbeth and about herself? Macbeth is ambitious, but an idealist. Now, Lady Macbeth is ambitious also, as the whole soliloquy sufficiently shows. But the tone of contempt in "holily"—extraordinary word!—tells us that she not only possesses no such double nature herself but complains of it in him. Lady Macbeth's character—about which so much has been written—is very simple. She is unscrupulous, but short-winded. No doubts beset her, except about the steadfastness of her accomplice. Single-natured, she is even willing to lose the nature she has ("unsex me here") in order to accomplish her purpose. But nihilistic, she has no staying power. Macbeth stays the course. By Act III she has already ceased to matter, weary, plunging towards insanity and suicide. The nature was shallow from the beginning, with its confidence that "A little water clears us of this deed"; only ambition mobilizes it, and only the horror of guilt can deepen it. There are just enough touches of sensibility—her analysis of her husband, and "Had he not resembled/My father as he slept I had done't"—to make her seem lifelike.

Lady Macbeth, in short, has no idea of what she is getting into. Now the reason she is conceived in this way, of course, is that she may throw a contrasting light on her husband, who is double-natured, heroic, uncertainly wicked, both loyal and faithless, meditative and violent, and *does* know what he is getting into. This knowledge of his is the real burden of the great soliloquy in I.vii:

> If it were done when 'tis done, then 'twere well
> It were done quickly . . .

The first "done" here means "finished," and the lines that follow show that what Macbeth has in mind is far deeper and more savage than any mere not-getting-away-with-the-murder, so to speak. Macbeth believes in "justice," and is afraid of teaching his own assassin (later) what to do; and he believes in eternal life, punishment, and would like to *skip* it ("jump the life to come"). He *believes*. His wife believes in nothing except her own ambition and her own guilt. He is also given to us as "brave," and "deserving" to be so called, and "worthy," and "frank," and he is full of scruples. But he has another nature. He is envious, ambitious, and hypocritical (the reasons he gives his wife, at I.vii.31ff., for not proceeding are quite different from the reasons he has just given himself). Therefore, he can be tempted. Shakespeare holds the balance exquisitely even between supernatural *solicitation* to evil (original) and supernatural *encouragement* to evil (secondary), as in Macbeth's line to the apparitional dagger: "Thou marshall'st me the way that I was going . . . " Holding the balance even is really to ask: Does it matter? Does it matter, that is, whether man falls in with temptation or just falls? The world is certainly full of temptations, whether created by nature or by the underworld of man's nature.

This duality of Macbeth is what makes the play possible; it also accounts for the ambiguity, the mystery, that characterizes the play throughout. But it only partly accounts for his hold upon the audience's or reader's sympathy. This is primarily a response to the imagination with which his creator has endowed Macbeth. His imagination mediates between his two natures, expressing and accounting for both, and projecting itself also into the future, in a way inaccessible to Lady Macbeth. One minute before she is bleating about "A little water," he has said:

> Will all great Neptune's ocean wash this blood
> Clean from my hand? No, this my hand will rather
> The multitudinous seas incarnadine.
> Making the green one red.

His mysterious brooding has scarcely a parallel elsewhere, even in Shakespeare's work. Increasingly, as the play advances, its antithetical subjects are cruelty and his own suffering; hand in hand these move, until the universe seems to consist of nothing else. There is nothing in *Macbeth* so intolerable as the last act of *Othello*, but no other Shakespearean tragedy is so desolate, and this desolation is conveyed to us through the fantastic imagination of its hero.

The course of action adopted by Macbeth, however, changes his nature, as we saw earlier, and the celebrated description of life as meaningless (at V.v.19ff.)—which has been so often and foolishly taken for Shakespeare's own conviction—is that of a man who is sickening to his end, who has ceased to be a man, who has acted himself—so to speak—out of his beliefs.

Duncan's character is fundamental also to Macbeth's fate. His mark is generosity, trust—even to foolishness, as is made plain at once, when he says of Cawdor the traitor:

> He was a gentleman on whom I built
> An absolute trust . . .

Such trust, Shakespeare is suggesting, *invites* treachery; so that, in some degree, Macbeth is merely cooperating. Such foolish trust leads also to the necessity of the depth of morbid *distrust* Duncan's son Malcolm feels obliged to display in Act IV. A certain natural suspicion, we may generalize, is a reasonable attribute in a ruler.

EVERY READER OF *Macbeth* notices the word "blood." From "What bloody man is that?" (I.ii.1) to "thou bloodier villain/Than terms can give thee out!" (V.viii.7) the noun and its derivatives darken the play. Critics have given statistics for it; all you have to do is count the number of occurrences in John Bartlett's *Concordance to Shakespeare's Works* (1894). But more important than statistics are: one particular way in which it is used, and the fact that it is often suggested without being stated. In the witches' dialogue (I.iii.1–2) we hear:

> Where hast thou been, sister?
> Killing swine.

Though the word does not even occur, the idea or *image* is present even to inundation, a flood of blood, such as spurts from a stuck pig. The same thing is true of Lady Macbeth's ghastly "Yet who would have thought the old man to have had so much blood in him?" (V.i.45), and accounts—along with the coarse insolence of her reference to the King, guest, benefactor, as "old man"—for the power of this celebrated line. We have blood not only everywhere, then, but swarming. Moreover, in a number of other very powerful passages, the audience or reader is compelled to imagine blood for itself even more specifically than in the "swine" passage. "It will have blood, they say; blood will have blood," Macbeth mutters to himself

(III.iv.122). Here the mysterious "It" is explained immediately—murder cries out for retribution—and yet the force of its initial, dreadful vagueness is not dissipated by the explanation. The horrible suggestion is in fact made by the explanation that anything in the universe not at once identified as something else *is blood*; and iteration of the actual word thrice in one line assists the suggestion. As a man thinks of his wife not by name but as "she" and "her," so Macbeth thinks of *his* topic—blood, the murder—as "it": central, permanent, a point to which other things are referred. The implied picture of his mind makes one shudder. This is psychological. The physical counterpart we hear at V.ii.16–17 with Angus's

> Now does he feel
> His secret murders sticking on his hands . . .

This can only be blood, as private as the floods of blood just discussed were public, blood ineradicable, intimate (and one thinks of Lady Macbeth's "A little water" and Macbeth's "this my hand will rather/ The multitudinous seas incarnadine"); you notice that the verb is practically a pun—what sticks cannot be got rid of.

Now, an ordinary play just tells its story, more or less efficiently. Clearly a Shakespearean play is concerned with something different as well: the presentment and enforcing, through imagery as well as through action and character, of a human experience complex and drenched, so to speak, as well as of a view of it similarly complex. Among the most brilliant results of twentieth-century Shakespearean criticism have been the studies of his imagery by Caroline Spurgeon, Msgr. F. C. Kolbe, Wolfgang Clemen, Edward A. Armstrong, and others.[2] These studies have been little hampered by the fact that no satisfactory definition of "imagery" is really possible; thus also have modern astronomers been able to learn a good deal about a universe which they are quite unable to define. We would *like* to take the word to refer to any representation in language of that which makes its appeal primarily to the *senses*. One *feels*, for instance, the word "sticking" as one does not feel, say, the word "as," which is a purely relational term. "Blood" is seen, smelled, felt, can even be tasted, as the word "position," say, cannot. But language, representing or embodying as it does the operations of the human mind, does not lend itself easily to these pigeonholes. Take the word "sleep": is it abstract or sensual? Shakespeare makes it, in *Macbeth*, sensual enough, and we get an elaborate image pattern. Worse still, a clear abstraction, like the word or idea "confusion," can be treated so obsessively and dramatically, as it is in *Macbeth*, that one has an impression that one is experiencing images. For example: "incarnadine" is plainly, or presents plainly, an image, visual, whereas "multitudinous" does not— or does it? The sensing and reflecting aspects of the mind are not so readily distinguished, except at their outer edges.

Just so, the reader responds both emotionally and intellectually to the image patterns. One both suffers and enjoys (understands) the blood image pattern: one recoils emotionally, *and* sees its point—that "blood will have blood," there is nemesis, and this is satisfying, in a world so terrifying and chaotic as the world of Macbeth.

But the blood image pattern is not of course given to us in isolation. There are other patterns, in the absence of which, indeed, the blood pattern itself would have much less than its actual effectiveness and meaning. One critic (Msgr. F. C. Kolbe, in *Shakespeare's Way: A Psychological Study*) connects the blood pattern with the sleep pattern, which not only forms the burden of several overwhelming speeches by Macbeth and of the Sleepwalking scene but receives heavy emphasis in speeches by Banquo (II.i.4–10), the witches (I.iii.19ff.), and others; and with these two patterns he associates what he calls a dark pattern—one of the most striking things in the play, of which the reader will easily discover examples for himself. These he generalizes very simply as resulting from the nature of the crime: "Duncan's *blood* was shed during his *sleep* in the middle of the *night*" (p. 10). But all this is still preparatory.

Msgr. Kolbe has half a dozen pages of quotation showing that ambiguity, confusion, *resulting* from this threefold nature of the crime, "is even more pervasive . . . than . . . Blood" (p. 11): "Fair is foul . . . broil . . . his country's wrack . . ."

> Shakes so my single state of man, that function
> Is smother'd in surmise, and nothing is
> But what is not . . .

"Unsex me here"—these from Act I alone. He notes, of "Double, double toil and trouble," in Act IV, that "the ingredients of the cauldron form a hell-broth of chaotic incongruities" (p. 14). (The Cambridge editors' brilliant conjecture "and none," for the folio's "and move" at IV.ii.22, accepted now by Dover Wilson and Peter Alexander, has really to be studied in this context of Msgr. Kolbe's:

> when we hold rumour
> From what we fear, yet know not what we fear
> But float upon a wild and violent sea
> Each way and none . . .

These three patterns are then explained by the critic as follows: "In this story of a great Temptation issuing in a great Crime, resulting in a great Retribution, Shakespeare has intensely individualised the sinners and the sin, but has universalised the consequences of the sin" (p. 20). Is a framework discernible for the patterns so far discovered? Msgr. Kolbe finds one in the antithesis throughout between the forces of Sin (witches, demons, spells, damnation, curses, hell, falsehood, doom) and the forces of Grace (angels, mercy, pity, justice, prayer, blessing, providence, truth). Again the reader will want to follow the development of the antithesis for himself in the text. But at least two parallelisms ought to be noted briefly. Behind Macbeth stand the witches, behind Malcolm the "gracious" (the word is from "grace," of course, which then itself occurs, IV.iii.189) King of England; and the expression "By the worst means, the worst" near the beginning is exactly balanced by the extraordinary phrase "by the grace of Grace" as almost the last words of the play (V.viii.72).

Clearly, the study of imagery emerges even more directly and rapidly into *theme* than does the study of plot or of character. The reason for this is that both plot and character tend to be more explicitly formulated in the artist's mind than either theme or imagery. In the case of a play like *Macbeth*, no formulation can ever hope to exhaust either theme or imagery. It will hardly be wrong, however, to suggest that one of the major themes of *Macbeth* is the exploration, in a very gifted and ambiguous and active man, of man's possibilities downward. It is *our* lower nature, as well as our higher, to which we attend in Macbeth; hence our sympathy. One critic (the late Donald Stauffer) once remarked that the king murder obviously symbolizes Macbeth's murder of his own higher faculties.[3] He picks his line—for evil—and is thenceforward committed to it. How briefly evil flourishes, how rapidly it succumbs to exhaustion (leaving out of account altogether, here, the *narrative* element of its overthrow from outside), is one of the dramatist's cardinal points, even in the dark state of mind in which Shakespeare was when he wrote this play. (The evil which in his directly preceding tragedy, *King Lear*, is reserved to definite villains—Edmund, the elder sisters, Cornwall—is here incorporated with his hero and heroine; and his next work was one of almost universal disillusion, *Antony and Cleopatra*.) Macbeth has no emotion left even for the death of his wife (the contrast here is with

Macduff's reception of *his* news). Evil dehumanizes and wears itself out.

Needless to say, the image patterns we have glanced at here are not the only ones in the play. Others that have been particularly studied are the clothes pattern, the animal pattern, the disease pattern, the discord-concord pattern. This last pattern is so closely associated with Msgr. Kolbe's confusion pattern that perhaps they ought to be identified. One theme in this pattern is worth special notice: the images of milk. "I fear thy nature," Lady Macbeth says,

> It is too full o' the milk of human kindness
> To catch the nearest way . . .

Two minutes later:

> Come to my woman's breasts,
> And take my milk for gall, you murd'ring ministers . . .

Malcolm, in his pretence to Macduff, says:

> Nay, had I pow'r, I should
> Pour the sweet milk of concord into hell . . .

Here we have a triple association of that which *nourishes* and is bound to the ideas of "kindness" and "concord" with the ideas "fear," "gall," "hell," producing, for the reader, a sense of chaos, of the unnatural, which is fundamental to the play. We begin, as human beings, with milk—we end, in this play, in blood—and the patterns are set against each other in such a way as to suggest that the whole spectrum of human possibilities is being explored with dismay. Images of courtship, procreation, infancy, allied to the milk pattern, intensify the irony, as in Banquo's speech on arriving at Macbeth's castle: "wooingly . . . bed . . . procreant cradle" (I.vi.6–8)—the birthing here is to be a murder—and Macbeth's

> Pity, like a naked new-born babe,
> Striding the blast . . .

and Lady Macbeth's terrifying

> I have given suck, and know
> How tender 'tis to love the babe that milks me:
> I would, while it was smiling in my face,

Have plucked my nipple from his boneless gums,
And dashed the brains out, had I so sworn
As you have done to this.

Images—and ideas, as in this solemn undertaking of Macbeth's to do evil—which in nature are wholly separate and opposed are joined by the dramatist. The interweaving of the consequent patterns is one of the aspects of this tragedy the reader will want to explore for himself.

1960

Shakespeare's Poor Relation:

2 Henry IV

PRODUCERS, CRITICS, AND MERE READERS have not been kind to *Part II, Henry IV*. In thirty-five years of playgoing I have seen it performed only once. The single quarto of 1600 was never reprinted, so far as we know, and one may doubt whether one in fifty readers of *Part I* go on to *Part II*. As for critics, they have mostly considered the two plays together, with very little said about the second. But it happens that in recent years half a dozen of them have bestirred themselves on its behalf, some on the unity of the giant double play considered as a whole, some on the unity of *Part II* taken alone as a sequel to the immensely successful *Part I*. It forms no part of my present purpose to canvas these views, though of course I shall refer to them now and again. My purpose is to account for the relative inferiority of *Part II* and then to make some remarks in mitigation of that argument: that is, to try to say why spectators and readers who do push on to it find themselves disappointed, in spite of the obviously great self-confidence and competence of the play and its occasional glories. Let me say first, though, that I cannot agree with those who see the two plays as a whole, and I feel no affinity with those who are surprised and depressed by the final rejection of Falstaff.

Shakespeare faced two problems. Hotspur was gone, and the relations between Prince Henry and Falstaff clearly had to deteriorate if the rejection was not to chill the reader wholly. The greatest dramatist the world has ever known took steps.

He kept the *spirit* of Hotspur going with two fine elegiac scenes.

And in an attempt to replace him with some character *inward* among the nobles, he took special pains with poor ill old Northumberland —well done, but hardly a substitute for the vaulting Harry Percy. One critic, Clifford Leech, remarks that this is a play about *old* men[1]; to this may be added that there is no fighting—the faith breech at Gaultree Forest compares miserably with Shrewsbury. The world where Hotspur flourished is gone, and his father Northumberland's betrayal bears on one less than his betrayal in *Part I*. Everything is cheapened and darkened in the play. One sees this in the women, in what we may call the love interest. Kate Percy being now merely a widow (a splendidly articulate one), it is Doll Tearsheet who replaces her, with Falstaff ("I am old, I am old"), and Doll is no chicken. The love scenes in the two parts are correlated: both begin with abuse and wind up in reconciliation. But what a world of difference there is between

> *Fal.* . . . the rogue fled from me like quicksilver.
> *Doll.* Yfaith, and thou followedst him like a church, thou
> horson little tydee Bartholomew borepigge, when wilt
> thou leave fighting a daies and foyning a nights, and
> begin to patch up thine old body for heauen.
> *Fal.* Peace good Doll, do not speake like a deaths head, do
> not bid me remember mine end.

and Lady Percy's "I faith, I'll break thy little finger, Harry." Both passages delight, but one also with sadness (church, heaven), the other purely with young love's mockery. One can hardly imagine the Welsh lady and her song and her "lap" (so attractive to Hotspur) in 2 *Henry IV*. The loves here are remembered loves, Justice Shallow's senile exploration with Falstaff of their early exploits imaginary and unsatisfactory. Falstaff despises Shallow (though with a grand gesture Shakespeare gives him one enlarged acknowledgement: "We haue heard the chimes at midnight, M. Shallow") and has a horrid description of him. No one in this play likes anyone else very much.

Names matter, for instance. Prince Hal of *Part I* is not "Hal" through four long acts (this is Shakespeare's longest play so far except *Richard III*, 3,180 lines in Hart's count, suggesting his deep interest in its themes): he only becomes so in Falstaff's mouth in the final scene of entreaty and rebuke and loss. Prince Henry's intimate in this play is, surprisingly, Poinz, and the nearest one gets to the old *Part I* is their disguised overspying of Falstaff at the Boar's Head. Exploits like the Gadshill robbery are out of the question. In fact, Prince

Shakespeare's Poor Relation: *2 Henry IV*

Henry does not figure largely in this play, except for the scene with his dying father and the chastisement, after his coronation, of Falstaff. It takes place in the world that he will transform—another play about him is promised by the Epilogue—after his change. This observation leads us in two directions. First, the failure to develop Henry in an intimate way, before his explanation to his father about the taking away of the crown, is certainly one of its author's gravest omissions. Shakespeare even takes the trouble to darken the stain on the whole royal family, by altering Holinshed to make Prince John of Lancaster responsible for the ghastly, Machiavellian business at Gaultree Forest.

Second, both D. A. Traversi ("Henry IV—Part II," *Scrutiny*, XV:2 [Spring 1948], pp. 117–27) and Leech (*Shakespeare Survey*, 1953) connect this play with *Troilus and Cressida* and other later works of profound disillusion, with images of sickness and so on, and raise the question of whether a *personal* reorientation towards the world and towards human nature distinguishes *Part II* from *Part I*—in short, whether we are not looking partly forward to the tragic period beginning with *Hamlet* two years hence in 1600.

Surely there is some truth in this view, just as surely as it is exaggerated. In Chambers's chronology, *Much Ado*, *As You Like It*, and *Twelfth Night* shine at us between *2 Henry IV* and the tragic period. (I may remark in passing that Chambers's classical chronology of 1930 and J. McManaway's remarks about it in *Shakespeare Survey*[2] are strictly out of date, as I hope to demonstrate in later papers.) But certain meannesses there are which claim notice here. The worst is the hideous little scene where Mistress Quickly and Doll are dragged off to gaol, just before Falstaff's downfall and consequent inability to help them—indeed, he is arrested himself, and no spectator or reader likes this—surely the new King's tirade was enough punishment for —for what?—for whatever his sins may have been. What are his sins, anyway? Certainly he has been a highway robber. Certainly, in this play, a poor comedown, he allows Bardolph to allow two men to buy their way out of the draft. But really it is for his *way of life* that he is banished and then arrested.

He has run away from armed combat. He has gloriously lied about it. He seeks credit (at Shrewsbury) for what he has not done in the way of battle. He is prepared to steal horses in order to get to his friend's coronation. He looks on companions as prey: of Shallow he says: "If the yong Dace be a baite for the old Pike, I see no reason in the law of nature but I may snap at him." The very sharp word "snap" defeats any Huckleberry Finn view of Falstaff. And yet does all this misdoing amount to much? Is it worth punishment? One feels

a certain coldness in the young King's speech, put there by Shakespeare to swerve part of the audience's sympathy away from the King
to Falstaff:

> I haue long dreampt of such a kind of man,
> So surfet-sweld, so old, and so prophane:
> But being awakt, I do despise my dreame,
> Make lesse thy body (hence) and more thy grace.

From a partaker in these riots, this is *good,* or seems so to us; I doubt
that an Elizabethan playgoer would feel any sanctimoniousness here,
being committed to monarchism (and nervous already about the succession to Elizabeth's throne). One might argue, even, that this word
"grace" is too often at Shakespeare's disposal for this kind of situation—Caliban you remember promises to be wiser thereafter and
"seek for grace."

I HAVE PUT THE CASE AGAINST the play as strongly as I could.
Let me now argue that a play containing the line "My father is gone
wild into his graue" (V.ii.128) cannot be negligible. This is Prince
Henry speaking to the Lord Chief Justice, and it might as well be
Dylan Thomas three and a half centuries later. Less remarkable but
valuable are some lines cut from the quarto, appearing only in the
folio:

> It was your presurmize,
> That in the dole of blowes, your Son might drop . . .

(anything like this is inconceivable in the early histories), and

> Thou (beastly Feeder) art so full of him,
> That thou prouok'st thy selfe to cast him vp

(the Archbishop about Henry IV) and "Their eyes of fire, sparkling
through sights of Steele."
   But the argument from style will concentrate rightly upon prose,
and in fact upon Falstaff's second speech: "Men of all sorts take a
pride to gird at me: the braine of this foolish compounded clay-man
is not able to inuent any thing that intends to laughter, more than I
inuent, or is inuented on me, I am not only witty in my selfe, but
the cause that wit is in other men." This really does have the tone
of *Hamlet,* and since Shakespeare's prose developed much more

slowly than his verse, it is remarkable. As in *Part I* he was merciless on Honour, so now he bandies back and forth "securitie," which he detests (having no credit rating), and his dialogue with the Justice is so funny that it has to be read to be believed.

I cannot tell, vertue is of so little regard in these costar-mongers times, that true valour is turn Berod [bear-herd]. Pregnancie is made a Tapster, & his quick wit wasted in giuing reckonings, all the other giftes appertinent to man, as the malice of his age shapes them, are not worth a goosbery, you that are old consider not the capacities of vs that are yong, you doe measure the heate of our liuers with the bitternesse of your galles, and we that are in the vaward of our youth, I must confesse are wagges too.

Only Thomas Nashe could have replied to this.

I would I might neuer spit white again: there is not a dangerous action can peepe out his head, but I am thrust vpon it. Wel, I cannot last euer, but it was always yet the tricke of our English nation, if they haue a good thing, to make it too common.

(I.ii.236)

To pass from style to incident: the little passage of Colevile of the Dale has always interested me. Falstaff on the battlefield recognizes this gentleman as a worthy foe, but on being recognized himself, Colevile yields without a blow. Falstaff shepherds him to where the leaders are, and not only does he receive no reward or thanks from Prince John, but John orders Colevile and others to "present execution." Shakespeare is full of instruction and I suppose we are bound to interpret. Falstaff *was* once such a warrior that his name suffices to convict; in short, his braggardism is diminished for us. Now the world is such that he receives for his exploit: nothing; hence his frequent complaints against the world have some foundation in fact. Third, Colevile having so nobly (to our hero) surrendered that it strikes one as an extreme of butchery that he should immediately be slain or murdered; a sympathy from his association with Falstaff—and his testimony, as it were, to Falstaff's valour—well, his death hurts us, and our feelings about Lancaster (no one has ever liked Lancaster) harden.

To pass from incident to motive. Falstaff somewhere contends [*Unfinished*]

1969–70

APPENDIX

Shakespeare's Reality

SOME PROBLEMS: POINTS OF ENTRY

SOME PROBLEMS: POINTS OF ENTRY

SHAKESPEARE NO DOUBT is incomprehensible, like other things (work and man) out of the usual scale, whether too large (like Dante, Shakespeare, Rembrandt, Beethoven) or too small (like Vermeer, Wordsworth, Thoreau). The natural scientists, too, remain baffled by the ultra-large and the ultra-small; but we may gain some confidence from their growing sense of a significant spectacular relation between those two ends: expressed by F. Hoyle (1955) as "ten" followed by thirteen zeros, a number which closely resembles (1) the ratio of the electrical force between a proton and an electron to the gravitational force between them, (2) the square root of the number of hydrogen atoms within the Olbers limit, and (3) the ratio of the density in the central region of a supernova to the average density of material in the universe. A layman, though lost here, cannot but be interested. A poet deals with two things, The I and The Other. It may appear, at a glance, that the purely lyric poet deals only with The I and the purely dramatic poet only with The Other, and that any enquiry into Shakespeare, who was both—sublimely both, and both in no apparent relation to each other—is foredoomed. It seems to me, on the contrary, that if we can establish a relation, in him, between his projection of The I and his introjection of The Other, each will appear less mysterious. Admittedly, this looks an ambitious enterprise, and its exposition, alas, has got to be serial, so I begin with some confessions.

Twenty years ago, in a Hodder lecture at Princeton and an article ["Shakespeare at Thirty," above] in *The Hudson Review*, I drew attention to Richard III's line *"Richard* loues *Richard,* that is, I am I." I was not yet in a position to understand this line, either in its expression of The I or in its expression of The Other, but at least I isolated it (and was encouraged, fumblingly, by Edmund Wilson's surprise at its brilliance). I even applied to it a capital formulation which I did not understand either, calling it an instance of "the unique stroking of presentment that drove Coleridge to one of his deepest conceptions, that of an 'ensouling of experience by meditation.' Now if we take "ensouling" to relate to The Other, as imagined—from "experience" both of the self and of others—by The I in "meditation," this seems to me to describe exactly what happens.

The King is in crisis, his unique self-confidence shaken during the night before the crucial battle, by the eleven frightful apparitions of his victims, even to doubt of who he is. So he gives himself a basal reassurance: at least he *loves* himself. At the dramatic level, we read this as: at any rate (however others may hate him, and however justly) *he* loves himself—and Shakespeareans will recall Eliot's interpretation of Othello as, in his final speech, "cheering himself up" (a view foreshadowed, we note, by Dr. Johnson's remark that Shakespeare's tragic heroes have yet left, in their end, "a miserable conceit"). At the metaphysical level, we gloss Richard's despair with an opinion of Whitehead's: that "as a first approximation the notion of life implies a certain absoluteness of self-enjoyment"; this is still available to the King, though Whitehead's other requirements (self-creation, creative advance, aim) are not, and so he is doomed. The philosophical reading, then—he *loves* himself—underlies, is deeper than, the dramatic. This is what we would expect. The poet is reading life, in the person of his shattered monarch in Act V.

The pivoting of the line after its fifth syllable has no parallel at this date, which is not (*pace* Chambers) 1592 but 1590. It obliges us to contrast three heavy first words, a strong unit, with the hesitant traipsing that follows. Greene, Peele, Lodge, and the rest were incapable of course of this concision and brooding force. But those qualities, as well as the metrical achievement, are rivalled by Marlowe, several years later, at the climax of *Dr. Faustus*: "See see where Christs blood / / streames in the firmament"—a line as resonant Other-ly as Shakespeare's inwardly. Having now listened to Professor Erikson, we can say with confidence that what is in question here is an unmasterable identity crisis, and see that the unprecedented labour of the dramatist's accumulation (*Richard III* is more than half again as long as the non-Shakespearean plays of its period) of an imperturbable and omnipotent ego for Richard, destroying without strain foe upon foe, wooing them even (Anne) into his evil bosom, was undertaken just toward this last-ditch line, where the rocking, unstable, unconvincing, double self-assertion suddenly reverses the process and he goes to pieces. Both in form and conception the line is integral with its play. During the course of our large study of Shakespeare's identity crises, we will generally find this to be the case, though not always so centrally.

But my other passage for investigation here at the outset is antithetical: it performs no apparent function in its play, *All's Well that Ends Well*. Count Bertram comes to the French court to seek service. The King is old and ill and good-natured:

> Youth, thou bear'st thy Fathers face,
> Franke Nature rather curious then in hast
> Hath well compos'd thee: Thy Fathers morall parts
> Maist thou inherit too: Welcome to *Paris*.
> *Ber.* My thankes and dutie are your Maiesties.
> *King.* I would I had that corporall soundnesse now,
> As when thy father, and my selfe, in friendship
> First tride our souldiership: he did looke farre
> Into the seruice of the time, and was
> Discipled of the brauest. He lasted long,
> But on vs both did haggish Age steale on,
> And wore vs out of act: It much repaires me
> To talke of your good father; in his youth
> He had the wit, which I can well obserue
> To day in our yong Lords: but they may iest
> Till their owne scorne returne to them vnnoted
> Ere they can hide their leuitie in honour
> So like a Courtier: contempt nor bitternesse
> Were in his pride, or sharpnesse; if they were,
> His equall had awak'd them, and his honour
> Clocke to it selfe, knew the true minute when
> Exception bid him speake: and at this time
> His tongue obey'd his hand. Who were below him,
> He vs'd as creatures of a nigher place,
> And bow'd his eminent top to their low rankes,
> Making them proud of his humilitie,
> In their poore praise be-humbled: Such a man
> Might be a copie to these yonger times;
> Which followed well, would demonstrate them now
> But goers backward.

Berryman's Shakespeare

Bertram sounds overwhelmed:

> His good remembrance sir
> Lies richer in your thoughts then on his tombe:
> So in approofe liues not his Epitaph,
> As in your royall speech.

The King has not heard:

> Would I were with him! He would alwaies say,
> (Me thinkes I heare him now) his plausiue words
> He scatter'd not in eares, but grafted them
> To grow there and to beare: Let me not liue,
> Thus his good melancholly often began
> On the Catastrophe and heele of pastime
> When it was out: Let me not liue (quoth hee)
> After my flame lackes oyle, to be the snuffe
> Of yonger spirits, whose apprehensiue senses
> All but new things disdaine; whose iudgements are
> Meere fathers of their garments: whose constancies
> Expire before their fashions: this he wish'd.
> I after him, do after him wish too:
> Since I nor waxe nor honie can bring home,
> I quickly were dissoluded from my hiue
> To giue some Labourers roome.[1]

At this point, Shakespeare remembered he was writing a play, and went curtly back to work:

> *L. 2. E.*[2] Y'are loued Sir,
> They that least lend it you, shall lacke you first.
> *King.* I fill a place I know't.

Here, first, after a gritty, tiresome opening scene, the great poet's imagination fires, and except for one moment of Parolles's identity crisis (of which a word later), it never fully does again in this justly neglected comedy. What ignited it? To what impulse do we owe this protracted marvel of ungovernable re-creation and mourning, richer I think than Dante's of Brunetto, the most remarkable tribute in the whole Shakespearean canon, unless we decide to couple it with Hamlet's to Horatio? But that is a young man's of a young man, face to face, and it has half a dozen varieties of importance in *Hamlet*: creating an ally in the hostile court, displaying the Prince's selfless passionate generosity, highlighting the treachery of his other young friends, establishing a Renaissance norm for the courtier (Castiglione much in Shakespeare's mind through adult life), to which then he himself both approximates and savagely does not. Here we have an old man remembering another old man, now at last dead, both highborn (as Horatio was not), lifelong friends allied in courage, "service," pride, *noblesse oblige*, and a horror of superannuation. Nearly fifty lines, contributing nothing to the play. There is no hint for it, no hint even of *a* character for the father, in Shakespeare's source. Surely even the stunted readers who actually imagine that Shakespeare in his heights never wrote out of his own heart (let me commend to them a lecture called "The Mythical Sorrows of Shakespeare," following which I awaited with true *Schadenfreude* Professor Sisson's studies of the mythical sorrows of St. Paul, Villon, Dostoevsky, Father Hopkins, and Hart Crane, but the eminent scholar perished some years ago, after a life of no sorrows) will concede that we have come on a subject deserving of explanation, if any can be proposed.

What is the subject? A mourning, in age, of the recent loss of an old colleague in virtues and also in a quirk, by no means universal, presented as a crowning virtue: an anxiety not to stand in the way of the next generation. Can we, after these centuries, discover any avenue of approach to this? Well, one stares us in the face, broad and singular—though over nearly forty years of Shakespearean reading I cannot recall one remark of its singularity. It is a fact that Shakespeare retired from the theatrical world early, at about forty-seven, at a peak moreover of his dramatic power, bidding London farewell with *The Tempest* itself, and retiring to Stratford to walk up and down in his orchard. My god, what a vision. There will be a great deal to say about this in the end. What concerns us just now is the fact, and the oddness of the fact, both suggesting very energetically indeed that Shakespeare shared the anxiety of his French King's equally imaginary friend. Perhaps we can now say we know something about him.

Why is it, shall we ask in passing, that nobody, of all those who have attended to this man's career, has expressed any wonder at its abrupt end? Who can imagine Rembrandt or Beethoven quitting in mid-career, that is to say, *ever*, just abandoning art? and loafing? Yet we feel very comfortable with this view of Shakespeare. It is no good dismissing it as the mere butcher's-son-goes-to-city-makes-good-gets-out image conveyed by his biographers Sidney Lee and J. Q. Adams. The delusion, frankly, is as old as his own time. We meet it first in his intimate Ben Jonson: "That Shakespeare wanted Arte"—so Drummond of Hawthornden reports him, possibly drunk; and this version of the delusion was shared by another perfectionist, John Milton (born a few hundred yards from Shakespeare's lodgings in the year of *Coriolanus* and the death of Shakespeare's mother), who groaned in 1630: "whilst to th'shame of slow-endeavouring art,/Thy easie numbers flow." The sense of the *inscrutable* Shakespeare begins there, which Wordsworth was concerned even to defend, which finds its ripest expression in Arnold's ineffable "Others abide our question. Thou art free," and which is with us still in E. A. Robinson's wide-ranging sharp-eyed poem "Ben Jonson Entertains a Man from Stratford":

> To me it looks as if the power that made him,
> For fear of giving all things to one creature,
> Left out the first,—faith, innocence, illusion,
> Whatever 'tis that keeps us out of Bedlam,—
> And thereby, for his too consuming vision
> Empowered him out of nature

and

> "No, Ben," he mused; "it's nothing. It's all nothing"

and

> O Lord, that House in Stratford!

Perhaps we may pause a little longer to comment on one of these delusions. That Jonson, though jealous, valued Shakespeare passionately enough, his great threnody proves; but himself a "classic," devoted to imitative punctilious crafting labour, he never really approved of the author of the careless dialogue that opens *Timon of Athens*:

> *Painter* You are rapt sir, in some worke, some Dedication
> To the great Lord.
> *Poet* A thing slipt idlely from me.
> Our poesie is as a Gumme, which oozes
> From whence 'tis nourished: the Fire i'the'flint
> Shewes not, till it be strooke: our gentle flame
> Prouokes it selfe, and like the currant flyes
> Each bound it chafes. What haue you there?

> *Painter* A Picture sir . . .
> It is a pretty mocking of the life:
> Heare is a touch: Is't good?
> *Poet*   I will say of it,
> It tutors Nature, Artificiall strife
> Liues in these toutches, liuelier then life.[3]

There is posing in "idly," true enough, like Kierkegaard's ten-minute appearances at the theatre to chat *in the intervals*, persuading Copenhagen of his idleness, when actually he was not at the play, he was home writing six books at once to flood forth pseudonymously. But Shakespeare's preternatural fluency was real too, as his friends Heminge and Condell tell us in the folio: "His mind and hand went together: And what he thought, he uttered with that easinesse, that wee haue scarse receiued from him a blot in his papers." Note "scarce," though, and even so, they exaggerate: the British Museum manuscript of his scene for *Sir Thomas More* shows a score of blots. He wrote rapidly, Mozart wrote rapidly—after long hours of patient immobile attention: only when all was clear began the faultless hand his father taught him. Manuscripts witness simply to manual labours like Housman's pyramiding of epithets.

The avenue invites us backward in Time. But what point is this from which we are starting? How near this end—the retirement—are we?

Unfortunately, the dating of *All's Well* is one of the most vexed of canonical topics. Malone put it in 1606, Delius in 1598, Coleridge changed his great mind again and again. It was F. G. Fleay (1878) who, linking it with *Measure for Measure* (1604), inserted it in the tragic period, between *Hamlet* and *Othello*, though he found in it remains (I.i.230–44, I.iii.133–42, II.i.130–214, III.iii.80–210, III.iv's sonnet and end) of very early work, which he assigned to 1591–92. There, for a century now, I am afraid the matter has stuck. Dover Wilson, predictably, escalated the revision theory, while Chambers, predictably, was rejecting it (though allowing, weirdly, in parts I–V "a quality which for whatever reason approximates to that of the blank verse of Chapman"). No record of performance survives, parallels to other plays remain controversial, and discussion had been bedevilled by a confusion of this comedy, or its first version, with the mysterious *Love's Labour's Won* (pre-1598). Meanwhile, confident studies of Shakespeare's "Problem Comedies"—*Troilus* adjoined with *All's Well* and *Measure*—proliferate. Yet what really links the latter two but the bed trick, a straw as frail as this linkage to *The Merchant of Venice*

(1596) by the ring trick? Let us nod to this pathetic history and start enquiry afresh.

The base style must be very late. Versification, diction, phrasing, syntax, tone, all more or less forbid the accepted "1602–3." Scientific metrical study began with Charles Bathurst (1857), who found the style of *All's Well* "harsh" and *"uneasy"* and later than *King Lear*—bravo, old pioneer who did not even sign your book. Its results were tabled by Chambers in 1930, with much labour, many improvements, and this made possible H. D. Gray's decisive advance. Gray insists (*MLN* 1931, p. 148) on an *average* of the three percentages of: double endings, run-on lines, speeches ending in-line. His chronological results, for the thirty-one plays considered "normal" (eight rank as "abnormal"), can only be called uncanny. With just three exceptions, the plays of the canon march in gorgeous and pleasing procession from 8.7 (*2 Henry VI*) to 53.8 (*The Tempest*)—a magnificent confirmation of the overall rightness of the end-product of the labours of a dozen generations of scholarship. *All's Well* is *the* exception; at 43.9 it "belongs" after *Lear*, just where Bathurst put it. No triumph, this, merely a suggested *terminus a quo*, and that merely for a play which is half prose, besides being possibly of two dates; but encouraging surely, hostile to "1602–3." So is the character of hendiadys: instead of *Hamlet's* characteristic "Out of the shot and danger of desire," we have not only the French King's more daring "Catastrophe and heele of pastime" already cited, but "captious and intenible Sieue," "the staggers and the carelesse lapse/Of youth and ignorance," and Helena's exquisite

> 'twere all one,
> That I should loue a bright particular starre,
> And think to wed it, he is so aboue me:
> In his bright radience and colaterall light
> Must I be comforted, not in his sphere.

Both in abstract diction and convoluted syntax—twice in his sixteen-line speech the King interrupts himself at length, expressing finely his special absorption as well as the general inconsequence of age—this style is to 1600 as is the style of *The Golden Bowl* to *The Portrait of a Lady*'s. A movement towards complexity accompanies regularly in the works of aged artists—the *Paradiso* (for instance xi, 28ff. on St. Francis), Beethoven's quartets (Op. 127 through 135)—an even more drastic movement towards simplicity. *The Tempest* fulfils this counterpoint, but we must be on the way there, well along too.

One would welcome a historical fact at this point, and happily some are available, heretofore neglected. The actors indicated by "G" and "E" at the end of I.ii and in IV.iii ought to be Robert Gough and John Edmans, legatees in 1604 of Shakespeare's long-time fellow (since, in fact, Lord Strange's Men) Thomas Pope. Gough too was with Strange's and then the King's Men, married Augustine Phillips's sister in 1603, played Memphronius in *The Second Maiden's Tragedy* (1611), and is in the folio "Names of the Principall Actors in all these Playes." Edmans is not (but note "Principall"); he married a fellow legatee of Pope's—all these men were far more closely connected than scholars have been willing to recognize—and begot children from 1605 to 1615, being a Globe lessee in 1612. William Ecclestone, of the folio list, has been proposed for "E": he had married Anne Jacob in the year 1603 at St. Saviour's, Southwark, just one week after Gough's marriage there. That same week a termer noted in his diary (February 12, 1603) that "Ben Jonson the poet now lives upon one [Aurelian] Townesend and scornes the world" (*John Manningham's Diary*, p. 130). Ecclestone played in *The Alchemist* and *Catiline* in 1610–11; he'd do us too. One begins to feel at home, indeed, in that remote world.

March 1971

NOTES

INTRODUCTION

[1] See "Shakespeare's Text," *The Nation*, August 21, 1943, pp. 218–19.

[2] All quotations for which no specific source is given relate to papers in the John Berryman Papers, Manuscripts Division, University of Minnesota Libraries—the principal source for all the writings included in this volume.

[3] René Weis, *King Lear: A Parallel Text Edition* (Harlow, Essex: Longman, 1993), p. 3.

[4] Heminge and Condell, "To the Great Variety of Readers," folio signature A3ʳ.

[5] Jay L. Halio's edition for the New Cambridge series, *The First Quarto of King Lear* (Cambridge University Press, 1994), opts to modernize spelling, regularize abbreviations and punctuation, and correct mislineation (see "Note on the Text," p. 27)—though all of Q's mislineations are recorded in his collation. (Hereinafter abbreviated as Halio, *First Quarto*.)

[6] See Edward Hubler, "The Verse Lining of the First Quarto of *King Lear*," in *Essays in Dramatic Literature: The Parrott Presentation Volume*, ed. Hardin Craig (Princeton University Press, 1935), p. 427.

[7] See the detailed and authoritative analysis by Peter W.M. Blayney, *The Texts of "King Lear" and Their Origins*, Vol. I: *Nicholas Okes and the First Quarto* (Cambridge University Press, 1982). Blayney describes the punctuation of Q *Lear* as "notoriously inadequate, erratic, and often insane" (p. 181).

[8] W. W. Greg, *The Variants in the First Quarto of "King Lear": A Bibliographical and Critical Inquiry*, supplement to the Bibliographical Society's Transactions, no. 15 (Oxford: Bibliographical Society, 1940), pp. 15, 50 (Greg identified in addition nineteen "consequential" variants); Weis, *King Lear*, p. 4.

[9] Alice Walker, *"King Lear": Textual Problems of the First Folio* (Cambridge University Press, 1953).

[10] Blayney, *Nicholas Okes and the First Quarto*, p. 81.

[11] But see MacD. P. Jackson's full analysis of the changes in this scene, "Fluctuating Variation: Author, Annotator, or Actor?" in *The Division of the Kingdoms: Shakespeare's Two Versions of "King Lear*," eds. Gary Taylor and Michael Warren (Oxford: Clarendon Press, 1983, reprinted new as paperback, 1986), pp. 332–39; and a succinct essay by John Kerrigan, "Shakespeare as Reviser," in the *Sphere History of Literature*, Vol. 3: *English Drama to 1710*, ed.

C. Ricks (1971; rev. edn., London: Sphere Reference, 1987), pp. 255–75, which argues that the quarto version uses "state" to mean "condition," "of" as "off"; F makes the line less ambiguous, while transforming "all cares . . . of our state" into one phrase in a two-line parenthesis opened after "Tell me my daughters" (p. 272). The changes are far from random, Kerrigan argues further, but serve to focus the political issues of the play.

¹² I take the terms from Weis, *King Lear*, p. 3. Weis, who favours the latter set, charts "the main areas of differences between Q 1608 and F 1623" on pp. 5–7.

¹³ Halio, *First Quarto*, p. 24.

¹⁴ See the contributions by Roger Warren, Michael Warren, Thomas Clayton, Beth Goldring, Randall McLeod, John Kerrigan, and Gary Taylor, in *The Division of the Kingdoms* (1983, 1986). Compare Richard Knowles, "The Case for Two Lears," *Shakespeare Quarterly* 36 (1985), pp. 115–20. Textual and critical developments are explored by Jay L. Halio, *The Tragedy of King Lear*, New Cambridge Shakespeare (Cambridge University Press, 1992), pp. 58–80 (hereinafter abbreviated as Halio, *Tragedy*); and summarized in Halio, *First Quarto*, pp. 24–26.

¹⁵ See Roger Warren, "The Folio Omission of the Mock Trial: Motives and Consequences," in *The Division of the Kingdoms*, pp. 45–57; Gary Taylor, "Monopolies, Show Trials, Disaster, and Invasion: *King Lear* and Censorship," in *Division*, pp. 88–101. Compare David Richman, "The *King Lear* Quarto in Rehearsal and Performance," *Shakespeare Quarterly* 37 (1986), pp. 381–82; Weis, *King Lear*, p. 23; Graham Holderness and Naomi Carter, "The King's Two Bodies: Text and Genre in *King Lear*," *English* 45:181 (1996), pp. 20–25; R. A. Foakes (ed.), *King Lear*, Arden Shakespeare, 3rd series (Walton-on-Thames, Surrey: Thomas Nelson and Sons, 1997), pp. 132–33, 135–36.

¹⁶ Gary Taylor, "*King Lear*: The Date and Authorship of the Folio Version," in *Division*, p. 424.

¹⁷ Weis, *King Lear*, p. 25. Compare Halio, *Tragedy*, pp. 270–71.

¹⁸ Grace Iopollo, "Revising *King Lear* and Revising 'Theory,'" in her *Revising Shakespeare* (Harvard University Press, 1991), pp. 161–87 (quoted from pp. 167, 169–70, 173, 177).

¹⁹ Graham Holderness and Naomi Carter, "The King's Two Bodies," pp. 9, 10, 15, 16. Holderness and Carter conclude with this self-confirming passage of jargon: "The textual destabilisation enacted by contemporary bibliography thus opens up further possibilities for an interpretative deconstruction of the 'Lear'-texts in terms of their openness to the manifold generic possibilities active in the collective body of Lear-narratives." The substance of Holderness's introduction to his edition of the quarto in the series cannily called "Shakespearean Originals: First Editions" (Hemel Hempstead, Herts.: Prentice Hall/Harvester Wheatsheaf, 1995) is virtually the same as that of the article co-written with Naomi Carter; my page citations refer to the article. (See also Graham Holderness, Bryan Loughrey, and Andrew Murphy, " 'What's the Matter?' Shakespeare and Textual Theory," *Textual Practice* 9:1 [1995], pp. 93–119.) Halio characterizes the scene at quarto IV.iii as "essentially a lyric interlude" (*Tragedy*, p. 77; see also p. 272).

²⁰ JB, letter to Kenneth Sisam (Oxford University Press), May 8, 1946.

²¹ For an outline of the New Bibliography, see G. Blakemore Evans, "Shakespeare's Text," in the *Riverside Shakespeare* (Boston: Houghton Mifflin, 1974), pp. 34–39; and Laurie E. Maguire, "The Rise of the New Bibliography," in her *Shakespearean Suspect Texts: The "Bad" Quartos and Their Contexts* (Cambridge University Press, 1996), pp. 21–71. Maguire satirically characterizes the New Bibliography as "that ambitious and sustained project of syntagmatic ratiocination" which aspired to "revolutionise the study of English literature by banishing sciolism, impressionism, and ignorance" (p. 40); and discusses Greg's "desire for one original text" on pp. 51–52. Greg "denied himself the option of revision" (p. 56). See also an important essay by T. H. Howard-Hill, "Modern Textual Theories and the Editing of Plays," *The Library*, 6th series, XI:2 (June 1989), pp. 89–115, which also takes issue with Greg.

Notes

²² Alexander Schmidt, *Zur Textkritik des "King Lear"* (Berlin, 1879); see H. H. Furness's *New Variorum* edition of *King Lear* (1880), pp. 367–70.

²³ E. K. Chambers, *William Shakespeare: A Study of Facts and Problems* (Oxford: Clarendon Press, 1930), Vol. I, (Hereinafter abbreviated as Chambers, *WS.*), pp. 465–66. Greg had written in an early essay: "I find it quite impossible to believe . . . that any writer, however familiar with the stage he might be, would in composition either deliberately or unconsciously introduce these features, which unnerve his language and destroy his verse, and then prune them away in revising the acting version" ("The Function of Literary Criticism Illustrated in a Study of the Text of *King Lear*," *Neophilologus* XVIII [1932–33], pp. 241–62; in *Collected Papers*, ed. J. C. Maxwell [Oxford: Clarendon Press, 1966], pp. 267–97 [quoted from p. 253]). In *The Shakespeare First Folio: Its Bibliographical and Textual History* (Oxford: Clarendon Press, 1955) Greg was to reject the very idea that Shakespeare, "at the height of his powers, could ever have written the clumsy and fumbling lines we find in Q, or that these could in general represent a stage in the development of F" (p. 379). Steven Urkowitz points out in *Shakespeare's Revision of "King Lear"* (Princeton University Press, 1980) that Shakespeare's hand in *Sir Thomas More* "is positively aggressive in its inconsistency and abhorrence of rule" (p. 132); he further urges: "The agent most likely to have produced the spelling, spacing, lineation, textual illegibility, verbal structures, patterns of dialogue, and dramatic designs in the Quarto of *King Lear* is Shakespeare himself" (p. 140).

²⁴ W. W. Greg, "*King Lear*—Mislineation and Stenography," *The Library*, 4th series, XVII (1936–37), p. 180.

²⁵ Greg, *The Variants in the First Quarto of "King Lear,"* p. 138.

²⁶ W. W. Greg, *The Shakespeare First Folio: Its Bibliographical and Textual History* (Oxford: Clarendon Press, 1955), p. 378.

²⁷ See Greg, *Variants*, p. 164; Blayney, *Nicholas Okes and the First Quarto*, pp. 248–49; Halio, *First Quarto*, p. 16.

²⁸ Madeleine Doran, *The Text of "King Lear"* (Stanford University Press, 1931). Ten years later, however, in a review of Greg's *Variants* for the *Review of English Studies* XVII (1941), pp. 468–74, Doran surrendered her own position on the status of the quarto: "That it represents Shakespeare's much-revised autograph, now appears to me dubious."

²⁹ The most concerted contribution to the debate is *The Division of the Kingdoms* (1983, 1986)—notably reviewed by T. H. Howard-Hill, "The Challenge of *King Lear*," *The Library*, 6th series, VII:2 (June 1985), pp. 161–79. In recent years, only P.W.K. Stone has argued that Q represents a theatrical report—specifically a longhand report (*The Textual History of "King Lear"* (London: Scolar Press, 1980). The change in fortunes for a theory of revision between Q and F dates from Michael J. Warren's essay "Quarto and Folio *King Lear* and the Interpretation of Albany and Edgar" (in *Shakespeare: Pattern of Excelling Nature*, eds. David Bevington and Jay L. Halio [University of Delaware Press, 1978]; though kindred arguments had been adumbrated by Kristian Smidt ("The Quarto and the Folio *Lear*: Another Look at the Theories of Textual Derivation," *English Studies* 45 [1964], pp. 149–62), and E.A.J. Honigmann (*The Stability of Shakespeare's Text* [London: Edward Arnold, 1965], pp. 121–28). Urkowitz pressed the case for an authorial quarto, and for authorial revision, in *Shakespeare's Revision of "King Lear"* (1980), as had Hardin Craig in "The Composition of *King Lear*," *Renaissance Papers* (1961), pp. 57–61. See also Gary Taylor, "The War in *King Lear*," *Shakespeare Survey* 33, ed. Kenneth Muir (Cambridge University Press, 1980), pp. 27–34; Honigmann, "Shakespeare's Revised Plays: *King Lear* and *Othello*," *The Library*, 6th series, IV (1982), pp. 142–73; Gary Taylor, "*King Lear*: The Date and Authorship of the Folio Version," in *Division*, pp. 351–468 (esp. 395–401); Stanley Wells and Gary Taylor, *William Shakespeare: A Textual Companion* (Oxford: Clarendon Press, 1987); Halio, *Tragedy*, 288–89. R. A. Foakes, while accepting the case for revision, dissents from the "two-text" consensus: "The reworking of *King Lear* is not

so thorough as to mean that we have to think of two plays" (*"Hamlet" versus "Lear": Cultural Politics and Shakespeare's Art* [Cambridge University Press, 1993], p. 111); see also Foakes (ed.), *King Lear*, Arden Shakespeare, p. 129: "I regard *King Lear* as a single work that is extant in two versions that differ in various ways." The scholarly arguments are reviewed by G. R. Hibbard, " 'King Lear': A Retrospect, 1939–79," in *Aspects of "King Lear": Articles Reprinted from "Shakespeare Survey,"* eds. Kenneth Muir and Stanley Wells (Cambridge University Press, 1982), pp. 1–12; Stanley Wells, "Introduction: The Once and Future *King Lear,*" in *Division*, pp. 1–22; Michael Warren in *The Parallel King Lear, 1608–1623* (University of California Press, 1989), which includes a good "Annotated Bibliography, 1885–1986"; and Iopollo, *Revising Shakespeare*, pp. 162–66. Larry S. Champion provides an annotated bibliography of studies published between 1930 and 1979 in Section IV, "Textual Studies," of *"King Lear": An Annotated Bibliography* (New York and London: Garland Publishing, 1980), Vol. II, pp. 49–84. See also Paul Werstine's sceptical view of quartos as "foul" papers or final drafts, "Narratives about Printed Shakespeare Texts: 'Foul Papers' and 'Bad' Quartos," *Shakespeare Quarterly* 41 (1990), pp. 65–86; Robert Clare, " 'Who is it that can tell me who I am?' ": The Theory of Authorial Revision between the Quarto and Folio Texts of *King Lear,*" *The Library*, 6th series, 17 (1995), pp. 34–59; Sidney Thomas, "Shakespeare's Supposed Revision of *King Lear,*" *Shakespeare Quarterly* 35 (1984), pp. 506–11.

[30] JB to Marshall, July 11, 1945 (copy in JB Papers). For Kirschbaum, see further Maguire, *Shakespearean Suspect Texts*, pp. 85–89. In his analyses of Q/F variants, Kirschbaum offers "a series of exercises in practical criticism which betray literary predilection rather than bibliographic deduction," writes Maguire (p. 86); and again: "Kirschbaum's method of diagnosis was impressionistic."

[31] JB, letter to C. K. Ogden, July 6, 1946.

[32] Maguire, *Shakespearean Suspect Texts*, p. 18. See also Maguire's interesting and critical chapters: (4) "Reporting Speech, Reconstructing Texts" and (7) "Diagnosing Memorial Reconstruction: The Poem, the Play, the Text." W. W. Greg, in a preface to the second edition of his *Editorial Problem* (Oxford, 1951), accepted Duthie's "dismissal of shorthand . . . cheerfully." Greg had reviewed G. I. Duthie's edition of *King Lear* in *Modern Language Review* XLIV (1949), pp. 397–400. See also James G. McManaway's critical notice of Duthie in "The Year's Contribution to Shakespearian Study: Textual Studies (1948–1965)," in *Studies in Shakespeare, Bibliography, and Theater*, eds. Richard Hosley, Arthur C. Kirsch, and John W. Velz (New York: Shakespeare Association of America, 1969), pp. 305–83.

[33] David Lyall Patrick, *The Textual History of "Richard III,"* Stanford University Publications: Language and Literature, VI:1 (1936). See George Ian Duthie, *King Lear: A Critical Edition* (Oxford: Basil Blackwell, 1949), pp. 6, 21–116.

[34] Walker, *Textual Problems of the First Folio*; *King Lear*, New Shakespeare edition by George Ian Duthie and John Dover Wilson (Cambridge University Press, 1960), p. 139.

[35] Chambers, *WS*, I, p. 465.

[36] Berryman is taking a side glance at G. I. Duthie's previous monograph, *The "Bad" Quarto of "Hamlet"* (Cambridge University Press, 1941).

[37] JB, letter to Sisam, May 8, 1946. Berryman is referring here to the work of J. Q. Adams, on Timothy Bright's stenographic system called Charactery (1588), in *Modern Philology* XXXIII (1935–36), pp. 139ff.

[38] Duthie, letter to JB, May 22, 1946.

[39] JB, letter to Duthie, July 8, 1946.

[40] JB, letter to Sisam, July 8, 1946.

[41] See also William Empson, " 'This' a Good Block," *TLS* (December 19, 1952), p. 837.

[42] Berryman added in another note: "The question is whether it is really, as it claims to be,

Notes

a 'critical' edition . . . And one wonders, finally, whether in the present stage of Shakespearean investigation, an editor can hope to fix a text without explaining it." Compare Foakes, *"Hamlet" versus "Lear,"* who argues among other things—while unfortunately mistranscribing the quarto participle "tottered" as "tattered"; an error not perpetuated in his Arden edition (1977), p. 339—that the alteration "clarifies the point that the vices of the poor are treated as great, while the rich and powerful escape" (p. 111).

43 While Stone, *The Textual History of "King Lear,"* p. 189, for example, regards the emendation "parti-ey'd" as "bizarre," R. A. Foakes, in the Arden edition (1977), p. 304, is content to gloss the F phrase "poorly led": "in a way unworthy of his rank, and by a poor man," with the rather weak further comment that F makes good dramatic sense "as Edgar first sees his father in surprisingly mean company, and only later, at 27–28, realizes also that Gloucester is blind." Kenneth Muir, in the Arden edition, second series (1952), conjectured "poorly rayd." See also Michael J.B. Allen and Kenneth Muir, *Shakespeare's Plays in Quarto* (University of California Press, 1981), p. xx; Halio, *Tragedy,* pp. 203–4; Weis, *King Lear,* pp. 214–15. R.J.C. Watt argues for "gory-eyed" ("Neither parti-eyed nor poorly led: Edgar Meets the Blind Gloucester," *RES,* new series, XLVIII:189 [1997], pp. 51–56).

44 Duthie, *King Lear,* p. 403.

45 Duthie explained his emendation in this fashion: "The 'eyd' seems convincing and the mis-correction of 'poorlie' to 'parti' may be explained if the Q copy read 'porly.' " Ann Thompson was later to remark of the Duthie–Wilson edition (1960): "The Notes suffer from serving as both collation and commentary, an especially difficult typographical and expository problem in view of the play's complex textual situations. These conventions make it impossible to re-create separately either the Quarto or the Folio versions" (*Which Shakespeare? A User's Guide to Editions* [Milton Keynes and Philadelphia: Open University Press, 1992], p. 95).

46 Notebook in William Empson Papers, Houghton Library, Harvard University. Empson added, "Edgar is always snobbish—cf. 'improper for a slave' . . . Gloucester's eyes are not bandaged as on the modern stage, but were plastered with white stuff."

47 JB, letter to John Marshall and Dr. Stevens, February 17, 1949. Even twenty-two years later, Berryman was still smarting from the damage he believed Duthie had done, as he asserted in his application for a senior fellowship from the National Endowment for the Humanities dated May 31, 1971: "I had established the whole text and apparatus criticus and was in III.vi with my full commentary when G. I. Duthie wrote from Scotland to say that his edition was in the printer's hands . . . and clearly I would have to take account of his findings; so, exhausted anyway after two years of 15-hrs-a-day, I laid my edition aside to wait for him. I waited years, and found it grossly unsatisfactory. His critics hit him on details, such as neglect of Folio variants, but what was really grotesque was his attempt to establish a text without defending it (he has no substantial commentary at all!), and his editorial timidity, in a situation almost uniquely requiring the daring Greg had called for (in a lecture in Holland) in 1933."

48 JB, letter to Sisam, May 8, 1946.

49 The phrase is from Paul Werstine, "Narratives About Printed Texts: 'Foul Papers' and 'Bad' Quartos," *Shakespeare Quarterly* 41 (1990), p. 86; quoted in Maguire, p. 25.

50 Halio (*First Quarto,* 1994) confirms Berryman's deduction: "Commas were sometimes used to indicate hyphens, as apparently at 4.1.7, where the uncorrected quarto (Q uncorr.) has 'poorlie, leed' . . ." (p. 7).

51 Duthie and Wilson, *King Lear,* p. 231.

52 JB, letter to Stevens and Marshall, March 14, 1946; he corrected himself, at the end: "Greg is the greatest living textual critic but he is never 'eloquent,' as I said he was above." For a while in the mid-1940s, Berryman proposed to write a monograph for the Clarendon Press to be entitled *On Emendation: The Shakespearean Cruxes.*

[53] Blayney, *Nicholas Okes and the First Quarto*, p. 2.

[54] That Berryman initially swallowed Greg's line of assertion can be seen in the fact that he refers, in his early review of Greg's *The Editorial Problem in Shakespeare* (Oxford: Clarendon Press, 1942), to the "inferior" quarto text ("Shakespeare's Text," *The Nation*, August 21, 1943, p. 218).

[55] Maguire, *Shakespearean Suspect Texts*, pp. 46, 51.

[56] Ibid., p. 53. "Interpretation was not Greg's strong point," Maguire alleges. "If Bradley was literal, Greg was even more so. A play was not a fiction; it was a bibliographical and historical narrative . . . As such, it was a subject (or substitute) for bibliography" (p. 48). "Greg presents his interpretive predilections as if they are bibliographically obvious facts, and so creates the impression that the issue is not open to debate" (p. 50). "It is easy to reverse the terms of many of Greg's statements and so show them for the interpretive options which they are, rather than the textual deductions which they claim to be" (p. 51).

[57] JB, letter to Marshall and Stevens, February 17, 1949. As Berryman made plain in the same letter (quoted above), his categories "critical" and "aesthetic" included the theatrical; but, as Maguire highlights, Greg and the New Bibliographers were "blatantly anti-theatrical": for Greg, the text was a "book" rather than a "play" (pp. 56–57). See also Howard-Hill, "Modern Textual Theories and the Editing of Plays," esp. pp. 103–8.

[58] JB, letter to Greg, February 16, 1946.

[59] JB, letter to Sisam, July 8, 1946. He went on in the same letter: "In general I take a view of the Folio's sophistication such that I have made a text altogether more eclectic . . . than I should expect from another critic. And, the transmitted texts being very corrupt, there is emendation." Since neither Q nor F can be relied upon to give us exactly what Shakespeare wrote (at any stage of the authorial process)—no one has disputed the fact that the copy for Q must have been execrable—Berryman, like most modern editors—including the editors of the Arden (1963, 1997) and the New Penguin (1972), as well as Alexander and Riverside—favoured the option of a conflated text. But Grace Iopollo asserts, "Any edition of *King Lear* which conflates the Quarto and Folio texts" creates "a counterfeit and non-Shakespearean foundation upon which only the most limited literary interpretation and meaning can be built." She goes on: "Many modern editors, who insist on reconstructing a copy-text, have ignored critical bibliography, which can point toward revision as a cause of variant, and instead have focused on their own taste and judgment in dismissing variants which they consider inferior or un-Shakespearean. And many eclectic editions present a text as the product of the printing process, utterly discounting it as the product of the author and as a work which underwent different authorial stages of composition and paths of transmission. This type of editorial treatment must be recognized as fraudulent and presumptuous; editors cannot claim that Shakespeare did not revise and at the same time revise for him. Textual critics cannot preserve Shakespeare's individual sanctity and his canonical importance only by presenting the integrity of *each* of his texts" (*Revising Shakespeare*, pp. 181, 184–85). (Wells and Taylor, in their *Textual Companion*, p. 510, speak of Q as "a legitimate early version" of the play, and support the notion of "the separate integrity" of Q and F. But compare Holderness and Carter, "The King's Two Bodies," p. 26: "Revisionist bibliography . . . needs the outdated critical concept of authorial intention.") Iopollo's declaration is handsomely said, but it is also unfair, misleading, and tendentious: it overlooks the fact that neither quarto nor folio *King Lear* can be said to be "authorized" by Shakespeare, and that many of the botched lines and variants, with vagaries of spelling and syntax, and seemingly impenetrable constructions, were quite evidently produced by the printers, as much as by Shakespeare's horrible handwriting (or perhaps, in places, as Berryman would have it, a scribbling thief's?); and the reference to Shakespeare's "sanctity" and "canonical importance" implies that conflationist editors are simpleminded and yet opportunistic bardo-

laters. Despite its honourable pretensions, the new orthodoxy, which exalts textual plurality and hence textual and narrative instability and indeterminacy, actually works to favour the critic over the author. Like William Empson, Berryman did place a value on "taste and judgement," but his attempts at conjectural emendation, which he believed should be rigorously defended by all the available evidence, textual and contextual, aimed to revise not Shakespeare but the erroneous printed embodiments of his work. Taylor and Warren (*The Division of the Kingdoms*, p. vii) remark—in a way Berryman would have applauded—that "any comprehensive defence of the Quarto's authority would have to provide . . . a detailed critical consideration of many individual variants." See also Marion Trousdale's salutary essay, "A Trip Through the Divided Kingdoms," *Shakespeare Quarterly* 37 (1986), pp. 218–23.

⁶⁰ McLeod, "*Gon.* No more, the text is foolish," in *Division*, p. 153. Likewise, G. R. Hibbard, writing in 1980, called Duthie's edition of 1949 "the most scholarly we have" (" 'King Lear': A Retrospect, 1939–79," p. 3).

⁶¹ To cite just two examples: Anne Bradstreet's lines in *Homage*, "Crumpling plunge of a pestle, bray" (36.4), and "a male great pestle smashes/small women swarming towards the mortar's rim in vain" (37.7–8), derive from Kent's asseveration apropos Oswald: "My lord, if you'll give me leave, I will tread this unbolted villain into mortar" (II.ii.59–60)—which itself took off from an old proverb, "to bray a fool in a mortar"; likewise, when Berryman's Bradstreet implores "Eat my sore breath, Black Angel. Let me die" (47.5), she is grimly (but perhaps unknowingly?) echoing Edgar's allusion (in the quarto only) to Samuel Harsnett's *A Declaration of Egregious Popish Impostures*: "Croak not, black angel: I have no food for thee" (III.vi.28–29).

⁶² Copy in John Berryman Papers.

⁶³ Elizabeth Bettmann, letter to Haffenden, n.d.

⁶⁴ Letter to Henry Allen Moe, John Simon Guggenheim Memorial Foundation, January 22, 1953; with John Berryman Papers.

⁶⁵ In comparison with his theory as to a link between *The Taming of the Shrew* and William Haughton, Berryman's speculation that *The Rare Triumphs of Love and Fortune* (first printed 1589; edited by W. W. Greg, 1930; and excerpted in Volume 8 of Geoffrey Bullough's *Narrative and Dramatic Sources of Shakespeare* [London: Routledge & Kegan Paul, 1975]) may have been written by Shakespeare himself at the age of eighteen is incredibly bold. He seems to have relied on his reading of internal evidence for proof of the claim. "It is an interesting play anyway, in some respects the first real Elizabethan play, and I mean to go into it. I have already made a full study of the diction, which promises. But some of the style is even more promising." He cites two instances of close similarity, the first between Juliet's "O comfortable friar, where is my lord?" and this line—"O comfortable words, were they but true!"—spoken by the character Hermione in *The Rare Triumphs*. "But," he goes on, "Bomelio's Lear-like distractions—sexual, and 'Come, Bess, let's go sleep. Come, Bess; together, together'—that does not sound to me like an accident at all, but either the closest imitation (at how many years' distance) or the same mind." Bullough gives his view in these terms: "This play has so many minor points of resemblance to *Cymbeline* that it is tempting to regard it as an influence on Shakespeare, by contra-suggestion rather than by direct imitation." J. M. Nosworthy (New Arden Shakespeare), writing two years after Berryman, coolly insisted on the reservation "that Shakespeare relied on memories and suggestions rather than on detailed study. Precisely what led Shakespeare to this ramshackle old play in the first place, I do not pretend to know." He goes on to surmise that it was "expedient for the King's Players to contemplate the revival of some of the romantic comedies that had been popular ten or twenty years earlier," and that Shakespeare would have read over *The Rare Triumphs* (even though it was not ultimately revived). Whatever the facts of the matter, Nosworthy's halfheartedness is usefully counterbalanced by Berryman's enthusi-

astic attribution. "And why," Berryman pertinently asked, "should a 30-year-old play have obsessed the end of his career, as no other play in his entire career ever did? The mere possibility, at any rate, of its being his, seems to me to deserve investigation." W. T. Jewkes (*Act Division in Elizabethan and Jacobean Plays, 1583–1616* [Hamden, Conn.: The Shoe String Press, 1958], p. 53) assigns *Love and Fortune* to Thomas Kyd; though Gary Taylor and John Jowett, who believe the play must have boasted more than one author, find the attribution implausible (*Shakespeare Reshaped 1606–1623* [Oxford: Clarendon Press, 1993], p. 27).

In an undated letter (*c.* January 1953), Berryman wrote further to his Princeton colleague G. E. Bentley on the subject of "Fletcher's *Women Pleased*, which on various grounds I think may be a recast of a lost play of 1597 by William Haughton."

⁶⁶ Berryman was encouraged to believe that Weever was well acquainted with London theatre folk by his understanding that epigram 5.24, "Ad Henricum Porter," referred to the playwright Henry Porter, author of *The Two Angry Women of Abingdon* (1599), who was to die in a duel with the playwright John Day on June 6/7, 1599 (see Leslie Hotson, *Shakespeare's Sonnets Dated* [London: Oxford University Press, 1949], pp. 193–203; Mark Eccles, "Brief Lives: Tudor and Stuart Authors," *Studies in Philology* 79:4 [Fall 1982], pp. 106–17); but in fact, as Honigmann discloses, the Henry Porter in question was vicar of Lancaster (1582–1600), a friend of Weever's family. Berryman might have reckoned that something was amiss with his identification from the fact that in 6.2 Weever explicitly states that during the fifth week of the sequence, "in dead mens praise" he had not spent "one line"—though it is possible that Weever's *Epigrammes* had gone to press before Porter's death in June. (McKerrow had doubted whether Henry Porter referred to the dramatist.)

⁶⁷ Albert Croll Baugh, *William Haughton's "Englishmen for My Money, or A Woman Will Have Her Will"* (Ph.D. thesis, University of Pennsylvania, 1917), p. 12; hereinafter abbreviated as Baugh, *Englishmen*. There is no reason to connect Haughton with the Houghton family, Baugh noted; "although that he was *not* connected with them is, of course, equally incapable of proof" (p. 13). *Englishmen* was earlier prepared by W. W. Greg for the Malone Society Reprints, 1912.

⁶⁸ The theory relies heavily on the belief that the Shakespeare family at some time used "Shakeshafte" as a variant, and was for long disfavoured—as by Professor S. Schoenbaum in *William Shakespeare: A Compact Documentary Life* (1977). However, in a succinct review of Honigmann's *Shakespeare: The "Lost" Years*, Schoenbaum concluded: "I am now persuaded that I had best revise my pages on Shakeshafte and the Hoghtons for the next impression of my *Compact Documentary Life*." ("A Detour into Lancashire," *TLS*, April 19, 1985, p. 424). All the same, the farthest that Schoenbaum would go, six years later, in the new edition of his *Shakespeare's Lives*, was to acknowledge with recovered scepticism: "The case for a Lancastrian connection for Shakespeare has been put forward by Honigmann with renewed vigour. Still, if Shakespeare was at seventeen in Hoghton's service, he would have had to be back in Stratford to woo, impregnate, and marry Anne Hathaway before his nineteenth birthday, not—on the face of it—the most plausible of scenarios" (Oxford: Clarendon Press, 1991, p. 536).

⁶⁹ Chambers, *WS*, II, pp. 371–75. See also an anonymous review, "Shakeshafte and Shakespeare," *TLS*, March 26, 1954.

⁷⁰ E. K. Chambers, *Shakespearean Gleanings* (Oxford: Clarendon Press, 1944), pp. 52–56. See also Alan Keen and Roger Lubbock, *The Annotator* (London: Putnam; N.Y: Macmillan, 1954). The Haughton-Houghton business, including later contributions by Pohl and Fleissner, is reviewed by Hugh Calvert in Chapter 11 of *Shakespeare's Sonnets and Problems of Autobiography* (Braunton, Devon: Merlin Books, 1987), pp. 143–53.

⁷¹ E.A.J. Honigmann, *Shakespeare: The "Lost" Years* (Manchester University Press, 1985); Honigmann, *John Weever: A Biography of a Literary Associate of Shakespeare and Jonson, To-*

Notes

gether with a Photographic Facsimile of Weever's "Epigrammes" (1599) (Manchester University Press, 1987).

[72] For identification of Foke (or Fulke) Gyllome as a guild player, see a letter from Alan Keen, "Shakespeare's Northern Apprenticeship," *TLS*, November 18, 1955. See also Keen's letter on "Shakespeare and the Chester Players," *TLS*, March 30, 1956, p. 195.

[73] The phrasing "if he be minded to keep & do keep players" is nonetheless singular; if it is not formulary (as it does not seem to be), it might suggest that Alexander was not even close enough to his half brother and heir to know whether or not he kept players or even desired to—though Bryne-Scoules is only a few miles from Lea. Berryman remarked in his notes, "The will *does* suggest that Hesketh *did* keep players; whereas no evid. that half-bro. Tho. did."

[74] Cf. H. A. Shield, who is keen to advance, with the support of the Stanley Papers, the claims of William Hughes as "Mr. W.H." ("Links with Shakespeare VI," *Notes & Queries* 195: 10 [May 13, 1950], pp. 205–6).

[75] See, for example, an excellent contribution by Robert Stevenson in Chapter VI, "William Shakespeare and William Shakeshafte: A Study of Religious Affiliations," of his *Shakespeare's Religious Frontier* (The Hague: Martinus Nijhoff, 1958), pp. 67–83; and Richard Wilson, "Shakespeare and the Jesuits," *TLS*, December 19, 1997, pp. 11–13. Muriel Bradbrook remarked in a review of Honigmann's *Shakespeare*, "The religious conflicts that tore families apart make a solid historical contribution" ("Shakeshafte Revisited," *The Guardian*, April 25, 1985, p. 10).

[76] See Chapter 15, "Strange's/Derby's Men, 1564–1620, and Pembroke's Men, 1591–1601," and Chapter 16, "Hunsdon's/Chamberlain's/King's Men, 1594–1608," in Andrew Gurr, *The Shakespearian Playing Companies* (Oxford: Clarendon Press, 1996).

[77] Leslie Hotson, "John Jackson and Thomas Savage," in his *Shakespeare's Sonnets Dated* (London: Oxford University Press, 1949), pp. 125–40. See also E.A.J. Honigmann and Susan Brock, *Playhouse Wills, 1558–1642* (Manchester University Press, 1993), pp. 85–88.

[78] The passage quoted by Berryman is from Keen and Lubbock, *The Annotator* (London: Putnam, 1954), p. 120.

[79] Cf. Honigmann, *Shakespeare*, p. 24: "Alexander Hoghton's family and friends seem to have had an active interest in education; in addition to their unlicensed schoolmasters in Lancashire, they even played their part abroad. Thomas I greatly assisted his friend, the later Cardinal Allen, in founding Douay College. It is almost inconceivable that Thomas's brother, Alexander, did not maintain a schoolmaster when he became head of the family, considering that his less affluent relatives thought it their duty to do so." See also Honigmann, *John Weever*, p. 92.

[80] The subtitle seems just as facetious, albeit opaque: "A *twice seven houres (in so many weekes) studie: No longer (like the fashion) not unlike to continue.*"

[81] Honigmann, *Shakespeare*, p. 158, n. 7. However, Honigmann does make this crucial point in the text of his subsequent *John Weever*, p. 91.

[82] As Katherine Duncan-Jones has pointed out, Richard Barnfield had—already?—praised Shakespeare's "hony-flowing vaine" in his *Poems: In Divers Humours* (1598). (See Chambers, *WS*, II, p. 195; and compare E.A.J. Honigmann, *Shakespeare's Impact on His Contemporaries* [Totowa, N.J.: Barnes & Noble, 1982], pp. 14–16.) Duncan-Jones goes on: "Also, the fact that Meres named twelve of Shakespeare's plays and Weever only two—'Romea Richard; more whose names I know not'—can most readily be explained by the assumption that Weever was not such a close student of Shakespeare's work as Meres" ("Intimation of Immortality," *TLS*, October 23–29, 1987).

[83] Frederick J. Pohl, *Like to the Lark* (London: Davis-Poynter, 1972), pp. 118–25. However, Pohl does issue a warning against identifying Houghton and Haughton.

[84] See Frederick Gard Fleay, *A Biographical Chronicle of the English Drama 1559–1642*

(London: Reeves and Turner, 2 vols., 1891), pp. 270–74; E. K. Chambers, *The Elizabethan Stage,* III (London: Oxford University Press, 1923), pp. 334–36.

[85] Honigmann and Brock, *Playhouse Wills, 1558–1642,* pp. 75–76.

[86] Taylor and Jowett describe *The Spanish Moor's Tragedy,* which might be the same as *Lust's Dominion* (printed in 1657), as "a Marlowe play revamped for Henslowe"; they add: "Scattered evidence of Dekker's and Marston's presence can certainly be found; Day and Haughton, however, are either not present or impossible to identify" (*Shakespeare Reshaped,* p. 43).

[87] Baugh, *Englishmen,* p. 18.

[88] Ibid., pp. 76–77.

[89] On Frederick Gard Fleay, see Hugh Grady, "Disintegration and Its Reverberations," in *The Appropriation of Shakespeare: Post-Renaissance Reconstructions of the Works and the Myth,* ed. Jean I. Marsden (Hemel Hempstead, Herts.: Harvester Wheatsheaf, 1991), pp. 111–27. E. K. Chambers, in a British Academy lecture, had attacked "The Disintegration of Shakespeare"; compare Taylor and Jowett's dignified defence: "Upon reflection we must realize that this metaphor emotionally maligns a legitimate and indeed necessary activity. Disintegrators do not disintegrate Shakespeare, but the accepted Shakespeare canon; they do so not in order to evaporate a solid presence, but to dislodge in particular cases the foreign accretions which encrust an ancient original. Properly and cautiously conducted, the disintegration of the Shakespeare canon permits and contributes to the reintegration of Shakespeare" (*Shakespeare Reshaped,* p. 233).

[90] William M. Baillie, "The Date and Authorship of *Grim the Collier of Croydon,*" *Modern Philology* 76 (November 1978), p. 183. See also Jewkes, *Act Division in Elizabethan and Jacobean Plays,* pp. 299–300; and David J. Lake, *The Canon of Thomas Middleton's Plays: Internal Evidence for the Major Problems of Authorship* (Cambridge University Press, 1975).

[91] Dugdale Sykes, "The Authorship of *Grim, the Collier of Croydon,*" *Modern Language Review* 14 (1919), pp. 245–53.

[92] William M. Baillie (ed.), *A Choice Ternary of English Plays: "Gratiæ Theatrales"* (1662) (Binghamton, N.Y.: Medieval & Renaissance Texts & Studies, Vol. 26, 1984), p. 176. Baillie's edition of *Grim the Collier of Croydon,* included in this volume, is full of sound information and good judgement.

[93] Baugh, *Englishmen,* pp. 31–32.

[94] K. M. Briggs, *The Anatomy of Puck: An Examination of Fairy Beliefs among Shakespeare's Contemporaries and Successors* (London: Routledge & Kegan Paul, 1959), pp. 77–79.

[95] *Wily Beguiled 1606* (The Malone Society Reprints, 1912), p. vii. By way of answering the supposition that the text of *Wily Beguiled* is a "bad" quarto (i.e., based not on an authorial manuscript but on a report), Berryman remarked in his notes: "If Q *Wily* is 'bad' (see Kirschbaum etc), the report of 1606 might naturally echo later plays (v. interesting if *Sh'n* plays predominate—suggesting that the reporter, & so the *play,* was King's) without *Wily* itself being later than 1596. The positive (earliest) allusions—as to Cadiz—govern 'reports' better than echoes."

[96] T. W. Baldwin, *On the Literary Genetics of Shakspeare's Poems and Sonnets* (Urbana: University of Illinois Press, 1950), pp. 251–53. Clifford Leech was sceptical of Baldwin's findings ("Shakespeare's Life, Times and Stage," *Shakespeare Survey* 5 [1952], pp. 137–38).

[97] M. M. Mahood, "Talk of the Devil" (letter to the editor), *TLS,* June 16, 1966, p. 541; see also Mahood's New Penguin edition of *Twelfth Night* (1968), p. 138.

[98] G. K. Hunter, *Dramatic Identities and Cultural Tradition: Studies in Shakespeare and his Contemporaries* (Liverpool University Press, 1978), p. 16.

[99] Marliss C. Desens, *The Bed-Trick in English Renaissance Drama: Explorations in Gender, Sexuality, and Power* (London and Toronto: Associated University Presses, 1994), pp. 57–58.

[100] J. Payne Collier, *The History of Dramatic Poetry to the Time of Shakespeare* (new edn., London: George Bell & Sons, 1879), p. 462.

[101] On the New Shakspere Society (1873–1894) and its founder, Frederick James Furnivall, see Grady, "Disintegration and Its Reverberations," pp. 112–13.

[102] A. C. Swinburne, *A Study of Shakespeare* (London: Chatto & Windus, 1880), pp. 127, 280.

[103] Chambers, *WS*, I, p. 324.

[104] Compare R. W. Dent, *Shakespeare's Proverbial Language: An Index* (Berkeley: University of California Press, 1981).

[105] A. H. Tolman, in *PMLA* V (1890), likewise observed that no other play by Shakespeare opens thus.

[106] It could be argued, however, that Meres erred not so much on the side of comprehensiveness as of symmetry: he names six comedies and six tragedies (the obvious omissions being the *Henry VI* plays and *The Taming of the Shrew*). Andrew Gurr suggests that Meres "must have acquired most of his titles from playbills rather than printed quartos, since six of the twelve plays named had not yet appeared in print" (*The Shakespearian Playing Companies*, p. 281).

[107] Roslyn L. Knutson, "Influence of the Repertory System on the Revival and Revision of *The Spanish Tragedy* and *Dr. Faustus*," *English Literary Renaissance* 18:2 (Spring 1988), pp. 267–68, n. 19.

[108] Peter Berek, "Text, Gender, and Genre in *The Taming of the Shrew*," in *"Bad" Shakespeare: Revaluations of the Shakespeare Canon*, ed. Maurice Charney (London and Toronto: Associated University Presses, 1988), p. 91.

[109] See also Alexander, "The Original Ending of *The Taming of the Shrew*," *Shakespeare Quarterly* 20:2 (Spring 1969), pp. 111–16.

[110] Richard Hosley, "Sources and Analogues of *The Taming of the Shrew*," *The Huntington Library Quarterly* 27:3 (May 1964), pp. 289–308; J. Dover Wilson (ed.), *The Taming of the Shrew*, New Cambridge Shakespeare (Cambridge University Press, 1928); G. R. Hibbard (ed.), *The Taming of the Shrew*, New Penguin Shakespeare (Harmondsworth, Middx.: Penguin, 1968); Brian Morris (ed.), *The Taming of the Shrew*, Arden Shakespeare (London: Methuen, 1981); H. J. Oliver (ed.), *The Taming of the Shrew*, Oxford Shakespeare (Oxford University Press, 1984); Ann Thompson (ed.), *The Taming of the Shrew*, New Cambridge Shakespeare (Cambridge University Press, 1984). Michael J.B. Warren and Kenneth Muir unpersuasively concur: "We side with the majority opinion, which argues that *A Shrew* was written after *The Shrew*, probably by the dramatist of a rival company who was urged to compose it" (*Shakespeare's Plays in Quarto* [Berkeley and Los Angeles: University of California Press, 1981], p. xiv). Tori Haring-Smith rehearses as if it were established fact the suppositious scenario of an early *Shrew*, in the opening paragraph of her Chapter I—"The Early Stage History of *The Taming of the Shrew* (1594–1800)"—of *From Farce to Metadrama: A Stage History of "The Taming of the Shrew," 1594–1983* (Westport, Conn.: Greenwood Press, 1985), p. 7. Graham Holderness and Bryan Loughrey defend the honour of *A Shrew* in their edition of the quarto in the equivocally titled series "Shakespearean Originals: First Editions" (Hemel Hempstead, Herts.: Harvester Wheatsheaf, 1992).

[111] Compare Chambers, *WS*, I, p. 324; G. I. Duthie, *"The Taming of a Shrew"* and *The Taming of the Shrew*, *Review of English Studies* 19 (1943), pp. 337–56. Geoffrey Bullough observes: "My own view is that QI is a badly printed version of the old play which Shakespeare used as his main source for *The Shrew* . . . Despite resemblances between the two plays the differences cannot be explained away by any theory of abridgement or piracy by memorizing or by putting together actors' parts . . . *A Shrew* may not be so much the source-play as Shakespeare's first shot at the theme" (*Narrative and Dramatic Sources of Shakespeare*, Vol. I

[London: Routledge & Kegan Paul; New York: Columbia University Press, 1966], pp. 57–58).

112 See William H. Moore, "An Allusion in 1593 to *The Taming of the Shrew*," *Shakespeare Quarterly* 15 (1964), pp. 55–60. Morris (Arden, p. 64), Oliver (Oxford, 1982, p. 32), and Thompson (New Cambridge, p. 3) dismiss the possibility that Chute's verse could be alluding to *A Shrew*.

113 *The Riverside Shakespeare*, ed. G. Blakemore Evans (Boston: Houghton Mifflin, 1974), p. 140.

114 Kathleen O. Irace, *Reforming the "Bad" Quartos: Performance and Provenance of Six Shakespearean First Editions* (London and Toronto: Associated University Presses, 1994), pp. 18–19.

115 Chambers, WS, I, p. 327.

116 Wells and Taylor, *William Shakespeare: A Textual Companion*, p. 170. In an article published the same year, Wells and Taylor observe, "So far, everything we have seen in Shakespeare's play can be explained as the product of a foul-paper manuscript representing the play as it stood at the end (or nearly the end) of a single sustained period of composition, but still containing various inconsistencies and false starts, some or all of which would probably be rectified in the preparation of a fair copy or prompt-book." As to *A Shrew*, they decline to commit themselves on the question of priority; all they will say is that the quarto, whether or not it is by an "adapter"—"author, copywriter, reporter—call him what you will"—is not a "bad" text but a good one ("No Shrew, A Shrew, and The Shrew: Internal Revision in *The Taming of the Shrew*," in *Shakespeare: Text, Language, Criticism*, eds. Bernhard Fabian and Kurt Tetzel von Rosador [Hildesheim: Olms-Weidmann, 1987], pp. 366, 368).

117 Chambers, WS, I, p. 324. Thomas Marc Parrott argued similarly: "The underplot . . . is the work of the collaborator, who perhaps . . . lifted the plot from Gascoigne's prose comedy, *The Supposes*, and turned it into such tame flat verse that it seems impossible that Shakespeare could have written it . . . Yet the two plots are so well woven together that we must assume that Shakespeare planned and directed the whole work" (*William Shakespeare: A Handbook* [New York: Charles Scribner's Sons, 1934, p. 144]).

118 Oliver, p. 28. Even Eric Sams repeats this supposed fact, declaring of *A Shrew*: "The underplot . . . was drawn entire from Gascoigne's *Supposes* . . . No other play of the period is thus indebted, save the Folio text of *The Shrew*" (*The Real Shakespeare*, p. 140). Reaching behind Gascoigne and Ariosto, however, Shakespeare (like Haughton) owes much to the tricks and devices of classical comedy: see Robert S. Miola, *Shakespeare and Classical Comedy: The Influence of Plautus and Terence* (Oxford: Clarendon Press, 1994), esp. pp. 62–79.

119 Baugh, *Englishmen*, p. 31.

120 Robert F. Fleissner, in "A Plausible Mr. W.H." (*Notes & Queries*, n.s. 16:4 [ccxiv] [April 1969], p. 129), advanced the claims of Haughton as the "friend" on the grounds that Haughton, as obtainer rather than inspirer of the sonnets, might have had more or less direct access to Shakespeare's publisher, Thomas Thorpe (who had brought out Jonson's *Volpone* in 1607). Haughton was an "intimate" of the playwright Henry Chettle (who had professed to admire Shakespeare) and collaborated with him, and Chettle was himself also a printer: Chettle "could easily have been acquainted with Thorpe, their both being printers, and so could have been the *liaison* between Haughton and Thorpe." Fleissner supposed, after Pohl (see above), that the dramatist Haughton could be readily identified with the Lancashire Houghton; but unlike Berryman, he made no attempt to explore the evidence. If Katherine Duncan-Jones is correct in her conjecture that many of Shakespeare's sonnets are later than critics have generally believed, and that internal and external evidence "points to 1603–4 as initiating an intense period of writing (and perhaps revising)" (Arden Shakespeare, Third Series [London: Thomas Nelson & Sons, 1997], p. 28), her argument certainly allows Haughton to re-enter the frame as a

possible Mr. W.H., since he was still alive at that date—though I would personally tend to concur with her presentation of the evidence for William Herbert (1580–1630), Third Earl of Pembroke.

¹²¹ Baugh, *Englishmen*, p. 43.

¹²² JB, holograph letter to Russell Cooper, June 19, 1958 (probably unsent).

¹²³ Compare a letter to Robert Giroux (August 3, 1955) in which Berryman had remarked about his biography in the form it took at that date: "A number of passages in my book go into this strange & unattractive moral smoothness of Shakespeare's."

¹²⁴ The work was to be fundamentally informed, as he explained in his application form, by "post-Freudian developments: Jung etc. Erikson etc, Schachtel: the socialization, even the environmentalization as it might be called, of psychoanalysis has made it much more fruitful for an author as fully socialized as Shakespeare."

¹²⁵ Mark Van Doren, letter to JB, June 18, 1971.

¹²⁶ JB, letter to Mark Van Doren, "Mpls, Tues morning." He had long admired Housman: in a preface to an early version of his critical biography of Shakespeare, dated August 27, 1960, for example, he had likewise concluded: "Housman's work was my model." In terms of biography, he explained in his application form to the NEH, "I admire particularly Gow's little memoir of Housman."

¹²⁷ JB, letter to Mr. Best, July 19, 1951.

SHAKESPEARE'S EARLY COMEDY

¹ E. K. Chambers, *William Shakespeare: A Study of Facts and Problems* (Oxford: Clarendon Press, 1930), II, p. 354. Hereinafter cited as Chambers, WS.

² [JB] When he was born nobody knows. The date April 23 is popular because it is St. George's Day, the patron saint of England, and because Shakespeare died on that date in 1616; that a coincidence with the date of death should have gone unnoticed for a century suggests that it is wrong. Evidently he was fifty-two when he died, though there are difficulties even about this. Thomas De Quincey fancied that the date of his granddaughter's first marriage, April 22, 1626, memorialized the poet's birthday.

³ Compare S. Schoenbaum, *Shakespeare's Lives*, new edition (Oxford: Clarendon Press, 1991), p. 292.

⁴ T. W. Baldwin, *William Shakspere's Small Latine & Lesse Greeke*, 2 vols. (Urbana: University of Illinois Press, 1944); Baldwin, *Shakspere's Five-Act Structure* (Urbana: University of Illinois Press, 1947). See also Penry Williams, "Art, Power and the Social Order," in *The New Oxford History of England*, Vol. II: *The Later Tudors: England, 1547–1603* (Oxford University Press, 1995).

⁵ T. S. Baynes, *Shakespeare Studies* (London: Longmans, Green, 1894). See also Virgil K. Whitaker, *Shakespeare's Use of Learning* (Huntington Library Publications, 1953).

⁶ But now see D. L. Thomas and N. E. Evans, "John Shakespeare in the Exchequer," *Shakespeare Quarterly* 35 (1984), pp. 315–18.

⁷ See also James G. McManaway, "John Shakespeare's 'Spiritual Testament,' " *Shakespeare Quarterly* 18 (1967), pp. 197–205; Gary Taylor, "Forms of Opposition: Shakespeare and Middleton," *English Literary Renaissance* 24:2 (Spring 1994), pp. 283–314, esp. 290–95.

⁸ John Henry de Groot, *The Shakespeares and "The Old Faith"* (New York: King's Crown Press, 1946); and see H. Mutschmann and K. Wentersdorf, *Shakespeare and Catholicism* (New York: Sheed & Ward, 1952). The evidence for identifying Shakespeare as a Catholic is rehearsed by Eamon Duffy, "Was Shakespeare a Catholic?," *The Tablet* (April 27, 1996), pp. 536–38. See also Father Peter Milward, *Shakespeare's Religious Background* (London: Sidg-

Notes

wick & Jackson, 1973); Milward, " 'The Papist and His Poet'—The Jesuit Background to Shakespeare's Plays," *The Renaissance Bulletin* (Tokyo), 20 (1993), pp. 1–33; Taylor, "Forms of Opposition," p. 293.

[9] See Oliver Baker, *In Shakespeare's Warwickshire and the Unknown Years* (London: Simpkin Marshall, 1937), pp. 294–95; Alan Keen and Roger Lubbock, *The Annotator: The Pursuit of an Elizabethan Reader of Halle's Chronicle Involving Some Surmises about the Early Life of William Shakespeare* (London: Putnam, 1954), pp. 77–79.

[10] Chambers, WS, II, p. 253.

[11] [JB] November 28, 1582, by two Shottery friends of Anne Hathaway's father, Richard; clearly, to ensure that Shakespeare *would* marry her. [See Sir Sidney Lee, *A Life of William Shakespeare*, London: Smith, Elder & Co. (1898), new edn., 1915, pp. 27–29.] The puzzling marriage license issued at the same registry just the day before, for a union of "William Shakespeare" and "Anne Whateley of Temple Grafton," is taken by Lee [*A Life of William Shakespeare*, Chapter 3, pp. 30–31] to refer to two different persons, though it has been argued that the clerk's entry merely blundered. Where and when the poet's marriage took place is not known.

[12] See also *The Riverside Shakespeare*, ed. G. Blakemore Evans (Boston: Houghton Mifflin, 1974), p. 1829.

[13] Chambers, WS, II, pp. 176–77; B. R. Lewis, *The Shakespeare Documents: Facsimiles, Transliterations and Commentary* (Stanford University Press, 1940), II, pp. 471–507; Richard Wilson, "A Constant Will to Publish: Shakespeare's Dead Hand," in his *Will Power: Essays on Shakespearean Authority* (Hemel Hempstead, Herts.: Harvester Wheatsheaf, 1993), pp. 184–234. Compare E.A.J. Honigmann, "The Second-Best Bed," *The New York Review of Books* 38: 18 (November 7, 1991), pp. 27–30.

[14] Chambers, WS, II, p. 254.

[15] Ibid., p. 284.

[16] Nicholas Rowe, "Some Account of the Life &c. of Mr. William Shakespear," in D. Nichol Smith (ed.), *Eighteenth Century Essays on Shakespeare* (Glasgow: James MacLehose & Sons, 1903), p. 3; Chambers, WS, II, p. 265.

[17] Chambers, WS, II, p. 257; Schoenbaum, *Shakespeare's Lives*, pp. 68–72.

[18] E. K. Chambers, *The Elizabethan Stage* (Oxford: Clarendon Press, 1923), I, p. 280; Baker, *In Shakespeare's Warwickshire and the Unknown Years*, pp. 298–301; Chambers, *Shakespearean Gleanings* (Oxford University Press, 1944), pp. 52–56; Russell Fraser, *Young Shakespeare* (New York: Columbia University Press, 1988), pp. 74–75. Anthony Wagner pointed out that Shakeshafte was a well-established surname at Preston, and that more than one William Shakeshafte is mentioned in local records ("Shakeshafte and Shakespeare," *TLS*, May 5, 1940).

[19] See Keen and Lubbock, *The Annotator*, p. 47.

[20] Chambers, *The Elizabethan Stage*, II, pp. 118–27. See also Alan Keen, "Shakespeare and the Chester Players" (a letter), *TLS*, March 30, 1956, p. 195.

[21] R. A. Foakes and R. T. Rickert (eds.), *Henslowe's Diary* (1961), pp. 16–19. See also Michael Hattaway (ed.), *The First Part of King Henry VI*, New Cambridge Shakespeare (Cambridge University Press, 1990), pp. 34–41.

[22] See further the essay on "Shakespeare's Friend" below.

[23] Mark Eccles, "Chapman's Early Years," *Studies in Philology* XLIII:2 (April 1946), pp. 176–93.

[24] [JB] Neither Alan Keen's earlier articles nor Moray McLaren's book *"By Me . . .": A Report Upon the Apparent Discovery of Some Working Notes of William Shakespeare in a Sixteenth Century Book* (London: John Redington, 1949) had much value except descriptive. [See Keen,

Notes

"Hall and Shakespeare," *TLS*, April 26, 1947, p. 197; "A Shakespearian Riddle," *TLS*, April 21, 1950, p. 252.] Keen's last, in the *Bulletin of the John Rylands Library*, March 1951, though unreliable, is better. It is the handwriting that is fundamental; a matter for experts. But I will give one example of other indications that require study. Objecting to Hall's use of an authority, the annotator writes: "The Author (if he dyd write it) wrote in the afternoone." Probably this means: napping. Shakespeare regularly sees the afternoon as a time to sleep (*Hamlet*, I.v.60, *All's Well*, V.iii.66, *Tempest*, III.ii.96) and even uses the phrase "a sleepy language." [But now see the more detailed account by Alan Keen and Roger Lubbock, *The Annotator*—though S. Schoenbaum dismisses the question of "the suppositious Shakespearian annotations" as an "unilluminating" controversy (*Shakespeare's Lives*, p. x).] I may mention that neither of the copies of Holinshed's chronicle claimed as Shakespeare's in 1938 by Mme de Chambrun has yet been critically examined: a mutilated 1577 edition in the Folger "which remained in his sister's family long after the poet's death," and a Stratford-owned, annotated 1587 edition in which the reigns from Richard II to Henry VII are worn thin at the bottom from thumbing. [Clara Longworth, Comtesse de Chambrun, *Shakespeare Rediscovered by Means of Public Records, Secret Reports and Private Correspondence Newly Set Forth as Evidence on His Life and Work* (New York: Scribner's, 1938), pp. 260, 246.] G. B. Harrison [in a preface for the Comtesse's volume] was impressed by the case for the latter. Some critics have long thought Shakespeare used both editions of Holinshed.

[25] D. H. Madden, *The Diary of Master William Silence: A Study of Shakespeare and of Elizabethan Sport* (London: Longmans, Green, 1897); Caroline Spurgeon, *Shakespeare's Imagery and What It Tells Us* (Cambridge University Press, 1935).

[26] A. W. Pollard, "Introduction," in Peter Alexander, *Shakespeare's "Henry VI" and "Richard III"* (Cambridge University Press, 1929), pp. 13–21. See also G. M. Pinciss, "Shakespeare, Her Majesty's Players, and Pembroke's Men," *Shakespeare Survey* 27 (1974), pp. 129–36. But Honigmann's recent evidence points firmly to Shakespeare's association during the 1580s not with the Queen's Men but with the rival Strange's Men (*Shakespeare: The "Lost Years"* [Manchester University Press, 1985], pp. 59–76).

[27] Edward Dowden, *Shakspere: A Critical Study of His Mind and Art* (New York, 1875), p. 160.

[28] E.M.W. Tillyard, *Shakespeare's History Plays* (London: Chatto & Windus, 1946), p. 176.

[29] John Dover Wilson (ed.), *The Second Part of King Henry VI*, New Shakespeare (Cambridge University Press, 1952).

[30] Chambers, WS, I, p. 293.

[31] Ibid., p. 291.

[32] Ibid., p. 316.

[33] Francis Meres, *Palladis Tamia* (London, 1598); Chambers, WS, II, p. 194; *Riverside Shakespeare*, p. 1844.

[34] Mark Van Doren, *Shakespeare* (New York: Henry Holt, 1939), p. 39.

[35] Hardin Craig, *An Interpretation of Shakespeare* (Columbia, Mo.: Lucas Brothers, 1948), p. 41.

[36] [JB] M. C. Bradbrook, *Shakespeare and Elizabethan Poetry* (London: Chatto & Windus, 1951), p. 110. Thomas P. Harrison finds this later image in *King Lear* and has an interesting comparison of the plays (*Shakespearian Essays*, eds. Alwin Thaler and Norman Sanders, 1964, p. 121).

[37] Cf. Paul E. Bennett, "An Apparent Allusion to *Titus Andronicus*," *Notes & Queries* 200 (October 1955), pp. 422–24; and "The Word *Goths* in *A Knack to Know a Knave*," *Notes & Queries* 200 (1955), pp. 462–63. See also the introductory remarks (including an indication of possible authorship) by G. R. Proudfoot in *A Knack to Know a Knave (1594)*, Malone Society Reprints, 1963 (1964).

[38] Chambers, *WS*, I, p. 316; C. H. Herford and P. Simpson (eds.), *Ben Jonson* (Oxford University Press, 1938), VI, p. 16.

[39] T. M. Raysor (ed.), *Coleridge's Shakespearean Criticism* (London: Constable, 1930), II, p. 287; R. A. Foakes (ed.), *Coleridge's Criticism of Shakespeare: A Selection* (London: The Athlone Press, 1989), p. 182.

[40] Walter Pater, *Appreciations* (London, 1895), p. 194.

[41] E. K. Chambers, *Shakespeare: A Survey* (London, 1935), p. 99.

[42] Two articles in *TLS*, November 13 and 20, 1930; Chambers, *WS*, I, p. 366.

[43] John Dover Wilson (ed.), *King John*, New Shakespeare (Cambridge University Press, 1936), pp. liv–lvii; E.A.J. Honigmann (ed.), *King John*, Arden Shakespeare (London: Methuen, 1954), pp. xliii–lviii; Honigmann, *Shakespeare's Impact on His Contemporaries* (Totowa, N.J.: Barnes & Noble, 1982), pp. 56–66, 78–88, 132–33. See also Peter Alexander, *Shakespeare's Life and Art* (London: J. Nisbet, 1939). Eliot Slater reports that in the course of his stylometric research on the putatively anonymous *The Reign of Edward III* "a close correlation between the vocabularies of part A of *Edward III* and *King John* was discovered, supporting the early dating Honigmann prefers" (*The Problem of "The Reign of King Edward III": A Statistical Approach* [Cambridge University Press, 1988], p. 98).

[44] H. Dugdale Sykes, *Sidelights on Shakespeare* (London, 1919), pp. 99ff.

[45] Alfred Harbage, "A Contemporary Attack upon Shakspere?," *Shakespeare Association Bulletin* XVI:1 (January 1941), pp. 42–49.

[46] See further Berryman's essay on *King John* below.

[47] Peele's *Works*, ed. A. Dyce (1861), p. 386; Chambers, *WS*, I, p. 84.

[48] A. W. Pollard, "Introduction," in Peter Alexander, *Shakespeare's "Henry VI" and "Richard III"* (Cambridge University Press, 1929), pp. 18–19. (The supposed allusion was first noticed by F. G. Fleay, *A Biographical Chronicle of the English Drama 1559–1642* [London, 1891], II, p. 157.)

[49] *Greene, Groats-worth of Witte* (London, 1592), signatures F1ᵛ–F2; Chambers, *WS*, II, p. 188.

[50] See Peter Alexander, "Greene's Quotation from 3 *Henry VI*," *Shakespeare's Henry VI and Richard III*, pp. 39–50; Robert Greene, *The Scottish History of James the Fourth*, New Mermaids, ed. J. A. Lavin (London: Ernest Benn, 1967), pp. x–xi; Honigmann, *Shakespeare's Impact on His Contemporaries*, pp. 1–14—though Honigmann does not seem to be aware (pp. 6, 141) that the putative pun on Greene's name in Shakespeare's "o'er-green" (Sonnet 112:4) had been proposed by Edgar I. Fripp, *Shakespeare, Man and Artist* (London: Oxford University Press, 1938), I, p. 311; D. Allen Carroll, "Greene's 'vpstart crow' Passage: A Survey of Commentary," *Research Opportunities in Renaissance Drama* 28 (1985), pp. 111–27; also Barbara Everett's comment that while Greene's attack "may impute plagiarism, its chief animus is social—that a mere common player has won where gentlemen lose" ("Shakespeare's Greening," *TLS*, July 8, 1994, p. 13).

[51] H[enry] C[hettle], *Kind-Harts Dreame* (London, n.d.), sigs. A3ᵛ–4; Chambers, *WS*, II, p. 189.

[52] Chambers, *WS*, II, p. 190.

[53] "Facetious" derives from Latin *facetus* (*OED* cites Chettle). See also William A. Ringler, Jr., "Spenser, Shakespeare, Honor, and Worship," *Renaissance News* XIV (1961), pp. 159–61; Honigmann, *Shakespeare's Impact on His Contemporaries*, Appendix A and p. 142n.

[54] A. P. Rossiter, *English Drama from Early Times to the Elizabethans* (London: Hutchinson, 1950, 3rd imp., 1958), p. 153.

[55] Ashley H. Thorndike, *English Comedy* (New York: Macmillan, 1929), p. 96.

[56] John Dover Wilson (ed.), *King John* (Cambridge University Press, 1936), p. lii; R. A. Foakes (ed.), *The Comedy of Errors*, Arden Shakespeare (London: Methuen, 1962), p. 2.

⁵⁷ Thomas Whitfield Baldwin, *William Shakespeare Adapts a Hanging* (Princeton University Press, 1931).

⁵⁸ See also Foakes (ed.), *The Comedy of Errors*, p. xxxiv.

⁵⁹ See also Peter Lindenbaum, "Education in *The Two Gentlemen of Verona*," *Studies in English Literature* 15 (1975), pp. 229–44; Camille Wells Slights, "*The Two Gentlemen of Verona* and the Courtesy Book Tradition," *Shakespeare Studies* 16 (1983), pp. 13–31.

⁶⁰ F. G. Fleay, *Shakespeare Manual* (London, 1876), p. 29.

⁶¹ H. B. Charlton, *Shakespearian Comedy* (London: Methuen & Co., 1938), p. 27.

⁶² Van Doren, *Shakespeare*, pp. 53, 57. See also Stanley Wells, "The Failure of *The Two Gentlemen of Verona*," *Shakespeare Jahrbuch* 99 (1963), pp. 161–73.

⁶³ Chambers, WS, I, p. 331; *Elizabethan Stage*, IV, p. 160. See also T. P. Harrison, Jr., "Shakespeare and Montemayor's *Diana*," *Texas University Studies in English* 5 and 6 (1925–26), pp. 72–120; Honigmann, *Shakespeare's Impact on His Contemporaries*, p. 88; Kurt Schlueter (ed.), *The Two Gentlemen of Verona* (Cambridge University Press, 1990), pp. 1–2.

SHAKESPEARE AT THIRTY

¹ Chambers, WS, II, pp. 186–87.

² See Schoenbaum, *Shakespeare's Lives*, p. 54.

³ Ibid.

⁴ [JB] Earlier speculation has been superseded by J. Hoops of Heidelberg in *Studies for William A. Read*, 1940; even Henry Bradley's.

⁵ See Edgar I. Fripp, *Shakespeare, Man and Artist* (London: Oxford University Press, 1938), I, p. 311.

⁶ [JB] Chettle does not name the men, but their identities, which are unmistakable, have not been doubted.

⁷ Compare Honigmann, *Shakespeare's Impact on His Contemporaries*, pp. 1–14.

⁸ [JB] The clearest reproduction I have seen, though small, is that of the Bodleian copy in E. K. Chambers.

⁹ Sir John Mennis, quoted by Thomas Plume (c. 1657); Chambers, WS, II, p. 247.

¹⁰ See further *Willobie His Avisa*, ed. G. B. Harrison (London, 1926); Chambers, WS, I, pp. 569–70; II, p. 191; B. N. De Luna, *The Queen Declined: An Interpretation of "Willobie His Avisa"* (Oxford, 1970); *Riverside Shakespeare*, p. 1836; Schoenbaum, *William Shakespeare*, pp. 180–82.

¹¹ See Schoenbaum, *Shakespeare's Lives*, p. 65.

PATHOS AND DREAM

¹ Chambers, WS, II, p. 249.

² [JB] Among them allusions to Henri IV's conversion in July (IV.i.21–33), to Gabriel Harvey's *Pierces Supererogation* of this year (IV.ii.89), to Chapman's poem *The Shadow of Night*, evidently seen in manuscript (Field printed it), for it was registered on December 31 (IV.iii.346–47, 255), besides plague allusions and "*Lord haue mercie on vs*" (V.ii.419).

³ [JB] A garden performance of the comedy a mile away at Ashford Chace in 1937, by a group from Cambridge, confirmed my impression of its private character and fadeless radiance.

⁴ [JB] Cf. G. B. Harrison, *An Elizabethan Journal*, 1929, p. 422. The chief modern discussions of the play's topicality are the introduction to the edition (1923) by Quiller-Couch and Dover Wilson; Frances A. Yates's *A Study of "Love's Labour's Lost"* (Cambridge University Press, 1936), M. C. Bradbrook's *The School of Night* (Cambridge University Press, 1936),

Notes

Eleanor Grace Clark's *Ralegh and Marlowe* (New York: Fordham University Press, 1941). A reaction is under way against their exaggerated claims.

⁵ See H. B. Charlton, *Shakespearian Tragedy* (Cambridge University Press, 1948), pp. 69–82.

⁶ Richard G. Moulton, *The Moral System of Shakespeare* (New York: Macmillan, 1903), p. 360.

⁷ Chambers, WS, II, pp. 319–20.

⁸ E. K. Chambers, *Review of English Studies*, I, 1925, pp. 75–76; Chambers, WS, II, pp. 320–21; *Riverside Shakespeare*, p. 1839.

⁹ Chambers, WS, I, pp. 358–59. Compare Paul N. Siegel, "A *Midsummer Night's Dream* and the Wedding Guests," *Shakespeare Quarterly* IV (1953), pp. 139–44; Paul A. Olson, "A *Midsummer Night's Dream* and the Meaning of Court Marriage," *Journal of English Literary History* XXIV (1957), pp. 95–119; John Dover Wilson, "Variations on the Theme of A *Midsummer Night's Dream*" (*Shakespeare's Happy Comedies* [London: Faber & Faber, 1962], esp. pp. 191–207); Brooks, Arden Shakespeare, p. lvi; Foakes, New Cambridge Shakespeare, pp. 3, 68; Marion Colthorpe, "Queen Elizabeth I and A *Midsummer Night's Dream*," *Notes and Queries*, n.s. 34:2 (June 1987), pp. 205–7. William B. Hunter, who perceives that "the artificial verse of the play seems to me to come from an earlier period in Shakespeare's development," believes it may have been written for the Southampton–Heneage wedding on May 2, 1594, and revised for the Berkeley–Carey wedding in February 1596 ("The First Performance of A *Midsummer Night's Dream*," *Notes and Queries*, n.s. 32:1 [March 1985], pp. 45–47). Steven W. May finds the play full of topical allusions to the Careys ("A *Midsummer Night's Dream* and the Carey-Berkeley Wedding," in *Renaissance Papers* 1983, eds. A. Leigh Daneef and M. Thomas Hester [Raleigh, N.C., 1984], pp. 43–52). J.J.M. Tobin argues for the Berkeley–Carey wedding because A *Midsummer Night's Dream* exploits numerous borrowings from *The Terrors of the Night* (1584), by Thomas Nashe ("Nashe and Shakespeare: Some Further Borrowings," *Notes and Queries*, n.s. 39:3 [September 1992], pp. 309–12). E.A.J. Honigmann has urged the occasion of the Vere–Derby wedding (*Shakespeare: The "Lost Years*," pp. 150–53); but John Idris Jones, while agreeing with the occasion, contends that E. K. Chambers mistranscribed the date of that wedding, which should be June 26, 1594, two days after midsummer's night, and not June 26, 1595 (Alison Roberts, "Why Bard Dreamt Up Midsummer Title," *The Times*, March 5, 1994). Stanley Wells is sceptical about the wedding-play theory ("A *Midsummer Night's Dream* Revisited," *Critical Survey* 3:1 [1991], pp. 14–18).

¹⁰ In holograph notes of a later date, Berryman remarked: "*Merchant* is immensely skilful & effective. Shakespeare had never before so adroitly exercised his formidable powers to overcome & resolve the problems of his themes, but it remains a deeply divided, even a schizophrenic work of art, in my judgement, and I have never much *liked* it. This is a confession, and the present chapter will have to take the form of an attempt frankly to expound & perhaps exorcise my prejudice. I was unlucky certainly in my first view of the play, a toneless school performance, and in my second view, a production by an abysmal touring company when I was an undergraduate at Cambridge. I walked out on this, but such impressions are hard to efface. But I also saw a perfectly brilliant mounting of it in London in the spring of 1937, with Gielgud as Shylock and Peggy Ashcroft's Portia, and I cannot honestly say that it reconciled me to the play . . . I despise Bassanio, a one-dimensional fortune-hunter who never from beginning to end says a striking thing. Even Bertram in *All's Well* is not more despicable. Even Bassanio's choice of the right casket is made *for* him, as R. Noble pointed out in *Shakespeare's Use of Song* [1923]: the rhymes insist on 'lead.' We may then admire the playwright's cunning but the character is not thereby endeared to us." Shylock "sticks out of the plot, like Mercutio," he added; and Shakespeare may be thought "in the end a little heartless?" Shylock is "simple,

after all, a mere triple compound of vindictiveness, avarice, Hebr. self-pity." On the other hand, Shakespeare's prose, he considered, showed "intensity, variety."

[11] John Dryden, from *Essay on the Dramatique Poetry of the Last Age* (1672); Chambers, *WS*, II, p. 251.

THE WORLD OF ACTION

[1] Raysor (ed.), *Coleridge's Shakespearean Criticism*, II, pp. 357–58.

[2] John Aubrey, *Brief Lives*; Bodleian MS Aubrey 6, fol. 109; Chambers, *WS*, II, p. 252.

[3] Leslie Hotson, *Shakespeare versus Shallow* (London: Nonesuch, 1931). See also Honigmann, *Shakespeare's Impact on His Contemporaries*, pp. 11–12.

[4] Cf. Hattaway (ed.), *The First Part of King Henry VI*, pp. 41–43.

[5] In his application for a senior fellowship from the National Endowment for the Humanities, in May 1971, Berryman recalled too: "Gielgud was incredible (that is, credible) both as weak lyrical Richard II and animal Shylock."

[6] John Palmer, *Political and Comic Characters of Shakespeare* (London: Macmillan, 1962), pp. 102–3.

[7] F. Liebermann, *Shakespeare als Bearbeiter des King John* (1921–22), *Archiv*, CXLII, p. 177; CXLIII, pp. 17, 190 (Chambers, *WS*, I, p. 365).

[8] Maurice Morgann, "An Essay on the Dramatic Character of Sir John Falstaff," in *Eighteenth Century Essays on Shakespeare*; Maurice Morgann, *Shakespearian Criticism*, ed. Daniel A. Fineman (Oxford University Press, 1972).

[9] See G. Wilson Knight, *The Olive and the Sword* (Oxford University Press, 1944).

[10] Lord Raglan, *The Hero* (London: Methuen, 1936).

[11] See Peter Corbin and Douglas Sedge (eds.), *The Oldcastle Controversy*, Revels Plays Companion Library (Manchester University Press, 1991).

[12] Chambers, *WS*, I, p. 434; Schoenbaum, *Shakespeare's Lives*, p. 51.

[13] See Chambers, *WS*, II, p. 247.

[14] M. W. MacCallum, *Shakespeare's Roman Plays and Their Background* (London: Macmillan, 1925), pp. 197–98.

[15] Nicholas Rowe, "Some Account of the Life &c. of Mr. William Shakespear" (1709), in Smith, *Eighteenth Century Essays on Shakespeare*, pp. 7–9.

ALL'S WELL

[1] A. C. Bradley, "Shakespeare the Man," *Oxford Lectures on Poetry* (1909) (London: Macmillan, 1965), pp. 354–55.

[2] In a letter to Robert Giroux, dated August 3, 1955, Berryman was further to observe about this famous passage: "This is one of the most formidable immediate warnings anyone ever received. Essex paid no heed & did not live long. It is also to the point that, as Chambers says (who doubts the allusion, but I don't, given the v. close dating & the linkage thro Southampton), such an allusion wd. be v. dangerous for the playwright."

[3] Chambers, *WS*, I, p. 385.

[4] See Enid Welsford, *The Fool* (London, 1935; rpt. 1961), pp. 245–46; David Wiles, *Shakespeare's Clown: Actor and Text in the Elizabethan Playhouse* (Cambridge University Press, 1987), pp. 144–58.

[5] Chambers, *WS*, II, p. 253; I, p. 388.

[6] John Wilcox, "Putting Jaques into 'As You Like It,' " *Modern Language Review* 36:3 (July 1941), p. 389.

Notes

7 T. W. Baldwin, *The Organization and Personnel of the Shakespearean Company* (New York: Russell & Russell, 1961), p. 246.

8 G. B. Harrison, *Shakespeare at Work 1592–1603* (London: Routledge & Sons, 1933), pp. 172–73. Lytton Strachey called the title "a crowningly deplorable pun" ("Sir John Harington" [1923], reprinted in *The Shorter Strachey*, eds. Michael Holroyd and Paul Levy [Oxford University Press, 1980], p. 212).

9 Helge Kökeritz, *Shakespeare's Pronunciation* (New Haven: Yale University Press, 1953), pp. 58, 91, 118.

10 Alfred Harbage, *Shakespeare's Audience* (New York: Columbia University Press, 1941), p. 11.

11 In some separate (undated) notes, Berryman wrote further: "In four decades of playgoing on three continents the Shakespearean moment sharpest for me is Alec Guinness's rendering of 'Sometimes I think I have no more wit than a Christian or an ordinary man has' at the Old Vic [in] 1937; he brought the house down, and Sir Andrew Aguecheek came into his own. Tyrone Guthrie directed him, and the fake swordplay . . . was worth an hour with the Marx Brothers. Guinness looked exactly like Stan Laurel, with a forelock standing straight up and an amazed expression. Malvolio's love, even Malvolio's love, in the production was tender."

12 Edgar Fripp, *Master Richard Quyny* (London, 1924), pp. 137–38; Fripp, *Shakespeare, Man and Artist*, II, p. 499; Chambers, WS, II, p. 102; Lewis, *The Shakespeare Documents*, I, pp. 226, 229; Mark Eccles, *Shakespeare in Warwickshire* (Madison, Wis., 1961), p. 93; *Riverside Shakespeare*, pp. 1831–32; Schoenbaum, *William Shakespeare: A Documentary Life*, p. 180; Herbert Berry, "Shakespeare, Richard Quiney, and the Cheshire Cheese" (with a new transcription of the letter), *Shakespeare Bulletin* 9:1 (Winter 1991), pp. 29–30.

13 Cited first by J. O. Halliwell, *New Boke about Shakespeare and Stratford-on-Avon* (1850); Fripp, *Shakespeare*, I, p. 408; Schoenbaum, *Shakespeare's Lives*, pp. 294–95.

14 Giles E. Dawson, "Authenticity and Attribution of Written Matter," *English Institute Annual* (1942) (New York: Columbia University Press, 1943), p. 100; J. Q. Adams, "A New Signature of Shakespeare?," *Bulletin of the John Rylands Library* XXVII (1943), pp. 256–59; "One of Shakespeare's Books?," *TLS*, May 1, 1943, p. 216; S. Schoenbaum, *William Shakespeare: Records and Images* (New York: Oxford University Press, 1981), pp. 104–9; Joyce Rogers, *The Second Best Bed: Shakespeare's Will in a New Light* (Westport, Conn.: Greenwood Press, 1993), pp. 58–62. Charles Hamilton, an autograph dealer and scholar, thinks the signature a forgery (*In Search of Shakespeare: A Reconnaissance into the Poet's Life and Handwriting* [New York: Harcourt Brace, 1985], p. 240). Hamilton endorses (pp. 163–67) the putative discovery by the Countess Clara Longworth de Chambrun of Shakespeare's own copy, with his marginal annotations, of the second edition of Holinshed's *Chronicles of England* (1587). Giles Dawson maintains the authenticity of the signature in *Archaionomia* ("A Seventh Signature for Shakespeare," *Shakespeare Quarterly* [Spring 1992], pp. 72–79). See also Eric Sams, "The Hand of a Lawyer's Clerk?," *TLS*, December 24, 1993, p. 4.

15 Chambers, WS, I, pp. 341–45.

16 See David Lyall Patrick, *The Textual History of "Richard III,"* Stanford University Publications: Language and Literature, VI:1 (1936).

17 Chambers, WS, I, p. 145.

18 Compare Giorgio Melchiori, who argues that the additions predate the interventions of the Master of the Revels ("The Master of the Revels and the Date of the Additions to *The Book of Sir Thomas More*," in *Shakespeare: Text, Language, Criticism*, eds. Bernhard Fabian and Kurt Tetzeli von Rosador [Hildesheim: Olms-Weidmann, 1987], pp. 164–79).

19 See Thomas Clayton, *The "Shakespearean" Additions in The Booke of Sir Thomas Moore: Some Aids to Scholarly and Critical Shakespearean Studies*, Shakespeare Studies, Monograph

Series I (Dubuque, Iowa, 1969); G. Blakemore Evans, *"Sir Thomas More*: The Additions Ascribed to Shakespeare," *The Riverside Shakespeare* (Boston: Houghton Mifflin, 1974), pp. 1683–97 (which includes a parallel-text transliteration and a modernized version); Gary Taylor (ed.), Oxford Shakespeare, 1986; Scott McMillin, *The Elizabethan Theatre & "The Book of Sir Thomas More"* (Ithaca, N.Y.: Cornell University Press, 1987); *Shakespeare and "Sir Thomas More": Essays on the Play and Its Shakespearian Interest*, ed. T. H. Howard-Hill (Cambridge University Press, 1989); Giles E. Dawson, "Shakespeare's Handwriting," *Shakespeare Survey* 42 (1989), pp. 119–28; G. Harold Metz's excellent introduction to *Sir Thomas More* in his edition of *Sources of Four Plays Ascribed to Shakespeare* (Columbia: University of Missouri Press, 1989), pp. 3–42; Anthony Munday and Others, *Sir Thomas More* (Revels Plays), eds. Vittorio Gabrieli and Giorgio Melchiori (Manchester University Press, 1990); and John Jones's appealing argument in "The One Manuscript: Sir Thomas More" (also with a modernized transcription), in his *Shakespeare at Work* (Oxford: Clarendon Press, 1995), pp. 7–35.

[20] JB's source here is probably R. C. Bald, *"The Booke of Sir Thomas More* and Its Problems," *Shakespeare Survey* 2 (1949), pp. 44–61. Charles Hamilton, who endorses the argument that Hand D is Shakespeare's, reviews the evidence, with supporting illustrations, in *In Search of Shakespeare*, pp. 105–15.

[21] L. Schücking, "Shakespeare and *Sir Thomas More*," *Review of English Studies* I (1925), pp. 40–59. Actually, as G. Blakemore Evans notes, the critical consensus still favours an earlier date between 1590 and 1593 for the original play and of 1594 or 1595 for the revisions (*Riverside Shakespeare*, p. 1684).

[22] Chambers, WS, I, pp. 353–55; *The Elizabethan Stage*, II, pp. 204–7. See also Leeds Barroll, "A New History for Shakespeare and his Time," *Shakespeare Quarterly* 39 (1988), pp. 441–64; James R. Siemon, " 'Word Itself against the Word': Close Reading after Voloshinov," in *Shakespeare Reread: The Texts in New Contexts*, ed. Russ McDonald (Ithaca, N.Y.: Cornell University Press, 1994), pp. 226–58; Gurr, *The Shakespearian Playing Companies*, pp. 288–89.

[23] See also John Dover Wilson, *The Essential Shakespeare: A Biographical Adventure* (Cambridge University Press, 1932), p. 36.

THE CRISIS

[1] Chambers, WS, II, pp. 95–99, 107–13, 118–27.

[2] Ibid., pp. 18–32.

[3] John Nichols, *The Progresses and Public Processions of Queen Elizabeth* (London: John Nichols, 1823), III, p. 552.

[4] Chambers, WS, I, pp. 353–55; II, p. 325; *The Elizabethan Stage*, II, pp. 204–7. See also Alfred Hart, *Shakespeare and the Homilies* (Melbourne University Press, 1934), pp. 170–71.

[5] Chambers, WS, II, p. 329.

[6] Ibid., p. 332.

[7] Ibid., pp. 194–95.

[8] Ibid., p. 197.

[9] See further Johannes Fabricius, *Syphilis in Shakespeare's England* (London: Jessica Kingsley, 1994) (reviewed by John L. Flood, "The Winchester Geese," *TLS*, January 13, 1995, p. 12), and Berryman's remarks on *Timon of Athens* below.

[10] See Harley Granville-Barker, *Prefaces to Shakespeare*, third series: *Hamlet* (London: Sidgwick & Jackson, 1936).

[11] See Philip Edwards (ed.), *Hamlet, Prince of Denmark*, New Cambridge Shakespeare (Cam-

bridge University Press, 1985), pp. 3–7, for an account of the relations between *The Spanish Tragedy*, *Hamlet*, and *Antonio's Revenge*.

¹² Chambers, *WS*, II, p. 332; John Dover Wilson (ed.), *Love's Labour's Lost*, New Shakespeare (Cambridge University Press, 2nd edn., 1962), p. lx.

¹³ Chambers, *WS*, II, pp. 228–29.

¹⁴ Compare Berryman's remarks about this speech, in "Shakespeare's Reality" (appendix).

¹⁵ Chambers, *WS*, II, p. 253.

¹⁶ Ibid., p. 73.

¹⁷ Charles William Wallace, "New Shakespeare Discoveries: Shakespeare as a Man among Men," *Harper's Monthly Magazine* CXX (March 1910), pp. 489–510; "Shakespeare and His London Associates as Revealed in Recently Discovered Documents," *University Studies of the University of Nebraska* 10:4 (October 1910), pp. 261–300; Chambers, *WS*, II, pp. 90–95.

¹⁸ Chambers, *WS*, II, p. 212.

¹⁹ Ibid., p. 254; Schoenbaum, *Shakespeare's Lives*, pp. 62–63. Compare Mary Edmond's judicious biography in the Revels Plays Companion Library series, *Rare Sir William Davenant* (Manchester University Press, 1987).

²⁰ Chambers, *WS*, II, p. 98.

²¹ Groot, *The Shakespeares and "The Old Faith."*

²² Raysor, *Coleridge's Shakespearean Criticism*, I, p. 35.

²³ Wolfgang H. Clemen, *The Development of Shakespeare's Imagery* (Cambridge, Mass.: Harvard University Press, 1951), pp. 112–14.

²⁴ A. C. Bradley, *Shakespearean Tragedy* (London: Macmillan, 1904), p. 93.

²⁵ G. R. Levy, *The Gate of Horn* (London: Faber & Faber, 1948), p. 327.

²⁶ Nicholas Rowe, "Some Account of the Life &c. of Mr. William Shakespeare," in *The Works of Mr. William Shakespeare, in Six Volumes* (London: Jacob Tonson, 1709), I, p. vi; reprinted in Smith, *Eighteenth Century Essays on Shakespeare*, p. 4.

²⁷ Berryman noted this quotation from an article in *The New York Times*, May 7, 1951. A fussier and less affecting version is in *The Complete Letters of Sigmund Freud to Wilhelm Fliess, 1887–1904*, trans. and ed. by Jeffrey Moussaieff Masson (Cambridge, Mass.: The Belknap Press of Harvard University Press, 1985), p. 202.

²⁸ George L. Craik, *The English of Shakespeare Illustrated in a Philological Commentary on His "Julius Caesar"* (London: Chapman & Hall, 1864).

²⁹ See for convenience T.J.B. Spencer, *Shakespeare's Plutarch* (Harmondsworth, Middx.: Penguin, 1964), p. 106.

THE TRAGIC SUBSTANCE

¹ Alfred Hart, "The Date of *Othello*," *TLS*, October 10, 1935, p. 631. For a useful discussion of the dating of *Othello*, see Marvin Rosenberg, *The Masks of Othello* (Berkeley and Los Angeles: University of California Press, 1961), pp. 257–58, n. 1.

² Giraldi Cinthio, *Hecatommithi*, quoted in *Othello*, New Variorum, ed. H. H. Furness (Philadelphia: J. B. Lippincott, 1886), p. 377.

³ Chambers, *WS*, II, p. 261.

⁴ See Chambers, *WS*, I, p. 461.

⁵ Raysor (ed.), *Coleridge's Shakespearean Criticism*, I, p. 225.

⁶ Arthur Sherbo (ed.), *Johnson on Shakespeare* (New Haven: Yale University Press, 1968) (Yale Edition of the Works of Samuel Johnson, Vol. VII), II, p. 1045.

⁷ On a separate manuscript page, Berryman added: "I said 'Iago-like' plot, but Edmund is really more like R III than he is like Iago: he has a *cause* for special ambition & villainy, his

bastardy, like R's deformity, and to tell the truth he is *likeable* as Iago is not. The superb transition from the evil agents of the main plot to the evil agent of the underplot, as we move into the 2nd. sc. of Act I, is worth attention. It is a positive relief to enter on the enthusiastic & specific ambition of Edmund, after the resentful & ambiguous malice of Gon. & Reg., who are much *more unnatural* than he is; his feelings during the opening lines of the play (as we imagine them—'why brand they us . . .' clearly refers back) have given us a certain sympathy w. him—after all, why *shd* a bastard be penalized?—and his invocation to nature does not strike us as displeasing after the violations visited on that goddess by Lear, and esp., just now, by Gon. & Reg. His victim Edgar we've not met yet & care nothing for. Finally, no small point, after the extravagant passions of Lear, Edmund is agreeably *businesslike*; it is quite imposs. to imagine Edmund ever angry. This seems to me one of the subtlest transitions in all drama."

⁸ In his application for a senior fellowship from the National Endowment for the Humanities (May 1971), Berryman recalled: "Joyce Bland was magnificent both as Imogen and as Goneril in the awful Komisarjevski *Lear* with knights chorusing, Fool squealing & plump, wing's thunder starting too early so that five minutes' dialogue was lost." On Komisarjevsky's *King Lear*, see also Ralph Berry, "Komisarjevsky at Stratford-upon-Avon," *Shakespeare Survey* 36 (1983), pp. 78–81.

⁹ Henry N. Paul, *The Royal Play of "Macbeth"* (New York: Macmillan, 1950). Compare Jonathan Goldberg, "Speculations: *Macbeth* and Source," in *Post-Structuralist Readings of English Poetry*, eds. Richard Machin and Christopher Norris (Cambridge University Press, 1987), pp. 38–58; Leeds Barroll, *Politics, Plague, and Shakespeare's Theater: The Stuart Years* (Ithaca, N.Y.: Cornell University Press, 1991), pp. 133–52.

¹⁰ Chambers, *The Elizabethan Stage* (1923), I, p. 130; III, p. 332; WS, I, p. 474.

¹¹ Chambers, *WS*, II, p. 201.

¹² Ibid., p. 333.

¹³ G. Wilson Knight, "*Macbeth* and the Metaphysic of Evil," *The Wheel of Fire* (1930), 4th edn. reprinted with corrections (London: Methuen, 1954), pp. 142–43.

¹⁴ Walter Clyde Curry, *Shakespeare's Philosophical Patterns* (Baton Rouge: Louisiana State University Press, 1937; 2nd edn., 1959), p. 40 (see also Chapter IV, "Macbeth's Changing Character").

THE END

¹ Chambers, *WS*, II, p. 253.

² See Chambers, *WS*, I, p. 483. Compare J. C. Maxwell (ed.), *Timon of Athens* (Cambridge University Press, 1968); Eliot Slater ("Word Links between *Timon of Athens* and *King Lear*," *Notes & Queries* 223 [1978], pp. 147–49), whose study of rare words in *Timon* and *Lear* "support[s] the view . . . that *Timon* was written at about the same time as *Lear*, or rather earlier; and it is a massive item of evidence against the Chambers view of *Timon* as a later play than *Coriolanus*" (p. 149); Slater's findings are summarized in *The Problem of "The Reign of King Edward III*," p. 86.

³ H. Mutschmann and K. Wentersdorf, *Shakespeare and Catholicism* (New York: Sheed and Ward, 1952), p. 192; M. M. Reese, *Shakespeare, His World and His Work* (London: Edward Arnold, 1953; rev. edn., 1980), p. 249.

⁴ A large body of opinion now reckons the play to be a collaboration between Shakespeare and Thomas Middleton: see David J. Lake, *The Canon of Thomas Middleton's Plays* (Cambridge University Press, 1975), pp. 279–86; MacD. P. Jackson, *Studies in Attribution: Middleton and Shakespeare*, Jacobean Drama Studies 79 (Salzburg, 1979), pp. 54–66; R. V. Holdsworth, *Middleton and Shakespeare: The Case for Middleton's Hand in "Timon of Athens"* (Ph.D. thesis,

Notes

University of Manchester, 1982); Stanley Wells and Gary Taylor, *William Shakespeare: A Textual Companion* (Oxford University Press, 1987), pp. 127–28, 501–2. Jonathan Hope, making use of what he terms "quantitative socio-historical linguistic methods," finds evidence giving "broad support for the notion" of such a collaboration (*The Authorship of Shakespeare's Plays: A Socio-linguistic Study* [Cambridge University Press, 1994], pp. 100–4, 151).

[5] John W. Draper, "The Theme of 'Timon of Athens,'" *Modern Language Review* 29 (1934), p. 28; E. C. Pettet, "*Timon of Athens*: The Disruption of Feudal Morality," *Review of English Studies* XXIII (October 1947), pp. 321–36.

[6] Andrew H. Woods, "Syphilis in Shakespeare's Timon of Athens," *The American Journal of Psychiatry* 91:1 (July 1934), p. 104.

[7] See also Fabricius, *Syphilis in Shakespeare's England*, reviewed by John L. Flood, "The Winchester Geese," *TLS*, January 13, 1995, p. 12.

[8] Jonathan Hope's evidence now supports the theory that *Pericles* is a collaboration between Shakespeare and George Wilkins (*The Authorship of Shakespeare's Plays*, pp. 106–13, 151–52).

[9] Chambers, *WS*, II, p. 218.

[10] Ibid., p. 96.

[11] Ibid., I, p. 559; II, p. 221.

[12] See Harley Granville-Barker, *Prefaces to Shakespeare*.

[13] Colin Still, *Shakespeare's Mystery Play: A Study of "The Tempest"* (London: Cecil Palmer, 1921).

[14] Compare Charles Norman (Berryman's source here): "The Baconian methods are sometimes surprising: *e.g.*, for the authority of *Psalm* 46 (King James version) read down 46 words, then up 46 words (omitting "Selah" at end)" (*So Worthy a Friend: William Shakespeare* [New York: Rinehart & Co., 1947], p. 297).

[15] See Charles William Wallace, "Shakespeare and His London Associates as Revealed in Recently Discovered Documents," *University Studies of the University of Nebraska* 10:4 (October 1910), p. 263; Chambers, *WS*, II, pp. 90–95. Shakespeare's deposition in the Belott–Mountjoy suit is transcribed anew in *Shakespeare Survey* 3 (1950), p. 13.

[16] J. O. Halliwell-Phillips, *Life of William Shakespeare* (1848), II, p. 244. Joyce Rogers observes, "It is of some interest that this boy was at the time the same age as Shakespeare's own son, Hamnet, upon his death on August 11, 1596" (*The Second Best Bed*, p. 3).

[17] See among other critical appraisals, Kenneth Muir, "Cardenio," in *Shakespeare as Collaborator* (London: Methuen, 1960), pp. 148–60; John Freehafer, "Cardenio, by Shakespeare and Fletcher," *PMLA* 84 (1969), pp. 501–13. G. Harold Metz rehearses the critical history and reception of the putative play and decides that it probably was a Shakespeare–Fletcher manuscript of a play entitled *The History of Cardenio*, written during the summer of 1612, that Humphrey Moseley "manifestly" entered on the Stationers' Register on September 9, 1653. While Jonathan Hope (who summarizes scholarly findings to date and provides an excellent bibliography) endorses the likelihood of these plays being Shakespeare–Fletcher collaborations (*The Authorship of Shakespeare's Plays*, pp. 67–100, 150–51), Robert F. Fleissner yet renews the case against *Cardenio*: "'The Likely Misascription of 'Cardenio' (and thereby 'Double Falsehood') in Part to Shakespeare," *Neuphilologische Mitteilungen* XCVII:2 (1996), pp. 217–30. See also William Shakespeare and John Fletcher, "Cardenio," or, "The Second Maiden's Tragedy," ed. Charles Hamilton (Lakewood, Colo.: Glenbridge, 1994). On Shakespeare's authentic share in *The Two Noble Kinsmen* see Alfred Hart, "Shakespeare and the Vocabulary of *The Two Noble Kinsmen*," *Review of English Studies* 10 (1934), pp. 274–87; Marco Mincoff, "The Authorship of *The Two Noble Kinsmen*," *English Studies* 33 (1952), pp. 97–115; Kenneth Muir, *Shakespeare as Collaborator*, Chapter 6; Cyrus Hoy, "The Shares of Fletcher and His Collaborators in the Beaumont and Fletcher Canon (VII)," *Studies in Bibliography* 15 (1962), pp. 71–90.

¹⁸ Chambers, *WS*, II, p. 153.

¹⁹ Ibid., pp. 12–13.

²⁰ Ibid., p. 153.

²¹ Ibid., pp. 141–52.

²² Ibid., p. 230.

²³ Ibid., p. 250.

²⁴ Ibid., pp. 7–8.

²⁵ Cf. Ibid., pp. 169–80 (175–76 relate to Judith); E.A.J. Honigmann and Susan Brock, *Playhouse Wills, 1558–1642* (Manchester University Press, 1993), pp. 105–9. See also Hugh A. Hanley, "Shakespeare's Family in Stratford Records," *TLS*, May 21, 1964, p. 441. Compare Rogers, *The Second Best Bed*, pp. 2–34; Richard Wilson, "A Constant Will to Publish: Shakespeare's Dead Hand," in his *Will Power*, pp. 184–234.

²⁶ Chambers, *WS*, II, p. 181.

²⁷ Ibid., p. 257.

²⁸ John Dryden, *An Essay of Dramatick Poesie* (1668), pp. 47–48; *Riverside Shakespeare*, p. 1848.

²⁹ According to William Hall in 1694; see Chambers, *WS*, II, p. 261.

SHAKESPEARE'S LAST WORD

¹ [JB] The word is taken over from the passage in Golding's *Ovid*, where its use is commonplace.

² Wolfgang Clemen, *The Development of Shakespeare's Imagery*, pp. 182–83.

³ Chambers, *WS*, II, p. 96.

⁴ The Belott–Mountjoy Suit, in ibid., pp. 90–95 (Shakespeare's deposition on pp. 91–92).

⁵ See *Johnson on Shakespeare*, I, p. 135.

⁶ See Schoenbaum, *Shakespeare: A Compact Documentary Life*, pp. 289–90.

PROJECT: AN EDITION OF *King Lear*

[*In this section the majority of the notes on* King Lear *are by Berryman himself; additional notes by Haffenden are given in square brackets.*]

¹ W. W. Greg, "The Function of Bibliography in Literary Criticism Illustrated in a Study of the Text of *King Lear*," *Neophilologus* 18 (1932–33), pp. 241–62; *The Editorial Problem in Shakespeare: A Survey of the Foundations of the Text* (Oxford: Clarendon Press, 1942).

² *King Lear*, 1608 (Pied Bull Quarto), *Shakespeare Quarto Facsimiles* (London: Shakespeare Association/Sidgwick & Jackson, 1939); C. T. Onions, *Shakespeare Glossary* (1911); Samuel A. Tannenbaum, *Shakspere's "King Lear": A Concise Bibliography*, Elizabethan Bibliographies, no. 16 (New York: Author, 1940); R. B. McKerrow, *Prolegomena for the Oxford Shakespeare* (Oxford: Clarendon Press, 1939).

³ Leon Kellner, *Restoring Shakespeare: A Critical Analysis of the Misreadings in Shakespeare's Works* (New York: Alfred A. Knopf, 1925).

TEXTUAL INTRODUCTION

¹ Running titles. See Dr. W. W. Greg's bibliography, 1939–44, for full descriptions of the two substantive editions.

² Both these matters have been misconceived. Of course the presumption that Q was unauthorized will not tell us whether it presents a good text or not (cf., *Q Troilus and Cressida*,

which although unauthorized gives us a text preferable on the whole in my opinion to F). But it is important to understand that entrance on the Stationers' Register—I quote McKerrow—"had, primarily at least, no reference to the abstract right of anyone to put the book into print . . . No *other* member of the Company might print it (and in general no one not a member might print at all); the entry did not necessarily imply that the printing of the book was sanctioned by the Licensing Authorities, nor that the enterer had any legal right to the possession of the copy" (R. B. McKerrow, *An Introduction to Bibliography for Literary Students* [Oxford: Clarendon Press, 1927], pp. 136–37). Dr. Greg notes that 151 of 464 individual plays published between 1581 and 1640 were unregistered, and says, "The proportion of Shakespeare's works entered is unusually high. This accident has led to too much reliance being placed on non-entrance as a criterion of irregular publication" (W. W. Greg, "Entrance, Licence, and Publication," *The Library*, Fourth Series, XXV:1,2 [June, September 1944], pp. 6–7).

King Lear, however, was entered as licensed by Buc. Sir George Buc had been Acting Master of the Revels since 1603. (It is true that Mark Eccles, who knows Buc's career better probably than anyone else, is doubtful of this in *Thomas Lodge and Other Elizabethans*, ed. C. J. Sisson [Cambridge, Mass.: Harvard University Press, 1933], esp. pp. 434–35, but I think the reservation needless; in view of the patent of reversion *and* commission of June 23, 1603, paralleling Tyllney's of 1581, I follow Chambers and Greg and take Buc to have been exercising most of the functions of the office by 1605–6, when *Lear* would have come before him for an acting license.) R. Crompton Rhodes [*Shakespeare's First Folio* (Oxford: Basil Blackwell, 1923), pp. 27–31, cited in Greg, "Entrance, Licence, and Publication," p. 11] argued that in such instances the Master's license for printing was really the original acting license—which would appear to guarantee as authorized the copy submitted for entrance; Chambers and Greg took up the suggestion with various degrees of confidence, and I was prepared to rely heavily on Buc's hand for the mutilated text of Fulke Greville's unperformed *Mustapha* published by Butter in 1609, when Dr. Greg abandoned Rhodes's hypothesis and showed conclusively that it cannot be maintained for a particular case (*The Library* XXV [1944], pp. 11–14). We are left simply with the license to print; and I agree with Dr. McKerrow that it cannot be relied on. Having examined plays already for the stage, Buc, as he says, "was not in the least likely to want to read them again for the press" (R. B. McKerrow, "The Elizabethan Printer and Dramatic Manuscripts," *The Library*, Fourth Series, XII:3 [December 1931], p. 268).

A suggestion by Joseph Quincy Adams (*A Life of Shakespeare* [Boston and New York: Houghton Mifflin, 1923], p. 521) rests on an error of fact, like his statement ("The Quarto of *King Lear* and Shorthand," *Modern Philology* XXXI:2 [November 1933], p. 135) that Butter had pirated *Hamlet*. A very tentative notion of Pollard's (Arthur W. Pollard, *Shakespeare's Fight with the Pirates and the Problems of the Transmission of His Text* [Cambridge University Press, 1920], p. 51; 1909, p. 53) seems to me even less plausible than it seemed to its distinguished author.

[3] (1) "It hath bin the height of our care, who are the Presenters, to make the present worthy"; (2) "The faults ours, if any be committed, by a payre so carefull"; (3) "We pray you do not envie his Friends, the office of their care, and paine, to haue collected & publish'd them."

[4] [*Ben Jonson*, eds. C. H. Herford and Percy Simpson (Oxford: Clarendon Press, 1927, 1954), p. 96.]

[5] D = Greg's suggestion ("The Function of Bibliography in Literary Criticism Illustrated in a Study of the Text of *King Lear*," *Neophilologus* XVII [1933], p. 253); but cf. p. 36.

[6] These figures, like all those to come for which no source is given, are based on my own exact counts, but the figures are themselves approximate. Enumeration cannot really express either lineation or variants. Where I differ therefore from earlier critics, as Miss Doran [*The Text of "King Lear"* (Stanford University Press, 1931)] and Mr. Hubler ["The Verse Lining of

the First Quarto of *King Lear*," in *Essays in Dramatic Literature: The Parrott Presentation Volume*, ed. Hardin Craig (Princeton University Press, 1935), pp. 421–41], neither of us is necessarily wrong. For general counts I follow Chambers and Hart.

⁷ Lines 318 and 321 are two of the fifty-eight that F splits for typographical nicety.

⁸ Cf. Chambers, WS, I, pp. 118ff., and especially Greg (1942) *passim*.

⁹ My precise view of the nature of the F copy was partly anticipated by Fleay in 1879 (Frederick Gard Fleay, "On the 1608 (Quarto) and 1623 (Folio) Editions of *The Tragedy of King Lear*," *Robinson's Epitome of Literature* [August 1, 1879], pp. 119–20). (See also: "The Quarto *Lear* abounds with errors of ear, and was clearly surreptitiously taken down by notes at the theatre"—Fleay, *Shakespeare Manual*, p. 62.)

¹⁰ *M. William Shak-speare's "King Lear": The First Quarto 1608*, a facsimile by Charles Praetorius, with an introduction by P. A. Daniel (London: C. Praetorius, 1885), p. x.

¹¹ [See Greg, *Variants*, pp. 140–41. Compare Stone, pp. 151, 237, 250; Duthie, *Shakespeare's "King Lear*," p. 10; Taylor, *Division*, p. 359; T. H. Howard-Hill, "Q1 and the Copy for Folio *Lear*," *Papers of the Bibliographical Society of America* 80 (1986), pp. 427–35; Halio, *Tragedy*, pp. 67–68; R. A. Foakes (ed.), *King Lear*, Arden Shakespeare, 3rd series (Walton-on-Thames, Surrey: Thomas Nelson and Sons, 1997), pp. 123–25.]

¹² W. W. Greg, "The Function of Bibliography in Literary Criticism Illustrated in a Study of the Text of *King Lear*," *Neophilologus* 18 (1933), p. 258. I should add that *p:x*, although for some reason not recognized by Kellner (he omits also *o:u*, *r:w*, and other well-known similarities), is one of the easiest misreadings in English hands of the period; and *l:t* confusion is very common in the quarto. The conjecture may be regarded as certain. As Greg notes, the Q corrector evidently made out the copy correctly but used a form he liked better; cf. Q "taske" for F "taxe" III.ii.16. [See also Berryman's letter to Greg, February 16, 1946, and Greg's response of February 28, 1946, below; and Greg, *Variants*, pp. 141–42; *Editorial Problem*, pp. 98–99. Compare Duthie, *King Lear*, pp. 12–13, 172; Duthie (1960), pp. 123–24; Stone, pp. 41, 83, 134, 193, 249; Taylor, *Division*, pp. 357–58, 431; Howard-Hill, "Q1 and the Copy for Folio *Lear*," p. 426.]

¹³ [John Dover Wilson, *The Manuscript of Shakespeare's "Hamlet" and the Problems of Its Transmission*, Vol. II: *Editorial Problems and Solutions* (Cambridge University Press, 1934), Chapter XVII: "Variants Proper."]

¹⁴ Editors, following Q, have ignored the ugly vowel clash of "clay, yea." Q has "yea" again, intolerably, at II.iv.134 for the folio's "O"—again in Lear's part.

¹⁵ Behind the general preference for F's phrase in this passage lies the last of the four chief canons of textual criticism, which may be stated briefly as follows: Other things being equal, one prefers (1) the more difficult reading, (2) the shorter reading, (3) the metrical reading, (4) the varied reading. Since, of several reasons why existing editions of *King Lear* are so extremely uncritical, I think inattention to these principles really is foremost, they require a little explanation. We prefer the harder reading on the ground that an author worth editing at all is likely to use expressions which will be *eased* into commonplace, inadvertently or deliberately, by scribes and actors and prompters and printers; thus "ponderous" is eased into "richer," "distaste" into "dislike," "threat-enraged" into "thereat enraged" (I.i.80, I.iii.14, IV.ii.75). The shorter reading is preferred on the ground that memory (of scribe or actor or compositor) dilutes and makes obvious what is compact and indirect in an author; the expansion of "Ha! Waking? Tis not so" into "sleeping, or wake-/ing; ha! sure tis not so" (I.iv.249) is a good example. This also illustrates the preference of metrical readings, which, when other things are equal, one follows on the ground that the author is a poet and his scribes and printers are not; a corollary of this canon, seldom mentioned, is that his editor should be a poet also, if possible not a bad one, and at any rate not one who, like Pope, imposes upon his author an alien metric. The varied

reading is preferred to repetition, because the eyes and memories of scribes and compositors are influenced by neighbouring lections into repetition of them, whereas the author varies his diction and phrasing. It should, but cannot, go without saying that these canons must be applied critically. Errors often produce readings as "hard" as they are unreal (for instance, Q at III.vii.43 and 59), genuine matter is omitted inadvertently and deliberately, scribes sometimes regulate an author's metre (so do actors, and it would be an insensitive editor who followed Q III.vii.70 in omitting Cordelia's repeated "I am," which makes the line one of Shakespeare's split alexandrines instead of a split pentameter), and authors repeat themselves. The present passage is a prime instance of one that needs care, knowledge, and a critical faculty. Let us suppose that a critic has observed not only that the Q phrase repeats Lear's earlier in the scene (I.iv.276) but also that F repeats Lear's at I.i.110, "Let it be so, thy truth then be thy dower." He has still to note that "yet haue I left a daughter" is simply a working phrase with nothing characteristic about it—one that would be repeated by Shakespeare fifty lines later only by inadvertence, and if so repeated, one hardly likely to be changed to "I haue another daughter" by anyone else (that there is no evidence of revision by the author I have said already). But "Let it be so" is a phrase of some power characteristic of Lear early in the play adjusting himself to violent disappointment, first at Cordelia's falling off, then at Goneril's; even without the syntactical lacuna, the metrical lacuna, and the folio's authority, its place in this dramatic pattern would guarantee it genuine. The critic will also know, and allow for in his decision against "yea" (see note above), the folio's curious dislike elsewhere of "yea," which in a few lines of 1 *Henry IV* it once sophisticates to "I" and once omits (I.ii.196, 204). [Compare Stone, p. 234; Werstine, *Division*, p. 279.]

[16] [Compare Urkowitz, *Revision*, pp. 44–46; McLeod, *Division*, pp. 176–77; Halio, *Tragedy*, p. 73.]

[17] [Compare McLeod, *Division*, pp. 177–79.]

[18] [Compare Duthie, *King Lear*, pp. 22–24; Duthie (1960), p. 133; Stone, p. 67; Jackson, *Division*, pp. 333–34, 344; Taylor, *Division*, pp. 381–82; Halio, *Tragedy*, pp. 72–73.]

[19] [Compare Duthie, *King Lear*, p. 30. Taylor (*Division*, pp. 367–68) observes: "But, aside from the fact that 'how, how' is not 'how now,' Q itself (but not F) had already used *Leir's* 'how' in Lear's preceding speech ('How, nothing can come of nothing, speake againe'). What happens between Q and F is simply a repositioning of the interjection, a postponement of Lear's first emotional burst—which hardly presupposes consultation or memory of the original source."]

[20] [Compare Duthie (1960), p. 133; Jackson, *Division*, pp. 333–34, 336.]

[21] I.i.85, 92, 115–16; II.ii.83. Although each case has been adjudged to F on its own merits, the four passages reinforce each other, of course, against Q. At IV.ii.29 the Q press reader similarly reverted to the proverbial form, the Q copy presumably being correct and agreeing with F.

[22] Alexander Schmidt's ingenious suggestion [*Zur Textkritik des "King Lear"* (Konigsberg: Dalkowski, 1879), in Furness, *Variorum*, V (1880), p. 15] that the actor of Lear was influenced here by the line he had spoken in *Julius Caesar* is weakened by the probability that Burbage played Brutus (cf., Baldwin, *The Organization and Personnel of the Shakespearean Company*, pp. 237–38) and strengthened again by his being onstage while Antony is speaking; but he would know the proverb. [Compare Duthie, *King Lear*, pp. 25–28; Jackson, *Division*, pp. 334–35, 339. Grace Iopollo persuasively argues: "In the Quarto, 'least' appears to mean 'not least in Lear's love,' while in the Folio, 'least' is used to mean 'youngest,' so that Lear offers her his affection in the Quarto and offers her affection to France and Burgundy in the Folio" ("Revising *King Lear* and Revising 'Theory,'" in her *Revising Shakespeare* [Cambridge, Mass.: Harvard University Press, 1991], p. 170). Laurie E. Maguire (*Shakespearean Suspect Texts: The "Bad"*

Quartos and Their Contexts [Cambridge University Press, 1996], p. 50) criticizes Greg's presumptuous confidence in "the impartiality of his interpretive sense": "Greg believes Q to be a memorial 'perversion' of F, rather than F a revision of Q. Rejecting Madeleine Doran's argument in favour of revision, he simply cites the above passages with the laconic challenge, 'If anybody can see revision in this passage his conception of poetical composition must be radically different from my own.' "]

²³ On May 24, 1946, in New York, for instance, the Old Vic actor of Pistol gave *2 Henry IV* II.iv.179 as "That cannot go but *more than* thirty mile a day."

²⁴ M. R. Ridley ([New Temple Shakespeare (London: Dent; New York: Dutton & Co., 1935)—an edition based on the quarto], p. x) thinks Q shows "vigorous brevity" here and calls F "polished." With such taste, as with the illiterate pronouncements of B.A.P. Van Dam (who reproaches Dr. Greg, for instance, for not seeing that Q II.iv.225, quoted above, is quite all right but for the "unpoetically applied word *rather*," which he therefore omits [Van Dam, *The Text of Shakespeare's "Lear*," Materials for the Study of the Old English Drama, new series, Vol. 10 (Louvain: Librairie Universitaire/Uystpruyst, 1935), p. 94]), argument is impossible; and I have thought it my duty to ignore criticism which showed plainly that its author was not a critic. Still, a fact is a fact, and for once I will point it out. The fact is that F is proved genuine by the necessity of Lear's "downe," without which the Fool's following speech is meaningless ("Cry to it Nunckle, as the Cockney did . . . downe wantons, downe").

²⁵ [Compare Duthie, *King Lear*, pp. 44–45; Stone, p. 51.]

²⁶ To diagnose any single reading as a coincidence of course will not affect the argument; the critic who is willing to rely on chance must be willing to ascribe to it the major portion of the readings cited. I may add that at every stage of the enquiry I have been alive to the possibility of all these, and other, corruptions in F.

²⁷ Anyone who thinks Q may be genuine should examine Bartlett [*A Complete Concordance or Verbal Index to Words, Phrases and Passages in the Dramatic Works of Shakespeare* (New York and London: Macmillan, 1896)] under the heads *Hundred* and *Twenty*.

²⁸ Greg, *Editorial Problem*, p. 91. Cf. *Hamlet* III.ii.37: "I haue thought some of Natures Iornimen had made men, and not made them well." [Compare Maguire, *Shakespearean Suspect Texts*, p. 50: "Given that a craftsman's apprenticeship lasted seven years, Q's reading is the greater insult. Greg rejects it in favour of F's 'sober sense': 'Shakespeare knows that art is long.' The tell-tale present tense ('art is long') . . . shows that we are not dealing with detached analysis. Instead, personal moral outlook is being passed off as textual logic. (And confidence in his personal moral outlook encourages Greg to assert textual certainty when he might better have rested in doubt.)"]

²⁹ Schmidt, *Zur Textkritik des "King Lear"* (1879); see Furness, *New Variorum*, pp. 367–70.

³⁰ [Greg, "The Function of Bibliography" (1933); *Variants* (1940); *Editorial Problem* (1942).] Almost our whole knowledge which is true, that is. The exceptions to this generalization are P. A. Daniel [in his introduction to *M. William Shak-speare's "King Lear": The First Quarto 1608*, a facsimile by C. Praetorius (1885)] and Miss Madeleine Doran [*The Text of "King Lear."*]

³¹ "Oft" and "nought" rime in *Passionate Pilgrim* 339–40.

³² [Compare Greg, *Variants*, p. 94; Duthie, *King Lear*, pp. 41–42 ("I find it much easier to hold a reporter responsible than to hold a scribe or the compositor responsible"); Greg, *The Shakespeare First Folio* (Oxford: Clarendon Press, 1955), p. 378; Stone, p. 15 ("just conceivably, misreadings"), p. 198; Urkowitz, pp. 132–33 ("Greg fails to recognize that the difference between 'a dogge, so bade in office' from the Quarto and 'a dog's obeyed in office' is more likely caused by graphical confusion (i.e., related to the written forms of the words) rather than phonetic error during dictation (caused by similarity of sounds). The two versions have distinct speech stresses and pauses and distinguishable consonant sounds when read aloud"); René

Notes

Weis, *King Lear: A Parallel Text Edition* (Harlow, Essex: Longman, 1993), p. 252 ("Q's version *a dogge, so bade in office* may suggest an auditory error, since its phonetic pattern is virtually identical to that of F's correct reading, perhaps because a compositor carried the line in his head and misremembered it"); and Maguire, *Shakespearean Suspect Texts*, p. 197 ("aural errors . . . can arise in almost any mode of transmission. We cannot exclude the possibility of mishearing by a scribe of a dictator, or by a compositor of himself"). See also Walker, *Textual Problems*, pp. 40–44. Urkowitz adds: "An explanation less exotic than surreptitious dictation can account for the Quarto text's 'mishearing' of 'in sight' for 'incite' . . . 'In sight' appears as one of the rhyming words in an exit-couplet, Cordelia's last speech in 4.4 . . . In its poetic context, the mishearing turns out to be an instance of eye-rhyming. In fact, the Folio prints the rhyming words as 'incite' and 'Rite.' The Quarto and Folio spellings seem much more likely to be products of the poet or the compositor than the products of dictation and mishearing."]

[33] McKerrow (*An Introduction to Bibliography*, 1927, pp. 241–46) has an admirable summary.

[34] As "strangenesse" for "strange Newes," II.i.89, and compare the next page. [Compare Trevor Howard-Hill, "The Problem of Manuscript Copy for Folio *King Lear*," *The Library*, 6th series, 4 (1982), pp. 1–24; Jay L. Halio, *The Tragedy of King Lear*: Cambridge University Press, 1992), pp. 65–68.]

[35] [Compare Duthie, p. 180; Stone, pp. 60, 101, 220.]

[36] V.iii.229. Goneril's call to Oswald might be considered a displacement.

[37] Greg, "The Function of Bibliography," 1933, p. 256. Dr. Leo Kirschbaum in a recent study (*The True Text of "King Lear"* [Baltimore: The Johns Hopkins Press, 1945]) thinks Q a memorial reconstruction of this simple type, but since he makes no attempt to account for the absence in Q of the four characteristics listed above, the opinion need not be taken seriously. It is based, I believe, on two misconceptions: (1) an impression that one can argue from the *communal* memorial reconstruction theory for the *Richard III* quarto (to be discussed shortly) to a *single* reporter for *Lear*; (2) an impression that wrongly assigned speeches rule out short-hand. But Dr. Kirschbaum is so categorical that he may mislead some students, and I think I must give some warning against his methods by citing one or two examples of them. Of "Hornes wealk'd and waued like the enridged Sea" he says: "Q's 'enridged' for F's (IV.vi.71) 'enraged' seems definitely more poetic—but it is a mishearing by the reporter and is not Shakespeare's" (p. 56). This is formula, not criticism. "Enridged" in such a context is really not the sort of word that *can* be a corruption; but if a critic should become doubtful, it is readily and amply supported by Nashe's "ridged tides" (iii.198) and Shakespeare's frequent nonce words, in plays of this period, in "en-," esp. enlink'd, entrenched, enclouded. Dr. Kirschbaum should have known this or found it out, but the truth is that he never troubles with evidence nor is troubled by doubt. "Enraged" is the deliberate sophistication of an unfamiliar word, like too many others in the First Folio. Dr. Kirschbaum knows nothing of this process either, and nothing of misreading (see his pp. 34, 66), and indeed it would be difficult to discover what he knows.

[38] Ms. in the Northwestern University Library. If this had been published in the dark age of criticism, when it was written, it might have done great good; and McJohnston deserves honour, not only as the author of the first detailed study of the *Lear* texts not based upon a fantasy of revision, but also as a pioneer in methods then I think quite unknown: analysis of stage directions, of actors' parts, even of spelling. He was the first critic to cite many errors in Q which have since become well known. Unluckily I secured a microfilm of his thesis only after my work was largely done, and the statement in it most suggestive to me, that Q omission occurs more frequently in prose than in verse, is not borne out by my figures (35:76).

[39] J. Q. Adams, "The Quarto of *King Lear* and Shorthand," *Modern Philology* XXXI:2 (November 1933), pp. 135–63; Oskar Stössel, *Stenographische Studien zu Shakespeares "King Lear"*

(Wurzburg: Richard Mayr, 1937); Madeleine Doran, "The Quarto of *King Lear* and Bright's Shorthand," *Modern Philology* XXXIII (1935), pp. 139–57.

⁴⁰ W. Matthews: On Charactery, "Shorthand and the Bad Shakespeare Quartos," *Modern Language Review* XXVII:3 (July 1932), pp. 243–62, and "Shakespeare and the Reporters," *The Library* XV:4 (March 1935), pp. 481–500; the arguments from reported sermons, chiefly by H. T. Price, are here reviewed and qualified out of existence. On Brachygraphy, "Peter Bales, Timothy Bright and William Shakespeare," *JEGP* XXXIV:4 (October 1935), pp. 483–510.

⁴¹ 538 characters are reproduced with Max Förster's "Zur Shakespeare-Stenographie," *Shakespeare-Jahrbuch* LXVIII (1932), pp. 87–102, which also lists the enthusiastic German studies of Charactery.

⁴² Both men perhaps had earlier systems, presumably cruder, than those they published (cf. William J. Carlton, *Timothe Bright, Doctor of Phisicke: A Memoir of "the Father of Modern Shorthand"* [London: Elliott Stock, 1911], pp. 65–66, and *DNB* on Bales). Bales's third edition, called *A New Year's Gift to England* (1600), is described by the only critic who has examined it as "not really a stenographic system at all, but a system of abbreviations . . . merely a kind of advertisement to arouse interest in Brachygraphy" (Harry R. Hoppe, "The Third (1600) Edition of Bales's *Brachygraphy*," in *JEGP* XXXVII:4 [October 1938], pp. 537–41); the one copy known is in Paris.

⁴³ So that Dr. Adams's citation for instance of "Leige:Lord" (I.i.36) is inadmissible. Miss Doran, in her patient and admirable refutation of his claims for Charactery, is more careful than are any of the advocates whom I have read; even Dr. Adams ignores the related corruption surrounding some of his examples and relies continually upon the most hypothetical explanations as if they were *evidence*.

⁴⁴ David Lyall Patrick, *The Textual History of "Richard III,"* Publications: Stanford University VI:1 (1936).

⁴⁵ A paragraph of G. I. Duthie's untitled review of Greg, *The Editorial Problem in Shakespeare* (Oxford, 1942), in *Modern Language Review* XXXVIII:3 (July 1943), pp. 256–57. I believe Dr. Duthie is at present elaborating this view; but meanwhile of course he must not be held responsible for my development and criticism of it, development which I hope he will better and criticism to which I hope he will conclusively reply. (See Duthie, *Elizabethan Shorthand and the First Quarto of "King Lear"* [Oxford: Basil Blackwell, 1949].)

⁴⁶ Greg, *Editorial Problem*, p. 86. Patrick (*The Textual History of "Richard III,"* p. 148) does not attempt to decide.

⁴⁷ The change in the company's policy appears to be marked by the order in the Stationers' Register, August 4, 1600, to "stay" the printing of three of Shakespeare's plays. It is less interesting that this order did not save *Henry V*, which was pirated the same year, than that evidently it did save *As You Like It*, which never appeared in quarto. The third, *Much Ado*, was one of the last group of four "good" texts, all released in the autumn of 1600; owing no doubt to the competition of the boys' companies during 1599–1600 and the order of June 22, 1600, limiting performances to two a week, the Chamberlain's Men were pressed for money and sold printing rights. Then they clamped down.

⁴⁸ Butter's early career has been touched on and will be developed; on Busby (the elder) see W. W. Greg, "The Two John Busby's," *The Library* XXIV:1, 2 (June, September 1943), pp. 81–86. That Henry Gosson did not enter *Pericles* himself means little, but that he published it after Blount's entry makes the publication suspicious. I don't think Blount's registration of *Pericles* and *Antony and Cleopatra* on May 20, 1608, can be considered evidence for relaxation on the part of the players. What appear to be receipt marks for the entrance fees are deleted in the Register, presumably cancelling the entries (Greg, *Editorial Problem*, 1942, p. 20¹). The King's Men bore the expense of part of a heavy fine at about the time of the entry (Chambers,

Notes

The Elizabethan Stage, II, pp. 213, 53, and I, p. 327); it is possible that they considered selling the right to print two Shakespearean plays, let Blount enter them, and then decided against it.

[49] Quoted by Sisson ("Shakespeare Quartos as Prompt-Copies, with Some Account of Cholmeley's Players and a New Shakespeare Allusion," *Review of English Studies* XVII:70 [April 1942], pp. 129–43) from St. Ch. 8, 19–20. The evidence supports an old suggestion of Greg's in an untitled review of E. M. Albright, *Dramatic Publications in England, 1580–1640* (1927), in *RES* IV:13 (January 1928), p. 96. I agree with Professor Sisson in thinking there is no likelihood that Sir Richard Cholmeley's Players (as he calls them) were using the old *Leir.*

[50] *Q Lear* could be played if necessary by a dozen actors, Edgar doubling Burgundy, Oswald France, and the Gentlemen, Messengers, etc., being divided among Cornwall (obit III.vii), Albany (absent during most of II, III, IV), and the Fool (obit III.vi).

[51] Leicester (August 1606) seems to be the northernmost visit recorded. Curiously, there is a mention in 1629 of "his Majesty's servants for the city of York" (Bentley, pp. 271–73).

[52] Dr. Greg, in a passage (*Editorial Problem,* pp. 43–44) written before Sisson's publication, is dubious about the companies' view of piracy; but the passage is a little rhetorical, being directed against "continuous copy." Weight must be given to Heywood's well-known statement of 1633: "Others of [my plays] are still retained in the hands of some Actors, who thinke it against their peculiar profit to haue them come in Print."

[53] A 3,071-line text of *King Lear* at the Old Vic played 3 hours, 11 minutes (Chambers, *Shakespearean Gleanings,* p. 40); Elizabethans would be faster.

[54] Alfred Hart, *Shakespeare and the Homilies,* pp. 77–153; reprinted from *RES* (1932 and 1934).

[55] F 2 *Henry VI,* F 2 *Henry IV,* F *Hamlet, Cymbeline.*

[56] "I can offer no explanation why the folio texts of these four plays [*Richard III, 2 Henry IV, Othello, Troilus and Cressida*] should be greater than those of the respective quarto texts, except that Heminge and Condell tried to offer them to the readers 'cur'd, and perfect of their limbes'; nor do I attempt to explain why the folio *Hamlet* and *King Lear* should have omitted so many lines already published. Any explanation is a guess" (Hart, *Stolne and Surreptitious Copies: A Comparative Study of Shakespeare's Bad Quartos* [Melbourne University Press, 1942], p. 136).

[57] Chambers, *Shakespearean Gleanings,* pp. 39–40.

[58] Chambers, *The Elizabethan Stage,* II, p. 543.

[59] From the entry on the Stationers' Register (November 26, 1607): "A booke called. Mr William Shakespeare his historye of Kynge Lear as yt was played before the kinges maiestie at Whitehall vppon St Stephans night at christmas Last"; and the records of court performances (Chambers, *WS,* II, p. 334).

[60] They seem to have begun at ten o'clock (one at court on January 7, 1610, did). One, one-thirty, and 2 a.m. are recorded for court and private endings in Elizabeth's reign; on May 20, 1619, a night of very elaborate feasting, *Pericles* lasted till two in the King's great chamber. At the Bishop of Lincoln's in September 1631 a "playe or tragidie" with an ass's head (not certainly *A Midsummer Night's Dream*) "began aboute tenn of the clocke at night, and ended about two or three of the clock in the morning" (Chambers, *Elizabethan Stage,* I, p. 225; *William Shakespeare,* II, pp. 346, 350). Feasting and some dancing aside, but hardly a jig (for Hart the jig is "invariable," but as usual his confidence exceeds the evidence, and I do not myself trust even Knolles's remark of 1606—for which see Baskervill [Charles Read Baskervill, *The Elizabethan Jig and Related Song Drama* (University of Chicago Press, 1929), p. 114]); three hours were certainly available.

Hart has made Chambers doubtful, it is true, even about three-hour performances at court —why I do not know—except that it rather suits Sir Edmund's mood in this admirable essay ("William Shakespeare: An Epilogue") to subordinate the playmaker to the artist. Is he prepared, I wonder, to abandon his views of *Q Lear,* F *Hamlet, Q Richard III,* etc.?

Notes

[61] Greg, *Editorial Problem*, p. 96.

[62] John Tucker Murray, *English Dramatic Companies, 1558–1642*, Vol. I: *London Companies, 1558–1642* (London: Constable, 1910), p. 151; Chambers, WS, I, p. 78.

[63] Chambers, WS, II, p. 334.

[64] Nichols, *The Progresses, Processions, and Magnificent Festivities*, II, p. 145.

[65] Not much more is known now than when Chambers wrote, reviewing Greg: "I do not think that there is anything which shows that the conditions of provincial performance or the tastes of provincial audiences entailed shorter plays than were customary in London. There is not much evidence one way or the other. There are examples of local regulations requiring performances to be over by 5, 6, 7 or 9 o'clock. In one case it is 5 in winter and 6 in summer. A late 'bill' of 1624 advertised a performance to begin at 1 o'clock. Clearly there is margin here for a three-hour play" (Chambers, untitled review of W. W. Greg, *Two Elizabethan Stage Abridgements* [1923], in *The Library* IV:3 [December 1, 1923], p. 245). When the available *cast* was reduced, of course abridgement was necessary. F *Lear* is clearly such a text.

[66] In *King Lear* this problem is difficult.

[67] *If* we should suppose this, it facilitates the discarded copy's getting to a publisher.

[68] Duthie, untitled review, *Modern Language Review* XXXVIII:3 (July 1943), p. 257.

[69] I.i.191 may be another late arrangement in F.

[70] In general, I have tried to avoid citing editors of the play either for support or for refutation, because their support, resting upon very incomplete analysis, is ambiguous, and their errors—it is best to speak frankly—are legion. Capell, Dyce, Furness, I think, are most often critical, and there is scarcely any editor who is not praiseworthy in some details; but I have an impression that *King Lear* confused, puzzled, and wearied them all. The Cambridge text can only be called shocking, as distinct from its collation; a distinction critics would gain by making.

[71] By a conjecture in which I am anticipated by Furness [H. H. Furness, *A New Variorum Edition of Shakespeare*, V: *King Lear*, Philadelphia, 1880], the same thing happened at III.vii.77 and the error was reproduced by F.

[72] It is irrelevant that F, which has been cutting in this passage, omits the preceding line.

[73] The plausibility of this explanation cannot be estimated without a knowledge of the press reader's activities. [Compare Duthie, *King Lear*, pp. 88, 392–93; Duthie, *Elizabethan Shorthand*, p. 46, 72; Urkowitz, *Revision*, pp. 36–38; Halio, *Tragedy*, p. 73; Foakes, *King Lear*, pp. 131–32. McLeod (*Division*, pp. 180–82, 192–93) derides Duthie's allegation of scribal error as "one of his most convoluted and fantastic editorial flights."]

[74] Perhaps worse than the vagueness I have noted in Q with regard to Oswald is its definiteness: he gets his name only in the prefixes to I.iv.358 (condemned) and 360, immediately after being *named by Goneril* for the first time (F 336 lost in Q). I suspect that Q knew who Curan is (II.i.1) only because he is named at once. This evidence is hard on dictation. [See also Stone, *Textual History*, pp. 21–22.]

[75] Twenty-eight of these are marked in F, all the others (save five, in which Q may be supposed to have influenced F) being for attendants.

[76] See note on the S.D. [stage direction] in F.

[77] Some even of these directions may have been added to Q in the printing house: III.iii.20 "Exit" is off-line in the margin of a narrow measure passage in Q, no doubt added, and the press reader added "A Letter" at IV.vi.266. These may not have stood in the copy, and conceivably the marginal notes at I.ii.145 and II.iv.297 were not. But the argument is frail, since the compositor may have omitted directions, both these and others.

[78] [Compare Foakes, *King Lear* (1997), pp. 401–2.]

[79] Taken over verbatim by F.

[80] Vague for F, which deletes; cf. "with Torches" F II.i.38, III.iv.115.

[81] "Leister" is the compositor's blunder; he expanded contractions wrongly in IV.vi.1 and

IV.ii.15 ("Edmund" for Edgar, and vice versa). [See also Wells and Taylor, *William Shake-speare: A Textual Companion*, p. 510; Maguire, *Shakespearean Suspect Texts*, p. 270.]

[82] J. Q. Adams's interesting collection of verbal similarities between Q directions like this and those of the reported 1 *If You Know Not Me, You Know Nobody* can prove nothing since he relies on similarities which are meaningless and ignores the much more definite character of S.D.'s in the Heywood report ("The Quarto of *King Lear* and Shorthand," *Modern Philology* XXXI:2 [November 1933], pp. 141–43).

[83] Hypocritically.

[84] Owing to the persistence of authors' directions and to general human impredicability. Cf. Greg, *Editorial Problem*, pp. 36ff. [Stone (*Textual History*, pp. 20–22) likewise stresses that "the character of the stage directions . . . indicates that they originated with a spectator"; while Taylor (*Division*, p. 404) nonchalantly remarks: "Q, characteristically of a foul-paper text, often fails to supply necessary entrances and exits . . . F, characteristically of a prompt-book, supplies almost all such necessary directions." Maguire (*Shakespearean Suspect Texts*, pp. 216–21) argues that it is misleading to equate descriptive stage directions with a reported text—though even she feels suspicious of the "additive" and "indeterminate" style of stage directions in the case, for example, of *The Taming of a Shrew* (p. 309). Weis remarks, in *King Lear: A Parallel Text Edition*, "The Q stage directions can with reasonable confidence be taken to point to holograph copy" (p. 36).]

[85] "and for you her owne for Venter": see note on IV.vi.276 [unavailable]. The compositor is probably responsible for this corruption.

[86] In this very unlikely event, however, the variant "in the hoast" would become worse for dictation than for performance. I may note that unluckily *Richard III* has no scroll pieces to serve for comparison, unless a couplet may be thought to.

[87] One historian, an advocate, however, says that "for upwards of 230 years no successful attempt was made seriously to exceed the limits [in the application of phonetic knowledge to the problems of speed-writing] he adopted in 1602" (A. T. Wright, *John Willis and Edmond Willis*, The Willis-Byrom Club, 1926, p. 70). Contrast a writer in *Encyclopaedia Britannica* (1911), XXIV, p. 1009.

[88] This is the apt description of a critic who has no faith in shorthand, Miss Madeleine Doran ("The Quarto of *King Lear* and Bright's Shorthand," *Modern Philology* XXXIII:2 [November 1935], pp. 139–57).

[89] Since all the early shorthand books are very rare, I may mention that I have deposited my transcript of the relevant parts of Willis (1602) in the Princeton University Library.

[90] W. Matthews, "A Postscript to 'Shorthand and the Bad Shakespeare Quartos,' " *Modern Language Review* XXVIII:1 [January 1933], p. 83 (which refers back to an article in *MLR* XXVII [July 1932], pp. 243ff.). Mr. W. J. Carlton had then recently purchased the manuscript; so far as I know, it has not been examined in print, and it should be, although without a parallel good text such study is always inconclusive.

[91] John Willis disclaims teaching shorthand, and Bright was a Yorkshire parson; the statement cannot refer only to Bales.

[92] [See Chambers, *Elizabethan Stage*, III, p. 342; WS, I, p. 147; Heywood, *Pleasant Dialogues and Dramas*, R5ʳ, in *If You Know Not Me, You Know Nobody*, ed. Madeleine Doran (Malone Society Reprints, 1934), p. xxxviii; G. N. Giordano-Orsini, "Thomas Heywood's Play on *The Troubles of Queen Elizabeth*," *The Library*, 4th series, 14 (1933–34), p. 338.]

[93] To G. N. Giordano-Orsini's demonstration ["Thomas Heywood's Play on *The Troubles of Queen Elizabeth*"] in *The Library*, 4th series, 14 (1933), pp. 313–38, add the evidence on p. xvii of the Malone Society reprint of the play (1934) edited by Miss Doran and Dr. Greg.

Notes

⁹⁴ [Compare Maguire (*Shakespearean Suspect Texts*, p. 103), who remarks that it is "the belatedness of Heywood's testimony"—which actually dates from 1637, not 1630–32—"that renders it less reliable than it might have been thirty years earlier. Our confidence in the statement also depends on whether it should be taken literally as a reference to the plot, for surely longhand would suffice for a scenario? In his analysis of Q1 *If You Know Not Me* Giordano-Orsini concludes that the text is a memorial reconstruction; Heywood, he says, was mistaken in his suggestion of shorthand, or, if shorthand were used, it was supplemented by other means."]

⁹⁵ [See John Webster, *The Devil's Law Case*, New Mermaids, ed. Elizabeth M. Brennan (London: Ernest Benn, 1975), IV.ii.26–27.]

⁹⁶ Cf. Mathews, "Shakespeare and the Reporters," *The Library* XV:4 (March 1935), p. 487: "The efficiency of a stenography depends upon its being mechanical. When a stenographer has to pen words at an average rate of three per second, he has no opportunity to consider meanings . . . One seldom remembers what one has written." [Compare also Duthie, *Elizabethan Shorthand*, pp. 23–24: "There can be no doubt that the words 'treatable' and 'treatably' refer to utterance of exceptional clarity, distinctness, and slowness . . . It is safe, I imagine, to suppose that the King's Men would not speak very much of *King Lear* treatably. Yet Willis demands treatable speech for *verbatim* reporting."]

⁹⁷ *The Tragedy of King Richard II* (1598), reproduced in facsimile, with an introduction by Alfred W. Pollard (London: Bernard Quaritch, 1916), p. 64. Dover Wilson thinks the copy was probably "composite in origin" (*King Richard II*, ed. John Dover Wilson [Cambridge University Press, 1939], p. 113), a notion for which I find no real evidence and cannot help thinking, in so short a copy, very implausible. Neither examines the passage in detail.

⁹⁸ IV.vi.180, 220. I cannot forbear to mention that the Cambridge editors, whose judgement in this scene was faultier than usual, actually print "Henry" at 180 and "Harry" at 220.

⁹⁹ The exception is "all" omitted in 237. F's addition "me" to this line is, I am afraid, a sophistication; see Abbott no. 192.

¹⁰⁰ Some of Q4's lining is like the worst passages in *Lear*; I doubt its copy had any division.

¹⁰¹ I dare not hope that it will prevent Dr. Kirschbaum from thinking the passage, on no evidence, a memorial reconstruction.

¹⁰² Miss Madeleine Doran writes of *Lear*: "It is interesting to compare the situation with that in *Troilus and Cressida*, which comes nearest of the good texts (barring *Richard III*) to K.L. in abundance of variation. There are about half as many variants in *T.C.* (621) as in *K.L.* (1382) and the proportion holds roughly for nearly every type of variant. Such constancy in proportion is remarkable if a very different factor . . . has entered into the element of variation in one of the plays" ("The Quarto of *King Lear* and Bright's Shorthand," p. 142). I agree that this would be remarkable, even in bodies of variation differing so decisively in *bulk*, and I am bound to report that my own studies have given different results. But more instructive than mathematics are the following textual facts: (1) *Lear* shows nothing resembling the hundred continuous lines in *Troilus* (II.ii.108–208) with only one variant, a singular-plural one; (2) *Troilus* displays, so far as I can discover, no patterns of interpolation remotely similar to Goneril's *Come sir*'s; nor (3) have I found in it the distant anticipations and recollections which prove *Lear* an actor's text. [For *Othello*, see E.A.J. Honigmann, *The Texts of "Othello" and Shakespearian Revision* (London: Routledge, 1996); notably reviewed by John Jowett, "The Milk of the Wood," *TLS*, August 23, 1996, pp. 13–14.]

¹⁰³ III.iv.39. F's entry for Edgar and the Fool is proved to be as usual too early by the Fool's "Come not *in* heere Nuncle" (40).

¹⁰⁴ I think the Fool's final line and Lear's dying words, both no doubt spoken weakly, and both missing in Q, are further examples (III.vi.92, V.iii.310–11).

¹⁰⁵ The objections to the dictation theory, that is, which I have set out; I do not think it impossible.

¹⁰⁶ II.iv.238. My statement has no references to the passages cut in F; lines may be lost irretrievably in IV.iii.

STAGING

¹ [See below for JB's letters to W. W. Greg of December 14, 1945, and February 16, 1946, with Greg's replies of January 6, February 28, and March 1, 1946.]

² Capell described the character cut from F as a "Physician," but the Globe's normalization "Doct." can scarcely deprive him of the emendation.

³ By "F authority" I mean the authority of regular transmission which determines readings in favour of F when proper editorial decision is impossible. Shakespeare, who elided a good deal, may here have written "of his sleepe," correctly spoken by the actor, taken by the reporter, and reproduced by the Q compositor—to be deleted on metrical grounds by the folio editor, or reduced to "*of 's*" by him and misunderstood by F compositor as deleted altogether. Or Shakespeare may have written "of 's," or, as in F, "of." The last seems to me most likely. But all judgement can tell us is that we have no real ground for decision here except in recension; there is insufficient reason in this phrase even to *suspect, much less to convict*, F *of* corruption or sophistication, and we follow it. Q order in 23 is condemned by cadence as well as authority.

⁴ It may be noted that F2 independently corrected to "doubt not of."

⁵ The book keeper "is careful to add missing entries. He does not trouble about exits, and many, clearly required by the action, remain unnoted" (Chambers, *WS*, I, p. 120).

⁶ Considering F's addition of noises, it is very unlikely that a direction "Musick" is omitted inadvertently. (Is *any* obvious noise omitted??) F's direction is new, not from Q.

⁷ For a different account, which I believe is incompatible with the text, see G. F. Reynolds, *Staging of Elizabethan Plays* (1940), p. 83. Reynolds does not notice that Sir Thomas is put into the stocks onstage: "I haue a warrant here," says the Jailor, "to make two knots to tye your ancles in . . . heere they are ready, sir./*Sir Tho.* How, slaue?/*Iay.* Nay, come, resist not . . . put in your bearers." See Bullen's edition of the play, pp. 76–80, in *Works of John Day* (1881). Reynolds notes that this is *the only* Red Bull play which appears to use stocks.

⁸ [Compare William A. Ringler, Jr., "Shakespeare and His Actors: Some Remarks on *King Lear*," in *Shakespeare's Art from a Comparative Perspective*, ed. Wendell M. Aycock (Lubbock, Tex.: Tech Press, 1981), pp. 183–94; John Meagher, "Economy and Recognition: Thirteen Shakespearean Puzzles," *Shakespeare Quarterly* 35 (1984), pp. 7–21; Richard Abrams, "The Double Casting of Cordelia and Lear's Fool," *Texas Studies in Literature and Language* 27 (1985), pp. 354–68; Skiles Howard, "Attendants and Others in Shakespeare's Margins: Doubling in the Two Texts of *King Lear*," *Theatre Survey* 32 (1991), pp. 187–213; Halio, *Tragedy*, pp. 34–35; Foakes, *King Lear*, pp. 146–48.]

⁹ Edgar's greeting him below with "Haile gentle Sir" does not really controvert this, and is taken from Q, in which arrangement the Gentleman had someone to address *besides* Edgar.

THE CONCEIVING OF *King Lear*

¹ [Compare Martin Mueller, "From Leir to Lear," *Philological Quarterly* 73:2 (Spring 1994), pp. 195–217.]

² [Wilfrid Perrett, *The Story of King Lear from Geoffrey of Monmouth to Shakespeare* (Berlin: Mayer & Müller, 1904 [*Palaestra* XXXV]). Kenneth Muir did not much consider Camden in his Arden edition of *King Lear* (1952, p. xxxvi note), but added a footnote to the corrected

Notes

edition (1972, pp. xxxii–xxxiii), referring in particular to S. Musgrove ("The Nomenclature of *King Lear*," *RES* VII:27 [July 1956], pp. 294–98), who argues that Shakespeare chose the Anglo-Saxon names from Camden principally because of their etymological significance. See also *Essays in Criticism* XLIII:1 (January 1993), pp. 10–11.]

³ [See R. A. Law in *PMLA* XXVII [n.s. XX] (1912), pp. 117–41.]

⁴ [Perrett, *The Story of King Lear*, pp. 121–23. On Camden (who admired Shakespeare), see Sir Maurice Powicke, "William Camden," in *English Studies 1948*, ed. F. P. Wilson.]

⁵ [As Berryman noted in another draft of this essay, Shakespeare took none of his names from Sidney's *Arcadia*.]

LETTERS ON *Lear*

¹ See JB's essay "Staging" (above), which was probably not yet written at this date.

² Greg discusses the emendation "alapt:ataxt" in "The Function of Bibliography in Literary Criticism Illustrated in a Study of the Text of *King Lear*," *Neophilogus* 18 (1933), p. 258. His review of Kellner, *Restoring Shakespeare*, appeared in *RES* I (1925), pp. 463–78. See Berryman's "Textual Introduction," p. 179.

³ See W. W. Greg, *The Variants in the First Quarto of "King Lear": A Bibliographical and Critical Inquiry*, supplement to the Bibliographical Society's Transactions, no. 15 (London: Bibliographical Society, 1940), p. 174; Weis, *King Lear*, p. 226.

⁴ See Hart, *Shakespeare and the Homilies*.

⁵ McKerrow, *Prolegomena for the Oxford Shakespeare*.

⁶ Alexander Schmidt, *Shakespeare-Lexicon* (2 vols., 1874–75; 3rd edn., 1902); Onions, *A Shakespeare Glossary*.

WILLIAM HOUGHTON, WILLIAM HAUGHTON, *The Shrew*, AND THE *Sonnets*

¹ Charles William Wallace, "New Shakespeare Discoveries: Shakespeare as a Man among Men," *Harper's Monthly Magazine* CXX (March 1910), pp. 489–510; "Shakespeare and His London Associates as Revealed in Recently Discovered Documents," *University Studies of the University of Nebraska* 10:4 (October 1910), pp. 261–300.

² Hotson, *Shakespeare versus Shallow*.

³ Charles J. Sisson (ed.), *Thomas Lodge and Other Elizabethans* (Cambridge, Mass.: Harvard University Press, 1933), p. v.

⁴ Perrett, *The Story of King Lear from Geoffrey of Monmouth to Shakespeare*, pp. 121–24, 238–39.

⁵ The remainder of this paragraph notably anticipates S. Musgrove, "The Nomenclature of *King Lear*," *Review of English Studies* VII:27 (July 1956), pp. 294–98. See also "The Conceiving of *King Lear*" above.

⁶ J. W. Lever, "Three Notes on Shakespeare's Plants," *Review of English Studies*, n.s. III:10 (1952), pp. 117–20.

⁷ Chambers, *WS*, II, p. 215; Holland's verses "Vpon the Lines and Life of the Famous Scenicke Poet, Master WILLIAM SHAKESPEARE" are quoted on p. 231.

⁸ DeWitt T. Starnes, "Shakespeare and Apuleius," *PMLA* LX (1945), pp. 1021–50.

⁹ Alfred Harbage, "Dating Shakespeare's Sonnets," *Shakespeare Quarterly* 1 (1950), pp. 57–63; Leslie Hotson, *Shakespeare's Sonnets Dated, and Other Essays* (London: Rupert Hart-Davis; New York: Oxford University Press; Toronto: Clarke, Irwin & Co., 1949). See also Edward Hubler, "Shakespeare's Sonnets Dated," *Shakespeare Quarterly* 1 (1950), pp. 78–83.

¹⁰ James G. McManaway, "Recent Studies in Shakespeare's Chronology," *Shakespeare Survey* 3 (1950), p. 31.

¹¹ James G. McManaway, "The Year's Contributions to Shakespearian Study: 3. Textual Studies," *Shakespeare Survey* 4 (1951), pp. 153–56 (citing Harbage on p. 155).

¹² Clifford Leech, "The Year's Contributions to Shakespearian Study: 2. Shakespeare's Life, Times and Stage," *Shakespeare Survey* 5 (1952), p. 138.

¹³ Harbage, "Dating Shakespeare's Sonnets," p. 58.

¹⁴ *The Sonnets*, New Variorum, ed. Hyder Edwin Rollins (Philadelphia and London: J. B. Lippincott Company, 2 vols., 1944).

¹⁵ See William Minto, *The Characteristics of English Poets* (1885), p. 371; Chambers, WS, I, p. 555. See also Robert Giroux, *The Book Known as Q: A Consideration of Shakespeare's Sonnets* (London: Weidenfeld and Nicolson, 1982), pp. 120–24.

¹⁶ See the *Riverside Shakespeare*, ed. G. Blakemore Evans (1974), p. 1844.

¹⁷ See Rollins, *The Sonnets*, I, pp. 147–49.

¹⁸ Thomas H. McNeal, " 'Every Man out of His Humour' and Shakespeare's 'Sonnets,' " *Notes and Queries* 197 (August 30, 1952), p. 376.

¹⁹ See too Arthur Platt, "*Edward III* and Shakespeare's Sonnets," *Modern Language Review* 6 (1911), pp. 511–13; *Shakespeare's Sonnets*, ed. C. F. Tucker Brooke (London: Oxford University Press, 1936); *Sonnets*, New Variorum, ed. Rollins, I, pp. 96, 170, 234–35, 290, 364; Claes Schaar, *Elizabethan Sonnet Themes and the Dating of Shakespeare's "Sonnets"* (Lund: Ohlsson, 1962); Giorgio Melchiori, *Shakespeare's Dramatic Meditations: An Experiment in Criticism* (Oxford: Clarendon Press, 1976).

²⁰ See Chambers, WS, I, pp. 515–18. Compare Kenneth Muir, "Shakespeare's Hand in *Edward III*," *Shakespeare as Collaborator*, pp. 10–30; Richard Proudfoot, who presents what he calls "a strong positive case" for Shakespeare's authorship ("*The Reign of King Edward the Third* (1596) and Shakespeare," *Proceedings of the British Academy* LXXI (Oxford University Press, 1986, pp. 159–85); John Kerrigan (ed.), *The Sonnets and A Lover's Complaint* (Harmondsworth, Middlesex: Penguin, 1986), pp. 293–95 (note on Sonnet 94.14); and Eliot Slater, whose stylometric analyses throw up the fascinating finding that Shakespeare did write the play, though he probably tackled Part A and Part B at different times (*The Problem of "The Reign of King Edward III": A Statistical Approach* [Cambridge University Press, 1988]). Jonathan Hope, who summarizes the evidence and arguments to date, and who adduces what he terms "quantitative socio-historical linguistic evidence," considers *Edward III* "the best candidate from the apocryphal plays for inclusion in the canon" (*The Authorship of Shakespeare's Plays: A Sociolinguistic Study*, pp. 133–37, 154). See also *Sources of Four Plays Ascribed to Shakespeare*, ed. G. Harold Metz (Columbia: University of Missouri Press, 1989), pp. 3–42; Giorgio Melchiori, *Shakespeare's Garter Plays: "Edward III" to "Merry Wives of Windsor"* (Newark: University of Delaware Press, 1994).

²¹ Rollins, II, p. 327; I, p. 62.

²² Ibid., I, p. 364.

²³ Ibid., p. 255.

²⁴ [JB] Malone noticed this, quoting *Odes*, Book IV, 29: "Les Muses lièrent un iour/De chaisnes de roses, Amour . . . l'emprissonerent." [Compare John Roe (ed.), *The Poems*, New Cambridge Shakespeare (Cambridge University Press, 1992, p. 85).] Ronsard had visited England; Watson and Sidney used him, Puttenham by 1589 was denouncing plagiarisms from him, but Daniel, Lodge, and Drayton kept eagerly on. There is no longer much question as to whether Shakespeare could read French. It is quite possible that Sonnets 24, 100, 122 borrow from Ronsard, and certain that *Timon* (IV.iii.438–45) uses the ode next but one after this used in *Venus and Adonis*.

²⁵ Chambers, *WS*, I, p. 324.

²⁶ Compare T. W. Baldwin, *Shakspeare's Love's Labour's Won: New Evidence from the Account Books of an Elizabethan Bookseller* (Carbondale: Southern Illinois University Press, 1957); but see also Eliot Slater, "Word Links with *All's Well that Ends Well*," *Notes & Queries* 222 (1977), pp. 109–12, and *The Problem of "The Reign of King Edward III*," pp. 84–85. Berryman's point here is supported by Roslyn L. Knutson's argument that Elizabethan theatre companies commonly duplicated play materials by means of sequels: "*Love's Labour's Lost* and *Love's Labour's Won* may have been genuine sequels. If Shakespeare changed the title of *Love's Labour's Won* to that of a now-extant play such as *AWW*, his doing so was at odds with a commercial practice that encouraged title echoes whether warranted or not" ("Influence of the Repertory System on the Revival and Revision of *The Spanish Tragedy* and *Dr. Faustus*," *English Literary Renaissance* 18:2 [Spring 1988], pp. 267–68 n. 19).

²⁷ See also E.A.J. Honigmann's detailed account: *John Weever: A Biography of a Literary Associate of Shakespeare and Jonson, Together with a Photographic Facsimile of Weever's "Epigrammes" (1599)* (Manchester University Press, 1987).

²⁸ Chambers, *The Elizabethan Stage*, III, p. 334.

²⁹ Alan Keen ("A Shakespearian Riddle," *TLS*, April 21, 1950) nominated the selfsame "William Hoghton" as a likely "W.H."

³⁰ John Weever, *Epigrammes in the Oldest Cut and Newest Fashion* (London: McKerrow/ Sidgwick & Jackson, 1911).

³¹ Berryman slightly misremembers the quotation, though he has the spirit of it. "Was then William Shakshafte," asked Chambers, "a player in 1581?" (*The Elizabethan Stage*, I, p. 280).

³² Chambers, *WS*, I, p. 324.

³³ C. H. Herford (ed.), *The Works of Shakespeare* (London: Macmillan, 1899), II, p. 4.

³⁴ Ibid.

³⁵ H. D. Gray, "Chronology of Shakespeare's Plays," *Modern Language Notes* XLVI (1931), pp. 147–50.

³⁶ JB's figure corresponds, albeit roughly, with what Kenneth Muir designated as the Shakespearean Part A (928 lines in sum) of *Edward III*, viz. I.ii.90ff., II, and IV.iv ("A Reconsideration of *Edward III*," *Shakespeare Survey* 6 [1953], pp. 39–48). See also Hart, "The Vocabulary of *Edward III*," *Shakespeare and the Homilies*, pp. 219–41; Muir, "Shakespeare's Hand in *Edward III*," *Shakespeare as Collaborator*, pp. 10–30; and see further below.

³⁷ Levin L. Schücking, "Shakespeare and *Sir Thomas More*," *Review of English Studies* 1 (1925), pp. 40–59. See also Thomas Clayton, "The 'Shakespearean' Addition in the Booke of Sir Thomas Moore: Some Aids to Scholarly and Critical Shakespearean Studies," *Shakespeare Studies Monograph Series* no. 1 (Vanderbilt University: The Center for Shakespeare Studies, 1969); Wells and Taylor, *William Shakespeare: The Complete Works*, pp. 124–25; G. Metz, " 'Voyce and Credyt': The Scholars and *Sir Thomas More*," in T. Howard-Hill (ed.), *Shakespeare and Sir Thomas More: Essays on the Play and Its Shakespearean Interest* (Cambridge University Press, 1989). M.W.A. Smith takes issue with the claim by Thomas Merriam ("Chettle, Munday, Shakespeare and *Sir Thomas More*," *Notes & Queries* 237 [1992], pp. 336–41; "Shakespeare, Stylometry and *Sir Thomas More*," *Studies in Philology* 89 [1992], pp. 434–44) that stylometry has revealed that *Sir Thomas More* should no longer be ascribed to Anthony Munday and that most of the play is by Shakespeare.

³⁸ *Johnson on Shakespeare*, I, p. 351.

³⁹ Now available as *The Diary of John Manningham of the Middle Temple, 1602–1603*, ed. R. W. Sorlien (Hanover, N.H.: University Press of New England, 1976).

⁴⁰ Professor G. E. ("Ged") Bentley (1901–94) was Murray Professor of English at Princeton University from 1945 to 1970. Born in Indiana, he had taken his doctorate on theatre history

with Allardyce Nicoll at London University, and taught for some years at Chicago. In 1941 he published the first two volumes of *The Jacobean and Caroline Stage*; by 1968 there would be seven volumes of the work, which was compared favourably with the achievement of Sir Edmund Chambers's *The Elizabethan Stage* (4 vols., 1923). His other publications include *Shakespeare and Jonson* (1945, 1965), *Shakespeare: A Biographical Handbook* (1961), *The Profession of Dramatist in Shakespeare's Time* (1964), *The Revels History of Drama in English* (Vol. IV, 1981), and *The Profession of Player in Shakespeare's Time* (1984).

THE *Sonnets*

¹ George Steevens (1780), quoted in *The Sonnets*, ed. Rollins, II, p. 336.

² Edmund Malone, *Supplement to the Edition of Shakespeare's Plays Published in 1778*, I (1780): Edward Dowden, *Sonnets* (1881); both quoted in Rollins, II, pp. 117–18.

³ Sidney Lee, *A Life of William Shakespeare* (London: Smith, Elder & Co., 1898), p. 154; quoted in Rollins, I, p. 113.

⁴ Rollins, II, p. 132.

⁵ Hotson, *Shakespeare's Sonnets Dated*.

⁶ James G. McManaway, "Recent Studies in Shakespeare's Chronology," *Shakespeare Survey* 3 (1950), p. 31.

⁷ Fripp, *Shakespeare, Man and Artist*, I, p. 311. See also Barbara Everett, "Shakespeare's Greening," *TLS*, July 8, 1994, pp. 11–13.

⁸ In other (undated) notes, Berryman reviewed the evidence as follows:

The first of our many questions about the sonnets is whether their publication by T. Thorpe in 1609 was authorized by the poet. I think the evidence suggests that it was.

1. Shakespeare was interested in fame. He'd published *Ven & Luc*, and many of the sonnets are about artistic immortality.

2. Who else wd have had so many, and addressed *both* to the young man and to the woman, to give a printer? Some had circulated among Shakespeare's friends for at least ten years, but so large a collection?

3. Who else would have had "A Lover's Complaint"?

4. No evidence of Shakespeare's resentment—as with Jaggard's *Passionate Pilgrimage*.

5. 1601—planned to retire?

Q *Troil*; Sh "Works"—Drummond 7H

6. A good text.

7. Why would anyone but the poet *want* them published?

Against all this can be set only the intensely personal, humiliating, and scandalous aspects of many of the sonnets—such that a man as sensitive & proud as Shakespeare may have not wanted to make them public. He certainly had hesitated long enough to do so. And why Thorpe? Richard Field had been a fellow townsman.

⁹ Rollins, I, p. 56.

¹⁰ Ibid., p. 176.

¹¹ But now compare Katherine Duncan-Jones, *Shakespeare's Sonnets*, Arden Shakespeare, 3rd series (Walton-on-Thames, Surrey: Thomas Nelson and Sons, 1997). See also *The Sonnets and A Lover's Complaint*, ed. John Kerrigan. Critical and biographical theories are fairly reviewed by Hugh Calvert, *Shakespeare's Sonnets, and Problems of Autobiography* (Braunton, Devon: Merlin Books, 1987)—though his conclusions are open to question.

¹² Rollins, II, pp. 284–88.

¹³ Ibid., I, p. 29.

¹⁴ Ibid., p. 55.

¹⁵ Ibid., p. 9.

Notes

[16] Ibid., p. 74.

[17] First noticed by Malone (ed. 1780); Rollins, I, p. 104.

[18] Rollins, I, p. 258.

[19] Ibid., p. 306.

The Comedy of Errors

[1] Chambers, WS, I, p. 311.

[2] Thomas Whitfield Baldwin, *William Shakespeare Adapts a Hanging* (Princeton University Press, 1931).

[3] Raysor (ed.), *Coleridge's Shakespearean Criticism*, I, p. 99.

1590: King John

[1] See E.A.J. Honigmann (ed.), *King John*, New Arden Shakespeare (London: Methuen, 1964). See also Brian Boyd, "*King John* and *The Troublesome Raigne*: Sources, Structure, Sequence," *Philological Quarterly* 74:1 (1995), pp. 37–56.

[2] Honigmann, p. xiv.

[3] J. Q. Adams, "A New Signature of Shakespeare?," *Bulletin of the John Rylands Library* XXVII (1943), pp. 256–59.

[4] Friedrick Kreyssig, *Vorlesungen über Shakespeare*, I (Berlin, 1877).

[5] [JB] One of these extraordinary coincidences that haunt Shakespearean studies is here too odd to neglect. Warburton, admitting the *Soliman and Perseda* connexion discovered by Theobald: "But the beauty of the passage consists in his alluding, at the same time, to his high original. His father, Richard I, was surnamed Coeur-de-Lion. And the *Cor Leonis*, a fixed star of the first magnitude, in the sign Leo, is called Basilisco(-us)." (This is quite true.) Johnson added: "Could one have thought it!"

[6] "Why on earth is 'James Gurney' so carefully named, by the way?" Berryman worried in his notes. "His part is *4 words*."

[7] Emrys Jones comments on the Bastard's reference to Colbrand in *Guy of Warwick*: "Such romance associations are not accidental. The Bastard *is* a folk-hero" (*The Origins of Shakespeare* [Oxford: Clarendon Press, 1977], p. 249).

[8] Alfred Harbage, "A Contemporary Attack upon Shakspere?," *The Shakespeare Association Bulletin* 16:1 (January 1941), pp. 42–49.

3 Henry VI

[1] Thomas V.N. Merriam and Robert A.J. Matthews, in "Neural Computation in Stylometry II: An Application to the Works of Shakespeare and Marlowe" (*Literary and Linguistic Computing* 9:1 [1994], pp. 1–6), argue from an analysis of stylometric characteristics that the anonymous plays *The Contention* and *The True Tragedy of Richard Duke of York* (1595) are by Marlowe, and that *3 Henry VI* "is a Shakespearean revision of a Marlovian original"; their findings thus support the claims put forward by C. F. Tucker Brooke, "The Authorship of the Second and Third Parts of 'King Henry VI,'" *Transactions of the Connecticut Academy of Arts and Sciences* 47 [1912], pp. 145–211.

The Two Gentlemen of Verona

[1] James G. McManaway, "Recent Studies in Shakespeare's Chronology," *Shakespeare Survey* 3 (1950), p. 25.

² R. Warwick Bond (ed.), *The Complete Works of John Lyly*, Vol. III (Oxford: Clarendon Press, 1902), pp. 232–34.

³ Our only text, F, is based on a transcript made thirty years later and can tell us little about the play's early conditions.

ON *Macbeth*

¹ See David Masson (ed.), *The Collected Writings of Thomas De Quincey*, Vol. X (London: A. & C. Black, 1897).

² Spurgeon, *Shakespeare's Imagery and What It Tells Us*; F.C. Kolbe, *Shakespeare's Way: A Psychological Study* (London: Sheed & Ward, 1930); Wolfgang H. Clemen, *The Development of Shakespeare's Imagery* (Cambridge, Mass.: Harvard University Press, 1951); Edward A. Armstrong, *Shakespeare's Imagination: A Study of the Psychology of Association and Inspiration* (London: Lindsay Drummond, 1946).

³ Donald A. Stauffer, *Shakespeare's World of Images* (New York: W. W. Norton, 1949), p. 212.

SHAKESPEARE'S POOR RELATION: *2 Henry IV*

¹ Clifford Leech, "The Unity of 2 *Henry IV*," *Shakespeare Survey* 6 (1953), pp. 16–24.

² McManaway, "Recent Studies in Shakespeare's Chronology," pp. 22–33.

SHAKESPEARE'S REALITY

¹ [JB] I have accepted "a nigher" (Dover Wilson conj.), "be-humbled" (Staunton conj.), and "Thus" (Pope), for F "another," "he humbled," and "This" in 43, 46, 57.

² [JB] That is, 2nd Lord (Ecclestone or Edmans—actors). Shakespeare wrote with his company in mind; Dogberry's speeches in Q *Much Ado*, which like F *All's Well* was printed from his "foul" papers (holograph copy), often are headed "Kemp," the famous clown Shakespeare created the part for. But the initial may have been added, as Chambers suggests, by the book keeper; if so, before production. The lack of pointing in the King's last line here is probably authentic.

³ [JB] Accepting Pope's "Gumme," Johnson's "oozes," Theobald's "chafes," for F *Gowne, vses, chases*.